THE HISTORY OF ENGLAND

VOLUME IV

MACMILLAN AND CO., Limited
LONDON · BOMBAY · CALCUTTA
MELBOURNE

THE MACMILLAN COMPANY
NEW YORK · BOSTON · CHICAGO
DALLAS · SAN FRANCISCO

THE MACMILLAN CO. OF CANADA, Ltd.
TORONTO

JOHN GRAHAM OF CLAVERHOUSE, 1st VISCOUNT DUNDEE.

From a painting by Sir Peter Lely, in the possession of the Earl of Strathmore.

THE HISTORY OF
ENGLAND

FROM THE ACCESSION OF JAMES THE SECOND

BY

LORD MACAULAY

EDITED BY

CHARLES HARDING FIRTH, M.A.

REGIUS PROFESSOR OF MODERN HISTORY IN THE
UNIVERSITY OF OXFORD

IN SIX VOLUMES

VOLUME IV

MACMILLAN AND CO., LIMITED
ST. MARTIN'S STREET, LONDON
1914

CONTENTS OF THE FOURTH VOLUME

CHAPTER XIII

PAGE

The Revolution more violent in Scotland than in England   1533

Elections for the Convention   1534

Rabbling of the Episcopal Clergy   1536

State of Edinburgh   1538

Question of an Union between England and Scotland raised   1540

Wish of the English Low Churchmen to preserve Episcopacy in Scotland   1544

Opinions of William about Church Government in Scotland   1545

Comparative strength of Religious Parties in Scotland   1546

Letter from William to the Scotch Convention ; William's Instructions to his Agents in Scotland   1547

The Dalrymples   1548

Melville   1551

James's Agents in Scotland : Dundee ; Balcarras   1552

Meeting of the Convention   1556

Hamilton elected President   1558

Committee of Elections ; Edinburgh Castle summoned ; Dundee threatened by the Covenanters   1560

Letter from James to the Convention   1562

Effect of James's Letter   1563

Flight of Dundee ; Tumultuous Sitting of the Convention   1564

A Committee appointed to frame a Plan of Government   1566

Resolutions proposed by the Committee   1570

William and Mary proclaimed ; The Claim of Right ; Abolition of Episcopacy   1572

Torture   1574

William and Mary accept the Crown of Scotland   1576

Discontent of the Covenanters   1577

Ministerial Arrangements in Scotland ; Hamilton ; Crawford   1578

The Dalrymples ; Lockhart ; Montgomery   1579

Melville ; Carstairs   1580

The Club formed ; Annandale ; Ross ; Hume ; Fletcher of Saltoun   1582

War breaks out in the Highlands ; State of the Highlands   1583

CONTENTS

	PAGE
Peculiar Nature of Jacobitism in the Highlands	1592
Jealousy of the Ascendency of the Campbells	1593
The Stewarts and Macnaghtens	1596
The Macleans; The Camerons; Lochiel	1597
The Macdonalds	1600
Feud between the Macdonalds and Mackintoshes; Inverness	1601
Inverness threatened by Macdonald of Keppoch	1602
Dundee appears in Keppoch's Camp	1604
Insurrection of the Clans hostile to the Campbells	1606
Tarbet's Advice to the Government	1608
Indecisive Campaign in the Highlands	1610
Military Character of the Highlanders	1611
Quarrels in the Highland Army	1614
Dundee applies to James for Assistance; The War in the Highlands suspended	1616
Scruples of the Covenanters about taking arms for King William; The Cameronian Regiment raised	1617
Edinburgh Castle surrenders	1618
Session of Parliament at Edinburgh; Ascendency of the Club	1620
Troubles in Athol	1623
The War breaks out again in the Highlands	1626
Death of Dundee; Retreat of Mackay	1634
Effect of the Battle of Killiecrankie	1635
The Scottish Parliament adjourned	1636
The Highland Army reinforced	1639
Skirmish at Saint Johnston's; Disorders in the Highland Army	1642
Mackay's Advice disregarded by the Scotch Ministers; The Cameronians stationed at Dunkeld	1643
The Highlanders attack the Cameronians and are repulsed	1644
Dissolution of the Highland Army; Intrigues of the Club; State of the Lowlands	1647

CHAPTER XIV

	PAGE
Disputes in the English Parliament; The Attainder of Russell reversed	1649
Other Attainders reversed; Case of Samuel Johnson	1652
Case of Devonshire; Case of Oates	1654
Bill of Rights	1663
Disputes about a Bill of Indemnity	1666
Last Days of Jeffreys	1668
The Whigs dissatisfied with the King	1673
Intemperance of Howe; Attack on Caermarthen	1674
Attack on Halifax	1675
Preparations for a Campaign in Ireland	1678
Schomberg	1679
Recess of the Parliament; State of Ireland. Advice of Avaux	1680
Dismission of Melfort; Schomberg lands in Ulster	1685

CONTENTS

PAGE

Carrickfergus taken ; Schomberg advances into Leinster 1686
The English and Irish Armies encamp near each other ; Schomberg
    declines a Battle 1688
Frauds of the English Commissariat 1689
Conspiracy among the French Troops in the English Service 1690
Pestilence in the English Army 1692
The English and Irish Armies go into Winter Quarters ; Various
    Opinions about Schomberg's Conduct 1694
Maritime Affairs ; Maladministration of Torrington 1696
Continental Affairs 1698
Skirmish at Walcourt ; Imputations thrown on Marlborough 1702
Pope Innocent XI succeeded by Alexander VIII 1704
The High Church Clergy divided on the Subject of the Oaths 1706
Arguments for taking the Oaths 1707
Arguments against taking the Oaths 1709
A great Majority of the Clergy take the Oaths 1713
The Nonjurors ; Ken 1714
Leslie 1717
Sherlock 1718
Hickes ; Collier 1720
Dodwell 1724
Kettlewell ; Fitzwilliam 1726
General Character of the nonjuring Clergy 1728
The Plan of Comprehension ; Tillotson 1732
An Ecclesiastical Commission issued 1734
Proceedings of the Commission 1736
The Convocation of the Province of Canterbury summoned. Temper
    of the Clergy 1742
The Clergy ill affected towards the King 1743
The Clergy exasperated against the Dissenters by the Proceedings of
    the Scotch Presbyterians 1746
Constitution of the Convocation 1749
Election of Members of Convocation; Ecclesiastical Preferments bestowed 1750
Compton discontented 1752
The Convocation meets 1753
The High Churchmen a Majority of the Lower House of Convocation 1754
Difference between the two Houses of Convocation 1756
The Lower House of Convocation proves unmanageable 1757
The Convocation prorogued 1758

CHAPTER XV

The Parliament meets. Retirement of Halifax 1760
Supplies voted ; The Bill of Rights passed 1762
Enquiry into Naval Abuses ; Enquiry into the Conduct of the Irish War 1764

CONTENTS

	PAGE
Reception of Walker in England	1765
Edmund Ludlow	1768
Violence of the Whigs; Impeachments	1772
Committee of Murder	1773
Malevolence of John Hampden	1774
1690. The Corporation Bill	1779
Debates on the Indemnity Bill	1784
Case of Sir Robert Sawyer	1786
The King purposes to retire to Holland	1789
He is induced to change his Intention	1790
The Whigs oppose his going to Ireland; He prorogues the Parliament	1791
Joy of the Tories	1792
Dissolution and General Election	1793
Changes in the Executive Departments	1795
Caermarthen Chief Minister	1796
Sir John Lowther	1797
Rise and Progress of Parliamentary Corruption in England	1798
Sir John Trevor	1803
Godolphin retires	1804
Changes at the Admiralty; Changes in the Commissions of Lieutenancy	1806
Temper of the Whigs	1810
Dealings of some Whigs with Saint Germains: Shrewsbury; Ferguson	1811
Hopes of the Jacobites; Meeting of the new Parliament; Settlement of the Revenue	1812
Provision for the Princess of Denmark	1816
Bill declaring the Acts of the preceding Parliament valid	1821
Debate on the Changes in the Lieutenancy of London	1822
Abjuration Bill	1823
The Parliament prorogued; Preparations for the first War	1830
Administration of James at Dublin	1831
An Auxiliary Force sent from France to Ireland	1832
Plan of the English Jacobites; Clarendon; Ailesbury; Dartmouth; Penn	1836
Preston	1837
The Jacobites betrayed by Fuller	1838
Crone arrested	1840
Difficulties of William	1841
Conduct of Shrewsbury	1842
The Council of Nine	1844
Conduct of Clarendon; Penn held to Bail	1846
Interview between William and Burnet; William sets out for Ireland	1847
Trial of Crone	1848
Danger of Invasion and Insurrection; Tourville's Fleet in the Channel	1850
Arrests of Suspected Persons; Torrington ordered to give Battle to Tourville	1852
Battle of Beachy Head	1856

CONTENTS

PAGE

Alarm in London ; Battle of Fleurus   1857
Spirit of the Nation   1858
Conduct of Shrewsbury   1860

CHAPTER XVI

William lands at Carrickfergus and proceeds to Belfast   1864
State of Dublin   1865
William's Military Arrangements   1868
William marches southward   1869
The Irish Army retreats   1870
The Irish make a stand at the Boyne ; The Army of James   1872
The Army of William   1874
Walker, now Bishop of Derry, accompanies the Army   1875
William reconnoitres the Irish Position ; William is wounded   1876
Battle of the Boyne   1878
Flight of James   1883
Loss of the two Armies   1885
Fall of Drogheda ; State of Dublin   1886
James flies to France   1888
Dublin evacuated by the French and Irish Troops   1889
Entry of William into Dublin ; Effect produced in France by the News
    from Ireland   1890
Effect produced at Rome by the News from Ireland ; Effect produced
    in London by the News from Ireland   1892
James arrives in France : His Reception there   1896
Tourville attempts a Descent on England   1898
Teignmouth destroyed   1900
Excitement of the English Nation against the French   1902
The Jacobite Press ; The Jacobite Form of Prayer and Humiliation   1905
Clamour against the nonjuring Bishops   1906
Military Operations in Ireland : Waterford taken   1908
The Irish Army collected at Limerick ; Lauzun pronounces that the
    place cannot be defended   1911
The Irish insist on defending Limerick   1912
Tyrconnel is against defending Limerick   1913
Limerick defended by the Irish alone   1914
Sarsfield surprises the English Artillery   1916
Arrival of Baldearg O'Donnel at Limerick   1917
The Besiegers suffer from the Rains   1918
Unsuccessful Assault on Limerick ; The Siege raised   1919
Tyrconnel and Lauzun go to France   1920
William returns to England ; Reception of William in England   1922
Expedition to the South of Ireland ; Marlborough takes Cork   1924
Marlborough takes Kinsale   1926

	PAGE
Affairs of Scotland ; Intrigues of Montgomery with the Jacobites	1928
War in the Highlands	1929
Fort William built	1930
Meeting of the Scottish Parliament ; Melville Lord High Commissioner ; The Government obtains a Majority	1932
Ecclesiastical Legislation	1934
The Coalition between the Club and the Jacobites dissolved	1938
The Chiefs of the Club betray each other	1940
General acquiescence in the new Ecclesiastical Polity ; Complaints of the Episcopalians	1943
The Presbyterian Nonjurors	1945
William dissatisfied with the Ecclesiastical Arrangements in Scotland ; Meeting of the General Assembly of the Church of Scotland	1948
State of Affairs on the Continent ; The Duke of Savoy joins the Coalition	1949
Supplies voted ; Ways and Means	1952
Proceedings against Torrington	1955
Torrington's Trial and Acquittal	1956
Animosity of the Whigs against Caermarthen	1958
A Jacobite Plot	1960
Meeting of the leading Conspirators	1961
The Conspirators determine to send Preston to Saint Germains	1962
Papers entrusted to Preston	1964
Information of the Plot given to Caermarthen	1965
Arrest of Preston and his Companions	1966

CHAPTER XVII

1691. William's Voyage to Holland	1968
William's Entrance into the Hague	1970
Congress at the Hague	1974
William his own Minister for Foreign Affairs	1978
William obtains a Toleration for the Waldenses	1979
Vices inherent in the Nature of Coalitions	1980
Siege and Fall of Mons	1982
William returns to England ; Trials of Preston and Ashton	1984
Execution of Ashton ; Preston's Irresolution and Confessions	1988
Lenity shown to the Conspirators ; Dartmouth	1990
Turner ; Penn ; Death of George Fox : his Character	1991
Interview between Penn and Sidney	1997
Preston pardoned ; Joy of the Jacobites at the Fall of Mons	1999
The vacant Sees filled	2000
Tillotson Archbishop of Canterbury	2001
Conduct of Sancroft	2004
Difference between Sancroft and Ken	2006

CONTENTS

PAGE

Hatred of Sancroft to the Established Church.　He provides for the
Episcopal Succession among the Nonjurors 2008

The New Bishops 2010

Sherlock, Dean of Saint Paul's 2012

Treachery of some of William's Servants 2018

Russell 2020

Godolphin 2022

Marlborough 2023

William returns to the Continent 2028

The Campaign of 1691 in Flanders 2029

The War in Ireland; State of the English Part of Ireland 2030

State of the Part of Ireland which was subject to James 2034

Dissensions among the Irish at Limerick 2037

Return of Tyrconnel to Ireland 2040

Arrival of a French Fleet at Limerick: Saint Ruth 2042

The English take the Field; Fall of Ballymore 2043

Siege and Fall of Athlone 2044

Retreat of the Irish Army 2052

Saint Ruth determines to fight 2054

Battle of Aghrim 2056

Fall of Galway 2059

Death of Tyrconnel 2062

Second Siege of Limerick 2063

The Irish desirous to capitulate; Negotiations between the Irish
Chiefs and the Besiegers 2066

The Capitulation of Limerick 2068

The Irish Troops required to make their Election between their Country
and France 2070

Most of the Irish Troops volunteer for France 2072

Many of the Irish who had volunteered for France desert 2073

The last Division of the Irish Army sails from Cork for France 2074

State of Ireland after the War   . 2076

LIST OF ILLUSTRATIONS

PAGE

THE PARLIAMENT HOUSE, EDINBURGH, ABOUT 1647   1535
From a drawing by James Gordon of Rothiemay

GLASGOW, FROM THE NORTH-EAST   1539
From Slezer's Theatrum Scotiae, 1693

EDINBURGH CASTLE   1541
From Slezer's Theatrum Scotiae, 1693

JAMES DALRYMPLE, FIRST VISCOUNT STAIR   1549
From an engraving in the Sutherland Collection

GEORGE, FIRST EARL OF MELVILLE   1553
From an engraving by R. White, after a painting by J. B. de Medina

COLIN LINDSAY, THIRD EARL OF BALCARRES   1555
From a miniature in the possession of the Earl of Crawford

WILLIAM, THIRD DUKE OF HAMILTON   1557
From an engraving by P. Vandrebanc, after a painting by Sir G. Kneller

THE INTERIOR OF THE PARLIAMENT HOUSE IN 1912   1559
From a photograph by Valentine & Sons

STIRLING CASTLE   1565
From Slezer's Theatrum Scotiae, 1693

EDINBURGH, FROM THE NORTH-WEST   1567
From Slezer's Theatrum Scotiae, 1693

MAJOR GENERAL HUGH MACKAY   1569
From an engraving of the portrait in the possession of Lord Reay, prefixed to
Mackay's Memoirs

THE CITY CROSS, EDINBURGH, IN 1750   1571
From an engraving

LORD PRESIDENT SIR GEORGE LOCKHART   1575
From the Scottish National Portrait Gallery.   Artist unknown

WILLIAM CARSTAIRS   1581
From the portrait by William Aikman, in the possession of the University of
Edinburgh

PAGE

MAP TO ILLUSTRATE DUNDEE'S CAMPAIGN IN 1689   1595
Based on the Map contained in Professor C. S. Terry's Life of Dundee

SIR EWAN CAMERON OF LOCHIEL   1599
From a contemporary engraving.

VIEW OF INVERNESS   1603
From Slezer's Theatrum Scotiae, 1693

GEORGE MACKENZIE, VISCOUNT TARBET   1609
From an engraving by P. Vandrebanc, after a painting by J. B. de Medina

JAMES DOUGLAS, EARL OF ANGUS   1619
From a painting in the possession of the Earl of Mar and Kellie

GEORGE, FIRST DUKE OF GORDON   1621
From an engraving by J. Sauvé, in the Sutherland Collection

JOHN MURRAY, FIRST MARQUIS OF ATHOLL   1625
From a painting in the possession of Macleod of Macleod

JOHN, LORD MURRAY, AFTERWARDS FIRST DUKE OF ATHOLL   1627
From a painting in the possession of the present duke

JOHN GRAHAM OF CLAVERHOUSE, FIRST VISCOUNT DUNDEE   1633
From a mezzotint by R. Williams

SCOTCH PROTESTANTS' COURAGE   1637
From the Pepysian Collection of Ballads

ALEXANDER ROBERTSON OF STRUAN   1641
From the painting in the National Portrait Gallery of Scotland. Artist unknown

VIEW OF DUNKELD   1645
From Slezer's Theatrum Scotiae, 1693

THE DEATH OF THE EARL OF ESSEX   1651
From a pamphlet entitled Essex's Innocency and Honour Vindicated

RACHEL, LADY RUSSELL   1653
From the painting by Sir G. Kneller, in the possession of the Duke of Bedford

TITUS OATES IN THE PILLORY   1655
Number 1135 in the British Museum Catalogue of Satirical Prints

SIR ROBERT HOWARD   1659
From an engraving by R. White, after a painting by Sir G. Kneller

THE PRINCESS SOPHIA OF HANOVER   1665
From a mezzotint by W. Faithorne, in the Sutherland Collection

WILLIAM, DUKE OF GLOUCESTER   1667
From a mezzotint by J. Smith, after a painting by Sir G. Kneller

THE CHANCELLOR'S RESOLUTION   1669
From the Pepysian Collection of Ballads

FREDERICK, DUKE OF SCHOMBERG   1681
From a mezzotint by W. Faithorne, after a painting by M. Dahl

LIST OF ILLUSTRATIONS

	PAGE
MAP OF CARRICKFERGUS AND THE ADJACENT COUNTRY From George Story's Impartial History of the Wars of Ireland, 1693	1687
THE ENGLISH CAMP NEAR DUNDALK From Walter Harris's Life of William III, 1749	1691
SIR CLOUDESLEY SHOVELL From a mezzotint by J. Smith, after a painting by W. de Rijck	1697
ARTHUR HERBERT, EARL OF TORRINGTON From an engraving by R. White, after a painting by J. Riley	1699
CHARLES V, DUKE OF LORRAINE From a French engraving in the Sutherland Collection	1701
GEORGE FREDERICK, PRINCE OF WALDECK From an engraving by Marrebeek, in the Sutherland Collection	1703
POPE ALEXANDER VIII From an engraving by N. Visscher, in the Sutherland Collection	1705
THOMAS KEN, BISHOP OF BATH AND WELLS From a painting at New College, Oxford	1715
CHARLES LESLIE From a mezzotint by G. White, in the Sutherland Collection	1719
GEORGE HICKES, DEAN OF WORCESTER From an engraving by R. White	1721
JEREMY COLLIER From a mezzotint by W. Faithorne, after a painting by E. Lely	1723
HENRY DODWELL, CAMDEN PROFESSOR OF ANCIENT HISTORY From an engraving by M. van der Gucht	1725
JOHN KETTLEWELL From an engraving by G. Vertue, after a painting by H. Tilson	1727
COLLEY CIBBER From a mezzotint by J. Simon, after a painting by Grisoni	1731
A CARICATURE AGAINST THE NON-JURORS, PUBLISHED IN 1718 Number 1146 in the British Museum Catalogue of Satirical Prints	1733
HENRY ALDRICH, D.D., DEAN OF CHRIST CHURCH From the painting by Sir G. Kneller, in the possession of the Governing Body of Christ Church, Oxford	1735
WILLIAM JANE From a painting by W. Gandy, in the Bodleian Library	1737
THE JERUSALEM CHAMBER, WESTMINSTER ABBEY From a photograph	1739
EDWARD STILLINGFLEET, BISHOP OF WORCESTER From an engraving by R. White, after a painting by Mary Beale	1741
THE MANNER OF HIS MAJESTY'S CURING THE DISEASE CALLED THE KING'S EVIL From a broadside in the Bodleian Library, published in 1679	1745

PAGE

REDUCED FACSIMILE OF THE FIRST PAGE OF THE LONDON GAZETTE
    FOR JANUARY 28, 1683   1747

JOHN LAKE, BISHOP OF CHICHESTER   1751
    From an engraving by D. Loggan

VIEW OF THE INTERIOR OF HENRY VII'S CHAPEL IN WESTMINSTER
    ABBEY   1755
    From an engraving in the British Museum

GEORGE SAVILE, MARQUIS OF HALIFAX   1761
    From the painting by Sir P. Lely in the possession of the Duke of Devonshire

THE REVEREND AND VALIANT MR. GEORGE WALKER   1767
    From an engraving by P. Vandrebanc, after a painting by Sir G. Kneller

MAJOR-GENERAL EDMUND LUDLOW   1769
    From an engraving by Robert White prefixed to Ludlow's Memoirs

A DIALOGUE BETWEEN FATHER GIFFORD AND OBADIAH WALKER   1775
    From a pamphlet in the Bodleian Library

THE WHIG MARTYRS   1777
    From an engraving in the Sutherland Collection

WILLIAM SACHEVERELL   1781
    From a portrait prefixed to Sir G. Sitwell's The First Whig

SIR ROBERT SAWYER   1785
    From a painting in the possession of the Earl of Carnarvon
        (From Dasent's Speakers of the House of Commons, 1911, by permission of Mr. John Lane)

SIR THOMAS ARMSTRONG   1787
    From a mezzotint in the Sutherland Collection

SIR JOHN LOWTHER   1799
    From a mezzotint by Alexander Browne, after a painting by Sir P. Lely

SIR JOHN TREVOR, MASTER OF THE ROLLS   1805
    From an engraving by W. Bond in the Sutherland Collection

THOMAS HERBERT, EIGHTH EARL OF PEMBROKE   1807
    From a mezzotint by J. Smith, after a painting by W. Wissing

HENRY COMPTON, BISHOP OF LONDON   1809
    From a mezzotint by J. Simon, after a painting by J. Hargrave

SIR CHARLES SEDLEY   1813
    From a sketch in the Sutherland Collection, by Thomas Athow, of a painting
        at Knole

PHILIP, FOURTH LORD WHARTON   1827
    From the painting by Van Dyck in the Hermitage Gallery, St. Petersburg

PLAN OF CHARLEMONT   1835
    From George Story's Impartial History of the Wars of Ireland, 1693

WILLIAM FULLER   1839
    From an engraving in the British Museum

QUEEN MARY II   1845
    From a mezzotint by J. Faber, after a painting by Sir G. Kneller

PAGE

ANNE HILARION DE COTENTIN, COUNT DE TOURVILLE 1849
From an engraving by S. Gantrel, after a painting by M. Menard

ADMIRAL CORNELIS EVERTSEN 1851
From a painting by N. Maes in the Rijks Museum at Amsterdam

REDUCED FACSIMILE OF THE ORDERS SENT TO THE EARL OF TOR-
RINGTON ON 29 JUNE, 1690 1853
From the British Museum. (Egerton MS. 2621, f. 91)

PLAN OF THE BATTLE OF BEACHY HEAD 1855
From an engraving in the Sutherland Collection

LOUIS DE CREVANT D'HUMIÈRES, MARSHAL OF FRANCE 1859
From an engraving by J. Lubin, after a painting by F. Voet

FRENCH MEDALS COMMEMORATING THE BATTLES OF BEACHY HEAD
AND FLEURUS 1861

SIR RICHARD HADDOCK 1863
From an engraving by W. Faithorne, after a painting by J. Closterman

PLAN OF BELFAST IN 1685, BY THOMAS PHILLIPS 1866-1867
From the British Museum

MAP ILLUSTRATING THE CAMPAIGN OF WILLIAM III IN IRELAND 1871

PLAN OF THE BATTLE OF THE BOYNE 1873
From George Story's Impartial History of the Wars of Ireland, 1693

VIEW OF THE OBELISK ERECTED AT THE BOYNE IN 1736 1877
From a mezzotint by Brookes and Croft, after a painting by Tudor

MEDAL REPRESENTING WILLIAM III AT THE BATTLE OF THE BOYNE 1879

MEDAL COMMEMORATING THE DUKE OF SCHOMBERG 1883
(The head resembles Ginkel rather than Schomberg)

MEDALS REPRESENTING WILLIAM III AND JAMES II 1885

THE PROTESTANT TRIUMPH 1887
From the Pepysian Collection of Ballads

A FRENCH CARICATURE REPRESENTING THE FUNERAL OF WILLIAM III 1891
Number 1242 in the British Museum Catalogue of Satirical Prints

A DUTCH CARICATURE REPRESENTING THE DEATH-BED OF LEWIS XIV 1893
Number 1245 in the British Museum Catalogue of Satirical Prints

A DUTCH CARICATURE REPRESENTING LEWIS XIV RECEIVING THE
NEWS FROM IRELAND 1895
Number 1246 in the British Museum Catalogue of Satirical Prints

LEWIS XIV 1897
From an engraving by N. Habert in the Sutherland Collection

THE DEVONSHIRE BOYS' COURAGE 1901
From the Roxburghe Ballads

THE ATTACK ON TEIGNMOUTH 1903
From a drawing by B. Chasse in the Cabinet des Estampes

PAGE

VIEW OF KILKENNY CASTLE   1909
From an engraving by W. Taylor in the British Museum

A PROSPECT OF LIMERICK   1915
From George Story's Impartial History of the Wars of Ireland, 1693

MEDAL COMMEMORATING THE SUBJUGATION OF IRELAND BY WILLIAM III   1919

THE ROYAL SALUTATION   1921
From the Pepysian Collection of Ballads

A VIEW OF THE FIREWORKS IN COVENT GARDEN   1923
From a mezzotint by B. Lens in the British Museum

PLAN OF CORK   1925
From George Story's Impartial History of the Wars of Ireland, 1693

PLAN OF KINSALE.   1927
From George Story's Impartial History of the Wars of Ireland, 1693

VIEW OF FORT WILLIAM   1931
From an engraving published by Robert Sayer

WILLIAM JOHNSTONE, MARQUIS OF ANNANDALE   1941
From a mezzotint by J. Smith, after a painting by Sir G. Kneller

VICTOR AMADEUS, DUKE OF SAVOY   1951
From an engraving by A. Moetjens in the Sutherland Collection

PRINCE EUGENE OF SAVOY   1953
From a mezzotint by J. Smith, after a painting by D. Richter

THE EARL OF TORRINGTON   1957
From a Dutch mezzotint in the Sutherland Collection

HENRY SIDNEY, FIRST EARL OF ROMNEY   1961
From a drawing by G. P. Harding of a painting in the possession of Lord De Lisle

JOHN ASHTON   1963
From an engraving in the Sutherland Collection, after a painting by J. Riley

MEDAL REPRESENTING THE LANDING OF WILLIAM IN HOLLAND   1969

THE ENTRANCE OF WILLIAM III INTO THE HAGUE   1971
From an engraving by I. Tangena

MEDALS COMMEMORATING WILLIAM'S RECEPTION AND VOYAGE   1972

EZECHIEL SPANHEIM   1973
From a mezzotint by J. Simon, after a painting by B. Artaud

FREDERIC, ELECTOR OF BRANDENBURG   1975
From a mezzotint by G. Valck

MEDALS COMMEMORATING THE CONGRESS AT THE HAGUE   1977

LEWIS XIV   1981
From an engraving by G. Edelinck of a painting by J. de la Haye

LEWIS XIV IN THE TRENCHES BEFORE MONS   1983
From an engraving in the Cabinet des Estampes

PAGE

MEDALS COMMEMORATING THE CAPTURE OF MONS BY LEWIS XIV   1985

CHIEF-JUSTICE SIR JOHN HOLT   1987
From an engraving in the Sutherland Collection

GEORGE FOX   1993
From a painting in Swarthmore College, Pennsylvania

WILLIAM PENN   1997
From a portrait carved in ivory by Silvanus Beavan in the possession of Mrs. Alfred Waterhouse

JOHN TILLOTSON, ARCHBISHOP OF CANTERBURY   2003
From an engraving by G. Vertue of a painting by Mary Beale (?) attributed to Sir G. Kneller

FACSIMILE OF A LETTER FROM THOMAS KEN, BISHOP OF BATH AND WELLS, TO GEORGE HARBIN   2005
From the British Museum. (Add. MS. 32095, f. 401)

TOMB OF ARCHBISHOP SANCROFT   2007
From an engraving by F. van Hove in the Sutherland Collection

RICHARD CUMBERLAND, BISHOP OF PETERBOROUGH   2009
From a mezzotint by J. Smith, after a painting by T. Murray

JOHN SHARP, ARCHBISHOP OF YORK   2011
From a mezzotint by F. Kyte

WILLIAM SHERLOCK, DEAN OF ST. PAUL'S   2013
From an engraving by R. White

ADMIRAL EDWARD RUSSELL   2021
From an engraving by W. Elder, after a painting by W. Wissing

CHARLES DE LORRAINE, PRINCE OF VAUDEMONT   2027
From an engraving by N. de Larmessin, after a painting by Ranc

PRINCE LEWIS OF BADEN   2031
From a mezzotint by J. Gole

GODARD VAN REEDE, BARON DE GINKEL, AFTERWARDS EARL OF ATHLONE   2035
From a mezzotint by R. Williams, after a painting by T. Hill

JAMES FITZJAMES, DUKE OF BERWICK   2039
From a French engraving in the Sutherland Collection

MAJOR-GENERAL THOMAS MAXWELL   2041
From a mezzotint by J. Smith, after a painting by J. Closterman

PLAN OF THE FORT OF BALLYMORE   2045
From George Story's Impartial History of the Wars of Ireland, 1693

PLAN OF ATHLONE   2047
From George Story's Impartial History of the Wars of Ireland, 1693

PRINCE GEORGE OF HESSE DARMSTADT   2049
From a mezzotint by J. Smith, after a painting by T. Murray

GUSTAVUS HAMILTON, FIRST VISCOUNT BOYNE   2051
From a painting in the possession of Viscount Boyne

PAGE

THE STORMING OF ATHLONE   2053
     From an engraving by Tangena in the Sutherland Collection

PLAN OF THE BATTLE OF AGHRIM   2057
     From George Story's Impartial History of the Wars of Ireland, 1693

MEDAL ON THE BATTLE OF AGHRIM   2059

PLAN OF GALWAY   2061
     From George Story's Impartial History of the Wars of Ireland, 1693

PLAN OF LIMERICK   2065
     From George Story's Impartial History of the Wars of Ireland, 1693

THE TRIUMPH OF IRELAND   2071
     From the Pepysian Collection of Ballads

PATRICK SARSFIELD, EARL OF LUCAN   2075
     From an engraving by F. Tilliard of a painting by Lady Bingham

TWO MEDALS CELEBRATING THE CAPTURE OF LIMERICK   2077

THE STATUE OF WILLIAM III ON COLLEGE GREEN, DUBLIN   2079
     From a photograph

MEDAL PRESENTED BY WILLIAM III TO THE CITY OF DUBLIN   2081

FULL PAGE PLATES IN COLOUR

JOHN GRAHAM OF CLAVERHOUSE, FIRST VISCOUNT DUNDEE   *Frontispiece*
     From a painting by Sir Peter Lely in the possession of the Earl of Strathmore

THE PASS OF KILLIECRANKIE   *facing* 1628
     From a water-colour drawing by G. F. Robson in the Sutherland Collection

JAMES II, 1633-1701   ,, 1682
     From the painting by John Riley in the National Portrait Gallery

SIMON PATRICK, BISHOP OF ELY   ,, 1742
     From a drawing by R. White in the Sutherland Collection

SARAH JENNINGS, DUCHESS OF MARLBOROUGH, 1660-1744   ,, 1816
     From the painting by M. Dahl in the National Portrait Gallery

WILLIAM III, 1650-1702, AT THE BATTLE OF THE BOYNE   ,, 1878
     From the painting by Jan Wyck in the National Portrait Gallery

RICHARD GRAHAM, VISCOUNT PRESTON, 1648-1695   ,, 1988
     From the painting in the National Portrait Gallery. (Artist unknown)

HISTORY OF ENGLAND

CHAPTER XIII

THE violence of revolutions is generally proportioned to the degree of the maladministration which has produced them. It is therefore not strange that the government of Scotland, having been during many years far more oppressive and corrupt than the government of England, should have fallen with a far heavier ruin. The movement against the last king of the House of Stuart was in England conservative, in Scotland destructive. The English complained, not of the law, but of the violation of the law. They rose up against the first magistrate merely in order to assert the supremacy of the law. They were for the most part strongly attached to the Church established by law. Even in applying that extraordinary remedy to which an extraordinary emergency compelled them to have recourse, they deviated as little as possible from the ordinary methods prescribed by the law. The Convention which met at Westminster, though summoned by irregular writs, was constituted on the exact model of a regular Great Council of the Realm. No man was invited to the Upper House whose right to sit there was not clear. The knights and burgesses of the Lower House were chosen by those electors who would have been entitled to send members to a Parliament called under the great seal. The franchises of the forty shilling freeholder, of the householder paying scot and lot, of the burgage tenant, of the liveryman of London, of the Master of Arts of Oxford, were respected. The sense of the constituent bodies was taken with as little violence on the part of mobs, with as little trickery on the part of returning officers, as at any general election of that age. When at length the Estates met, their deliberations were carried on with perfect freedom and in strict accordance with ancient forms. There was indeed, after the first flight of James, an alarming anarchy in London and in some parts of the country. But that anarchy nowhere lasted longer than forty eight hours. From the day on which William reached Saint James's, not even the most unpopular agents of

[margin note:] The Revolution more violent in Scotland than in England

the fallen government, not even the ministers of the Roman Catholic Church, had anything to fear from the fury of the populace.

In Scotland the course of events was very different. There the law itself was a grievance; and James had perhaps incurred more unpopularity by enforcing it than by violating it. The Church established by law was the most odious institution in the realm. The tribunals had pronounced some sentences so flagitious, the Parliament had passed some Acts so oppressive, that, unless those sentences and those Acts were treated as nullities, it would be impossible to bring together a Convention commanding the public respect and expressing the public opinion. It was hardly to be expected, for example, that the Whigs, in this day of their power, would endure to see their hereditary leader, the son of a martyr, the grandson of a martyr, excluded from the Parliament House in which nine of his ancestors had sate as Earls of Argyle, and excluded by a judgment on which the whole kingdom cried shame. Still less was it to be expected that they would suffer the election of members for counties and towns to be conducted according to the provisions of the existing law. For under the existing law no elector could vote without swearing that he renounced the Covenant, and that he acknowledged the Royal supremacy in matters ecclesiastical.[1] Such an oath no rigid Presbyterian could take. If such an oath had been exacted, the constituent bodies would have been merely small knots of prelatists: the business of devising securities against oppression would have been left to the oppressors; and the great party which had been most active in effecting the Revolution would, in an assembly sprung from the Revolution, have had not a single representative.[2]

William saw that he must not think of paying to the laws of Scotland that scrupulous respect which he had wisely and righteously paid to the laws of England. It was absolutely necessary that he should determine by his own authority how that Convention which was to meet at Edinburgh should be chosen, and that he should assume the power of annulling some judgments and some statutes. He accordingly summoned to the Parliament House several Lords who had been deprived of their honours by sentences which the general voice loudly condemned as unjust; and he took on himself to dispense with the Act which deprived Presbyterians of the elective franchise.

Elections for the Convention   The consequence was that the choice of almost all the shires and burghs fell on Whig candidates. The defeated party complained loudly of foul play, of the rudeness of the populace, and of the partiality of the presiding magistrates; and these

---

[1] Act. Parl. Scot., Aug. 31. 1681.

[2] Balcarras's Memoirs; Short History of the Revolution in Scotland in a letter from a Scotch gentleman in Amsterdam to his friend in London, 1712.

CVRIA Supremi Conventus Ordinum Regni Scotiæ,
Vulgo Domus Parliamenti.
The Parliament House in Edinborrough by J.G.

THE PARLIAMENT HOUSE, EDINBURGH, ABOUT 1647

From a drawing by James Gordon of Rothiemay

complaints were in many cases well founded. It is not under such rulers as Lauderdale and Dundee that nations learn justice and moderation.[1]

Nor was it only at the elections that the popular feeling, so long and so severely compressed, exploded with violence. The heads and the hands of the martyred Whigs were taken down from the gates of Edinburgh, carried in procession by great multitudes to the cemeteries, and laid in the earth with solemn respect.[2]

Rabbling of the Episcopal Clergy

It would have been well if the public enthusiasm had manifested itself in no less praiseworthy form. Unhappily throughout a large part of Scotland the clergy of the Established Church were, to use the phrase then common, rabbled. The morning of Christmas day was fixed for the commencement of these outrages. For nothing disgusted the rigid Covenanter more than the reverence paid by the prelatist to the ancient holidays of the Church. That such reverence may be carried to an absurd extreme is true. But a philosopher may perhaps be inclined to think the opposite extreme not less absurd, and may ask why religion should reject the aid of associations which exist in every nation sufficiently civilised to have a calendar, and which are found by experience to have a powerful and often a salutary effect. The Puritan, who was, in general, but too ready to follow precedents and analogies drawn from the history and jurisprudence of the Jews, might have found in the Old Testament quite as clear warrant for keeping festivals in honour of great events as for assassinating bishops and refusing quarter to captives. He certainly did not learn from his master, Calvin, to hold such festivals in abhorrence ; for it was in consequence of the strenuous exertions of Calvin that Christmas was, after an interval of some years, again observed by the citizens of Geneva.[3] But there had arisen in Scotland Calvinists who were to Calvin what Calvin was to Laud. To these austere fanatics a holiday was an object of positive disgust and hatred. They long continued in their solemn manifestoes to reckon it among the sins which would one day bring down some fearful judgment on the land that the Court of Session took a vacation in the last week of December.[4]

---

[1] Balcarras's Memoirs ; Life of James, ii. 341.

[2] A Memorial for His Highness the Prince of Orange in relation to the Affairs of Scotland, by two Persons of Quality, 1689.

[3] See Calvin's letter to Haller, iv. Non. Jan. 1551 : "Priusquam urbem unquam ingrederer, nullæ prorsus erant feriæ præter diem Dominicum. Ex quo sum revocatus hoc temperamentum quæsivi, ut Christi natalis celebraretur."

[4] In the Act, Declaration, and Testimony of the Seceders, dated in December 1736, it is said that "countenance is given by authority of Parliament to the observation of holidays in Scotland, by the vacation of our most considerable Courts of Justice in the latter end of December." This is declared to be a national sin, and a ground of the Lord's indignation. In March 1758, the Associate Synod addressed a Solemn Warning to the nation, in which the same complaint was repeated. A poor crazy creature, whose nonsense has been thought worthy of being reprinted

On Christmas day, therefore, the Covenanters held armed musters by concert in many parts of the western shires. Each band marched to the nearest manse, and sacked the cellar and larder of the minister, which at that season were probably better stocked than usual. The priest of Baal was reviled and insulted, sometimes beaten, sometimes ducked. His furniture was thrown out of the windows; his wife and children turned out of doors in the snow. He was then carried to the marketplace, and exposed during some time as a malefactor. His gown was torn to shreds over his head : if he had a prayer book in his pocket it was burned ; and he was dismissed with a charge, never, as he valued his life, to officiate in the parish again. The work of reformation having been thus completed, the reformers locked up the church and departed with the keys. In fairness to these men it must be owned that they had suffered such oppression as may excuse, though it cannot justify, their violence ; and that, though they were rude even to brutality, they do not appear to have been guilty of any intentional injury to life or limb.[1]

The disorder spread fast. In Ayrshire, Clydesdale, Nithisdale, Annandale, every parish was visited by these turbulent zealots. About two hundred curates,—so the episcopal parish priests were called,— were expelled. The graver Covenanters, while they applauded the fervour of their riotous brethren, were apprehensive that proceedings so irregular might give scandal, and learned, with especial concern, that here and there an Achan had disgraced the good cause by stooping to plunder the Canaanites whom he ought only to have smitten. A general meeting of ministers and elders was called for the purpose of preventing such discreditable excesses. In this meeting it was determined that, for the future, the ejection of the established clergy should be performed in a more ceremonious manner. A form of notice was drawn up and served on every curate in the Western Lowlands who had not yet been rabbled. This notice was simply a threatening letter, commanding him to quit his parish peaceably, on pain of being turned out by force.[2]

The Scottish Bishops, in great dismay, sent the Dean of Glasgow to plead the cause of their persecuted Church at Westminster. The outrages committed by the Covenanters were in the highest degree

even in our own time, says : " I leave my testimony against the abominable Act of the pretended Queen Anne and her pretended British, really Brutish Parliament, for enacting the observance of that which is called the Yule Vacance."—The Dying Testimony of William Wilson, sometime Schoolmaster in Park, in the Parish of Douglas, aged 68, who died in 1757.

[1] An Account of the Present Persecution of the Church in Scotland, in several Letters, 1690 ; The Case of the afflicted Clergy in Scotland truly represented, 1690 ; Faithful Contendings Displayed ; Burnet, i. 805.

[2] The form of notice will be found in the book entitled Faithful Contendings Displayed.

offensive to William, who had, in the south of the island, protected even Benedictines and Franciscans from insult and spoliation. But, though he had, at the request of a large number of the noblemen and gentlemen of Scotland, taken on himself provisionally the executive administration of that kingdom, the means of maintaining order there were not at his command. He had not a single regiment north of the Tweed, or indeed within many miles of that river. It was vain to hope that mere words would quiet a nation which had not, in any age, been very amenable to control, and which was now agitated by hopes and resentments, such as great revolutions, following great oppressions, naturally engender. A proclamation was however put forth, directing that all people should lay down their arms, and that, till the Convention should have settled the government, the clergy of the Established Church should be suffered to reside on their cures without molestation. But this proclamation, not being supported by troops, was little regarded. On the very day after it was published at Glasgow, the venerable Cathedral of that city, almost the only fine church of the middle ages which stands uninjured in Scotland, was attacked by a crowd of Presbyterians from the meeting houses, with whom were mingled many of their fiercer brethren from the hills. It was a Sunday : but to rabble a congregation of prelatists was held to be a work of necessity and mercy. The worshippers were dispersed, beaten, and pelted with snowballs. It was indeed asserted that some wounds were inflicted with much more formidable weapons.[1]

Edinburgh, the seat of government, was in a state of anarchy. The Castle, which commanded the whole city, was still held for James by
State of Edinburgh   the Duke of Gordon. The common people were generally Whigs. The College of Justice, a great forensic society composed of judges, advocates, writers to the signet, and solicitors, was the stronghold of Toryism : for a rigid test had during some years excluded Presbyterians from all the departments of the legal profession. The lawyers, some hundreds in number, formed themselves into a battalion of infantry, and for a time effectually kept down the multitude. They paid, however, so much respect to William's authority as to disband themselves when his proclamation was published. But the example of obedience which they had set was not imitated. Scarcely had they laid down their weapons, when Covenanters from the west, who had done all that was to be done in the way of pelting and hustling the curates of their own neighbourhood, came dropping into Edinburgh, by tens and twenties, for the purpose of protecting, or, if need should

---

[1] Account of the Present Persecution, 1690 ; Case of the afflicted Clergy, 1690 ; A true Account of that Interruption that was made of the Service of God on Sunday last, being the 17th of February, 1689, signed by James Gibson, acting for the Lord Provost of Glasgow.

Facies Civitatis GLASGOW ab Oriente Estore. The Prospect Sy y Town of GLASGOW from y North East

GLASGOW, FROM THE NORTH-EAST

From Slezer's Theatrum Scotiae, 1693

be, of overawing the Convention. Glasgow alone sent four hundred of these men. It could hardly be doubted that they were directed by some leader of great weight. They showed themselves little in any public place : but it was known that every cellar was filled with them ; and it might well be apprehended that, at the first signal, they would pour forth from their caverns, and appear armed round the Parliament House.[1]

It might have been expected that every patriotic and enlightened Scotchman would have earnestly desired to see the agitation appeased,

Question of an Union between England and Scotland raised and some government established which might be able to protect property and to enforce the law. An imperfect settlement which could be speedily made might well appear to such a man preferable to a perfect settlement which must be the work of time. Just at this moment, however, a party, strong both in numbers and in abilities, raised a new and most important question, which seemed not unlikely to prolong the interregnum till the autumn. This party maintained that the Estates ought not immediately to declare William and Mary King and Queen, but to propose to England a treaty of union, and to keep the throne vacant till such a treaty should be concluded on terms advantageous to Scotland.[2]

It may seem strange that a large portion of a people, whose patriotism, exhibited, often in a heroic, and sometimes in a comic form, has long been proverbial, should have been willing, nay impatient, to surrender an independence which had been, through many ages, dearly prized and manfully defended. The truth is that the stubborn spirit which the arms of the Plantagenets and Tudors had been unable to subdue had begun to yield to a very different kind of force. Custom-houses and tariffs were rapidly doing what the carnage of Falkirk and Halidon, of Flodden and Pinkie, had failed to do. Scotland had some experience of the effects of an union. She had, near forty years before, been united to England on such terms as England, flushed with conquest, chose to dictate. That union was inseparably associated in the minds of the vanquished people with defeat and humiliation. And yet even that union, cruelly as it had wounded the pride of the Scots, had promoted their prosperity. Cromwell, with wisdom and liberality rare in his age, had established the most complete freedom of trade between the dominant and the subject country. While he governed, no prohibition, no duty, impeded the transit of commodities from any part of the island to any other. His navigation laws imposed no restraint on the trade of Scotland. A Scotch vessel was at liberty to carry a Scotch cargo to Barbadoes, and to bring the sugars of Barbadoes into the port of London.[3] The rule of the Protector therefore had been

[1] Balcarras's Memoirs ; Mackay's Memoirs.   [2] Burnet, ii. 21.

[3] Scobell, 1654, cap. 9. ; and Oliver's Ordinance in Council of the 12th of April in the same year.

The North East View of EDINBURGH CASTLE.

EDINBURGH CASTLE

From Slezer's Theatrum Scotiae, 1693

propitious to the industry and to the physical wellbeing of the Scottish people.   Hating him and cursing him, they could not help thriving under him, and often, during the administration of their legitimate princes, looked back with regret to the golden days of the usurper.[1]

The Restoration came, and changed everything.   The Scots regained their independence, and soon began to find that independence had its discomfort as well as its dignity.   The English Parliament treated them as aliens and as rivals.   A new Navigation Act put them on almost the same footing with the Dutch.   High duties, and in some cases pro-hibitory duties, were imposed on the products of Scottish industry.   It is not wonderful that a nation eminently industrious, shrewd, and enter-prising, a nation which, having been long kept back by a sterile soil and a severe climate, was just beginning to prosper in spite of these dis-advantages, and which found its progress suddenly stopped, should think itself cruelly treated.   Yet there was no help.   Complaint was vain. Retaliation was impossible.   The Sovereign, even if he had the wish, had not the power, to bear himself evenly between his large and his small kingdom, between the kingdom from which he drew an annual revenue of a million and a half and the kingdom from which he drew an annual revenue of little more than sixty thousand pounds.   He dared neither to refuse his assent to any English law injurious to the trade of Scotland, nor to give his assent to any Scotch law injurious to the trade of England.

The complaints of the Scotch, however, were so loud that Charles, in 1667, appointed Commissioners to arrange the terms of a commercial treaty between the two British kingdoms.   The conferences were soon broken off; and all that passed while they continued proved that there was only one way in which Scotland could obtain a share of the com-mercial prosperity which England at that time enjoyed.[2]   The Scotch

---

[1] Burnet and Fletcher of Saltoun mention the prosperity of Scotland under the Protector, but ascribe it to a cause quite inadequate to the production of such an effect.   "There was," says Burnet, "a considerable force of about seven or eight thousand men kept in Scotland.   The pay of the army brought so much money into the kingdom that it continued all that while in a very flourishing state. . . .   We always reckon those eight years of usurpation a time of great peace and prosperity."   "During the time of the usurper Cromwell," says Fletcher, "we imagined ourselves to be in a tolerable condition with respect to the last particular (trade and money) by reason of that expense which was made in the realm by those forces that kept us in subjection."   The true explanation of the phænomena about which Burnet and Fletcher blundered so grossly will be found in a pamphlet entitled, "Some seasonable and modest Thoughts partly occasioned by and partly concerning the Scotch East India Company,' Edinburgh, 1696.   See the proceedings of the Wednesday Club in Friday Street, upon the subject of an Union with Scotland, December 1705.   See also the seventh Chapter of Mr. Burton's valuable History of Scotland.

[2] See the paper in which the demands of the Scotch Commissioners are set forth.   It will be found in the Appendix to De Foe's History of the Union, No. 13.

must become one people with the English. The Parliament which had hitherto sate at Edinburgh must be incorporated with the Parliament which sate at Westminster. The sacrifice could not but be painfully felt by a brave and haughty people, who had, during twelve generations, regarded the southern domination with deadly aversion, and whose hearts still swelled at the thought of the death of Wallace and of the triumphs of Bruce. There were doubtless many punctilious patriots who would have strenuously opposed an union even if they could have foreseen that the effect of an union would be to make Glasgow a greater city than Amsterdam, and to cover the dreary Lothians with harvests and woods, neat farmhouses and stately mansions. But there was also a large class which was not disposed to throw away great and substantial advantages in order to preserve mere names and ceremonies ; and the influence of this class was such that, in the year 1670, the Scotch Parliament made direct overtures to England.[1] The King undertook the office of mediator ; and negotiators were named on both sides : but nothing was concluded.

The question, having slept during eighteen years, was suddenly revived by the Revolution. Different classes, impelled by different motives, concurred on this point. With merchants, eager to share in the advantages of the West Indian Trade, were joined active and aspiring politicians who wished to exhibit their abilities in a more conspicuous theatre than the Scottish Parliament House, and to collect riches from a more copious source than the Scottish treasury. The cry for union was swelled by the voices of some artful Jacobites, who merely wished to cause discord and delay, and who hoped to attain this end by mixing up with the difficult question which it was the especial business of the Convention to settle another question more difficult still. It is probable that some who disliked the ascetic habits and rigid discipline of the Presbyterians wished for an union as the only mode of maintaining prelacy in the northern part of the island. In an united Parliament the English members must greatly preponderate ; and in England the Bishops were held in high honour by the great majority of the population. The Episcopal Church of Scotland, it was plain, rested on a narrow basis, and would fall before the first attack. The Episcopal Church of Great Britain might have a foundation broad and solid enough to withstand all assaults.

Whether, in 1689, it would have been possible to effect a civil union without a religious union may well be doubted. But there can be no doubt that a religious union would have been one of the greatest calamities that could have befallen either kingdom. The union accomplished in 1707 has indeed been a great blessing both to England and

[1] Act. Parl. Scot., July 30. 1670.

to Scotland. But it has been a blessing because, in constituting one State, it left two Churches. The political interest of the contracting parties was the same : but the ecclesiastical dispute between them was one which admitted of no compromise. They could therefore preserve harmony only by agreeing to differ. Had there been an amalgamation of the hierarchies, there never would have been an amalgamation of the nations. Successive Mitchells would have fired at successive Sharpes. Five generations of Claverhouses would have butchered five generations of Camerons. Those marvellous improvements which have changed the face of Scotland would never have been effected. Plains now rich with harvests would have remained barren moors. Waterfalls which now turn the wheels of immense factories would have resounded in a wilderness. New Lanark would still have been a sheepwalk, and Greenock a fishing hamlet. What little strength Scotland could, under such a system, have possessed must, in an estimate of the resources of Great Britain, have been, not added, but deducted. So encumbered, our country never could have held, either in peace or in war, a place in the first rank of nations. We are unfortunately not without the means of judging of the effect which may be produced on the moral and physical state of a people by establishing, in the exclusive enjoyment of riches and dignity, a Church loved and reverenced only by the few, and regarded by the many with religious and national aversion. One such Church is quite burden enough for the energies of one empire.

But these things, which to us, who have been taught by a bitter experience, seem clear, were by no means clear in 1689, even to very tolerant and enlightened politicians. In truth the English Low Churchmen were, if possible, more anxious than the English High Churchmen to preserve Episcopacy in Scotland. It is a remarkable fact that Burnet, who was always accused of wishing to establish the Calvinistic discipline in the south of the island, incurred great unpopularity among his own countrymen by his efforts to uphold prelacy in the north. He was doubtless in error : but his error is to be attributed to a cause which does him no discredit. His favourite object, an object unattainable indeed, yet such as might well fascinate a large intellect and a benevolent heart, had long been an honourable treaty between the Anglican Church and the Nonconformists. He thought it most unfortunate that one opportunity of concluding such a treaty should have been lost at the time of the Restoration. It seemed to him that another opportunity was afforded by the Revolution. He and his friends were eagerly pushing forward Nottingham's Comprehension Bill, and were flattering themselves with vain hopes of success. But they felt that there could hardly be a Comprehension in one of the two British kingdoms, unless there were also a Comprehension in the

Wish of the English Low Churchmen to preserve Episcopacy in Scotland

other. Concession must be purchased by concession. If the Presbyterian pertinaciously refused to listen to any terms of compromise where
he was strong, it would be almost impossible to obtain for him liberal
terms of compromise where he was weak. Bishops must therefore be
allowed to keep their sees in Scotland, in order that divines not ordained
by Bishops might be allowed to hold rectories and canonries in
England.

Thus the cause of the Episcopalians in the north and the cause
of the Presbyterians in the south were bound up together in a manner
which might well perplex even a skilful statesman. It was
happy for our country that the momentous question which
excited so many strong passions, and which presented itself
in so many different points of view, was to be decided by
such a man as William. He listened to Episcopalians, to
Latitudinarians, to Presbyterians, to the Dean of Glasgow who pleaded
for the apostolical succession, to Burnet who represented the danger of
alienating the Anglican clergy, to Carstairs who hated prelacy with
the hatred of a man whose thumbs were deeply marked by the screws
of prelatists. Surrounded by these eager advocates, William remained
calm and impartial. He was indeed eminently qualified by his situation as well as by his personal qualities to be the umpire in that great
contention. He was the King of a prelatical kingdom. He was the
Prime Minister of a presbyterian republic. His unwillingness to offend
the Anglican Church of which he was the head, and his unwillingness
to offend the reformed Churches of the Continent which regarded him
as a champion divinely sent to protect them against the French
tyranny, balanced each other, and kept him from leaning unduly to
either side. His conscience was perfectly neutral. For it was his
deliberate opinion that no form of ecclesiastical polity was of divine
institution. He dissented equally from the school of Laud and from
the school of Cameron, from the men who held that there could not be
a Christian Church without Bishops, and from the men who held that
there could not be a Christian Church without synods. Which form of
government should be adopted was in his judgment a question of mere
expediency. He would probably have preferred a temper between the
two rival systems, a hierarchy in which the chief spiritual functionaries
should have been something more than moderators and something less
than prelates. But he was far too wise a man to think of settling such a
matter according to his own personal tastes. He determined therefore
that, if there was on both sides a disposition to compromise, he would
act as mediator. But, if it should appear that the public mind of
England and the public mind of Scotland had taken the ply strongly
in opposite directions, he would not attempt to force either nation into

Opinions of William about Church government in Scotland

conformity with the opinion of the other. He would suffer each to have its own church, and would content himself with restraining both churches from persecuting nonconformists, and from encroaching on the functions of the civil magistrate.

The language which he held to those Scottish Episcopalians who complained to him of their sufferings and implored his protection was well weighed and well guarded, but clear and ingenuous. He wished, he said, to preserve, if possible, the institution to which they were so much attached, and to grant, at the same time, entire liberty of conscience to that party which could not be reconciled to any deviation from the Presbyterian model. But the Bishops must take care that they did not, by their own rashness and obstinacy, put it out of his power to be of any use to them. They must also distinctly understand that he was resolved not to force on Scotland by the sword a form of ecclesiastical government which she detested. If, therefore, it should be found that prelacy could be maintained only by arms, he should yield to the general sentiment, and should merely do his best to obtain for the Episcopalian minority permission to worship God in freedom and safety.[1]

It is not likely that, even if the Scottish Bishops had, as William recommended, done all that meekness and prudence could do to conciliate their countrymen, episcopacy could, under any modification, have been maintained. It was indeed asserted by writers of that generation, and has been repeated by writers of our generation, that the Presbyterians were not, before the Revolution, the majority of the people of Scotland.[2] But in this assertion there is an obvious fallacy. The effective strength of sects is not to be ascertained merely by counting heads. An established church, a dominant church, a church which has the exclusive possession of civil honours and emoluments, will always rank among its nominal members multitudes who have no religion at all; multitudes who, though not destitute of religion, attend little to theological disputes, and have no scruple about conforming to the mode of worship which happens to be established; and multitudes who have scruples about conforming, but whose scruples have yielded to worldly motives. On the other hand, every member of an oppressed church is a man who has a very decided preference for that church. Every person who,

Comparative strength of religious parties in Scotland

---

[1] Burnet, ii. 23.

[2] See, for example, a pamphlet entitled "Some questions resolved concerning episcopal and presbyterian government in Scotland, 1690." One of the questions is, whether Scottish presbytery be agreeable to the general inclinations of that people. The author answers the question in the negative, on the ground that the upper and middle classes had generally conformed to the episcopal Church before the Revolution.

in the time of Diocletian, joined in celebrating the Christian mysteries might reasonably be supposed to be a firm believer in Christ. But it may well be doubted whether one single Pontiff or Augur in the Roman Senate was a firm believer in Jupiter. In Mary's reign, everybody who attended the secret meetings of the Protestants was a real Protestant : but hundreds of thousands went to mass, who, as appeared before she had been dead a month, were not real Roman Catholics. If, under the Kings of the House of Stuart, when a Presbyterian was excluded from political power and from the learned professions, was daily annoyed by informers, by tyrannical magistrates, by licentious dragoons, and was in danger of being hanged if he heard a sermon in the open air, the population of Scotland was not very unequally divided between Episcopalians and Presbyterians, the rational inference is that more than nineteen twentieths of those Scotchmen whose conscience was interested in the matter were Presbyterians, and that the Scotchmen, who were decidedly and on conviction Episcopalians, were a small minority. Against such odds the Bishops had but little chance ; and whatever chance they had they made haste to throw away ; some of them because they sincerely believed that their allegiance was still due to James ; others probably because they apprehended that William would not have the power, even if he had the will, to serve them, and that nothing but a counterrevolution in the State could avert a revolution in the Church.

As the new King of England could not be at Edinburgh during the sitting of the Scottish Convention, a letter from him to the Estates was prepared with great skill. In this document he professed warm attachment to the Protestant religion, but gave no opinion touching those questions about which Protestants were divided. He had observed, he said, with great satisfaction that many of the Scottish nobility and gentry with whom he had conferred in London were inclined to an union of the two British kingdoms. He was sensible how much such an union would conduce to the happiness of both ; and he would do all in his power towards the accomplishing of so good a work. *Letter from William to the Scotch Convention*

It was necessary that he should allow a large discretion to his confidential agents at Edinburgh. The private instructions with which he furnished those persons could not be minute, but were highly judicious. He charged them to ascertain to the best of their power the real sense of the Convention, and to be guided by it. They must remember that the first object was to settle the government. To that object every other object, even the union, must be postponed. A treaty between two independent legislatures, distant from each other several days' journey, must necessarily be a *William's instructions to his agents in Scotland* work of time; and the throne could not safely remain vacant while the negotiations were pending. It was therefore important that His Majesty's agents should be on their guard against the arts of persons who, under pretence of promoting the union, might really be contriving only to prolong the interregnum. If the Convention should be bent on establishing the Presbyterian form of church government, William desired that his friends would do all in their power to prevent the triumphant sect from retaliating what it had suffered.[1]

The person by whose advice William appears to have been at this time chiefly guided as to Scotch politics was a Scotchman of great abilities and attainments, Sir James Dalrymple of Stair, the founder of a family eminently distinguished at the bar, on the bench, in the senate, in diplomacy, in arms, and in letters, but distinguished also by misfortunes and misdeeds which have furnished poets and novelists with materials for the darkest and most heartrending tales. Already Sir James had been in mourning for more than one strange and terrible death. One of his sons had died by poison. One of his daughters had poniarded her bridegroom on the wedding night. One of his grandsons had in boyish sport been slain by another. Savage libellers asserted, and some of the superstitious vulgar believed, that calamities so portentous were the consequences of some connection between the unhappy race and the powers of darkness. Sir James had a wry neck; and he was reproached with this misfortune as if it had been a crime, and was told that it marked him out as a man doomed to the gallows. His wife, a woman of great ability, art, and spirit, was popularly nicknamed the Witch of Endor. It was gravely said that she had cast fearful spells on those whom she hated, and that she had been seen in the likeness of a cat seated on the cloth of state by the side of the Lord High Commissioner. The man, however, over whose roof so many curses appeared to hang, did not, as far as we can now judge, fall short of that very low standard of morality which was generally attained by politicians of his age and nation. In force of mind and extent of knowledge he was superior to them all. In his youth he had borne arms: he had then been a professor of philosophy: he had then studied law, and had become, by general acknowledgment, the greatest jurist that his country had produced. In the days of the Protectorate, he had been a judge. After the Restoration, he had made his peace with the royal family, had sate in the Privy Council, and had presided with unrivalled ability in the Court of Session. He had doubtless borne a share in

The marginal note reads: **The Dalrymples**

---

[1] The instructions are in the Leven and Melville Papers. They bear date March 7. 168⅞. On the first occasion on which I quote this most valuable collection, I cannot refrain from acknowledging the obligations under which I, and all who take an interest in the history of our island, lie to the gentleman who has performed so well the duty of an editor.

JAMES DALRYMPLE, FIRST VISCOUNT STAIR

From an engraving in the Sutherland Collection

many unjustifiable acts; but there were limits which he never passed. He had a wonderful power of giving to any proposition which it suited him to maintain a plausible aspect of legality and even of justice; and this power he frequently abused. But he was not, like many of those among whom he lived, impudently and unscrupulously servile. Shame and conscience generally restrained him from committing any bad action for which his rare ingenuity could not frame a specious defence; and he was seldom in his place at the council board when anything outrageously unjust or cruel was to be done. His moderation at length gave offence to the Court. He was deprived of his high office, and found himself in so disagreeable a situation that he retired to Holland. There he employed himself in correcting the great work on jurisprudence which has preserved his memory fresh down to our own time. In his banishment he tried to gain the favour of his fellow exiles, who naturally regarded him with suspicion. He protested, and perhaps with truth, that his hands were pure from the blood of the persecuted Covenanters. He made a high profession of religion, prayed much, and observed weekly days of fasting and humiliation. He even consented, after much hesitation, to assist with his advice and his credit the unfortunate enterprise of Argyle. When that enterprise had failed, a prosecution was instituted at Edinburgh against Dalrymple; and his estates would doubtless have been confiscated, had they not been saved by an artifice which subsequently became common among the politicians of Scotland. His eldest son and heir apparent, John, took the side of the government, supported the dispensing power, declared against the Test, and accepted the place of Lord Advocate, when Sir George Mackenzie, after holding out through ten years of foul drudgery, at length showed signs of flagging. The services of the younger Dalrymple were rewarded by a remission of the forfeiture which the offences of the elder had incurred. Those services indeed were not to be despised. For Sir John, though inferior to his father in depth and extent of legal learning, was no common man. His knowledge was great and various: his parts were quick; and his eloquence was singularly ready and graceful. To sanctity he made no pretensions. Indeed Episcopalians and Presbyterians agreed in regarding him as little better than an atheist. During some months Sir John at Edinburgh affected to condemn the disloyalty of his unhappy parent Sir James; and Sir James at Leyden told his Puritan friends how deeply he lamented the wicked compliances of his unhappy child Sir John.

The Revolution came, and brought a large increase of wealth and honours to the House of Stair. The son promptly changed sides, and cooperated ably and zealously with the father. Sir James established himself in London for the purpose of giving advice to William on

Scotch affairs. Sir John's post was in the Parliament House at Edinburgh. He was not likely to find any equal among the debaters there, and was prepared to exert all his powers against the dynasty which he had lately served.[1]

By the large party which was zealous for the Calvinistic church government John Dalrymple was regarded with incurable distrust and dislike. It was therefore necessary that another agent should be employed to manage that party. Such an agent was George Melville, Lord Melville, a nobleman connected by affinity with the unfortunate Monmouth, and with that Leslie who had, in 1640, invaded England at the head of a Scottish army. Melville had always been accounted a Whig and a Presbyterian. Those who speak of him most favourably have not ventured to ascribe to him eminent intellectual endowments or exalted public spirit. But he appears from his letters to have been by no means deficient in that homely prudence the want of which has often been fatal to men of brighter genius and of purer virtue. That prudence had restrained him from going very far in opposition to the tyranny of the Stuarts : but he had listened while his friends talked about resistance, and therefore, when the Rye House plot was discovered, thought it expedient to retire to the Continent. In his absence he was accused of treason, and was convicted on evidence which would not have satisfied any impartial tribunal. He was condemned to death : his honours and lands were declared forfeit : his arms were torn with contumely out of the Heralds' Book ; and his domains swelled the estate of the cruel and rapacious Perth. The fugitive meanwhile, with characteristic wariness, lived quietly on the Continent, and discountenanced the unhappy projects of his kinsman Monmouth, but cordially approved of the enterprise of the Prince of Orange.

Illness had prevented Melville from sailing with the Dutch expedition : but he arrived in London a few hours after the new Sovereigns had been proclaimed there. William instantly sent him down to Edinburgh, in the hope, as it should seem, that the Presbyterians would be disposed to listen to moderate counsels proceeding from a man who was attached to their cause, and who had suffered for it. Melville's second son, David, who had inherited, through his mother, the title of Earl of Leven, and who had acquired some military experience in the

Melville

---

[1] As to the Dalrymples, see the Lord President's own writings, and among them his Vindication of the Divine Perfections ; Wodrow's Analecta ; Douglas's Peerage ; Lockhart's Memoirs ; the Satyre on the Familie of Stairs ; the Satyric Lines upon the long wished for and timely Death of the Right Honourable Lady Stairs ; Law's Memorials ; and the Hyndford Papers, written in 170⅘ and printed with the Letters of Carstairs. Lockhart, though a mortal enemy of John Dalrymple, says, " There was none in the parliament capable to take up the cudgels with him."

service of the Elector of Brandenburgh, had the honour of being the bearer of a letter from the new King of England to the Scottish Convention.[1]

James had entrusted the conduct of his affairs in Scotland to John Graham, Viscount Dundee, and Colin Lindsay, Earl of Balcarras.

James's agents in Scotland: Dundee; Balcarras

Dundee had commanded a body of Scottish troops which had marched into England to oppose the Dutch: but he had found, in the inglorious campaign which had been fatal to the dynasty of Stuart, no opportunity of displaying the courage and military skill which those who most detest his merciless nature allow him to have possessed. He lay with his forces not far from Watford, when he was informed that James had fled from Whitehall, and that Feversham had ordered all the royal army to disband. The Scottish regiments were thus left, without pay or provisions, in the midst of a foreign and indeed a hostile nation. Dundee, it is said, wept with grief and rage. Soon, however, more cheering intelligence arrived from various quarters. William wrote a few lines to say that, if the Scots would remain quiet, he would pledge his honour for their safety; and, some hours later, it was known that James had returned to his capital. Dundee repaired instantly to London.[2] There he met his friend Balcarras, who had just arrived from Edinburgh. Balcarras, a man distinguished by his handsome person and by his accomplishments, had, in his youth, affected the character of a patriot, but had deserted the popular cause, had accepted a seat in the Privy Council, had become a tool of Perth and Melfort, and had been one of the Commissioners who were appointed to execute the office of Treasurer when Queensberry was disgraced for refusing to betray the interests of the Protestant religion.[3]

Dundee and Balcarras went together to Whitehall, and had the honour of accompanying James in his last walk up and down the Mall. He told them that he intended to put his affairs in Scotland under their management. "You, my Lord Balcarras, must undertake the civil business: and you, my Lord Dundee, shall have a commission from me to command the troops." The two noblemen vowed that they would prove themselves deserving of his confidence, and disclaimed all thought of making their peace with the Prince of Orange.[4]

On the following day James left Whitehall for ever; and the Prince of Orange arrived at Saint James's. Both Dundee and Balcarras swelled the crowd which thronged to greet the deliverer, and were not

---

[1] As to Melville, see the Leven and Melville Papers, *passim*, and the preface; the Act. Parl. Scot., June 16. 1685; and the Appendix, June 13.; Burnet, ii. 24.; and the Burnet MS. Harl. 6584.

[2] Creichton's Memoirs.   [3] Mackay's Memoirs.   [4] Memoirs of the Lindsays.

ungraciously received.   Both were well known to him.   Dundee had
served under him on the Continent[1]; and the first wife of Balcarras
had been a lady of the House of Orange, and had worn, on her wedding
day, a superb pair of emerald earrings, the gift of her cousin the
Prince.[2]

The Scottish Whigs, then assembled in great numbers at Westminster, earnestly pressed William to proscribe by name four or five
men who had, during the evil times, borne a conspicuous part in the
proceedings of the Privy Council at Edinburgh.   Dundee and Balcarras
were particularly mentioned.   But the Prince had determined that, as
far as his power extended, all the past should be covered with a general
amnesty, and absolutely refused to make any declaration which could
drive to despair even the most guilty of his uncle's servants.

Balcarras went repeatedly to Saint James's, had several audiences
of William, professed deep respect for His Highness, and owned that
King James had committed great errors, but would not promise to
concur in a vote of deposition.   William gave no signs of displeasure,
but said at parting; "Take care, my Lord, that you keep within the
law; for, if you break it, you must expect to be left to it."[3]

Dundee seems to have been less ingenuous.   He employed the
mediation of Burnet, opened a negotiation with Saint James's, declared
himself willing to acquiesce in the new order of things, obtained from
William a promise of protection, and promised in return to live peaceably.   Such credit was given to his professions, that he was suffered to
travel down to Scotland under the escort of a troop of cavalry.   Without such an escort the man of blood, whose name was never mentioned

[1] About the early relation between William and Dundee, some Jacobite, many years after
they were both dead, invented a story which by successive embellishments was at last improved
into a romance such as it seems strange that even a child should believe to be true.   The last
edition runs thus.   William's horse was killed under him at Seneff, and his life was in imminent
danger.   Dundee, then Captain Graham, mounted His Highness again.   William promised to reward
this service with promotion, but broke his word, and gave to another the commission which Graham
had been led to expect.   The injured hero went to Loo.   There he met his successful competitor
and gave him a box on the ear.   The punishment for striking in the palace was the loss of the
offending right hand; but this punishment the Prince of Orange ungraciously remitted.   "You,"
he said, "saved my life: I spare your right hand; and now we are quits."

Those who, down to our own time, have repeated this nonsense seem to have thought, first,
that the Act of Henry the Eighth "for punishment of murder and malicious bloodshed within
the King's Court" (Stat. 33 Hen. VIII. c. 2.) was law in Guelders; and, secondly, that, in 1674,
William was a King, and his house a King's Court.   They were also not aware that he did
not purchase Loo till long after Dundee had left the Netherlands.   See Harris's Description of
Loo, 1699.

This legend, of which I have not been able to discover the slightest trace in the voluminous
Jacobite literature of William's reign, seems to have originated about a quarter of a century after
Dundee's death, and to have attained its full absurdity in another quarter or a century.

[2] Memoirs of the Lindsays.   [3] Ibid.

but with a shudder at the hearth of any Presbyterian family, would, at that conjuncture, have had but a perilous journey through Berwickshire and the Lothians.[1]

February was drawing to a close when Dundee and Balcarras reached Edinburgh. They had some hope that they might be at the head of a majority in the Convention. They therefore exerted them-

COLIN LINDSAY, THIRD EARL OF BALCARRES

From a miniature in the possession of the Earl of Crawford

selves vigorously to consolidate and animate their party. They assured the rigid royalists, who had a scruple about sitting in an assembly convoked by an usurper, that the rightful King particularly wished no friend of hereditary monarchy to be absent. More than one waverer was kept steady by being assured, in confident terms, that a speedy restoration was inevitable. Gordon had determined to surrender the

[1] Burnet, ii. 22. ; Memoirs of the Lindsays.

castle, and had begun to remove his furniture : but Dundee and Balcarras prevailed on him to hold out some time longer. They informed him that they had received from Saint Germains full powers to adjourn the Convention to Stirling, and that, if things went ill at Edinburgh, those powers would be used.[1]

At length the fourteenth of March, the day fixed for the meeting of the Estates, arrived, and the Parliament House was crowded. Nine prelates were in their places. When Argyle presented himself, a single lord protested against the admission of a person whom a legal sentence, passed in due form, and still unreversed, had deprived of the honours of the peerage. But this objection was overruled by the general sense of the assembly. When Melville appeared, no voice was raised against his admission. The Bishop of Edinburgh officiated as chaplain, and made it one of his petitions that God would help and restore King James.[2] It soon appeared that the general feeling of the Convention was by no means in harmony with this prayer. The first matter to be decided was the choice of a President. The Duke of Hamilton was supported by the Whigs, the Marquess of Athol by the Jacobites. Neither candidate possessed, and neither deserved, the entire confidence of his supporters. Hamilton had been a Privy Councillor of James, had borne a part in many unjustifiable acts, and had offered but a very cautious and languid opposition to the most daring attacks on the laws and religion of Scotland. Not till the Dutch guards were at Whitehall had he ventured to speak out. Then he had joined the victorious party, and had assured the Whigs that he had pretended to be their enemy, only in order that he might, without incurring suspicion, act as their friend. Athol was still less to be trusted. His abilities were mean, his temper false, pusillanimous, and cruel. In the late reign he had gained a dishonourable notoriety by the barbarous actions of which he had been guilty in Argyleshire. He had turned with the turn of fortune, and had paid servile court to the Prince of Orange, but had been coldly received, and had now, from mere mortification, come back to the party which he had deserted.[3] Neither of the rival noblemen had chosen to stake the dignities and lands of his house on the issue of the contention between the rival Kings. The eldest son of Hamilton had declared for James, and the eldest son of Athol for William, so that, in any event, both coronets and both estates were safe.

Meeting of the Convention

[1] Balcarras's Memoirs.

[2] Act. Parl. Scot., Mar. 14. 1689 ; History of the late Revolution in Scotland, 1690 ; An Account of the Proceedings of the Estates of Scotland, fol. Lond. 1689.

[3] Balcarras's narrative exhibits both Hamilton and Athol in a most unfavourable light. See also the Life of James, ii. 338, 339.

WILLIAM, THIRD DUKE OF HAMILTON

From an engraving by P. Vandrebanc. after a painting by Sir G. Kneller

But in Scotland the fashionable notions touching political morality were lax; and the aristocratical sentiment was strong. The Whigs were therefore willing to forget that Hamilton had lately sate in the council of James. The Jacobites were equally willing to forget that Athol had lately fawned on William. In political inconsistency those two great lords were far indeed from standing by themselves; but in dignity and power they had scarcely an equal in the assembly. Their descent was eminently illustrious: their influence was immense: one of them could raise the Western Lowlands; the other could bring into the field an army of northern mountaineers. Round these chiefs therefore the hostile factions gathered.

The votes were counted; and it appeared that Hamilton had a majority of forty. The consequence was that about twenty of the defeated party instantly passed over to the victors.[1] At West-minster such a defection would have been thought strange; but it seems to have caused little surprise at Edinburgh. It

Hamilton elected President

is a remarkable circumstance that the same country should have produced in the same age the most wonderful specimens of both extremes of human nature. No class of men mentioned in history has ever adhered to a principle with more inflexible pertinacity than was found among the Scotch Puritans. Fine and imprisonment, the sheers and the branding iron, the boot, the thumbscrew, and the gallows could not extort from the stubborn Covenanter one evasive word on which it was possible to put a sense inconsistent with his theological system. Even in things indifferent he would hear of no compromise; and he was but too ready to consider all who recommended prudence and charity as traitors to the cause of truth. On the other hand, the Scotchmen of that generation who made a figure in the Parliament House and in the Council Chamber were the most dishonest and unblushing timeservers that the world has ever seen. The English marvelled alike at both classes. There were indeed many stouthearted nonconformists in the South; but scarcely any who in obstinacy, pugnacity, and hardihood could bear a comparison with the men of the school of Cameron. There were many knavish politicians in the South; but few so utterly destitute of morality, and still fewer so utterly destitute of shame, as the men of the school of Lauderdale. Perhaps it is natural that the most callous and impudent vice should be found in the near neighbourhood of unreasonable and impracticable virtue. Where enthusiasts are ready to destroy or to be destroyed for trifles magnified into importance by a squeamish conscience, it is not strange that the very name of conscience should become a byword of contempt to cool and shrewd men of business.

[1] Act. Parl. Scot., March 14. 168⅝; Balcarras's Memoirs; History of the late Revolution in Scotland; Life of James, ii. 342.

THE INTERIOR OF THE PARLIAMENT HOUSE IN 1912

From a photograph by Valentine & Sons

The majority, reinforced by the crowd of deserters from the minority, proceeded to name a Committee of Elections. Fifteen persons were Committee chosen, and it soon appeared that twelve of these were not of Elections disposed to examine severely into the regularity of any proceeding of which the result had been to send up a Whig to the Parliament House. The Duke of Hamilton is said to have been disgusted by the gross partiality of his own followers, and to have exerted himself, with but little success, to restrain their violence.[1]

Before the Estates proceeded to deliberate on the business for which they had met, they thought it necessary to provide for their own security. Edinburgh They could not be perfectly at ease while the roof under which Castle sum- they sate was commanded by the batteries of the Castle. moned A deputation was therefore sent to inform Gordon that the Convention required him to evacuate the fortress within twenty four hours, and that if he complied, his past conduct should not be remembered against him. He asked a night for consideration. During that night his wavering mind was confirmed by the exhortations of Dundee and Balcarras. On the morrow he sent an answer drawn in respectful but evasive terms. He was very far, he declared, from meditating harm to the City of Edinburgh. Least of all could he harbour any thought of molesting an august assembly which he regarded with profound reverence. He would willingly give bond for his good behaviour to the amount of twenty thousand pounds sterling. But he was in communication with the government now established in England. He was in hourly expectation of important despatches from that government; and, till they arrived, he should not feel himself justified in resigning his command. These excuses were not admitted. Heralds and trumpeters were sent to summon the Castle in form, and to denounce the penalties of high treason against those who should continue to occupy that fortress in defiance of the authority of the Estates. Guards were at the same time posted to intercept all communication between the garrison and the city.[2]

Two days had been spent in these preludes; and it was expected that on the third morning the great contest would begin. Meanwhile Dundee the population of Edinburgh was in an excited state. It had threatened been discovered that Dundee had paid visits to the castle; by the Covenanters and it was believed that his exhortations had induced the garrison to hold out. His own soldiers were known to be gathering round him; and it might well be apprehended that he would make some

[1] Balcarras's Memoirs; History of the late Revolution in Scotland, 1690.

[2] Act. Parl. Scot., March 14. and 15. 1689; Balcarras's Memoirs; London Gaz. March 25; History of the late Revolution in Scotland, 1690; Account of the Proceedings of the Estates of Scotland, 1689.

desperate attempt. He, on the other hand, had been informed that the Western Covenanters who filled the cellars of the city had vowed vengeance on him : and, in truth, when we consider that their temper was singularly savage and implacable, that they had been taught to regard the slaying of a persecutor as a duty, that no examples furnished by Holy Writ had been more frequently held up to their admiration than Ehud stabbing Eglon and Samuel hewing Agag limb from limb, that they had never heard any achievement in the history of their own country more warmly praised by their favourite teachers than the butchery of Cardinal Beatoun and of Archbishop Sharpe, we may well wonder that a man who had shed the blood of the saints like water should have been able to walk the High Street in safety during a single day. The enemy whom Dundee had most reason to fear was a youth of distinguished courage and abilities named William Cleland. Cleland had, when little more than sixteen years old, borne arms in that insurrection which had been put down at Bothwell Bridge. He had since disgusted some virulent fanatics by his humanity and moderation. But with the great body of Presbyterians his name stood high. For with the strict morality and ardent zeal of a Puritan he united some accomplishments of which few Puritans could boast. His manners were polished, and his literary and scientific attainments respectable. He was a linguist, a mathematician, and a poet. It is true that his hymns, odes, ballads, and Hudibrastic satires are of very little intrinsic value ; but, when it is considered that he was a mere boy when most of them were written, it must be admitted that they show considerable vigour of mind. He was now at Edinburgh : his influence among the West Country Whigs assembled there was great : he hated Dundee with deadly hatred, and was believed to be meditating some act of violence.[1]

On the fifteenth of March Dundee received information that some of the Covenanters had bound themselves together to slay him and Sir

[1] See Cleland's Poems, and the commendatory poems contained in the same volume, Edinburgh, 1697. It has been repeatedly asserted that this William Cleland was the father of William Cleland, the Commissioner of Taxes, who was well known twenty years later in the literary society of London, who rendered some not very reputable services to Pope, and whose son John was the author of an infamous book but too widely celebrated. This is an entire mistake. William Cleland, who fought at Bothwell Bridge, was not twenty eight when he was killed in August 1689 ; and William Cleland, the Commissioner of Taxes, died at sixty seven in September 1741. The former therefore cannot have been the father of the latter. See the Exact Narrative of the battle of Dunkeld ; the Gentleman's Magazine for 1740 ; and Warburton's note on the Letter to the Publisher of the Dunciad, a letter signed W. Cleland, but really written by Pope. In a paper drawn up by Sir Robert Hamilton, the oracle of the extreme Covenanters, and a bloodthirsty ruffian, Cleland is mentioned as having been once leagued with those fanatics, but afterwards a great opposer of their testimony. Cleland probably did not agree with Hamilton in thinking it a sacred duty to cut the throats of prisoners of war who had been received to quarter. See Hamilton's Letter to the Societies, Dec. 7. 1685.

George Mackenzie, whose eloquence and learning, long prostituted to the service of tyranny, had made him more odious to the Presbyterians than any other man of the gown. Dundee applied to Hamilton for protection; and Hamilton advised him to bring the matter under the consideration of the Convention at the next sitting.[1]

Before that sitting, a person named Crane arrived from France, with a letter addressed by the fugitive King to the Estates. The letter was sealed: the bearer, strange to say, was not furnished with a copy for the information of the heads of the Jacobite party; nor did he bring any message, written or verbal, to either of James's agents. Balcarras and Dundee were mortified by finding that so little confidence was reposed in them, and were harassed by painful doubts touching the contents of the document on which so much depended. They were willing, however, to hope for the best. King James could not, situated as he was, be so ill advised as to act in direct opposition to the counsel and entreaties of his friends. His letter, when opened, must be found to contain such gracious assurances as would animate the royalists and conciliate the moderate Whigs. His adherents, therefore, determined that it should be produced.

Letter from James to the Convention

When the Convention reassembled on the morning of Saturday the sixteenth of March, it was proposed that measures should be taken for the personal security of the members. It was alleged that the life of Dundee had been threatened; that two men of sinister appearance had been watching the house where he lodged, and had been heard to say that they would use the dog as he had used them. Mackenzie complained that he too was in danger, and, with his usual copiousness and force of language, demanded the protection of the Estates. But the matter was lightly treated by the majority: and the Convention passed on to other business.[2]

It was then announced that Crane was at the door of the Parliament House. He was admitted. The paper of which he was in charge was laid on the table. Hamilton remarked that there was, in the hands of the Earl of Leven, a communication from the Prince by whose authority the Estates had been convoked. That communication seemed to be entitled to precedence. The Convention was of the same opinion; and the well weighed and prudent letter of William was read.

It was then moved that the letter of James should be opened. The Whigs objected that it might possibly contain a mandate dissolving the

---

[1] Balcarras's Memoirs.

[2] Balcarras's Memoirs. But the fullest account of these proceedings is furnished by some manuscript notes which are in the library of the Faculty of Advocates. Balcarras's dates are not quite exact. He probably trusted to his memory for them. I have corrected them from the parliamentary records.

Convention.   They therefore proposed that, before the seal was broken, the Estates should resolve to continue sitting, notwithstanding any such mandate.   The Jacobites, who knew no more than the Whigs what was in the letter, and were impatient to have it read, eagerly assented.   A vote was passed by which the members bound themselves to consider any order which should command them to separate as a nullity, and to remain assembled till they should have accomplished the work of securing the liberty and religion of Scotland.   This vote was signed by almost all the lords and gentlemen who were present.   Seven out of nine bishops subscribed it.   The names of Dundee and Balcarras, written by their own hands, may still be seen on the original roll. Balcarras afterwards excused what, on his principles, was, beyond all dispute, a flagrant act of treason, by saying that he and his friends had, from zeal for their master's interest, concurred in a declaration of rebellion against their master's authority ; that they had anticipated the most salutary effects from the letter ; and that, if they had not made some concession to the majority, the letter would not have been opened.

In a few minutes the hopes of Balcarras were grievously disappointed.   The letter from which so much had been hoped and feared was read with all the honours which Scottish Parliaments were in the habit of paying to royal communications : but every word carried despair to the hearts of the Jacobites.   It was plain that adversity had taught James neither wisdom nor mercy. All was obstinacy, cruelty, insolence.   A pardon was promised to those traitors who should return to their allegiance within a fortnight. Against all others unsparing vengeance was denounced.   Not only was no sorrow expressed for past offences : but the letter was itself a new offence : for it was written and countersigned by the apostate Melfort, who was, by the statutes of the realm, incapable of holding the office of Secretary, and who was not less abhorred by the Protestant Tories than by the Whigs.   The hall was in a tumult.   The enemies of James were loud and vehement.   His friends, angry with him, and ashamed of him, saw that it was vain to think of continuing the struggle in the Convention.   Every vote which had been doubtful when his letter was unsealed was now irrecoverably lost.   The sitting closed in great agitation.[1]

It was Saturday afternoon.   There was to be no other meeting till Monday morning.   The Jacobite leaders held a consultation, and came to the conclusion that it was necessary to take a decided step.   Dundee and Balcarras must use the powers with which they had been entrusted. The minority must forthwith leave Edinburgh and assemble at Stirling.

Effect of James's letter

[1]Act. Parl. Scot., March 16. 168⅚ ; Balcarras's Memoirs ; History of the late Revolution in Scotland, 1690 ; Account of the Proceedings of the Estates of Scotland, 1689 ; London Gaz., March 25. 1689 ; Life of James, ii. 342.   Burnet blunders strangely about these transactions.

Athol assented, and undertook to bring a great body of his clansmen from the Highlands to protect the deliberations of the Royalist Convention. Everything was arranged for the secession; but, in a few hours, the tardiness of one man and the haste of another ruined the whole plan.

The Monday came. The Jacobite lords and gentlemen were actually taking horse for Stirling, when Athol asked for a delay of twenty four hours. He had no personal reason to be in haste. By staying he ran no risk of being assassinated. By going he incurred the risks inseparable from civil war. The members of his party, unwilling to separate from him, consented to the postponement which he requested, and repaired once more to the Parliament House. Dundee alone refused to stay a moment longer. His life was in danger. The Convention had refused to protect him. He would not remain to be a mark for the pistols and daggers of murderers. Balcarras expostulated to no purpose. " By departing alone," he said, " you will give the alarm and break up the whole scheme." But Dundee was obstinate. Brave as he undoubtedly was, he seems, like many other brave men, to have been less proof against the danger of assassination than against any other form of danger. He knew what the hatred of the Covenanters was : he knew how well he had earned their hatred ; and he was haunted by that consciousness of inexpiable guilt, and by that dread of a terrible retribution, which the ancient polytheists personified under the awful name of the Furies. His old troopers, the Satans and Beelzebubs who had shared his crimes, and who now shared his perils, were ready to be the companions of his flight.

Flight of Dundee

Meanwhile the Convention had assembled. Mackenzie was on his legs, and was pathetically lamenting the hard condition of the Estates, at once commanded by the guns of a fortress and menaced by a fanatical rabble, when he was interrupted by some sentinels who came running from the posts near the Castle. They had seen Dundee at the head of fifty horse on the Stirling road. That road ran close under the huge rock on which the citadel is built. Gordon had appeared on the ramparts, and had made a sign that he had something to say. Dundee had climbed high enough to hear and to be heard, and was then actually conferring with the Duke. Up to that moment the hatred with which the Presbyterian members of the assembly regarded the merciless persecutor of their brethren in the faith had been restrained by the decorous forms of parliamentary deliberation. But now the explosion was terrible. Hamilton himself, who, by the acknowledgment of his opponents, had hitherto performed the duties of President with gravity and impartiality, was the loudest and fiercest man in the hall. " It is high time," he cried, " that we should look to ourselves. The enemies of our religion and of our civil freedom are

Tumultuous sitting of the Convention

The Prospect of their Maties Castle of Sterling. ARCIS REGIÆ STERLINENSIS PROSPECTUS.

STIRLING CASTLE

From Slezer's Theatrum Scotiae, 1693

mustering all around us ; and we may well suspect that they have accomplices even here.   Lock the doors.   Lay the keys on the table. Let nobody go out but those lords and gentlemen whom we shall appoint to call the citizens to arms.   There are some good men from the West in Edinburgh, men for whom I can answer."   The assembly raised a general cry of assent.   Several members of the majority boasted that they too had brought with them trusty retainers who would turn out at a moment's notice against Claverhouse and his dragoons.   All that Hamilton proposed was instantly done.   The Jacobites, silent and unresisting, became prisoners.   Leven went forth and ordered the drums to beat.   The Covenanters of Lanarkshire and Ayrshire promptly obeyed the signal.   The force thus assembled had indeed no very military appearance, but was amply sufficient to overawe the adherents of the House of Stuart.   From Dundee nothing was to be hoped or feared.   He had already scrambled down the Castle hill, rejoined his troopers, and galloped westward.   Hamilton now ordered the doors to be opened.   The suspected members were at liberty to depart.   Humbled and brokenspirited, yet glad that they had come off so well, they stole forth through the crowd of stern fanatics which filled the High Street. All thought of secession was at an end.[1]

On the following day it was resolved that the kingdom should be put into a posture of defence.   The preamble of this resolution contained a severe reflection on the perfidy of the traitor who, within a few hours after he had, by an engagement subscribed with his own hand, bound himself not to quit his post in the Convention, had set the example of desertion, and given the signal of civil war.   All Protestants, from sixteen to sixty, were ordered to hold themselves in readiness to assemble in arms at the first summons ; and, that none might pretend ignorance, it was directed that the edict should be proclaimed at all the market crosses throughout the realm.[2]

The Estates then proceeded to send a letter of thanks to William. To this letter were attached the signatures of many noblemen and gentlemen who were in the interest of the banished King.   The Bishops however unanimously refused to subscribe their names.

It had long been the custom of the Parliaments of Scotland to entrust the preparation of Acts to a select number of members who A Committee appointed to frame a plan of government were designated as the Lords of Articles.   In conformity with this usage, the business of framing a plan for the settling of the government was now confided to a Committee of twenty four.   Of the twenty four eight were peers, eight representatives of counties, and eight representatives of towns.   The

[1] Balcarras's Memoirs ; MS. in the Library of the Faculty of Advocates.
[2] Act. Parl. Scot., March 19. 168⅝ ; History of the late Revolution in Scotland, 1690.

Prospectus Orientalis EDINBURGENA prope DEANdicto. The Prospect of EDINBURGH from ye DEAN ...

EDINBURGH, FROM THE NORTH-WEST

From Slezer's Theatrum Scotiae, 1693

majority of the Committee were Whigs; and not a single prelate had a seat.

The spirit of the Jacobites, broken by a succession of disasters, was, about this time, for a moment revived by the arrival of the Duke of Queensberry from London. His rank was high: his influence was great: his character, by comparison with the characters of those who surrounded him, was fair. When Popery was in the ascendent, he had been true to the cause of the Protestant Church; and, since Whiggism had been in the ascendent, he had been true to the cause of hereditary monarchy. Some thought that, if he had been earlier in his place, he might have been able to render important service to the House of Stuart.[1] Even now the stimulants which he applied to his torpid and feeble party produced some faint symptoms of returning animation. Means were found of communicating with Gordon; and he was earnestly solicited to fire on the city. The Jacobites hoped that, as soon as the cannon balls had beaten down a few chimneys, the Estates would adjourn to Glasgow. Time would thus be gained; and the royalists might be able to execute their old project of meeting in a separate convention. Gordon however positively refused to take on himself so grave a responsibility on no better warrant than the request of a small cabal.[2]

By this time the Estates had a guard on which they could rely more firmly than on the undisciplined and turbulent Covenanters of the West. A squadron of English men of war from the Thames had arrived in the Frith of Forth. On board were the three Scottish regiments which had accompanied William from Holland. He had, with great judgment, selected them to protect the assembly which was to settle the government of their country; and, that no cause of jealousy might be given to a people exquisitely sensitive on points of national honour, he had purged the ranks of all Dutch soldiers, and had thus reduced the number of men to about eleven hundred. This little force was commanded by Hugh Mackay, a Highlander of noble descent, who had long served on the Continent, and who was distinguished by courage of the truest temper, and by a piety such as is seldom found in soldiers of fortune. The Convention passed a resolution appointing Mackay general of their forces. When the question was put on this resolution, the Archbishop of Glasgow, unwilling doubtless to be a party to such an usurpation of powers which belonged to the King alone, begged that the prelates might be excused from voting. Divines, he said, had nothing to do with military arrangements. "The Fathers of the Church," answered a member very keenly, "have been lately favoured with a new light. I have myself seen military orders signed by the

[1] Balcarras.   [2] Ibid.

Most Reverend person who has suddenly become so scrupulous. There was indeed one difference: those orders were for dragooning Protestants; and the resolution before us is meant to protect us from Papists." [1]

MAJOR GENERAL HUGH MACKAY

From an engraving of the portrait in the possession of Lord Reay, prefixed to Mackay's Memoirs

The arrival of Mackay's troops, and the determination of Gordon to remain inactive, quelled the spirit of the Jacobites. They had indeed

[1] Act. Parl. Scot. ; History of the late Revolution, 1690 ; Memoirs of North Britain, 1715.

one chance left.   They might possibly, by joining with those Whigs who were bent on an union with England, have postponed during a considerable time the settlement of the government.   A negotiation was actually opened with this view, but was speedily broken off.   For it soon appeared that the party which was for James was really hostile to the union, and that the party which was for the union was really hostile to James.   As these two parties had no object in common, the only effect of a coalition between them must have been that one of them would have become the tool of the other.   The question of the union therefore was not raised.[1]   Some Jacobites retired to their country seats: others, though they remained at Edinburgh, ceased to show themselves in the Parliament House : many passed over to the winning side ; and, when at length the resolutions prepared by the Twenty Four were submitted to the Convention, it appeared that the great body which on the first day of the session had rallied round Athol had dwindled away to nothing.

The resolutions had been framed, as far as possible, in conformity with the example recently set at Westminster.   In one important point, Resolutions however, it was absolutely necessary that the copy should proposed by deviate from the original.   The Estates of England had the Com-
mittee   brought two charges against James, his misgovernment and his flight, and had, by using the soft word " Abdication," evaded, with some sacrifice of verbal precision, the question whether subjects may lawfully depose a bad prince.   That question the Estates of Scotland could not evade.   They could not pretend that James had deserted his post.   For he had never, since he came to the throne, resided in Scotland.   During many years that kingdom had been ruled by sovereigns who dwelt in another land.   The whole machinery of the administration had been constructed on the supposition that the King would be absent, and was therefore not necessarily deranged by that flight which had, in the south of the island, dissolved all government, and suspended the ordinary course of justice.   It was only by letter that the King could, when he was at Whitehall, communicate with the Council and the Parliament at Edinburgh ; and by letter he could communicate with them when he was at Saint Germains or at Dublin. The Twenty Four were therefore forced to propose to the Estates a resolution distinctly declaring that James the Seventh had by his mis-conduct forfeited the crown.   Many writers have inferred from the language of this resolution that sound political principles had made a greater progress in Scotland than in England.   But the whole history of the two countries from the Restoration to the Union proves this inference to be erroneous.   The Scottish Estates used plain language,

[1] Balcarras.

simply because it was impossible for them, situated as they were, to use evasive language.

The person who bore the chief part in framing the resolution, and in defending it, was Sir John Dalrymple, who had recently held the high office of Lord Advocate, and had been an accomplice in some of

A Prospect of yͤ Mercat Crosse of Edinͬ. 1750.

THE CITY CROSS, EDINBURGH, IN 1750

From an engraving

the misdeeds which he now arraigned with great force of reasoning and eloquence. He was strenuously supported by Sir James Montgomery, member for Ayrshire, a man of considerable abilities, but of loose principles, turbulent temper, insatiable cupidity, and implacable malevolence. The Archbishop of Glasgow and Sir George Mackenzie spoke on the other side : but the only effect of their oratory was to deprive their party of the advantage of being able to allege that the Estates were under duress, and that liberty of speech had been denied to the defenders of hereditary monarchy.

When the question was put, Athol, Queensberry, and some of their friends withdrew. Only five members voted against the resolution which pronounced that James had forfeited his right to the allegiance of his subjects. When it was moved that the Crown of Scotland should be settled as the Crown of England had been settled, Athol and Queensberry reappeared in the hall. They had doubted, they said, whether they could justifiably declare the throne vacant. But, since it had been declared vacant, they felt no doubt that William and Mary were the persons who ought to fill it.

The Convention then went forth in procession to the High Street. Several great nobles, attended by the Lord Provost of the capital and **William and Mary proclaimed** by the heralds, ascended the octagon tower from which rose the city cross surmounted by the unicorn of Scotland.[1] Hamilton read the vote of the Convention ; and a King at Arms proclaimed the new Sovereigns with sound of trumpet. On the same day the Estates issued an order that the parochial clergy should, on pain of deprivation, publish from their pulpits the proclamation which had just been read at the city cross, and should pray for King William and Queen Mary.

Still the interregnum was not at an end. Though the new Sovereigns had been proclaimed, they had not yet been put into **The Claim of Right** possession of the royal authority by a formal tender and a formal acceptance. At Edinburgh, as at Westminster, it was thought necessary that the instrument which settled the government should clearly define and solemnly assert those privileges of the people which the Stuarts had illegally infringed. A Claim of Right was therefore drawn up by the Twenty Four, and adopted by the Convention. To this Claim, which purported to be merely declaratory of the law as it stood, was added a supplementary paper containing a list of grievances which could be remedied only by new laws. One most important **Abolition of Episcopacy** article which we should naturally expect to find at the head of such a list, the Convention, with great practical prudence, but in defiance of notorious facts and of unanswerable arguments, placed in the Claim of Right. Nobody could deny that prelacy was established by Act of Parliament. The power exercised by the Bishops might be pernicious, unscriptural, antichristian : but illegal it certainly was not ; and to pronounce it illegal was to outrage common sense. The Whig leaders however were much more desirous to get rid of episcopacy than to prove themselves consummate publicists and logicians.

---

[1] Every reader will remember the malediction which Sir Walter Scott, in the Fifth Canto of Marmion, pronounced on the dunces who removed this interesting monument.

If they made the abolition of episcopacy an article of the contract by which William was to hold the crown, they attained their end, though doubtless in a manner open to much criticism. If, on the other hand, they contented themselves with resolving that episcopacy was a noxious institution which at some future time the legislature would do well to abolish, they might find that their resolution, though unobjectionable in form, was barren of consequences. They knew that William by no means sympathised with their dislike of Bishops, and that, even had he been much more zealous for the Calvinistic model than he was, the relation in which he stood to the Anglican Church would make it difficult and dangerous for him to declare himself hostile to a fundamental part of the constitution of that Church. If he should become King of Scotland without being fettered by any pledge on this subject, it might well be apprehended that he would hesitate about passing an Act which would be regarded with abhorrence by a large body of his subjects in the south of the island. It was therefore most desirable that the question should be settled while the throne was still vacant. In this opinion many politicians concurred, who had no dislike to rochets and mitres, but who wished that William might have a quiet and prosperous reign. The Scottish people,—so these men reasoned,—hated episcopacy. The English loved it. To leave William any voice in the matter was to put him under the necessity of deeply wounding the strongest feelings of one of the nations which he governed. It was therefore plainly for his own interest that the question, which he could not settle in any manner without incurring a fearful amount of obloquy, should be settled for him by others who were exposed to no such danger. He was not yet Sovereign of Scotland. While the interregnum lasted, the supreme power belonged to the Estates; and for what the Estates might do the prelatists of his southern kingdom could not hold him responsible. The elder Dalrymple wrote strongly from London to this effect; and there can be little doubt that he expressed the sentiments of his master. William would have sincerely rejoiced if the Scots could have been reconciled to a modified episcopacy. But, since that could not be, it was manifestly desirable that they should themselves, while there was yet no King over them, pronounce the irrevocable doom of the institution which they abhorred.[1]

The Convention, therefore, with little debate as it should seem, inserted in the Claim of Right a clause declaring that prelacy was an insupportable burden to the kingdom, that it had been long odious to the body of the people, and that it ought to be abolished.

---

[1] " It will be neither secuir nor kynd to the King to expect it be (by) Act of Parliament after the setlement, which will lay it at his door."—Dalrymple to Melville, 5 April, 1689; Leven and Melville Papers.

Nothing in the proceedings at Edinburgh astonishes an Englishman more than the manner in which the Estates dealt with the practice of torture. In England torture had always been illegal. In the most servile times the judges had unanimously pronounced it so. Those rulers who had occasionally resorted to it had, as far as was possible, used it in secret, had never pretended that they had acted in conformity with either statute law or common law, and had excused themselves by saying that the extraordinary peril to which the state was exposed had forced them to take on themselves the responsibility of employing extraordinary means of defence. It had therefore never been thought necessary by any English Parliament to pass any Act or resolution touching this matter. The torture was not mentioned in the Petition of Right, or in any of the statutes framed by the Long Parliament. No member of the Convention of 1689 dreamed of proposing that the instrument which called the Prince and Princess of Orange to the throne should contain a declaration against the using of racks and thumb-screws for the purpose of forcing prisoners to accuse themselves. Such a declaration would have been justly regarded as weakening rather than strengthening a rule which, as far back as the days of the Plantagenets, had been proudly declared by the most illustrious sages of Westminster Hall to be a distinguishing feature of the English jurisprudence.[1] In the Scottish Claim of Right, the use of torture, without evidence, or in ordinary cases, was declared to be contrary to law. The use of torture, therefore, where there was strong evidence, and where the crime was extraordinary, was, by the plainest implication, declared to be according to law; nor did the Estates mention the use of torture among the grievances which required a legislative remedy. In truth, they could not condemn the use of torture without condemning themselves. It had chanced that, while they were employed in settling the government, the eloquent and learned Lord President Lockhart had been foully murdered in a public street through which he was returning from church on a Sunday. The murderer was seized, and proved to be a wretch who, having treated his wife barbarously and turned her out of doors, had been compelled by a decree of the Court of Session to provide for her. A savage hatred of the Judges by whom she had been protected had taken possession of his mind, and had goaded him to a horrible crime and a horrible fate. It was natural that an assassination attended by so many circumstances of aggravation should move the indignation of the members of the Convention. Yet they should have considered the gravity of the conjuncture and the importance of their own mission. They unfortunately, in the heat of passion, directed the magistrates of Edinburgh to strike the prisoner in

Torture

---

[1] There is a striking passage on this subject in Fortescue.

the boots, and named a Committee to superintend the operation. But for this unhappy event, it is probable that the law of Scotland con-

LORD PRESIDENT SIR GEORGE LOCKHART

From the Scottish National Portrait Gallery. Artist unknown

cerning torture would have been immediately assimilated to the law of England.[1]

[1] Act. Parl. Scot., April 1. 1689; Orders of Committee of Estates, May 16. 1689; London Gazette, April 11.

Having settled the Claim of Right, the Convention proceeded to revise the Coronation oath. When this had been done, three members were appointed to carry the Instrument of Government to London. Argyle, though not, in strictness of law, a Peer, was chosen to represent the Peers: Sir James Montgomery represented the Commissioners of Shires, and Sir John Dalrymple the Commissioners of Towns.

The Estates then adjourned for a few weeks, having first passed a vote which empowered Hamilton to take such measures as might be necessary for the preservation of the public peace till the end of the interregnum.

The ceremony of the inauguration was distinguished from ordinary pageants by some highly interesting circumstances. On the eleventh of May the three Commissioners came to the Council Chamber at Whitehall, and thence, attended by almost all the Scotchmen of note who were then in London, proceeded to the Banqueting House. There William and Mary appeared seated under a canopy. A splendid circle of English nobles and statesmen stood round the throne: but the sword of state was committed to a Scotch lord; and the oath of office was administered after the Scotch fashion. Argyle recited the words slowly. The royal pair, holding up their hands towards heaven, repeated after him till they came to the last clause. There William paused. That clause contained a promise that he would root out all heretics and all enemies of the true worship of God; and it was notorious that, in the opinion of many Scotchmen, not only all Roman Catholics, but all Protestant Episcopalians, all Independents, Baptists, and Quakers, all Lutherans, nay all British Presbyterians who did not hold themselves bound by the Solemn League and Covenant, were enemies of the true worship of God.[1] The King had apprised the Commissioners that he could not take this part of the oath without a distinct and public explanation; and they had

William and Mary accept the Crown of Scotland

---

[1] As it has lately been denied that the extreme Presbyterians entertained an unfavourable opinion of the Lutherans, I will give two decisive proofs of the truth of what I have asserted in the text. In the book entitled Faithful Contendings Displayed is a report of what passed at the General Meeting of the United Societies of Covenanters on the 24th of October 1688. The question was propounded whether there should be an association with the Dutch. "It was concluded unanimously," says the Clerk of the Societies, "that we could not have an association with the Dutch in one body, nor come formally under their conduct, being such a promiscuous conjunction of reformed Lutheran malignants and sectaries, to join with whom were repugnant to the testimony of the Church of Scotland." In the Protestation and Testimony drawn up on the 2nd of October 1707, the United Societies complain that the crown has been settled on "the Prince of Hanover, who has been bred and brought up in the Lutheran religion, which is not only different from, but even in many things contrary unto that purity in doctrine, reformation, and religion, we in these nations had attained unto, as is very well known." They add: "The admitting such a person to reign over us is not only contrary to our Solemn League and Covenant, but to the very Word of God itself, Deut. xvii."

been authorised by the Convention to give such an explanation as would satisfy him. "I will not," he now said, "lay myself under any obligation to be a persecutor." "Neither the words of this oath," said one of the Commissioners, "nor the laws of Scotland, lay any such obligation on Your Majesty." "In that sense, then, I swear," said William; "and I desire you all, my lords and gentlemen, to witness that I do so." Even his detractors have generally admitted that on this great occasion he acted with uprightness, dignity, and wisdom.[1]

As King of Scotland, he soon found himself embarrassed at every step by all the difficulties which had embarrassed him as King of England, and by other difficulties which in England were **Discontent** happily unknown. In the north of the island, no class was **of the Cove-** more dissatisfied with the Revolution than the class which **nanters** owed most to the Revolution. The manner in which the Convention had decided the question of ecclesiastical polity had not been more offensive to the Bishops themselves than to those fiery Covenanters who had long, in defiance of sword and carbine, boot and gibbet, worshipped their Maker after their own fashion in caverns and on mountain tops. Was there ever, these zealots exclaimed, such a halting between two opinions, such a compromise between the Lord and Baal? The Estates ought to have said that episcopacy was an abomination in God's sight, and that, in obedience to his word, and from fear of his righteous judgment, they were determined to deal with this great national sin and scandal after the fashion of those saintly rulers who of old cut down the groves and demolished the altars of Chemosh and Astarte. Unhappily, Scotland was ruled, not by pious Josiahs, but by careless Gallios. The antichristian hierarchy was to be abolished, not because it was an insult to heaven, but because it was felt as a burden on earth; not because it was hateful to the great Head of the Church, but because it was hateful to the people. Was public opinion, then, the test of right and wrong in religion? Was not the order which Christ had established in his own house to be held equally sacred in all countries and through all ages? And was there no reason for following that order in Scotland, except a reason which might be urged with equal force for maintaining Prelacy in England, Popery in Spain, and Mahometanism in Turkey? Why, too, was nothing said of those Covenants which the nation had so generally subscribed and so generally violated? Why was it not distinctly affirmed that the promises set down in those rolls were still binding, and would to the end of time be binding, on the kingdom? Were these truths to be suppressed from regard for the feelings and

---

[1] History of the late Revolution in Scotland; London Gazette, May 16. 1689. The official account of what passed was evidently drawn up with great care. See also the Royal Diary, 1702. The writer of this work professes to have derived his information from a divine who was present.

interests of a prince who was all things to all men, an ally of the idolatrous Spaniard and of the Lutheran Dane, a presbyterian at the Hague and a prelatist at Whitehall?　He, like Jehu in ancient times, had doubtless so far done well that he had been the scourge of the idolatrous House of Ahab.　But he, like Jehu, had not taken heed to walk in the divine law with his whole heart, but had tolerated and practised impieties differing only in degree from those of which he had declared himself the enemy.　It would have better become godly senators to remonstrate with him on the sin which he was committing by conforming to the Anglican ritual, and by maintaining the Anglican Church government, than to flatter him by using a phraseology which seemed to indicate that they were as deeply tainted with Erastianism as himself.　Many of those who held this language refused to do any act which could be construed into a recognition of the new Sovereigns, and would rather have been fired upon by files of musketeers, or tied to stakes within low water mark, than have uttered a prayer that God would bless William and Mary.

Yet the King had less to fear from the pertinacious adherence of these men to their absurd principles than from the ambition and avarice **Ministerial arrangements in Scotland** of another set of men who had no principles at all.　It was necessary that he should immediately name ministers to conduct the government of Scotland; and, name whom he might, he could not fail to disappoint and irritate a multitude of expectants.　Scotland was one of the least wealthy countries in Europe: yet no country in Europe contained a greater number of clever and selfish politicians.　The places in the gift of the Crown were not enough to satisfy one twentieth part of the placehunters, every one of whom thought that his own services had been preeminent, and that, whoever might be passed by, he ought to be remembered.　William did his best to satisfy these innumerable and insatiable claimants by putting many offices into commission.　There were however a few great posts which **Hamilton** it was impossible to divide.　Hamilton was declared Lord High Commissioner, in the hope that immense pecuniary allowances, a residence in Holyrood Palace, and a pomp and dignity little less than regal, would content him.　The Earl of Crawford **Crawford** was appointed President of the Parliament; and it was supposed that this appointment would conciliate the rigid Presbyterians: for Crawford was what they called a professor.　His letters and speeches are, to use his own phraseology, exceeding savoury.　Alone, or almost alone, among the prominent politicians of that time, he retained the style which had been fashionable in the preceding generation.　He had a text from the Pentateuch or the Prophets ready for every occasion. He filled his despatches with allusions to Ishmael and Hagar, Hannah

and Eli, Elijah, Nehemiah, and Zerubbabel, and adorned his oratory
with quotations from Ezra and Haggai.   It is a circumstance strikingly
characteristic of the man, and of the school in which he had been trained,
that, in all the mass of his writing which has come down to us, there is
not a single word indicating that he had ever in his life heard of the
New Testament.   Even in our own time some persons of a peculiar
taste have been so much delighted by the rich unction of his eloquence,
that they have confidently pronounced him a saint.   To those whose
habit is to judge of a man rather by his actions than by his words,
Crawford will appear to have been a selfish, cruel, politician, who was
not at all the dupe of his own cant, and whose zeal against episcopal
government was not a little whetted by his desire to obtain a grant of
Episcopal domains.   In excuse for his greediness, it ought to be said
that he was the poorest noble of a poor nobility, and that before the
Revolution he was sometimes at a loss for a meal and a suit of clothes.[1]

The ablest of Scottish politicians and debaters, Sir John Dalrymple,
was appointed Lord Advocate.   His father, Sir James, the The Dal-
greatest of Scottish jurists, was placed at the head of the rymples
Court of Session.   Sir William Lockhart, a man whose letters Lockhart
prove him to have possessed considerable ability, became Solicitor
General.

Sir James Montgomery had flattered himself that he should be the
chief minister.   He had distinguished himself highly in the Convention.
He had been one of the Commissioners who had tendered Mont-
the Crown and administered the oath to the new Sovereigns. gomery
In parliamentary ability and eloquence he had no superior among his
countrymen, except the new Lord Advocate.   The Secretaryship was,
not indeed in dignity, but in real power, the highest office in the Scottish government ; and this office was the reward to which Montgomery
thought himself entitled.   But the Episcopalians and the moderate
Presbyterians dreaded him as a man of extreme opinions and of bitter
spirit.   He had been a chief of the Covenanters : he had been prosecuted at one time for holding conventicles, and at another time for

[1] See Crawford's Letters and Speeches, *passim*. His style of begging for a place was peculiar.
After owning, not without reason, that his heart was deceitful and desperately wicked, he
proceeded thus : " The same Omnipotent Being who hath said, when the poor and needy seek
water and there is none, and their tongue faileth for thirst, he will not forsake them, notwithstanding of my present low condition, can build me a house if He think fit."—Letter to Melville,
of May 28. 1689. As to Crawford's poverty and his passion for Bishops' lands, see his letter to
Melville of the 4th of December 1690. As to his humanity, see his letter to Melville, Dec. 11.
1690. All these letters are among the Leven and Melville Papers. The author of An Account
of the Late Establishment of Presbyterian Government says of a person who had taken a bribe of
ten or twelve pounds, " Had he been as poor as my Lord Crawford, perhaps he had been the
more excusable." See also the dedication of the celebrated tract entitled Scotch Presbyterian
Eloquence Displayed.

harbouring rebels : he had been fined : he had been imprisoned : he had been almost driven to take refuge from his enemies beyond the Atlantic in the infant settlement of New Jersey.   It was apprehended that, if he were now armed with the whole power of the Crown, he would exact a terrible retribution for what he had suffered.[1]   William therefore pre-

Melville   ferred Melville, who, though not a man of eminent talents, was regarded by the Presbyterians as a thoroughgoing friend, and yet not regarded by the Episcopalians as an implacable enemy. Melville fixed his residence at the English Court, and became the regular organ of communication between Kensington and the authorities at Edinburgh.

William had, however, one Scottish adviser who deserved and possessed more influence than any of the ostensible ministers.   This

Carstairs   was Carstairs, one of the most remarkable men of that age. He united great scholastic attainments with great aptitude for civil business, and the firm faith and ardent zeal of a martyr with the shrewdness and suppleness of a consummate politician.   In courage and fidelity he resembled Burnet ; but he had, what Burnet wanted, judgment, selfcommand, and a singular power of keeping secrets.   There was no post to which he might not have aspired if he had been a layman, or a priest of the Church of England.   But a Presbyterian clergyman could not hope to attain any high dignity either in the north or in the south of the island.   Carstairs was forced to content himself with the substance of power, and to leave the semblance to others.   He was named Chaplain to Their Majesties for Scotland : but wherever the King was, in England, in Ireland, in the Netherlands, there was this most trusty and most prudent of courtiers.   He obtained from the royal bounty a modest competence ; and he desired no more.   But it was well known that he could be as useful a friend and as formidable an enemy as any member of the cabinet ; and he was designated at the public offices and in the antechambers of the palace by the significant nickname of the Cardinal.[2]

To Montgomery was offered the place of Lord Justice Clerk.   But that place, though high and honourable, he thought below his merits and his capacity ; and he returned from London to Scotland with a heart ulcerated by hatred of his ungrateful master and of his successful rivals.

---

[1] Burnet, ii. 23, 24. ; Fountainhall Papers, 13. Aug. 1684, 14. and 15. Oct. 1684, 3. May 1685 ; Montgomery to Melville, June 23. 1689, in the Leven and Melville Papers ; Pretences of the French Invasion Examined, licensed May 25. 1692.

[2] See the life and correspondence of Carstairs, and the interesting memorials of him in the Caldwell Papers, printed in 1854. See also Mackay's character of him, and Swift's note. Swift's word is not to be taken against a Scotchman and a Presbyterian. I believe, however, that Carstairs, though an honest and pious man in essentials, had his full share of the wisdom of the serpent.

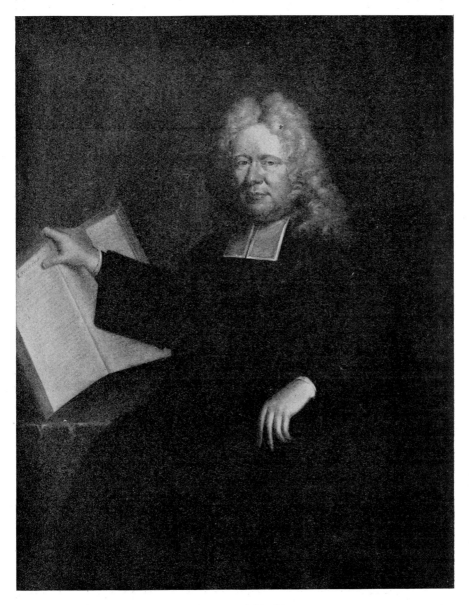

WILLIAM CARSTAIRS

From the portrait by William Aikman, in the possession of the University of Edinburgh

At Edinburgh a knot of Whigs, as severely disappointed as himself
by the new arrangements, readily submitted to the guidance of so bold
The Club and able a leader.   Under his direction these men, among
formed : whom the Earl of Annandale and Lord Ross were the most
Annandale ;
Ross conspicuous, formed themselves into a society called the Club,
appointed a clerk, and met daily at a tavern to concert plans of opposition.   Round this nucleus soon gathered a great body of greedy and
angry politicians.[1]   With these dishonest malecontents, whose object
was merely to annoy the government and to get places, were leagued
other malecontents, who, in the course of a long resistance to tyranny,
had become so perverse and irritable that they were unable to live con-
tentedly even under the mildest and most constitutional rule.   Such a
Hume man was Sir Patrick Hume.   He had returned from exile, as
litigious, as impracticable, as morbidly jealous of all superior
authority, and as fond of haranguing, as he had been four years before,
and was as much bent on making a merely nominal sovereign of William
as he had formerly been bent on making a merely nominal general of
Argyle.[2]   A man far superior morally and intellectually to Hume,
Fletcher of Fletcher of Saltoun, belonged to the same party.   Though
Saltoun not a member of the Convention, he was a most active member of the Club.[3]   He hated monarchy : he hated democracy : his
favourite project was to make Scotland an oligarchical republic.   The
King, if there must be a King, was to be a mere pageant.   The lowest
class of the people were to be bondsmen.   The whole power, legislative
and executive, was to be in the hands of the Parliament.   In other
words, the country was to be absolutely governed by a hereditary aris-
-tocracy, the most needy, the most haughty, and the most quarrelsome
in Europe.   Under such a polity there could have been neither freedom
nor tranquillity.   Trade, industry, science, would have languished ; and
Scotland would have been a smaller Poland, with a puppet sovereign, a
turbulent diet, and an enslaved people.   With unsuccessful candidates
for office, and with honest but wrongheaded republicans, were mingled
politicians whose course was determined merely by fear.   Many sycophants, who were conscious that they had, in the evil time, done what
deserved punishment, were desirous to make their peace with the powerful and vindictive Club, and were glad to be permitted to atone for their

[1] Sir John Dalrymple to Lord Melville, June 18. 20. 25. 1689 ; Leven and Melville Papers.

[2] There is an amusing description of Sir Patrick in the Hyndford MS., written about 1704,
and printed among the Carstairs Papers.   " He is a lover of set speeches, and can hardly give
audience to private friends without them."

[3] "No man, though not a member, busier than Saltoun."—Lockhart to Melville, July 11.
1689 ; Leven and Melville Papers.   See Fletcher's own works, and the descriptions of him in
Lockhart's and Mackay's Memoirs.

servility to James by their opposition to William.[1]   The great body of Jacobites meanwhile stood aloof, saw with delight the enemies of the House of Stuart divided against one another, and indulged the hope that the confusion would end in the restoration of the banished king.[2]

While Montgomery was labouring to form out of various materials a party which might, when the Convention should reassemble, be powerful enough to dictate to the throne, an enemy still more formidable than Montgomery had set up the standard of civil war in a region about which the politicians of West-minster, and indeed most of the politicians of Edinburgh, knew no more than about Abyssinia or Japan. *War breaks out in the Highlands*

It is not easy for a modern Englishman, who can pass in a day from his club in Saint James's Street to his shooting box among the Grampians, and who finds in his shooting box all the comforts and luxuries of his club, to believe that, in the time of his greatgrandfathers, Saint James's Street had as little connection with the Grampians as with the Andes.   Yet so it was.   In the south of our island scarcely any thing was known about the Celtic part of Scotland ; and what was known excited no feeling but contempt and loathing. The crags and the glens, the woods and the waters, were indeed the same that now swarm every autumn with admiring gazers and sketchers. The Trosachs wound as now between gigantic walls of rock tapestried with broom and wild roses : Foyers came headlong down through the birchwood with the same leap and the same roar with which he still rushes to Loch Ness ; and, in defiance of the sun of June, the snowy scalp of Ben Cruachan rose, as it still rises, over the willowy islets of Loch Awe.   Yet none of these sights had power, till a recent period, to attract a single poet or painter from more opulent and more tranquil regions.   Indeed, law and police, trade and industry, have done far more than people of romantic dispositions will readily admit, to develope in our minds a sense of the wilder beauties of nature.   A traveller must be freed from all apprehension of being murdered or starved before he can be charmed by the bold outlines and rich tints of the hills.   He is not likely to be thrown into ecstasies by the abruptness of a precipice from which he is in imminent danger of falling two thousand feet perpendicular ; by the boiling waves of a torrent which suddenly whirls away his baggage and forces him to run for his life ; by the gloomy grandeur of a pass where he finds a corpse which marauders have just stripped and mangled ; or by the screams of those eagles whose next meal may probably be on his own eyes.   About the year 1730, Captain *State of the Highlands*

---

[1] Dalrymple says, in a letter of the 5th of June, " All the malignants, for fear, are come into the Club ; and they all vote alike."

[2] Balcarras.

Burt, one of the first Englishmen who caught a glimpse of the spots which now allure tourists from every part of the civilised world, wrote an account of his wanderings.   He was evidently a man of a quick, an observant, and a cultivated mind, and would doubtless, had he lived in our age, have looked with mingled awe and delight on the mountains of Invernessshire.   But, writing with the feeling which was universal in his own age, he pronounced those mountains monstrous excrescences. Their deformity, he said, was such that the most sterile plains seemed lovely by comparison.   Fine weather, he complained, only made bad worse ; for, the clearer the day, the more disagreeably did those mis-shapen masses of gloomy brown and dirty purple affect the eye.   What a contrast, he exclaimed, between these horrible prospects and the beauties of Richmond Hill ![1]   Some persons may think that Burt was a man of vulgar and prosaical mind : but they will scarcely venture to pass a similar judgment on Oliver Goldsmith.   Goldsmith was one of the very few Saxons who, more than a century ago, ventured to explore the Highlands.   He was disgusted by the hideous wilderness, and declared that he greatly preferred the charming country round Leyden, the vast expanse of verdant meadow, and the villas with their statues and grottoes, trim flower beds, and rectilinear avenues.   Yet it is difficult to believe that the author of the Traveller and of the Deserted Village was naturally inferior in taste and sensibility to the thousands of clerks and milliners who are now thrown into raptures by the sight of Loch Katrine and Loch Lomond.[2]   His feelings may easily be explained. It was not till roads had been cut out of the rocks, till bridges had been flung over the courses of the rivulets, till inns had succeeded to dens of

[1] Captain Burt's Letters from Scotland.

[2] " Shall I tire you with a description of this unfruitful country, where I must lead you over their hills all brown with heath, or their valleys scarce able to feed a rabbit ? . . .   Every part of the country presents the same dismal landscape.   No grove or brook lend their music to cheer the stranger."—Goldsmith to Bryanton, Edinburgh, Sept. 26. 1753.   In a letter written soon after from Leyden to the Reverend Thomas Contarine, Goldsmith says, " I was wholly taken up in observing the face of the country.   Nothing can equal its beauty.   Wherever I turned my eye, fine houses, elegant gardens, statues, grottos, vistas presented themselves. Scotland and this country bear the highest contrast : there, hills and rocks intercept every prospect ; here it is all a continued plain."   See Appendix C. to the First Volume of Mr. Forster's Life of Goldsmith.   I will cite the testimony of another man of genius in support of the doctrine propounded in the text.   No human being has ever had a finer sense of the beauties of nature than Gray.   No prospect surpasses in grandeur and loveliness the first view of Italy from Mount Cenis.   Had Gray enjoyed that view from the magnificent road constructed in this century, he would undoubtedly have been in raptures.   But in his time the descent was performed with extreme inconvenience and with not a little peril.   He therefore, instead of breaking forth into ejaculations of admiration and delight, says most unpoetically, " Mount Cenis, I confess, carries the permission mountains have of being frightful rather too far ; and its horrors were accompanied with too much danger to give one time to reflect upon their beauties."—Gray to West, Nov. 16. 1739.

robbers, till there was as little danger of being slain or plundered in the wildest defile of Badenoch or Lochaber as in Cornhill, that strangers could be enchanted by the blue dimples of the lakes and by the rainbows which overhung the waterfalls, and could derive a solemn pleasure even from the clouds and tempests which lowered on the mountain tops.

The change in the feeling with which the Lowlanders regarded the Highland scenery was closely connected with a change not less remarkable in the feeling with which they regarded the Highland race. It is not strange that the Wild Scotch, as they were sometimes called, should, in the seventeenth century, have been considered by the Saxons as mere savages. But it is surely strange that, considered as savages, they should not have been objects of interest and curiosity. The English were then abundantly inquisitive about the manners of rude nations separated from our island by great continents and oceans. Numerous books were printed describing the laws, the superstitions, the cabins, the repasts, the dresses, the marriages, the funerals of Laplanders and Hottentots, Mohawks and Malays. The plays and poems of that age are full of allusions to the usages of the black men of Africa and of the red men of America. The only barbarian about whom there was no wish to have any information was the Highlander. Five or six years after the Revolution, an indefatigable angler published an account of Scotland. He boasted that, in the course of his rambles from lake to lake, and from brook to brook, he had left scarcely a nook of the kingdom unexplored. But, when we examine his narrative, we find that he had never ventured beyond the extreme skirts of the Celtic region. He tells us that even from the people who lived close to the passes he could learn little or nothing about the Gaelic population. Few Englishmen, he says, had ever seen Inverary. All beyond Inverary was chaos.[1] In the reign of George the First, a work was published which professed to give a most exact account of Scotland; and in this work, consisting of more than three hundred pages, two contemptuous paragraphs were thought sufficient for the Highlands and the Highlanders.[2] We may well doubt whether, in 1689, one in twenty of the well read gentlemen who assembled at Will's coffeehouse knew that, within the four seas, and at the distance of less than five hundred miles from London, were many miniature courts, in each of which a petty prince, attended by guards, by armour bearers, by musicians, by a hereditary orator, by a hereditary poet laureate, kept a rude state, dispensed a rude

[1] Northern Memoirs, by R. Franck Philanthropus, 1694. The author had caught a few glimpses of Highland scenery, and speaks of it much as Burt spoke in the following generation: "It is a part of the creation left undressed; rubbish thrown aside when the magnificent fabric of the world was created; as void of form as the natives are indigent of morals and good manners."

[2] Journey through Scotland, by the author of the Journey through England, 1723.

justice, waged wars, and concluded treaties. While the old Gaelic institutions were in full vigour, no account of them was given by any observer, qualified to judge of them fairly. Had such an observer studied the character of the Highlanders, he would doubtless have found in it closely intermingled the good and the bad qualities of an uncivilised nation. He would have found that the people had no love for their country or for their king ; that they had no attachment to any commonwealth larger than the clan, or to any magistrate superior to the chief. He would have found that life was governed by a code of morality and honour widely different from that which is established in peaceful and prosperous societies. He would have learned that a stab in the back, or a shot from behind a fragment of rock, were approved modes of taking satisfaction for insults. He would have heard men relate boastfully how they or their fathers had wreaked on hereditary enemies in a neighbouring valley such vengeance as would have made old soldiers of the Thirty Years' War shudder. He would have found that robbery was held to be a calling, not merely innocent, but honourable. He would have seen, wherever he turned, that dislike of steady industry, and that disposition to throw on the weaker sex the heaviest part of manual labour, which are characteristic of savages. He would have been struck by the spectacle of athletic men basking in the sun, angling for salmon, or taking aim at grouse, while their aged mothers, their pregnant wives, their tender daughters, were reaping the scanty harvest of oats. Nor did the women repine at their hard lot. In their view it was quite fit that a man, especially if he assumed the aristocratic title of Duinhe Wassel and adorned his bonnet with the eagle's feather, should take his ease, except when he was fighting, hunting, or marauding. To mention the name of such a man in connection with commerce or with any mechanical art was an insult. Agriculture was indeed less despised. Yet a highborn warrior was much more becomingly employed in plundering the land of others than in tilling his own. The religion of the greater part of the Highlands was a rude mixture of Popery and Paganism. The symbol of redemption was associated with heathen sacrifices and incantations. Baptised men poured libations of ale to one Dæmon, and set out drink offerings of milk for another. Seers wrapped themselves up in bulls' hides, and awaited, in that vesture, the inspiration which was to reveal the future. Even among those minstrels and genealogists whose hereditary vocation was to preserve the memory of past events, an enquirer would have found very few who could read. In truth, he might easily have journeyed from sea to sea without discovering a page of Gaelic printed or written. The price which he would have had to pay for his knowledge of the country would have been heavy. He would have had to endure hardships as great as if he had sojourned among the Esquimaux or the Samoyeds. Here and there, indeed, at the castle of some great lord who had a seat in the Parliament and Privy Council, and who was accustomed to pass a large part of his life in the cities of the South, might have been found wigs and embroidered coats, plate and fine linen, lace and jewels, French dishes and French wines. But, in general, the traveller would have been forced to content himself with very different quarters. In many dwellings the furniture, the food, the clothing, nay the very hair and skin of his hosts, would have put his philosophy to the proof. His lodging would sometimes have been in a hut of which every nook would have swarmed with vermin. He would have inhaled an atmosphere thick with peat smoke, and foul with a hundred noisome exhalations. At supper grain fit only for horses would have been set before him, accompanied by a cake of blood drawn from living cows. Some of the company with which he would have feasted would have been covered with cutaneous eruptions, and others would have been smeared with tar like sheep. His couch would have been the bare earth, dry or wet as the weather might be ; and from that couch he would have risen half poisoned with stench, half blind with the reek of turf, and half mad with the itch.[1]

This is not an attractive picture. And yet an enlightened and dis-passionate observer would have found in the character and manners of this rude people something which might well excite admiration and a good hope. Their courage was what great exploits achieved in all the four quarters of the globe have since proved it to be. Their intense attachment to their own tribe and to their own patriarch, though politically a great evil, partook of the nature of virtue. The sentiment was misdirected and ill regulated ; but still it was heroic. There must be some elevation of soul in a man who loves the society of which he is a member and the leader whom he follows with a love stronger than the love of life. It was true that the Highlander had few scruples about shedding the blood of an enemy : but it was not less true that he had high notions of the duty of observing faith to allies and hospitality to guests. It was true that his predatory habits were most pernicious to the commonwealth. Yet those erred greatly who imagined that he bore any resemblance to villains who, in rich and well governed com-munities, live by stealing. When he drove before him the herds of Lowland farmers up the pass which led to his native glen, he no more considered himself as a thief than the Raleighs and Drakes considered

---

[1] Almost all these circumstances are taken from Burt's Letters. For the tar, I am indebted to Cleland's poetry. In his verses on the "Highland Host" he says :

"The reason is, they're smeared with tar,
Which doth defend their head and neck,
Just as it doth their sheep protect."

themselves as thieves when they divided the cargoes of Spanish galleons. He was a warrior seizing lawful prize of war, of war never once intermitted during the thirty five generations which had passed away since the Teutonic invaders had driven the children of the soil to the mountains. That, if he was caught robbing on such principles, he should, for the protection of peaceful industry, be punished with the utmost rigour of the law was perfectly just. But it was not just to class him morally with the pickpockets who infested Drury Lane Theatre, or the highwaymen who stopped coaches on Blackheath. His inordinate pride of birth and his contempt for labour and trade were indeed great weaknesses, and had done far more than the inclemency of the air and the sterility of the soil to keep his country poor and rude. Yet even here there was some compensation. It must in fairness be acknowledged that the patrician virtues were not less widely diffused among the population of the Highlands than the patrician vices. As there was no other part of the island where men, sordidly clothed, lodged, and fed, indulged themselves to such a degree in the idle sauntering habits of an aristocracy, so there was no other part of the island where such men had in such a degree the better qualities of an aristocracy, grace and dignity of manner, selfrespect, and that noble sensibility which makes dishonour more terrible than death. A gentleman of Sky or Lochaber, whose clothes were begrimed with the accumulated filth of years, and whose hovel smelt worse than an English hogstye, would often do the honours of that hovel with a lofty courtesy worthy of the splendid circle of Versailles. Though he had as little booklearning as the most stupid ploughboys of England, it would have been a great error to put him in the same intellectual rank with such ploughboys. It is indeed only by reading that men can become profoundly acquainted with any science. But the arts of poetry and rhetoric may be carried near to absolute perfection, and may exercise a mighty influence on the public mind, in an age in which books are wholly or almost wholly unknown. The first great painter of life and manners has described, with a vivacity which makes it impossible to doubt that he was copying from nature, the effect produced by eloquence and song on audiences ignorant of the alphabet. It is probable that, in the Highland councils, men who would not have been qualified for the duty of parish clerks sometimes argued questions of peace and war, of tribute and homage, with ability worthy of Halifax and Caermarthen, and that, at the Highland banquets, minstrels who did not know their letters sometimes poured forth rhapsodies in which a discerning critic might have found passages such as would have reminded him of the tenderness of Otway or of the vigour of Dryden.

There was therefore even then evidence sufficient to justify the belief that no natural inferiority had kept the Celt far behind the Saxon.

It might safely have been predicted that, if ever an efficient police should make it impossible for the Highlander to avenge his wrongs by violence and to supply his wants by rapine, if ever his faculties should be developed by the civilising influence of the Protestant religion and of the English language, if ever he should transfer to his country and to her lawful magistrates the affection and respect with which he had been taught to regard his own petty community and his own petty prince, the kingdom would obtain an immense accession of strength for all the purposes both of peace and of war.

Such would doubtless have been the decision of a well informed and impartial judge. But no such judge was then to be found. The Saxons who dwelt far from the Gaelic provinces could not be well informed. The Saxons who dwelt near those provinces could not be impartial. National enmities have always been fiercest among borderers ; and the enmity between the Highland borderer and the Lowland borderer along the whole frontier was the growth of ages, and was kept fresh by constant injuries. One day many square miles of pasture land were swept bare by armed plunderers from the hills. Another day a score of plaids dangled in a row on the gallows of Crieff or Stirling. Fairs were indeed held on the debatable land for the necessary interchange of commodities. But to those fairs both parties came prepared for battle ; and the day often ended in bloodshed. Thus the Highlander was an object of hatred to his Saxon neighbours ; and from his Saxon neighbours those Saxons who dwelt far from him learned the very little that they cared to know about his habits. When the English condescended to think of him at all,—and it was seldom that they did so,—they considered him as a filthy abject savage, a slave, a Papist, a cutthroat, and a thief.[1]

[1] A striking illustration of the opinion which was entertained of the Highlander by his Lowland neighbours, and which was by them communicated to the English, will be found in a volume of Miscellanies published by Afra Behn in 1685. One of the most curious pieces in the collection is a coarse and profane Scotch poem entitled, " How the first Hielandman was made." How and of what materials he was made I shall not venture to relate. The dialogue which immediately follows his creation may be quoted, I hope, without much offence.

> " Says God to the Hielandman, ' Quhair wilt thou now ? '
> ' I will down to the Lowlands, Lord, and there steal a cow.'
> ' Ffy,' quod St. Peter, ' thou wilt never do weel,
> ' An thou, but new made, so sune gais to steal.'
> ' Umff,' quod the Hielandman, and swore by yon kirk,
> ' So long as I may geir get to steal, will I nevir work.' "

An eminent Lowland Scot, the brave Colonel Cleland, about the same time, described the Highlander in the same manner :

> " For a misobliging word
> She'll dirk her neighbour o'er the board.
> If any ask her of her drift,
> Forsooth, her nainself lives by theft."

Much to the same effect are the very few words which Franck Philanthropus (1694) spares to

This contemptuous loathing lasted till the year 1745, and was then for a moment succeeded by intense fear and rage. England, thoroughly alarmed, put forth her whole strength. The Highlands were subjugated rapidly, completely, and for ever. During a short time the English nation, still heated by the recent conflict, breathed nothing but vengeance. The slaughter on the field of battle and on the scaffold was not sufficient to slake the public thirst for blood. The sight of the tartan inflamed the populace of London with hatred, which showed itself by unmanly outrages to defenceless captives. A political and social revolution took place through the whole Celtic region. The power of the chiefs was destroyed : the people were disarmed : the use of the old national garb was interdicted : the old predatory habits were effectually broken ; and scarcely had this change been accomplished when a strange reflux of public feeling began. Pity succeeded to aversion. The nation execrated the cruelties which had been committed on the Highlanders, and forgot that for those cruelties it was itself answerable. Those very Londoners, who, while the memory of the march to Derby was still fresh, had thronged to hoot and pelt the rebel prisoners, now fastened on the prince who had put down the rebellion the nickname of Butcher. Those barbarous institutions and usages, which, while they were in full force, no Saxon had thought worthy of serious examination, or had mentioned except with contempt, had no sooner ceased to exist than they became objects of curiosity, of interest, even of admiration. Scarcely had the chiefs been turned into mere landlords, when it became the fashion to draw invidious comparisons between the rapacity of the landlord and the indulgence of the chief. Men seemed to have forgotten that the ancient Gaelic polity had been found to be incompatible with the authority of law, had obstructed the progress of civilisation, had more than once brought on the empire the curse of civil war. As they had formerly seen only the odious side of that polity, they could now see only the pleasing side. The old tie, they said, had been parental : the new tie was purely commercial. What could be more lamentable than that the head of a tribe should eject, for a paltry arrear of rent, tenants who were his own flesh and blood, tenants whose forefathers had often with their bodies covered his forefathers on the field of battle ? As long as there were Gaelic marauders, they had been regarded by the Saxon population as hateful vermin who ought to be exterminated without mercy. As soon as the extermination had been accomplished,

the Highlanders : "They live like lairds and die like loons, hating to work and no credit to borrow : they make depredations and rob their neighbours." In the History of the Revolution in Scotland, printed at Edinburgh in 1690, is the following passage : "The Highlanders of Scotland are a sort of wretches that have no other consideration of honour, friendship, obedience, or government, than as, by any alteration of affairs or revolution in the government, they can improve to themselves an opportunity of robbing or plundering their bordering neighbours."

as soon as cattle were as safe in the Perthshire passes as in Smithfield market, the freebooter was exalted into a hero of romance. As long as the Gaelic dress was worn, the Saxons had pronounced it hideous, ridiculous, nay, grossly indecent. Soon after it had been prohibited, they discovered that it was the most graceful drapery in Europe. The Gaelic monuments, the Gaelic usages, the Gaelic superstitions, the Gaelic verses, disdainfully neglected during many ages, began to attract the attention of the learned from the moment at which the peculiarities of the Gaelic race began to disappear. So strong was this impulse that, where the Highlands were concerned, men of sense gave ready credence to stories without evidence, and men of taste gave rapturous applause to compositions without merit. Epic poems, which any skilful and dispassionate critic would at a glance have perceived to be almost entirely modern, and which, if they had been published as modern, would have instantly found their proper place in company with Blackmore's Alfred and Wilkie's Epigoniad, were pronounced to be fifteen hundred years old, and were gravely classed with the Iliad. Writers of a very different order from the impostor who fabricated these forgeries saw how striking an effect might be produced by skilful pictures of the old Highland life. Whatever was repulsive was softened down : whatever was graceful and noble was brought prominently forward. Some of these works were executed with such admirable art that, like the historical plays of Shakspeare, they superseded history. The visions of the poet were realities to his readers. The places which he described became holy ground, and were visited by thousands of pilgrims. Soon the vulgar imagination was so completely occupied by plaids, targets, and claymores, that, by most Englishmen, Scotchman and Highlander were regarded as synonymous words. Few people seemed to be aware that, at no remote period, a Macdonald or a Macgregor in his tartan was to a citizen of Edinburgh or Glasgow what an Indian hunter in his war paint is to an inhabitant of Philadelphia or Boston. Artists and actors represented Bruce and Douglas in striped petticoats. They might as well have represented Washington brandishing a tomahawk, and girt with a string of scalps. At length this fashion reached a point beyond which it was not easy to proceed. The last British King who held a court in Holyrood thought that he could not give a more striking proof of his respect for the usages which had prevailed in Scotland before the Union, than by disguising himself in what, before the Union, was considered by nine Scotchmen out of ten as the dress of a thief.

    Thus it has chanced that the old Gaelic institutions and manners have never been exhibited in the simple light of truth. Up to the middle of the last century, they were seen through one false medium : they have since been seen through another. Once they loomed dimly through an obscuring and distorting haze of prejudice ; and no sooner had that fog dispersed than they appeared bright with all the richest tints of poetry.   The time when a perfectly fair picture could have been painted has now passed away.   The original has long disappeared : no authentic effigy exists : and all that is possible is to produce an imperfect likeness by the help of two portraits, of which one is a coarse caricature and the other a masterpiece of flattery.

Among the erroneous notions which have been commonly received concerning the history and character of the Highlanders is one which it is especially necessary to correct.   During the century which commenced with the campaign of Montrose, and terminated with the campaign of the young Pretender, every great military exploit which was achieved on British ground in the cause of the House of Stuart was achieved by the valour of Gaelic tribes. The English have therefore very naturally ascribed to those tribes the feelings of English cavaliers, profound reverence for the royal office, and enthusiastic attachment to the royal family.   A close enquiry however will show that the strength of these feelings among the Celtic clans has been greatly exaggerated.

Peculiar nature of Jacobitism in the Highlands

In studying the history of our civil contentions, we must never forget that the same names, badges, and warcries had very different meanings in different parts of the British isles.   We have already seen how little there was in common between the Jacobitism of Ireland and the Jacobitism of England.   The Jacobitism of the Scotch Highlander was, at least in the seventeenth century, a third variety, quite distinct from the other two.   The Gaelic population was far indeed from holding the doctrines of passive obedience and nonresistance.   In fact disobedience and resistance made up the ordinary life of that population.   Some of those very clans which it has been the fashion to describe as so enthusiastically loyal that they were prepared to stand by James to the death, even when he was in the wrong, had never, while he was on the throne, paid the smallest respect to his authority, even when he was clearly in the right.   Their practice, their calling, had been to disobey and to defy him.   Some of them had actually been proscribed by sound of horn for the crime of withstanding his lawful commands, and would have torn to pieces without scruple any of his officers who had dared to venture beyond the passes for the purpose of executing his warrant.   The English Whigs were accused by their opponents of holding doctrines dangerously lax touching the obedience due to the chief magistrate.   Yet no respectable English Whig ever defended rebellion, except as a rare and extreme remedy for rare and extreme evils.   But among those Celtic chiefs whose loyalty has been the theme of so much warm eulogy were some whose whole existence from boyhood upwards had been one long rebellion.

Such men, it is evident, were not likely to see the Revolution in the light in which it appeared to an Oxonian nonjuror. On the other hand they were not, like the aboriginal Irish, urged to take arms by impatience of Saxon domination. To such domination the Scottish Celt had never been subjected. He occupied his own wild and sterile region, and followed his own national usages. In his dealings with the Saxons, he was rather the oppressor than the oppressed. He exacted black mail from them : he drove away their flocks and herds ; and they seldom dared to pursue him to his native wilderness. They had never portioned out among themselves his dreary region of moor and shingle. He had never seen the tower of his hereditary chieftains occupied by an usurper who could not speak Gaelic, and who looked on all who spoke it as brutes and slaves ; nor had his national and religious feelings ever been outraged by the power and splendour of a church which he regarded as at once foreign and heretical.

The real explanation of the readiness with which a large part of the population of the Highlands, twice in the seventeenth century, drew the sword for the Stuarts is to be found in the internal quarrels which divided the commonwealth of clans. For there was a commonwealth of clans, the image, on a reduced scale, of the great commonwealth of European nations. In the smaller of these two commonwealths, as in the larger, there were wars, treaties, alliances, disputes about territory and precedence, a system of public law, a balance of power. There was one inexhaustible source of discontents and quarrels. The feudal system had, some centuries before, been introduced into the hill country, but had neither destroyed the patriarchal system nor amalgamated completely with it. In general he who was lord in the Norman polity was also chief in the Celtic polity ; and, when this was the case, there was no conflict. But, when the two characters were separated, all the willing and loyal obedience was reserved for the chief. The lord had only what he could get and hold by force. If he was able, by the help of his own tribe, to keep in subjection tenants who were not of his own tribe, there was a tyranny of clan over clan, the most galling, perhaps, of all forms of tyranny. At different times different races had risen to an authority which had produced general fear and envy. The Macdonalds had once possessed, in the Hebrides and throughout the mountain country of Argyleshire and Invernessshire, an ascendency similar to that which the House of Austria had once possessed in Christendom. But the ascendency of the Macdonalds had, like the ascendency of the House of Austria, passed away ; and the Campbells, the children of Diarmid, had become in the Highlands what the Bourbons had become in Europe.[1] The parallel might

Jealousy of the ascendency of the Campbells

---

[1] Since this passage was written I was much pleased by finding that Lord Fountainhall used, in July 1676, exactly the same illustration which had occurred to me. He says that " Argyle's

be carried far. Imputations similar to those which it was the fashion to throw on the French government were thrown on the Campbells. A peculiar dexterity, a peculiar plausibility of address, a peculiar contempt for the obligations of plighted faith, were ascribed, with or without reason, to the dreaded race. " Fair and false like a Campbell " became a proverb. It was said that Mac Callum More after Mac Callum More had, with unwearied, unscrupulous, and unrelenting ambition, annexed mountain after mountain and island after island to the original domains of his House. Some tribes had been expelled from their territory, some compelled to pay tribute, some incorporated with the conquerors. At length the number of fighting men who bore the name of Campbell was sufficient to meet in the field of battle the combined forces of all the other western clans. It was during those civil troubles which commenced in 1638 that the power of this aspiring family reached the zenith. The Marquess of Argyle was the head of a party as well as the head of a tribe. Possessed of two different kinds of authority, he used each of them in such a way as to extend and fortify the other. The knowledge that he could bring into the field the claymores of five thousand half heathen mountaineers added to his influence among the austere Presbyterians who filled the Privy Council and the General Assembly at Edinburgh. His influence at Edinburgh added to the terror which he inspired among the mountains. Of all the Highland Princes whose history is well known to us he was the greatest and most dreaded. It was while his neighbours were watching the increase of his power with hatred which fear could scarcely keep down that Montrose called them to arms. The call was promptly obeyed. A powerful coalition of clans waged war, nominally for King Charles, but really against Mac Callum More. It is not easy for any person who has studied the history of that contest to doubt that, if Argyle had supported the cause of monarchy, his neighbours would have declared against it. Grave writers tell of the victory gained at Inverlochy by the royalists over the rebels. But the peasants who dwell near the spot speak more accurately. They talk of the great battle won there by the Macdonalds over the Campbells.

The feelings which had produced the coalition against the Marquess of Argyle retained their force long after his death. His son, Earl Archibald, though a man of many eminent virtues, inherited, with the ascendency of his ancestors, the unpopularity which such ascendency could scarcely fail to produce. In 1675, several warlike tribes formed a confederacy against him, but were compelled to submit to the superior

ambitious grasping at the mastery of the Highlands and Western Islands of Mull, Ila, &c., stirred up other clans to enter into a combination for bearing him downe, like the confederat forces of Germanie, Spain, Holland, &c., against the growth of the French."

Map to illustrate
DUNDEE'S CAMPAIGN
April–July, 1689

English Miles
0 5 10   20   30   40   50

Dundee's Route shown thus:-

Emery Walker sc.

MAP TO ILLUSTRATE DUNDEE'S CAMPAIGN IN 1689

Based on the Map contained in Professor C. S. Terry's Life of Dundee force which was at his command. There was therefore great joy from sea to sea when, in 1681, he was arraigned on a futile charge, condemned to death, driven into exile, and deprived of his dignities : there was great alarm when, in 1685, he returned from banishment, and sent forth the fiery cross to summon his kinsmen to his standard ; and there was again great joy when his enterprise had failed, when his army had melted away, when his head had been fixed on the Tolbooth of Edinburgh, and when those chiefs who had regarded him as an oppressor had obtained from the Crown, on easy terms, remissions of old debts and grants of new titles. While England and Scotland generally were execrating the tyranny of James, he was honoured as a deliverer in Appin and Lochaber, in Glenroy and Glenmore.[1] The hatred excited by the power and ambition of the House of Argyle was not satisfied even when the head of that House had perished, when his children were fugitives, when strangers garrisoned the castle of Inverary, and when the whole shore of Loch Fyne had been laid waste by fire and sword. It was said that the terrible precedent which had been set in the case of the Macgregors ought to be followed, and that it ought to be made a crime to bear the odious name of Campbell.

On a sudden all was changed. The Revolution came. The heir of Argyle returned in triumph. He was, as his predecessors had been, the head, not only of a tribe, but of a party. The sentence which had deprived him of his estate and of his honours was treated by the majority of the Convention as a nullity. The doors of the Parliament House were thrown open to him : he was selected from the whole body of Scottish nobles to administer the oath of office to the new Sovereigns ; and he was authorised to raise an army on his domains for the service of the Crown. He would now, doubtless, be as powerful as the most powerful of his ancestors. Backed by the strength of the Government, he would demand all the long and heavy arrears of rent and tribute which were due to him from his neighbours, and would exact revenge for all the injuries and insults which his family had suffered. There was

The Stewarts and Macnaghtens terror and agitation in the castles of twenty petty kings. The uneasiness was great among the Stewarts of Appin, whose territory was close pressed by the sea on one side, and by the race of Diarmid on the other. The Macnaghtens were still more alarmed. Once they had been the masters of those beautiful valleys through which the Ara and the Shira flow into Loch Fyne. But the

---

[1] In the introduction to the Memoirs of Sir Ewan Cameron is a very sensible remark : " It may appear paradoxical ; but the editor cannot help hazarding the conjecture that the motives which prompted the Highlanders to support King James were substantially the same as those by which the promoters of the Revolution were actuated." The whole introduction, indeed, well deserves to be read.

Campbells had prevailed. The Macnaghtens had been reduced to subjection, and had, generation after generation, looked up with awe and detestation to the neighbouring Castle of Inverary. They had recently been promised a complete emancipation. A grant, by virtue of which their chief would have held his estate immediately from the Crown, had been prepared, and was about to pass the seals, when the Revolution suddenly extinguished a hope which amounted almost to certainty.[1]

The Macleans remembered that, only fourteen years before, their lands had been invaded and the seat of their chief taken and garrisoned by the Campbells.[2] Even before William and Mary had been proclaimed at Edinburgh, a Maclean, deputed doubtless by the head of his tribe, had crossed the sea to Dublin, and had assured James that, if two or three battalions from Ireland landed in Argyleshire, they would be immediately joined by four thousand four hundred claymores.[3]

The Macleans

A similar spirit animated the Camerons. Their ruler, Sir Ewan Cameron, of Lochiel, surnamed the Black, was in personal qualities unrivalled among the Celtic princes. He was a gracious master, a trusty ally, a terrible enemy. His countenance and bearing were singularly noble. Some persons who had been at Versailles, and among them the shrewd and observant Simon Lord Lovat, said that there was, in person and manner, a most striking resemblance between Lewis the Fourteenth and Lochiel; and whoever compares the portraits of the two will perceive that there really was some likeness. In stature the difference was great. Lewis, in spite of highheeled shoes and a towering wig, hardly reached the middle size. Lochiel was tall and strongly built. In agility and skill at his weapons he had few equals among the inhabitants of the hills. He had repeatedly been victorious in single combat. He was a hunter of great fame. He made vigorous war on the wolves which, down to his time, preyed on the red deer of the Grampians; and by his hand perished

The Camerons; Lochiel

---

[1] Skene's Highlanders of Scotland; Douglas's Baronage of Scotland.

[2] See the Memoirs of the Life of Sir Ewan Cameron, and the Historical and Genealogical Account of the Clan Maclean, by a Senachie. Though this last work was published so late as 1838, the writer seems to have been inflamed by animosity as fierce as that with which the Macleans of the seventeenth century regarded the Campbells. In the short compass of one page the Marquess of Argyle is designated as "the diabolical Scotch Cromwell," "the vile vindictive persecutor," "the base traitor," and "the Argyle impostor." In another page he is "the insidious Campbell, fertile in villany," "the avaricious slave," "the coward of Argyle," and "the Scotch traitor." In the next page he is "the base and vindictive enemy of the House of Maclean," "the hypocritical Covenanter," "the incorrigible traitor," "the cowardly and malignant enemy." It is a happy thing that passions so violent can now vent themselves only in scolding.

[3] Letter of Avaux to Louvois, April $\frac{6}{16}$. 1689, enclosing a paper entitled Mémoire du Chevalier Macklean.

the last of the ferocious breed which is known to have wandered at large in our island.   Nor was Lochiel less distinguished by intellectual than by bodily vigour.   He might indeed have seemed ignorant to educated and travelled Englishmen, who had studied the classics under Busby at Westminster and under Aldrich at Oxford, who had learned something about the sciences among Fellows of the Royal Society, and something about the fine arts in the galleries of Florence and Rome. But though Lochiel had very little knowledge of books, he was eminently wise in council, eloquent in debate, ready in devising expedients, and skilful in managing the minds of men.   His understanding preserved him from those follies into which pride and anger frequently hurried his brother chieftains.   Many, therefore, who regarded his brother chieftains as mere barbarians, mentioned him with respect. Even at the Dutch Embassy in Saint James's Square he was spoken of as a man of such capacity and courage that it would not be easy to find his equal.   As a patron of literature, he ranks with the magnificent Dorset.   If Dorset out of his own purse allowed Dryden a pension equal to the profits of the Laureateship, Lochiel is said to have bestowed on a celebrated bard, who had been plundered by marauders, and who implored alms in a pathetic Gaelic ode, three cows and the almost incredible sum of fifteen pounds sterling.   In truth, the character of this great chief was depicted two thousand five hundred years before his birth, and depicted,—such is the power of genius,—in colours which will .be fresh as many years after his death.   He was the Ulysses of the Highlands.[1]

He held a large territory peopled by a race which reverenced no lord, no king but himself.   For that territory, however, he owed homage to the House of Argyle ; and he was deeply in debt to his feudal superiors for rent.   This vassalage he had doubtless been early taught to consider as degrading and unjust.   In his minority he had been the ward in chivalry of the politic Marquess, and had been educated at the Castle of Inverary. But at eighteen the boy broke loose from the authority of his guardian, and fought bravely both for Charles the First and for Charles the Second.   He was therefore considered by the English as a Cavalier, was well received at Whitehall after the Restoration, and was knighted

---

[1] See the singularly interesting Memoirs of Sir Ewan Cameron of Lochiel, printed at Edinburgh for the Abbotsford Club in 1842.   The MS. must have been at least a century older. See also in the same volume the account of Sir Ewan's death, copied from the Balhadie papers. I ought to say that the author of the Memoirs of Sir Ewan, though evidently well informed about the affairs of the Highlands and the characters of the most distinguished chiefs, was grossly ignorant of English politics and history.   I will quote what Van Citters wrote to the States General about Lochiel, $\frac{Nov. 26.}{Dec. 6.}$ 1689 : "Sir Evan Cameron, Lord Locheale, een man,—soo ik hoor van die hem lange gekent en dagelyk hebben mede omgegaan,—van so groot verstant, courage, en beleyt, als weyniges syns gelycke syn."

Sr Ewen Cameron *Chief of the* Clan-Cameron

The Honest Man, whom Virtue sways.
His GOD adores, His KING obeys;
Does factious Mens rebellious pride
And threatning Tyrants rage deride
Honour's his Wealth, his Rule, his Aime
Unshaken, fixt, & still the same.

SIR EWAN CAMERON OF LOCHIEL

From a contemporary engraving

by the hand of James. The compliment, however, which was paid to him, on one of his appearances at the English Court, would not have seemed very flattering to a Saxon. "Take care of your pockets, my lords," cried His Majesty; "here comes the king of the thieves." The loyalty of Lochiel is almost proverbial: but it was very unlike what was called loyalty in England. In the records of the Scottish Parliament he was, in the days of Charles the Second, described as a lawless and rebellious man, who held lands masterfully and in high contempt of the royal authority.[1] On one occasion the Sheriff of Invernessshire was directed by King James to hold a court in Lochaber. Lochiel, jealous of this interference with his own patriarchal despotism, came to the tribunal at the head of four hundred armed Camerons. He affected great reverence for the royal commission, but he dropped three or four words which were perfectly understood by the pages and armour-bearers who watched every turn of his eye. "Is none of my lads so clever as to send this judge packing? I have seen them get up a quarrel when there was less need of one." In a moment a brawl began in the crowd, none could say how or where. Hundreds of dirks were out: cries of "Help" and "Murder" were raised on all sides: many wounds were inflicted: two men were killed: the sitting broke up in tumult; and the terrified Sheriff was forced to put himself under the protection of the chief, who, with a plausible show of respect and concern, escorted him safe home. It is amusing to think that the man who performed this feat is constantly extolled as the most faithful and dutiful of subjects by writers who blame Somers and Burnet as contemners of the legitimate authority of Sovereigns. Lochiel would undoubtedly have laughed the doctrine of nonresistance to scorn. But scarcely any chief in Invernessshire had gained more than he by the downfall of the House of Argyle, or had more reason than he to dread the restoration of that House. Scarcely any chief in Invernessshire, therefore, was more alarmed and disgusted by the proceedings of the Convention.

But of all those Highlanders who looked on the recent turn of fortune with painful apprehension the fiercest and the most powerful The Mac- were the Macdonalds. More than one of the magnates who donalds bore that widespread name laid claim to the honour of being the rightful successor of those Lords of the Isles, who, as late as the fifteenth century, disputed the preeminence of the Kings of Scotland. This genealogical controversy, which has lasted down to our own time, caused much bickering among the competitors. But they all agreed in regretting the past splendour of their dynasty, and in detesting the upstart race of Campbell. The old feud had never

[1] Act. Parl., July 5. 1661.

slumbered.   It was still constantly repeated, in verse and prose, that the finest part of the domain belonging to the ancient heads of the Gaelic nation, Islay, where they had lived with the pomp of royalty, Iona, where they had been interred with the pomp of religion, the paps of Jura, the rich peninsula of Kintyre, had been transferred from the legitimate possessors to the insatiable Mac Callum More.   Since the downfall of the House of Argyle, the Macdonalds, if they had not regained their ancient superiority, might at least boast that they had now no superior.   Relieved from the fear of their mighty enemy in the West, they had turned their arms against weaker enemies in the East, against the clan of Mackintosh and against the town of Inverness.

The clan of Mackintosh, a branch of an ancient and renowned tribe which took its name and badge from the wild cat of the forests, had a dispute with the Macdonalds, which originated, if tradition may be believed, in those dark times when the Danish pirates wasted the coasts of Scotland.   Inverness was a Saxon colony among the Celts, a hive of traders and artisans in the midst *Feud between the Macdonalds and Mackintoshes* of a population of loungers and plunderers, a solitary outpost of civilisation in a region of barbarians.   Though the buildings covered but a small part of the space over which they now extend ; though the arrival of a brig in the port was a rare event ; though the *Inverness* Exchange was the middle of a miry street, in which stood a market cross much resembling a broken milestone ; though the sittings of the municipal council were held in a filthy den with a roughcast wall ; though the best houses were such as would now be called hovels ; though the best roofs were of thatch ; though the best ceilings were of bare rafters ; though the best windows were, in bad weather, closed with shutters for want of glass ; though the humbler dwellings were mere heaps of turf, in which barrels with the bottoms knocked out served the purpose of chimneys ; yet to the mountaineer of the Grampians this city was as Babylon or as Tyre.   Nowhere else had he seen four or five hundred houses, two churches, twelve maltkilns, crowded close together.   Nowhere else had he been dazzled by the splendour of rows of booths, where knives, horn spoons, tin kettles, and gaudy ribands were exposed to sale.   Nowhere else had he been on board of one of those huge ships which brought sugar and wine over the sea from countries far beyond the limits of his geography.[1]   It is not strange that the haughty and warlike Macdonalds, despising peaceful

---

[1] See Burt's Third and Fourth Letters.   In the early editions is an engraving of the market cross of Inverness, and of that part of the street where the merchants congregated.

I ought here to acknowledge my obligations to Mr. Robert Carruthers, who kindly furnished me with much curious information about Inverness, and with some extracts from the municipal records.

industry, yet envying the fruits of that industry, should have fastened a succession of quarrels on the people of Inverness. In the reign of Charles the Second, it had been apprehended that the town would be stormed and plundered by those rude neighbours. The terms of peace which they offered showed how little they regarded the authority of the prince and of the law. Their demand was that a heavy tribute should be paid to them, that the municipal magistrates should bind themselves by an oath to deliver up to the vengeance of the clan every burgher who should shed the blood of a Macdonald, and that every burgher who should anywhere meet a person wearing the Macdonald tartan should ground arms in token of submission. Never did Lewis the Fourteenth, not even when he was encamped between Utrecht and Amsterdam, treat the States General with such despotic insolence.[1] By the intervention of the Privy Council of Scotland a compromise was effected : but the old animosity was undiminished.

Common enmities and common apprehensions produced a good understanding between the town and the clan of Mackintosh. The foe

Inverness threatened by Macdonald of Keppoch most hated and dreaded by both was Colin Macdonald of Keppoch, an excellent specimen of the genuine Highland Jacobite. Keppoch's whole life had been passed in insulting and resisting the authority of the Crown. He had been repeatedly charged on his allegiance to desist from his lawless practices, but had treated every admonition with contempt. The government, however, was not willing to resort to extremities against him ; and he long continued to rule undisturbed the stormy peaks of Coryarrick, and the gigantic terraces which still mark the limits of what was once the Lake of Glenroy. He was famed for his knowledge of all the ravines and caverns of that dreary region ; and such was the skill with which he could track a herd of cattle to the most secret hidingplace that he was known by the nickname of Coll of the Cows.[2] At length his outrageous violations of all law compelled the Privy Council to take decided steps. He was proclaimed a rebel : letters of fire and sword were issued against him under the seal of James ; and, a few weeks before the Revolution, a body of royal troops, supported by the whole strength of the Mackintoshes, marched into Keppoch's territories. Keppoch gave battle to the invaders, and was victorious. The King's forces were put to flight ; the King's captain was slain ; and this by a hero whose loyalty to the King many writers have very complacently contrasted with the factious turbulence of the Whigs.[3]

[1] I am indebted to Mr. Carruthers for a copy of the demands of the Macdonalds, and of the answer of the Town Council.

[2] Colt's Deposition, Appendix to the Act. Parl. of July 14. 1690.

[3] See the Life of Sir Ewan Cameron.

VIEW OF INVERNESS

From Slezer's Theatrum Scotiae, 1693

If Keppoch had ever stood in any awe of the government, he was completely relieved from that feeling by the general anarchy which followed the Revolution.   He wasted the lands of the Mackintoshes, advanced to Inverness, and threatened the town with destruction.   The danger was extreme.   The houses were surrounded only by a wall which time and weather had so loosened that it shook in every storm.   Yet the inhabitants showed a bold front ; and their courage was stimulated by their preachers.   Sunday the twenty-eighth of April was a day of alarm and confusion.   The savages went round and round the small colony of Saxons like a troop of famished wolves round a sheepfold.   Keppoch threatened and blustered.   He would come in with all his men.   He would sack the place.   The burghers meanwhile mustered in arms round the market cross to listen to the oratory of their ministers.   The day closed without an assault: the Monday and the Tuesday passed away in intense anxiety ; and then an unexpected mediator made his appearance.

Dundee, after his flight from Edinburgh, had retired to his country seat in that valley through which the Glamis descends to the ancient

Dundee appears in Keppoch's camp

castle of Macbeth.   Here he remained quiet during some time. He protested that he had no intention of opposing the new government.   He declared himself ready to return to Edinburgh, if only he could be assured that he should be protected against lawless violence ; and he offered to give his word of honour, or, if that were not sufficient, to give bail, that he would keep the peace.   Some of his old soldiers had accompanied him, and formed a garrison sufficient to protect his house against the Presbyterians of the neighbourhood. Here he might possibly have remained unharmed and harmless, had not an event for which he was not answerable made his enemies implacable, and made him desperate.[1]

An emissary of James had crossed from Ireland to Scotland with letters addressed to Dundee and Balcarras.   Suspicion was excited. The messenger was arrested, interrogated, and searched ; and the letters were found.   Some of them proved to be from Melfort, and were worthy of him.   Every line indicated those qualities which had made him the abhorrence of his country, and the favourite of his master.   He announced with delight the near approach of the day of vengeance and rapine, of the day when the estates of the seditious would be divided among the loyal, and when many who had been great and prosperous would be exiles and beggars.   The King, Melfort said, was determined to be severe.   Experience had at length convinced His Majesty that mercy would be weakness.   Even the Jacobites were disgusted by learning that a restoration would be immediately followed by a confiscation and a proscription.   Some of them pretended to suspect a forgery.

[1] Balcarras's Memoirs ; History of the late Revolution in Scotland.

Others did not hesitate to say that Melfort was a villain, that he wished to ruin Dundee and Balcarras, and that, for that end, he had written these odious despatches, and had employed a messenger who had very dexterously managed to be caught. It is however quite certain that Melfort never disavowed these papers, and that, after they were published, he continued to stand as high as ever in the favour of James. It can therefore hardly be doubted that, in those passages which shocked even the zealous supporters of hereditary right, the Secretary merely expressed with fidelity the feelings and intentions of his master.[1] Hamilton, by virtue of the powers which the Estates had, before their adjournment, confided to him, ordered Balcarras and Dundee to be arrested. Balcarras was taken, and was confined, first in his own house, and then in the Tolbooth of Edinburgh. But to seize Dundee was not so easy an enterprise. As soon as he heard that warrants were out against him, he crossed the Dee with his followers, and remained a short time in the wild domains of the House of Gordon. There he held some communication with the Macdonalds and Camerons about a rising. But he seems at this time to have known little and cared little about the Highlanders. For their national character he probably felt the dislike of a Saxon, for their military character the contempt of a professional soldier. He soon returned to the Lowlands, and stayed there till he learned that a considerable body of troops had been sent to apprehend him.[2] He then betook himself to the hill country as his last refuge, pushed northward through Strathdon and Strathbogie, crossed the Spey, and, on the morning of the first of May, arrived with a small band of horsemen at the camp of Keppoch before Inverness.

The new situation in which Dundee was now placed, the new view of society which was presented to him, naturally suggested new projects to his inventive and enterprising spirit. The hundreds of athletic Celts whom he saw in their national order of battle were evidently not allies to be despised. If he could form a great coalition of clans, if he could muster under one banner ten or twelve thousand of those hardy warriors, if he could induce them to submit to the restraints of discipline, what a career might be before him !

A commission from King James, even when King James was securely seated on the throne, had never been regarded with much respect by

---

[1] There is among the Nairne Papers in the Bodleian Library a curious MS. entitled "Journal de ce qui s'est passé en Irlande depuis l'arrivée de Sa Majesté." In this journal there are notes and corrections in English and French ; the English in the handwriting of James, the French in the handwriting of Melfort. The letters intercepted by Hamilton are mentioned, and mentioned in a way which plainly shows that they were genuine ; nor is there the least sign that James disapproved of them.

[2] " Nor did ever," says Balcarras, addressing James, " the Viscount of Dundee think of going to the Highlands without further orders from you, till a party was sent to apprehend him."

Coll of the Cows. That chief, however, hated the Campbells with all the hatred of a Macdonald, and promptly gave in his adhesion to the cause of the House of Stuart. Dundee undertook to settle the dispute between Keppoch and Inverness. The town agreed to pay two thousand dollars, a sum which, small as it might be in the estimation of the goldsmiths of Lombard Street, probably exceeded any treasure that had ever been carried into the wilds of Coryarrick. Half the sum was raised, not without difficulty, by the inhabitants; and Dundee is said to have passed his word for the remainder.[1]

He next tried to reconcile the Macdonalds with the Mackintoshes, and flattered himself that the two warlike tribes, lately arrayed against each other, might be willing to fight side by side under his command. But he soon found that it was no light matter to take up a Highland feud. About the rights of the contending Kings neither clan knew anything or cared anything. The conduct of both is to be ascribed to local passions and interests. What Argyle was to Keppoch, Keppoch was to the Mackintoshes. The Mackintoshes therefore remained neutral; and their example was followed by the Macphersons, another branch of the race of the wild cat. This was not Dundee's only disappointment. The Mackenzies, the Frasers, the Grants, the Munros, the Mackays, the Macleods, dwelt at a great distance from the territory of Mac Callum More. They had no dispute with him; they owed no debt to him; and they had no reason to dread the increase of his power. They therefore did not sympathise with his alarmed and exasperated neighbours, and could not be induced to join the confederacy against him.[2] Those chiefs, **Insurrection of the clans hostile to the Campbells** on the other hand, who lived nearer to Inverary, and to whom the name of Campbell had long been terrible and hateful, greeted Dundee eagerly, and promised to meet him at the head of their followers on the eighteenth of May. During the fortnight which preceded that day, he traversed Badenoch and Athol, and exhorted the inhabitants of those districts to rise in arms. He dashed into the Lowlands with his horsemen, surprised Perth, and carried off some Whig gentlemen prisoners to the mountains. Meanwhile the fiery crosses had been wandering from hamlet to hamlet over all the heaths and mountains thirty miles round Ben Nevis; and when he reached the trysting place in Lochaber he found that the gathering had begun. The head quarters were fixed close to Lochiel's house, a large pile built entirely of fir wood, and considered in the Highlands as

---

[1] See the narrative sent to James in Ireland and received by him July 7. 1689. It is among the Nairne Papers. See also the Memoirs of Dundee, 1714; Memoirs of Sir Ewan Cameron; Balcarras's Memoirs; Mackay's Memoirs. These narratives do not perfectly agree with each other, or with the information which I obtained from Inverness.

[2] Memoirs of Dundee: Tarbet to Melville, 1st June 1689, in the Leven and Melville Papers.

a superb palace. Lochiel, surrounded by more than six hundred broadswords, was there to receive his guests. Macnaghten of Macnaghten and Stewart of Appin were at the muster with their little clans. Macdonald of Keppoch led the warriors who had, a few months before, under his command, put to flight the musketeers of King James. Macdonald of Clanronald was of tender years : but he was brought to the camp by his uncle, who acted as Regent during the minority. The youth was attended by a picked body guard composed of his own cousins, all comely in appearance, and good men of their hands. Macdonald of Glengarry, conspicuous by his dark brow and his lofty stature, came from that great valley where a chain of lakes, then unknown to fame, and scarcely set down in maps, is now the daily highway of steam vessels passing and repassing between the Atlantic and the German Ocean. None of the rulers of the mountains had a higher sense of his personal dignity, or was more frequently engaged in disputes with other chiefs. He generally affected in his manners and in his housekeeping a rudeness beyond that of his rude neighbours, and professed to regard the very few luxuries which had then found their way from the civilised parts of the world into the Highlands as signs of the effeminacy and degeneracy of the Gaelic race. But on this occasion he chose to imitate the splendour of Saxon warriors, and rode on horseback before his four hundred plaided clansmen in a steel cuirass and a coat embroidered with gold lace. Another Macdonald, destined to a lamentable and horrible end, led a band of hardy freebooters from the dreary pass of Glencoe. Somewhat later came the great Hebridean potentates. Macdonald of Sleat, the most opulent and powerful of all the grandees who laid claim to the lofty title of Lord of the Isles, arrived at the head of seven hundred fighting men from Sky. A fleet of long boats brought five hundred Macleans from Mull under the command of their chief, Sir John of Duart. A far more formidable array had in old times followed his forefathers to battle. But the power, though not the spirit, of the clan had been broken by the arts and arms of the Campbells. Another band of Macleans arrived under a valiant leader, who took his title from Lochbuy, which is, being interpreted, the Yellow Lake.[1]

[1] Narrative in the Nairne Papers ; Depositions of Colt, Osburne, Malcolm, and Stewart of Ballachan in the Appendix to the Act. Parl. of July 14. 1690 ; Memoirs of Sir Ewan Cameron. A few touches I have taken from an English translation of some passages in a lost epic poem written in Latin, and called the Grameis. The writer was a zealous Jacobite named Phillipps. I have seldom made use of the Memoirs of Dundee, printed in 1714, and never without some misgiving. The writer was certainly not, as he pretends, one of Dundee's officers, but a stupid and ignorant Grub Street garreteer. He is utterly wrong both as to the place and as to the time of the most important of all the events which he relates, the battle of Killiecrankie. He says that it was fought on the banks of the Tummell, and on the 13th of June. It was fought on the banks of the Garry, and on the 27th of July. After giving such a specimen of inaccuracy as this, it would be idle to point out minor blunders.

It does not appear that a single chief who had not some special cause to dread and detest the House of Argyle obeyed Dundee's sum-

Tarbet's advice to the government mons. There is indeed strong reason to believe that the chiefs who came would have remained quietly at home if the government had understood the politics of the Highlands. Those politics were thoroughly understood by one able and experienced statesman, sprung from the great Highland family of Mackenzie, the Viscount Tarbet. He at this conjuncture pointed out to Melville by letter, and to Mackay in conversation, both the cause and the remedy of the distempers which seemed likely to bring on Scotland the calamities of civil war. There was, Tarbet said, no general disposition to insurrection among the Gael. Little was to be apprehended even from those popish clans which were under no apprehension of being subjected to the yoke of the Campbells. It was notorious that the ablest and most active of the discontented chiefs troubled themselves not at all about the questions which were in dispute between the Whigs and the Tories. Lochiel in particular, whose eminent personal qualities made him the most important man among the mountaineers, cared no more for James than for William. If the Camerons, the Macdonalds, and the Macleans could be convinced that, under the new government, their estates and their dignities would be safe, if Mac Callum More would make some concessions, if Their Majesties would take on themselves the payment of some arrears of rent, Dundee might call the clans to arms : but he would call to little purpose. Five thousand pounds, Tarbet thought, would be sufficient to quiet all the Celtic magnates ; and in truth, though that sum might seem ludicrously small to the politicians of Westminster, though it was not larger than the annual gains of the Groom of the Stole, or of the Paymaster of the Forces, it might well be thought immense by a barbarous potentate who, while he ruled hundreds of square miles, and could bring hundreds of warriors into the field, had perhaps never had fifty guineas at once in his coffers.[1]

Though Tarbet was considered by the Scottish ministers of the new Sovereigns as a very doubtful friend, his advice was not altogether neglected. It was resolved that overtures such as he recommended should be made to the malecontents. Much depended on the choice of an agent ; and unfortunately the choice showed how little the prejudices of the wild tribes of the hills were understood at Edinburgh. A Campbell was selected for the office of gaining over to the cause of King William men whose only quarrel to King William was that he

---

[1] From a letter of Archibald Earl of Argyle to Lauderdale, which bears date the 25th of June 1664, it appears that a hundred thousand marks Scots, little more than five thousand pounds sterling, would, at that time, have very nearly satisfied all the claims of Mac Callum More on his neighbours.

GEORGE MACKENZIE, VISCOUNT TARBET

From an engraving by Vandrebanc, after a painting by J. B. de Medina countenanced the Campbells. Offers made through such a channel were naturally regarded as at once snares and insults. After this it was to no purpose that Tarbet wrote to Lochiel and Mackay to Glengarry. Lochiel returned no answer to Tarbet; and Glengarry returned to Mackay a coldly civil answer, in which the general was advised to imitate the example of Monk.[1]

Mackay, meanwhile, wasted some weeks in marching, in counter-marching, and in indecisive skirmishing. He afterwards honestly admitted that the knowledge which he had acquired, during thirty years of military service on the Continent, was, in the new situation in which he was placed, useless to him. It was difficult in such a country to track the enemy. It was impossible to drive him to bay. Food for an invading army was not to be found in the wilderness of heath and shingle; nor could supplies for many days be transported far over quaking bogs and up precipitous ascents. The general found that he had tired his men and their horses almost to death, and yet had effected nothing. Highland auxiliaries might have been of the greatest use to him : but he had few such auxiliaries. The chief of the Grants, indeed, who had been persecuted by the late government, and had been accused of conspiring with the unfortunate Earl of Argyle, was zealous on the side of the Revolution. Two hundred Mackays, animated probably by family feeling, came from the northern extremity of our island, where at midsummer there is no night, to fight under a commander of their own name : but in general the clans which took no part in the insurrection awaited the event with cold indifference, and pleased themselves with the hope that they should easily make their peace with the conquerors, and be permitted to assist in plundering the conquered.

Indecisive campaign in the Highlands

An experience of little more than a month satisfied Mackay that there was only one way in which the Highlands could be subdued. It was idle to run after the mountaineers up and down their mountains. A chain of fortresses must be built in the most important situations, and must be well garrisoned. The place with which the general proposed to begin was Inverlochy, where the huge remains of an ancient castle stood and still stand. This post was close to an arm of the sea, and was in the heart of the country occupied by the discontented clans. A strong force stationed there, and supported, if necessary, by ships of war, would effectually overawe at once the Macdonalds, the Camerons, and the Macleans.[2]

While Mackay was representing in his letters to the council at Edinburgh the necessity of adopting this plan, Dundee was contending

---

[1] Mackay's Memoirs; Tarbet to Melville, June 1. 1689, in the Leven and Melville Papers; Dundee to Melfort, June 27, in the Nairne Papers.

[2] See Mackay's Memoirs, and his letter to Hamilton of the 14th of June 1689.

with difficulties which all his energy and dexterity could not completely overcome.

The Highlanders, while they continued to be a nation living under a peculiar polity, were in one sense better and in another sense worse fitted for military purposes than any other nation in Europe. **Military character of the Highlanders** The individual Celt was morally and physically well qualified for war, and especially for war in so wild and rugged a country as his own. He was intrepid, strong, fleet, patient of cold, of hunger, and of fatigue. Up steep crags, and over treacherous morasses, he moved as easily as the French household troops paced along the great road from Versailles to Marli. He was accustomed to the use of weapons and to the sight of blood : he was a fencer : he was a marksman ; and, before he had ever stood in the ranks, he was already more than half a soldier.

As the individual Celt was easily turned into a soldier, so a tribe of Celts was easily turned into a battalion of soldiers. All that was necessary was that the military organisation should be conformed to the patriarchal organisation. The Chief must be Colonel : his uncle or his brother must be Major : the tacksmen, who formed what may be called the peerage of the little community, must be the Captains : the company of each Captain must consist of those peasants who lived on his land, and whose names, faces, connections, and characters were perfectly known to him : the subaltern officers must be selected among the Duinhe Wassels, proud of the eagle's feather : the henchman was an excellent orderly : the hereditary piper and his sons formed the band ; and the clan became at once a regiment. In such a regiment was found from the first moment that exact order and prompt obedience in which the strength of regular armies consists. Every man, from the highest to the lowest, was in his proper place, and knew that place perfectly. It was not necessary to impress by threats or by punishment on the newly enlisted troops the duty of regarding as their head him whom they had regarded as their head ever since they could remember anything. Every private had, from infancy, respected his corporal much and his Captain more, and had almost adored his Colonel. There was therefore no danger of mutiny. There was as little danger of desertion. Indeed the very feelings which most powerfully impel other soldiers to desert kept the Highlander to his standard. If he left it, whither was he to go ? All his kinsmen, all his friends, were arrayed round it. To separate himself from it was to separate himself for ever from his family, and to incur all the misery of that very homesickness which, in regular armies, drives so many recruits to abscond at the risk of stripes and of death. When these things are fairly considered, it will not be thought strange that the Highland clans should have occasionally achieved great martial exploits.

But those very institutions which made a tribe of Highlanders, all bearing the same name, and all subject to the same ruler, so formidable in battle, disqualified the nation for war on a large scale. Nothing was easier than to turn clans into efficient regiments; but nothing was more difficult than to combine these regiments in such a manner as to form an efficient army. From the shepherds and herdsmen who fought in the ranks up to the chiefs, all was harmony and order. Every man looked up to his immediate superior; and all looked up to the common head. But with the chief this chain of subordination ended. He knew only how to govern, and had never learned to obey. Even to royal proclamations, even to Acts of Parliament, he was accustomed to yield obedience only when they were in perfect accordance with his own inclinations. It was not to be expected that he would pay to any delegated authority a respect which he was in the habit of refusing to the supreme authority. He thought himself entitled to judge of the propriety of every order which he received. Of his brother chiefs, some were his enemies and some his rivals. It was hardly possible to keep him from affronting them, or to convince him that they were not affronting him. All his followers sympathised with all his animosities, considered his honour as their own, and were ready at his whistle to array themselves round him in arms against the commander in chief. There was therefore very little chance that by any contrivance any five clans could be induced to cooperate heartily with one another during a long campaign. The best chance, however, was when they were led by a Saxon. It is remarkable that none of the great actions performed by the Highlanders during our civil wars was performed under the command of a Highlander. Some writers have mentioned it as a proof of the extraordinary genius of Montrose and Dundee that those captains, though not themselves of Gaelic race or speech, should have been able to form and direct confederacies of Gaelic tribes. But in truth it was precisely because Montrose and Dundee were not Highlanders that they were able to lead armies composed of Highland clans. Had Montrose been chief of the Camerons, the Macdonalds would never have submitted to his authority. Had Dundee been chief of Clanronald, he would never have been obeyed by Glengarry. Haughty and punctilious men, who scarcely acknowledged the King to be their superior, would not have endured the superiority of a neighbour, an equal, a competitor. They could far more easily bear the preeminence of a distinguished stranger. Yet even to such a stranger they would allow only a very limited and a very precarious authority. To bring a chief before a court martial, to shoot him, to cashier him, to degrade him, to reprimand him publicly, was impossible. Macdonald of Keppoch or Maclean of Duart would have struck dead any officer who had demanded his sword, and told him to consider himself as under arrest; and hundreds of claymores would instantly have been drawn to protect the murderer. All that was left to the commander under whom these potentates condescended to serve was to argue with them, to supplicate them, to flatter them, to bribe them; and it was only during a short time that any human skill could preserve harmony by these means. For every chief thought himself entitled to peculiar observance; and it was therefore impossible to pay marked court to any one without disobliging the rest. The general found himself merely the president of a congress of petty kings. He was perpetually called upon to hear and to compose disputes about pedigrees, about precedence, about the division of spoil. His decision, be it what it might, must offend somebody. At any moment he might hear that his right wing had fired on his centre in pursuance of some quarrel two hundred years old, or that a whole battalion had marched back to its native glen, because another battalion had been put in the post of honour. A Highland bard might easily have found in the history of the year 1689 subjects very similar to those with which the war of Troy furnished the great poets of antiquity. One day Achilles is sullen, keeps his tent, and announces his intention to depart with all his men. The next day Ajax is storming about the camp, and threatening to cut the throat of Ulysses.

Hence it was that, though the Highlanders achieved some great exploits in the civil wars of the seventeenth century, those exploits left no trace which could be discerned after the lapse of a few weeks. Victories of strange and almost portentous splendour produced all the consequences of defeat. Veteran soldiers and statesmen were bewildered by those sudden turns of fortune. It was incredible that undisciplined men should have performed such feats of arms. It was incredible that such feats of arms, having been performed, should be immediately followed by the triumph of the conquered and the submission of the conquerors. Montrose, having passed rapidly from victory to victory, was, in the full career of success, suddenly abandoned by his followers. Local jealousies and local interests had brought his army together. Local jealousies and local interests dissolved it. The Gordons left him because they fancied that he neglected them for the Macdonalds. The Macdonalds left him because they wanted to plunder the Campbells. The force which had once seemed sufficient to decide the fate of a kingdom melted away in a few days: and the victories of Tippermuir and Kilsyth were followed by the disaster of Philiphaugh. Dundee did not live long enough to experience a similar reverse of fortune;

H.E. IV   F

but there is every reason to believe that, had his life been prolonged one fortnight, his history would have been the history of Montrose retold.

Dundee made one attempt, soon after the gathering of the clans in Lochaber, to induce them to submit to the discipline of a regular army. He called a council of war to consider this subject. His opinion was supported by all the officers who had joined him from the low country. Distinguished among them were James Seton, Earl of Dunfermline, and James Galloway, Lord Dunkeld. The Celtic chiefs took the other side. Lochiel, the ablest among them, was their spokesman, and argued the point with much ingenuity and natural eloquence. "Our system,"—such was the substance of his reasoning,—"may not be the best : but we were bred to it from childhood : we understand it perfectly : it is suited to our peculiar institutions, feelings, and manners. Making war after our own fashion, we have the expertness and coolness of veterans. Making war in any other way, we shall be raw and awkward recruits. To turn us into soldiers like those of Cromwell and Turenne would be the business of years : and we have not even weeks to spare. We have time enough to unlearn our own discipline, but not time enough to learn yours." Dundee, with high compliments to Lochiel, declared himself convinced, and perhaps was convinced : for the reasonings of the wise old chief were by no means without weight.[1]

Yet some Celtic usages of war were such as Dundee could not tolerate. Cruel as he was, his cruelty always had a method and a purpose. He still hoped that he might be able to win some chiefs who remained neutral ; and he carefully avoided every act which could goad them into open hostility. This was undoubtedly a policy likely to promote the interest of James ; but the interest of James was nothing to the wild marauders who used his name and rallied round his banner merely for the purpose of making profitable forays and wreaking old grudges. Keppoch especially, who hated the Mackintoshes much more than he loved the Stuarts, not only plundered the territory of his enemies, but burned whatever he could not carry away. Dundee was moved to great wrath by the sight of the blazing dwellings. "I would rather," he said, "carry a musket in a respectable regiment than be captain of such a gang of thieves." Punishment was of course out of the question. Indeed it may be considered as a remarkable proof of the general's influence that Coll of the Cows deigned to apologise for conduct for which, in a well governed army, he would have been shot.[2]

As the Grants were in arms for King William, their property was

Quarrels in the Highland army

---

[1] Memoirs of Sir Ewan Cameron.   [2] Ibid.

considered as fair prize. Their territory was invaded by a party of Camerons : a skirmish took place : some blood was shed ; and many cattle were carried off to Dundee's camp, where provisions were greatly needed. This raid produced a quarrel, the history of which illustrates in the most striking manner the character of a Highland army. Among those who were slain in resisting the Camerons was a Macdonald of the Glengarry branch, who had long resided among the Grants, had become in feelings and opinions a Grant, and had absented himself from the muster of his tribe. Though he had been guilty of a high offence against the Gaelic code of honour and morality, his kinsmen remembered the sacred tie which he had forgotten. Good or bad, he was bone of their bone : he was flesh of their flesh ; and he should have been reserved for their justice. The name which he bore, the blood of the Lords of the Isles, should have been his protection. Glengarry in a rage went to Dundee and demanded vengeance on Lochiel and the whole race of Cameron. Dundee replied that the unfortunate gentleman who had fallen was a traitor to the clan as well as to the King. Was it ever heard of in war that the person of an enemy, a combatant in arms, was to be held inviolable on account of his name and descent ? And, even if wrong had been done, how was it to be redressed ? Half the army must slaughter the other half before a finger could be laid on Lochiel. Glengarry went away raging like a madman. Since his complaints were disregarded by those who ought to right him, he would right himself : he would draw out his men, and fall sword in hand on the murderers of his cousin. During some time he would listen to no expostulation. When he was reminded that Lochiel's followers were in number nearly double of the Glengarry men, " No matter," he cried, " one Macdonald is worth two Camerons." Had Lochiel been equally irritable and boastful, it is probable that the Highland insurrection would have given little more trouble to the government, and that the rebels would have perished obscurely in the wilderness by one another's claymores. But nature had bestowed on him in large measure the qualities of a statesman, though fortune had hidden those qualities in an obscure corner of the world. He saw that this was not a time for brawling : his own character for courage had long been established ; and his temper was under strict government. The fury of Glengarry, not being inflamed by any fresh provocation, rapidly abated. Indeed there were some who suspected that he had never been quite so pugnacious as he had affected to be, and that his bluster was meant only to keep up his own dignity in the eyes of his retainers. However this might be, the quarrel was composed ; and the two chiefs met, with the outward show of civility, at the general's table.[1]

[1] Memoirs of Sir Ewan Cameron.

What Dundee saw of his Celtic allies must have made him desirous to have in his army some troops on whose obedience he could depend, **Dundee applies to James for assistance** and who would not, at a signal from their colonel, turn their arms against their general and their king. He accordingly, during the months of May and June, sent to Dublin a succession of letters earnestly imploring assistance. If six thousand, four thousand, three thousand, regular soldiers were now sent to Lochaber, he trusted that His Majesty would soon hold a court in Holyrood. That such a force might be spared hardly admitted of a doubt. The authority of James was at that time acknowledged in every part of Ireland, except on the shores of Lough Erne and behind the ramparts of Londonderry. He had in that kingdom an army of forty thousand men. An eighth part of such an army would scarcely be missed there, and might, united with the clans which were in insurrection, effect great things in Scotland.

Dundee received such answers to his applications as encouraged him to hope that a large and well appointed force would soon be sent from Ulster to join him. He did not wish to try the chance of battle before these succours arrived.[1] Mackay, on the other hand, was weary of marching to and fro in a desert. His men were exhausted and out of heart. He thought it desirable that they should withdraw from the hill country ; and William was of the same opinion.

In June therefore the civil war was, as if by concert between the generals, completely suspended. Dundee remained in Lochaber, im- **The war in the Highlands suspended** patiently awaiting the arrival of troops and supplies from Ireland. It was impossible for him to keep his Highlanders together in a state of inactivity. A vast extent of moor and mountain was required to furnish food for so many mouths. The clans therefore went back to their own glens, having promised to reassemble on the first summons.

Meanwhile Mackay's soldiers, exhausted by severe exertions and privations, were taking their ease in quarters scattered over the low country from Aberdeen to Stirling. Mackay himself was at Edinburgh, and was urging the ministers there to furnish him with the means of constructing a chain of fortifications among the Grampians. The ministers had, it should seem, miscalculated their military resources. It had been expected that the Campbells would take the field in such force as would balance the whole strength of the clans which marched under Dundee. It had also been expected that the Covenanters of the West would hasten to swell the ranks of the army of King William. Both expectations were disappointed. Argyle had found his principality devastated, and his tribe disarmed and disorganised. A considerable time must elapse before his standard would be surrounded by an array

[1] Dundee to Melfort, June 27. 1689.

such as his forefathers had led to battle. The Covenanters of the West were in general unwilling to enlist. They were assuredly not wanting in courage; and they hated Dundee with deadly hatred. Scruples of the Covenanters about taking arms for King William In their part of the country the memory of his cruelty was still fresh. Every village had its own tale of blood. The greyheaded father was missed in one dwelling, the hopeful stripling in another. It was remembered but too well how the dragoons had stalked into the peasant's cottage, cursing and damning him, themselves, and each other at every second word, pushing from the ingle nook his grandmother of eighty, and thrusting their hands into the bosom of his daughter of sixteen; how the abjuration had been tendered to him; how he had folded his arms and said "God's will be done"; how the Colonel had called for a file with loaded muskets; and how in three minutes the goodman of the house had been wallowing in a pool of blood at his own door. The seat of the martyr was still vacant at the fireside; and every child could point out his grave still green amidst the heath. When the people of this region called their oppressor a servant of the devil, they were not speaking figuratively. They believed that between the bad man and the bad angel there was a close alliance on definite terms; that Dundee had bound himself to do the work of hell on earth, and that, for high purposes, hell was permitted to protect its slave till the measure of his guilt should be full. But, intensely as these men abhorred Dundee, most of them had a scruple about drawing the sword for William. A great meeting was held in the parish church of Douglas; and the question was propounded, whether, at a time when war was in the land, and when an Irish invasion was expected, it were not a duty to take arms. The debate was sharp and tumultuous. The orators on one side adjured their brethren not to incur the curse denounced against the inhabitants of Meroz, who came not to the help of the Lord against the mighty. The orators on the other side thundered against sinful associations. There were malignants in William's army: Mackay's own orthodoxy was problematical: to take military service with such comrades, and under such a general, would be a sinful association. At length, after much wrangling, and amidst great confusion, a vote was taken; and the majority pronounced that to take military service would be a sinful association. There was however a The Cameronian regiment raised large minority; and, from among the members of this minority, the Earl of Angus was able to raise a body of infantry, which is still, after the lapse of more than a hundred and sixty years, known by the name of the Cameronian Regiment. The first Lieutenant Colonel was Cleland, that implacable avenger of blood who had driven Dundee from the Convention. There was no small difficulty in filling the ranks; for many West country Whigs, who did not think it absolutely sinful to

enlist, stood out for terms subversive of all military discipline. Some
would not serve under any colonel, major, captain, serjeant, or corporal,
who was not ready to sign the Covenant. Others insisted that, if it
should be found absolutely necessary to appoint any officer who had
taken the tests imposed in the late reign, he should at least qualify himself for command by publicly confessing his sin at the head of the
regiment. Most of the enthusiasts who had proposed these conditions
were induced by dexterous management to abate much of their demands.
Yet the new regiment had a very peculiar character. The soldiers were
all rigid Puritans. One of their first acts was to petition the Parliament
that all drunkenness, licentiousness, and profaneness might be severely
punished. Their own conduct must have been exemplary : for the worst
crime which the most austere bigotry could impute to them was that of
huzzaing on the King's birthday. It was originally intended that with
the military organisation of the corps should be interwoven the organisation of a Presbyterian congregation. Each company was to furnish an
elder ; and the elders were, with the chaplain, to form an ecclesiastical
court for the suppression of immorality and heresy. Elders, however,
were not appointed : but a noted hill preacher, Alexander Shields, was
called to the office of chaplain. It is not easy to conceive that fanaticism
can be heated to a higher temperature than that which is indicated by
the writings of Shields. According to him, it should seem to be the
first duty of a Christian ruler to persecute to the death every heterodox
subject, and the first duty of a Christian subject to poniard a heterodox
ruler. Yet there was then in Scotland an enthusiasm compared with
which the enthusiasm even of this man was lukewarm. The extreme
Covenanters protested against his defection as vehemently as he had
protested against the Black Indulgence and the oath of supremacy, and
pronounced every man who entered Angus's regiment guilty of a wicked
confederacy with malignants.[1]

Meanwhile Edinburgh Castle had fallen, after holding out more than
two months. Both the defence and the attack had been languidly conducted. The Duke of Gordon, unwilling to incur the mortal
hatred of those at whose mercy his lands and life might soon
be, did not choose to batter the city. The assailants, on the
other hand, carried on their operations with so little energy and so little

Edinburgh
Castle
surrenders

[1] See Faithful Contendings Displayed, particularly the proceedings of April 29. and 30. and
of May 13. and 14. 1689 ; the petition to Parliament drawn up by the regiment, on July 18. 1689 ;
the protestation of Sir Robert Hamilton of November 6. 1689 ; and the admonitory Epistle to
the Regiment, dated March 27. 1690. The Society people, as they called themselves, seem to
have been especially shocked by the way in which the King's birthday had been kept. " We
hope," they wrote, " ye are against observing anniversary days as well as we, and that ye will
mourn for what ye have done." As to the opinions and temper of Alexander Shields, see his
Hind Let Loose.

vigilance that a constant communication was kept up between the Jacobites within the citadel and the Jacobites without. Strange stories were told of the polite and facetious messages which passed between the

JAMES DOUGLAS, EARL OF ANGUS

From a painting in the possession of the Earl of Mar and Kellie

besieged and the besiegers. On one occasion Gordon sent to inform the magistrates that he was going to fire a salute on account of some news which he had received from Ireland, but that the good town need not be alarmed, for that his guns would not be loaded with ball. On another occasion, his drums beat a parley : the white flag was hung out : a conference took place ; and he gravely informed the enemy that all his cards had been thumbed to pieces, and begged to have a few more packs. His friends established a telegraph by means of which they conversed with him across the lines of sentinels. From a window in the top story of one of the loftiest of those gigantic houses, a few of which still darken the High Street, a white cloth was hung out when all was well, and a black cloth when things went ill. If it was necessary to give more detailed information, a board was held up inscribed with capital letters so large that they could, by the help of a telescope, be read on the ramparts of the castle. Agents laden with letters and fresh provisions managed, in various disguises and by various shifts, to cross the sheet of water which then lay on the north of the fortress and to clamber up the precipitous ascent. The peal of a musket from a particular half moon was the signal which announced to the friends of the House of Stuart that another of their emissaries had got safe up the rock. But at length the supplies were exhausted ; and it was necessary to capitulate. Favourable terms were readily granted : the garrison marched out ; and the keys were delivered up amidst the acclamations of a great multitude of burghers.[1]

But the government had far more acrimonious and more pertinacious enemies in the Parliament House than in the Castle. When the Estates **Session of** reassembled after their adjournment, the crown and sceptre of **Parliament at Edin-** Scotland were displayed with the wonted pomp in the hall as **burgh** types of the absent sovereign. Hamilton rode in state from Holyrood up the High Street as Lord High Commissioner ; and Crawford took the chair as President. Two Acts, one turning the Convention into a Parliament, the other recognising William and Mary as King and Queen, were rapidly passed and touched with the sceptre ; and then the conflict of factions began.[2]

It speedily appeared that the opposition which Montgomery had organised was irresistibly strong. Though made up of many conflicting **Ascendency** elements, Republicans, Whigs, Tories, zealous Presbyterians, **of the Club** bigoted Prelatists, it acted for a time as one man, and drew to itself a multitude of those mean and timid politicians who naturally gravitate towards the stronger party. The friends of the government were few and disunited. Hamilton brought but half a heart to the discharge of his duties. He had always been unstable ; and he was now discontented. He held indeed the highest place to which a subject

---

[1] Siege of the Castle of Edinburgh, printed for the Bannatyne Club ; Lond. Gaz., June $\frac{10}{20}$. 1689.

[2] Act. Parl. Scot., June 5. June 17. 1689.

could aspire. But he imagined that he had only the show of power while others enjoyed the substance, and was not sorry to see those of whom he was jealous thwarted and annoyed. He did not absolutely betray the prince whom he represented : but he sometimes tampered

GEORGE, FIRST DUKE OF GORDON

From an engraving by J. Sauvé, in the Sutherland Collection

with the chiefs of the Club, and sometimes did sly ill turns to those who were joined with him in the service of the Crown.

His instructions directed him to give the royal assent to laws for the mitigating or removing of numerous grievances, and particularly to a law restricting the power and reforming the constitution of the Committee of Articles, and to a law establishing the Presbyterian Church Government.[1] But it mattered not what his instructions were. The chiefs of the Club were bent on finding a cause of quarrel. The propositions of the Government touching the Lords of the Articles were contemptuously rejected. Hamilton wrote to London for fresh directions ; and soon a second plan, which left little more than the name of the once despotic Committee, was sent back. But the second plan, though such as would have contented judicious and temperate reformers, shared the fate of the first. Meanwhile the chiefs of the Club laid on the table a law which interdicted the King from ever employing in any public office any person who had ever borne any part in any proceeding inconsistent with the Claim of Right, or who had ever obstructed or retarded any good design of the Estates. This law, uniting, within a very short compass, almost all the faults which a law can have, was well known to be aimed at the Lord President of the Court of Session, and at his son the Lord Advocate. Their prosperity and power made them objects of envy to every disappointed candidate for office. That they were new men, the first of their race who had risen to distinction, and that nevertheless they had, by the mere force of ability, become as important in the state as the Duke of Hamilton or the Earl of Argyle, was a thought which galled the hearts of many needy and haughty patricians. To the Whigs of Scotland the Dalrymples were what Halifax and Caermarthen were to the Whigs of England. Neither the exile of Sir James, nor the zeal with which Sir John had promoted the Revolution, was received as an atonement for old delinquency. They had both served the bloody and idolatrous House. They had both oppressed the people of God. Their late repentance might perhaps give them a fair claim to pardon, but surely gave them no right to honours and rewards.

The friends of the government in vain attempted to divert the attention of the Parliament from the business of persecuting the Dalrymple family to the important and pressing question of Church Government. They said that the old system had been abolished ; that no other system had been substituted ; that it was impossible to say what was the established religion of the kingdom ; and that the first duty of the legislature was to put an end to an anarchy which was daily producing disasters and crimes. The leaders of the Club were not to be so drawn away from their object. It was moved and resolved that the consideration of ecclesiastical affairs should be postponed till secular affairs had been settled. The unjust and absurd Act of Incapacitation was carried by seventy four voices to twenty

---

[1] The instructions will be found among the Somers Tracts.

four.   Another vote still more obviously aimed at the House of
Stair speedily followed.   The Parliament laid claim to a Veto on the
nomination of the Judges, and assumed the power of stopping the
signet, in other words, of suspending the whole administration of justice,
till this claim should be allowed.   It was plain from what passed in
debate that, though the chiefs of the Club had begun with the Court of
Session, they did not mean to end there.   The arguments used by Sir
Patrick Hume and others led directly to the conclusion that the King
ought not to have the appointment of any great public functionary.   Sir
Patrick indeed avowed, both in speech and in writing, his opinion that the
whole patronage of the realm ought to be transferred from the Crown to
the Estates.   When the place of Treasurer, of Chancellor, of Secretary, was
vacant, the Parliament ought to submit two or three names to His Majesty;
and one of those names His Majesty ought to be bound to select.[1]

All this time the Estates obstinately refused to grant any supply
till their Acts should have been touched with the sceptre.   The Lord
High Commissioner was at length so much provoked by their perverseness that, after long temporising, he refused to touch even Acts which
were in themselves unobjectionable, and to which his instructions
empowered him to consent.   This state of things would have ended in
some great convulsion, if the King of Scotland had not been also King
of a much greater and more opulent kingdom.   Charles the First had
never found any parliament at Westminster more unmanageable than
William, during this session, found the parliament at Edinburgh.   But
it was not in the power of the parliament at Edinburgh to put
on William such a pressure as the parliament at Westminster had put
on Charles.   A refusal of supplies at Westminster was a serious thing,
and left the Sovereign no choice except to yield, or to raise money by
unconstitutional means.   But a refusal of supplies at Edinburgh reduced
him to no such dilemma.   The largest sum that he could hope to
receive from Scotland in a year was less than what he received from
England every fortnight.   He had therefore only to entrench himself
within the limits of his undoubted prerogative, and there to remain on
the defensive, till some favourable conjuncture should arrive.[2]

While these things were passing in the Parliament House, the civil
war in the Highlands, having been during a few weeks suspended,
broke forth again more violently than before.   Since the   **Troubles**
splendour of the House of Argyle had been eclipsed, no   **in Athol**
Gaelic chief could vie in power with the Marquess of Athol.   The

---

[1] As to Sir Patrick's views, see his letter of the 7th of June, and Lockhart's letter of the 11th
of July, in the Leven and Melville Papers.

[2] My chief materials for the history of this session have been the Acts, the Minutes, and the
Leven and Melville Papers.

district from which he took his title, and of which he might almost be called the sovereign, was in extent larger than an ordinary county, and was more fertile, more diligently cultivated, and more thickly peopled than the greater part of the Highlands. The men who followed his banner were supposed to be not less numerous than all the Macdonalds and Macleans united, and were, in strength and courage, inferior to no tribe in the mountains. But the clan had been made insignificant by the insignificance of the chief. The Marquess was the falsest, the most fickle, the most pusillanimous, of mankind. Already, in the short space of six months, he had been several times a Jacobite, and several times a Williamite. Both Jacobites and Williamites regarded him with contempt and distrust, which respect for his immense power prevented them from fully expressing. After repeatedly vowing fidelity to both parties, and repeatedly betraying both, he began to think that he should best provide for his safety by abdicating the functions both of a peer and of a chieftain, by absenting himself both from the Parliament House at Edinburgh and from his castle in the mountains, and by quitting the country to which he was bound by every tie of duty and honour at the very crisis of her fate. While all Scotland was waiting with impatience and anxiety to see in which army his numerous retainers would be arrayed, he stole away to England, settled himself at Bath, and pretended to drink the waters.[1] His principality, left without a head, was divided against itself. The general leaning of the Athol men was towards King James. For they had been employed by him, only four years before, as the ministers of his vengeance against the House of Argyle. They had garrisoned Inverary: they had ravaged Lorn: they had demolished houses, cut down fruit trees, burned fishing boats, broken millstones, hanged Campbells, and were therefore not likely to be pleased by the prospect of Mac Callum More's restoration. One word from the Marquess would have sent two thousand claymores to the Jacobite side. But that word he would not speak; and the consequence was, that the conduct of his followers was as irresolute and inconsistent as his own.

While they were waiting for some indication of his wishes, they were called to arms at once by two leaders, either of whom might, with some show of reason, claim to be considered as the representative of the absent chief. Lord Murray, the Marquess's eldest son, who was married to a daughter of the Duke of Hamilton, declared for King William. Stewart of Ballenach, the Marquess's confidential agent, declared for King James. The people knew not which summons to obey. He whose

---

[1] "Athol," says Dundee contemptuously, "is gone to England, who did not know what to do."—Dundee to Melfort, June 27. 1689. See Athol's letters to Melville of the 21st of May and the 8th of June, in the Leven and Melville Papers.

authority would have been held in profound reverence had plighted faith to both sides, and had then run away for fear of being under the neces-

JOHN MURRAY, FIRST MARQUIS OF ATHOLL
From a painting in the possession of Macleod of Macleod

sity of joining either ; nor was it very easy to say whether the place which he had left vacant belonged to his steward or to his heir apparent.

The most important military post in Athol was Blair Castle. The house which now bears that name is not distinguished by any striking peculiarity from other country seats of the aristocracy. The old building was a lofty tower of rude architecture which commanded a vale watered by the Garry. The walls would have offered very little resistance to a battering train, but were quite strong enough to keep the herdsmen of the Grampians in awe. About five miles south of this stronghold, the valley of the Garry contracts itself into the celebrated glen of Killiecrankie. At present a highway as smooth as any road in Middlesex ascends gently from the low country to the summit of the defile. White villas peep from the birch forest ; and, on a fine summer day, there is scarcely a turn of the pass at which may not be seen some angler casting his fly on the foam of the river, some artist sketching a pinnacle of rock, or some party of pleasure banqueting on the turf in the fretwork of shade and sunshine. But, in the days of William the Third, Killiecrankie was mentioned with horror by the peaceful and industrious inhabitants of the Perthshire lowlands. It was deemed the most perilous of all those dark ravines through which the marauders of the hills were wont to sally forth. The sound, so musical to modern ears, of the river brawling round the mossy rocks and among the smooth pebbles, the masses of grey crag and dark verdure worthy of the pencil of Wilson, the fantastic peaks bathed, at sunrise and sunset, with light rich as that which glows on the canvass of Claude, suggested to our ancestors thoughts of murderous ambuscades, and of bodies stripped, gashed, and abandoned to the birds of prey. The only path was narrow and rugged : a horse could with difficulty be led up : two men could hardly walk abreast ; and, in some places, the way ran so close by the precipice that the traveller had great need of a steady eye and foot. Many years later, the first Duke of Athol constructed a road up which it was just possible to drag his coach. But even that road was so steep and so strait that a handful of resolute men might have defended it against an army ;[1] nor did any Saxon consider a visit to Killiecrankie as a pleasure, till experience had taught the English Government that the weapons by which the Celtic clans could be most effectually subdued were the pickaxe and the spade.

The country which lay just above this pass was now the theatre of a war such as the Highlands had not often witnessed. Men wearing **The war breaks out again in the Highlands** the same tartan, and attached to the same lord, were arrayed against each other. The name of the absent chief was used, with some show of reason, on both sides. Ballenach, at the head of a body of vassals who considered him as the representative of the Marquess, occupied Blair Castle. Murray, with twelve hundred

[1] Memoirs of Sir Ewan Cameron.

followers, appeared before the walls, and demanded to be admitted into the mansion of his family, the mansion which would one day be his

JOHN, LORD MURRAY, AFTERWARDS FIRST DUKE OF ATHOLL

From a painting in the possession of the present duke

own.   The garrison refused to open the gates.   Messages were sent off by the besiegers to Edinburgh, and by the besieged to Lochaber.[1]   In

[1] Mackay's Memoirs.

both places the tidings produced great agitation. Mackay and Dundee agreed in thinking that the crisis required prompt and strenuous exertion. On the fate of Blair Castle probably depended the fate of all Athol. On the fate of Athol might depend the fate of Scotland. Mackay hastened northward, and ordered his troops to assemble in the low country of Perthshire. Some of them were quartered at such a distance that they did not arrive in time. He soon, however, had with him the three Scotch regiments which had served in Holland, and which bore the names of their colonels, Mackay himself, Balfour, and Ramsay. There was also a gallant regiment of infantry from England, then called Hastings's, but now known as the thirteenth of the line. With these old troops were joined two regiments newly levied in the Lowlands. One of them was commanded by Lord Kenmore; the other, which had been raised on the Border, and which is still styled the King's Own Borderers, by Lord Leven. Two troops of horse, Lord Annandale's and Lord Belhaven's, probably made up the army to the number of above three thousand men. Belhaven rode at the head of his troop: but Annandale, the most factious of all Montgomery's followers, preferred the Club and the Parliament House to the field.[1]

Dundee, meanwhile, had summoned all the clans which acknowledged his commission to assemble for an expedition into Athol. His exertions were strenuously seconded by Lochiel. The fiery crosses were sent again in all haste through Appin and Ardnamurchan, up Glenmore, and along Loch Leven. But the call was so unexpected, and the time allowed was so short, that the muster was not a very full one. The whole number of broadswords seems to have been under three thousand. With this force, such as it was, Dundee set forth. On his march he was joined by succours which had just arrived from Ulster. They consisted of little more than three hundred Irish foot, ill armed, ill clothed, and ill disciplined. Their commander was an officer named Cannon, who had seen service in the Netherlands, and who might perhaps have acquitted himself well in a subordinate post and in a regular army, but who was altogether unequal to the part now assigned to him.[2] He had already loitered among the Hebrides so long that some ships which had been sent with him, and which were laden with stores, had been taken by English cruisers. He and his soldiers had with difficulty escaped the same fate. Incompetent as he was, he bore a commission which gave him military rank in Scotland next to Dundee.

The disappointment was severe. In truth James would have done better to withhold all assistance from the Highlanders than to mock them by sending them, instead of the well appointed army which they had asked and expected, a rabble contemptible in numbers and

[1] Mackay's Memoirs.   [2] Van Odyck to the Greffier of the States General, Aug. $\frac{2}{12}$. 1689.

THE PASS OF KILLIECRANKIE.

From a water-colour drawing by G. F. Robson, in the Sutherland Collection.

appearance.　It was now evident that whatever was done for his cause in Scotland must be done by Scottish hands.[1]

While Mackay from one side, and Dundee from the other, were advancing towards Blair Castle, important events had taken place there. Murray's adherents soon began to waver in their fidelity to him.　They had an old antipathy to Whigs; for they considered the name of Whig as synonymous with the name of Campbell.　They saw arrayed against them a large number of their kinsmen, commanded by a gentleman who was supposed to possess the confidence of the Marquess.　The besieging army therefore melted rapidly away.　Many returned home on the plea that, as their neighbourhood was about to be the seat of war, they must place their families and cattle in security.　Others more ingenuously declared that they would not fight in such a quarrel.　One large body went to a brook, filled their bonnets with water, drank a health to King James, and then dispersed.[2]　Their zeal for King James, however, did not induce them to join the standard of his general.　They lurked among the rocks and thickets which overhang the Garry, in the hope that there would soon be a battle, and that, whatever might be the event, there would be fugitives and corpses to plunder.

Murray was in a strait.　His force had dwindled to three or four hundred men: even in those men he could put little trust; and the Macdonalds and Camerons were advancing fast.　He therefore raised the siege of Blair Castle, and retired with a few followers into the defile of Killiecrankie.　There he was soon joined by a detachment of two hundred fusileers whom Mackay had sent forward to secure the pass. The main body of the Lowland army speedily followed.[3]

Early in the morning of Saturday the twenty-seventh of July, Dundee arrived at Blair Castle.　There he learned that Mackay's troops were already in the ravine of Killiecrankie.　It was necessary to come to a prompt decision.　A council of war was held.　The Saxon officers were generally against hazarding a battle.　The Celtic chiefs were of a different opinion.　Glengarry and Lochiel were now both of a mind. "Fight, my Lord," said Lochiel with his usual energy: "fight immediately: fight, if you have only one to three.　Our men are in heart. Their only fear is that the enemy should escape.　Give them their way; and be assured that they will either perish or gain a complete victory. But if you restrain them, if you force them to remain on the defensive, I answer for nothing.　If we do not fight, we had better break up and retire to our mountains."[4]

Dundee's countenance brightened.　"You hear, gentlemen," he said to his Lowland officers, "you hear the opinion of one who understands

[1] Memoirs of Sir Ewan Cameron.
[2] Balcarras's Memoirs.
[3] Mackay's Short Relation, dated Aug. 17. 1689.
[4] Memoirs of Sir Ewan Cameron.

Highland war better than any of us." No voice was raised on the other side. It was determined to fight ; and the confederated clans in high spirits set forward to encounter the enemy.

The enemy meanwhile had made his way up the pass. The ascent had been long and toilsome : for even the foot had to climb by twos and threes ; and the baggage horses, twelve hundred in number, could mount only one at a time. No wheeled carriage had ever been tugged up that arduous path. The head of the column had emerged and was on the table land, while the rearguard was still in the plain below. At length the passage was effected ; and the troops found themselves in a valley of no great extent. Their right was flanked by a rising ground, their left by the Garry. Wearied with the morning's work, they threw themselves on the grass to take some rest and refreshment.

Early in the afternoon, they were roused by an alarm that the Highlanders were approaching. Regiment after regiment started up and got into order. In a little while the summit of an ascent which was about a musket shot before them was covered with bonnets and plaids. Dundee rode forward for the purpose of surveying the force with which he was to contend, and then drew up his own men with as much skill as their peculiar character permitted him to exert. It was desirable to keep the clans distinct. Each tribe, large or small, formed a column separated from the next column by a wide interval. One of these battalions might contain seven hundred men, while another consisted of only a hundred and twenty. Lochiel had represented that it was impossible to mix men of different tribes without destroying all that constituted the peculiar strength of a Highland army.[1]

On the right, close to the Garry, were the Macleans. Nearest to them were Cannon and his Irish foot. Next stood the Macdonalds of Clanronald, commanded by the guardian of their young prince. On their left were other bands of Macdonalds. At the head of one large battalion towered the stately form of Glengarry, who bore in his hand the royal standard of King James the Seventh.[2] Still further to the left were the cavalry, a small squadron, consisting of some Jacobite gentlemen who had fled from the Lowlands to the mountains, and of about forty of Dundee's old troopers. The horses had been ill fed and ill tended among the Grampians, and looked miserably lean and feeble. Beyond them was Lochiel with his Camerons. On the extreme left, the men of Sky were marshalled by Macdonald of Sleat.[3]

In the Highlands, as in all countries where war has not become a science, men thought it the most important duty of a commander to set an example of personal courage and of bodily exertion. Lochiel was

[1] Memoirs of Sir Ewan Cameron ; Mackay's Memoirs.
[2] Douglas's Baronage of Scotland.   [3] Memoirs of Sir Ewan Cameron.

especially renowned for his physical prowess. His clansmen looked big with pride when they related how he had himself broken hostile ranks and hewn down tall warriors. He probably owed quite as much of his influence to these achievements as to the high qualities which, if fortune had placed him in the English Parliament or at the French court, would have made him one of the foremost men of his age. He had the sense however to perceive how erroneous was the notion which his countrymen had formed. He knew that to give and to take blows was not the business of a general. He knew with how much difficulty Dundee had been able to keep together, during a few days, an army composed of several clans ; and he knew that what Dundee had effected with difficulty Cannon would not be able to effect at all. The life on which so much depended must not be sacrificed to a barbarous prejudice. Lochiel therefore adjured Dundee not to run into any unnecessary danger. " Your Lordship's business," he said, " is to overlook everything, and to issue your commands. Our business is to execute those commands bravely and promptly." Dundee answered with calm magnanimity that there was much weight in what his friend Sir Ewan had urged, but that no general could effect anything great without possessing the confidence of his men. " I must establish my character for courage. Your people expect to see their leaders in the thickest of the battle ; and to day they shall see me there. I promise you, on my honour, that in future fights I will take more care of myself."

Meanwhile a fire of musketry was kept up on both sides, but more skilfully and more steadily by the regular soldiers than by the mountaineers. The space between the armies was one cloud of smoke. Not a few Highlanders dropped ; and the clans grew impatient. The sun however was low in the west before Dundee gave the order to prepare for action. His men raised a great shout. The enemy, probably exhausted by the toil of the day, returned a feeble and wavering cheer. " We shall do it now," said Lochiel : " that is not the cry of men who are going to win." He had walked through all his ranks, had addressed a few words to every Cameron, and had taken from every Cameron a promise to conquer or die.[1]

It was past seven o'clock. Dundee gave the word. The Highlanders dropped their plaids. The few who were so luxurious as to wear rude socks of untanned hide spurned them away. It was long remembered in Lochaber that Lochiel took off what probably was the only pair of shoes in his clan, and charged barefoot at the head of his men. The whole line advanced firing. The enemy returned the fire and did much execution. When only a small space was left between the armies, the Highlanders suddenly flung away their firelocks, drew

---

[1] Memoirs of Sir Ewan Cameron.

their broadswords, and rushed forward with a fearful yell. The Lowlanders prepared to receive the shock : but this was then a long and
awkward process ; and the soldiers were still fumbling with the muzzles
of their guns and the handles of their bayonets when the whole flood
of Macleans, Macdonalds, and Camerons came down. In two minutes
the battle was lost and won. The ranks of Balfour's regiment broke.
He was cloven down while struggling in the press. Ramsay's men
turned their backs and dropped their arms. Mackay's own foot were
swept away by the furious onset of the Camerons. His brother and
nephew exerted themselves in vain to rally the men. The former
was laid dead on the ground by a stroke from a claymore. The latter,
with eight wounds on his body, made his way through the tumult and
carnage to his uncle's side. Even in that extremity Mackay retained
all his selfpossession. He had still one hope. A charge of horse might
recover the day ; for of horse the bravest Highlanders were supposed to
stand in awe. But he called on the horse in vain. Belhaven indeed
behaved like a gallant gentleman : but his troopers, appalled by the
rout of the infantry, galloped off in disorder: Annandale's men followed :
all was over; and the mingled torrent of redcoats and tartans went raving
down the valley to the gorge of Killiecrankie.

Mackay, accompanied by one trusty servant, spurred bravely through
the thickest of the claymores and targets, and reached a point from
which he had a view of the field. His whole army had disappeared,
with the exception of some Borderers whom Leven had kept together, and of the English regiment, which had poured a murderous
fire into the Celtic ranks, and which still kept unbroken order. All the
men that could be collected were only a few hundreds. The general
made haste to lead them across the Garry, and, having put that river
between them and the enemy, paused for a moment to meditate on his
situation.

He could hardly understand how the conquerors could be so unwise
as to allow him even that moment for deliberation. They might with
ease have killed or taken all who were with him before the night closed
in. But the energy of the Celtic warriors had spent itself in one furious
rush and one short struggle. The pass was choked by the twelve
hundred beasts of burden which carried the provisions and baggage of
the vanquished army. Such a booty was irresistibly tempting to men
who were impelled to war quite as much by the desire of rapine as by the
desire of glory. It is probable that few even of the chiefs were disposed to
leave so rich a prize for the sake of King James. Dundee himself might
at that moment have been unable to persuade his followers to quit the
heaps of spoil, and to complete the great work of the day ; and Dundee
was no more.

At the beginning of the action he had taken his place in front of his little band of cavalry. He bade them follow him, and rode forward.

The Vis- count Dundee

JOHN GRAHAM OF CLAVERHOUSE, FIRST VISCOUNT DUNDEE

From a mezzotint by R. Williams

But it seemed to be decreed that, on that day, the Lowland Scotch should in both armies appear to disadvantage. The horse hesitated. Dundee turned round, stood up in his stirrups, and, waving his hat,

invited them to come on.   As he lifted his arm, his cuirass rose, and exposed the lower part of his left side.   A musket ball struck him : his horse

Death of   sprang forward and plunged into a cloud of smoke and dust,
Dundee   which hid from both armies the fall of the victorious general.
A person named Johnstone was near him, and caught him as he sank
down from the saddle.   " How goes the day ? " said Dundee.   " Well
for King James ; " answered Johnstone : " but I am sorry for Your Lordship."   " If it is well for him," answered the dying man, " it matters the
less for me."   He never spoke again : but when, half an hour later, Lord
Dunfermline and some other friends came to the spot, they thought that
they could still discern some faint remains of life.   The body, wrapped
in two plaids, was carried to the Castle of Blair.[1]

Mackay, who was ignorant of Dundee's fate, and well acquainted
with Dundee's skill and activity, expected to be instantly and hotly

Retreat of   pursued, and had very little expectation of being able to save
Mackay   the scanty remains of the vanquished army.   He could not
retreat by the pass : for the Highlanders were already there.   He therefore resolved to push across the mountains towards the valley of the
Tay.   He soon overtook two or three hundred of his runaways who had
taken the same road.   Most of them belonged to Ramsay's regiment,
and must have seen service.   But they were unarmed : they were utterly
bewildered by the recent disaster ; and the general could find among
them no remains either of martial discipline or of martial spirit.   His
situation was one which must have severely tried the firmest nerves.
Night had set in : he was in a desert : he had no guide : a victorious
enemy was, in all human probability, on his track ; and he had to provide for the safety of a crowd of men who had lost both head and heart.
He had just suffered a defeat of all defeats the most painful and humiliating.   His domestic feelings had been not less severely wounded than
his professional feelings.   One dear kinsman had just been struck dead
before his eyes.   Another, bleeding from many wounds, moved feebly
at his side.   But the unfortunate general's courage was sustained by a
firm faith in God, and a high sense of duty to the state.   In the midst of
misery and disgrace, he still held his head nobly erect, and found fortitude,
not only for himself, but for all around him.   His first care was to be
sure of his road.   A solitary light which twinkled through the darkness

---

[1] As to the battle, see Mackay's Memoirs, Letters, and Short Relation ; the Memoirs of Dundee ; Memoirs of Sir Ewan Cameron ; Nisbet's and Osburne's depositions in the Appendix to the
Act. Parl. of July 14. 1690.   See also the account of the battle in one of Burt's Letters.   Macpherson printed a letter from Dundee to James dated the day after the battle.   I need not say
that it is as impudent a forgery as Fingal.   The author of the Memoirs of Dundee says that Lord
Leven was scared by the sight of the Highland weapons, and set the example of flight.   This
is a spiteful falsehood.   That Leven behaved remarkably well is proved by Mackay's Letters,
Memoirs, and Short Relation.

guided him to a small hovel. The inmates spoke no tongue but the Gaelic, and were at first scared by the appearance of uniforms and arms. But Mackay's gentle manner removed their apprehension : their language had been familiar to him in childhood ; and he retained enough of it to communicate with them. By their directions, and by the help of a pocket map, in which the routes through that wild country were roughly laid down, he was able to find his way. He marched all night. When day broke his task was more difficult than ever. Light increased the terror of his companions. Hastings's men and Leven's men indeed still behaved themselves like soldiers. But the fugitives from Ramsay's were a mere rabble. They had flung away their muskets. The broadswords from which they had fled were ever in their eyes. Every fresh object caused a fresh panic. A company of herdsmen in plaids driving cattle was magnified by imagination into a host of Celtic warriors. Some of the runaways left the main body and fled to the hills, where their cowardice met with a proper punishment. They were killed for their coats and shoes ; and their naked carcasses were left for a prey to the eagles of Ben Lawers. The desertion would have been much greater, had not Mackay and his officers, pistol in hand, threatened to blow out the brains of any man whom they caught attempting to steal off.

At length the weary fugitives came in sight of Weem Castle. The proprietor of the mansion was a friend to the new government, and extended to them such hospitality as was in his power. His stores of oatmeal were brought out : kine were slaughtered ; and a rude and hasty meal was set before the numerous guests. Thus refreshed, they again set forth, and marched all day over bog, moor, and mountain. Thinly inhabited as the country was, they could plainly see that the report of their disaster had already spread far, and that the population was everywhere in a state of great excitement. Late at night they reached Castle Drummond, which was held for King William by a small garrison ; and, on the following day, they proceeded with less difficulty to Stirling.[1]

The tidings of their defeat had outrun them. All Scotland was in a ferment. The disaster had indeed been great : but it was exaggerated by the wild hopes of one party and by the wild fears of the   **Effect of** other. It was at first believed that the whole army of King   **the battle** William had perished ; that Mackay himself had fallen ; that   **crankie** Dundee, at the head of a great host of barbarians, flushed with victory and impatient for spoil, had already descended from the hills ; that he was master of the whole country beyond the Forth ; that Fife was up to join him ; that in three days he would be at Stirling ; that in a week

[1] Mackay's Memoirs ; Life of General Hugh Mackay by J. Mackay of Rockfield.

he would be at Holyrood. Messengers were sent to urge a regiment which lay in Northumberland to hasten across the border. Others carried to London earnest entreaties that His Majesty would instantly send every soldier that could be spared, nay, that he would come himself to save his northern kingdom. The factions of the Parliament

The Scottish Parliament adjourned House, awestruck by the common danger, forgot to wrangle. Courtiers and malecontents with one voice implored the Lord High Commissioner to close the session, and to dismiss them from a place where their deliberations might soon be interrupted by the mountaineers. It was seriously considered whether it might not be expedient to abandon Edinburgh, to send the numerous state prisoners who were in the Castle and the Tolbooth on board of a man of war which lay off Leith, and to transfer the seat of government to Glasgow.

The news of Dundee's victory was everywhere speedily followed by the news of his death ; and it is a strong proof of the extent and vigour of his faculties that his death seems everywhere to have been regarded as a complete set off against his victory. Hamilton, before he adjourned the Estates, informed them that he had good tidings for them, that Dundee was certainly dead, and that therefore the rebels had on the whole sustained a defeat. In several letters written at that conjuncture by able and experienced politicians a similar opinion is expressed. The messenger who rode with the news of the battle to the English capital was fast followed by another who carried a despatch for the King, and, not finding His Majesty at Saint James's, galloped to Hampton Court. Nobody in the capital ventured to break the seal ; but fortunately, after the letter had been closed, some friendly hand had hastily written on the outside a few words of comfort : " Dundee is killed. Mackay has got to Stirling :" and these words seem to have quieted the minds of the Londoners.[1]

From the pass of Killiecrankie the Highlanders had retired, proud of their victory, and laden with spoil, to the Castle of Blair. They boasted that the field of battle was covered with heaps of Saxon soldiers, and that the appearance of the corpses bore ample testimony to the power of a good Gaelic broadsword in a good Gaelic right hand. Heads were found cloven down to the throat, and skulls struck clean off just above the ears. The conquerors however had bought their victory dear. While they were advancing, they had been much galled by the musketry of the enemy ; and, even after the decisive charge, Hastings's Englishmen and some of Leven's Borderers had continued to keep up a steady fire. A hundred and twenty Camerons had been slain : the loss of the

---

[1] Letter of the Extraordinary Ambassadors to the Greffier of the States General, August $\frac{2}{12}$. 1689 ; and a letter of the same date from Van Odyck, who was at Hampton Court.

THE
Scotch Protestants Courage:
OR,
The Destruction, Death, and Downfall
OF
DUNDEE.

To the Tune of, *Billy and Molly.*   *Licensed according to Order.*

HEre's joyful tydings now we bring
from the spite Scottish Nation,
The fame of Protestants Bell ring,
though Town and Corporation:
The Rebell which did lead the Van,
and o're the Mountains scour'd,
At length brave Borgis dead and gone,
and all his Forces rout'd.

The Protestant great General,
upon his men to Battel,
Although on both sides some did fall,
We made Dundee in field to March,
while Guns and Drums did rattle.

In noble shining Armour bright,
four fade both brisk and airy
March'd with Mackay in field to fight,
for William and Queen Mary;
Alas the fray near lasted long,
when once we went about it,
Dundee was slain in all the throng,
likewise his Rebells rout'd.

Though he at first rid up in state,
too soon did Mars his Glory,
a Pistol Bullet sent him strait
from honor, to Purgatory:
His Rebells they did likewise run,
and though the Gallies scour'd,
So oft each man and mothers son
by Protestants were rout'd.

The Clans and the Mackdonells too,
and all the Heathen faction;
When they had told that this was true
they all were in distraction;
There hearts were still with fear and dread,
as through the Walls they scour'd;
Still crying out, Dundee is dead,
and we shall all be rout'd.

The fight they bravely did maintain
and while they were about it;
Dundee in field was fairly slain,
and all his Rebells routed.

Mackay he did the Rebells face,
that valiant stout Commander;
And for his Courage seem'd to trace
the steps of Alexander:
His forces he drew up with speed,
although the Papists scour'd;
He made Dundee in field to March,
and all his forces routed.

Five hundred Rebells, Foot and Horse,
one had a Town did plunder,
Bur Mackay hearing of that loss,
strait after them did Thunder:
He charg'd and fir'd in the Re-
as they before him scour'd,
Till he at last the Coast did clear,
and they were more than rout'd.

We cut them down as they did fly
and stoutly follow'd after,
The Noise smote them hip and Thigh,
I saith with a great slaughter:
There some was slain, the rest was tak
who on our Forces scour'd,
In this sharp fray, we gave the Day
and all the Rebells rout'd.

Some say Dundee has fled his wrath,
and sie to Purgatory,
But some are of another mind,
enjoying the same a story;
They heard him tell his spirit trade,
upon the Scotish Borders,
While he said God was for'd to take
away to Hell for others.

Printed for P. Brooksby, J. Deacon, J. Blare, and I. Back.

SCOTCH PROTESTANTS' COURAGE

From the Pepysian Collection of Ballads

Macdonalds had been still greater; and several gentlemen of birth and note had fallen.[1]

Dundee was buried in the church of Blair Athol: but no monument was erected over his grave; and the church itself has long disappeared. A rude stone on the field of battle marks, if local tradition can be trusted, the place where he fell.[2] During the last three months of his life he had approved himself a great warrior and politician; and his name is therefore mentioned with respect by that large class of persons who think that there is no excess of wickedness for which courage and ability do not atone.

It is curious that the two most remarkable battles that perhaps were ever gained by irregular over regular troops should have been fought in the same week; the battle of Killiecrankie, and the battle of Newton Butler. In both battles the success of the irregular troops was singularly rapid and complete. In both battles the panic of the regular troops, in spite of the conspicuous example of courage set by their generals, was singularly disgraceful. It ought also to be noted that, of these extraordinary victories, one was gained by Celts over Saxons, and the other by Saxons over Celts. The victory of Killiecrankie indeed, though neither more splendid nor more important than the victory of Newton Butler, is far more widely renowned; and the reason is evident. The Anglosaxon and the Celt have been reconciled in Scotland, and have never been reconciled in Ireland. In Scotland all the great actions of both races are thrown into a common stock, and are considered as making up the glory which belongs to the whole country. So completely has the old antipathy been extinguished that nothing is more usual than to hear a Lowlander talk with complacency and even with pride of the most humiliating defeat that his ancestors ever underwent. It would be difficult to name any eminent man in whom national feeling and clannish feeling were stronger than in Sir Walter Scott. Yet when Sir Walter Scott mentioned Killiecrankie, he seemed utterly to forget that he was a Saxon, that he was of the same blood and of the same speech with Ramsay's foot and Annandale's horse. His heart swelled with triumph when he related how his own kindred had fled like hares before a smaller number of warriors of a different breed and of a different tongue.

In Ireland the feud remains unhealed. The name of Newton Butler, insultingly repeated by a minority, is hateful to the great majority of the population. If a monument were set up on the field of battle, it would probably be defaced: if a festival were held in Cork or Waterford on

[1] Memoirs of Sir Ewan Cameron; Memoirs of Dundee.

[2] The tradition is certainly much more than a hundred and twenty years old. The stone was pointed out to Burt.

the anniversary of the battle, it would probably be interrupted by violence. The most illustrious Irish poet of our time would have thought it treason to his country to sing the praises of the conquerors. One of the most learned and diligent Irish archæologists of our time has laboured, not indeed very successfully, to prove that the event of the day was decided by a mere accident from which the Englishry could derive no glory. We cannot wonder that the victory of the Highlanders should be more celebrated than the victory of the Enniskilleners when we consider that the victory of the Highlanders is matter of boast to all Scotland, and that the victory of the Enniskilleners is matter of shame to three fourths of Ireland.

As far as the great interests of the State were concerned, it mattered not at all whether the battle of Killiecrankie were lost or won. It is very improbable that even Dundee, if he had survived the most glorious day of his life, could have surmounted those difficulties which sprang from the peculiar nature of his army, and which would have increased tenfold as soon as the war was transferred to the Lowlands. It is certain that his successor was altogether unequal to the task. During a day or two, indeed, the new general might flatter himself that all would go well. His army was rapidly swollen to near double the number of claymores that Dundee had commanded. The Stewarts of Appin, who, though full of zeal, had not been able to come up in time for the battle, were among the first who arrived. Several clans who had hitherto waited to see which side was the stronger, were now eager to descend on the Lowlands under the standard of King James the Seventh. The Grants indeed continued to bear true allegiance to William and Mary; and the Mackintoshes were kept neutral by unconquerable aversion to Keppoch. But Macphersons, Farquharsons, and Frasers came in crowds to the camp at Blair. The hesitation of the Athol men was at an end. Many of them had lurked, during the fight, among the crags and birch trees of Killiecrankie, and, as soon as the event of the day was decided, had emerged from those hiding places to strip and butcher the fugitives who tried to escape by the pass. The Robertsons, a Gaelic race, though bearing a Saxon name, gave in at this conjuncture their adhesion to the cause of the exiled King. Their chief Alexander, who took his appellation from his lordship of Struan, was a very young man and a student at the University of Saint Andrew's. He had there acquired a smattering of letters, and had been initiated much more deeply into Tory politics. He now joined the Highland army, and continued, through a long life, to be constant to the Jacobite cause. His part, however, in public affairs was so insignificant that his name would not now be remembered, if he had not left a volume of poems, always very stupid and often very profligate. Had this book

The High-land army reinforced

been manufactured in Grub Street, it would scarcely have been honoured with a quarter of a line in the Dunciad. But it attracted some notice on account of the situation of the writer. For, a hundred and twenty years ago, an eclogue or a lampoon written by a Highland chief was a literary portent.[1]

But, though the numerical strength of Cannon's forces was increasing, their efficiency was diminishing. Every new tribe which joined the camp brought with it some new cause of dissension. In the hour of peril, the most arrogant and mutinous spirits will often submit to the guidance of superior genius. Yet, even in the hour of peril, and even to the genius of Dundee, the Celtic chiefs had yielded but a precarious and imperfect obedience. To restrain them, when intoxicated with success and confident of their strength, would probably have been too hard a task even for him, as it had been, in the preceding generation, too hard a task for Montrose. The new general did nothing but hesitate and blunder. One of his first acts was to send a large body of men, chiefly Robertsons, down into the low country for the purpose of collecting provisions. He seems to have supposed that this detachment would without difficulty occupy Perth. But Mackay had already restored order among the remains of his army : he had assembled round him some troops which had not shared in the disgrace of the late defeat ; and he was again ready for action. Cruel as his sufferings had been, he had wisely and magnanimously resolved not to punish what was past. To distinguish between degrees of guilt was not easy. To decimate the guilty would have been to commit a frightful massacre. His habitual piety too led him to consider the unexampled panic which had seized his soldiers as a proof rather of the divine displeasure than of their cowardice. He acknowledged with heroic humility that the singular firmness which he had himself displayed in the midst of the confusion and havoc was not his own, and that he might well, but for the support of a higher power, have behaved as pusillanimously as any of the wretched runaways who had thrown away their weapons and implored quarter in vain from the barbarous marauders of Athol. His dependence on heaven did not, however, prevent him from applying himself vigorously to the work of providing, as far as human prudence could provide, against the recurrence of such a calamity as that which he had just experienced. The immediate cause of the late defeat was the difficulty of fixing bayonets. The firelock of the Highlander was quite distinct from the weapon which he used in close fight. He discharged his shot, threw

[1] See the History prefixed to the poems of Alexander Robertson. In this history he is represented as having joined before the battle of Killiecrankie. But it appears from the evidence which is in the Appendix to the Act. Parl. Scot. of July 14. 1690, that he came in on the following day.

away his gun, and fell on with his sword. This was the work of a moment. It took the regular musketeer two or three minutes to alter

ALEXANDER ROBERTSON OF STRUAN

From the painting in the National Portrait Gallery of Scotland. Artist unknown

his missile weapon into a weapon with which he could encounter an enemy hand to hand ; and during these two or three minutes the event of the battle of Killiecrankie had been decided. Mackay therefore ordered all his bayonets to be so formed that they might be screwed upon the barrel without stopping it up, and that his men might be able to receive a charge the very instant after firing.[1]

As soon as he learned that a detachment of the Gaelic army was advancing towards Perth, he hastened to meet them at the head of a body of dragoons who had not been in the battle, and whose spirit was therefore unbroken. On Wednesday the thirty-first of July, only four days after his defeat, he fell in with the Robertsons, attacked them, routed them, killed a hundred and twenty of them, and took thirty prisoners, with the loss of only a single soldier.[2] This skirmish produced an effect quite out of proportion to the number of the combatants or of the slain. The reputation of the Celtic arms went down almost as fast as it had risen. During two or three days it had been everywhere imagined that those arms were invincible. There was now a reaction. It was perceived that what had happened at Killiecrankie was an exception to ordinary rules, and that the Highlanders were not, except in very peculiar circumstances, a match for good regular troops.

Skirmish at Saint Johnston's

Meanwhile the disorders of Cannon's camp went on increasing. He called a council of war to consider what course it would be advisable to take. But, as soon as the council had met, a preliminary question was raised. Who were entitled to be consulted? The army was almost exclusively a Highland army. The recent victory had been won exclusively by Highland warriors. Great chiefs, who had brought six or seven hundred fighting men into the field, did not think it fair that they should be outvoted by gentlemen from Ireland and from the low country, who bore indeed King James's commission, and were called Colonels and Captains, but who were Colonels without regiments and Captains without companies. Lochiel spoke strongly in behalf of the class to which he belonged: but Cannon decided that the votes of the Saxon officers should be reckoned.[3]

Disorders in the Highland army

It was next considered what was to be the plan of the campaign. Lochiel was for advancing, for marching towards Mackay wherever Mackay might be, and for giving battle again. It can hardly be supposed that success had so turned the head of the wise chief of the Camerons as to make him insensible of the danger of the course which he recommended. But he probably conceived that nothing but a choice between dangers was left to him. His notion was that vigorous action was necessary to the very being of a Highland army,

---

[1] Mackay's Memoirs.   [2] Mackay's Memoirs ; Memoirs of Sir Ewan Cameron.
[3] Memoirs of Sir Ewan Cameron.

and that the coalition of clans would last only while they were impatiently pushing forward from battlefield to battlefield. He was again overruled. All his hopes of success were now at an end. His pride was severely wounded. He had submitted to the ascendency of a great captain : but he cared as little as any Whig for a royal commission. He had been willing to be the right hand of Dundee : but he would not be ordered about by Cannon. He quitted the camp, and retired to Lochaber. He indeed directed his clan to remain. But the clan, deprived of the leader whom it adored, and aware that he had withdrawn himself in ill humour, was no longer the same terrible column which had a few days before kept so well the vow to perish or to conquer. Macdonald of Sleat, whose forces exceeded in number those of any other of the confederate chiefs, followed Lochiel's example and returned to Sky.[1]

Mackay's arrangements were by this time complete ; and he had little doubt that, if the rebels came down to attack him, the regular army would retrieve the honour which had been lost at Killiecrankie. His chief difficulties arose from the unwise interference of the ministers of the Crown at Edinburgh with matters which ought to have been left to his direction. The **Mackay's advice disregarded by the Scotch ministers** truth seems to be that they, after the ordinary fashion of men who, having no military experience, sit in judgment on military operations, considered success as the only test of the ability of a commander. Whoever wins a battle is, in the estimation of such persons, a great general : whoever is beaten is a bad general ; and no general had ever been more completely beaten than Mackay. William, on the other hand, continued to place entire confidence in his unfortunate lieutenant. To the disparaging remarks of critics who had never seen a skirmish, Portland replied, by his master's orders, that Mackay was perfectly trustworthy, that he was brave, that he understood war better than any other officer in Scotland, and that it was much to be regretted that any prejudice should exist against so good a man and so good a soldier.[2]

The unjust contempt with which the Scotch Privy Councillors regarded Mackay led them into a great error which might well have caused a great disaster. The Cameronian regiment was **The Cameronians stationed at Dunkeld** sent to garrison Dunkeld. Of this arrangement Mackay altogether disapproved. He knew that at Dunkeld these troops would be near the enemy ; that they would be far from all assistance ; that they would be in an open town ; that they would be

[1] Memoirs of Sir Ewan Cameron.

[2] See Portland's Letters to Melville of April 22. and May 15. 1690, in the Leven and Melville Papers.

surrounded by a hostile population ; that they were very imperfectly disciplined, though doubtless brave and zealous ; that they were regarded by the whole Jacobite party throughout Scotland with peculiar malevolence ; and that in all probability some great effort would be made to disgrace and destroy them.[1]

The General's opinion was disregarded ; and the Cameronians occupied the post assigned to them. It soon appeared that his forebodings were just. The inhabitants of the country round Dunkeld furnished Cannon with intelligence, and urged him to make a bold push. The peasantry of Athol, impatient for spoil, came in great numbers to swell his army. The regiment hourly expected to be attacked, and became discontented and turbulent. The men, intrepid, indeed, both from constitution and from enthusiasm, but not yet broken to habits of military submission, expostulated with Cleland, who commanded them. They had, they imagined, been recklessly, if not perfidiously, sent to certain destruction. They were protected by no ramparts : they had a very scanty stock of ammunition : they were hemmed in by enemies. An officer might mount and gallop beyond reach of danger in an hour : but the private soldier must stay and be butchered. " Neither I," said Cleland, " nor any of my officers will, in any extremity, abandon you. Bring out my horse, all our horses : they shall be shot dead." These words produced a complete change of feeling. The men answered that the horses should not be shot, that they wanted no pledge from their brave Colonel except his word, and that they would run the last hazard with him. They kept their promise well. The Puritan blood was now thoroughly up ; and what that blood was when it was up had been proved on many fields of battle.

That night the regiment passed under arms. On the morning of the following day, the twenty-first of August, all the hills round **The Highlanders attack the Cameronians and are repulsed** Dunkeld were alive with bonnets and plaids. Cannon's army was much larger than that which Dundee had commanded, and was accompanied by more than a thousand horses laden with baggage. Both the horses and baggage were probably part of the booty of Killiecrankie. The whole number of Highlanders was estimated by those who saw them at from four to five thousand men. They came furiously on. The outposts of the Cameronians were speedily driven in. The assailants came pouring on every side into the streets. The church, however, held out obstinately But the greater part of the regiment made its stand behind a wall which surrounded a house belonging to the Marquess of Athol. This wall, which had two or three days before been hastily repaired with

---

[1] Mackay's Memoirs ; Memoirs of Sir Ewan Cameron.

Prospectus, Civitatis CALIDONIÆ The Prospect of the Town of DUNKELD

VIEW OF DUNKELD

From Slezer's Theatrum Scotiae, 1693

timber and loose stones, the soldiers defended desperately with musket, pike, and halbert. Their bullets were soon spent; but some of the men were employed in cutting lead from the roof of the Marquess's house and shaping it into slugs. Meanwhile all the neighbouring houses were crowded from top to bottom with Highlanders, who kept up a galling fire from the windows. Cleland, while encouraging his men, was shot dead. The command devolved on Major Henderson. In another minute Henderson fell pierced with three mortal wounds. His place was supplied by Captain Munro, and the contest went on with undiminished fury. A party of the Cameronians sallied forth, set fire to the houses from which the fatal shots had come, and turned the keys in the doors. In one single dwelling sixteen of the enemy were burnt alive. Those who were in the fight described it as a terrible initiation for recruits. Half the town was blazing; and with the incessant roar of the guns were mingled the piercing shrieks of wretches perishing in the flames. The struggle lasted four hours. By that time the Cameronians were reduced nearly to their last flask of powder: but their spirit never flagged. "The enemy will soon carry the wall. Be it so. We will retreat into the house: we will defend it to the last; and, if they force their way into it, we will burn it over their heads and our own." But, while they were revolving these desperate projects, they observed that the fury of the assault slackened. Soon the Highlanders began to fall back: disorder visibly spread among them; and whole bands began to march off to the hills. It was in vain that their general ordered them to return to the attack. Perseverance was not one of their military virtues. The Cameronians meanwhile, with shouts of defiance, invited Amalek and Moab to come back and to try another chance with the chosen people. But these exhortations had as little effect as those of Cannon. In a short time the whole Gaelic army was in full retreat towards Blair. Then the drums struck up: the victorious Puritans threw their caps into the air, raised, with one voice, a psalm of triumph and thanksgiving, and waved their colours, colours which were on that day unfurled for the first time in the face of an enemy, but which have since been proudly borne in every quarter of the world, and which are now embellished with the Sphinx and the Dragon, emblems of brave actions achieved in Egypt and in China.[1]

The Cameronians had good reason to be joyful and thankful; for

---

[1] Exact Narrative of the Conflict at Dunkeld between the Earl of Angus's Regiment and the Rebels, collected from several Officers of that Regiment who were Actors in or Eye-witnesses of all that's here narrated in Reference to those Actions; Letter of Lieutenant Blackader to his brother, dated Dunkeld, Aug. 21. 1689; Faithful Contendings Displayed; Minute of the Scotch Privy Council of August 28., quoted by Mr. Burton.

they had finished the war. In the rebel camp all was discord and dejection. The Highlanders blamed Cannon: Cannon blamed the Highlanders; and the host which had been the terror of Scotland melted fast away. The confederate chiefs signed **Dissolution of the Highland army** an association by which they declared themselves faithful subjects of King James, and bound themselves to meet again at a future time. Having gone through this form,—for it was no more,—they departed, each to his home. Cannon and his Irishmen retired to the Isle of Mull. The Lowlanders who had followed Dundee to the mountains shifted for themselves as they best could. On the twenty-fourth of August, exactly four weeks after the Gaelic army had won the battle of Killiecrankie, that army ceased to exist. It ceased to exist, as the army of Montrose had, more than forty years earlier, ceased to exist, not in consequence of any great blow from without, but by a natural dissolution, the effect of internal malformation. All the fruits of victory were gathered by the vanquished. The Castle of Blair, which had been the immediate object of the contest, opened its gates to Mackay; and a chain of military posts, extending northward as far as Inverness, protected the cultivators of the plains against the predatory inroads of the mountaineers.

During the autumn the government was much more annoyed by the Whigs of the low country, than by the Jacobites of the hills. The Club, which had, in the late session of Parliament, attempted **Intrigues of the Club: state of the Lowlands** to turn the kingdom into an oligarchical republic, and which had induced the Estates to refuse supplies and to stop the administration of justice, continued to sit during the recess, and harassed the ministers of the Crown by systematic agitation. The organisation of this body, contemptible as it may appear to the generation which has seen the Roman Catholic Association and the League against the Corn Laws, was then thought marvellous and formidable. The leaders of the confederacy boasted that they would force the King to do them right. They got up petitions and addresses, tried to inflame the populace by means of the press and the pulpit, employed emissaries among the soldiers, and talked of bringing up a large body of Covenanters from the west to overawe the Privy Council. In spite of every artifice, however, the ferment of the public mind gradually subsided. The government, after some hesitation, ventured to open the Courts of Justice which the Estates had closed. The Lords of Session appointed by the King took their seats; and Sir James Dalrymple presided. The Club attempted to induce the advocates to absent themselves from the bar, and entertained some hope that the mob would pull the judges from the bench. But it speedily became clear that there was much more likely to be a scarcity of fees than of lawyers to take them : the common people of Edinburgh were well pleased to see again a tribunal associated in their imagination with the dignity and prosperity of their city; and by many signs it appeared that the false and greedy faction which had commanded a majority of the legislature did not command a majority of the nation.[1]

[1] The history of Scotland during this autumn will be best studied in the Leven and Melville Papers.

CHAPTER XIV

TWENTY FOUR hours before the war in Scotland was brought to a close by the discomfiture of the Celtic army at Dunkeld, the Parliament broke up at Westminster. The Houses had sate Disputes in the English Parliament ever since January without a recess. The Commons, who were cooped up in a narrow space, had suffered severely from heat and discomfort ; and the health of many members had given way. The fruit however had not been proportioned to the toil. The last three months of the session had been almost entirely wasted in disputes, which have left no trace in the Statute Book. The progress of salutary laws had been impeded, sometimes by bickerings between the Whigs and the Tories, and sometimes by bickerings between the Lords and the Commons.

The Revolution had scarcely been accomplished when it appeared that the supporters of the Exclusion Bill had not forgotten what they had suffered during the ascendency of their enemies, and were bent on obtaining both reparation and revenge. Even before the throne was filled, the Lords appointed a committee to examine into the truth of the frightful stories which had been circulated concerning the death of Essex. The Committee, which consisted of zealous Whigs, continued its enquiries till all reasonable men were convinced that he had fallen by his own hand, and till his wife, his brother, and his most intimate friends were desirous that the investigation should be carried no further.[1] Atonement was made, without any opposition on the part of the Tories, to the memory and the families of some victims, who were themselves beyond the reach of human power. Soon after The attainder of Russell reversed the Convention had been turned into a Parliament, a bill for reversing the attainder of Lord Russell was presented to the Peers, was speedily passed by them, was sent down to the Lower

---

[1] See the Lords' Journals of Feb. 5. 168⅚, and of many subsequent days ; Braddon's pamphlet, entitled the Earl of Essex's Memory and Honour Vindicated, 1690 ; and the London Gazettes of July 31. and August 4. and 7. 1690, in which Lady Essex and Burnet publicly contradicted Braddon.

House, and was welcomed there with no common signs of emotion. Many of the members had sate in that very chamber with Russell. He had long exercised there an influence resembling the influence which, within the memory of this generation, belonged to the upright and benevolent Althorpe ; an influence derived, not from superior skill in debate or in declamation, but from spotless integrity, from plain good sense, and from that frankness, that simplicity, that good nature, which are singularly graceful and winning in a man raised by birth and fortune high above his fellows. By the Whigs Russell had been honoured as a chief ; and his political adversaries had admitted that, when he was not misled by associates less respectable and more artful than himself, he was as honest and kindhearted a gentleman as any in England. The manly firmness and Christian meekness with which he had met death, the desolation of his noble house, the misery of the bereaved father, the blighted prospects of the orphan children,[1] above all, the union of womanly tenderness and angelic patience in her who had been dearest to the brave sufferer, who had sate, with the pen in her hand, by his side at the bar, who had cheered the gloom of his cell, and who, on his last day, had shared with him the memorials of the great sacrifice, had softened the hearts of many who were little in the habit of pitying an opponent. That Russell had many good qualities, that he had meant well, that he had been hardly used, was now admitted even by courtly lawyers who had assisted in shedding his blood, and by courtly divines who had done their worst to blacken his reputation. When, therefore, the parchment which annulled his sentence was laid on the table of that assembly in which, eight years before, his face and his voice had been so well known, the excitement was great. One old Whig member tried to speak, but was overcome by his feelings. " I cannot," he faltered out, " name my Lord Russell without disorder. It is enough to name him. I am not able to say more." Many eyes were directed towards that part of the house where Finch sate. The highly honourable manner in which he had quitted a lucrative office, as soon as he had found that he could not keep it without supporting the dispensing power, and the conspicuous part which he had borne in the defence of the Bishops, had done much to atone for his faults. Yet, on this day, it could not be forgotten that he had strenuously exerted himself, as counsel for the Crown, to obtain

---

[1] Whether the attainder of Lord Russell would, if unreversed, have prevented his son from succeeding to the earldom of Bedford, is a difficult question. The old Earl collected the opinions of the greatest lawyers of the age, which may still be seen among the archives at Woburn. It is remarkable that one of these opinions is signed by Pemberton, who had presided at the trial. This circumstance seems to prove that the family did not impute to him any injustice or cruelty; and in truth he had behaved as well as any judge, before the Revolution, ever behaved on a similar occasion.

THE DEATH OF THE EARL OF ESSEX

From a pamphlet entitled Essex's Innocency and Honour Vindicated that judgment which was now to be solemnly revoked. He rose, and attempted to defend his conduct: but neither his legal acuteness, nor that fluent and sonorous elocution which was in his family a hereditary gift, and of which none of his family had a larger share than himself, availed him on this occasion. The House was in no humour to hear him, and repeatedly interrupted him by cries of "Order." He had been treated, he was told, with great indulgence. No accusation had been brought against him. Why then should he, under pretence of vindicating himself, attempt to throw dishonourable imputations on an illustrious name, and to apologise for a judicial murder? He was forced to sit down, after declaring that he meant only to clear himself from the charge of having exceeded the limits of his professional duty, that he disclaimed all intention of attacking the memory of Lord Russell, and that he should sincerely rejoice at the reversing of the attainder. Before the House rose the bill was read a second time, and would have been instantly read a third time and passed, had not some additions and omissions been proposed, which would, it was thought, make the reparation more complete. The amendments were prepared with great expedition: the Lords agreed to them; and the King gladly gave his assent.[1]

Other attainders reversed

This bill was soon followed by three other bills which annulled three wicked and infamous judgments, the judgment against Sidney, the judgment against Cornish, and the judgment against Alice Lisle.[2]

Case of Samuel Johnson

Some living Whigs obtained without difficulty redress for injuries which they had suffered in the late reign. The sentence of Samuel Johnson was taken into consideration by the House of Commons. It was resolved that the scourging which he had undergone was cruel, and that his degradation was of no legal effect. The latter proposition admitted of no dispute: for he had been degraded by the prelates who had been appointed to govern the diocese of London during Compton's suspension. Compton had been suspended by a decree of the High Commission; and the decrees of the High Commission were universally acknowledged to be nullities. Johnson had therefore been stripped of his robe by persons who had no jurisdiction over him. The Commons requested the King to compensate the sufferer by some ecclesiastical preferment.[3] William, however, found that he could not, without great inconvenience, grant this request. For

[1] Grey's Debates, March 168⅞.

[2] The Acts which reversed the attainders of Russell, Sidney, Cornish, and Alice Lisle were private Acts. Only the titles therefore are printed in the Statute Book: but the Acts will be found in Howell's Collection of State Trials.

[3] Commons' Journals, June 24. 1689.

Johnson, though brave, honest, and religious, had always been rash,
mutinous, and quarrelsome ; and, since he had endured for his opinions

RACHEL, LADY RUSSELL

From the painting by Sir G. Kneller, in the possession of the Duke of Bedford

a martyrdom more terrible than death, the infirmities of his temper and
understanding had increased to such a degree that he was as offensive
to Low Churchmen as to High Churchmen. Like too many other men,

who are not to be turned from the path of right by pleasure, by lucre, or by danger, he mistook the impulses of his pride and resentment for the monitions of conscience, and deceived himself into a belief that, in treating friends and foes with indiscriminate insolence and asperity, he was merely showing his Christian faithfulness and courage. Burnet, by exhorting him to patience and forgiveness of injuries, made him a mortal enemy. " Tell His Lordship," said the inflexible priest, " to mind his own business, and to let me look after mine." [1] It soon began to be whispered that Johnson was mad. He accused Burnet of being the author of the report, and avenged himself by writing libels so violent that they strongly confirmed the imputation which they were meant to refute. The King thought it better to give out of his own revenue a liberal compensation for the wrongs which the Commons had brought to his notice than to place an eccentric and irritable man in a situation of dignity and public trust. Johnson was gratified with a present of a thousand pounds, and a pension of three hundred a year for two lives. His son was also provided for in the public service.[2]

While the Commons were considering the case of Johnson, the Lords were scrutinising with severity the proceedings which had, in the **Case of Devonshire** late reign, been instituted against one of their own order, the Earl of Devonshire. The judges who had passed sentence on him were strictly interrogated ; and a resolution was passed declaring that in his case the privileges of the peerage had been infringed, and that the Court of King's Bench, in punishing a hasty blow by a fine of thirty thousand pounds, had violated common justice and the Great Charter.[3]

In the cases which have been mentioned, all parties seem to have agreed in thinking that some public reparation was due. But the fiercest **Case of Oates** passions both of Whigs and Tories were soon roused by the noisy claims of a wretch whose sufferings, great as they might seem, had been trifling when compared with his crimes. Oates had come back, like a ghost from the place of punishment, to haunt the spots which had been polluted by his guilt. The three years and a half which followed his scourging he had passed in one of the cells of Newgate, except when on certain days, the anniversaries of his perjuries, he had been brought forth and set on the pillory. He was still, however, regarded by many fanatics as a martyr ; and it was said that they were able so far to corrupt his keepers that, in spite of positive

---

[1] Johnson tells this story himself in his strange pamphlet entitled, Notes upon the Phœnix Edition of the Pastoral Letter, 1694.

[2] Some Memorials of the Reverend Samuel Johnson, prefixed to the folio edition of his works, 1710.

[3] Lords' Journals, May 15. 1689.

TESTIS OVAT

Titus Oates, *Anagr.* Teſtis Ovat.

Teſtis ovat falſæ fruitur dum Crimine linguæ,
Et referens Sceleris præmia Teſtis ovat.
Teſtis ovat, plorent liceat tria Regna, doloris
Author quam Sicco lumine Teſtis ovat.
Teſtis ovat, quòd Ierna perit, ruit Anglia, vires
Quòd minuit proprias Scotia, Teſtis ovat.
Teſtis ovat lætus magnos disjungere Fratres,
Et pulſo è Patria Caſtore Teſtis ovat.
Teſtis ovat nocui dum pœna plectitur infons;
Ebrius innocuo Sanguine Teſtis ovat.
Teſtis ovat; falſæ ſed qualis ovatio linguæ;
Qui quod iniquus, ovat, quam male Teſtis ovat.

Thus rendred.

Paid for his Crimes the Perjur'd Witneſs ſwears,
    And ſhews what for rewards his falſe Tongue dare
Swears till three Kingdoms mourn; whilſt o'er the prize
Our Witneſs triumphs with relentleſs Eyes.
Swears on till *Ireland* periſh, *England* fall,
And *Scotland* in one common Funeral.
Swears ſtill, dreadleſs of Hell, nor fearing Heaven,
Till the great *TORK* be from his Countrey driven.
Wrong'd Innocence by Perjur'd Witneſs dies,
Who drunk with guiltleſs Bloud ſtill ſwears and lies.
Then ſince our Witneſs has this hardned face,
Let the falſe Wretch the Pillory diſgrace.

London, Printed for *J. Hindmarſh,* at the *Golden Ball* over againſt the *Royal Exchange.* 1685.

TITUS OATES IN THE PILLORY

Number 1135 in the British Museum Catalogue of Satirical Prints

orders from the government, his sufferings were mitigated by many indulgences. While offenders, who, compared with him, were innocent, grew lean on the prison allowance, his cheer was mended by turkeys and chines, capons and sucking pigs, venison pasties and hampers of claret, the offerings of zealous Protestants.[1] When James had fled from Whitehall, and when London was in confusion, it was moved, in the Council of Lords which had provisionally assumed the direction of affairs, that Oates should be set at liberty. The motion was rejected :[2] but the gaolers, not knowing whom to obey in that time of anarchy, and desiring to conciliate a man who had once been, and might perhaps again be, a terrible enemy, allowed their prisoner to go freely about the town.[3] His uneven legs and his hideous face, made more hideous by the shearing which his ears had undergone, were now again seen every day in Westminster Hall and the Court of Requests.[4] He fastened himself on his old patrons, and, in that drawl which he affected as a mark of gentility, gave them the history of his wrongs and of his hopes. It was impossible, he said, that now, when the good cause was triumphant, the discoverer of the plot could be overlooked. "Charles gave me nine hundred pounds a year. Sure William will give me more."[5]

In a few weeks he brought his sentence before the House of Lords by a writ of error. This is a species of appeal which raises no question of fact. The Lords, while sitting judicially on the writ of error, were not competent to examine whether the verdict which pronounced Oates guilty was or was not according to the evidence. All that they had to consider was whether, the verdict being supposed to be according to the evidence, the judgment was legal. But it would have been difficult even for a tribunal composed of veteran magistrates, and was almost impossible for an assembly of noblemen who were all strongly biassed on one side or on the other, and among whom there was at that time not a single person whose mind had been disciplined by the study of juris-prudence, to look steadily at the mere point of law, abstracted from the

---

[1] North's Examen, 224. North's evidence is confirmed by several contemporary squibs in prose and verse. See also the εἰκὼν βροτολοίγου, 1697.

[2] Halifax MS. in the British Museum.   [3] Epistle Dedicatory to Oates's εἰκὼν βασιλική.

[4] In a ballad of the time are the following lines :

> " Come listen, ye Whigs, to my pitiful moan,
>   All you that have ears, when the Doctor has none."

These lines must have been in Mason's head when he wrote the couplet—

> " Witness, ye Hills, ye Johnsons, Scots, Shebbeares ;
>   Hark to my call : for some of you have ears."

[5] North's Examen, 224. 254. North says "six hundred a year." But I have taken the larger sum from the impudent petition which Oates addressed to the Commons, July 25. 1689. See the Journals.

special circumstances of the case. In the view of one party, a party which even among the Whig peers was probably a small minority, the appellant was a man who had rendered inestimable services to the cause of liberty and religion, and who had been requited by long confinement, by degrading exposure, and by torture not to be thought of without a shudder. The majority of the House more justly regarded him as the falsest, the most malignant, and the most impudent being that had ever disgraced the human form. The sight of that brazen forehead, the accents of that lying tongue, deprived them of all mastery over themselves. Many of them doubtless remembered with shame and remorse that they had been his dupes, and that, on the very last occasion on which he had stood before them, he had by perjury induced them to shed the blood of one of their own illustrious order. It was not to be expected that a crowd of gentlemen under the influence of feelings like these would act with the cold impartiality of a court of justice. Before they came to any decision on the legal question which Titus had brought before them, they picked a succession of quarrels with him. He had published a paper magnifying his merits and his sufferings. The Lords found out some pretence for calling this publication a breach of privilege, and sent him to the Marshalsea. He petitioned to be released : but an objection was raised to his petition. He had described himself as a Doctor of Divinity ; and their lordships refused to acknowledge him as such. He was brought to their bar, and asked where he had graduated. He answered, " At the university of Salamanca." This was no new instance of his mendacity and effrontery. His Salamanca degree had been, during many years, a favourite theme of all the Tory satirists from Dryden downwards ; and even on the Continent the Salamanca Doctor was a nickname in ordinary use.[1] The Lords, in their hatred of Oates, so far forgot their own dignity as to treat this ridiculous matter seriously. They ordered him to efface from his petition the words " Doctor of Divinity." He replied that he could not in conscience do it ; and he was accordingly sent back to gaol.[2]

These preliminary proceedings indicated, not obscurely, what the fate of the writ of error would be. The counsel for Oates had been heard. No counsel appeared against him. The Judges were required to give their opinions. Nine of them were in attendance ; and among the nine were the Chiefs of the three Courts of Common Law. The unanimous answer of these grave, learned, and upright magistrates was that the Court of King's Bench was not competent to degrade a priest from his sacred office, or to pass a sentence of perpetual imprisonment ;

[1] Van Citters, in his despatches to the States General, uses this nickname quite gravely.
[2] Lords' Journals, May 30. 1689.

and that therefore the judgment against Oates was contrary to law, and ought to be reversed. The Lords should undoubtedly have considered themselves as bound by this opinion. That they knew Oates to be the worst of men was nothing to the purpose. To them, sitting as a court of justice, he ought to have been merely a John of Styles, or a John of Nokes. But their indignation was violently excited. Their habits were not those which fit men for the discharge of judicial duties. The debate turned almost entirely on matters to which no allusion ought to have been made. Not a single peer ventured to affirm that the judgment was legal : but much was said about the odious character of the appellant, about the impudent accusation which he had brought against Catharine of Braganza, and about the evil consequences which might follow if so bad a man were capable of being a witness. " There is only one way," said the Lord President, " in which I can consent to reverse the fellow's sentence. He has been whipped from Aldgate to Tyburn. He ought to be whipped from Tyburn back to Aldgate." The question was put. Twenty three peers voted for reversing the judgment ; thirty five for affirming it.[1]

This decision produced a great sensation, and not without reason. A question was now raised which might justly excite the anxiety of every man in the kingdom. That question was whether the highest tribunal, the tribunal on which, in the last resort, depended the most precious interests of every English subject, was at liberty to decide judicial questions on other than judicial grounds, and to withhold from a suitor what was admitted to be his legal right, on account of the depravity of his moral character. That the supreme Court of Appeal ought not to be suffered to exercise arbitrary power, under the forms of ordinary justice, was strongly felt by the ablest men in the House of Commons, and by none more strongly than by Somers. With him, and with those who reasoned like him, were, on this occasion, allied all the weak and hotheaded zealots who still regarded Oates as a public bene-factor, and who imagined that to question the existence of the Popish plot was to question the truth of the Protestant religion. On the very morning after the decision of the Peers had been pronounced, keen reflections were thrown, in the House of Commons, on the justice of their lordships. Three days later, the subject was brought forward by a Whig Privy Councillor, Sir Robert Howard, member for Castle Rising. He was one of the Berkshire branch of his noble family, a branch which enjoyed, in that age, the unenviable distinction of being wonderfully fertile of bad rhymers. The poetry of the Berkshire Howards was the jest of three generations of satirists. The mirth began with the first

[1] Lords' Journals, May 31. 1689 ; Commons' Journals, Aug. 2. ; North's Examen, 234. ; Luttrell's Diary.

G. Kneller Eques pinxit   R. White Sculpsit

The Hon.ble Sr Robert Howard.

SIR ROBERT HOWARD

From an engraving by R. White, after a painting by Sir G. Kneller representation of the Rehearsal, and continued down to the last edition of the Dunciad.[1]   But Sir Robert, in spite of his bad verses, and of some foibles and vanities which had caused him to be brought on the stage under the name of Sir Positive Atall, had in parliament the weight which a stanch party man, of ample fortune, of illustrious name, of ready utterance, and of resolute spirit, can scarcely fail to possess.[2]   When he rose to call the attention of the Commons to the case of Oates, some Tories, animated by the same passions which had prevailed in the other House, received him with loud hisses.   In spite of this most unparliamentary insult, he persevered ; and it soon appeared that the majority was with him.   Some orators extolled the patriotism and courage of Oates : others dwelt much on a prevailing rumour, that the solicitors who were employed against him on behalf of the Crown had distributed large sums of money among the jurymen.   These were topics on which there was much difference of opinion.   But that the sentence was illegal was a proposition which admitted of no dispute.   The most eminent lawyers in the House of Commons declared that, on this point, they entirely concurred in the opinion given by the Judges in the House of Lords.   Those who had hissed when the subject was introduced were so effectually cowed that they did not venture to demand a division ; and a bill annulling the sentence was brought in, without any opposition.[3]

The Lords were in an embarrassing situation.   To retract was not pleasant.   To engage in a contest with the Lower House, on a question on which that House was clearly in the right, and was backed at once by the opinions of the sages of the law, and by the passions of the populace, might be dangerous.   It was thought expedient to take a middle course. An address was presented to the King, requesting him to pardon Oates.[4] But this concession only made bad worse.   Titus had, like every other human being, a right to justice : but he was not a proper object of mercy.   If the judgment against him was illegal, it ought to have been reversed.   If it was legal, there was no ground for remitting any portion of it.   The Commons, very properly, persisted, passed their bill, and

[1] Sir Robert was the original hero of the Rehearsal, and was called Bilboa.   In the remodelled Dunciad, Pope inserted the lines—

" And highborn Howard, more majestic sire,
With Fool of Quality completes the quire."

Pope's highborn Howard was Edward Howard, the author of the British Princes.   Dorset ridiculed Edward Howard's poetry in a short satire, in which thought and wit are packed as close as in the finest passages of Hudibras.

[2] Key to the Rehearsal ; Shadwell's Sullen Lovers ; Pepys, May 5. 8. 1668 ; Evelyn, Feb. 16. 168⅘.

[3] Grey's Debates and Commons' Journals, June 4. and 11. 1689.

[4] Lords' Journals, June 6. 1689.

sent it up to the Peers.   Of this bill the only objectionable part was the
preamble, which asserted, not only that the judgment was illegal, a proposition which appeared on the face of the record to be true, but also
that the verdict was corrupt, a proposition which, whether true or false,
was certainly not proved.

The Lords were in a great strait.   They knew that they were
in the wrong.   Yet they were determined not to proclaim, in their
legislative capacity, that they had, in their judicial capacity, been
guilty of injustice.   They again tried a middle course.   The preamble
was softened down : a clause was added which provided that Oates
should still remain incapable of being a witness ; and the bill thus
altered was returned to the Commons.

The Commons were not satisfied.   They rejected the amendments,
and demanded a free conference.   Two eminent Tories, Rochester and
Nottingham, took their seats in the Painted Chamber as managers
for the Lords.   With them was joined Burnet, whose well known
hatred of Popery was likely to give weight to what he might say on
such an occasion.   Somers was the chief orator on the other side ; and
to his pen we owe a singularly lucid and interesting abstract of
the debate.

The Lords frankly owned that the judgment of the Court of King's
Bench could not be defended.   They knew it to be illegal, and had
known it to be so even when they affirmed it.   But they had acted for
the best.   They accused Oates of bringing an impudently false accusation against Queen Catharine : they mentioned other instances of
his villany ; and they asked whether such a man ought still to be
capable of giving testimony in a court of justice.   The only excuse
which, in their opinion, could be made for him was, that he was insane ;
and in truth, the incredible insolence and absurdity of his behaviour
when he was last before them seemed to warrant the belief that his
brain had been turned, and that he was not to be trusted with the
lives of other men.   The Lords could not therefore degrade themselves
by expressly rescinding what they had done; nor could they consent to
pronounce the verdict corrupt on no better evidence than common report.

The reply was complete and triumphant.   "Oates is now the
smallest part of the question.   He has, Your Lordships say, falsely
accused the Queen Dowager and other innocent persons.   Be it so.
This bill gives him no indemnity.   We are quite willing that, if
he is guilty, he shall be punished.   But for him, and for all Englishmen, we demand that punishment shall be regulated by law, and not by
the arbitrary discretion of any tribunal.   We demand that, when
a writ of error is before Your Lordships, you shall give judgment on it
according to the known customs and statutes of the realm.   We

H.E. IV   I

deny that you have any right, on such an occasion, to take into consideration the moral character of a plaintiff or the political effect of a decision. It is acknowledged by yourselves that you have, merely because you thought ill of this man, affirmed a judgment which you knew to be illegal. Against this assumption of arbitrary power the Commons protest; and they hope that you will now redeem what you must feel to be an error. Your Lordships intimate a suspicion that Oates is mad. That a man is mad may be a very good reason for not punishing him at all. But how it can be a reason for inflicting on him a punishment which would be illegal even if he were sane, the Commons do not comprehend. Your Lordships think that you should not be justified in calling a verdict corrupt which has not been legally proved to be so. Suffer us to remind you that you have two distinct functions to perform. You are judges; and you are legislators. When you judge, your duty is strictly to follow the law. When you legislate, you may properly take facts from common fame. You invert this rule. You are lax in the wrong place, and scrupulous in the wrong place. As judges, you break through the law for the sake of a supposed convenience. As legislators, you will not admit any fact without such technical proof as it is rarely possible for legislators to obtain.[1]

This reasoning was not and could not be answered. The Commons were evidently flushed with their victory in the argument, and proud of the appearance which Somers had made in the Painted Chamber. They particularly charged him to see that the report which he had made of the conference was accurately entered in the Journals. The Lords very wisely abstained from inserting in their records an account of a debate in which they had been so signally discomfited. But, though conscious of their fault and ashamed of it, they could not be brought to do public penance by owning, in the preamble of the Act, that they had been guilty of injustice. The minority was, however, strong. The resolution to adhere was carried by only twelve votes, of which ten were proxies.[2] Twenty one Peers protested. The bill dropped. Two Masters in Chancery were sent to announce to the Commons the final resolution of the Peers. The Commons thought this proceeding unjustifiable in substance and uncourteous in form. They determined to remonstrate; and Somers drew up an excellent manifesto, in which the vile name of Oates was scarcely mentioned, and in which the Upper House was with great earnestness and gravity exhorted to treat judicial questions judicially, and not, under pretence of administering

---

[1] Commons' Journals, Aug. 2. 1689; Dutch Ambassadors Extraordinary to the States General, $\frac{\text{July 30.}}{\text{Aug. 9.}}$

[2] Lords' Journals, July 30. 1689; Luttrell's Diary; Clarendon's Diary, July 31. 1689.

law, to make law.[1] The wretched man, who had now a second time thrown the political world into confusion, received a pardon, and was set at liberty. His friends in the Lower House moved an address to the Throne, requesting that a pension sufficient for his support might be granted to him.[2] He was consequently allowed about three hundred a year, a sum which he thought unworthy of his acceptance, and which he took with the savage snarl of disappointed greediness.

From the dispute about Oates sprang another dispute, which might have produced very serious consequences. The instrument which had declared William and Mary King and Queen was a   **Bill of** revolutionary instrument. It had been drawn up by an   **Rights** assembly unknown to the ordinary law, and had never received the royal sanction. It was evidently desirable that this great contract between the governors and the governed, this title-deed by which the King held his throne and the people their liberties, should be put into a strictly regular form. The Declaration of Rights was therefore turned into a Bill of Rights ; and the Bill of Rights speedily passed the Commons : but in the Lords difficulties arose.

The Declaration had settled the crown, first on William and Mary jointly, then on the survivor of the two, then on Mary's posterity, then on Anne and her posterity, and, lastly, on the posterity of William by any other wife than Mary. The Bill had been drawn in exact conformity with the Declaration. Who was to succeed if Mary, Anne, and William should all die without posterity, was left in uncertainty. Yet the event for which no provision was made was far from improbable. Indeed it really came to pass. William had never had a child. Anne had repeatedly been a mother, but had no child living. It would not be very strange if, in a few months, disease, war, or treason should remove all those who stood in the entail. In what state would the country then be left ? To whom would allegiance be due ? The bill indeed contained a clause which excluded Papists from the throne. But would such a clause supply the place of a clause designating the successor by name ? What if the next heir should be a prince of the House of Savoy not three months old ? It would be absurd to call such an infant a Papist. Was he then to be proclaimed King ? Or was the crown to be in abeyance till he came to an age at which he might be capable of choosing a religion ? Might not the most honest and the most intelligent men be in doubt whether they ought to regard him as their Sovereign ? And to whom could they look for a solution of this doubt ? Parliament there would be none : for the Parliament would expire with the prince who had convoked it. There would be

[1] See the Commons' Journals of July 31. and August 13. 1689.
[2] Commons' Journals, Aug. 20.

mere anarchy, anarchy which might end in the destruction of the monarchy, or in the destruction of public liberty. For these weighty reasons, Burnet, at William's suggestion, proposed in the House of Lords that the crown should, failing heirs of His Majesty's body, be entailed on an undoubted Protestant, Sophia, Duchess of Brunswick Lunenburg, granddaughter of James the First, and daughter of Elizabeth, Queen of Bohemia.

The Lords unanimously assented to this amendment: but the Commons unanimously rejected it. The cause of the rejection no contemporary writer has satisfactorily explained. One Whig historian talks of the machinations of the republicans, another of the machinations of the Jacobites. But it is quite certain that four fifths of the representatives of the people were neither Jacobites nor republicans. Yet not a single voice was raised in the Lower House in favour of the clause which in the Upper House had been carried by acclamation.[1] The most probable explanation seems to be that the gross injustice which had been committed in the case of Oates had irritated the Commons to such a degree that they were glad of an opportunity to quarrel with the Peers. A conference was held. Neither assembly would give way. While the dispute was hottest, an event took place which, it might have been thought, would have restored harmony. Anne gave birth to a son. The child was baptised at Hampton Court with great pomp, and with many signs of public joy. William was one of the sponsors. The other was the accomplished Dorset, whose roof had given shelter to the Princess in her distress. The King bestowed his own name on his godson, and announced to the splendid circle assembled round the font that the little William was henceforth to be called Duke of Gloucester.[2] The birth of this child had greatly diminished the risk against which the Lords had thought it necessary to guard. They might therefore have retracted with a good grace. But their pride had been wounded by the severity with which their decision on Oates's writ of error had been censured in the Painted Chamber. They had been plainly told across the table that they were unjust judges; and the imputation was not the less irritating because they were conscious that it was deserved. They refused to make any concession; and the Bill of Rights was suffered to drop.[3]

---

[1] Oldmixon accuses the Jacobites, Burnet the republicans. Though Burnet took a prominent part in the discussion of this question, his account of what passed is grossly inaccurate. He says that the clause was warmly debated in the Commons, and that Hampden spoke strongly for it. But we learn from the Journals (June 19. 1689) that it was rejected *nemine contradicente*. The Dutch Ambassadors describe it as "een propositie 'twelck geen ingressie schÿnt te sullen vinden."

[2] London Gazette, Aug. 1. 1689; Luttrell's Diary.

[3] The history of this Bill may be traced in the Journals of the two Houses, and in Grey's Debates.

The true Effigies of the Most Illustrious Princess Anna Sophia of Hanover declared by a late Act of Parliament for settling the Succession in y.º Protestant line to succeed to the Crown of England after Her Matie Queen Ann and her Royal Issue.
Done from y.º Original brought from Hanover by y.º R.º Honble The L.º Raby and dedicated to his Lordshipp by his most humble Servant. E.C.

W.ᵐ Faithorne fec: Cum Privilegio   Sold by E. Cooper at the 3 Pigeons in Bedford street

THE PRINCESS SOPHIA OF HANOVER

From a mezzotint by W. Faithorne, in the Sutherland Collection

But the most exciting question of this long and stormy session was, what punishment should be inflicted on those men who had, during the **Disputes about a Bill of Indemnity** interval between the dissolution of the Oxford Parliament and the Revolution, been the advisers or the tools of Charles and James. It was happy for England that, at this crisis, a prince who belonged to neither of her factions, who loved neither, who hated neither, and who, for the accomplishment of a great design wished to make use of both, was the moderator between them.

The two parties were now in a position closely resembling that in which they had been twenty eight years before. The party indeed which had then been undermost was now uppermost : but the analogy between the situations is one of the most perfect that can be found in history. Both the Restoration and the Revolution were accomplished by coalitions. At the Restoration, those politicians who were peculiarly zealous for liberty assisted to reestablish monarchy : at the Revolution those politicians who were peculiarly zealous for monarchy assisted to vindicate liberty. The Cavalier would, at the former conjuncture, have been able to effect nothing without the help of Puritans who had fought for the Covenant ; nor would the Whig, at the latter conjuncture, have offered a successful resistance to arbitrary power, had he not been backed by men who had a very short time before condemned resistance to arbitrary power as a deadly sin. Conspicuous among those by whom, in 1660, the royal family was brought back, were Hollis, who had, in the days of the tyranny of Charles the First, held down the Speaker in the chair by main force, while Black Rod knocked for admission in vain ; Ingoldsby, whose name was subscribed to the memorable death warrant ; and Prynne, whose ears Laud had cut off, and who, in return, had borne the chief part in cutting off Laud's head. Among the seven who, in 1688, signed the invitation to William, were Compton, who had long enforced the duty of obeying Nero ; Danby, who had been impeached for endeavouring to establish military despotism ; and Lumley, whose bloodhounds had tracked Monmouth to that last sad hiding-place among the fern. Both in 1660 and in 1688, while the fate of the nation still hung in the balance, forgiveness was exchanged between the hostile factions. On both occasions the reconciliation, which had seemed to be cordial in the hour of danger, proved false and hollow in the hour of triumph. As soon as Charles the Second was at Whitehall, the Cavalier forgot the good service recently done by the Presbyterians, and remembered only their old offences. As soon as William was King, too many of the Whigs began to demand vengeance for all that they had, in the days of the Rye House plot, suffered at the hands of the Tories. On both occasions the Sovereign found it difficult to save the vanquished party from the fury of his triumphant

His Highness The Duke of Glocester

I. Kneller ad vivum pinxit   I Smith fecit & excudit

WILLIAM, DUKE OF GLOUCESTER

From a mezzotint by J. Smith, after a painting by Sir G. Kneller supporters ; and on both occasions those whom he had disappointed of their revenge murmured bitterly against the government which had been so weak and ungrateful as to protect its foes against its friends.

So early as the twenty-fifth of March, William called the attention of the Commons to the expediency of quieting the public mind by an amnesty. He expressed his hope that a bill of general pardon and oblivion would be as speedily as possible presented for his sanction, and that no exceptions would be made, except such as were absolutely necessary for the vindication of public justice and for the safety of the state. The Commons unanimously agreed to thank him for this instance of his paternal kindness : but they suffered many weeks to pass without taking any step towards the accomplishment of his wish. When at length the subject was resumed, it was resumed in such a manner as plainly showed that the majority had no real intention of putting an end to the suspense which embittered the lives of all those Tories who were conscious that, in their zeal for prerogative, they had sometimes overstepped the exact line traced by law. Twelve categories were framed, some of which were so extensive as to include tens of thousands of delinquents; and the House resolved that, under every one of these categories, some exceptions should be made. Then came the examination into the cases of individuals. Numerous culprits and witnesses were summoned to the bar. The debates were long and sharp ; and it soon became evident that the work was interminable. The summer glided away : the autumn was approaching : the session could not last much longer ; and of the twelve distinct inquisitions, which the Commons had resolved to institute, only three had been brought to a close. It was necessary to let the bill drop for that year.[1]

Among the many offenders whose names were mentioned in the course of these enquiries, was one who stood alone and unapproached in **Last days of** guilt and infamy, and whom Whigs and Tories were equally **Jeffreys** willing to leave to the extreme rigour of the law. On that terrible day which was succeeded by the Irish Night, the roar of a great city disappointed of its revenge had followed Jeffreys to the drawbridge of the Tower. His imprisonment was not strictly legal : but he at first accepted with thanks and blessings the protection which those dark walls, made famous by so many crimes and sorrows, afforded him against the fury of the multitude.[2] Soon, however, he became sensible that his life was still in imminent peril. For a time he flattered himself with the hope that a writ of Habeas Corpus would liberate him from his confinement, and that he should be able to steal away to some foreign country,

[1] See Grey's debates, and the Commons' Journals from March to July. The twelve categories will be found in the Journals of the 23rd and 29th of May and of the 8th of June.

[2] Halifax MS. in the British Museum.

The Chancellors Resolution.

O R,

His Last Sayings a little before his Death.

To the Tune of, Lilli-bolero.

I have been long in Custody here,
  Being pack't always with a fear,
  that I should live to swing at the last;
  Peter was slain thus requited.
  sorrow and grief my senses does seize;
I never was sixty'd, but faith I have stirr'd
  the Hang-man, and cozen'd him of his fees.

I have been made the scorn of the Town,
  who was of late next man to a Throne;
Every Rascal's running me down,
  so that I may look pittiful now;

There's a thousand deaths inherited,
  for honest George, who them did displease;
But to their vexation, I shall cheat the Nation,
  and likewise the Hang-man of all his fees.

I was the whipping Scourge of this age,
  causing good men to suffer with shame,
Therefore the Land is as in a Rage,
  wishing I might partake of the same;
Some say I run of me, others hang me,
  thus they are condemning as they please;
But my speech does flatter, I shall scape the Matter,
  and cozen the Hang-man of all his fees.

I wish the rest would murder the Tree,
  this is a Crime which none would excuse;
And the good Actions that lie in the West,
  hopes they shall see me ope in my speech;
But they will not have their wishes,
  conjuring Death does Chancellor seize;
Or let them not Cavil, the Gout and the Gravel,
  will cozen the Hang-man of all his fees.

Ever since I have lain in this Den,
  faith I have lost the Court and the Pen,
And am cried abroad amongst Men,
  under the terms of shame and disgrace;
Some say hang me, others free me,
  and twenty Deaths more cruel then these;
But here I am trying, upon my Bed dying,
  I'll cozen the Hang-man of all his fees.

William and Mary being Proclaim'd,
  thus like an Arrow went to my heart;
I with a Feavour straight was inflam'd,
  fearing I soon should have my Desert;
Thousands waited for my Trial,
  a shameful merry Rabble may'd please,
Tho' they do escape it, they never shall have it,
  I'll cozen the Hang-man of all his fees.

Now when I heard King William was Crown'd,
  and that the loud-mouth'd Cannons did roar,
Presently I fell into a Swound,
  never was man so daunted before;
And my Stony old Distemper,
  violently my Body did seize,
'Tis no feigned Story, but in this I glory,
  to cozen the Hang-man of all his fees.

Some did declare I must look my Head,
  others said hanging would be my Doom,
'Cause I for Romance had been misled,
  pleading always for Treacherous Rome;
But faith they're disappointed,
  conjuring Death my Spirits does seize,
I'll make such a War, and straight ways expire,
  to cozen the Hang-man of all his fees.

FINIS.

Printed in the Year 1689.

THE CHANCELLOR'S RESOLUTION

From the Pepysian Collection of Ballads

and to hide himself with part of his ill gotten wealth from the detestation of mankind : but, till the government was settled, there was no
Court competent to grant a writ of Habeas Corpus ; and, as soon as the
government had been settled, the Habeas Corpus Act was suspended.[1]
Whether the legal guilt of murder could be brought home to Jeffreys
may be doubted. But he was morally guilty of so many murders that,
if there had been no other way of reaching his life, a retrospective Act
of Attainder would have been clamorously demanded by the whole
nation. A disposition to triumph over the fallen has never been one of
the besetting sins of Englishmen : but the hatred of which Jeffreys was
the object was without a parallel in our history, and partook but too
largely of the savageness of his own nature. The people, where he was
concerned, were as cruel as himself, and exulted in his misery as he had
been accustomed to exult in the misery of convicts listening to the
sentence of death, and of families clad in mourning. The rabble congregated before his deserted mansion in Duke Street, and read on the
door, with shouts of laughter, the bills which announced the sale of his
property. Even delicate women, who had tears for highwaymen and
housebreakers, breathed nothing but vengeance against him. The
lampoons on him which were hawked about the town were distinguished
by an atrocity rare even in those days.[2] Hanging would be too mild a
death for him : a grave under the gibbet would be too respectable a
resting place : he ought to be whipped to death at the cart's tail : he
ought to be tortured like an Indian : he ought to be devoured alive.
The street poets portioned out all his joints with cannibal ferocity, and
computed how many pounds of steaks might be cut from his well
fattened carcass. Nay, the rage of his enemies was such that, in
language seldom heard in England, they proclaimed their wish that he
might go to the place of wailing and gnashing of teeth, to the worm
that never dies, to the fire that is never quenched. They exhorted him
to hang himself in his garters, and to cut his throat with his razor.
They put up horrible prayers that he might not be able to repent, that
he might die the same hard-hearted, wicked Jeffreys that he had lived.
His spirit, as mean in adversity as insolent and inhuman in prosperity,
sank down under the load of public abhorrence. His constitution,
originally bad, and much impaired by intemperance, was completely

---

[1] The Life and Death of George Lord Jeffreys ; Finch's speech in Grey's Debates, March 1.
168⅞.

[2] See, among many other pieces, Jeffreys's Elegy, the Letter to the Lord Chancellor exposing
to him the sentiments of the people, the Elegy on Dangerfield, Dangerfield's Ghost to Jeffreys,
the Humble Petition of Widows and fatherless Children in the West, the Lord Chancellor's Discovery and Confession made in the Time of his Sickness in the Tower ; Hickeringill's Ceremony-
monger ; a broadside entitled "O rare show ! O rare sight ! O strange monster ! The like not
in Europe ! To be seen near Tower Hill, a few doors beyond the Lion's den."

broken by distress and anxiety.   He was tormented by a cruel internal disease, which the most skilful surgeons of that age were seldom able to relieve.   One solace was left to him, brandy.   Even when he had causes to try and councils to attend, he had seldom gone to bed sober.   Now, when he had nothing to occupy his mind save terrible recollections and terrible forebodings, he abandoned himself without reserve to his favourite vice.   Many believed him to be bent on shortening his life by excess. He thought it better, they said, to go off in a drunken fit than to be hacked by Ketch, or torn limb from limb by the populace.

Once he was roused from a state of abject despondency by an agreeable sensation, speedily followed by a mortifying disappointment. A parcel had been left for him at the Tower.   It appeared to be a barrel of Colchester oysters, his favourite dainties.   He was greatly moved : for there are moments when those who least deserve affection are pleased to think that they inspire it.   " Thank God," he exclaimed, " I have still some friends left."   He opened the barrel ; and from among a heap of shells out tumbled a stout halter.[1]

It does not appear that one of the flatterers or buffoons whom he had enriched out of the plunder of his victims came to comfort him in the day of trouble.   But he was not left in utter solitude.   John Tutchin, whom he had sentenced to be flogged every fortnight for seven years, made his way into the Tower, and presented himself before the fallen oppressor.   Poor Jeffreys, humbled to the dust, behaved with abject civility, and called for wine.   " I am glad, sir," he said, " to see you." " And I am glad," answered the resentful Whig, " to see Your Lordship in this place."   " I served my master," said Jeffreys : " I was bound in conscience to do so."   " Where was your conscience," said Tutchin, " when you passed that sentence on me at Dorchester ? "   " It was set down in my instructions," answered Jeffreys, fawningly, " that I was to show no mercy to men like you, men of parts and courage.   When I went back to court I was reprimanded for my lenity." [2]   Even Tutchin, acrimonious as was his nature, and great as were his wrongs, seems to have been a little mollified by the pitiable spectacle which he had at first contemplated with vindictive pleasure.   He always denied the truth of the report that he was the person who sent the Colchester barrel to the Tower.

A more benevolent man, John Sharp, the excellent Dean of Norwich, forced himself to visit the prisoner.   It was a painful task : but Sharp had been treated by Jeffreys, in old times, as kindly as it was in the nature of Jeffreys to treat anybody, and had once or twice been able, by patiently waiting till the storm of curses and invec-

[1] Life and Death of George Lord Jeffreys.
[2] Tutchin himself gives this narrative in the Bloody Assizes.

tives had spent itself, and by dexterously seizing the moment of good humour, to obtain for unhappy families some mitigation of their sufferings. The prisoner was surprised and pleased. " What," he said, " dare you own me now ? " It was in vain, however, that the amiable divine tried to give salutary pain to that seared conscience. Jeffreys, instead of acknowledging his guilt, exclaimed vehemently against the injustice of mankind. " People call me a murderer for doing what at the time was applauded by some who are now high in public favour. They call me a drunkard because I take punch to relieve me in my agony." He would not admit that, as President of the High Commission, he had done anything that deserved reproach. His colleagues, he said, were the real criminals ; and now they threw all the blame on him. He spoke with peculiar asperity of Sprat, who had undoubtedly been the most humane and moderate member of the board.

It soon became clear that the wicked judge was fast sinking under the weight of bodily and mental suffering. Doctor John Scott, prebendary of Saint Paul's, a clergyman of great sanctity, and author of the Christian Life, a treatise once widely renowned, was summoned, probably on the recommendation of his intimate friend Sharp, to the bedside of the dying man. It was in vain, however, that Scott spoke, as Sharp had already spoken, of the hideous butcheries of Dorchester and Taunton. To the last Jeffreys continued to repeat that those who thought him cruel did not know what his orders were, that he deserved praise instead of blame, and that his clemency had drawn on him the extreme displeasure of his master.[1]

Disease, assisted by strong drink and by misery, did its work fast. The patient's stomach rejected all nourishment. He dwindled in a few weeks from a portly and even corpulent man to a skeleton. On the eighteenth of April he died, in the forty-first year of his age. He had been Chief Justice of the King's bench at thirty five, and Lord Chancellor at thirty seven. In the whole history of the English bar there is no other instance of so rapid an elevation, or of so terrible a fall. The emaciated corpse was laid, with all privacy, next to the corpse of Monmouth in the chapel of the Tower.[2]

[1] See the Life of Archbishop Sharp by his son. What passed between Scott and Jeffreys was related by Scott to Sir Joseph Jekyl. See Tindal's History ; Eachard, iii. 932. Eachard's informant, who is not named, but who seems to have had good opportunities of knowing the truth, said that Jeffreys died, not, as the vulgar believed, of drink, but of the stone. The distinction is of little importance. It is certain that Jeffreys was grossly intemperate ; and his malady was one which intemperance notoriously tends to aggravate.

[2] See a Full and True Account of the Death of George Lord Jeffreys, licensed on the day of his death. The wretched Le Noble was never weary of repeating that Jeffreys was poisoned by the usurper. I will give a short passage as a specimen of the calumnies of which William was

The fall of this man, once so great and so much dreaded, the horror with which he was regarded by all the respectable members of his own party, the manner in which the least respectable members of that party renounced fellowship with him in his distress, and threw on him the whole blame of crimes which they had encouraged him to commit, ought to have been a lesson to those intemperate friends of liberty who were clamouring for a new proscription. But it was a lesson which too many of them disregarded. The King had, at the very commencement of his reign, displeased them by appointing a few Tories and Trimmers to high offices ; and the discontent excited by these appointments had been inflamed by his attempt to obtain a general amnesty for the vanquished. He was in truth not a man to be popular with the vindictive zealots of any faction. For among his peculiarities was a certain ungracious humanity which rarely conciliated his foes, which often provoked his adherents, but in which he doggedly persisted, without troubling himself either about the thanklessness of those whom he had saved from destruction, or about the rage of those whom he had disappointed of their revenge. Some of the Whigs now spoke of him as bitterly as they had ever spoken of either of his uncles. He was a Stuart after all, and was not a Stuart for nothing. Like the rest of the race, he loved arbitrary power. In Holland, he had succeeded in making himself, under the forms of a republican polity, scarcely less absolute than the old hereditary Counts had been. In consequence of a strange combination of circumstances, his interest had, during a short time, coincided with the interest of the English people : but, though he had been a deliverer by accident, he was a despot by nature. He had no sympathy with the just resentments of the Whigs. He had objects in view which the Whigs would not willingly suffer any Sovereign to attain. He knew that the Tories were the only tools for his purpose. He had, therefore, from the moment at which he took his seat on the throne, favoured them unduly. He was now trying to procure an indemnity for those very delinquents whom he had, a few months before, described in his Declaration as deserving of exemplary punishment. In November

The Whigs dissatisfied with the King

the object. " Il envoya," says Pasquin, " ce fin ragoût de champignons au Chancelier Jeffreys, prisonnier dans la Tour, qui les trouva du même goust, et du même assaisonnement que furent les derniers dont Agrippine regala le bon-homme Claudius son époux, et que Neron appella depuis la viande de Dieux." Marforio asks : " Le Chancelier est donc mort dans la Tour ?" Pasquin answers : " Il estoit trop fidèle à son Roi légitime, et trop habile dans les loix du royaume, pour échapper à l'Usurpateur qu'il ne vouloit point reconnoistre. Guillemot prit soin de faire publier que ce malheureux prisonnier estoit attaqué d'une fièvre maligne : mais, à parler franchement, il vivroit peut-estre encore, s'il n'avoit rien mangé que de la main de ses anciens cuisiniers "—Le Festin de Guillemot, 1689. Dangeau (May 7.) mentions a report that Jeffreys had poisoned himself. In 1693 the corpse of Jeffreys was, by the royal permission, removed from the chapel of the Tower, and laid in the church of St. Mary Aldermary.

he had told the world that the crimes in which these men had borne a part had made it the duty of subjects to violate their oath of allegiance, of soldiers to desert their standards, of children to make war on their parents. With what consistency then could he recommend that such crimes should be covered by a general oblivion? And was there not too much reason to fear that he wished to save the agents of tyranny from the fate which they merited, in the hope that, at some future time, they might serve him as unscrupulously as they had served his father in law?[1]

Of the members of the House of Commons who were animated by these feelings, the fiercest and most audacious was Howe. He went so far

Intemperance of Howe

on one occasion as to move that an enquiry should be instituted into the proceedings of the Parliament of 1685, and that some note of infamy should be put on all who, in that Parliament, had voted with the Court. This absurd and mischievous motion was discountenanced by all the most respectable Whigs, and strongly opposed by Birch and Maynard.[2] Howe was forced to give way : but he was a man whom no check could abash ; and he was encouraged by the applause of many hotheaded members of his party, who were far from foreseeing that he would, after having been the most rancorous and unprincipled of Whigs, become, at no distant time, the most rancorous and unprincipled of Tories.

This quickwitted, restless, and malignant politician, though himself occupying a lucrative place in the royal household, declaimed, day after

Attack on Caermarthen

day, against the manner in which the great offices of state were filled ; and his declamations were echoed, in tones somewhat less sharp and vehement, by other orators. No man, they said, who had been a minister of Charles or of James ought to be a minister of William. The first attack was directed against the Lord President Caermarthen. Howe moved that an address should be presented to the King, requesting that all persons who had ever been impeached by the Commons might be dismissed from His Majesty's counsels and presence. The debate on this motion was repeatedly adjourned. While the event was doubtful, William sent Dykvelt to

---

[1] Among the numerous pieces in which the malecontent Whigs vented their anger, none is more curious than the poem entitled the Ghost of Charles the Second. Charles addresses William thus :

> " Hail, my blest Nephew, whom the fates ordain
> To fill the measure of the Stuarts' reign,
> That all the ills by our whole race designed
> In thee their full accomplishment might find :
> 'Tis thou that art decreed this point to clear,
> Which we have laboured for these fourscore year."

[2] Grey's Debates, June 12. 1689.

expostulate with Howe. Howe was obdurate. He was what is vulgarly called a disinterested man ; that is to say, he valued money less than the pleasure of venting his spleen and of making a sensation. " I am doing the King a service," he said : " I am rescuing him from false friends ; and, as to my place, that shall never be a gag to prevent me from speaking my mind." The motion was made, but completely failed. In truth the proposition, that mere accusation, never prosecuted to conviction, ought to be considered as a decisive proof of guilt, was shocking to natural justice. The faults of Caermarthen had doubtless been great; but they had been exaggerated by party spirit, had been expiated by severe suffering, and had been redeemed by recent and eminent services. At the time when he raised the great county of York in arms against Popery and tyranny, he had been assured by some of the most eminent Whigs that all old quarrels were forgotten. Howe indeed maintained that the civilities which had passed in the moment of peril signified nothing. " When a viper is on my hand," he said, " I am very tender of him : but as soon as I have him on the ground, I set my foot on him and crush him." The Lord President, however, was so strongly supported that, after a discussion which lasted three days, his enemies did not venture to take the sense of the House on the motion against him. In the course of the debate a grave constitutional question was incidentally raised. This question was whether a pardon could be pleaded in bar of a parliamentary impeachment. The Commons resolved, without a division, that a pardon could not be so pleaded.[1]

The next attack was made on Halifax. He was in a much more invidious position than Caermarthen, who had, under pretence of ill health, withdrawn himself almost entirely from business. **Attack on** Halifax was generally regarded as the chief adviser of the **Halifax** Crown, and was in an especial manner held responsible for all the faults which had been committed with respect to Ireland. The evils which had brought that kingdom to ruin might, it was said, have been averted by timely precaution, or remedied by vigorous exertion. But the government had foreseen nothing : it had done little ; and that little had been done neither at the right time nor in the right way. Negotiation had been employed instead of troops, when a few troops might have sufficed. A few troops had been sent when many were needed. The troops that had been sent had been ill equipped and ill commanded. Such, the vehement Whigs exclaimed, were the natural fruits of that great error which King William had committed on the first day of his reign. He had placed in Tories and Trimmers a confidence which

[1] See Commons' Journals, and Grey's Debates, June 1. 3. and 4. 1689 ; Life of William, 1704.

they did not deserve. He had, in a peculiar manner, entrusted the direction of Irish affairs to the Trimmer of Trimmers, to a man whose ability nobody disputed, but who was not firmly attached to the new government, who, indeed, was incapable of being firmly attached to any government, who had always halted between two opinions, and who, till the moment of the flight of James, had not given up the hope that the discontents of the nation might be quieted without a change of dynasty. Howe, on twenty occasions, designated Halifax as the cause of all the calamities of the country. Monmouth held similar language in the House of Peers. Though First Lord of the Treasury, he paid no attention to financial business, for which he was altogether unfit, and of which he had very soon become weary. His whole heart was in the work of persecuting the Tories. He plainly told the King that nobody who was not a Whig ought to be employed in the public service. William's answer was cool and determined. " I have done as much for your friends as I can do without danger to the state ; and I will do no more."[1] The only effect of this reprimand was to make Monmouth more factious than ever. Against Halifax especially he intrigued and harangued with indefatigable animosity. The other Whig Lords of the Treasury, Delamere and Capel, were scarcely less eager to drive the Lord Privy Seal from office ; and personal jealousy and antipathy impelled the Lord President to conspire with his own accusers against his rival.

What foundation there may have been for the imputations thrown at this time on Halifax cannot now be fully ascertained. His enemies, though they interrogated numerous witnesses, and though they obtained William's reluctant permission to inspect the minutes of the Privy Council, could find no evidence which would support a definite charge.[2] But it was undeniable that the Lord Privy Seal had acted as minister for Ireland, and that Ireland was all but lost. It is unnecessary, and indeed absurd, to suppose, as many Whigs supposed, that his administration was unsuccessful because he did not wish it to be successful. The truth seems to be that the difficulties of the situation were great, and that he, with all his ingenuity and eloquence, was ill qualified to cope with those difficulties. The whole machinery of government was out of joint ; and he was not the man to set it right. What was wanted was not what he had in large measure, wit, taste, amplitude of comprehension, subtlety in drawing distinctions ; but what he had not, prompt decision, indefatigable energy, and stubborn resolution. His mind was at best of too soft a temper for such work as he had now

[1] Burnet MS. Harl. 6584. ; Avaux to De Croissy, June $\frac{16}{28}$. 1689.

[2] As to the minutes of the Privy Council, see the Commons' Journals of June 22. and 28., and of July 3. 5. 13. and 16.

to do, and had been recently made softer by severe affliction. He had lost two sons in less than twelve months. A letter is still extant, in which he at this time complained to his honoured friend Lady Russell of the desolation of his hearth and of the cruel ingratitude of the Whigs. We possess, also, the answer, in which she gently exhorted him to seek for consolation where she had found it under trials not less severe than his.[1]

The first attack on him was made in the Upper House. Some Whig Peers, among whom the wayward and petulant First Lord of the Treasury was conspicuous, proposed that the King should be requested to appoint a new Speaker. The friends of Halifax moved and carried the previous question.[2] About three weeks later his persecutors brought forward, in a Committee of the whole House of Commons, a resolution which imputed to him no particular crime either of omission or of commission, but which simply declared it to be advisable that he should be dismissed from the service of the Crown. The debate was warm. Moderate politicians of both parties were unwilling to put a stigma on a man, not indeed faultless, but distinguished both by his abilities and by his amiable qualities. His accusers saw that they could not carry their point, and tried to escape from a decision which was certain to be adverse to them, by proposing that the Chairman should report progress. But their tactics were disconcerted by the judicious and spirited conduct of Lord Eland, now the Marquess's only son. "My father has not deserved," said the young nobleman, "to be thus trifled with. If you think him culpable, say so. He will at once submit to your verdict. Dismission from Court has no terrors for him. He is raised, by the goodness of God, above the necessity of looking to office for the means of supporting his rank." The Committee divided, and Halifax was absolved by a majority of fourteen.[3]

---

[1] The letter of Halifax to Lady Russell is dated on the 23d of July 1689, about a fortnight after the attack on him in the Lords, and about a week before the attack on him in the Commons.

[2] See the Lords' Journals of July 10. 1689, and a letter from London dated July $\frac{11}{21}$., and transmitted by Croissy to Avaux. Don Pedro de Ronquillo mentions this attack of the Whig Lords on Halifax in a despatch of which I cannot make out the date.

[3] This was on Saturday the 3d of August. As the division was in Committee, the numbers do not appear in the Journals. Clarendon, in his Diary, says that the majority was eleven. But Narcissus Luttrell, Oldmixon, and Tindal agree in putting it at fourteen. Most of the little information which I have been able to find about the debate is contained in a despatch of Don Pedro de Ronquillo. "Se resolvio," he says, "que el sabado, en comity de toda la casa, se tratasse del estado de la nacion para representarle al Rey. Empezose por acusar al Marques de Olifax ; y reconociendo sus emulos que no tenian partido bastante, quisieron remitir para otro dia esta mocion : pero el Conde de Elan, primogenito del Marques de Olifax, miembro de la casa, les dijo que su padre no era hombre para andar peloteando con el, y que se tubiesse culpa lo acabasen de castigar, que el no havia menester estar en la corte para portarse conforme á su

Had the division been postponed a few hours, the majority would probably have been much greater. The Commons voted under the impression that Londonderry had fallen, and that all Ireland was lost. Scarcely had the House risen when a courier arrived with news that the boom on the Foyle had been broken. He was speedily followed by a second, who announced the raising of the siege, and by a third who brought the tidings of the battle of Newton Butler. Hope and exultation succeeded to discontent and dismay.[1] Ulster was safe ; and it was confidently expected that Schomberg would speedily reconquer Leinster, Connaught, and Munster. He was now ready to set out. The port of Chester was the place from which he was to take his departure. The army which he was to command had assembled there ; and the Dee was crowded with men of war and transports. Unfortunately almost all those English soldiers who had seen war had been sent to Flanders. The bulk of the force destined for Ireland consisted of men just taken from the plough and the threshing floor. There was, however, an excellent brigade of Dutch troops under the command of an experienced officer, the Count of Solmes. Four regiments, one of cavalry and three of infantry, had been formed out of the French refugees, many of whom had borne arms with credit. No person did more to promote the raising of these regiments than the Marquess of Ruvigny. He had been during many years an eminently faithful and useful servant of the French government. So highly was his merit appreciated at Versailles that he had been solicited to accept indulgences which scarcely any other heretic could by any solicitation obtain. Had he chosen to remain in his native country, he and his household would have been permitted to worship God privately according to their own forms. But Ruvigny rejected all offers, cast in his lot with his brethren, and, at upwards of eighty years of age, quitted Versailles, where he might still have been a favourite, for a modest dwelling at Greenwich. That dwelling was, during the last months of his life, the resort of all that was most distinguished among his fellow exiles. His abilities, his experience, and his munificent kindness, made him the undisputed chief of the refugees. He was at the same time half an Englishman : for his sister had been Countess of Southampton, and he was uncle of Lady Russell. He was long past the time of action. But his two sons, both men of eminent courage, devoted their swords to the service of William. The younger son, who

Prepara-
tions
for a cam-
paign
in Ireland

---

estado, pues Dios le havia dado abundamente para poderlo hazer ; con que por pluralidad de voces vencio su partido." I suspect that Lord Eland meant to sneer at the poverty of some of his father's persecutors, and at the greediness of others.

[1] This change of feeling, immediately following the debate on the motion for removing Halifax, is noticed by Ronquillo.

bore the name of Caillemot, was appointed colonel of one of the Huguenot regiments of foot. The two other regiments of foot were commanded by La Melloniere and Cambon, officers of high reputation. The regiment of horse was raised by Schomberg himself, and bore his name. Ruvigny lived just long enough to see these arrangements complete.[1]

The general to whom the direction of the expedition against Ireland was confided had wonderfully succeeded in obtaining the affection and esteem of the English nation. He had been made a Duke, a Knight of the Garter, and Master of the Ordnance : he was now placed at the head of an army; and yet his elevation excited none of that jealousy which showed itself as often as any mark of royal favour was bestowed on Bentinck, on Zulestein, or on Auverquerque. Schomberg's military skill was universally acknowledged. He was regarded by all Protestants as a confessor who had endured everything short of martyrdom for the truth. For his religion he had resigned a splendid income, had laid down the truncheon of a Marshal of France, and had, at near eighty years of age, begun the world again as a needy soldier of fortune. As he had no connection with the United Provinces, and had never belonged to the little Court of the Hague, the preference given to him over English captains was justly ascribed, not to national or personal partiality, but to his virtues and his abilities. His deportment differed widely from that of the other foreigners who had just been created English peers. They, with many respectable qualities, were, in tastes, manners, and predilections, Dutchmen, and could not catch the tone of the society to which they had been transferred. He was a citizen of the world, had travelled over all Europe, had commanded armies on the Meuse, on the Ebro, and on the Tagus, had shone in the splendid circle of Versailles, and had been in high favour at the court of Berlin. He had often been taken by French noblemen for a French nobleman. He had passed some time in England, spoke English remarkably well, accommodated himself easily to English manners, and was often seen walking in the park with English companions. In youth his habits had been temperate ; and his temperance had its proper reward, a singularly green and vigorous old age. At fourscore he retained a strong relish for innocent pleasures : he conversed with great courtesy and sprightliness : nothing could be in better taste than his equipages and his table ; and every cornet of cavalry envied the grace and dignity with which the veteran appeared in Hyde Park on his

Schomberg

[1] As to Ruvigny, see Saint Simon's Memoirs of the year 1697 ; Burnet, i. 366. There is some interesting information about Ruvigny and about the Huguenot regiments in a narrative written by a French refugee of the name of Dumont. This narrative, which is in manuscript, and which I shall occasionally quote as the Dumont MS., was kindly lent to me by Dr. Vignoles, Dean of Ossory.

charger at the head of his regiment.[1] The House of Commons had, with general approbation, compensated his losses and rewarded his services by a grant of a hundred thousand pounds. Before he set out for Ireland, he requested permission to express his gratitude for this magnificent present. A chair was set for him within the bar. He took his seat there with the mace at his right hand, rose, and in a few graceful words returned his thanks and took his leave. The Speaker replied that the Commons could never forget the obligation under which they already lay to His Grace, that they saw him with pleasure at the head of an English army, that they felt entire confidence in his zeal and ability, and that, at whatever distance he might be, he would always be in a peculiar manner an object of their care. The precedent set on this interesting occasion was followed with the utmost minuteness, a hundred and twenty five years later, on an occasion more interesting still. Exactly on the same spot on which, in July 1689, Schomberg had acknowledged the liberality of the nation, a chair was set, in July 1814, for a still more illustrious warrior, who came to return thanks for a still more splendid mark of public gratitude. Few things illustrate more strikingly the peculiar character of the English government and people than the circumstance that the House of Commons, a popular assembly, should, even in a moment of joyous enthusiasm, have adhered to ancient forms with the punctilious accuracy of a College of Heralds ; that the sitting and rising, the covering and the uncovering, should have been regulated by exactly the same etiquette in the nineteenth century as in the seventeenth ; and that the same mace which had been held at the right hand of Schomberg should have been held in the same position at the right hand of Wellington.[2]

On the twentieth of August the Parliament, having been constantly engaged in business during seven months, broke up, by the royal command, for a short recess. The same Gazette which announced that the Houses had ceased to sit announced that Schomberg had landed in Ireland.[3]

Recess of the Parliament

During the three weeks which preceded his landing, the dismay and confusion at Dublin Castle had been extreme. Disaster had followed disaster so fast that the mind of James, never very firm, had been completely prostrated. He had learned first that Londonderry had been relieved ; then that one of his armies had been beaten by the Enniskilleners ; then that another of his armies was retreating, or rather flying, from Ulster, reduced in numbers and

State of Ireland. Advice of Avaux

---

[1] See the Abrégé de la Vie de Frederic Duc de Schomberg by Luzancy, 1690, the Memoirs of Count Dohna, and the note of Saint Simon on Dangeau's Journal, July 30. 1690.

[2] See the Commons' Journals of July 16. 1689, and of July 1. 1814.

[3] Journals of the Lords and Commons, Aug. 20. 1689 ; London Gazette, Aug. 22.

FREDERICK, DUKE OF SCHOMBERG

From an engraving by W. Faithorne, after a painting by M. Dahl.

broken in spirit; then that Sligo, the key of Connaught, had been abandoned to the Englishry. He had found it impossible to subdue the colonists, even when they were left almost unaided. He might therefore well doubt whether it would be possible for him to contend against them when they were backed by an English army, under the command of the greatest general living. The unhappy prince seemed, during some days, to be sunk in despondency. On Avaux the danger produced a very different effect. Now, he thought, was the time to turn the war between the English and the Irish into a war of extirpation, and to make it impossible that the two nations could ever be united under one government. With this view, he coolly submitted to the King a proposition of almost incredible atrocity. There must be a Saint Bartholomew. A pretext would easily be found. No doubt, when Schomberg was known to be in Ireland, there would be some excitement in those southern towns of which the population was chiefly English. Any disturbance, wherever it might take place, would furnish an excuse for a general massacre of the Protestants of Leinster, Munster, and Connaught.[1] As the King did not at first express any horror at this suggestion,[2] the Envoy, a few days later, returned to the subject, and pressed His Majesty to give the necessary orders. Then James, with a warmth which did him honour, declared that nothing should induce him to commit such a crime. " These people are my subjects : and I cannot be so cruel as to cut their throats while they live peaceably under my government." " There is nothing cruel," answered the callous diplomatist, " in what I recommend. Your Majesty ought to consider that mercy to Protestants is cruelty to Catholics." James, however, was not to be moved ; and Avaux retired in very bad humour. His belief was that the King's professions of humanity were hypocritical, and that, if the orders for the butchery were not given, they were not given only because His Majesty was confident that the Catholics all over the country would fall on the Protestants without waiting for orders.[3] But Avaux was entirely mistaken. That he should have supposed James to be as profoundly immoral as himself is not strange. But it is strange that so able a man should have forgotten that James and himself had quite different objects in view. The object of the Ambassador's politics was to make the separation between

---

[1] " J'estois d'avis qu', après que la descente seroit faite, si on apprenoit que des Protestans se fussent soulevez en quelques endroits du royaume, on fit main basse sur tous généralement."— Avaux, $\frac{\text{July 31.}}{\text{Aug. 1c.}}$ 1689.

[2] " Le Roy d'Angleterre m'avoit écouté assez paisiblement la première fois que je luy avois proposé ce qu'il y avoit à faire contre les Protestans."—Avaux, Aug. $\frac{4}{14}$.

[3] Avaux, Aug. $\frac{4}{14}$. He says, " Je m'imagine qu'il est persuadé que, quoiqu'il ne donne point d'ordre sur cela, la plupart des Catholiques de la campagne se jetteront sur les Protestans."

JAMES II., 1633-1701.

From the painting by John Riley, in the National Portrait Gallery.

England and Ireland eternal. The object of the King's politics was to unite England and Ireland under his own sceptre; and he could not but be aware that, if there should be a general massacre of the Protestants of three provinces, and he should be suspected of having authorised it or of having connived at it, there would in a fortnight be not a Jacobite left even at Oxford.[1]

Just at this time the prospects of James, which had seemed hopelessly dark, began to brighten. The danger which had unnerved him had roused the Irish people. They had, six months before, risen up as one man against the Saxons. The army which Tyrconnel had formed was, in proportion to the population from which it was taken, the largest that Europe had ever seen. But that army had sustained a long succession of defeats and disgraces, unredeemed by a single brilliant achievement. It was the fashion, both in England and on the Continent, to ascribe those defeats and disgraces to the pusillanimity of the Irish race.[2] That this was a great error is sufficiently proved by the history of every war which has been carried on in any part of Christendom during five generations. The raw material out of which a good army may be formed existed in great abundance among the Irish. Avaux informed his government that they were a remarkably handsome, tall, and well made race; that they were personally brave; that they were sincerely attached to the cause for which they were in arms; that they were violently exasperated against the colonists. After extolling their strength and spirit, he proceeded to explain why it was that, with all their strength and spirit, they were constantly beaten. It was vain, he said, to imagine that bodily prowess, animal courage, or patriotic enthusiasm would, in the day of battle, supply the place of discipline. The infantry were ill armed and ill trained. They were suffered to pillage wherever they went. They had contracted all the habits of banditti. There was among them scarcely one officer capable of showing them their duty. Their colonels were generally men of good family, but men who had never seen service. The captains were butchers, tailors, shoemakers. Hardly one of them troubled himself about the comforts, the accoutrements, or the drilling of those over whom he was placed.

---

[1] Lewis, $\frac{\text{Aug. 27.}}{\text{Sept. 6.}}$, reprimanded Avaux, though much too gently, for proposing to butcher the whole Protestant population of Leinster, Connaught, and Munster. "Je n'approuve pas cependant la proposition que vous faites de faire main basse sur tous les Protestans du royaume, du moment qu', en quelque endroit que ce soit, ils se seront soulevez: et, outre que la punition d'une infinité d'innocens pour peu de coupables ne seroit pas juste, d'ailleurs les représailles contre les Catholiques seroient d'autant plus dangereuses, que les premiers se trouveront mieux armez et soutenus de toutes les forces d'Angleterre."

[2] Ronquillo, Aug. $\frac{9}{19}$., speaking of the Siege of Londonderry, expresses his astonishment "que una plaza sin fortificazion y sin gentes de guerra aya hecho una defensa tan gloriosa, y que los sitiadores al contrario ayan sido tan poltrones."

The dragoons were little better than the infantry. But the horse were with some exceptions, excellent. Almost all the Irish gentlemen who had any military experience held commissions in the cavalry; and, by the exertions of these officers, some regiments had been raised and disciplined which Avaux pronounced equal to any that he had ever seen. It was therefore evident that the inefficiency of the foot and of the dragoons was to be ascribed to the vices, not of the Irish character but of the Irish administration.[1]

The events which took place in the autumn of 1689 sufficiently proved that the ill fated race, which enemies and allies generally agreed in regarding with unjust contempt, had, together with the faults insepar able from poverty, ignorance, and superstition, some fine qualities which have not always been found in more prosperous and more enlightened communities. The evil tidings which terrified and be-wildered James stirred the whole population of the southern provinces like the peal of a trumpet sounding to battle. That Ulster was lost, that the English were coming, that the death grapple between the two hostile nations was at hand, was proclaimed from all the altars of three and twenty counties. One last chance was left; and, if that chance failed, nothing remained but the despotic, the merciless, rule of the Saxon colony and of the heretical church. The Roman Catholic priest who had just taken possession of the glebe house and the chancel, the Roman Catholic squire who had just been carried back on the shoulders of the shouting tenantry into the hall of his fathers, would be driven forth to live on such alms as peasants, themselves oppressed and miser-able, could spare. A new confiscation would complete the work of the Act of Settlement; and the followers of William would seize whatever the followers of Cromwell had spared. These apprehensions produced such an outbreak of patriotic and religious enthusiasm as deferred for a

[1] This account of the Irish army is compiled from numerous letters written by Avaux to Lewis and to Lewis's ministers. I will quote a few of the most remarkable passages. " Les plus beaux hommes," Avaux says of the Irish, " qu'on peut voir. Il n'y en a presque point au dessous de cinq pieds cinq à six pouces." It will be remembered that the French foot is longer than ours. " Ils sont très bien faits : mais ils ne sont ny disciplinez ny armez, et de surplus sont de grands voleurs." " La plupart de ces régimens sont levez par des gentilshommes qui n'ont jamais esté à l'armée. Ce sont des tailleurs, des bouchers, des cordonniers, qui ont formé les compagnies et qui en sont les Capitaines." " Jamais troupes n'ont marché comme font celles-cy. Ils vont comme des bandits, et pillent tout ce qu'ils trouvent en chemin." " Quoiqu'il soit vrai que les soldats paroissent fort résolus à bien faire, et qu'ils soient fort animez contre les rebelles, néant-moins il ne suffit pas de cela pour combattre. . . . Les officiers subalternes sont mauvais, et, à la reserve d'un très petit nombre, il n'y en a point qui ayt soin des soldats, des armes, et de la disci-pline." " On a beaucoup plus de confiance en la cavalerie, dont la plus grande partie est assez bonne." Avaux mentions several regiments of horse with particular praise. Of two of these he says, " On ne peut voir de meilleur régiment." The correctness of the opinion which he had formed both of the infantry and of the cavalry was, after his departure from Ireland, signally proved at the Boyne.

time the inevitable day of subjugation.   Avaux was amazed by the energy which, in circumstances so trying, the Irish displayed.   It was indeed the wild and unsteady energy of a half barbarous people : it was transient : it was often misdirected : but, though transient and misdirected, it did wonders.   The French Ambassador was forced to own that those officers of whose incompetency and inactivity he had so often complained had suddenly shaken off their lethargy.   Recruits came in by thousands.   The ranks which had been thinned under the walls of Londonderry were soon again full to overflowing.   Great efforts were made to arm and clothe the troops ; and, in the short space of a fortnight, everything presented a new and cheering aspect.[1]

The Irish required of the King, in return for their strenuous exertions in his cause, one concession which was by no means agreeable to him.   The unpopularity of Melfort had become such that his person was scarcely safe.   He had no friend to speak a **Dismission of Melfort** word in his favour.   The French hated him.   In every letter which arrived at Dublin from England or from Scotland, he was described as the evil genius of the House of Stuart.   It was necessary for his own sake to dismiss him.   An honourable pretext was found.   He was ordered to repair to Versailles, to represent there the state of affairs in Ireland, and to implore the French government to send over without delay six or seven thousand veteran infantry.   He laid down the seals ; and they were, to the great delight of the Irish, put into the hands of an Irishman, Sir Richard Nagle, who had made himself conspicuous as Attorney General and Speaker of the House of Commons.   Melfort took his departure under cover of the night : for the rage of the populace against him was such that he could not without danger show himself in the streets of Dublin by day.   On the following morning James left his capital in the opposite direction to encounter Schomberg.[2]

Schomberg had landed in the north of Ulster.   The force which he had brought with him did not exceed ten thousand men.   But he expected to be joined by the armed colonists and by the **Schomberg** regiments which were under Kirke's command.   The coffee- **lands in** house politicians of London fully expected that such a **Ulster** general with such an army would speedily reconquer the island.

---

[1] I will quote a passage or two from the despatches written at this time by Avaux.   On September $\frac{7}{17}$. he says: " De quelque costé qu'on se tournât, on ne pouvoit rien prevoir que de désagréable.   Mais dans cette extrémité chacun s'est évertué.   Les officiers ont fait leurs recrues avec beaucoup de diligence."   Three days later he says: " Il y a quinze jours que nous n'espérions guère de pouvoir mettre les choses en si bon estat : mais my Lord Tyrconnel et tous les Irlandais ont travaillé avec tant d'empressement qu'on s'est mis en estat de deffense."

[2] Avaux, Aug. $\frac{2\,0}{3\,0}$. $\frac{\text{Aug. 25.}}{\text{Sept. 4.}}\frac{\text{Aug. 26.}}{\text{Sept. 5.}}$; Life of James, ii. 373.; Melfort's vindication of himself among the Nairne Papers.   Avaux says : " Il pourra partir ce soir à la nuit : car je vois bien qu'il apprehende qu'il ne sera pas sur pour luy de partir en plein jour."

Unhappily it soon appeared that the means which had been furnished to him were altogether inadequate to the work which he had to perform : of the greater part of these means he was speedily deprived by a succession of unforeseen calamities ; and the whole campaign was merely a long struggle maintained by his prudence and resolution against the utmost spite of fortune.

He marched first to Carrickfergus. That town was held for James by two regiments of infantry. Schomberg battered the walls ; and the Irish, after holding out a week, capitulated. He promised that they should depart unharmed ; but he found it no easy matter to keep his word. The people of the town and neighbourhood were generally Protestants of Scottish extraction. They had suffered much during the short ascendency of the native race ; and what they had suffered they were now eager to retaliate. They assembled in great multitudes, exclaiming that the capitulation was nothing to them, and that they would be revenged. They soon proceeded from words to blows. The Irish, disarmed, stripped, and hustled, clung for protection to the English officers and soldiers. Schomberg with difficulty prevented a massacre by spurring, pistol in hand, through the throng of enraged colonists.[1]

From Carrickfergus Schomberg proceeded to Lisburn, and thence, through towns left without an inhabitant, and over plains on which not a cow, nor a sheep, nor a stack of corn was to be seen, to Loughbrickland. Here he was joined by three regiments of Enniskilleners, whose dress, horses, and arms looked strange to eyes accustomed to the pomp of reviews, but who in natural courage were inferior to no troops in the world, and who had, during months of constant watching and skirmishing, acquired many of the essential qualities of soldiers.[2]

Schomberg continued to advance towards Dublin through a desert. The few Irish troops which remained in the south of Ulster retreated before him, destroying as they retreated. Newry, once a well built and thriving Protestant borough, he found a heap of smoking ashes. Carlingford too had perished. The spot where the town had once stood was marked only by the massy remains of the old Norman castle. Those who ventured to wander from the camp reported that the country, as far as they could explore it, was a wilderness. There were cabins, but no inmates : there was rich pasture, but neither flock nor herd : there were cornfields : but the harvest lay on the ground soaked with rain.[3]

While Schomberg was advancing through a vast solitude, the Irish

Carrickfergus taken

Schomberg advances into Leinster

---

[1] Story's Impartial History of the Wars of Ireland, 1693 ; Life of James, ii. 374. ; Avaux, Sept. $\frac{7}{17}$. 1689 ; Nihell's Journal, printed in 1689, and reprinted by Macpherson.

[2] Story's Impartial History.   [3] Ibid.

MAP OF CARRICKFERGUS AND THE ADJACENT COUNTRY

From George Story's Impartial History of the Wars of Ireland, 1693

forces were rapidly assembling from every quarter. On the tenth of September the royal standard of James was unfurled on the tower

The English and Irish armies encamp near each other of Drogheda; and beneath it were soon collected twenty thousand fighting men, the infantry generally bad, the cavalry generally good, but both infantry and cavalry full of zeal for their country and their religion.[1] The troops were attended as usual by a great multitude of camp followers, armed with scythes, half pikes, and skeans. By this time Schomberg had reached Dundalk. The distance between the two armies was not more than a long day's march. It was therefore generally expected that the fate of the island would speedily be decided by a pitched battle.

In both camps, all who did not understand war were eager to fight; and, in both camps, the few who had a high reputation for military science were against fighting. Neither Rosen nor Schomberg wished to put everything on a cast. Each of them knew intimately the defects of his own army; and neither of them was fully aware of the defects of the other's army. Rosen was certain that the Irish infantry were worse equipped, worse officered, and worse drilled, than any infantry that he had ever seen from the Gulf of Bothnia to the Atlantic; and he supposed that the English troops were well trained, and were, as they doubtless ought to have been, amply provided with everything necessary to their efficiency. Numbers, he rightly judged, would avail little against a great superiority of arms and discipline. He therefore advised James to fall back, and even to abandon Dublin to the enemy, rather than hazard a battle the loss of which would be the loss of all. Athlone was the best place in the kingdom for a determined stand. The passage of the Shannon might be defended till the succours which Melfort had been charged to solicit came from France; and those succours would change the whole character of the war. But the Irish, with Tyrconnel at their head, were unanimous against retreating. The blood of the whole nation was up. James was pleased with the enthusiasm of his subjects, and positively declared that he would not disgrace himself by leaving his capital to the invaders without a blow.[2]

In a few days it became clear that Schomberg had determined not to fight. His reasons were weighty. He had some good Dutch

Schomberg declines a battle and French troops. The Enniskilleners who had joined him had served a military apprenticeship, though not in a very regular manner. But the bulk of his army consisted of English peasants who had just left their cottages. His musketeers had

---

[1] Avaux, Sept. $\frac{18}{28}$. 1689; Story's Impartial History; Life of James, ii. 377, 378. Orig. Mem. Story and James agree in estimating the Irish army at about twenty thousand men. See also Dangeau, Oct. 28. 1689.

[2] Life of James, ii. 377, 378. Orig. Mem.

still to learn how to load their pieces : his dragoons had still to learn how to manage their horses ; and these inexperienced recruits were for the most part commanded by officers as inexperienced **Frauds of** as themselves. His troops were therefore not generally **the English Commis-** superior in discipline to the Irish, and were in number far **sariat** inferior. Nay, he found that his men were almost as ill armed, as ill lodged, and as ill clad, as the Celts to whom they were opposed. The wealth of the English nation and the liberal votes of the English parliament had entitled him to expect that he should be abundantly supplied with all the munitions of war. But he was cruelly disappointed. The administration had, ever since the death of Oliver, been constantly becoming more and more imbecile, more and more corrupt ; and now the Revolution reaped what the Restoration had sown. A crowd of negligent or ravenous functionaries, formed under Charles and James, plundered, starved, and poisoned the armies and fleets of William. Of these men the most important was Henry Shales, who, in the late reign, had been Commissary General to the camp at Hounslow. It is difficult to blame the new government for continuing to employ him : for, in his own department, his experience far surpassed that of any other Englishman. Unfortunately, in the same school in which he had acquired his experience, he had learned the whole art of peculation. The beef and brandy which he furnished were so bad that the soldiers turned from them with loathing : the tents were rotten : the clothing was scanty : the muskets broke in the handling. Great numbers of shoes were set down to the account of the government : but, two months after the Treasury had paid the bill, the shoes had not arrived in Ireland. The means of transporting baggage and artillery were almost entirely wanting. An ample number of horses had been pur- chased in England with the public money, and had been sent to the banks of the Dee. But Shales had let them out for harvest work to the farmers of Cheshire, had pocketed the hire, and had left the troops in Ulster to get on as they best might.[1] Schomberg thought that, if he should, with an ill trained and ill appointed army, risk a battle against a superior force, he might not improbably be defeated ; and he knew that a defeat might be followed by the loss of one kingdom, perhaps by the loss of three kingdoms. He therefore made up his mind to stand on the defensive till his men had been disciplined, and till reinforcements and supplies should arrive.

He entrenched himself near Dundalk in such a manner that he could not be forced to fight against his will. James, emboldened by the caution of his adversary, and disregarding the advice of Rosen, advanced

[1] See Grey's Debates, Nov. 26, 27, 28. 1689, and the Dialogue between a Lord Lieutenant and one of his Deputies, 1692.

to Ardee, appeared at the head of the whole Irish army before the English lines, drew up horse, foot, and artillery, in order of battle, and displayed his banner. The English were impatient to fall on. But their general had made up his mind, and was not to be moved by the bravadoes of the enemy or by the murmurs of his own soldiers. During some weeks he remained secure within his defences, while the Irish lay a few miles off. He set himself assiduously to drill those new levies which formed the greater part of his army. He ordered the musketeers to be constantly exercised in firing, sometimes at marks, and sometimes by platoons ; and, from the way in which they at first acquitted themselves, it plainly appeared that he had judged wisely in not leading them out to battle. It was found that not one in four of the English soldiers could manage his piece at all ; and whoever succeeded in discharging it, no matter in what direction, thought that he had performed a great feat.

While the Duke was thus employed, the Irish eyed his camp without daring to attack it. But within that camp soon appeared two evils

Conspiracy among the French troops in the English service

more terrible than the foe, treason and pestilence. Among the best troops under his command were the French exiles. And now a grave doubt arose touching their fidelity. The real Huguenot refugee indeed might safely be trusted. The dislike with which the most zealous English Protestant regarded the House of Bourbon and the Church of Rome was a lukewarm feeling when compared with that inextinguishable hatred which glowed in the bosom of the persecuted, dragooned, expatriated Calvinist of Languedoc. The Irish had already remarked that the French heretic neither gave nor took quarter.[1] Now, however, it was found that with those emigrants who had sacrificed everything for the reformed religion were intermingled emigrants of a very different sort, deserters who had run away from their standards in the Low Countries, and had coloured their crime by pretending that they were Protestants, and that their conscience would not suffer them to fight for the persecutor of their Church. Some of these men, hoping that by a second treason they might obtain both pardon and reward, opened a correspondence with Avaux. The letters were intercepted ; and a formidable plot was brought to light. It appeared that, if Schomberg had been weak enough to yield to the importunity of those who wished him to give battle, several French companies would, in the heat of the action, have fired on the English, and gone over to the enemy. Such a defection might well have produced a general panic in a better army than that which was encamped

[1] Nihell's Journal. A French officer, in a letter to Avaux, written soon after Schomberg's landing, says, " Les Huguenots font plus de mal que les Anglois, et tuent force Catholiques pour avoir fait résistance."

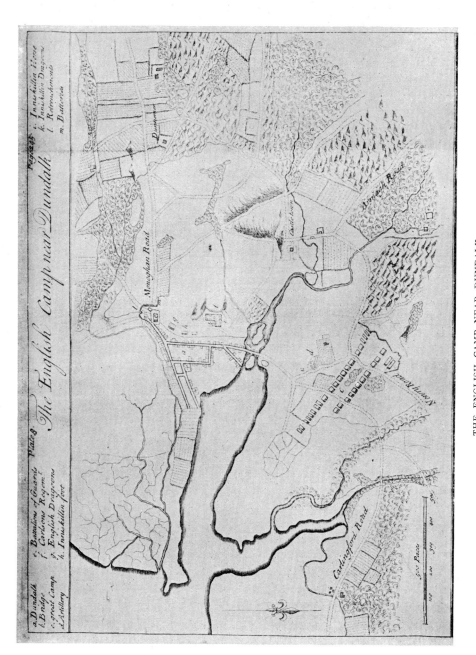

THE ENGLISH CAMP NEAR DUNDALK

From Walter Harris's Life of William III, 1749

under Dundalk.　It was necessary to be severe.　Six of the conspirators were hanged.　Two hundred of their accomplices were sent in irons to England.　Even after this winnowing, the refugees were long regarded by the rest of the army with unjust but not unnatural suspicion. During some days indeed there was great reason to fear that the enemy would be entertained with a bloody fight between the English soldiers and their French allies.[1]

A few hours before the execution of the chief conspirators, a general muster of the army was held ; and it was observed that the ranks of the English battalions looked thin.　From the first day of the campaign, there had been much sickness among the recruits : but it was not till the time of the equinox that the mortality became alarming.　The autumnal rains of Ireland are usually heavy ; and this year they were heavier than usual.　The whole country was deluged ; and the Duke's camp became a marsh.　The Enniskillen men were seasoned to the climate.　The Dutch were accustomed to live in a country which, as a wit of that age said, draws fifty feet of water.　They kept their huts dry and clean ; and they had experienced and careful officers who did not suffer them to omit any precaution. But the peasants of Yorkshire and Derbyshire had neither constitutions prepared to resist the pernicious influence, nor skill to protect themselves against it.　The bad provisions furnished by the Commissariat aggravated the maladies generated by the air.　Remedies were almost entirely wanting.　The surgeons were few.　The medicine chests contained little more than lint and plasters for wounds.　The English sickened and died by hundreds.　Even those who were not smitten by the pestilence were unnerved and dejected, and, instead of putting forth the energy which is the heritage of our race, awaited their fate with the helpless apathy of Asiatics.　It was in vain that Schomberg tried to teach them to improve their habitations, and to cover the wet earth with a thick carpet of fern.　Exertion had become more dreadful to them than death.　It was not to be expected that men who would not help themselves should help each other.　Nobody asked and nobody showed compassion.　Familiarity with ghastly spectacles produced a hardheartedness and a desperate impiety of which an example will not easily be found even in the history of infectious diseases.　The moans of the sick were drowned by the blasphemy and ribaldry of their comrades. Sometimes, seated on the body of a wretch who had died in the morning, might be seen a wretch destined to die before night, cursing, singing loose songs, and swallowing usquebaugh to the health of the devil.

Pestilence in the English army (marginal note)

---

[1] Story ; Narrative transmitted by Avaux to Seignelay, $\frac{\text{Nov. 26.}}{\text{Dec. 6.}}$ 1689 ; London Gazette, Oct. 14. 1689.　It is curious that, though Dumont was in the camp before Dundalk, there is in his MS. no mention of the conspiracy among the French.

When the corpses were taken away to be buried the survivors grumbled. A dead man, they said, was a good screen and a good stool. Why, when there was so abundant a supply of such useful articles of furniture, were people to be exposed to the cold air and forced to crouch on the moist ground.[1]

Many of the sick were sent by the English vessels which lay off the coast to Belfast, where a great hospital had been prepared. But scarce half of them lived to the end of the voyage. More than one ship lay long in the bay of Carrickfergus, heaped with carcasses, and exhaling the stench of death, without a living man on board.[2]

The Irish army suffered much less. The kerne of Munster or Connaught was quite as well off in the camp as if he had been in his own mud cabin inhaling the vapours of his own quagmire. He naturally exulted in the distress of the Saxon heretics, and flattered himself that they would be destroyed without a blow. He heard with delight the guns pealing all day over the graves of the English officers, till at length the funerals became too numerous to be celebrated with military pomp, and the mournful sounds were succeeded by a silence more mournful still.

The superiority of force was now so decidedly on the side of James that he could safely venture to detach five regiments from his army, and to send them into Connaught. Sarsfield commanded them. He did not, indeed, stand so high as he deserved in the royal estimation. The King, with an air of intellectual superiority which must have made Avaux and Rosen bite their lips, pronounced him a brave fellow, but very scantily supplied with brains. It was not without great difficulty that the Ambassador prevailed on His Majesty to raise the best officer in the Irish army to the rank of Brigadier. Sarsfield now fully vindicated the favourable opinion which his French patrons had formed of him. He dislodged the English from Sligo; and he effectually secured Galway, which had been in considerable danger.[3]

No attack, however, was made on the English entrenchments before Dundalk. In the midst of difficulties and disasters hourly multiplying, the great qualities of Schomberg appeared hourly more and more conspicuous. Not in the full tide of success, not on the field of Montes Claros, not under the walls of Maestricht, had he so well deserved the admiration of mankind. His resolution never gave way. His prudence never slept. His temper, in spite of manifold vexations and provocations,

---

[1] Story's Impartial History; Dumont MS. The profaneness and dissoluteness of the camp during the sickness are mentioned in many contemporary pamphlets both in verse and prose. See particularly a Satire entitled Reformation of Manners, part ii.

[2] Story's Impartial History.

[3] Avaux, Oct. $\frac{11}{21}$. Nov. $\frac{14}{24}$. 1689; Story's Impartial History; Life of James, ii. 382, 383. Orig. Mem.; Nihell's Journal.

was always cheerful and serene. The effective men under his command, even if all were reckoned as effective who were not stretched on the earth by fever, did not now exceed five thousand. These were hardly equal to their ordinary duty; and yet it was necessary to harass them with double duty. Nevertheless so masterly were the old man's dispositions that with this small force he faced during several weeks twenty thousand troops who were accompanied by a multitude of armed banditti. At length early in November the Irish dispersed, and went to winter quarters. The Duke then broke up his camp and retired into Ulster. Just as the remains of his army were about to move, a rumour spread that the enemy was approaching in great force. Had this rumour been true, the danger would have been extreme. But the English regiments, though they had been reduced to a third part of their complement, and though the men who were in best health were hardly able to shoulder arms, showed a strange joy and alacrity at the prospect of battle, and swore that the Papists should pay for all the misery of the last month. "We English," Schomberg said, identifying himself goodhumouredly with the people of the country which had adopted him, "we English have stomach enough for fighting. It is a pity that we are not as fond of some other parts of a soldier's business."

The alarm proved false: the Duke's army departed unmolested: but the highway along which he retired presented a piteous and hideous spectacle. A long train of waggons laden with the sick jolted over the rugged pavement. At every jolt some wretched man gave up the ghost. The corpse was flung out and left unburied to the foxes and crows. The whole number of those who died, in the camp at Dundalk, in the hospital at Belfast, on the road, and on the sea, amounted to above six thousand. The survivors were quartered for the winter in the towns and villages of Ulster. The general fixed his head quarters at Lisburn.[1]

His conduct was variously judged. Wise and candid men said that he had surpassed himself, and that there was no other captain in Europe who, with raw troops, with ignorant officers, with scanty stores, having to contend at once against a hostile army of greatly superior force, against a villanous commissariat, against a nest of traitors in his own camp, and against a disease more murderous than the sword, would have brought the

The English and Irish armies go into winter quarters

Various opinions about Schomberg's conduct

[1] Story's Impartial History; Schomberg's Despatches; Nihell's Journal, and James's Life; Burnet, ii. 20.; Dangeau's journal during this autumn; the Narrative sent by Avaux to Seignelay, and the Dumont MS. The lying of the London Gazette is monstrous. Through the whole autumn the troops are constantly said to be in good condition. In the absurd drama entitled the Royal Voyage, which was acted for the amusement of the rabble of London in 1689, the Irish are represented as attacking some of the sick English. The English put the assailants to the rout, and then drop down dead,

campaign to a close without the loss of a flag or a gun. On the other hand, many of those newly commissioned majors and captains, whose helplessness had increased all his perplexities, and who had not one qualification for their post except personal courage, grumbled at the skill and patience which had saved them from destruction. Their complaints were echoed on the other side of Saint George's Channel. Some of the murmuring, though unjust, was excusable. The parents, who had sent a gallant lad, in his first uniform, to fight his way to glory, might be pardoned if, when they learned that he had died on a wisp of straw without medical attendance, and had been buried in a swamp without any Christian or military ceremony, their affliction made them hasty and unreasonable. But with the cry of bereaved families was mingled another cry much less respectable. All the hearers and tellers of news abused the general who furnished them with so little news to hear and to tell. For men of that sort are so greedy after excitement that they far more readily forgive a commander who loses a battle than a commander who declines one. The politicians, who delivered their oracles from the thickest cloud of tobacco smoke at Garroway's, confidently asked, without knowing anything, either of war in general, or of Irish war in particular, why Schomberg did not fight. They could not venture to say that he did not understand his calling. He had, in his day, they acknowledged, been an excellent officer : but he was very old. He seemed to bear his years well : but his faculties were not what they had been : his memory was failing ; and it was well known that he sometimes forgot in the afternoon what he had done in the morning. It may be doubted whether there ever existed a human being whose mind was quite as firmly toned at eighty as at forty. But that Schomberg's intellectual powers had been little impaired by years is sufficiently proved by his despatches, which are still extant, and which are models of official writing, terse, perspicuous, full of important facts and weighty reasons, compressed into the smallest possible number of words. In those despatches he sometimes alluded, not angrily, but with calm disdain, to the censures thrown upon his conduct by shallow babblers, who, never having seen any military operation more important than the relieving of the guard at Whitehall, imagined that the easiest thing in the world was to gain great victories in any situation and against any odds, and by sturdy patriots who were convinced that one English carter or thresher, who had not yet learned how to load a gun or port a pike, was a match for any six musketeers of King Lewis's household,[1]

Unsatisfactory as had been the results of the campaign in Ireland, the results of the maritime operations of the year were more unsatis-

[1] See his despatches in the Appendix to Dalrymple's Memoirs.

factory still. It had been confidently expected that, on the sea, England, allied with Holland, would have been far more than a match for **Maritime affairs** the power of Lewis: but everything went wrong. Herbert had, after the unimportant skirmish of Bantry Bay, returned with his squadron to Portsmouth. There he found that he had not lost the good opinion either of the public or of the government. The House of Commons thanked him for his services; and he received signal marks of the favour of the Crown. He had not been at the coronation, and had therefore missed his share of the rewards which, at the time of that solemnity, had been distributed among the chief agents in the Revolution. The omission was now repaired; and he was created Earl of Torrington. The King went down to Portsmouth, dined on board of the Admiral's flag ship, expressed the fullest confidence in the valour and loyalty of the navy, knighted two gallant captains, Cloudesley Shovel and John Ashby, and ordered a donative to be divided among the seamen.[1]

We cannot justly blame William for having a high opinion of Torrington. For Torrington was generally regarded as one of the **Maladministration of Torrington** bravest and most skilful officers in the navy. He had been promoted to the rank of Rear Admiral of England by James, who, if he understood anything, understood maritime affairs. That place and other lucrative places Torrington had relinquished when he found that he could retain them only by submitting to be a tool of the Jesuitical cabal. No man had taken a more active, a more hazardous, or a more useful part in effecting the Revolution. It seemed, therefore, that no man had fairer pretensions to be put at the head of the naval administration. Yet no man could be more unfit for such a post. His morals had always been loose, so loose indeed that the firmness with which in the late reign he had adhered to his religion had excited much surprise. His glorious disgrace indeed seemed to have produced a salutary effect on his character. In poverty and exile he rose from a voluptuary into a hero. But, as soon as prosperity returned, the hero sank again into a voluptuary; and the relapse was deep and hopeless. The nerves of his mind, which had been during a short time braced to a high tone, were now so much relaxed by vice that he was utterly incapable of selfdenial or of strenuous exertion. The vulgar courage of a foremast man he still retained. But both as Admiral and as First Lord of the Admiralty he was utterly inefficient. Month after month the fleet which should have been the terror of the seas lay in harbour while he was diverting himself in London. The sailors, punning upon his new title, gave him the name of Lord Tarry-in-town. When he came on shipboard he was accompanied by a bevy of courtesans.

[1] London Gazette, May 20. 1689.

SIR CLOUDESLEY SHOVELL

From a mezzotint by J. Smith, after a painting by W. de Rijck

There was scarcely an hour of the day or of the night when he was not under the influence of claret. Being insatiable of pleasure, he necessarily became insatiable of wealth. Yet he loved flattery almost as much as either wealth or pleasure. He had long been in the habit of exacting the most abject homage from those who were under his command. His flag ship was a little Versailles. He expected his captains to attend him to his cabin when he went to bed, and to assemble every morning at his levee. He even suffered them to dress him. One of them combed his flowing wig ; another stood ready with the embroidered coat. Under such a chief there could be no discipline. His tars passed their time in rioting among the rabble of Portsmouth. Those officers who had won his favour by servility and adulation easily obtained leave of absence, and spent weeks in London, revelling in taverns, scouring the streets, or making love to the masked ladies in the pit of the theatre. The victuallers soon found out with whom they had to deal, and sent down to the fleet casks of meat which dogs would not touch, and barrels of beer which smelt worse than bilge water. Meanwhile the British Channel seemed to be abandoned to French rovers. Our merchantmen were boarded in sight of the ramparts of Plymouth. The sugar fleet from the West Indies lost seven ships. The whole value of the prizes taken by the cruisers of the enemy in the immediate neighbourhood of our island, while Torrington was engaged with his bottle and his haram, was estimated at six hundred thousand pounds. So difficult was it to obtain the convoy of a man of war, except by giving immense bribes, that our traders were forced to hire the services of Dutch privateers, and found these foreign mercenaries much more useful and much less greedy than the officers of our own royal navy.[1]

    The only department with which no fault could be found was the department of Foreign Affairs. There William was his own minister ;

Continental affairs — and, where he was his own minister, there were no delays, no blunders, no jobs, no treasons. The difficulties with which he had to contend were indeed great. Even at the Hague he had to encounter an opposition which all his wisdom and firmness could, with the strenuous support of Heinsius, scarcely overcome. The English were not aware that, while they were murmuring at their Sovereign's partiality for the land of his birth, a strong party in Holland was murmuring at his partiality for the land of his adoption. The Dutch ambassadors at Westminster complained that the terms of alliance which he proposed were derogatory to the dignity and prejudicial to the interests of the republic ; that wherever the honour of the English flag

---

[1] Commons' Journals, Nov. 13. 23. 1689 ; Grey's Debates, Nov. 13. 14. 18. 23. 1689. See, among numerous pasquinades, the Parable of the Bearbaiting, Reformation of Manners, a Satire, the Mock Mourners, a Satire. See also Pepys's Diary kept at Tangier, Oct. 15. 1683.

The Right Honble ARTHUR Earle of TORRINGTON,
Baron HERBERT of Torbay,
First Ld. of the Admiralty, ADMIRALL of their Maties Navy, & Capt Genll
of the Narrow Seas. 1689.

ARTHUR HERBERT, EARL OF TORRINGTON

From an engraving by R. White, after a painting by J. Riley

was concerned, he was punctilious and obstinate ; that he peremptorily insisted on an article which interdicted all trade with France, and which could not but be grievously felt on the Exchange of Amsterdam ; that, when they expressed a hope that the Navigation Act would be repealed, he burst out a laughing, and told them that the thing was not to be thought of. He carried all his points ; and a solemn contract was made by which England and the Batavian federation bound themselves to stand firmly by each other against France, and not to make peace except by mutual consent. But one of the Dutch plenipotentiaries declared that he was afraid of being one day held up to obloquy as a traitor for conceding so much ; and the signature of another plainly appeared to have been traced by a hand shaking with emotion.[1]

Meanwhile under William's skilful management a treaty of alliance had been concluded between the States General and the Emperor. To that treaty Spain and England gave in their adhesion ; and thus the four great powers which had long been bound together by a friendly understanding were bound together by a formal contract.[2]

But before that formal contract had been signed and sealed, all the contracting parties were in arms. Early in the year 1689 war was raging all over the Continent from the Hæmus to the Pyrenees. France, attacked at once on every side, made on every side a vigorous defence ; and her Turkish allies kept a great German force fully employed in Servia and Bulgaria. On the whole, the results of the military operations of the summer were not unfavourable to the confederates. Beyond the Danube, the Christians, under Prince Lewis of Baden, gained a succession of victories over the Mussulmans. In the passes of Roussillon, the French troops contended without any decisive advantage against the martial peasantry of Catalonia. One German army, led by the Elector of Bavaria, occupied the Archbishopric of Cologne. Another was commanded by Charles, Duke of Lorraine, a sovereign who, driven from his own dominions by the arms of France, had turned soldier of fortune, and had, as such, obtained both distinction and revenge. He marched against the devastators of the Palatinate, forced them to retire behind the Rhine, and, after a long siege, took the important and strongly fortified city of Mentz.

Between the Sambre and the Meuse the French, commanded by Marshal Humieres, were opposed to the Dutch, commanded by the

---

[1] The best account of these negotiations will be found in Wagenaar, lxi. He had access to Witsen's papers, and has quoted largely from them. It was Witsen who signed in violent agitation, "zo als," he says, " myne beevende hand getuigen kan." The treaties will be found in Dumont's Corps Diplomatique. They were signed in August 1689.

[2] The treaty between the Emperor and the States General is dated May 12. 1689. It will be found in Dumont's Corps Diplomatique.

CHARLES V, DUKE OF LORRAINE

From a French engraving in the Sutherland Collection

Prince of Waldeck, an officer who had long served the States General with fidelity and ability, though not always with good fortune, and who stood high in the estimation of William. Under Waldeck's orders was Marlborough, to whom William had confided an English brigade consisting of the best regiments of the old army of James. Second to Marlborough in command, and second also in professional skill, was Thomas Talmash, a brave soldier, destined to a fate never to be mentioned without shame and indignation. Between the army of Waldeck and the army of Humieres no general action took place : but in a succession **Skirmish at Walcourt** of combats the advantage was on the side of the confederates. Of these combats the most important took place at Walcourt on the fifth of August. The French attacked an outpost defended by the English brigade, were vigorously repulsed, and were forced to retreat in confusion, abandoning a few field pieces to the conquerors and leaving more than six hundred corpses on the ground. Marlborough, on this as on every similar occasion, acquitted himself like a valiant and skilful captain. The Coldstream Guards commanded by Talmash, and the regiment which is now called the sixteenth of the line, commanded by Colonel Robert Hodges, distinguished themselves highly. The Royal regiment too, which had a few months before set up the standard of rebellion at Ipswich, proved on this day that William, in freely pardoning that great fault, had acted not less wisely than generously. The testimony which Waldeck in his despatch bore to the gallant conduct of the islanders was read with delight by their countrymen. The fight indeed was no more than a skirmish : but it was a sharp and bloody skirmish. There had within living memory been no equally serious encounter between the English and French ; and our ancestors were naturally elated by finding that many years of inaction and vassalage did not appear to have enervated the courage of the nation.[1]

The Jacobites however discovered in the events of the campaign abundant matter for invective. Marlborough was, not without reason, **Imputations thrown on Marlborough** the object of their bitterest hatred. In his behaviour on a field of battle malice itself could find little to censure : but there were other parts of his conduct which presented a fair mark for obloquy. Avarice is rarely the vice of a young man : it is rarely the vice of a great man : but Marlborough was one of the few who have, in the bloom of youth, loved lucre more than wine or women, and who have, at the height of greatness, loved lucre more than power or fame. All the precious gifts which nature had lavished on him he valued chiefly for what they would fetch. At twenty he

---

[1] See the despatch of Waldeck in the London Gazette, Aug. 26. 1689 ; Historical Records of the First Regiment of Foot ; Dangeau, Aug. 28. ; Monthly Mercury, September 1689.

De prins van Waldek uit een overout geslagt,   Daar Zit de vorst te prijk voor d'eedle Batavier,
Bij 't duitze keizerrijk in 't krijgsampt hoog geägt,   'S Lantshelden kroontmen met den Helden lauwerier
Maarshalk van Hollants staat staat hier door kunst gedreven   't Ontschiet de braafste wel van 't toppunt 't lof te schieten
D'Ervarentheit heeft hem op 't Schilt van mars verheven   Geen Edelmoedig helt kan 't weldoen ooit verdrieten.

Marrebeek fecit

GEORGE FREDERICK, PRINCE OF WALDECK

From an engraving by Marrebeek, in the Sutherland Collection made money of his beauty and his vigour. At sixty he made money of his genius and his glory. The applauses which were justly due to his conduct at Walcourt could not altogether drown the voices of those who muttered that, wherever a broad piece was to be saved or got, this hero was a mere Euclio, a mere Harpagon ; that, though he drew a large allowance under pretence of keeping a public table, he never asked an officer to dinner ; that his muster rolls were fraudulently made up; that he pocketed pay in the names of men who had long been dead, of men who had been killed in his own sight four years before at Sedgemoor ; that there were twenty such names in one troop ; that there were thirty six in another. Nothing but the union of dauntless courage and commanding powers of mind with a bland temper and winning manners could have enabled him to gain and keep, in spite of faults eminently unsoldier-like, the good will of his soldiers.[1]

About the time at which the contending armies in every part of Europe were going into winter quarters, a new Pontiff ascended the chair of Saint Peter. Innocent the Eleventh was no more. His fate had been strange indeed. His conscientious and fervent attachment to the Church of which he was the head had induced him, at one of the most critical conjunctures in her history, to ally himself with her mortal enemies. The news of his decease was received with concern and alarm by Protestant princes and commonwealths, and with joy and hope at Versailles and Dublin. An extraordinary ambassador of high rank was instantly despatched by Lewis to Rome. The French garrison which had been placed in Avignon was withdrawn. When the votes of the Conclave had been united in favour of Peter Ottobuoni, an ancient Cardinal who assumed the appellation of Alexander the Eighth, the representative of France assisted at the installation, bore up the cope of the new Pontiff, and put into the hands of His Holiness a letter in which the Most Christian King declared that he renounced the odious privilege of protecting robbers and assassins. Alexander pressed the letter to his lips, embraced the bearer, and talked with rapture of the near prospect of reconciliation. Lewis began to entertain a hope that the influence of the Vatican might be exerted to dissolve the alliance between the House of Austria and the heretical usurper of the English throne. James was even more sanguine. He was foolish enough to expect that the new Pope would give him money, and ordered Melfort, who had now acquitted himself of his mission at Versailles, to hasten to Rome, and beg His Holiness to contribute something towards the good work of upholding pure

Pope Innocent XI succeeded by Alexander VIII

---

[1] See the Dear Bargain, a Jacobite pamphlet, clandestinely printed in 1690. "I have not patience," says the writer, "after this wretch (Marlborough) to mention any other. All are innocent comparatively, even Kirke himself."

POPE ALEXANDER VIII

From an engraving by N. Visscher, in the Sutherland Collection religion in the British islands. But it soon appeared that Alexander, though he might hold language different from that of his predecessor, was determined to follow in essentials his predecessor's policy. The original cause of the quarrel between the Holy See and Lewis was not removed. The King continued to appoint prelates : the Pope continued to refuse them institution ; and the consequence was that a fourth part of the dioceses of France had bishops who were incapable of performing any episcopal function.[1]

The Anglican Church was, at this time, not less distracted than the Gallican Church. The first of August had been fixed by Act of Parliament as the day before the close of which all beneficed clergymen and all persons holding academical offices must, on pain of suspension, swear allegiance to William and Mary. During the earlier part of the summer, the Jacobites had hoped that the number of nonjurors would be so considerable as seriously to alarm and embarrass the government. But this hope was disappointed. Few indeed of the clergy were Whigs. Few were Tories of that moderate school which acknowledged, reluctantly and with reserve, that extreme abuses might sometimes justify a nation in resorting to extreme remedies. The great majority of the profession still held the doctrine of passive obedience : but that majority was now divided into two sections. A question, which, before the Revolution, had been mere matter of speculation, and had therefore, though some-times incidentally raised, been, by most persons, very superficially considered, had now become practically most important. The doctrine of passive obedience being taken for granted, to whom was that obedience due? While the hereditary right and the possession were conjoined, there was no room for doubt : but the hereditary right and the possession were now separated. One prince, raised by the Revolution, was reigning at Westminster, passing laws, appointing magistrates and prelates, sending forth armies and fleets. His Judges decided causes. His Sheriffs arrested debtors, and executed criminals. Justice, order, property, would cease to exist, and society would be resolved into chaos, but for his Great Seal. Another prince, deposed by the Revolution, was living abroad. He could exercise none of the powers and perform none of the duties of a ruler, and could, as it seemed, be restored only by means as violent as those by which he had been displaced. To which of these two princes did Christian men owe allegiance?

The High Church clergy divided on the subject of the oaths

---

[1] See the Mercuries for September 1689, and the four following months. See also Wel-wood's Mercurius Reformatus of Sept. 18. Sept. 25. and Oct. 8. 1689. Melfort's Instructions, and his memorials to the Pope and the Cardinal of Este, are among the Nairne Papers ; and some extracts have been printed by Macpherson.

To a large part of the clergy it appeared that the plain letter of Scripture required them to submit to the Sovereign who was in possession, without troubling themselves about his title. The **Arguments for taking the oaths** powers which the Apostle, in the text most familiar to the Anglican divines of that age, pronounces to be ordained of God, are not the powers that can be traced back to a legitimate origin, but the powers that be. When Jesus was asked whether the chosen people might lawfully give tribute to Cæsar, he replied by asking the questioners, not whether Cæsar could make out a pedigree derived from the old royal house of Judah, but whether the coin which they scrupled to pay into Cæsar's treasury came from Cæsar's mint, in other words, whether Cæsar actually possessed the authority and performed the functions of a ruler.

It is generally held, with much appearance of reason, that the most trustworthy comment on the text of the Gospels and Epistles is to be found in the practice of the primitive Christians, when that practice can be satisfactorily ascertained ; and it so happened that the times during which the Church is universally acknowledged to have been in the highest state of purity were times of frequent and violent political change. One at least of the Apostles appears to have lived to see four Emperors pulled down in little more than a year. Of the martyrs of the third century a great proportion must have been able to remember ten or twelve revolutions. Those martyrs must have had occasion often to consider what was their duty towards a prince just raised to power by a successful insurrection. That they were, one and all, deterred by the fear of punishment from doing what they thought right, is an imputation which no candid infidel would throw on them. Yet, if there be any proposition which can with perfect confidence be affirmed touching the early Christians, it is this, that they never once refused obedience to any actual ruler on account of the illegitimacy of his title. At one time, indeed, the supreme power was claimed by twenty or thirty competitors. Every province from Britain to Egypt had its own Augustus. All these pretenders could not be rightful Emperors. Yet it does not appear that, in any place, the faithful had any scruple about submitting to the person who, in that place, exercised the imperial functions. While the Christian of Rome obeyed Aurelian, the Christian of Lyons obeyed Tetricus, and the Christian of Palmyra obeyed Zenobia. " Day and night,"—such were the words which the great Cyprian, Bishop of Carthage, addressed to the representative of Valerian and Gallienus,—" day and night do we Christians pray to the one true God for the safety of our Emperors." Yet those Emperors had a few months before pulled down their predecessor Æmilianus, who had pulled down his predecessor Gallus, who had climbed to power on the ruins of the house of his predecessor Decius, who had slain his predecessor Philip, who had slain his predecessor Gordian. Was it possible to believe that a saint, who had, in the short space of thirteen or fourteen years, borne true allegiance to this series of rebels and regicides, would have made a schism in the Christian body rather than acknowledge King William and Queen Mary? A hundred times those Anglican divines who had taken the oaths challenged their more scrupulous brethren to cite a single instance in which the primitive Church had refused obedience to a successful usurper; and a hundred times the challenge was evaded. The nonjurors had little to say on this head, except that precedents were of no force when opposed to principles, a proposition which came with but a bad grace from a school which had always professed an almost superstitious reverence for the authority of the Fathers.[1]

To precedents drawn from later and more corrupt times little respect was due. But, even in the history of later and more corrupt times, the nonjurors could not easily find any precedent that could serve their purpose. In our own country many Kings, who had not the hereditary right, had filled the throne: but it had never been thought inconsistent with the duty of a Christian to be a true liegeman to such Kings. The usurpation of Henry the Fourth, the more odious usurpation of Richard the Third, had produced no schism in the Church. As soon as the usurper was firm in his seat, Bishops had done homage to him for their domains: Convocations had presented addresses to him, and granted him supplies; nor had any casuist ever pronounced that such submission to a prince in possession was deadly sin.[2]

---

[1] See the Answer of a Nonjuror to the Bishop of Sarum's challenge in the Appendix to the Life of Kettlewell. Among the Tanner MSS. in the Bodleian Library is a paper which, as Sancroft thought it worth preserving, I venture to quote. The writer, a strong nonjuror, after trying to evade, by many pitiable shifts, the argument drawn by a more compliant divine from the practice of the primitive Church, proceeds thus: " Suppose the primitive Christians all along, from the time of the very Apostles, had been as regardless of their oaths by former princes as he suggests, will he therefore say that their practice is to be a rule? Ill things have been done, and very generally abetted, by men of otherwise very orthodox principles." The argument from the practice of the primitive Christians is very strongly put in a tract entitled The Doctrine of Nonresistance or Passive Obedience No Way concerned in the Controversies now depending between the Williamites and the Jacobites, by a Lay Gentleman, of the Communion of the Church of England, as by Law establish'd, 1689. The author of this tract was Edmund Bohun, whom I shall have occasion to mention hereafter.

[2] One of the most adulatory addresses ever voted by a Convocation was to Richard the Third. It will be found in Wilkins's Concilia. Dryden, in his fine *rifacimento* of one of the finest passages in the Prologue to the Canterbury Tales, represents the Good Parson as choosing to resign his benefice rather than acknowledge the Duke of Lancaster to be King of England. For this representation no warrant can be found in Chaucer's Poem, or anywhere else. Dryden wished to write something that would gall the clergy who had taken the oaths, and therefore attributed to a Roman Catholic priest of the fourteenth century a superstition which originated among the Anglican priests of the seventeenth century.

With the practice of the whole Christian world the authoritative teaching of the Church of England appeared to be in strict harmony. The Homily on Wilful Rebellion, a discourse which inculcates, in unmeasured terms, the duty of obeying rulers, speaks of none but actual rulers. Nay, the people are distinctly told in that Homily that they are bound to obey, not only their legitimate prince, but any usurper whom God shall in anger set over them for their sins. And surely it would be the height of absurdity to say that we must accept submissively such usurpers as God sends in anger, but must pertinaciously withhold our obedience from usurpers whom He sends in mercy. Grant that it was a crime to invite the Prince of Orange over, a crime to join him, a crime to make him King; yet what was the whole history of the Jewish nation and of the Christian Church but a record of cases in which Providence had brought good out of evil? And what theologian would assert that, in such cases, we ought, from abhorrence of the evil, to reject the good?

On these grounds a large body of divines, still asserting the doctrine that to resist the Sovereign must always be sinful, conceived that William was now the Sovereign whom it would be sinful to resist.

To these arguments the nonjurors replied that Saint Paul must have meant by the powers that be the rightful powers that be; and that to put any other interpretation on his words would be to outrage common sense, to dishonour religion, to give scandal to weak believers, to give an occasion of triumph to scoffers. The feelings of all mankind must be shocked by the proposition that, as soon as a King, however clear his title, however wise and good his administration, is expelled by traitors, all his servants are bound to abandon him, and to range themselves on the side of his enemies. In all ages and nations, fidelity to a good cause in adversity had been regarded as a virtue. In all ages and nations, the politician whose practice was always to be on the side which was uppermost had been despised. This new Toryism was worse than Whiggism. To break through the ties of allegiance because the Sovereign was a tyrant was doubtless a very great sin: but it was a sin for which specious names and pretexts might be found, and into which a brave and generous man, not instructed in divine truth and guarded by divine grace, might easily fall. But to break through the ties of allegiance merely because the Sovereign was unfortunate was not only wicked, but dirty. Could any unbeliever offer a greater insult to the Scriptures than by asserting that the Scriptures had enjoined on Christians as a sacred duty what the light of nature had taught heathens to regard as the last excess of baseness? In the Scriptures was to be found the history of a King of Israel, driven from his palace by an unnatural son, and compelled to

Arguments against taking the oaths

fly beyond Jordan. David, like James, had the right : Absalom, like William, had the possession. Would any student of the sacred writings dare to affirm that the conduct of Shimei on that occasion was proposed as a pattern to be imitated, and that Barzillai, who loyally adhered to his fugitive master, was resisting the ordinance of God, and receiving to himself damnation ? Would any true son of the Church of England seriously maintain that a man who was a strenuous royalist till after the battle of Naseby, who then went over to the Parliament, who, as soon as the Parliament had been purged, became an obsequious servant of the Rump, and who, as soon as the Rump had been ejected, professed himself a faithful subject of the Protector, was more deserving of the respect of Christian men than the stout old Cavalier who bore true fealty to Charles the First in prison and to Charles the Second in exile, and who was ready to put lands, liberty, life, in peril, rather than acknowledge, by word or act, the authority of any of the upstart governments which, during that evil time, obtained possession of a power not legitimately theirs ? And what distinction was there between that case and the case which had now arisen ? That Cromwell had actually enjoyed as much power as William, nay much more power than William, was quite certain. That the power of William, as well as the power of Cromwell, had an illegitimate origin, every divine who held the doctrine of nonresistance would admit. How then was it possible for such a divine to deny that obedience had been due to Cromwell, and yet to affirm that it was due to William ? To suppose that there could be such inconsistency without dishonesty would be, not charity, but weakness. Those who were determined to comply with the Act of Parliament would do better to speak out, and to say, what everybody knew, that they complied simply to save their benefices. The motive was no doubt strong. That a clergyman who was a husband and a father should look forward with dread to the first of August and the first of February was natural. But he would do well to remember that, however terrible might be the day of suspension and the day of deprivation, there would assuredly come two other days more terrible still, the day of death and the day of judgment.[1]

The swearing clergy, as they were called, were not a little perplexed by this reasoning. Nothing embarrassed them more than the analogy which the nonjurors were never weary of pointing out between the usurpation of Cromwell and the usurpation of William. For there was in that age no High Churchman who would not have thought himself reduced to an absurdity, if he had been reduced to the necessity of saying

---

[1] See the Defence of the Profession which the Right Reverend Father in God John Lake, Lord Bishop of Chichester, made upon his Deathbed concerning Passive Obedience and the New Oaths. 1690.

that the Church had commanded her sons to obey Cromwell. And yet it was impossible to prove that William was more fully in possession of supreme power than Cromwell had been. The swearers therefore avoided coming to close quarters with the nonjurors on this point, as carefully as the nonjurors avoided coming to close quarters with the swearers on the question touching the practice of the primitive Church.

The truth is that the theory of government which had long been taught by the clergy was so absurd that it could lead to nothing but absurdity. Whether the priest who adhered to that theory swore or refused to swear, he was alike unable to give a rational explanation of his conduct. If he swore, he could vindicate his swearing only by laying down propositions against which every honest heart instinctively revolts, only by proclaiming that Christ had commanded the Church to desert the righteous cause as soon as that cause ceased to prosper, and to strengthen the hands of successful villany against afflicted virtue. And yet, strong as were the objections to this doctrine, the objections to the doctrine of the nonjuror were, if possible, stronger still. According to him, a Christian nation ought always to be in a state of slavery or in a state of anarchy. Something is to be said for the man who sacrifices liberty to preserve order. Something is to be said for the man who sacrifices order to preserve liberty. For liberty and order are two of the greatest blessings which a society can enjoy ; and, when unfortunately they appear to be incompatible, much indulgence is due to those who take either side. But the nonjuror sacrificed, not liberty to order, not order to liberty, but both liberty and order to a superstition as stupid and degrading as the Egyptian worship of cats and onions. While a particular person, differing from other persons by the mere accident of birth, was on the throne, though he might be a Nero, there was to be no insubordination. When any other person was on the throne, though he might be an Alfred, there was to be no obedience. It mattered not how frantic and wicked might be the administration of the dynasty which had the hereditary title, or how wise and virtuous might be the administration of a government sprung from a revolution. Nor could any time of limitation be pleaded against the claim of the expelled family. The lapse of years, the lapse of ages, made no change. To the end of the world, Christians were to regulate their political conduct simply according to the pedigree of their ruler. The year 1800, the year 1900, might find princes who derived their title from the votes of the Convention reigning in peace and prosperity. No matter : they would still be usurpers ; and, if, in the twentieth or twenty-first century, any person who could make out a better right by blood to the crown should call on a late posterity to acknowledge him as King, the call must be obeyed on peril of eternal perdition.

A Whig might well enjoy the thought that the controversies which had arisen among his adversaries had established the soundness of his own political creed. The disputants who had long agreed in accusing him of an impious error had now effectually vindicated him, and refuted one another. The High Churchman who took the oaths had shown by irrefragable arguments from the Gospels and the Epistles, from the uniform practice of the primitive Church, and from the explicit declarations of the Anglican Church, that Christians were not in all cases bound to pay obedience to the prince who had the hereditary title. The High Churchman who would not take the oaths had shown as satisfactorily that Christians were not in all cases bound to pay obedience to the prince who was actually reigning. It followed that, to entitle a government to the allegiance of subjects, something was necessary different from mere legitimacy, and different also from mere possession. What that something was the Whigs had no difficulty in pronouncing. In their view, the end for which all governments had been instituted was the happiness of society. While the magistrate was, on the whole, notwithstanding some faults, a minister for good, Reason taught mankind to obey him ; and Religion, giving her solemn sanction to the teaching of Reason, commanded mankind to revere him as divinely commissioned. But if he proved to be a minister for evil, on what grounds was he to be considered as divinely commissioned ? The Tories who swore had proved that he ought not to be so considered on account of the origin of his power : the Tories who would not swear had proved as clearly that he ought not to be so considered on account of the existence of his power.

Some violent and acrimonious Whigs triumphed ostentatiously and with merciless insolence over the perplexed and divided priesthood. The nonjuror they generally affected to regard with contemptuous pity as a dull and perverse, but sincere, bigot, whose absurd practice was in harmony with his absurd theory, and who might plead, in excuse for the infatuation which impelled him to ruin his country, that the same infatuation had impelled him to ruin himself. They reserved their sharpest taunts for those divines who, having, in the days of the Exclusion Bill and the Rye House plot, been distinguished by zeal for the divine and indefeasible right of the hereditary Sovereign, were now ready to swear fealty to an usurper. Was this then the real sense of all those sublime phrases which had resounded during twenty nine years from innumerable pulpits ? Had the thousands of clergymen, who had so loudly boasted of the unchangeable loyalty of their order, really meant only that their loyalty would remain unchangeable till the next change of fortune ? It was idle, it was impudent in them to pretend that their present conduct was consistent with their former language. If any Reverend Doctor had at length been convinced that he had been in the wrong, he surely ought, by an open recantation, to make all the amends now possible to the persecuted, the calumniated, the murdered defenders of liberty. If he was still convinced that his old opinions were sound, he ought manfully to cast in his lot with the nonjurors. Respect, it was said, is due to him who ingenuously confesses an error : respect is due to him who courageously suffers for an error : but it is difficult to respect a minister of religion, who, while asserting that he still adheres to the principles of the Tories, saves his benefice by taking an oath which can be honestly taken only on the principles of the Whigs.

These reproaches, though perhaps not altogether unjust, were unseasonable. The wiser and more moderate Whigs, sensible that the throne of William could not stand firm if it had not a wider basis than their own party, abstained at this conjuncture from sneers and invectives, and exerted themselves to remove the scruples, and to soothe the irritated feelings of the clergy. The collective power of the rectors and vicars of England was immense ; and it was much better that they should swear for the most flimsy reason which could be devised by a sophist than that they should not swear at all.

It soon became clear that the arguments for swearing, backed as they were by some of the strongest motives which can influence the human mind, had prevailed. Above twenty nine thirtieths A great ma-
of the profession submitted to the law. Most of the divines jority of the
clergy take
of the capital, who then formed a separate class, and who the oaths
were as much distinguished from the rural clergy by liberality of sentiment as by eloquence and learning, gave in their adhesion to the govern-
ment early, and with every sign of cordial attachment. Eighty of them repaired together, in full term, to Westminster Hall, and were there sworn. The ceremony occupied so long a time that little else was done that day in the Courts of Chancery and King's Bench.[1] But in general the compliance was tardy, sad, and sullen. Many, no doubt, deliberately violated what they believed to be their duty. Conscience told them that they were committing a sin. But they had not fortitude to resign the parsonage, the garden, the glebe, and to go forth without knowing where to find a meal or a roof for themselves and their little ones. Many swore with doubts and misgivings.[2] Some declared, at the moment of taking the oath, that they did not mean to promise that they would not submit to James, if he should ever be in a condition to demand their allegiance.[3] Some clergymen in the North were, on the first of August,

---

[1] London Gazette, June 30. 1689 ; Luttrell's Diary. " The eminentest men," says Luttrell.

[2] See in Kettlewell's Life, iii. 72., the retractation drawn by him for a clergyman who had taken the oaths, and who afterwards repented of having done so.

[3] See the account of Dr. Dove's conduct in Clarendon's Diary, and the account of Dr. Marsh's conduct in the Life of Kettlewell.

going in a company to swear, when they were met on the road by the news of the battle which had been fought, four days before, in the pass of Killiecrankie. They immediately turned back, and did not again leave their homes on the same errand till it was clear that Dundee's victory had made no change in the state of public affairs.[1] Even of those whose understandings were fully convinced that obedience was due to the existing government, very few kissed the book with the heartiness with which they had formerly plighted their faith to Charles and James. Still the thing was done. Ten thousand clergymen had solemnly called heaven to attest their promise that they would be true liegemen to William ; and this promise, though it by no means warranted him in expecting that they would strenuously support him, had at least deprived them of a great part of their power to injure him. They could not, without entirely forfeiting that public respect on which their influence depended, attack, except in an indirect and timidly cautious manner, the throne of one whom they had, in the presence of God, vowed to obey as their King. Some of them, it is true, affected to read the prayers for the new Sovereigns in a peculiar tone which could not be misunderstood.[2] Others were guilty of still grosser indecency. Thus, one wretch, just after praying for William and Mary in the most solemn office of religion, took off a glass to their damnation. Another, after performing divine service on a fast day appointed by their authority, dined on a pigeon pie, and while he cut it up, uttered a wish that it was the usurper's heart. But such audacious wickedness was doubtless rare and was injurious rather to the Church than to the government.[3]

Those clergymen and members of the Universities who incurred the penalties of the law were about four hundred in number. Fore-

The non-jurors most in rank stood the Primate and six of his suffragans, Turner of Ely, Lloyd of Norwich, Frampton of Gloucester, Lake of Chichester, White of Peterborough, and Ken of Bath and Wells. Thomas of Worcester would have made a seventh : but he died three weeks before the day of suspension. On his deathbed he adjured his clergy to be true to the cause of hereditary right, and declared that those divines who tried to make out that the oaths might be taken without any departure from the loyal doctrines of the Church of England seemed to him to reason more Jesuitically than the Jesuits themselves.[4]

Ken, who, both in intellectual and in moral qualities, ranked highest among the nonjuring prelates, hesitated long. There were few clergymen who could have submitted to the new government with a better

Ken grace. For, when nonresistance and passive obedience were the favourite themes of his brethren, he had scarcely ever alluded to politics

---

[1] The Anatomy of a Jacobite Tory, 1690.　　[2] Dialogue between a Whig and a Tory.
[3] Luttrell's Diary, November 1691, February 1692.　　[4] Life of Kettlewell, iii. 4.

THOMAS KEN, BISHOP OF BATH AND WELLS

From a painting at New College, Oxford

in the pulpit. He owned that the arguments in favour of swearing were very strong. He went indeed so far as to say that his scruples would be completely removed, if he could be convinced that James had entered into engagements for ceding Ireland to the French King. It is evident therefore that the difference between Ken and the Whigs was not a difference of principle. He thought, with them, that misgovernment, carried to a certain point, justified a transfer of allegiance, and doubted only whether the misgovernment of James had been carried quite to that point. Nay, the good Bishop actually began to prepare a pastoral letter explaining his reasons for taking the oaths. But, before it was finished, he received information which convinced him that Ireland had not been made over to France : doubts came thick upon him : he threw his unfinished letter into the fire, and implored his less scrupulous friends not to urge him further. He was sure, he said, that they had acted uprightly : he was glad that they could do with a clear conscience what he shrank from doing : he felt the force of their reasoning : he was all but persuaded ; and he was afraid to listen longer lest he should be quite persuaded : for, if he should comply, and his misgivings should afterwards return, he should be the most miserable of men. Not for wealth, not for a palace, not for a peerage, would he run the smallest risk of ever feeling the torments of remorse. It is a curious fact that, of the seven nonjuring prelates, the only one whose name carries with it much weight was on the point of swearing, and was prevented from doing so, as he himself acknowledged, not by the force of reason, but by a morbid scrupulosity which he did not advise others to imitate.[1]

Among the priests who refused the oaths were some men eminent

---

[1] See Turner's Letter to Sancroft, dated on Ascension Day, 1689. The original is among the Tanner MSS. in the Bodleian Library. But the letter will be found, with much other curious matter, in the Life of Ken by a Layman, lately published. See also the Life of Kettlewell, iii. 95.; and Ken's Letter to Burnet, dated Oct. 5. 1689, in Hawkins's Life of Ken. "I am sure," Lady Russell wrote to Dr. Fitzwilliam, "the Bishop of Bath and Wells excited others to comply, when he could not bring himself to do so, but rejoiced when others did." Ken declared that he had advised nobody to take the oaths, and that his practice had been to remit those who asked his advice to their own studies and prayers. Lady Russell's assertion and Ken's denial will be found to come nearly to the same thing, when we make those allowances which ought to be made for situation and feeling, even in weighing the testimony of the most veracious witnesses. Ken, having at last determined to cast in his lot with the nonjurors, naturally tried to vindicate his consistency as far as he honestly could. Lady Russell, wishing to induce her friend to take the oaths, naturally made as much of Ken's disposition to compliance as she honestly could. She went too far in using the word "excited." On the other hand, it is clear that Ken, by remitting those who consulted him to their own studies and prayers, gave them to understand that, in his opinion, the oath was lawful to those who, after a serious enquiry, thought it lawful. If people had asked him whether they might lawfully commit perjury or adultery, he would assuredly have told them, not to consider the point maturely and to implore the divine direction, but to abstain on peril of their souls.

in the learned world, as grammarians, chronologists, canonists, and antiquaries, and a very few who were distinguished by wit and eloquence; but scarcely one can be named who was qualified to discuss any large question of morals or politics, scarcely one whose writings do not indicate either extreme feebleness or extreme flightiness of mind. Those who distrust the judgment of a Whig on this point will probably allow some weight to the opinion which was expressed, many years after the Revolution, by a philosopher of whom the Tories are justly proud. Johnson, after passing in review the celebrated divines who had thought it sinful to swear allegiance to William the Third and George the First, pronounced that, in the whole body of nonjurors, there was one, and one only, who could reason.[1]

The nonjuror in whose favour Johnson made this exception was Charles Leslie. Leslie had, before the Revolution, been Chancellor of the diocese of Connor in Ireland. He had been forward in opposition to Tyrconnel; had, as a justice of the peace for Monaghan, refused to acknowledge a papist as Sheriff of that county; and had been so courageous as to send some officers of the Irish army to prison for marauding. But the doctrine of nonresistance, such as it had been taught by Anglican divines in the days of the Rye House Plot, was immovably fixed in his mind. When the state of Ulster became such that a Protestant who remained there could hardly avoid being either a rebel or a martyr, Leslie fled to London. His abilities and his connections were such that he might easily have obtained high preferment in the Church of England. But he took his place in the front rank of the Jacobite body, and remained there steadfastly through all the dangers and vicissitudes of three and thirty troubled years. Though constantly engaged in theological controversy with Deists, Jews, Socinians, Presbyterians, Papists, and Quakers, he found time to be one of the most voluminous political writers of his age. Of all the nonjuring clergy he was the best qualified to discuss constitutional

Leslie

---

[1] See the conversation of June 9. 1784, in Boswell's Life of Johnson, and the note. Boswell, with his usual absurdity, is sure that Johnson could not have recollected " that the seven bishops, so justly celebrated for their magnanimous resistance to arbitrary power, were yet nonjurors." Only five of the seven were nonjurors; and anybody but Boswell would have known that a man may resist arbitrary power, and yet not be a good reasoner. Nay, the resistance which Sancroft and the other nonjuring bishops offered to arbitrary power, while they continued to hold the doctrine of nonresistance, is the most decisive proof that they were incapable of reasoning. It must be remembered that they were prepared to take the whole kingly power from James and to bestow it on William, with the title of Regent. Their scruple was merely about the word King.

I am surprised that Johnson should have pronounced William Law no reasoner. Law did indeed fall into great errors; but they were errors against which logic affords no security. In mere dialectical skill he had very few superiors. That he was more than once victorious over Hoadley no candid Whig will deny. But Law did not belong to the generation with which I have now to do.

questions. For, before he had taken orders, he had resided long in the Temple, and had been studying English history and law, while most of the other chiefs of the schism had been poring over the Acts of Chalcedon, or seeking for wisdom in the Targum of Onkelos.[1]

In 1689, however, Leslie was almost unknown in England. Among the divines who incurred suspension on the first of August in that year, the highest in popular estimation was without dispute Doctor William Sherlock. Perhaps no simple presbyter of the Church of England has ever possessed a greater authority over his brethren than belonged to Sherlock at the time of the Revolution. He was not of the first rank among his contemporaries as a scholar, as a preacher, as a writer on theology, or as a writer on politics: but in all the four characters he had distinguished himself. The perspicuity and liveliness of his style have been praised by Prior and Addison. The facility and assiduity with which he wrote are sufficiently proved by the bulk and the dates of his works. There were indeed among the clergy men of brighter genius and men of wider attainments: but during a long period there was none who more completely represented the order, none who, on all subjects, spoke more precisely the sense of the Anglican priesthood, without any taint of Latitudinarianism, of Puritanism, or of Popery. He had, in the days of the Exclusion Bill, when the power of the dissenters was very great in Parliament and in the country, written strongly against the sin of nonconformity. When the Rye House Plot was detected, he had zealously defended by tongue and pen the doctrine of nonresistance. His services to the cause of episcopacy and monarchy were so highly valued that he was made master of the Temple. A pension was also bestowed on him by Charles: but that pension James soon took away: for Sherlock, though he held himself bound to pay passive obedience to the civil power, held himself equally bound to combat religious errors, and was the keenest and most laborious of that host of controversialists who, in the day of peril, manfully defended the Protestant faith. In little more than two years he published sixteen treatises, some of them large books, against the high pretensions of Rome. Not content with the easy victories which he gained over such feeble antagonists as those who were quartered at Clerkenwell and the Savoy, he had the courage to measure his strength with no less a champion than Bossuet, and came out of the conflict without discredit. Nevertheless Sherlock still continued to maintain that no oppression could justify Christians in resisting the kingly authority. When the Convention was about to meet, he strongly recommended, in a tract which was considered as the manifesto of a large part of the clergy, that James should be invited to return on such conditions as might

Sherlock (margin note)

[1] Ware's History of the Writers of Ireland, continued by Harris.

secure the laws and religion of the nation.[1] The vote which placed William and Mary on the throne filled Sherlock with sorrow and anger. He is said to have exclaimed that if the Convention was deter-

Charles Leslie 1716

From a mezzotint by G. White, in the Sutherland Collection

mined on a revolution, the clergy would find forty thousand good Churchmen to effect a restoration.[2] Against the new oaths he gave his

[1] Letter to a member of the Convention, 1689.
[2] Johnson's Notes on the Phœnix Edition of Burnet's Pastoral Letter, 1692.

opinion plainly and warmly. He professed himself at a loss to understand how any honest man could doubt that, by the powers that be, Saint
Paul meant legitimate powers and no others. No name was in 1689
cited by the Jacobites more proudly or more fondly than that of Sherlock.
Before the end of 1690 that name excited very different feelings.

A few other nonjurors ought to be particularly noticed. High among
them in rank was George Hickes, Dean of Worcester. Of all the English-

Hickes   men of his time he was the most versed in the old Teutonic
languages ; and his knowledge of the early Christian literature was extensive. As to his capacity for political discussions, it may be
sufficient to say that his favourite argument for passive obedience
was drawn from the story of the Theban legion. He was the younger
brother of that unfortunate John Hickes who had been found hidden
in the malthouse of Alice Lisle. James had, in spite of all solicitation,
put both John Hickes and Alice Lisle to death. Persons who did not
know the strength of the Dean's principles thought that he might
possibly feel some resentment on this account : for he was of no gentle
or forgiving temper, and could retain during many years a bitter
remembrance of small injuries. But he was strong in his religious and
political faith : he reflected that the sufferers were dissenters ; and
he submitted to the will of the Lord's Anointed not only with patience
but with complacency. He became indeed a more loving subject than
ever from the time when his brother was hanged and his brother's
benefactress beheaded. While almost all other clergymen, appalled
by the Declaration of Indulgence and by the proceedings of the High
Commission, were beginning to think that they had pushed the doctrine
of nonresistance a little too far, he was writing a vindication of his
darling legend, and trying to convince the troops at Hounslow that,
if James should be pleased to massacre them all, as Maximian had
massacred the Theban legion, for refusing to commit idolatry, it would
be their duty to pile their arms, and meekly to receive the crown
of martyrdom. To do Hickes justice, his whole conduct after the
Revolution proved that his servility had sprung neither from fear nor
from cupidity, but from mere bigotry.[1]

Jeremy Collier, who was turned out of the preachership of the Rolls,
was a man of a much higher order. He is well entitled to grateful

Collier   and respectful mention : for to his eloquence and courage is
to be chiefly ascribed the purification of our lighter literature
from that foul taint which had been contracted during the Antipuritan

---

[1] The best notion of Hickes's character will be formed from his numerous controversial
writings, particularly his Jovian, written in 1684, his Thebæan Legion no Fable, written in 1687,
though not published till 1714, and his Discourses upon Dr. Burnet and Dr. Tillotson, 1695.
His literary fame rests on works of a very different kind.

ΗΙ ΚΑΝΟΤΗΣ   ΗΜΩΝ ΕΚ   ΤΟΥ ΘΕΟΥ

GEORGIUS HICKES S.T.P.
Non ita pridem Collegii Lincoln in Academia Oxon Socius, ex
Canonico Ecclesiæ Cathedr Wigorn factus Decanus Octobris die 13 A.D. 1683.

GEORGE HICKES, DEAN OF WORCESTER

From an engraving by R. White

reaction.   He was, in the full force of the words, a good man.   He was also a man of eminent abilities, a great master of sarcasm, a great master of rhetoric.[1]   His reading too, though undigested, was of immense extent.   But his mind was narrow : his reasoning, even when he was so fortunate as to have a good cause to defend, was singularly futile and inconclusive ; and his brain was almost turned by pride, not personal, but professional.   In his view, a priest was the highest of human beings, except a bishop.   Reverence and submission were due from the best and greatest of the laity to the least respectable of the clergy.   However ridiculous a man in holy orders might make himself, it was impiety to laugh at him.   So nervously sensitive indeed was Collier on this point that he thought it profane to throw any reflection even on the ministers of false religions.   He laid it down as a rule that Muftis and Augurs ought always to be mentioned with respect.   He blamed Dryden for sneering at the Hierophants of Apis. He praised Racine for giving dignity to the character of a priest of Baal. He praised Corneille for not bringing that learned and reverend divine Tiresias on the stage in the tragedy of Œdipus.   The omission, Collier owned, spoiled the dramatic effect of the piece : but the holy function was much too solemn to be played with.   Nay, incredible as it may seem, he thought it improper in the laity to sneer even at Presbyterian preachers.   Indeed his Jacobitism was little more than one of the forms in which his zeal for the dignity of his profession manifested itself.   He abhorred the Revolution less as a rising up of subjects against their King than as a rising up of the laity against the sacerdotal caste.   The doctrines which had been proclaimed from the pulpit during thirty years had been treated with contempt by the Convention.   A new government had been set up in opposition to the wishes of the spiritual peers in the House of Lords and of the priesthood through- out the country.   A secular assembly had taken upon itself to pass a law requiring archbishops and bishops, rectors and vicars, to abjure, on pain of deprivation, what they had been teaching all their lives.   Whatever meaner spirits might do, Collier was deter- mined not to be led in triumph by the victorious enemies of his order.   To the last he would confront, with the authoritative port of an ambassador of heaven, the anger of the powers and principalities of the earth.

In parts Collier was the first man among the nonjurors.   In eru- dition the first place must be assigned to Henry Dodwell, who, for the

---

[1] Collier's Tracts on the Stage are, on the whole, his best pieces.   But there is much that is striking in his political pamphlets.   His " Persuasive to Consideration, tendered to the Royalists, particularly those of the Church of England," seems to me one of the best productions of the Jacobite press.

Mr Jeremiah Collier.

JEREMY COLLIER

From a mezzotint by W. Faithorne, after a painting by E. Lely unpardonable crime of having a small estate in Mayo, had been attainted by the Popish Parliament at Dublin. He was Camdenian Professor of Ancient History in the University of Oxford, and had

Dodwell

already acquired considerable celebrity by chronological and geographical researches : but, though he never could be persuaded to take orders, theology was his favourite study. He was doubtless a pious and sincere man. He had perused innumerable volumes in various languages, and had indeed acquired more learning than his slender faculties were able to bear. The small intellectual spark which he possessed was put out by the fuel. Some of his books seem to have been written in a madhouse, and, though filled with proofs of his immense reading, degrade him to the level of James Naylor and Ludowick Muggleton. He began a dissertation intended to prove that the law of nations was a divine revelation made to the family which was preserved in the ark. He published a treatise in which he maintained that a marriage between a member of the Church of England and a dissenter was a nullity, and that the couple were, in the sight of heaven, guilty of adultery. He defended the use of instrumental music in public worship on the ground that the notes of the organ had a power to counteract the influence of devils on the spinal marrow of human beings. In his treatise on this subject he remarked that there was high authority for the opinion that the spinal marrow, when decomposed, became a serpent. Whether this opinion were or were not correct, he thought it unnecessary to decide. Perhaps, he said, the eminent men in whose works it was found had meant only to express figuratively the great truth, that the Old Serpent operates on us chiefly through the spinal marrow.[1] Dodwell's speculations on the state of human beings after death are, if possible, more extraordinary still. He tells us that our souls are naturally mortal. Annihilation is the fate of the greater part of mankind, of heathens, of Mahometans, of unchristened babes. The gift of immortality is conveyed in the sacrament of baptism : but to the efficacy of the sacrament it is absolutely necessary that the water be poured and the words pronounced by a minister who has been ordained by a bishop. In the natural course of things, therefore, all Presbyterians, Independents, Baptists, and Quakers would, like the inferior animals, cease to exist. But Dodwell was far too good a churchman to let off dissenters so easily. He informs them that, as they have had an opportunity of hearing the

---

[1] See Brokesby's Life of Dodwell. The Discourse against Marriages in different Communions is known to me, I ought to say, only from Brokesby's copious abstract. That Discourse is very rare. It was originally printed as an appendage to a sermon preached by Leslie. When Leslie collected his works he omitted the discourse, probably because he was ashamed of it. I have not been able to find it in the Library of the British Museum. The Treatise on the Lawfulness of Instrumental Music I have read ; and incredibly absurd it is.

Mr Henry Dodwell

obijt Jun: 7. A.D. 1711. Ætat: 70.

HENRY DODWELL, CAMDEN PROFESSOR OF ANCIENT HISTORY

From an engraving by M. van der Gucht

gospel preached, and might, but for their own perverseness, have received episcopalian baptism, God will, by a preternatural act of power, bestow immortality on them in order that they may be tormented for ever and ever.[1]

No man abhorred the growing latitudinarianism of those times more than Dodwell. Yet no man had more reason to rejoice in it. For, in the earlier part of the seventeenth century, a speculator who had dared to affirm that the human soul is by its nature mortal, and does, in the great majority of cases, actually die with the body, would have been burned alive in Smithfield. Even in days which Dodwell could well remember, such heretics as himself would have been thought fortunate if they escaped with life, their backs flayed, their ears clipped, their noses slit, their tongues bored through with red hot iron, and their eyes knocked out with brickbats. With the nonjurors, however, the author of this theory was still the great Mr. Dodwell ; and some, who thought it culpable lenity to tolerate a Presbyterian meeting, thought it at the same time gross illiberality to blame a learned and pious Jacobite for denying a doctrine so utterly unimportant in a religious point of view as that of the immortality of the soul.[2]

Two other nonjurors deserve special mention, less on account of their abilities and learning, than on account of their rare integrity, and **Kettlewell** of their not less rare candour. These were John Kettlewell, **Fitzwilliam** Rector of Coleshill, and John Fitzwilliam, Canon of Windsor. It is remarkable that both these men had seen much of Lord Russell, and that both, though differing from him in political opinions, and strongly disapproving the part which he had taken in the Whig plot, had thought highly of his character, and had been sincere mourners for his death. He had sent to Kettlewell an affectionate message from the scaffold in Lincoln's Inn Fields. Lady Russell, to her latest day, loved, trusted, and revered Fitzwilliam, who, when she was a girl, had been the friend of her father, the virtuous Southampton. The two clergymen agreed in refusing to swear : but they, from that moment, took different paths. Kettlewell was one of the most active members of his party : he declined no drudgery in the common cause, provided only that it were such drudgery as did not misbecome an honest man ; and he

---

[1] Dodwell tells us that the title of the work in which he first promulgated this theory was framed with great care and precision. I will therefore transcribe the title-page. "An Epistolary Discourse proving from Scripture and the First Fathers that the Soul is naturally Mortal, but Immortalized actually by the Pleasure of God to Punishment or to Reward, by its Union with the Divine Baptismal Spirit, wherein is proved that none have the Power of giving this Divine Immortalizing Spirit since the Apostles but only the Bishops. By H. Dodwell." Dr. Clarke, in a Letter to Dodwell (1706), says that this Epistolary Discourse is "a book at which all good men are sorry, and all profane men rejoice."

[2] See Leslie's Rehearsals, No. 286, 287.

Iohannes Kettlewell Obyt 12 Apr. 1695. Æta 42.

Who when he was reviled, reviled not again; when he suffered he threatned not, but committed himself to him that judgeth righteously. S.t Peter.

ὁ κακῶς τὸ κακῶς παθεῖν κακῶν ἐστι τὸ ποιῆσαι κακῶς. S. Chrysost:

JOHN KETTLEWELL

From an engraving by G. Vertue, after a painting by H. Tilson defended his opinions in several tracts, which give a much higher notion of his sincerity than of his judgment or acuteness.[1] Fitzwilliam thought that he had done enough in quitting his pleasant dwelling and garden under the shadow of Saint George's Chapel, and in betaking himself with his books to a small lodging in an attic. He could not with a safe conscience acknowledge William and Mary : but he did not conceive that he was bound to be always stirring up sedition against them ; and he passed the last years of his life, under the powerful protection of the House of Bedford, in innocent and studious repose.[2]

Among the less distinguished divines who forfeited their benefices, were doubtless many good men : but it is certain that the moral character of the nonjurors, as a class, did not stand high. It seems hard to impute laxity of principle to persons who undoubtedly made a great sacrifice to principle. And yet experience abundantly proves that many who are capable of making a great sacrifice, when their blood is heated by conflict, and when the public eye is fixed upon them, are not capable of persevering long in the daily practice of obscure virtues. It is by no means improbable that zealots may have given their lives for a religion which had never effectually restrained their vindictive or their licentious passions. We learn indeed from fathers of the highest authority that, even in the purest ages of the Church, some confessors, who had manfully refused to save themselves from torments and death by throwing frankincense on the altar of Jupiter, afterwards brought scandal on the Christian name by gross fraud and debauchery.[3] For the nonjuring divines great allowance must in fairness be made. They were doubtless in a most trying situation. In general, a schism, which divides a religious community, divides the laity as well as the clergy. The seceding pastors therefore carry with them a large part of their flocks, and are consequently assured of a main-

General character of the nonjuring clergy

[1] See his works, and the highly curious life of him which was compiled from the papers of his friends Hickes and Nelson.

[2] See Fitzwilliam's correspondence with Lady Russell, and his evidence on the trial of Ashton, in the State Trials. The only work which Fitzwilliam, as far as I have been able to discover, ever published was a sermon on the Rye House Plot, preached a few weeks after Russell's execution. There are some sentences in this sermon which I a little wonder that the widow and the family forgave.

[3] Cyprian, in one of his Epistles, addresses the confessors thus : " Quosdam audio inficere numerum vestrum, et laudem præcipui nominis prava sua conversatione destruere . . . Cum quanto nominis vestri pudore delinquitur quando alius aliquis temulentus et lasciviens demoratur ; alius in eam patriam unde extorris est regreditur, ut deprehensus non jam quasi Christianus, sed quasi nocens pereat." He uses still stronger language in the book de Unitate Ecclesiæ : " Neque enim confessio immunem facit ab insidiis diaboli, aut contra tentationes et pericula et incursus atque impetus sæculares adhuc in sæculo positum perpetua securitate defendit ; cæterum nunquam in confessoribus fraudes et stupra et adulteria postmodum videremus, quæ nunc in quibusdam videntes ingemiscimus et dolemus."

tenance. But the schism of 1689 scarcely extended beyond the clergy. The law required the rector to take the oaths, or to quit his living : but no oath, no acknowledgment of the title of the new King and Queen, was required from the parishioner as a qualification for attending divine service, or for receiving the Eucharist. Not one in fifty, therefore, of those laymen who disapproved of the Revolution thought himself bound to quit his pew in the old church, where the old liturgy was still read, and where the old vestments were still worn, and to follow the ejected priest to a conventicle, a conventicle, too, which was not protected by the Toleration Act. Thus the new sect was a sect of preachers without hearers ; and such preachers could not make a livelihood by preaching. In London indeed, and in some other large towns, those vehement Jacobites, whom nothing would satisfy but to hear King James and the Prince of Wales prayed for by name, were sufficiently numerous to make up a few small congregations, which met secretly, and under constant fear of the constables, in rooms so mean that the meeting houses of the Puritan dissenters might by comparison be called palaces. Even Collier, who had all the qualities which attract large audiences, was reduced to be the minister of a little knot of malecontents, whose oratory was on a second floor in the city. But the nonjuring clergymen who were able to obtain even a pittance by officiating at such places were very few. Of the rest some had independent means : some lived by literature : one or two practised physic. Thomas Wagstaffe, for example, who had been Chancellor of Lichfield, had many patients, and made himself conspicuous by always visiting them in full canonicals.[1] But these were exceptions. Industrious poverty is a state by no means unfavourable to virtue : but it is dangerous to be at once poor and idle ; and most of the clergymen who had refused to swear found themselves thrown on the world with nothing to eat and with nothing to do. They naturally became beggars and loungers. Considering themselves as martyrs suffering in a public cause, they were not ashamed to ask any good churchman for a guinea. Most of them passed their lives in running about from one Tory coffeehouse to another, abusing the Dutch, hearing and spreading reports that within a month His Majesty would certainly be on English ground, and wondering who would have Salisbury when Burnet was hanged. During the session of Parliament the lobbies and the Court of Requests were crowded with deprived parsons, asking who was up, and what the numbers were on the last division. Many of the ejected divines became domesticated, as chaplains, tutors, and spiritual directors, in the houses of opulent Jacobites. In a situation of

[1] Much curious information about the nonjurors will be found in the Biographical Memoirs of William Bowyer, Printer, which forms the first volume of Nichols's Literary Anecdotes of the eighteenth century. A specimen of Wagstaffe's prescriptions is in the Bodleian Library.

this kind, a man of pure and exalted character, such a man as Ken was among the nonjurors, and Watts among the nonconformists, may preserve his dignity, and may much more than repay by his example and his instructions the benefits which he receives. But to a person whose virtue is not high toned this way of life is full of peril. If he is of a quiet disposition, he is in danger of sinking into a servile, sensual, drowsy parasite. If he is of an active and aspiring nature, it may be feared that he will become expert in those bad arts by which, more easily than by faithful service, retainers make themselves agreeable or formidable. To discover the weak side of every character, to flatter every passion and prejudice, to sow discord and jealousy where love and confidence ought to exist, to watch the moment of indiscreet openness for the purpose of extracting secrets important to the prosperity and honour of families, such are the practices by which keen and restless spirits have too often avenged themselves for the humiliation of dependence. The public voice loudly accused many nonjurors of requiting the hospitality of their benefactors with villany as black as that of the hypocrite depicted in the masterpiece of Moliere. Indeed, when Cibber undertook to adapt that noble comedy to the English stage, he made his Tartuffe a non-juror : and Johnson, who cannot be supposed to have been prejudiced against the nonjurors, frankly owned that Cibber had done them no wrong.[1]

There can be no doubt that the schism caused by the oaths would have been far more formidable, if, at this crisis, any extensive change had been made in the government or in the ceremonial of the Established Church. It is a highly instructive fact that those en-lightened and tolerant divines who most ardently desired such a change

---

[1] Cibber's play, as Cibber wrote it, ceased to be popular when the Jacobites ceased to be formidable, and is now known only to the curious. In 1768 Bickerstaffe altered it into the Hypocrite, and substituted Dr. Cantwell, the Methodist, for Dr. Wolf, the Nonjuror. "I do not think," said Johnson, "the character of the Hypocrite justly applicable to the Methodists; but it was very applicable to the nonjurors." Boswell asked him if it were true that the nonjuring clergymen intrigued with the wives of their patrons. "I am afraid," said Johnson, " many of them did." This conversation took place on the 27th of March 1775. It was not merely in careless talk that Johnson expressed an unfavourable opinion of the nonjurors. In his Life of Fenton, who was a nonjuror, are these remarkable words : " It must be remembered that he kept his name unsullied, and never suffered himself to be reduced, like too many of the same sect, to mean arts and dishonourable shifts." See the character of a Jacobite, 1690. Even in Kettlewell's Life, compiled from the papers of his friends Hickes and Nelson, will be found admissions which show that, very soon after the schism, some of the nonjuring clergy fell into habits of idleness, dependence, and mendicancy, which lowered the character of the whole party. "Several unde-serving persons, who are always the most confident, by their going up and down, did much prejudice to the truly deserving, whose modesty would not suffer them to solicit for themselves. . . . . . Mr. Kettlewell was also very sensible that some of his brethren spent too much of their time in places of concourse and news, by depending for their subsistence upon those whom they there got acquainted with."

COLLEY CIBBER

From a mezzotint by J. Simon, after a painting by Grisoni

saw reason, not long afterwards, to be thankful that their favourite project had failed.

Whigs and Tories had in the late Session combined to get rid of Nottingham's Comprehension Bill by voting an address which requested

The plan of Compre-hension

the King to refer the whole subject to the Convocation. Burnet foresaw the effect of this vote. The whole scheme, he said, was utterly ruined.[1] Many of his friends, however, thought differently; and among these was Tillotson. Of all the members of the Low Church party Tillotson stood highest in general estimation.

Tillotson

As a preacher he was thought by his contemporaries to have surpassed all rivals living or dead. Posterity has reversed this judgment. Yet Tillotson still keeps his place as a legitimate English classic. His highest flights were indeed far below those of Taylor, of Barrow, and of South; but his oratory was more correct and equable than theirs. No quaint conceits, no pedantic quotations from Talmudists and scholiasts, no mean images, buffoon stories, scurrilous invectives, ever marred the effect of his grave and temperate discourses. His reasoning was just sufficiently profound and sufficiently refined to be followed by a popular audience with that slight degree of intellectual exertion which is a pleasure. His style is not brilliant; but it is pure, transparently clear, and equally free from the levity and from the stiffness which disfigure the sermons of some eminent divines of the seventeenth century. He is always serious: yet there is about his manner a certain graceful ease which marks him as a man who knows the world, who has lived in populous cities and in splendid courts, and who has conversed, not only with books, but with lawyers and merchants, wits and beauties, statesmen and princes. The greatest charm of his compositions, however, is derived from the benignity and candour which appear in every line, and which shone forth not less conspicuously in his life than in his writings.

As a theologian, Tillotson was certainly not less latitudinarian than Burnet. Yet many of those clergymen to whom Burnet was an object of implacable aversion spoke of Tillotson with tenderness and respect. It is therefore not strange that the two friends should have formed different estimates of the temper of the priesthood, and should have expected different results from the meeting of the Convocation. Tillotson was not displeased with the vote of the Commons. He conceived that changes made in religious institutions by mere secular authority might disgust many churchmen, who would yet be perfectly willing to vote, in an ecclesiastical synod, for changes more extensive still; and his opinion had great weight with the King.[2] It was resolved that the Convocation should meet at the beginning of the next session

---

[1] Reresby's Memoirs, 344.   [2] Birch's Life of Tillotson.

CONVERTE ANGLIAM

It is a foolish Sheep that makes the Wolf her Confessor

A CARICATURE AGAINST THE NON-JURORS, PUBLISHED IN 1718

Number 1146 in the British Museum Catalogue of Satirical Prints

of Parliament, and that in the mean time a commission should issue empowering some eminent divines to examine the Liturgy, the canons, and the whole system of jurisprudence administered by the Courts Christian, and to report on the alterations which it might be desirable to make.[1]

Most of the Bishops who had taken the oaths were in this commission : and with them were joined twenty priests of great note. Of the

An Ecclesi-astical Commission issued

twenty Tillotson was the most important : for he was known to speak the sense both of the King and of the Queen. Among those Commissioners who looked up to Tillotson as their chief were Stillingfleet, Dean of Saint Paul's, Sharp, Dean of Norwich, Patrick, Dean of Peterborough, Tenison, Rector of Saint Martin's, and Fowler, to whose judicious firmness was chiefly to be ascribed the determination of the London clergy not to read the Declaration of Indulgence.

With such men as those who have been named were mingled some divines who belonged to the High Church party. Conspicuous among these were two of the rulers of Oxford, Aldrich and Jane. Aldrich had recently been appointed Dean of Christchurch, in the room of the Papist Massey, whom James had, in direct violation of the laws, placed at the head of that great college. The new Dean was a polite, though not a profound, scholar, and a jovial, hospitable gentleman. He was the author of some theological tracts which have long been forgotten, and of a compendium of logic which is still used : but the best works which he has bequeathed to posterity are his catches. Jane, the King's Professor of Divinity, was a graver but a less estimable man. He had borne the chief part in framing that decree by which his University ordered the works of Milton and Buchanan to be publicly burned in the Schools. A few years later, irritated and alarmed by the persecution of the Bishops and by the confiscation of the revenues of Magdalene College, he had renounced the doctrine of nonresistance, had repaired to the head quarters of the Prince of Orange, and had assured His Highness that Oxford would willingly coin her plate for the support of the war against her oppressor. During a short time Jane was generally considered as a Whig, and was sharply lampooned by some of his old allies. He was so unfortunate as to have a name which was an excellent mark for the learned punsters of his University. Several epigrams were written on the doublefaced Janus, who, having got a professorship by looking one way, now hoped to get a bishopric by looking another. That he hoped to get a bishopric was perfectly true. He demanded the see of Exeter as a reward due to his services. He was refused : the refusal convinced him that the Church had as much to apprehend from Latitudinarianism as from Popery; and he speedily became a Tory again.[2]

---

[1] See the Discourse concerning the Ecclesiastical Commission, 1689.
[2] Birch's Life of Tillotson ; Life of Prideaux ; Gentleman's Magazine for June and July 1745.

Early in October the Commissioners assembled in the Jerusalem Chamber. At their first meeting they determined to propose that, in the public services of the Church, lessons taken from the canonical books of

Henry Aldrich, D.D.
Dean of Christ-Church.
1689.

From the painting by Sir G. Kneller, in the possession of the Governing Body of Christ Church, Oxford

Scripture should be substituted for the lessons taken from the Apocrypha.[1]

[1] Diary of the Proceedings of the Commissioners, taken by Dr. Williams, afterwards Bishop of Chichester, one of the Commissioners, every night after he went home from the several meetings. This most curious Diary was printed by order of the House of Commons in 1854.

At the second meeting a strange question was raised by the very last person who ought to have raised it. Sprat, Bishop of Rochester, **Proceedings of the Commission** had, without any scruple, sate, during two years, in the unconstitutional tribunal which had, in the late reign, oppressed and pillaged the Church of which he was a ruler. But he had now become scrupulous, and was not ashamed, after acting without hesitation under King James's commission, to express a doubt whether King William's commission were legal. To a plain understanding the doubt seems to be childish. King William's commission gave power neither to make laws nor to administer laws, but simply to enquire and to report. Even without a royal commission Tillotson, Patrick, and Stillingfleet might, with perfect propriety, have met to discuss the state and prospects of the Church, and to consider whether it would or would not be desirable to make some concession to the dissenters. And how could it be a crime for subjects to do at the request of their Sovereign that which it would have been innocent and laudable to do without any such request? Sprat however was seconded by Jane. There was a sharp altercation; and Lloyd, Bishop of Saint Asaph, who, with many good qualities, had an irritable temper, was provoked into saying something about spies. Sprat withdrew and came no more. His example was soon followed by Jane and Aldrich.[1] The Commissioners proceeded to take into consideration the question of the posture at the Eucharist. It was determined to recommend that a communicant, who, after conference with his minister, should declare that he could not conscientiously receive the bread and wine kneeling, might receive them sitting. Mew, Bishop of Winchester, an honest man, but illiterate, weak even in his best days, and now fast sinking into dotage, protested against this concession, and withdrew from the assembly. The other members continued to apply themselves vigorously to their task; and no more secessions took place, though there were great differences of opinion, and though the debates were sometimes warm. The highest churchmen who still remained were Doctor William Beveridge, Archdeacon of Colchester, who many years later became Bishop of Saint Asaph, and Doctor John Scott, the same who had prayed by the deathbed of Jeffreys. The most active among the Latitudinarians appear to have been Burnet, Fowler, and Tenison.

The baptismal service was repeatedly discussed. As to matter of form the Commissioners were disposed to be indulgent. They were generally willing to admit infants into the Church without sponsors and without the sign of the cross. But the majority, after much debate, steadily refused to soften down or explain away those words which, to all minds not sophisticated, appear to assert the regenerating virtue of the sacrament.[2]

[1] Williams's Diary.   [2] Ibid.

As to the surplice, the Commissioners determined to recommend that a large discretion should be left to the Bishops. Expedients were

WILLIAM JANE

From a painting by W. Gandy, in the Bodleian Library

devised by which a person who had received Presbyterian ordination might, without admitting, either expressly or by implication, the invalidity of that ordination, become a minister of the Church of England.[1]

The ecclesiastical calendar was carefully revised. The great festivals were retained. But it was not thought desirable that Saint Valentine, Saint Chad, Saint Swithin, Saint Edward King of the West Saxons, Saint Dunstan, and Saint Alphage, should share the honours of Saint John and Saint Paul ; or that the Church should appear to class the ridiculous fable of the discovery of the cross with facts so awfully important as the Nativity, the Passion, the Resurrection, and the Ascension of her Lord.[2]

The Athanasian Creed caused much perplexity. Most of the Commissioners were equally unwilling to give up the doctrinal clauses and to retain the damnatory clauses. Burnet, Fowler, and Tillotson were desirous to strike this famous symbol out of the Liturgy altogether. Burnet brought forward one argument, which to himself probably did not appear to have much weight, but which was admirably calculated to perplex his opponents, Beveridge and Scott. The Council of Ephesus had always been reverenced by Anglican divines as a synod which had truly represented the whole body of the faithful, and which had been divinely guided in the way of truth. The voice of that Council was the voice of the Holy Catholic and Apostolic Church, not yet corrupted by superstition, or rent asunder by schism. During more than twelve centuries the world had not seen an ecclesiastical assembly which had an equal claim to the respect of believers. The Council of Ephesus had, in the plainest terms, and under the most terrible penalties, forbidden Christians to frame or to impose on their brethren any creed other than the creed settled by the Nicene Fathers. It should seem therefore that, if the Council of Ephesus was really under the direction of the Holy Spirit, whoever uses the Athanasian Creed must, in the very act of uttering an anathema against his neighbours, bring down an anathema on his own head.[3] In spite of the authority of the Ephesian Fathers, the majority of the Commissioners determined to leave the Athanasian Creed in the Prayer Book : but

---

[1] Williams's Diary.

[2] See the alterations in the Book of Common Prayer prepared by the Royal Commissioners for the revision of the Liturgy in 1689, and printed by order of the House of Commons in 1854.

[3] It is difficult to conceive stronger or clearer language than that used by the Council. Τούτων τοίνυν ἀναγνωσθέντων, ὥρισεν ἡ ἁγία σύνοδος, ἑτέραν πίστιν μηδενὶ ἐξεῖναι προσφέρειν, ἤγουν συγγράφειν, ἢ συντιθέναι, παρὰ τὴν ὁρισθεῖσαν παρὰ τῶν ἁγίων πατέρων τῶν ἐν τῇ Νικαέων σινελθόντων σὺν ἁγίῳ πνεύματι· τοὺς δὲ τολμῶντας ἢ συντιθέναι πίστιν ἑτέραν, ἤγουν προκομίζειν, ἢ προσφέρειν τοῖς ἐθέλουσιν ἐπιστρέφειν εἰς ἐπίγνωσιν τῆς ἀληθείας, ἢ ἐξ Ἑλληνισμοῦ, ἢ ἐξ Ἰουδαϊσμοῦ, ἢ ἐξ αἱρέσεως οἱασδηποτοῦν, τούτους, εἰ μὲν εἶεν ἐπίσκοποι ἢ κληρικοί, ἀλλοτρίους εἶναι τοὺς ἐπισκόπους τῆς ἐπισκοπῆς, καὶ τοὺς κληρικοὺς τοῦ κλήρου, εἰ δὲ λαϊκοὶ εἶεν, ἀναθεματίζεσθαι. —Concil. Ephes. Actio VI.

THE JERUSALEM CHAMBER, WESTMINSTER ABBEY

From a photograph

they proposed to add a rubric drawn up by Stillingfleet, which declared that the damnatory clauses were to be understood to apply only to such as obstinately denied the substance of the Christian Faith. Obstinacy is of the nature of moral pravity, and is not imputable to a candid and modest enquirer who, from some defect or malformation of the intellect, is mistaken as to the comparative weight of opposite arguments or testimonies. Orthodox believers were therefore permitted to hope that the heretic who had honestly and humbly sought for truth would not be everlastingly punished for having failed to find it.[1]

Tenison was entrusted with the business of examining the Liturgy, and of collecting all those expressions to which objections had been made, either by theological or by literary critics. It was determined to remove some obvious blemishes. And it would have been wise in the Commissioners to stop here. Unfortunately they determined to rewrite a great part of the Prayer Book. It was a bold undertaking ; for in general the style of that volume is such as cannot be improved. The English Liturgy indeed gains by being compared even with those fine ancient Liturgies from which it is to a great extent taken. The essential qualities of devotional eloquence, conciseness, majestic simplicity, pathetic earnestness of supplication, sobered by a profound reverence, are common between the translations and the originals. But in the subordinate graces of diction the originals must be allowed to be far inferior to the translations. And the reason is obvious. The technical phraseology of Christianity did not become a part of the Latin language till that language had passed the age of maturity and was sinking into barbarism. But the technical phraseology of Christianity was found in the Anglosaxon and in the Norman French, long before the union of those two dialects had produced a third dialect superior to either. The Latin of the Roman Catholic services, therefore, is Latin in the last stage of decay. The English of our services is English in all the vigour and suppleness of early youth. To the great Latin writers, to Terence and Lucretius, to Cicero and Cæsar, to Tacitus and Quinctilian, the noblest compositions of Ambrose and Gregory would have seemed to be, not merely bad writing, but senseless gibberish.[2] The diction of our Book of Common Prayer, on the other hand, has directly or indirectly contributed to form the diction of almost every great English writer, and has extorted the admiration of the most

---

[1] Williams's Diary ; Alterations in the Book of Common Prayer.

[2] It is curious to consider how those great masters of the Latin tongue who used to sup with Mæcenas and Pollio would have been perplexed by " Tibi Cherubim et Seraphim incessabili voce proclamant, Sanctus, Sanctus, Sanctus, Dominus Deus Sabaoth ; " or by " Ideo cum angelis et archangelis, cum thronis et dominationibus."

The Right Reverend Father in God
EDWARD STILLINGFLEET D.D.
late Lord Bishop of Worcester.

Obijt March 27. 1699.

Ætatis Suæ 63.

M. Beal pinxit.

R. White sculpsit.

EDWARD STILLINGFLEET, BISHOP OF WORCESTER

From an engraving by R. White, after a painting by Mary Beale accomplished infidels and of the most accomplished nonconformists, of such men as David Hume and Robert Hall.

The style of the Liturgy, however, did not satisfy the Doctors of the Jerusalem Chamber. They voted the Collects too short and too dry ; and Patrick was entrusted with the duty of expanding and ornamenting them. In one respect, at least, the choice seems to have been unexceptionable ; for, if we judge by the way in which Patrick paraphrased the most sublime Hebrew poetry, we shall probably be of opinion that, whether he was or was not qualified to make the collects better, no man that ever lived was more competent to make them longer.[1]

It mattered little, however, whether the recommendations of the Commission were good or bad. They were all doomed before they were known. The writs summoning the Convocation of the Province of Canterbury had been issued ; and the clergy were everywhere in a state of violent excitement. They had just taken the oaths, and were smarting from the earnest reproofs of nonjurors, from the insolent taunts of Whigs, and often undoubtedly from the stings of remorse. The announcement that a Convocation was to sit for the purpose of deliberating on a plan of comprehension roused all the strongest passions of the priest who had just complied with the law, and was ill satisfied or half satisfied with himself for complying. He had an opportunity of contributing to defeat a favourite scheme of that government which had exacted from him, under severe penalties, a submission not easily to be reconciled to his conscience or his pride. He had an opportunity of signalising his zeal for that Church whose characteristic doctrines he had been accused of deserting for lucre. She was now, he conceived, threatened by a danger as great as that of the preceding year. The Latitudinarians of 1689 were not less eager to humble and to ruin her than the Jesuits of 1688 had been. The Toleration Act had done for the Dissenters quite

The Convocation of the Province of Canterbury summoned. Temper of the clergy

---

[1] I will give two specimens of Patrick's workmanship. "He maketh me," says David, "to lie down in green pastures : he leadeth me beside the still waters." Patrick's version is as follows : "For as a good shepherd leads his sheep in the violent heat to shady places, where they may lie down and feed (not in parched, but) in fresh and green pastures, and in the evening leads them (not to muddy and troubled waters, but) to pure and quiet streams ; so hath he already made a fair and plentiful provision for me, which I enjoy in peace without any disturbance."

In the Song of Solomon is an exquisitely beautiful verse. "I charge you, O daughters of Jerusalem, if ye find my beloved, that ye tell him that I am sick of love." Patrick's version runs thus : "So I turned myself to those of my neighbours and familiar acquaintance who were awakened by my cries to come and see what the matter was ; and conjured them, as they would answer it to God, that, if they met with my beloved, they would let him know—What shall I say ?—What shall I desire you to tell him but that I do not enjoy myself now that I want his company, nor can be well till I recover his love again ?"

SIMON PATRICK, BISHOP OF ELY.

From a drawing by R. White, in the Sutherland Collection.

as much as was compatible with her dignity and security ; and nothing more ought to be conceded, not the hem of one of her vestments, not an epithet from the beginning to the end of her Liturgy.   All the reproaches which had been thrown on the ecclesiastical commission of James were transferred to the ecclesiastical commission of William.   The two commissions indeed had nothing but the name in common.   But the name was associated with illegality and oppression, with the violation of dwellings and the confiscation of freeholds, and was therefore assiduously sounded with no small effect by the tongues of the spiteful in the ears of the ignorant.

The King too, it was said, was not sound.   He conformed indeed to the established worship ; but his was a local and occasional conformity.   For some ceremonies to which High Churchmen **The clergy** were attached he had a distaste which he was at no pains to **ill affected towards** conceal.   One of his first acts had been to give orders that **the King** in his private chapel the service should be said instead of being sung ; and this arrangement, though warranted by the rubric, caused much murmuring.[1]   It was known that he was so profane as to sneer at a practice which had been sanctioned by high ecclesiastical authority, the practice of touching for the scrofula.   This ceremony had come down almost unaltered from the darkest of the dark ages to the time of Newton and Locke.   The Stuarts frequently dispensed the healing influences in the Banqueting House.   The days on which this miracle was to be wrought were fixed at sittings of the Privy Council, and were solemnly notified by the clergy in all the parish churches of the realm.[2]   When the appointed time came, several divines in full canonicals stood round the canopy of state.   The surgeon of the royal household introduced the sick.   A passage from the sixteenth chapter of the Gospel of Saint Mark was read.   When the words, " They shall lay their hands on the sick, and they shall recover," had been pronounced, there was a pause ; and one of the sick was brought up to the King.   His Majesty stroked the ulcers and swellings, and hung round the patient's neck a white riband to which was fastened a gold coin.   The other sufferers were then led up in succession ; and, as each was touched, the chaplain repeated the incantation, " They shall lay their hands on the sick, and they shall recover."   Then came the epistle, prayers, antiphonies, and a benediction.   The service may still be found in the prayer books of the reign of Anne.   Indeed it was not till some time after the accession of George the First that the University of Oxford ceased to reprint the

[1] William's dislike of the Cathedral service is sarcastically noticed by Leslie in the Rehearsal, No. 7.   See also a Letter from a Member of the House of Commons to his Friend in the Country 1689, and Bisset's Modern Fanatic, 1710.

[2] See the Order in Council of Jan. 9. 1683.

Office of Healing together with the Liturgy.   Theologians of eminent
learning, ability, and virtue gave the sanction of their authority to this
mummery;[1] and, what is stranger still, medical men of high note
believed, or affected to believe, in the balsamic virtues of the royal hand.
We must suppose that every surgeon who attended Charles the Second
was a man of high repute for skill ; and more than one of the surgeons
who attended Charles the Second has left us a solemn profession of
faith in the King's miraculous power.   One of them is not ashamed to
tell us that the gift was communicated by the unction administered at
the coronation ; that the cures were so numerous and sometimes so
rapid that they could not be attributed to any natural cause ; that the
failures were to be ascribed to want of faith on the part of the patients;
that Charles once handled a scrofulous Quaker and made him a healthy
man and a sound Churchman in a moment ; that, if those who had been
healed lost or sold the piece of gold which had been hung round their
necks, the ulcers broke forth again, and could be removed only by a
second touch and a second talisman.   We cannot wonder that, when
men of science gravely repeated such nonsense, the vulgar should have
believed it.   Still less can we wonder that wretches tortured by a disease
over which natural remedies had no power should have eagerly drunk
in tales of preternatural cures : for nothing is so credulous as misery.
The crowds which repaired to the palace on the days of healing were
immense.   Charles the Second, in the course of his reign, touched near
a hundred thousand persons.   The number seems to have increased or
diminished as the king's popularity rose or fell.   During that Tory
reaction which followed the dissolution of the Oxford Parliament, the
press to get near him was terrific.   In 1682, he performed the rite
eight thousand five hundred times.   In 1684, the throng was such that
six or seven of the sick were trampled to death.   James, in one of his
progresses, touched eight hundred persons in the choir of the Cathedral
of Chester.   The expense of the ceremony was little less than ten
thousand pounds a year, and would have been much greater but for
the vigilance of the royal surgeons, whose business it was to examine
the applicants, and to distinguish those who came for the cure from
those who came for the gold.[2]

[1] See Collier's Desertion discussed, 1689.   Thomas Carte, who was a disciple, and, at one
time, an assistant, of Collier, inserted, so late as the year 1747, in a bulky History of England,
an exquisitely absurd note, in which he assured the world that, to his certain knowledge, the
Pretender had cured the scrofula, and very gravely inferred that the healing virtue was transmitted
by inheritance, and was quite independent of any unction.   See Carte's History of England,
vol. i. page 291.

[2] See the Preface to a Treatise on Wounds, by Richard Wiseman, Sergeant Chirurgeon to His
Majesty, 1676.   But the fullest information on this curious subject will be found in the Charisma
Basilicon, by John Browne, Chirurgeon in ordinary to His Majesty, 1684.   See also The

The Manner of His Majesties Curing the Diseaſe,

CALLED THE

KINGS-EVIL.

London Printed for Dorman Newman at the kings Armes in the Poultry W.   *F. H. van Houe Sculp.*

THE Miniſters of the Kings Majeſties Chappel reading the Common-Prayers and Liturgy allowed in the Church of England, when the Ordinary Prayers with the Epiſtle and Goſpel is ended, the diſeaſed perſons are brought by the Kings Chyrurgeons into His Majeſties preſence, where by Faith and fervent Prayer they deſire help. Then is read this Goſpel next following; and when theſe words are read, viz. They ſhall lay their hands, &c. The King layeth both his hands on the diſeaſed perſons, and with his bare hands doth ſtroke them: which being done, the diſeaſed perſons ſtand a little aſide. Then the reſt of this Goſpel is read, viz. So then when, &c.

The Goſpel written in the xvj of Mark.

IEſus appeared unto the eleven as they ſate at meat, and caſt in their teeth their unbelief and hardneſs of heart, becauſe they believed not them which had ſeen that he was riſen again from the dead. And he ſaid unto them, Go ye into all the world, and preach the Goſpel to all creatures: He that believeth and is baptized, ſhall be ſaved: but he that believeth not, ſhall be damned. And theſe tokens ſhall follow them that believe: In my Name they ſhall caſt out devils, they ſhall ſpeak with new tongues, they ſhall drive away ſerpents; and if they drink any deadly thing, it ſhall not hurt them: THEY SHALL LAY THEIR HANDS ON THE SICK, AND THEY SHALL RECOVER. So then when the Lord had ſpoken unto them, he was received into heaven, and is on the right hand of God. And they went forth, and preached every where, the Lord working with them, and confirming the word with miracles following.

Which Goſpel being read, then this Goſpel next following is alſo read: And when theſe words are read, That light was the true light, &c. The King ariſeth, and the diſeaſed are again brought before him; then he taketh a piece of Gold called an Angel, of the value of 10 ſhillings, with a hole made therein, and making the ſign of the Croſs on the diſeaſed place, with Prayer and Bleſſing, he hangeth the Gold in a Silk-ſtring about the Neck of every diſeaſed perſion. When the King hath ſo put an Angel of Gold about the Neck of every one of the diſeaſed perſons, then the reſt of this Goſpel is read, viz. He was in the world, &c. The diſeaſed perſons ſtanding in the mean time a little aſide.

The Goſpel written in the firſt of St. John.

IN the beginning was the Word, and the Word was with God, and God was the Word. The ſame was in the beginning with God. All things were made by it, and without it was made nothing that was made. In it was life, and the life was the light of men, and the light ſhineth in the darkneſs, and the darkneſs comprehended it not. There was ſent from God a man, whoſe name was John: He ſame came as a witneſs to bear witneſs of the light, that all men through him might believe. He was not that Light, but was ſent to bear witneſs of the light. THAT LIGHT WAS THE TRUE LIGHT, WHICH LIGHTETH EVERY MAN THAT COMETH INTO THE WORLD. He came among his own, and his own received him not. But as many as received him, to them gave he power to be made ſons of God, even them that believed on his Name, which were born, not of blood, nor of the will of the fleſh, nor yet of the will of man, but of God. And the ſame word became fleſh, and dwelt among us, and we ſaw the glory of it, as the glory of the only begotten Son of the Father, full of grace and truth.

This Goſpel being ended, then the King with the whole company of the Church upon their knees do pray thus:

LOrd have mercy upon us.   Chriſt have mercy upon us.   Lord have mercy upon us.
Our Father which art in Heaven, hallowed be thy Name, Thy Kingdom come, Thy will be done in Earth, as it is in Heaven, Give us this day our dayly bread, And forgive us our treſpaſſes, as we forgive them that treſpaſs againſt us, And lead us not into temptation: Anſwer. But deliver us from evil. Amen.
Miniſter, O Lord ſave thy ſervants   Anſwer. Which put their truſt in thee.
Min. Send unto them help from above.   Anſ. And evermore mightily defend them.
Min. Help us O God our Saviour.   Anſ. And for the glory of thy Names ſake deliver us, be merciful unto us ſinners for thy Names ſake.
Min. O Lord hear our prayers.   Anſ. And let our cry come unto thee.
ALmighty God, the eternal health of all ſuch as put their truſt in thee, hear we beſeech thee on the behalf of theſe thy ſervants for whom we call for thy merciful help, that they receiving health, may give thanks to thee in thy holy Church, through Jeſus Chriſt our Lord, Amen.

Then the Prayers are concluded with this Bleſſing, viz.

THE peace of God which paſſeth all underſtanding, keep your hearts and minds in the knowledg and love of God, and of his Son Jeſus Chriſt our Lord: And the bleſſing of God Almighty, the Father, the Son, and the HolyGhoſt, be amongſt you, and remain with you always. Amen.

Which being ended, the healed perſons depart, firſt giving thanks to God, and to the Kings Majeſty, and congratulating one another for their recovery.

LONDON. Printed for Dorman Newman, at the Kings-Arms in the Poultrey, MDCLXXIX.

THE MANNER OF HIS MAJESTY'S CURING THE DISEASE CALLED THE
KING'S EVIL

From a broadside in the Bodleian Library, published in 1679

William had too much sense to be duped, and too much honesty to bear a part in what he knew to be an imposture. " It is a silly superstition," he exclaimed, when he heard that, at the close of Lent, his palace was besieged by a crowd of the sick : " Give the poor creatures some money, and send them away." [1]   On one single occasion he was importuned into laying his hand on a patient. " God give you better health," he said, " and more sense."   The parents of scrofulous children cried out against his cruelty : bigots lifted up their hands and eyes in horror at his impiety : Jacobites sarcastically praised him for not presuming to arrogate to himself a power which belonged only to legitimate sovereigns ; and even some Whigs thought that he acted unwisely in treating with such marked contempt a superstition which had a strong hold on the vulgar mind : but William was not to be moved, and was accordingly set down by many High Churchmen as either an infidel or a puritan.[2]

The chief cause, however, which at this time made even the most moderate plan of comprehension hateful to the priesthood still remains to be mentioned.   What Burnet had foreseen and foretold had come to pass.   There was throughout the clerical profession a strong disposition to retaliate on the Presbyterians of England the wrongs of the Episcopalians of Scotland.   It could not be denied that even the highest churchmen had, in the summer of 1688, generally declared themselves willing to give up many things for the sake of union.   But it was said, and not without plausibility, that what was passing on the other side of the Border proved union on any reasonable terms to be impossible.   With what face, it was asked, can those who will make no concession to us where we are weak, blame us for refusing to make any concession to them where we are strong ?   We cannot judge correctly of the principles and feelings of a sect from the professions which it makes in a time of feebleness and suffering.   If we would know what the Puritan spirit really is, we must observe the Puritan when he is dominant.   He was dominant here in the last generation ; and his little finger was thicker than the loins of the prelates.   He drove hundreds of quiet students

The clergy exasperated against the Dissenters by the proceedings of the Scotch Presbyterians

---

Ceremonies used in the Time of King Henry VII. for the Healing of them that be Diseased with the King's Evil, published by His Majesty's Command, 1686 ; Evelyn's Diary, March 28. 1684 ; and Bishop Cartwright's Diary, August 28, 29, and 30. 1687.   It is incredible that so large a proportion of the population should have been really scrofulous.   No doubt many persons who had slight and transient maladies were brought to the king ; and the recovery of these persons kept up the vulgar belief in the efficacy of his touch.

[1] Paris Gazette, April 23. 1689.

[2] See Whiston's Life of himself.   Poor Whiston, who believed in everything but the Trinity, tells us gravely that the single person whom William touched was cured, notwithstanding His Majesty's want of faith.   See also the Athenian Mercury of January 16. 1691.

Numb. 1898

The London Gazette.

Published by Authority.

From **Thursday** January 24. to **Monday** January 28. 1683.

Whitehall, January 26.

THis day was published the following Order of Council.

At the Court at WHITEHALL,

The Ninth of *January*, 1683.

Present

The Kings most Excellent Majesty.

Lord *Keeper*	*Earl of* Nottingham
Lord *Privy Seal*	*Earl of* Rochester
Duke of Ormond	Lord *Bishop of* London.
Duke of Beaufort	Mr. *Secretary* Jenkins
Earl of Oxford	Mr. *Chancellor of the* Ex-
Earl of Huntingdon	chequer
Earl of Bridgwater	Mr. *Chancellor of the*
Earl of Peterborrow	Dutchy
Earl of Chesterfield	Lord *Chief* *Justice*
Earl of Clarendon	Jeffryes
Earl of Bathe	Mr. Godolphin.
Earl of Craven	

WHereas by the Grace and Blessing of God, the Kings and Queens of this Realm by many Ages past, have had the happiness by their Sacred Touch, and Invocation of the Name of God, to Cure those who are afflicted with the Disease called the Kings-Evil; And His Majesty is no less measure than any of His Royal Predecessors having had good success therein, and in His most Gracious and Pious disposition, being as ready and willing as any King or Queen of this Realm ever was in any thing to relieve the distresses and necessities of His good Subjects; Yet in His Princely Wisdom foreseeing that in this (as in all other things) Order is to be observed, and fit times are necessary to be appointed for the performing of this great work of Charity, His Majesty was therefore this day pleased to Declare in Council His Royal Will and Pleasure to be, That (in regard heretofore the usual times of presenting such persons for this purpose have been prefixed by His Royal Predecessors) the times of Publick Healings shall from henceforth be from the Feast of All Saints, commonly called Alhallontide, till a week before Christmas: and after Christmas until the First day of March, and then to cease till the Passion Week, being times most convenient both for the temperature of the season, and in respect of Contagion which may happen in this near access to His Majesty's Sacred Person. And when His Majesty shall at any time think fit to go any Progress, He will be pleased to appoint such other times for Healing as shall be most convenient: And His Majesty doth hereby accordingly Order and Command, That from the time of Publishing this His Majesty's Order, none presume to repair to His Majesty's Court to be Healed of the said Disease, but

only at, or within the times for that purpose hereby appointed as aforesaid. And His Majesty was further pleased to Order, That all such as hereafter shall come, or repair to the Court for this purpose, shall bring with them Certificates under the Hands and Seals of the Parson, Vicar, or Minister, and of both or one of the Churchwardens of the respective Parishes where they dwell, and from whence they come, testifying according to the truth, That they have not at any time before been touched by His Majesty to the intent to be healed of that Disease. And all Ministers and Churchwardens are hereby required to be very careful to examine into the truth before they give such Certificates, and also to keep a Register of all Certificates they shall from time to time give. And to the end that all His Majesty's Loving Subjects may the better take knowledge of this His Majesty's Command, His Majesty was pleased to Direct, That this His Order be Read publickly in all Parish-Churches, and then be affixt to some conspicuous place there; And that to that end the same be Printed, and a convenient Number of Copies sent to the most Reverend Fathers in God, the Lord Arch Bishop of Canterbury, and the Lord Arch Bishop of York, who are to take care that the same be distributed to all Parishes within their respective Provinces.

PHIL. LLOYD.

Lintz, January 4. The Lord *Landsdown* arrived here the last week with his Brother Mr. *Greenvile* from *Hungary*, having served this last Campagne first as a Voluntier, and afterwards, at the relief of *Vienna*, as a Captain of Horse, and at the Battle of *Barkan* commanding a Squadron, in Count *Taafs* Brigade. His Lordship was very well received at this Court, and the Emperor at his taking his Leave of him, was pleased to tell his Lordship, that he could not let him return for *England* from a Campagne, wherein he hath behaved himself with so much Gallantry, without a mark of Honour, and at the same time delivered to him a Warrant to the Elector of *Mentz*, Chancelor of *Germany*, to pass a Diploma constituting his Lordship a Count of the Empire. The Venetian Ambassador at this Court is often in Conference with the Imperial Ministers; And it is confidently reported that the League which is treating between the Pope, the Emperor, and the Republick of *Venice*, against the Turks, will be very suddenly concluded. The Marquis de *Seppeville*, Envoy Extraordinary from the Most Christian King, is preparing for his return home.

Ratisbonne, January 6. The Electoral Colledge continues to press for a Peace or Truce with *France*, upon the Conditions proposed by his Most Christian Majesty. We are assured the Elector of *Bavaria* will have an Army of 10000 men the next Summer; And it's said they will not be employed in *Hungary*, but that they are to act on this side, with the Troops

---

REDUCED FACSIMILE OF THE FIRST PAGE OF THE LONDON GAZETTE
FOR JANUARY 28, 1683

from their cloisters, and thousands of respectable divines from their parsonages, for the crime of refusing to sign his Covenant. No tenderness was shown to learning, to genius, or to sanctity. Such men as Hall and Sanderson, Chillingworth and Hammond, were not only plundered, but flung into prisons, and exposed to all the rudeness of brutal gaolers. It was made a crime to read fine psalms and prayers bequeathed to the faithful by Ambrose and Chrysostom. At length the nation became weary of the reign of the saints. The fallen dynasty and the fallen hierarchy were restored. The Puritan was in his turn subjected to disabilities and penalties; and he immediately found out that it was barbarous to punish men for entertaining conscientious scruples about a garb, about a ceremony, about the functions of ecclesiastical officers. His piteous complaints and his arguments in favour of toleration had at length imposed on many well meaning persons. Even zealous churchmen had begun to entertain a hope that the severe discipline which he had undergone had made him candid, moderate, charitable. Had this been really so, it would doubtless have been our duty to treat his scruples with extreme tenderness. But, while we were considering what we could do to meet his wishes in England, he had obtained ascendency in Scotland; and, in an instant, he was all himself again, bigoted, insolent, and cruel. Manses had been sacked; churches shut up; prayer books burned; sacred garments torn; congregations dispersed by violence; priests hustled, pelted, pilloried, driven forth, with their wives and babes, to beg or die of hunger. That these outrages were to be imputed, not to a few lawless marauders, but to the great body of the Presbyterians of Scotland, was evident from the fact that the government had not dared either to inflict punishment on the offenders or to grant relief to the sufferers. Was it not fit then that the Church of England should take warning? Was it reasonable to ask her to mutilate her apostolical polity and her beautiful ritual for the purpose of conciliating those who wanted nothing but power to rabble her as they had rabbled her sister? Already these men had obtained a boon which they ill deserved, and which they never would have granted. They worshipped God in perfect security. Their meeting houses were as effectually protected as the choirs of our cathedrals. While no episcopal minister could, without putting his life in jeopardy, officiate in Ayrshire or Renfrewshire, a hundred Presbyterian ministers preached unmolested every Sunday in Middlesex. The legislature had, with a generosity perhaps imprudent, granted toleration to the most intolerant of men; and with toleration it behoved them to be content.

Thus several causes conspired to inflame the parochial clergy against the scheme of comprehension. Their temper was such that, if the plan framed in the Jerusalem Chamber had been directly submitted to them, it would have been rejected by a majority of twenty to one. But in the Convocation their weight bore no proportion to their number.   The Convocation has, happily for our country, been so long utterly insignificant that, till a recent period, none but curious students cared to enquire how it was constituted ; and even now many persons, not generally ill informed, imagine it to be a council representing the Church of England.   In truth the Convocation so often mentioned in our ecclesiastical history is merely the synod of the Province of Canterbury, and never had a right to speak in the name of the whole clerical body.   The Province of York has also its Convocation : but, till the eighteenth century was far advanced, the Province of York was generally so poor, so rude, and so thinly peopled, that, in political importance, it could hardly be considered as more than a tenth part of the kingdom.   The sense of the Southern clergy was therefore popularly considered as the sense of the whole profession.   When the formal concurrence of the Northern clergy was required, it seems to have been given as a matter of course. Indeed the canons passed by the Convocation of Canterbury in 1604 were ratified by James the First, and were ordered to be strictly observed in every part of the kingdom, two years before the Convocation of York went through the form of approving them.   Since these ecclesiastical councils became mere names, a great change has taken place in the relative position of the two Archbishoprics.   In all the elements of power, the region beyond Trent is now at least a third part of England.   When in our own time the representative system was adjusted to the altered state of the country, almost all the small boroughs which it was necessary to disfranchise were in the south.   Two thirds of the new members given to great provincial towns were given to the north.   If therefore any English government should suffer the Convocations, as now constituted, to meet for the despatch of business, two independent synods would be legislating at the same time for one Church.   It is by no means impossible that one assembly might adopt canons which the other might reject, that one assembly might condemn as heretical propositions which the other might hold to be orthodox.[1]   In the seventeenth century no such danger was apprehended. So little indeed was the Convocation of York then considered, that the two Houses of Parliament had, in their address to William, spoken

Constitution of the Convocation

---

[1] In several recent publications the apprehension that differences might arise between the Convocation of York and the Convocation of Canterbury has been contemptuously pronounced chimerical.   But it is not easy to understand why two independent Convocations should be less likely to differ than two Houses of the same Convocation ; and it is matter of notoriety that, in the reigns of William the Third and Anne, the two Houses of the Convocation of Canterbury scarcely ever agreed.

only of one Convocation, which they called the Convocation of the Clergy of the Kingdom.

The body which they thus not very accurately designated is divided into two Houses. The Upper House is composed of the Bishops of the Province of Canterbury. The Lower House consisted, in 1689, of a hundred and forty four members. Twenty two Deans and fifty four Archdeacons sate there in virtue of their offices. Twenty four divines sate as proctors for twenty four chapters. Only forty four proctors were elected by the eight thousand parish priests of the twenty two dioceses. These forty four proctors, however, were almost all of one mind. The elections had in former times been conducted in the most quiet and decorous manner. But on this occasion the canvassing was eager : the contests were sharp : Clarendon, who had refused to take the oaths, and his brother Rochester, the leader of the party which in the House of Lords had opposed the Comprehension Bill, had gone to Oxford, the head quarters of that party, for the purpose of animating and organising the opposition.[1] The representatives of the parochial clergy must have been men whose chief distinction was their zeal : for in the whole list can be found not a single illustrious name, and very few names which are now known even to persons well read in ecclesiastical history.[2] The official members of the Lower House, among whom were many distinguished scholars and preachers, seem to have been not very unequally divided.

Election of members of Convocation

During the summer of 1689 several high spiritual dignities became vacant, and were bestowed on divines who were sitting in the Jerusalem Chamber. It has already been mentioned that Thomas, Bishop of Worcester, died just before the day fixed for taking the oaths. Lake, Bishop of Chichester, lived just long enough to refuse them, and with his last breath declared that he would maintain even at the stake the doctrine of indefeasible hereditary right. The see of Chichester was filled by Patrick, and that of Worcester by Stillingfleet ; and the deanery of Saint Paul's which Stillingfleet quitted was given to Tillotson. That Tillotson was not raised to the episcopal bench excited some surprise. But in truth it was because the government held his services in the highest estimation that he was suffered to remain a little longer a simple presbyter. The most important office in the Convocation was that of Prolocutor of the Lower House : the Prolocutor was to be chosen by the members ; and it was hoped at Court

Ecclesiastical preferments bestowed

---

[1] Birch's Life of Tillotson ; Life of Prideaux. From Clarendon's Diary, it appears that he and Rochester were at Oxford on the 23rd of September.

[2] See the Roll in the Historical Account of the present Convocation, appended to the second edition of Vox Cleri, 1690. The most considerable name that I perceive in the list of proctors chosen by the parochial clergy is that of Dr. John Mill, the editor of the Greek Testament.

Reverendus admodum in Christo pater Dominus IOHANNES LAKE
Permissione divinâ Cicestrensis Episcopus.

D. Loggan sculp 1688.

Sold by D.Loggan next dore to the goldenhead in Leicesterfeilds.

JOHN LAKE, BISHOP OF CHICHESTER

From an engraving by D. Loggan

that they would choose Tillotson. It had in fact been already determined that he should be the next Archbishop of Canterbury. When he went to kiss hands for his new deanery he warmly thanked the King. "Your Majesty has now set me at ease for the remainder of my life." "No such thing, Doctor, I assure you," said William. He then plainly intimated that, whenever Sancroft should cease to fill the highest ecclesiastical station, Tillotson would succeed to it. Tillotson stood aghast: for his nature was quiet and unambitious: he was beginning to feel the infirmities of old age: he cared little for rank or money: the worldly advantages which he most valued were an honest fame and the general good will of mankind: those advantages he already possessed; and he could not but be aware that, if he became primate, he should incur the bitterest hatred of a powerful party, and should become a mark for obloquy, from which his gentle and sensitive nature shrank as from the rack or the wheel. William was earnest and resolute. "It is necessary," he said, "for my service; and I must lay on your conscience the responsibility of refusing me your help." Here the conversation ended. It was, indeed, not necessary that the point should be immediately decided; for several months were still to elapse before the Archbishopric would be vacant.

Tillotson bemoaned himself with unfeigned anxiety and sorrow to Lady Russell, whom, of all human beings, he most honoured and trusted.[1] He hoped, he said, that he was not inclined to shrink from the service of the Church: but he was convinced that his present line of service was that in which he could be most useful. If he should be forced to accept so high and so invidious a post as the primacy, he should soon sink under the load of duties and anxieties too heavy for his strength. His spirits, and with his spirits his abilities, would fail him. He gently complained of Burnet, who loved and admired him with a truly generous heartiness, and who had laboured to persuade both the King and Queen that there was in England only one man fit for the highest ecclesiastical dignity. "The Bishop of Salisbury," said Tillotson, "is one of the best and worst friends that I know."

Nothing that was not a secret to Burnet was likely to be long a secret to anybody. It soon began to be whispered about that the King Compton dis- had fixed on Tillotson to fill the place of Sancroft. The news contented caused cruel mortification to Compton, who, not unnaturally, conceived that his own claims were unrivalled. He had educated the

---

[1] The letter in which Tillotson informed Lady Russell of the King's intentions is printed in Birch's book: but the date is clearly erroneous. Indeed I feel assured that parts of two distinct letters have been by some blunder joined together. In one passage Tillotson informs his correspondent that Stillingfleet is made Bishop of Worcester, and in another that Walker is made Bishop of Derry. Now Stillingfleet was consecrated Bishop of Worcester on the 13th of October 1689, and Walker was not made Bishop of Derry till June 1690.

Queen and her sister; and to the instruction which they had received from him might fairly be ascribed, at least in part, the firmness with which, in spite of the influence of their father, they had adhered to the established religion. Compton was, moreover, the only prelate who, during the late reign, had raised his voice in Parliament against the dispensing power, the only prelate who had been suspended by the High Commission, the only prelate who had signed the invitation to the Prince of Orange, the only prelate who had actually taken arms against Popery and arbitrary power, the only prelate, save one, who had voted against a Regency. Among the ecclesiastics of the Province of Canterbury who had taken the oaths, he was highest in rank. He had therefore held, during some months, a vicarious primacy: he had crowned the new Sovereigns: he had consecrated the new Bishops: he was about to preside in the Convocation. It may be added, that he was the son of an Earl, and that no person of equally high birth then sate, or had ever sate, since the Reformation, on the episcopal bench. That the government should put over his head a priest of his own diocese, who was the son of a Yorkshire clothier, and who was distinguished only by abilities and virtues, was provoking; and Compton, though by no means a badhearted man, was much provoked. Perhaps his vexation was increased by the reflection that he had, for the sake of those by whom he was thus slighted, done some things which had strained his conscience and sullied his reputation, that he had at one time practised the disingenuous arts of a diplomatist, and at another time given scandal to his brethren by wearing the buffcoat and jackboots of a trooper. He could not accuse Tillotson of inordinate ambition. But, though Tillotson was most unwilling to accept the Archbishopric himself, he did not use his influence in favour of Compton, but earnestly recommended Stillingfleet as the man fittest to preside over the Church of England. The consequence was that, on the eve of the meeting of Convocation, the Bishop who was to be at the head of the Upper House became the personal enemy of the presbyter whom the government wished to see at the head of the Lower House. This quarrel added new difficulties to difficulties which little needed any addition.[1]

It was not till the twentieth of November that the Convocation met for the despatch of business. The place of meeting had, in former times, been Saint Paul's Cathedral. But Saint Paul's The Convo-
Cathedral was slowly rising from its ruins: and, though the cation meets
dome already towered high above the hundred steeples of the City, the choir had not yet been opened for public worship. The assembly

---

[1] Birch's Life of Tillotson. The account there given of the coldness between Compton and Tillotson was taken by Birch from the MSS. of Henry Wharton, and is confirmed by many circumstances which are known from other sources of intelligence.

therefore sate at Westminster.[1]   A table was placed in the beautiful chapel of Henry the Seventh.   Compton was in the chair.   On his right and left those suffragans of Canterbury who had taken the oaths were ranged in gorgeous vestments of scarlet and miniver.   Below the table was assembled the crowd of presbyters.   Beveridge preached a Latin sermon, in which he warmly eulogised the existing system, and yet declared himself favourable to a moderate reform.   Ecclesiastical laws were, he said, of two kinds.   Some laws were fundamental and eternal: they derived their authority from God ; nor could any religious community abrogate them without ceasing to form a part of the universal Church.   Other laws were local and temporary.   They had been framed by human wisdom, and might be altered by human wisdom.   They ought not indeed to be altered without grave reasons.   But surely, at that moment, such reasons were not wanting.   To unite a scattered flock in one fold under one shepherd, to remove stumblingblocks from the path of the weak, to reconcile hearts long estranged, to restore spiritual discipline to its primitive vigour, to place the best and purest of Christian societies on a base broad enough to stand against all the attacks of earth and hell, these were objects which might well justify some modification, not of Catholic institutions, but of national or provincial usages.[2]

The Lower House, having heard this discourse, proceeded to appoint a Prolocutor.   Sharp, who was probably put forward by the members favourable to a comprehension as one of the highest churchmen among them, proposed Tillotson.   Jane, who had refused to act under the Royal Commission, was proposed on the other side.   After some animated discussion, Jane was elected by fifty five votes to twenty eight.[3]

The High Churchmen a majority of the Lower House of Convocation

The Prolocutor was formally presented to the Bishop of London, and made, according to ancient usage, a Latin oration.   In this oration the Anglican Church was extolled as the most perfect of all institutions. There was a very intelligible intimation that no change whatever in her doctrine, her discipline, or her ritual was required ; and the discourse concluded with a most significant sentence.   Compton, when a few months before he exhibited himself in the somewhat unclerical character of a colonel of horse, had ordered the colours of his regiment to be embroidered with the well-known words "Nolumus leges Angliæ mutari"; and with these words Jane closed his peroration.[4]

Still the Low Churchmen did not relinquish all hope.   They very

---

[1] Chamberlayne's State of England, 18th edition.

[2] Concio ad Synodum per Gulielmum Beveregium, 1689.

[3] Luttrell's Diary ; Historical Account of the Present Convocation.

[4] Kennet's History, iii. 552.

The Inside View of King Henry VII Chappel in Westminster Abbey. — _Une perspective de l'interieur de la Chappelle du Roy Henry VII dans l'Abbaye de Westminster._

Printed for K. Sheats & the Royal Wares in Cornhill

VIEW OF THE INTERIOR OF HENRY VII'S CHAPEL IN WESTMINSTER ABBEY

From an engraving in the British Museum

wisely determined to begin by proposing to substitute lessons taken from the canonical books for the lessons taken from the Apocrypha. It should seem that this was a suggestion which, even if there had not been a single dissenter in the kingdom, might well have been received with favour. For the Church had, in her sixth Article, declared that the canonical books were, and that the Apocryphal books were not, entitled to be called Holy Scriptures, and to be regarded as the rule of faith. Even this reform, however, the High Churchmen were determined to oppose. They asked, in pamphlets which covered the counters of Paternoster Row and Little Britain, why country congregations should be deprived of the pleasure of hearing about the ball of pitch with which Daniel choked the dragon, and about the fish whose liver gave forth such a fume as sent the devil flying from Ecbatana to Egypt. And were there not chapters of the Wisdom of the Son of Sirach far more interesting and edifying than the genealogies and muster rolls which made up a large part of the Chronicles of the Jewish Kings, and of the narrative of Nehemiah? No grave divine however would have liked to maintain, in Henry the Seventh's Chapel, that it was impossible to find, in many hundreds of pages dictated by the Holy Spirit, fifty or sixty chapters more edifying than anything which could be extracted from the works of the most respectable uninspired moralist or historian. The leaders of the majority therefore determined to shun a debate in which they must have been reduced to a disagreeable dilemma. Their plan was, not to reject the recommendations of the Commissioners, but to prevent those recommendations from being discussed; and with this view a system of tactics was adopted which proved successful.

The law, as it had been interpreted during a long course of years, prohibited the Convocation from even deliberating on any ecclesiastical ordinance without a previous warrant from the Crown. Such a warrant, sealed with the great seal, was brought in form to Henry the Seventh's Chapel by Nottingham. He at the same time delivered a message from the King. His Majesty exhorted the assembly to consider calmly and without prejudice the recommendations of the Commission, and declared that he had nothing in view but the honour and advantage of the Protestant religion in general, and of the Church of England in particular.[1]

The Bishops speedily agreed on an address of thanks for the royal message, and requested the concurrence of the Lower House. Jane and his adherents raised objection after objection. First they claimed the privilege of presenting a separate address. When they were forced to waive this claim, they refused to agree to any expression which imported that the Church of England had any fellowship with any other Protestant community. Amend-

Difference between the two Houses of Convocation

[1] Historical Account of the Present Convocation, 1689.

ments and reasons were sent backward and forward. Conferences were held at which Burnet on one side and Jane on the other were the chief speakers. At last, with great difficulty, a compromise was made ; and an address, cold and ungracious compared with that which the Bishops had framed, was presented to the King in the Banqueting House. He dissembled his vexation, returned a kind answer, and intimated a hope that the assembly would now at length proceed to consider the great question of Comprehension.[1]

Such however was not the intention of the leaders of the Lower House. As soon as they were again in Henry the Seventh's Chapel, one of them raised a debate about the nonjuring Bishops. In spite of the unfortunate scruple which those prelates enter- tained, they were learned and holy men. Their advice might, at this conjuncture, be of the greatest service to the Church. The Upper House was hardly an Upper House in the absence of the Primate and of many of his most respectable suffragans. Could nothing be done to remedy this evil ?[2] Another member complained of some pamphlets which had lately appeared, and in which the Convocation was not treated with proper deference. The assembly took fire. Was it not monstrous that this heretical and schismatical trash should be cried by the hawkers about the streets, and should be exposed to sale in the booths of Westminster Hall, within a hundred yards of the Prolocutor's chair? The work of mutilating the Liturgy and of turning cathedrals into conventicles might surely be postponed till the Synod had taken measures to protect its own freedom and dignity. It was then debated how the printing of such scandalous books should be prevented. Some were for indictments, some for ecclesiastical censures.[3] In such deliberations as these week after week passed away. Not a single proposition tending to a Comprehension had been even dis- cussed. Christmas was approaching. At Christmas there was to be a recess. The Bishops were desirous that, during the recess, a committee should sit to prepare business. The Lower House refused to consent.[4] That House, it was now evident, was fully determined not even to enter on the consideration of any part of the plan which had been framed by the Royal Commissioners. The proctors of the dioceses were in a worse humour than when they first came up to Westminster. Many of them had probably never before passed a week in the capital, and had not been aware how great the difference was between a town

The Lower House of Convoca- tion proves unmanage- able

[1] Historical Account of the Present Convocation ; Burnet, ii. 58. ; Kennet's History of the Reign of William and Mary.

[2] Historical Account of the Present Convocation ; Kennet's History.

[3] Historical Account of the Present Convocation ; Kennet.

[4] Historical Account of the Present Convocation.

divine and a country divine. The sight of the luxuries and comforts enjoyed by the popular preachers of the city raised, not unnaturally, some sore feeling in a Lincolnshire or Caernarvonshire vicar who was accustomed to live as hardly as a small farmer. The very circumstance that the London clergy were generally for a comprehension made the representatives of the rural clergy obstinate on the other side.[1] The prelates were, as a body, sincerely desirous that some concession might be made to the nonconformists. But the prelates were utterly unable to curb the mutinous democracy. They were few in number. Some of them were objects of extreme dislike to the parochial clergy. The President had not the full authority of a primate ; nor was he

The Convocation prorogued

sorry to see those who had, as he conceived, used him ill, thwarted and mortified. It was necessary to yield. The Convocation was prorogued for six weeks. When those six weeks had expired, it was prorogued again ; and many years elapsed before it was permitted to transact business.

So ended, and for ever, the hope that the Church of England might be induced to make some concession to the scruples of the nonconformists. A learned and respectable minority of the clerical order relinquished that hope with deep regret. Yet in a very short time even Burnet and Tillotson found reason to believe that their defeat was really an escape, and that victory would have been a disaster. A reform, such as, in the days of Elizabeth, would have united the great body of English Protestants, would, in the days of William, have alienated more hearts than it would have conciliated. The schism which the oaths had produced was, as yet, insignificant. Innovations such as those proposed by the Royal Commissioners would have given it a terrible importance. As yet a layman, though he might think the proceedings of the Convention unjustifiable, and though he might applaud the virtue of the nonjuring clergy, still continued to sit under the accustomed pulpit, and to kneel at the accustomed altar. But if, just at this conjuncture, while his mind was irritated by what he thought the wrong done to his favourite divines, and while he was perhaps doubting whether he ought not to follow them, his ears and eyes had

---

[1] That there was such a jealousy as I have described is admitted in the pamphlet entitled Vox Cleri. "Some country ministers, now of the Convocation, do now see in what great ease and plenty the City ministers live, who have their readers and lecturers, and frequent supplies, and sometimes tarry in the vestry till prayers be ended, and have great dignities in the Church, besides their rich parishes in the City." The author of this tract, once widely celebrated, was Thomas Long, proctor for the clergy of the diocese of Exeter. In another pamphlet, published at this time, the rural clergymen are said to have seen with an evil eye their London brethren refreshing themselves with sack after preaching. Several satirical allusions to the fable of the Town Mouse and the Country Mouse will be found in the pamphlets of that winter.

been shocked by changes in the worship to which he was fondly attached, if the compositions of the doctors of the Jerusalem Chamber had taken the place of the old collects, if he had seen clergymen without surplices carrying the chalice and the paten up and down the aisle to seated communicants, the tie which bound him to the Established Church would have been dissolved. He would have repaired to some nonjuring assembly, where the service which he loved was performed without mutilation. The new sect, which as yet consisted almost exclusively of priests, would soon have been swelled by numerous and large congregations; and in those congregations would have been found a much greater proportion of the opulent, of the highly descended, and of the highly educated, than any other body of dissenters could show. The Episcopal schismatics, thus reinforced, would probably have been as formidable to the new King and his successors as ever the Puritan schismatics had been to the princes of the House of Stuart. It is an indisputable and a most instructive fact, that we are, in a great measure, indebted for the civil and religious liberty which we enjoy to the pertinacity with which the High Church party, in the Convocation of 1689, refused even to deliberate on any plan of Comprehension.[1]

[1] Burnet, ii. 33, 34. The best narratives of what passed in this Convocation are the Historical Account appended to the second edition of Vox Cleri, and the passage in Kennet's History to which I have already referred the reader. The former narrative is by a very high churchman, the latter by a very low churchman. Those who are desirous of obtaining fuller information must consult the contemporary pamphlets. Among them are Vox Populi; Vox Laici; Vox Regis et Regni; the Healing Attempt; the Letter to a Friend, by Dean Prideaux; the Letter from a Minister in the Country to a Member of the Convocation; the Answer to the Merry Answer to Vox Cleri; the Remarks from the Country upon two Letters relating to the Convocation; the Vindication of the Letters in answer to Vox Cleri; the Answer to the Country Minister's Letter. All these tracts appeared late in 1689 or early in 1690.

CHAPTER XV

WHILE the Convocation was wrangling on one side of Old Palace Yard, the Parliament was wrangling even more fiercely on the other. The Houses, which had separated on the twentieth of August, had met again on the nineteenth of October. On the day of meeting an important change struck every eye. Halifax was no longer on the woolsack. He had reason to expect that the persecution, from which he had narrowly escaped in the summer, would be renewed. The events which had taken place during the recess, and especially the disasters of the campaign in Ireland, had furnished his enemies with fresh means of annoyance. His administration had not been successful; and, though his failure was partly to be ascribed to causes against which no human wisdom could have contended, it was also partly to be ascribed to the peculiarities of his temper and of his intellect. It was certain that a large party in the Commons would attempt to remove him; and he could no longer depend on the protection of his master. It was natural that a prince who was emphatically a man of action should become weary of a minister who was a man of speculation. Charles, who went to Council as he went to the play, solely to be amused, was delighted with an adviser who had a hundred pleasant and ingenious things to say on both sides of every question. But William had no taste for disquisitions and disputations, however lively and subtle, which occupied much time and led to no conclusion. It was reported, and is not improbable, that on one occasion he could not refrain from expressing in sharp terms at the council board his impatience at what seemed to him a morbid habit of indecision.[1] Halifax, mortified by his mischances in public life, dejected by domestic calamities, disturbed by apprehensions of an impeachment, and no longer supported by royal favour, became sick of public life, and began to pine for the silence and solitude of his seat in Nottinghamshire, an old

The Parliament meets. Retirement of Halifax

---

[1] " Halifax a eu une reprimande sévère publiquement dans le conseil par le Prince d'Orange pour avoir trop balancé."—Avaux to De Croissy, Dublin, June $\frac{16}{26}$. 1689. " His mercurial wit," says Burnet, ii. 4., "was not well suited with the King's phlegm."

GEORGE SAVILE, MARQUIS OF HALIFAX

From the painting by Sir P. Lely in the possession of the Duke of Devonshire

Cistercian Abbey buried deep among woods. Early in October it was known that he would no longer preside in the Upper House. It was at the same time whispered as a great secret that he meant to retire altogether from business, and that he retained the Privy Seal only till a successor should be named. Chief Baron Atkyns was appointed Speaker of the Lords.[1]

On some important points there appeared to be no difference of opinion in the legislature. The Commons unanimously resolved that

Supplies voted

they would stand by the King in the work of reconquering Ireland, and that they would enable him to prosecute with vigour the war against France.[2] With equal unanimity they voted an extraordinary supply of two millions.[3] It was determined that the greater part of this sum should be levied by an assessment on real property. The rest was to be raised partly by a poll tax, and partly by new duties on tea, coffee, and chocolate. It was proposed that a hundred thousand pounds should be exacted from the Jews; and this proposition was at first favourably received by the House: but difficulties arose. The Jews presented a petition in which they declared that they could not afford to pay such a sum, and that they would rather leave the kingdom than stay there to be ruined. Enlightened politicians could not but perceive that special taxation, laid on a small class which happens to be rich, unpopular, and defenceless, is really confiscation, and must ultimately impoverish rather than enrich the State. After some discussion, the Jew tax was abandoned.[4]

The Bill of Rights, which, in the last Session, had, after causing much altercation between the Houses, been suffered to drop, was again

The Bill of Rights passed

introduced, and was speedily passed. The peers no longer insisted that any person should be designated by name as successor to the crown, if Mary, Anne, and William should all die without posterity. During eleven years nothing more was heard of the claims of the House of Brunswick.

The Bill of Rights contained some provisions which deserve special mention. The Convention had resolved that it was contrary to the interest of the kingdom to be governed by a Papist, but had prescribed no test which could ascertain whether a prince was or was not a Papist. The defect was now supplied. It was enacted that every English Sovereign should, in full Parliament, and at the coronation, repeat and subscribe the Declaration against Transubstantiation.

---

[1] Clarendon's Diary, Oct. 10. 1689 ; Lords' Journals, Oct. 19. 1689.

[2] Commons' Journals, Oct. 24. 1689.   [3] Commons' Journals, Nov. 2. 1689.

[4] Commons' Journals, Nov. 7. 19., Dec. 30. 1689. The rule of the House then was that no petition could be received against the imposition of a tax. This rule was, after a very hard fight, rescinded in 1842. The petition of the Jews was not received, and is not mentioned in the Journals. But something may be learned about it from Luttrell's Diary and from Grey's Debates, Nov. 19. 1689.

It was also enacted that no person who should marry a Papist should be capable of reigning in England, and that, if the Sovereign should marry a Papist, the subject should be absolved from allegiance. Burnet boasts that this part of the Bill of Rights was his work. He had little reason to boast : for a more wretched specimen of legislative workmanship will not easily be found. In the first place, no test is prescribed. Whether the consort of a Sovereign has taken the oath of supremacy, has signed the declaration against transubstantiation, has communicated according to the ritual of the Church of England, are very simple issues of fact. But whether the consort of a Sovereign is or is not a Papist is a question about which people may argue for ever. What is a Papist? The word is not a word of definite signification either in law or in theology. It is merely a popular nickname, and means very different things in different mouths. Is every person a Papist who is willing to concede to the Bishop of Rome a primacy among Christian prelates? If so, James the First, Charles the First, Laud, Heylyn, were Papists.[1] Or is the appellation to be confined to persons who hold the ultramontane doctrines touching the authority of the Holy See? If so, neither Bossuet nor Pascal was a Papist.

What again is the legal effect of the words which absolve the subject from his allegiance? Is it meant that a person arraigned for high treason may tender evidence to prove that the Sovereign has married a Papist? Would Thistlewood, for example, have been entitled to an acquittal, if he could have proved that King George the Fourth had married Mrs. Fitzherbert, and that Mrs. Fitzherbert was a Papist? It is not easy to believe that any tribunal would have gone into such a question. Yet to what purpose is it to enact that, in a certain case, the subject shall be absolved from his allegiance, if the tribunal before which he is tried for a violation of his allegiance is not to go into the question whether that case has arisen?

The question of the dispensing power was treated in a very different manner, was fully considered, and was finally settled in the only way in which it could be settled. The Declaration of Right had gone no further than to pronounce that the dispensing power, as of late exercised, was illegal. That a certain dispensing power belonged to the Crown was a proposition sanctioned by authorities and precedents of which

---

[1] James, in the very treatise in which he tried to prove the Pope to be Antichrist, says : "For myself, if that were yet the question, I would with all my heart give my consent that the Bishop of Rome should have the first seat." There is a remarkable letter on this subject written by James to Charles and Buckingham, when they were in Spain. Heylyn, speaking of Laud's negotiation with Rome, says : "So that upon the point the Pope was to content himself among us in England with a priority instead of a superiority over other Bishops, and with a primacy instead of a supremacy in these parts of Christendom, which I conceive no man of learning and sobriety would have grudged to grant him."

even Whig lawyers could not speak without respect: but as to the precise extent of this power hardly any two jurists were agreed; and every attempt to frame a definition had failed. At length by the Bill of Rights the anomalous prerogative which had caused so many fierce disputes was absolutely and for ever taken away.[1]

In the House of Commons there was, as might have been expected, a series of sharp debates on the misfortunes of the autumn. The negli-

Enquiry into naval abuses gence or corruption of the Navy Board, the frauds of the contractors, the rapacity of the captains of the King's ships, the losses of the London merchants, were themes for many keen speeches. There was indeed reason for anger. A severe enquiry, conducted by William in person at the Treasury, had just elicited the fact that much of the salt with which the meat furnished to the fleet had been cured had been by accident mixed with galls such as are used for the purpose of making ink. The victuallers threw the blame on the rats, and maintained that the provisions thus seasoned, though certainly disagreeable to the palate, were not injurious to health.[2] The Commons were in no temper to listen to such excuses. Several persons who had been concerned in cheating the government and poisoning the seamen were taken into custody by the Serjeant.[3] But no censure was passed on the chief offender, Torrington; nor does it appear that a single voice was raised against him. He had personal friends in both parties. He had many popular qualities. Even his vices were not those which excite public hatred. The people readily forgave a courageous open-handed sailor for being too fond of his bottle, his boon companions, and his mistresses, and did not sufficiently consider how great must be the perils of a country of which the safety depends on a man sunk in indolence, stupified by wine, enervated by licentiousness, ruined by prodigality, and enslaved by sycophants and harlots.

The sufferings of the army in Ireland called forth strong expressions of sympathy and indignation. The Commons did justice to the

Enquiry into the conduct of the Irish war firmness and wisdom with which Schomberg had conducted the most arduous of all campaigns. That he had not achieved more was attributed chiefly to the villany of the Commissariat. The pestilence itself, it was said, would have been no serious calamity if it had not been aggravated by the wickedness of man. The disease had generally spared those who had warm garments and bedding, and had swept away by thousands those who were thinly clad and who slept on the wet ground. Immense sums had been drawn out of the Treasury: yet the pay of the troops was in arrear. Hundreds of horses, tens of thousands of shoes, had been paid for by the public: yet the baggage

---

[1] Stat. 1 W. & M. sess. 2. c. 2.   [2] Treasury Minute Book, Nov. 3. 1689.
[3] Commons' Journals and Grey's Debates, Nov. 13, 14. 18, 19. 23. 28. 1689.

was left behind for want of beasts to draw it ; and the soldiers were marching barefoot through the mire.　Seventeen hundred pounds had been charged to the government for medicines : yet the common drugs with which every apothecary in the smallest market town was provided were not to be found in the plague-stricken camp.　The cry against Shales was loud.　An address was carried to the throne, requesting that he might be sent for to England, and that his accounts and papers might be secured.　With this request the King readily complied : but the Whig majority was not satisfied.　By whom had Shales been recommended for so important a place as that of Commissary General ? He had been a favourite at Whitehall in the worst times.　He had been zealous for the Declaration of Indulgence.　Why had this creature of James been entrusted with the business of catering for the army of William ?　It was proposed by some of those who were bent on driving all Tories and Trimmers from office to ask His Majesty by whose advice a man so undeserving of the royal confidence had been employed. The most moderate and judicious Whigs pointed out the indecency and impolicy of interrogating the King, and of forcing him either to accuse his ministers or to quarrel with the representatives of his people. " Advise His Majesty, if you will," said Somers, " to withdraw his confidence from the counsellors who recommended this unfortunate appointment.　Such advice, given, as we should probably give it, unanimously, must have great weight with him.　But do not put to him a question such as no private gentleman would willingly answer.　Do not force him, in defence of his own personal dignity, to protect the very men whom you wish him to discard."　After a hard fight of two days, and several divisions, the address was carried by a hundred and ninety five votes to a hundred and forty six.[1]　The King, as might have been foreseen, coldly refused to turn informer ; and the House did not press him further.[2]　To another address, which requested that a Commission might be sent to examine into the state of things in Ireland, William returned a very gracious answer, and desired the Commons to name the Commissioners.　The Commons, not to be outdone in courtesy, excused themselves, and left it to His Majesty's wisdom to select the fittest persons.[3]

In the midst of the angry debates on the Irish war a pleasing incident produced for a moment goodhumour and unanimity.　Walker had arrived in London, and had been received there with boundless enthusiasm.　His face was in every print shop. Newsletters describing his person and his demeanour were sent to every corner of the kingdom.　Broadsides of prose and verse

Reception of Walker in England

---

[1] Commons' Journals and Grey's Debates, November 26. and 27. 1689.

[2] Commons' Journals, November 28., December 2. 1689.

[3] Commons' Journals and Grey's Debates, November 30., December 2. 1689.

written in his praise were cried in every street. The Companies of London feasted him splendidly in their halls. The common people crowded to gaze on him wherever he moved, and almost stifled him with rough caresses. Both the Universities offered him the degree of Doctor of Divinity. Some of his admirers advised him to present himself at the palace in that military garb in which he had repeatedly headed the sallies of his fellow townsmen. But, with a better judgment than he sometimes showed, he made his appearance at Hampton Court in the peaceful robe of his profession, was most graciously received, and was presented with an order for five thousand pounds. "And do not think, Doctor," William said, with great benignity, "that I offer you this sum as payment for your services. I assure you that I consider your claims on me as not at all diminished." [1]

It is true that amidst the general applause the voice of detraction made itself heard. The defenders of Londonderry were men of two nations and of two religions. During the siege, hatred of the Irishry had held together all Saxons; and hatred of Popery had held together all Protestants. But, when the danger was over, the Englishman and the Scotchman, the Episcopalian and the Presbyterian, began to wrangle about the distribution of praises and rewards. The dissenting preachers, who had zealously assisted Walker in the hour of peril, complained that, in the account which he had published of the siege, he had, though acknowledging that they had done good service, omitted to mention their names. The complaint was just, and, had it been made in a manner becoming Christians and gentlemen, would probably have produced a considerable effect on the public mind. But Walker's accusers in their resentment disregarded truth and decency, used scurrilous language, brought calumnious accusations which were triumphantly refuted, and thus threw away the advantage which they had possessed. Walker defended himself with moderation and candour. His friends fought his battle with vigour, and retaliated keenly on his assailants. At Edinburgh perhaps the public opinion might have been against him. But in London the controversy seems only to have raised his character. He was regarded as an Anglican divine of eminent merit, who, after having heroically defended his religion against an army of Irish Rapparees, was rabbled by a mob of Scotch Covenanters.[2]

---

[1] London Gazette, September 2. 1689; Observations upon Mr. Walker's Account of the Siege of Londonderry, licensed October 4. 1689; Luttrell's Diary; Mr. J. Mackenzie's Narrative a False Libel, a Defence of Mr. G. Walker written by his Friend in his Absence, 1690.

[2] Walker's True Account, 1689; An Apology for the Failures charged on the True Account, 1689; Reflections on the Apology, 1689; A Vindication of the True Account by Walker, 1689; Mackenzie's Narrative, 1690; Mr. Mackenzie's Narrative a False Libel, 1690; Dr. Walker's Invisible Champion foyled by Mackenzie, 1690; Welwood's Mercurius Reformatus, Dec. 4. and

THE REVEREND AND VALIANT MR. GEORGE WALKER

From an engraving by P. Vandrebanc, after a painting by Sir G. Kneller

He presented to the Commons a petition setting forth the destitute condition to which the widows and orphans of some brave men who had fallen during the siege were now reduced. The Commons instantly passed a vote of thanks to him, and resolved to present to the King an address requesting that ten thousand pounds might be distributed among the families whose sufferings had been so touchingly described. The next day it was rumoured about the benches that Walker was in the lobby. He was called in. The Speaker, with great dignity and grace, informed him that the House had made haste to comply with his request, commended him in high terms for having taken on himself to govern and defend a city betrayed by its proper governors and defenders, and charged him to tell those who had fought under him that their fidelity and valour would always be held in grateful remembrance by the Commons of England.[1]

About the same time the course of parliamentary business was diversified by another curious and interesting episode, which, like the **Edmund Ludlow** former, sprang out of the events of the Irish war. In the preceding spring, when every messenger from Ireland brought evil tidings, and when the authority of James was acknowledged in every part of that kingdom, except behind the ramparts of Londonderry and on the banks of Lough Erne, it was natural that Englishmen should remember with how terrible an energy the great Puritan warriors of the preceding generation had crushed the insurrection of the Celtic race. The names of Cromwell, of Ireton, and of the other chiefs of the conquering army, were in many mouths. One of those chiefs, Edmund Ludlow, was still living. At twenty two he had served as a volunteer in the parliamentary army: at thirty he had risen to the rank of Lieutenant General. He was now old: but the vigour of his mind was unimpaired. His courage was of the truest temper; his understanding strong, but narrow. What he saw he saw clearly: but he saw not much at a glance. In an age of perfidy and levity, he had, amidst manifold temptations and dangers, adhered firmly to the principles of his youth. His enemies could not deny that his life had been consistent, and that with the same spirit with which he had stood up against the Stuarts he had stood up against the Cromwells. There was but a single blemish on his fame: but that blemish, in the opinion of the great majority of his countrymen, was one for which no merit could compensate and which no time could efface. His name and seal were on the death warrant of Charles the First.

11. 1689. The Oxford editor of Burnet's History expresses his surprise at the silence which the Bishop observes about Walker. In the Burnet MS. Harl. 6584. there is an animated panegyric on Walker. Why that panegyric does not appear in the History, I am at a loss to explain.

[1] Commons' Journals, November 18. and 19. 1689 ; and Grey's Debates.

MAJOR-GENERAL EDMUND LUDLOW

From an engraving by Robert White prefixed to Ludlow's Memoirs

After the Restoration, Ludlow found a refuge on the shores of the Lake of Geneva. He was accompanied thither by another member of the High Court of Justice, John Lisle, the husband of that Alice Lisle whose death has left a lasting stain on the memory of James the Second. But even in Switzerland the regicides were not safe. A large price was set on their heads; and a succession of Irish adventurers, inflamed by national and religious animosity, attempted to earn the bribe. Lisle fell by the hand of one of these assassins. But Ludlow escaped unhurt from all the machinations of his enemies. A small knot of vehement and determined Whigs regarded him with a veneration, which increased as years rolled away, and left him almost the only survivor, certainly the most illustrious survivor, of a mighty race of men, the conquerors in a terrible civil war, the judges of a king, the founders of a republic. More than once he had been invited by the enemies of the House of Stuart to leave his asylum, to become their captain, and to give the signal for rebellion : but he had wisely refused to take any part in the desperate enterprises which the Wildmans and Fergusons were never weary of planning.[1]

The Revolution opened a new prospect to him. The right of the people to resist oppression, a right which, during many years, no man could assert without exposing himself to ecclesiastical anathemas and to civil penalties, had been solemnly recognised by the Estates of the realm, and had been proclaimed by Garter King at Arms on the very spot where the memorable scaffold had been set up forty years before. James had not, indeed, like Charles, died the death of a traitor. Yet the punishment of the son might seem to differ from the punishment of the father rather in degree than in principle. Those who had recently waged war on a tyrant, who had turned him out of his palace, who had frightened him out of his country, who had deprived him of his crown, might perhaps think that the crime of going one step further had been sufficiently expiated by thirty years of banishment. Ludlow's admirers, some of whom appear to have been in high public situations, assured him that he might safely venture over, nay, that he might expect to be sent in high command to Ireland, where his name was still cherished by his old soldiers and by their children.[2] He came; and early in September it was known that he was in London.[3] But it soon appeared that he and his friends had misunderstood the temper of the English people. By all, except a small extreme section of the Whig party, the act, in which he had borne a part never to be

[1] Wade's Confession, Harl. MS. 6845.

[2] See the Preface to the First Edition of his Memoirs, Vevay, 1698.

[3] "Colonel Ludlow, an old Oliverian, and one of King Charles the First his Judges, is arrived lately in this kingdom from Switzerland." Luttrell's Diary, September 1689.

forgotten, was regarded, not merely with the disapprobation due to a great violation of law and justice, but with horror such as even the Gunpowder Plot had not excited. The absurd and almost impious service which is still read in our churches on the thirtieth of January had produced in the minds of the vulgar a strange association of ideas. The sufferings of Charles were confounded with the sufferings of the Redeemer of mankind; and every regicide was a Judas, a Caiaphas, or a Herod. It was true that, when Ludlow sate on the tribunal in Westminster Hall, he was an ardent enthusiast of twenty eight, and that he now returned from exile a greyheaded and wrinkled man in his seventieth year. Perhaps, therefore, if he had been content to live in close retirement, and to shun places of public resort, even zealous Royalists might not have grudged the old Republican a grave in his native soil. But he had no thought of hiding himself. It was soon rumoured that one of those murderers, who had brought on England guilt, for which she annually, in sackcloth and ashes, implored God not to enter into judgment with her, was strutting about the streets of her capital and boasting that he should ere long command her armies. His lodgings, it was said, were the head quarters of the most noted enemies of monarchy and episcopacy.[1] The subject was brought before the House of Commons. The Tory members called loudly for justice on the traitor. None of the Whigs ventured to say a word in his defence. One or two faintly expressed a doubt whether the fact of his return had been proved by evidence such as would warrant a parliamentary proceeding. This objection was disregarded. It was resolved, without a division, that the King should be requested to issue a proclamation for the apprehending of Ludlow. Seymour presented the address; and the King promised to do what was asked. Some days however elapsed before the proclamation appeared.[2] Ludlow had time to make his escape, and hid himself in his Alpine retreat, never again to emerge. English travellers are still taken to see his house close to the lake, and his tomb in a church among the vineyards which overlook the little town of Vevay. On the house was formerly legible an inscription purporting that to him to whom God is a father every land is a fatherland;[3] and the epitaph on the tomb still attests the feelings with which the stern old Puritan to the last regarded the people of Ireland and the House of Stuart.

[1] Third Caveat against the Whigs, 1712.

[2] Commons' Journals, November 6. and 8. 1689; Grey's Debates; London Gazette, November 18.

[3] "Omne solum forti patria, quia patris." See Addison's Travels. It is a remarkable circumstance that Addison, though a Whig, speaks of Ludlow in language which would better have become a Tory, and sneers at the inscription as cant.

Tories and Whigs had concurred, or had affected to concur, in paying honour to Walker and in putting a brand on Ludlow. But the **Violence of the Whigs** feud between the two parties was more bitter than ever. The King had entertained a hope that, during the recess, the animosities which had in the preceding session prevented an Act of Indemnity from passing would have been mitigated. On the day on which the Houses reassembled, he had pressed them earnestly to put an end to the fear and discord which could never cease to exist, while great numbers held their property and their liberty, and not a few even their lives, by an uncertain tenure. His exhortation proved of no effect. October, November, December passed away; and nothing was done. An Indemnity Bill indeed had been brought in, and read once: but it had ever since lain neglected on the table of the House.[1] Vindictive as had been the mood in which the Whigs had left Westminster, the mood in which they returned was more vindictive still. Smarting from old sufferings, drunk with recent prosperity, burning with implacable resentment, confident of irresistible strength, they were not less rash and headstrong than in the days of the Exclusion Bill. Sixteen hundred and eighty was come again. Again all compromise was rejected. Again the voices of the wisest and most upright friends of liberty were drowned by the clamour of hotheaded and designing agitators. Again moderation was despised as cowardice, or execrated as treachery. All the lessons taught by a cruel experience were forgotten. The very same men who had expiated, by years of humiliation, of imprisonment, of penury, of exile, the folly with which they had misused the advantage given them by the Popish plot, now misused with equal folly the advantage given them by the Revolution. The second madness would, in all probability, like the first, have ended in their proscription, dispersion, decimation, but for the magnanimity and wisdom of that great prince, who, bent on fulfilling his mission, and insensible alike to flattery and to outrage, coldly and inflexibly saved them in their own despite.

It seemed that nothing but blood would satisfy them. The aspect and the temper of the House of Commons reminded men of the time **Impeachments** of the ascendency of Oates; and that nothing might be wanting to the resemblance, Oates himself was there. As a witness, indeed, he could now render no service: but he had caught the scent of carnage, and came to gloat on the butchery in which he could no longer take an active part. His loathsome features were again daily seen, and his well known "Ah Laard, ah Laard!" was again daily heard in the lobbies and in the gallery.[2] The House fell first on the renegades of the late reign. Of those renegades the Earls

---

[1] Commons' Journals, Nov. 1. 7. 1689.   [2] Roger North's Life of Dudley North.

of Peterborough and Salisbury were the highest in rank, but were also the lowest in intellect: for Salisbury had always been an idiot; and Peterborough had long been a dotard. It was however resolved by the Commons that both had, by joining the Church of Rome, committed high treason, and that both should be impeached.[1] A message to that effect was sent to the Lords. Poor old Peterborough was instantly taken into custody, and was sent tottering on a crutch, and wrapped up in woollen stuffs, to the Tower. The next day Salisbury was brought to the bar of his peers. He muttered something about his youth and his foreign education, and was then sent to bear Peterborough company.[2] The Commons had meanwhile passed on to offenders of humbler station and better understanding. Sir Edward Hales was brought before them. He had doubtless, by holding office in defiance of the Test Act, incurred heavy penalties. But these penalties fell far short of what the revengeful spirit of the victorious party demanded; and he was committed as a traitor.[3] Then Obadiah Walker was led in. He behaved with a pusillanimity and disingenuousness which deprived him of all claim to respect or pity. He protested that he had never changed his religion, that his opinions had always been and still were those of some highly respectable divines of the Church of England, and that there were points on which he differed from the Papists. In spite of this quibbling, he was pronounced guilty of high treason, and sent to prison.[4] Then Castelmaine was put to the bar, interrogated, and committed under a warrant which charged him with the capital crime of trying to reconcile the kingdom to the Church of Rome.[5]

In the meantime the Lords had appointed a Committee to enquire who were answerable for the deaths of Russell, of Sidney, and of some other eminent Whigs. Of this Committee, which was popularly called the Murder Committee, the Earl of Stamford, a Whig who had been deeply concerned in the plots formed by his party against the Stuarts, was chairman.[6] The books of the Council were inspected: the clerks of the Council were examined: some facts disgraceful to the Judges, to the Solicitors of the Treasury, to the witnesses for the Crown, and to the keepers of the state prisons, were elicited: but about the packing of the juries no evidence could be obtained.

Committee of Murder

---

[1] Commons' Journals, Oct. 26. 1689.   [2] Lords' Journals, October 26. and 27. 1689.

[3] Commons' Journals, Oct. 26. 1689.

[4] Commons' Journals, Oct. 26. 1689; Wood's Athenæ Oxonienses; Dod's Church History, VIII. ii. 3.

[5] Commons' Journals, October 28. 1689. The proceedings will be found in the collection of State Trials.

[6] Lords' Journals, Nov. 2. and 6. 1689.

The Sheriffs kept their own counsel.   Sir Dudley North, in particular, underwent a most severe cross examination with characteristic clearness of head and firmness of temper, and steadily asserted that he had never troubled himself about the political opinions of the persons whom he put on any panel, but had merely enquired whether they were substantial citizens.   He was undoubtedly lying; and so some of the Whig peers told him in very plain words and in very loud tones: but, though they were morally certain of his guilt, they could find no proofs which would support a criminal charge against him.   The indelible stain however remains on his memory, and is still a subject of lamentation to those who, while loathing his dishonesty and cruelty, cannot forget that he was one of the most original, profound, and accurate thinkers of his age.[1]

Halifax, more fortunate than Dudley North, was completely cleared, not only from legal, but also from moral guilt.   He was the chief object of attack; and yet a severe examination brought nothing to light that was not to his honour.   Tillotson was called as a witness. He swore that he had been the channel of communication between Halifax and Russell when Russell was a prisoner in the Tower.   "My Lord Halifax," said the Doctor, "showed a very compassionate concern for my Lord Russell; and my Lord Russell charged me with his last thanks for my Lord Halifax's humanity and kindness."   It was proved that the unfortunate Duke of Monmouth had borne similar testimony to Halifax's good nature.   One hostile witness indeed was produced, John Hampden, whose mean supplications and enormous bribes had saved his neck from the halter.   He was now a powerful and prosperous man: he was a leader of the dominant party in the House of Commons; and yet he was one of the most unhappy beings on the face of the earth.   The recollection of the pitiable figure which he had made at the bar of the Old Bailey embittered his temper and impelled him to avenge himself without mercy on those who had directly or indirectly contributed to his humiliation.   Of all the Whigs he was the most intolerant and the most obstinately hostile to all plans of amnesty.   The consciousness that he had disgraced himself made him jealous of his dignity and quick to take offence.   He constantly paraded his services and his sufferings, as if he hoped that this ostentatious display would hide from others the stain which nothing could hide from himself.   Having during many months harangued vehemently against Halifax in the House of Commons, he now came to swear against Halifax before the Lords.   The scene was curious.   The witness represented himself as having saved his country, as having planned the Revolution, as having placed Their Majesties on the throne.   He then gave evidence intended to show that his life had been endangered

Malevolence of John Hampden

[1] Lords' Journals, Dec. 20. 1689; Life of Dudley North.

A Dialogue between
Father GIFFORD,
The late Popiſh Preſident of *Maudlin,*
AND
OBADIAH WALKER
Maſter of *Univerſity,* upon their New *Colledge* Preferment in
NEWGATE,

Giff. **M**Y good old Friend Obadiah! *With what open Arms and joyful Embraces could I run to meet my dear Friend in any other place, but in this curſed Academy of* Newgate.

Obad. As curſed as 'tis, *old* Oxonian, *give me thy Paw.* Brothers in Affliction may have the pleaſure of ſhaking Hands ſure, though they met at the Devils together.

Giff. *But, prethee, Brother, What are we brought hither for!*

Obad. For our Sins, old Lad, our Sins.

Giff. *Sins! I know none I have committed: For hang me, Brother, if I can be convinced we are either of us in any Fault yet all this while. 'Tis true, I was a Popiſh Preſident of* Maudlin, *and You Maſter of* Univerſity, *and what then! Certainly whil'ſt the High Eccleſiaſtical Commiſſion ſtood ſtaunch, the Devil's in't if we Two could not make both upſtantial Heads of a* Colledge, *where the Chancellor was Head of a Church.*

Obad. Ah, Friend, now you talk of that Divine good Man the Chancellor, had his *Spiritual Supremacy* continued, we had all been Bleſt. What glorious Proſpects had we then in View! I tell thee, Friend, in thoſe Golden Days, had Matters went on, and the *Teſt* and *Penal* Diſſolution but brought the Church-Lands back again, I expected to be an Abbot at leaſt my ſelf. Nay, on my Veracity, to be plain with thee, I went as big with the hopes of a Cardinal's Cap, as e're the Queen went of a *Prince of Wales.*

Giff. *I can't tell what Preferment in Time we might have look'd for; but, for my part, I met with none extraordinary yet. E'ne much good may do 'em with their old Dr.* Hough, *and their Colledge again too, for any Profit I got by it. In troth, Brother, I was grown e'ne as weary on't, as* Trincalo *of his Dukedom; for, under the Roſe, I was almoſt ſtarv'd in't. We might call, and call again upon our Colledge Tenants, and* Dunn *for our Rents till our Hearts aked, and truly we might as well have demanded Peter-Pence of 'em; and they, in ſhort, thought it as downright* Popery *to pay it us. Then for Credit or Truſt with either Butcher, Brewer, or Baker, the Devil a Doit of Faith amongſt them all; on my Conſcience, had we wanted Bread-Corn enough but for 4* Wafer, *though we had loſt the making of a God by it, the* Heretick *Infidels would never have truſted us for it.* Maudlin Colledge, *quotha', if that were all our Preferment, our* Heretick *Enemies need neither have murmur'd nor envy'd at us. Alas! for all our great Colledge Lands and Livings, we might e'ne have ſet up for poor weeping* Maudlinites *after all, had not a ſweet Showre of Court* Manna *now and then been ſo kind as to relieve us.*

Obad. Court *Manna!* Ay, and Court *Fleſh-pots* too! Ah! our ſweet Bounteous *Whitehall* Maſter, what Golden Showrs that kind *Jove* deſcended in! Well, I'll ſay this for my Converſion, beſides many a private Dab that ſhall be nameleſs, it got me the ſweeteſt *Printing-Preſs.* Between Friends, I took as many Golden *Jacobus's* of him for thoſe lumping Impreſſions of *Eleemoſinary Legends, Roſaries, Virgin Pſalters, &c.* to be diſtributed amongſt the New Converts, as ever *Brent* and *Graham* took for
New

A DIALOGUE BETWEEN FATHER GIFFORD AND OBADIAH WALKER

From a pamphlet in the Bodleian Library

by the machinations of the Lord Privy Seal : but that evidence missed the mark at which it was aimed, and recoiled on him from whom it proceeded. Hampden was forced to acknowledge that he had sent his wife to implore the intercession of the man whom he was now perse- cuting. "Is it not strange," asked Halifax, "that you should have requested the good offices of one whose arts had brought your head into peril?" "Not at all," said Hampden : "to whom was I to apply except to the men who were in power? I applied to Lord Jeffreys : I applied to Father Petre ; and I paid them six thousand pounds for their services." "But did Lord Halifax take any money?" "No : I cannot say that he did." "And, Mr. Hampden, did not you after- wards send your wife to thank him for his kindness?" "Yes : I believe I did," answered Hampden : "but I know of no solid effects of that kindness. If there were any, I should be obliged to my Lord to tell me what they were." Disgraceful as had been the appearance which this degenerate heir of an illustrious name had made at the Old Bailey, the appearance which he made before the Committee of Murder was more disgraceful still.[1] It is pleasing to know that a person who had been far more cruelly wronged than he, but whose nature differed widely from his, the nobleminded Lady Russell, remonstrated against the injustice with which the extreme Whigs treated Halifax.[2]

The malice of John Hampden, however, was unwearied and un- abashed. A few days later, in a committee of the whole House of Commons on the state of the nation, he made a bitter speech, in which he ascribed all the disasters of the year to the influence of the men who had, in the days of the Exclusion Bill, been censured by Parlia- ments, of the men who had attempted to mediate between James and William. The King, he said, ought to dismiss from his counsels and presence all the three noblemen who had been sent to negotiate with him at Hungerford. He went on to speak of the danger of employing men of republican principles. He doubtless alluded to the chief object of his implacable malignity. For Halifax, though from temper averse to violent changes, was well known to be in speculation a republican, and often talked, with much ingenuity and pleasantry, against heredi- tary monarchy. The only effect, however, of the reflection now thrown on him was to call forth a roar of derision. That a Hampden, that the grandson of the great leader of the Long Parliament, that a man who boasted of having conspired with Algernon Sidney against the royal House, should use the word republican as a term of reproach! When

[1] The report is in the Lords' Journals, Dec. 20. 1689. Hampden's examination was on the 18th of November.

[2] This, I think, is clear from a letter of Lady Montague to Lady Russell, dated Dec. 23. 1689, three days after the Committee of Murder had reported.

THE WHIG MARTYRS

From an engraving in the Sutherland Collection

the storm of laughter had subsided, several members stood up to vindicate the accused statesmen.   Seymour declared that, much as he disapproved of the manner in which the administration had lately been
conducted, he could not concur in the vote which John Hampden had
proposed.   " Look where you will," he said, " to Ireland, to Scotland,
to the navy, to the army, you will find abundant proofs of mismanagement.   If the war is still to be conducted by the same hands, we can
expect nothing but a recurrence of the same disasters.   But I am not
prepared to proscribe men for the best thing that they ever did in their
lives, to proscribe men for attempting to avert a revolution by timely
mediation."   It was justly said by another speaker that Halifax and
Nottingham had been sent to the Dutch camp because they possessed the confidence of the nation, because they were universally
known to be hostile to the dispensing power, to the Popish religion,
and to the French ascendency.   It was at length resolved that
the King should be requested in general terms to find out and to
remove the authors of the late miscarriages.[1]   A committee was
appointed to prepare an Address.   John Hampden was chairman, and
drew up a representation in terms so bitter that, when it was reported
to the House, his own father expressed disapprobation, and one member
exclaimed : " This an address !   It is a libel."   After a sharp debate,
the Address was recommitted, and was not again mentioned.[2]

Indeed, the animosity which a large part of the House had felt
against Halifax was beginning to abate.   It was known that, though
he had not yet formally delivered up the Privy Seal, he had ceased to
be a confidential adviser of the Crown.   The power which he had
enjoyed during the first months of the reign of William and Mary had
passed to the more daring, more unscrupulous, and more practical
Caermarthen, against whose influence Shrewsbury contended in vain.
Personally Shrewsbury stood high in the royal favour : but he was
a leader of the Whigs, and, like all leaders of parties, was frequently
pushed forward against his will by those who seemed to follow him.
He was himself inclined to a mild and moderate policy : but he had
not sufficient firmness to withstand the clamorous importunity with
which such politicians as John Howe and John Hampden demanded
vengeance on their enemies.   His advice had therefore, at this time,
little weight with his master, who neither loved the Tories nor trusted
them, but who was fully determined not to proscribe them.

Meanwhile the Whigs, conscious that they had lately sunk in the
opinion both of the King and of the nation, resolved on making a bold
and crafty attempt to become independent of both.   A perfect account

[1] Commons' Journals, Dec. 14. 1689 ; Grey's Debates ; Boyer's Life of William.
[2] Commons' Journals, Dec. 21.; Grey's Debates ; Oldmixon.

of that attempt cannot be constructed out of the scanty and widely dispersed materials which have come down to us.   Yet the story, as it may still be put together, is both interesting and instructive.

A bill for restoring the rights of those corporations which had surrendered their charters to the Crown during the last two reigns had been brought into the House of Commons, had been received with general applause by men of all parties, had been read twice, and had been referred to a select committee, of which Somers was chairman.   On the second of January Somers brought up the report.   The attendance of Tories was scanty : for, as no important discussion was expected, many country gentlemen had left town, and were keeping a merry Christmas by the blazing chimneys of their manor houses.   The muster of zealous Whigs was strong.   As soon as the bill had been reported, Sacheverell, renowned in the stormy parliaments of the reign of Charles the Second as one of the ablest and keenest of the Exclusionists, stood up and moved to add a clause providing that every municipal functionary who had in any manner been a party to the surrendering of the franchises of a borough should be incapable for seven years of holding any office in that borough.   The constitution of almost every corporate town in England had been remodelled during that hot fit of loyalty which followed the detection of the Rye House Plot ; and, in almost every corporate town, the voice of the Tories had been for delivering up the charter, and for trusting everything to the paternal care of the Sovereign.   The effect of Sacheverell's clause, therefore, was to make some thousands of the most opulent and highly considered men in the kingdom incapable, during seven years, of bearing any part in the government of the places in which they resided, and to secure to the Whig party, during seven years, an overwhelming influence in borough elections.

1690.
The Cor-
poration Bill

The minority exclaimed against the gross injustice of passing, rapidly and by surprise, at a season when London was empty, a law of the highest importance, a law which retrospectively inflicted a severe penalty on many hundreds of respectable gentlemen, a law which would call forth the strongest passions in every town from Berwick to Saint Ives, a law which must have a serious effect on the composition of the House itself.   Common decency required at least an adjournment.   An adjournment was moved : but the motion was rejected by a hundred and twenty seven votes to eighty nine.   The question was then put that Sacheverell's clause should stand part of the bill, and was carried by a hundred and thirty three to sixty eight.   Sir Robert Howard immediately moved that every person who, being under Sacheverell's clause disqualified for municipal office, should presume to take any such office, should forfeit five hundred pounds, and should be for life incapable of holding any public employment whatever. The Tories did not venture to divide.[1] The rules of the House put it in the power of a minority to obstruct the progress of a bill ; and this was assuredly one of the very rare occasions on which that power would have been with great propriety exerted. It does not appear however that the parliamentary tacticians of the seventeenth century were aware of the extent to which a small number of members can, without violating any form, retard the course of business.

It was immediately resolved that the bill, enlarged by Sacheverell's and Howard's clauses, should be engrossed. The most vehement Whigs were bent on finally passing it within forty eight hours. The Lords, indeed, were not likely to regard it very favourably. But it should seem that some desperate men were prepared to withhold the supplies till it should pass, nay, even to tack it to the bill of supply, and thus to place the Upper House under the necessity of either consenting to a vast proscription of the Tories or refusing to the government the means of carrying on the war.[2] There were Whigs, however, honest enough to wish that fair play should be given to the hostile party, and prudent enough to know that an advantage obtained by violence and cunning could not be permanent. These men insisted that at least a week should be suffered to elapse before the third reading, and carried their point. Their less scrupulous associates complained bitterly that the good cause was betrayed. What new laws of war were these ? Why was chivalrous courtesy to be shown to foes who thought no stratagem immoral, and who had never given quarter ? And what had been done that was not in strict accordance with the law of Parliament ? That law knew nothing of short notices and long notices, of thin houses and full houses. It was the business of a representative of the people to be in his place. If he chose to shoot and guzzle at his country seat when important business was under consideration at Westminster, what right had he to murmur because more upright and laborious servants of the public passed, in his absence, a bill which appeared to them necessary to the public safety ? As however a postponement of a few days appeared to be inevitable, those who had intended to gain the victory by stealing a march now disclaimed that intention. They solemnly assured the King, who could not help showing some displeasure at their conduct, and who felt much more displeasure than he showed, that they had owed nothing to surprise, and that they were quite certain of a

---

[1] Commons' Journals, Jan. 2. 16$\frac{89}{90}$.

[2] Thus, I think, must be understood some remarkable words in a letter written by William to Portland, on the day after Sacheverell's bold and unexpected move. William calculates the amount of the supplies, and then says: " S'ils n'y mettent des conditions que vous savez, c'est une bonne affaire : mais les Wigges sont si glorieux d'avoir vaincu qu'ils entreprendront tout."

majority in the fullest house.   Sacheverell is said to have declared with great warmth that he would stake his seat on the issue, and that if he

Ætb 18.

William Sacheverell.

From a portrait prefixed to Sir G. Sitwell's The First Whig

found himself mistaken he would never show his face in Parliament again.   Indeed, the general opinion at first was that the Whigs would win the day. But it soon became clear that the fight would be a hard one. The mails had carried out along all the high roads the tidings that, on the second of January, the Commons had agreed to a retrospective penal law against the whole Tory party, and that, on the tenth, that law would be considered for the last time. The whole kingdom was moved from Northumberland to Cornwall. A hundred knights and squires left their halls hung with mistletoe and holly, and their boards groaning with brawn and plum porridge, and rode up post to town, cursing the short days, the cold weather, the miry roads, and the villanous Whigs. The Whigs, too, brought up reinforcements, but not to the same extent; for the clauses were generally unpopular, and not without good cause. Assuredly no reasonable man of any party will deny that the Tories, in surrendering to the Crown all the municipal franchises of the realm, and, with those franchises, the power of altering the constitution of the House of Commons, committed a great fault. But in that fault the nation itself had been an accomplice. If the Mayors and Aldermen whom it was now proposed to punish had, when the tide of loyal enthusiasm ran high, sturdily refused to comply with the wish of their Sovereign, they would have been pointed at in the street as Roundhead knaves, preached at by the Rector, lampooned in ballads, and probably burned in effigy before their own doors. That a community should be hurried into errors alternately by fear of tyranny and by fear of anarchy is doubtless a great evil. But the remedy for that evil is not to punish for such errors some persons who have merely erred with the rest, and who have since repented with the rest. Nor ought it to have been forgotten that the offenders against whom Sacheverell's clause was directed had, in 1688, made large atonement for the misconduct of which they had been guilty in 1683. They had, as a class, stood up firmly against the dispensing power; and most of them had actually been turned out of their municipal offices by James for refusing to support his policy. It is not strange therefore that the attempt to inflict on all these men without exception a degrading punishment should have raised such a storm of public indignation as many Whig members of parliament were unwilling to face.

As the decisive conflict drew near, and as the muster of the Tories became hourly stronger and stronger, the uneasiness of Sacheverell and of his confederates increased. They found that they could hardly hope for a complete victory. They must make some concession. They must propose to recommit the bill. They must declare themselves willing to consider whether any distinction could be made between the chief offenders and the multitudes who had been misled by evil example. But as the spirit of one party fell the spirit of the other rose. The

Tories, glowing with resentment which was but too just, were resolved to listen to no terms of compromise.

The tenth of January came ; and, before the late daybreak of that season, the House was crowded. More than a hundred and sixty members had come up to town within a week. From dawn till the candles had burned down to their sockets the ranks kept unbroken order ; and few members left their seats except for a minute to take a crust of bread or a glass of claret. Messengers were in waiting to carry the result to Kensington, where William, though shaken by a violent cough, sate up till midnight, anxiously expecting the news, and writing to Portland, whom he had sent on an important mission to the Hague.

The only remaining account of the debate is defective and confused : but from that account it appears that the excitement was great. Sharp things were said. One young Whig member used language so hot that he was in danger of being called to the bar. Some reflections were thrown on the Speaker for allowing too much licence to his own friends. But in truth it mattered little whether he called transgressors to order or not. The House had long been quite unmanageable ; and veteran members bitterly regretted the old gravity of debate and the old authority of the chair.[1] That Somers disapproved of the violence of the party to which he belonged may be inferred, both from the whole course of his public life, and from the very significant fact that, though he had charge of the Corporation Bill, he did not move the penal clauses, but left that ungracious office to men more impetuous and less sagacious than himself. He did not however abandon his allies in this emergency, but spoke for them, and tried to make the best of a very bad case. The House divided several times. On the first division a hundred and seventy four voted with Sacheverell, a hundred and seventy nine against him. Still the battle was stubbornly kept up ; but the majority increased from five to ten, from ten to twelve, and from twelve to eighteen. Then at length, after a stormy sitting of fourteen hours, the Whigs yielded. It was near midnight when, to the unspeakable joy and triumph of the Tories, the clerk tore away from the parchment on which the bill had been engrossed the odious clauses of Sacheverell and Howard.[2]

[1] " The authority of the chair, the awe and reverence to order, and the due method of debates being irrecoverably lost by the disorder and tumultuousness of the House."—Sir J. Trevor to the King, Appendix to Dalrymple's Memoirs, Part ii. Book 4.

[2] Commons' Journals, Jan. 10. 16$\frac{89}{90}$. I have done my best to frame an account of this contest out of very defective materials. Burnet's narrative contains more blunders than lines. He evidently trusted to his memory, and was completely deceived by it. My chief authorities are the Journals ; Grey's Debates ; William's Letters to Portland ; the Despatches of Van Citters ; a Letter concerning the Disabling Clauses, lately offered to the House of Commons, for regulating

Emboldened by this great victory, the Tories made an attempt to push forward the Indemnity Bill which had lain many weeks neglected on the table.[1] But the Whigs, notwithstanding their recent defeat, were still the majority of the House ; and many mem-

Debates on the Indemnity Bill

bers, who had shrunk from the unpopularity which they would have incurred by supporting the Sacheverell clause and the Howard clause, were perfectly willing to assist in retarding the general pardon. They still propounded their favourite dilemma. How, they asked, was it possible to defend this project of amnesty without condemning the Revolution ? Could it be contended that crimes which had been grave enough to justify rebellion had not been grave enough to deserve punishment ? And, if those crimes were of such magnitude that they could justly be visited on the Sovereign whom the Constitution had exempted from responsibility, on what principle was immunity to be granted to his advisers and tools, who were beyond all doubt responsible ? One facetious member put this argument in a singular form. He contrived to place in the Speaker's chair a paper which, when examined, appeared to be a Bill of Indemnity for King James, with a sneering preamble about the mercy which had, since the Revolution, been extended to more heinous offenders, and about the indulgence due to a King, who, in oppressing his people, had only acted after the fashion of all Kings.[2]

On the same day on which this mock Bill of Indemnity disturbed the gravity of the Commons, it was moved that the House should go into Committee on the real Bill. The Whigs threw the motion out by a hundred and ninety three votes to a hundred and fifty six. They then proceeded to resolve that a bill of pains and penalties against delinquents should be forthwith brought in, and engrafted on the Bill of Indemnity.[3]

Corporations, 1690 ; The True Friends to Corporations vindicated, in an answer to a letter concerning the Disabling Clauses, 1690 ; and Some Queries concerning the Election of Members for the ensuing Parliament, 1690. To this last pamphlet is appended a list of those who voted for the Sacheverell clause. See also Clarendon's Diary, Jan. 10. $16\frac{89}{90}$, and the Third Part of the Caveat against the Whigs, 1712. I will quote the last sentences of William's Letter of the 10th of January. The news of the first division only had reached Kensington. " Il est à présent onze eures de nuit, et à dix eures la Chambre Basse estoit encore ensemble. Ainsi je ne vous puis escrire par cette ordinaire l'issue de l'affaire. Les previos questions les Tories l'ont emporté de cinq vois. Ainsi vous pouvez voir que la chose est bien disputée. J'ay si grand somiel, et mon toux m'incomode que je ne vous en saurez dire d'avantage. Jusques à mourir à vous."

On the same night Van Citters wrote to the States General. The debate, he said, had been very sharp. The design of the Whigs, whom he calls the Presbyterians, had been nothing less than to exclude their opponents from all offices, and to obtain for themselves the exclusive possession of power.

[1] Commons' Journals, January 11. $16\frac{89}{90}$.

[2] Luttrell's Diary, Jan. 16. 1690 ; Van Citters to the States General, Jan. $\frac{21}{31}$.

[3] Commons' Journals, Jan. 16. $16\frac{89}{90}$.

SIR ROBERT SAWYER

From a painting in the possession of the Earl of Carnarvon

A few hours later a vote passed which showed more clearly than anything that had yet taken place how little chance there was that the public mind would be speedily quieted by an amnesty. Few persons stood higher in the estimation of the Tory party than Sir Robert Sawyer. He was a man of ample fortune and aristocratical connections, of orthodox opinions and regular life, an able and experienced lawyer, a well read scholar, and, in spite of a little pomposity, a good speaker. He had been Attorney General at the time of the detection of the Rye House Plot : he had been employed for the Crown in the prosecutions which followed ; and he had conducted those prosecutions with an eagerness which would, in our time, be called cruelty by all parties, but which, in his own time, and to his own party, seemed to be merely laudable zeal. His friends indeed asserted that he was conscientious even to scrupulosity in matters of life and death [1] : but this is an eulogy which persons who bring the feelings of the nineteenth century to the study of the State Trials of the seventeenth century will have some difficulty in understanding. The best excuse which can be made for this part of his life is that the stain of innocent blood was common to him with almost all the eminent public men of those evil days. When we blame him for prosecuting Russell, we must not forget that Russell had prosecuted Stafford.

Case of Sir Robert Sawyer

Great as Sawyer's offences were, he had made great atonement for them. He had stood up manfully against Popery and despotism : he had, in the very presence chamber, positively refused to draw warrants in contravention of Acts of Parliament : he had resigned his lucrative office rather than appear in Westminster Hall as the champion of the dispensing power : he had been the leading counsel for the seven Bishops ; and he had, on the day of their trial, done his duty ably, honestly, and fearlessly. He was therefore a favourite with High Churchmen, and might be thought to have fairly earned his pardon from the Whigs. But the Whigs were not in a pardoning mood ; and Sawyer was now called to account for his conduct in the case of Sir Thomas Armstrong.

If Armstrong was not belied, he was deep in the worst secrets of the Rye House Plot, and was one of those who undertook to slay the two royal brothers. When the conspiracy was discovered, he fled to the Continent and was outlawed. The magistrates of Leyden were induced by a bribe to deliver him up. He was hurried on board of an English ship, carried to London, and brought before the King's Bench. Sawyer moved the Court to award execution on the outlawry. Armstrong represented that a year had not yet elapsed since he had been outlawed, and that, by an Act passed in the reign of Edward the Sixth,

[1] Roger North's Life of Guildford.

an outlaw who yielded himself within the year was entitled to plead Not Guilty, and to put himself on his country. To this it was answered that Armstrong had not yielded himself, that he had been dragged to the bar a prisoner, and that he had no right to claim a privilege which

SIR THOMAS ARMSTRONG

From a mezzotint in the Sutherland Collection

was evidently meant to be given only to persons who voluntarily rendered themselves up to public justice. Jeffreys and the other judges unanimously overruled Armstrong's objection, and granted the award of execution. Then followed one of the most terrible of the many terrible scenes which, in those times, disgraced our Courts. The daughter of the unhappy man was at his side. "My Lord," she cried out, "you will not murder my father. This is murdering a man." "How now?"

roared the Chief Justice. " Who is this woman ?   Take her, Marshal. Take her away."   She was forced out, crying as she went, " God Almighty's judgments light on you ! "   " God Almighty's judgments," said Jeffreys, " will light on traitors.   Thank God, I am clamour proof." When she was gone, her father again insisted on what he conceived to be his right.   " I ask," he said, " only the benefit of the law."   " And, by the grace of God, you shall have it," said the judge.   " Mr. Sheriff, see that execution be done on Friday next.   There is the benefit of the law for you."   On the following Friday, Armstrong was hanged, drawn and quartered ; and his head was placed over Westminster Hall.[1]

The insolence and cruelty of Jeffreys excite, even at the distance of so many years, an indignation which makes it difficult to be just to him. Yet a perfectly dispassionate enquirer may perhaps think it by no means clear that the award of execution was illegal.   There was no precedent ; and the words of the Act of Edward the Sixth may, without any straining, be construed as the Court construed them.   Indeed, had the penalty been only fine and imprisonment, nobody would have seen anything reprehensible in the proceeding.   But to send a man to the gallows as a traitor, without confronting him with his accusers, without hearing his defence, solely because a timidity which is perfectly compatible with innocence has impelled him to hide himself, is surely a violation, if not of any written law, yet of those great principles to which all laws ought to conform.   The case was brought before the House of Commons.   The orphan daughter of Armstrong came to the bar to demand vengeance ; and a warm debate followed.   Sawyer was fiercely attacked, and strenuously defended.   The Tories declared that he appeared to them to have done only what, as counsel for the Crown, he was bound to do, and to have discharged his duty to God, to the King, and to the prisoner.   If the award was legal, nobody was to blame ; and, if the award was illegal, the blame lay, not with the Attorney General, but with the Judges.   There would be an end of all liberty of speech at the bar, if an advocate was to be punished for making a strictly regular application to a Court, and for arguing that certain words in a statute were to be understood in a certain sense. The Whigs called Sawyer murderer, bloodhound, hangman.   If the liberty of speech claimed by advocates meant the liberty of haranguing men to death, it was high time that the nation should rise up and exterminate the whole race of lawyers.   " Things will never be well done," said one orator, " till some of that profession be made examples."

---

[1] See the account of the proceedings in the collection of State Trials.   It has been asserted that I have committed an error here, and that Armstrong's head was placed on Temple Bar. The truth is that one of his quarters was placed on Temple Bar.   His head was on Westminster Hall.   See Luttrell's Diary, June 1684.

"No crime to demand execution!" exclaimed John Hampden. "We shall be told next that it was no crime in the Jews to cry out 'Crucify him.'" A wise and just man would probably have been of opinion that this was not a case for severity. Sawyer's conduct might have been, to a certain extent, culpable : but, if an Act of Indemnity was to be passed at all, it was to be passed for the benefit of persons whose conduct had been culpable. The question was not whether he was guiltless, but whether his guilt was of so peculiarly black a dye that he ought, not-withstanding all his sacrifices and services, to be excluded by name from the mercy which was to be granted to many thousands of offenders. This question calm and impartial judges would probably have decided in his favour. It was, however, resolved that he should be excepted from the Indemnity, and expelled from the House.[1]

On the morrow the Bill of Indemnity, now transformed into a Bill of Pains and Penalties, was again discussed. The Whigs consented to refer it to a Committee of the whole House, but proposed to instruct the Committee to begin its labours by making out a list of the offenders who were to be proscribed. The Tories moved the previous question. The House divided ; and the Whigs carried their point by a hundred and ninety votes to a hundred and seventy three.[2]

The King watched these events with painful anxiety. He was weary of his crown. He had tried to do justice to both the contending parties ; but justice would satisfy neither. The Tories hated him for protecting the Dissenters. The Whigs hated him for protecting the Tories. The amnesty seemed to be more remote than when, ten months before, he first recommended it from the throne. The last campaign in Ireland had been disastrous. It might well be that the next campaign would be more disastrous still. The malpractices, which had done more than the exhalations of the marshes of Dundalk to destroy the efficiency of the English troops, were likely to be as monstrous as ever. Every part of the administration was thoroughly disorganised ; and the people were surprised and angry because a foreigner, newly come among them, imperfectly acquainted with them, and constantly thwarted by them, had not, in a year, put the whole machine of government to rights. Most of his ministers, instead of assisting him, were trying to get up addresses and impeachments

The King purposes to retire to Holland

---

[1] Commons' Journals, Jan. 20. 168⁹⁄₉₀ ; Grey's Debates, Jan. 18. and 20.

[2] Commons' Journals, Jan. 21. 168⁸⁄₉. On the same day William wrote thus from Kensington to Portland : "C'est aujourd'hui le grand jour à l'éguard du Bill of Indemnité. Selon tout ce que je puis aprendre, il y aura beaucoup de chaleur, et rien déterminer ; et de la manière que la chose est entourré, il n'y a point d'aparence que cette affaire viene à aucune conclusion. Et ainsi il se pouroit que la cession fust fort courte ; n'ayant plus d'argent à espérer ; et les esprits s'aigrissent l'un contre l'autre de plus en plus." Three days later Van Citters informed the States General that the excitement about the Bill of Indemnity was extreme.

H.E. IV R

against each other. Yet if he employed his own countrymen, on whose fidelity and attachment he could rely, a general cry of rage was set up by all the English factions. The knavery of the English Commissariat had destroyed an army : yet a rumour that he intended to employ an able, experienced, and trusty Commissary from Holland had excited general discontent. The King felt that he could not, while thus situated, render any service to that great cause to which his whole soul was devoted. Already the glory which he had won by conducting to a successful issue the most important enterprise of that age was becoming dim. Even his friends had begun to doubt whether he really possessed all that sagacity and energy which had a few months before extorted the unwilling admiration of his enemies. But he would endure his splendid slavery no longer. He would return to his native country. He would content himself with being the first citizen of a commonwealth to which the name of Orange was dear. As such, he might still be foremost among those who were banded together in defence of the liberties of Europe. As for the turbulent and ungrateful islanders, who detested him because he would not let them tear each other in pieces, Mary must try what she could do with them. She was born on their soil. She spoke their language. She did not dislike some parts of their Liturgy, which they fancied to be essential, and which to him seemed at best harmless. If she had little knowledge of politics and war, she had what might be more useful, feminine grace and tact, a sweet temper, a smile and a kind word for everybody. She might be able to compose the disputes which distracted the State and the Church. Holland, under his government, and England, under hers, might act cordially together against the common enemy.

He secretly ordered preparations to be made for his voyage. Having done this, he called together a few of his chief counsellors, and told **He is induced to change his intention** them his purpose. A squadron, he said, was ready to convey him to his country. He had done with them. He hoped that the Queen would be more successful. The ministers were thunderstruck. For once all quarrels were suspended. The Tory Caermarthen on one side, the Whig Shrewsbury on the other, expostulated and implored with a pathetic vehemence rare in the conferences of statesmen. Many tears were shed. At length the King was induced to give up, at least for the present, his design of abdicating the government. But he announced another design which he was fully determined not to give up. Since he was still to remain at the head of the English administration, he would go himself to Ireland. He would try whether the whole royal authority, strenuously exerted on the spot where the fate of the empire was to be decided, would suffice to prevent peculation and to maintain discipline.[1]

[1] Burnet, ii. 39.; MS. Memoir written by the first Lord Lonsdale among the Mackintosh Papers.

That he had seriously meditated a retreat to Holland long continued to be a secret, not only to the multitude, but even to the Queen.[1]   That he had resolved to take the command of his army in Ireland   The Whigs was soon rumoured all over London.   It was known that his   oppose his going to camp furniture was making, and that Sir Christopher Wren   Ireland was busied in constructing a house of wood which was to travel about, packed in two waggons, and to be set up wherever His Majesty might fix his quarters.[2]   The Whigs raised a violent outcry against the whole scheme.   Not knowing, or affecting not to know, that it had been formed by William and by William alone, and that none of his ministers had dared to advise him to encounter the Irish swords and the Irish atmosphere, the whole party confidently affirmed that he had been misled by some traitor in the cabinet, by some Tory who hated the Revolution and all that had sprung from the Revolution.   Would any true friend have advised His Majesty, infirm in health as he was, to expose himself, not only to the dangers of war, but to the malignity of a climate which had recently been fatal to thousands of men much stronger than himself?   In private the King sneered bitterly at this anxiety for his safety.   It was merely, in his judgment, the anxiety which a hard master feels lest his slaves should become unfit for their drudgery.   The Whigs, he wrote to Portland, were afraid to lose their tool before they had done their work.   "As to their friendship," he added, "you know what it is worth."   His resolution, he told his friend, was unalterably fixed.   Everything was at stake ; and go he must, even though the Parliament should present an address imploring him to stay.[3]

He soon learned that such an address would be immediately moved in both Houses and supported by the whole strength of the Whig party. This intelligence satisfied him that it was time to take a   He pro- decisive step.   He would not discard the Whigs : but he   rogues the would give them a lesson of which they stood much in need.   Parliament He would break the chain in which they imagined that they had him fast.   He would not let them have the exclusive possession of power.

---

[1] Burnet, ii. 40.   [2] Luttrell's Diary, January and February.

[3] William to Portland, Jan. $\frac{19}{29}$. 1690.   "Les Wiges ont peur de me perdre trop tost, avant qu'ils n'ayent fait avec moy ce qu'ils veulent : car, pour leur amitié, vous savez ce qu'il y a à compter làdessus en ce pays icy."

Jan. $\frac{14}{24}$.   "Me voilà le plus embarassé du monde, ne sachant quel parti prendre, estant toujours persuadé que, sans que j'aille en Irlande, l'on n'y faira rien qui vaille.   Pour avoir du conseil en cette affaire, je n'en ay point à attendre, personne n'ausant dire ses sentimens.   Et l'on commence déjà à dire ouvertement que ce sont des traitres qui m'ont conseillé de prendre cette résolution."

Jan. $\frac{21}{31}$.   "Je n'ay encore rien dit,"—he means to the Parliament,—"de mon voyage pour l'Irlande.   Et je ne suis point encore déterminé si j'en parlerez : mais je crains que nonobstant j'aurez une adresse pour n'y point aller ; ce qui m'embarassera beaucoup, puis que c'est une nécessité absolue que j'y aille."

He would not let them persecute the vanquished party. In their despite, he would grant an amnesty to his people. In their despite, he would take the command of his army in Ireland. He arranged his plan with characteristic prudence, firmness, and secrecy. A single Englishman it was necessary to trust : for William was not sufficiently master of our language to address the Houses from the throne in his own words ; and, on very important occasions, his practice was to write his speech in French, and to employ a translator. It is certain that to one person, and to one only, the King confided the momentous resolution which he had taken ; and it can hardly be doubted that this person was Caermarthen.

On the twenty-seventh of January, Black Rod knocked at the door of the Commons. The Speaker and the members repaired to the House of Lords. The King was on the throne. He gave his assent to the Supply Bill, thanked the Houses for it, announced his intention of going to Ireland, and prorogued the Parliament. None could doubt that a dissolution would speedily follow. As the concluding words, " I have thought it convenient now to put an end to this session," were uttered, the Tories, both above and below the bar, broke forth into a shout of joy. The King meanwhile surveyed his audience from the throne with that bright eagle eye which nothing escaped. He might be pardoned if he felt some little vindictive pleasure in annoying those who had cruelly annoyed him. " I saw," he wrote to Portland the next day, " faces an ell long. I saw some of those men change colour twenty times while I was speaking." [1]

A few hours after the prorogation, a hundred and fifty Tory members of Parliament had a parting dinner together at the Apollo Tavern **Joy of the Tories** in Fleet Street, before they set out for their counties. They were in better temper with William than they had been since his father in law had been turned out of Whitehall. They had scarcely recovered from the joyful surprise with which they had heard it announced from the throne that the session was at an end. The recollection of their danger and the sense of their deliverance were still fresh. They talked of repairing to Court in a body to testify their gratitude : but they were induced to forego their intention ; and not without cause : for a great crowd of squires, after a revel, at which doubtless neither October nor claret had been spared, might have caused some inconvenience in the presence chamber. Sir John Lowther, who in wealth

---

[1] William to Portland, $\frac{\text{Jan. 28.}}{\text{Feb. 7.}}$ 1690 ; Van Citters to the States General, same date ; Evelyn's Diary ; Lords' Journals, Jan. 27. I will quote William's own words. "Vous vairez mon harangue imprimée : ainsi je ne vous en direz rien. Et pour les raisons qui m'y ont obligé, je les reserverez à vous les dire jusques à vostre retour. Il semble que les Toris en sont bien aise, mais point les Wiggs. Ils estoient tous fort surpris quand je leur parlois, n'ayant communiqué mon dessin qu'à une seule personne. Je vis des visages long comme un aune, changé de couleur vingt fois pendant que je parlois. Tous ces particularités jusques à vostre heureux retour."

and influence was inferior to no country gentleman of that age, was deputed to carry the thanks of the assembly to the palace. He spoke, he told the King, the sense of a great body of honest gentlemen. They begged His Majesty to be assured that they would in their counties do their best to serve him ; and they cordially wished him a safe voyage to Ireland, a complete victory, a speedy return, and a long and happy reign. During the following week, many, who had never shown their faces in the circle at Saint James's since the Revolution, went to kiss the King's hand. So warmly indeed did those who had hitherto been regarded as half Jacobites express their approbation of the policy of the government that the thoroughgoing Jacobites were much disgusted, and complained bitterly of the strange blindness which seemed to have come on the sons of the Church of England.[1]

All the acts of William, at this time, indicated his determination to restrain, steadily though gently, the violence of the Whigs, and to conciliate, if possible, the good will of the Tories. Several persons whom the Commons had thrown into prison for treason were set at liberty on bail.[2] The prelates who held that their allegiance was still due to James were treated with a tenderness rare in the history of revolutions. Within a week after the prorogation, the first of February came, the day on which those ecclesiastics who refused to take the oaths were to be finally deprived. Several of the suspended clergy, after holding out till the last moment, swore just in time to save themselves from beggary. But the Primate and five of his suffragans were still inflexible. They consequently forfeited their bishoprics : but Sancroft was informed that the King had not yet relinquished the hope of being able to make some arrangement which might avert the necessity of appointing successors, and that the nonjuring prelates might continue for the present to reside in their palaces. Their receivers were appointed receivers for the Crown, and continued to collect the revenues of the vacant sees.[3] Similar indulgence was shown to some divines of lower rank. Sherlock, in particular, continued, after his deprivation, to live unmolested in his official mansion close to the Temple Church.

And now appeared a proclamation dissolving the Parliament. The writs for a general election went out ; and soon every part of the kingdom was in a ferment. Van Citters, who had resided in England during many eventful years, declared that he had never seen London more violently agitated.[4] The excitement **Dissolution and general election** was kept up by compositions of all sorts, from sermons with sixteen

---

[1] Evelyn's Diary; Clarendon's Diary, Feb. 9. 1690; Van Citters to the States General, $\frac{Jan. 31.}{Feb. 10.}$; Lonsdale MS. quoted by Dalrymple.

[2] Narcissus Luttrell's Diary.   [3] Clarendon's Diary, Feb. 11. 1690.

[4] Van Citters to the States General, February $\frac{14}{24}$. 1690 ; Evelyn's Diary.

heads down to jingling street ballads. Lists of divisions were, for the first time in our history, printed and dispersed for the information of constituent bodies. Two of these lists may still be seen in old libraries. One of the two, circulated by the Whigs, contained the names of those Tories who had voted against declaring the throne vacant. The other, circulated by the Tories, contained the names of those Whigs who had supported the Sacheverell clause.

It soon became clear that public feeling had undergone a great change during the year which had elapsed since the Convention had met; and it is impossible to deny that this change was, at least in part, the natural consequence and the just punishment of the intemperate and vindictive conduct of the Whigs. Of the City of London they thought themselves sure. The livery had in the preceding year returned four zealous Whigs without a contest. But all the four had voted for the Sacheverell clause; and by that clause many of the merchant princes of Lombard Street and Cornhill, men powerful in the twelve great companies, men whom the goldsmiths followed humbly, hat in hand, up and down the arcades of the Royal Exchange, would have been turned with all indignity out of the Court of Aldermen and out of the Common Council. The struggle was for life or death. No exertions, no artifices, were spared. William wrote to Portland that the Whigs of the City, in their despair, stuck at nothing, and that, as they went on, they would soon stand as much in need of an Act of Indemnity as the Tories. Four Tories however were returned, and that by so decisive a majority that the Tory who stood lowest polled four hundred votes more than the Whig who stood highest.[1] The Sheriffs, desiring to defer as long as possible the triumph of their enemies, granted a scrutiny. But, though the majority was diminished, the result was not affected.[2] At Westminster, two opponents of the Sacheverell clause were elected without a contest.[3] But nothing indicated more strongly the disgust excited by the proceedings of the late House of Commons than what passed in the University of Cambridge. Newton retired to his quiet observatory over the gate of Trinity College. Two Tories were returned by an overwhelming majority. At the head of the poll was Sawyer, who had, but a few days before, been excepted from the Indemnity Bill and expelled from the House of Commons. The records of the University contain curious proofs that the unwise severity with which he had been treated had raised an enthusiastic feeling in his favour. Newton voted for Sawyer; and this remarkable fact justifies us in

[1] William to Portland, $\frac{\text{Feb. 28.}}{\text{March 10.}}$ 1690; Van Citters to the States General, March $\frac{4}{14}$.; Narcissus Luttrell's Diary.

[2] Van Citters, March $\frac{4}{14}$. 1690; Narcissus Luttrell's Diary.

[3] Van Citters to the States General, March $\frac{4}{14}$. 1690.

believing that the great philosopher, in whose genius and virtue the Whig party justly glories, had seen the headstrong and revengeful conduct of that party with concern and disapprobation.[1]

It was soon plain that the Tories would have a majority in the new House of Commons.[2] All the leading Whigs however obtained seats, with one exception. John Hampden was excluded, and was regretted only by the most intolerant and unreasonable members of his party.[3]

The King meanwhile was making, in almost every department of the executive government, a change corresponding to the change which the general election was making in the composition of the legislature. Still, however, he did not think of forming what is now called a ministry. He still reserved to himself more especially the direction of foreign affairs, and he superintended with minute attention all the preparations for the approaching campaign in Ireland. In his confidential letters he complained that he had to perform, with little or no assistance, the task of organising the disorganised military establishments of the kingdom. The work, he said, was heavy ; but it must be done ; for everything depended on it.[4] In general, the government was still a government by independent departments ; and in almost every department Whigs and Tories were still mingled, though not exactly in the old proportions. The Whig element had decidedly predominated in 1689. The Tory element predominated, though not very decidedly, in 1690.

Changes in the executive departments

Halifax had laid down the Privy Seal. It was offered to Chesterfield, a Tory who had voted in the Convention for a Regency. But

---

[1] The votes were for Sawyer 165, for Finch 141, for Bennet, whom I suppose to have been a Whig, 87. At the University every voter delivers his vote in writing. One of the votes given on this occasion is in the following words, " Henricus Jenkes, ex amore justitiæ, eligit virum consultissimum Robertum Sawyer."

[2] Van Citters to the States General, March $\frac{18}{28}$. 1690.

[3] It is amusing to see how absurdly foreign pamphleteers, ignorant of the real state of things in England, exaggerated the importance of John Hampden, whose name they could not spell. In a French Dialogue between William and the Ghost of Monmouth, William says, " Entre ces membres de la Chambre Basse étoit un certain homme hardy, opiniâtre, et zélé à l'excès pour sa créance ; on l'appelle Embden, également dangereux par son esprit et par son crédit. . . . Je ne trouvay point de chemin plus court pour me délivrer de cette traverse que de casser le parlement, en convoquer un autre, et empescher que cet homme, qui me faisoit tant d'ombrages, ne fust nommé pour un des deputez au nouvel parlement." " Ainsi," says the Ghost, " cette cassation de parlement qui a fait tant de bruit, et a produit tant de raisonnemens et de spéculations, n'estoit que pour exclure Embden. Mais s'il estoit si adroit et si zélé, comment as-tu pu trouver le moyen de le faire exclure du nombre des deputez ? " To this sensible question the King replies, not very explicitly, " Il m'a fallu faire d'étranges manœuvres pour en venir à bout."— L'Ombre de Monmouth, 1690.

[4] " A présent tout dépendra d'un bon succès en Irlande ; et à quoy il faut que je m'aplique entièrement pour régler le mieux que je puis toutte chose. . . . Je vous asseure que je n'ay pas peu sur les bras, estant aussi mal assisté que je suis."—William to Portland, $\frac{\text{Jan. 28.}}{\text{Feb. 7.}}$ 1690.

Chesterfield refused to quit his country house and gardens in Derbyshire for the Court and the Council Chamber; and the Privy Seal was
put into Commission.[1]   Caermarthen was now the chief adviser of the
crown on all matters relating to the internal administration and to the
management of the two Houses of Parliament.   The white staff, and
the immense power which accompanied the white staff, William was

**Caermar-
then chief
minister**

still determined never to entrust to any subject.   Caermarthen therefore continued to be Lord President; but he took
possession of a suite of apartments in Saint James's Palace
which was considered as peculiarly belonging to the Prime Minister.[2]
He had, during the preceding year, pleaded ill health as an excuse for
seldom appearing at the Council Board; and the plea was not without
foundation: for his digestive organs had some morbid peculiarities
which puzzled the whole College of Physicians: his complexion was
livid: his frame was meagre; and his face, handsome and intellectual as
it was, had a haggard look which indicated the restlessness of pain as
well as the restlessness of ambition.[3]   As soon, however, as he was
once more minister, he applied himself strenuously to business, and
toiled, every day, and all day long, with an energy which amazed
everybody who saw his ghastly countenance and tottering gait.

Though he could not obtain for himself the office of Lord Treasurer,
his influence at the Treasury was great.   Monmouth, the First Commissioner, and Delamere, the Chancellor of the Exchequer, two of the most
violent Whigs in England, quitted their seats.   On this, as on many
other occasions, it appeared that they had nothing but their Whiggism
in common.   The volatile Monmouth, sensible that he had none of the
qualities of a financier, seems to have taken no personal offence at
being removed from a place which he never ought to have occupied.
He thankfully accepted a pension, which his profuse habits made

---

[1] Van Citters, Feb. $\frac{14}{24}$. 16$\frac{89}{90}$; Memoir of the Earl of Chesterfield, by himself; Halifax to
Chesterfield, Feb. 6.; Chesterfield to Halifax, Feb. 8.   The editor of the letters of the second
Earl of Chesterfield, not allowing for the change of style, has misplaced this correspondence by a
year.

[2] Van Citters to the States General, Feb. $\frac{11}{21}$. 1690.

[3] A strange peculiarity of his constitution is mentioned in an account of him which was
published a few months after his death.   See the volume entitled "Lives and Characters of the
most Illustrious Persons, British and Foreign, who died in the year 1712."   So early as the days
of Charles the Second, the leanness and ghastliness of Caermarthen were among the favourite
topics of Whig satirists.   In a ballad entitled the Chequer Inn are these lines :

> "He is as stiff as any stake,
> And leaner, Dick, than any rake :
>   Envy is not so pale ;
> And though, by selling of us all,
> He has wrought himself into Whitehall,
>   He looks like bird of gaol."

necessary to him, and still continued to attend councils, to frequent the Court, and to discharge the duties of a Lord of the Bedchamber.[1] He also tried to make himself useful in military business, which he understood, if not well, yet better than most of his brother nobles; and he professed, during a few months, a great regard for Caermarthen. Delamere was in a very different mood. It was in vain that his services were overpaid with honours and riches. He was created Earl of Warrington. He obtained a grant of all the lands that could be discovered belonging to Jesuits in five or six counties. A demand made by him on account of expenses incurred at the time of the Revolution was allowed; and he carried with him into retirement as the reward of his patriotic exertions a large sum which the State could ill spare. But his anger was not to be so appeased; and to the end of his life he continued to complain bitterly of the ingratitude with which he and his party had been treated.[2]

Sir John Lowther became first Lord of the Treasury, and was the person on whom Caermarthen chiefly relied for the conduct of the ostensible business of the House of Commons. Lowther was **Sir John** a man of ancient descent, ample estate, and great parliamen- **Lowther** tary interest. Though not an old man, he was an old senator: for he had, before he was of age, succeeded his father as knight of the shire for Westmoreland. In truth the representation of Westmoreland was almost as much one of the hereditaments of the Lowther family as Lowther Hall. Sir John's abilities were respectable: his manners, though sarcastically noticed in contemporary lampoons as too formal, were eminently courteous: his personal courage he was but too ready to prove: his morals were irreproachable: his time was divided between respectable labours and respectable pleasures: his chief business was to attend the House of Commons and to preside on the Bench of Justice: his favourite amusements were reading and gardening. In opinions he was a very moderate Tory. He was attached to hereditary monarchy

---

[1] Monmouth's pension and the good understanding between him and the Court are mentioned in a letter from a Jacobite agent in England, which is in the Archives of the French War Office. The date is April $\frac{8}{18}$. 1690.

[2] The grants of land obtained by Delamere are mentioned by Narcissus Luttrell. It appears from the Treasury Letter Book of 1690 that Delamere continued to dun the government for money after his retirement. As to his general character it would not be safe to trust the representations of his enemies. But his own writings, and the admissions of the divine who preached his funeral sermon, show that his temper was not the most gentle. Clarendon remarks (Dec. 17. 1688) that a little thing sufficed to put Lord Delamere into a passion. In the poem entitled the King of Hearts, Delamere is described as—

"A restless malecontent even when preferred."

His countenance furnished a subject for satire:

"His boding looks a mind distracted show;
And envy sits engraved upon his brow."

and to the Established Church : but he had concurred in the Revolution : he had no misgivings touching the title of William and Mary : he had sworn allegiance to them without any mental reservation ; and he appears to have strictly kept his oath. Between him and Caermarthen there was a close connection. They had acted together cordially in the Northern insurrection ; and they agreed in their political views, as nearly as a very cunning statesman and a very honest country gentleman could be expected to agree.[1] By Caermarthen's influence Lowther was now raised to one of the most important places in the kingdom. Unfortunately it was a place requiring qualities very different from those which suffice to make a valuable county member and chairman of quarter sessions. The tongue of the new First Lord of the Treasury was not sufficiently ready, nor was his temper sufficiently callous for his post. He had neither adroitness to parry, nor fortitude to endure, the gibes and reproaches to which, in his new character of courtier and placeman, he was exposed. There was also something to be done which he was too scrupulous to do ; something which had never been done by Wolsey or Burleigh ; something which has never been done by any English statesman of our generation ; but which, from the time of Charles the Second to the time of George the Third, was one of the most important parts of the business of a minister.

The history of the rise, progress, and decline of parliamentary corruption in England still remains to be written. No subject has called

Rise and progress of parliamentary corruption in England forth a greater quantity of eloquent vituperation and stinging sarcasm. Three generations of serious and of sportive writers wept and laughed over the venality of the senate. That venality was denounced on the hustings, anathematised from the pulpit, and burlesqued on the stage ; was attacked by Pope in brilliant verse, and by Bolingbroke in stately prose, by Swift with savage hatred, and by Gay with festive malice. The voices of Tories and Whigs, of Johnson and Akenside, of Smollett and Fielding, contributed to swell the cry. But none of those who railed or of those who jested took the trouble to verify the phænomena, or to trace them to the real causes.

Sometimes the evil was imputed to the depravity of a particular minister : but, when he had been driven from power, and when those who had most loudly accused him governed in his stead, it was found

---

[1] My notion of Lowther's character has been chiefly formed from two papers written by himself, one of which has been printed, though I believe not published. A copy of the other is among the Mackintosh MSS. Something I have taken from contemporary satires. That Lowther was too ready to expose his life in private encounters is sufficiently proved by the fact that, when he was First Lord of the Treasury, he accepted a challenge from a custom house officer whom he had dismissed. There was a duel ; and Lowther was severely wounded. This event is mentioned in Luttrell's Diary, April 1691.

SIR JOHN LOWTHER

From a mezzotint by Alexander Browne, after a painting by Sir P. Lely that the change of men had produced no change of system. Some-times the evil was imputed to the degeneracy of the national character. Luxury and cupidity, it was said, had produced in our country the same effect which they had produced of old in the Roman republic. The modern Englishman was to the Englishman of the sixteenth cen-tury what Verres and Curio were to Dentatus and Fabricius. Those who held this language were as ignorant and shallow as people generally are who extol the past at the expense of the present. A man of sense would have perceived that, if the English of the time of George the Second had really been more sordid and dishonest than their forefathers, the deterioration would not have shown itself in one place alone. The progress of judicial venality and of official venality would have kept pace with the progress of parliamentary venality. But nothing is more certain than that, while the legislature was becoming more and more venal, the courts of law and the public offices were becoming purer and purer. The representatives of the people were undoubtedly more mer-cenary in the days of Hardwicke and Pelham than in the days of the Tudors. But the Chancellors of the Tudors took plate, jewels, and purses of broad pieces, from suitors without scruple or shame ; and Hardwicke would have committed for contempt any suitor who had dared to bring him a present. The Treasurers of the Tudors raised princely fortunes by the sale of places, titles, and pardons ; and Pelham would have ordered his servants to turn out of his house any man who had offered him money for a peerage or a commissionership of customs. It is evident, therefore, that the prevalence of corruption in the Parlia-ment cannot be ascribed to a general depravation of morals. The taint was local : we must look for some local cause ; and such a cause will without difficulty be found.

Under our ancient sovereigns the House of Commons rarely interfered with the executive administration. The Speaker was charged not to let the members meddle with matters of State. If any gentleman was very troublesome, he was cited before the Privy Council, interrogated, reprimanded, and sent to meditate on his undutiful conduct in the Tower. The Commons did their best to protect themselves by keeping their deliberations secret, by excluding strangers, by making it a crime to repeat out of doors what had passed within doors. But these precau-tions were of small avail. In so large an assembly there were always talebearers, ready to carry the evil report of their brethren to the palace. To oppose the Court was therefore a service of serious danger. In those days, of course, there was little or no buying of votes. For an honest man was not to be bought ; and it was much cheaper to intimi-date or to coerce a knave than to buy him.

For a very different reason there has been no direct buying of votes within the memory of the present generation. The House of Commons is now supreme in the State, but is accountable to the nation. Even those members who are not chosen by large constituent bodies are kept in awe by public opinion. Everything is printed : everything is discussed : every material word uttered in debate is read by a million of people on the morrow. Within a few hours after an important division, the lists of the majority and the minority are scanned and analysed in every town from Plymouth to Inverness. If a name be found where it ought not to be, the apostate is certain to be reminded in sharp language of the promises which he has broken, and of the professions which he has belied. At present, therefore, the best way in which a government can secure the support of a majority of the representative body is by gaining the confidence of the nation.

But between the time when our Parliaments ceased to be controlled by royal prerogative and the time when they began to be constantly and effectually controlled by public opinion there was a long interval. After the Restoration, no government ventured to return to those methods by which, before the civil war, the freedom of deliberation had been restrained. A member could no longer be called to account for his harangues or his votes. He might obstruct the passing of bills of supply : he might arraign the whole foreign policy of the country : he might lay on the table articles of impeachment against all the chief ministers ; and he ran not the smallest risk of being treated as Morrice had been treated by Elizabeth, or Eliot by Charles the First. The senator now stood in no awe of the Court. Nevertheless all the defences behind which the feeble Parliaments of the sixteenth century had entrenched themselves against the attacks of prerogative were not only still kept up, but were extended and strengthened. No politician seems to have been aware that these defences were no longer needed for their original purpose, and had begun to serve a purpose very different. The rules which had been originally designed to secure faithful representatives against the displeasure of the Sovereign, now operated to secure unfaithful representatives against the displeasure of the people, and proved much more effectual for the latter end than they had ever been for the former. It was natural, it was inevitable, that, in a legislative body emancipated from the restraints of the sixteenth century, and not yet subjected to the restraints of the nineteenth century, in a legislative body which feared neither the King nor the public, there should be corruption.

The plague spot began to be visible and palpable in the days of the Cabal. Clifford, the boldest and fiercest of the wicked Five, had the merit of discovering that a noisy patriot, whom it was no longer possible to send to prison, might be turned into a courtier by a goldsmith's note. Clifford's example was followed by his successors. It soon became a proverb that a Parliament resembled a pump. Often, the wits said, when a pump appears to be dry, if a very small quantity of water is poured in, a great quantity of water gushes out : and so, when a Parliament appears to be niggardly, ten thousand pounds judiciously given in bribes will often produce a million in supplies. The evil was not diminished, nay, it was aggravated, by that Revolution which freed our country from so many other evils. The House of Commons was now more powerful than ever as against the Crown, and yet was not more strictly responsible than formerly to the nation. The government had a new motive for buying the members ; and the members had no new motive for refusing to sell themselves. William, indeed, had an aversion to bribery : he resolved to abstain from it ; and, during the first year of his reign, he kept his resolution. Unhappily the events of that year did not encourage him to persevere in his good intentions. As soon as Caermarthen was placed at the head of the internal administration of the realm, a complete change took place. He was in truth no novice in the art of purchasing votes. He had, sixteen years before, succeeded Clifford at the Treasury, had inherited Clifford's tactics, had improved upon them, and had employed them to an extent which would have amazed the inventor. From the day on which Caermarthen was called a second time to the chief direction of affairs, parliamentary corruption continued to be practised, with scarcely any intermission, by a long succession of statesmen, till the close of the American war. Neither of the great English parties can justly charge the other with any peculiar guilt on this account. The Tories were the first who introduced the system and the last who clung to it : but it attained its greatest vigour in the time of Whig ascendency. The extent to which parliamentary support was bartered for money cannot be with any precision ascertained. But it seems probable that the number of hirelings was greatly exaggerated by vulgar report, and was never large, though often sufficient to turn the scale on important divisions. An unprincipled minister eagerly accepted the services of these mercenaries. An honest minister reluctantly submitted, for the sake of the commonwealth, to what he considered as a shameful and odious extortion. But during many years every minister, whatever his personal character might be, consented, willingly or unwillingly, to manage the Parliament in the only way in which the Parliament could then be managed. It at length became as notorious that there was a market for votes at the Treasury as that there was a market for cattle in Smithfield. Numerous demagogues out of power declaimed against this vile traffic : but every one of those demagogues, as soon as he was in power, found himself driven by a kind of fatality to engage in that traffic, or at least to connive at it. Now and then perhaps a man who had romantic notions of public virtue refused to be himself the pay-master of the corrupt crew, and averted his eyes while his less scrupu-lous colleagues did that which he knew to be indispensable, and yet felt to be degrading.   But the instances of this prudery were rare indeed. The doctrine generally received, even among upright and honourable politicians, was that it was shameful to receive bribes, but that it was necessary to distribute them.   It is a remarkable fact that the evil reached the greatest height during the administration of Henry Pelham, a statesman of good intentions, of spotless morals in private life, and of exemplary disinterestedness.   It is not difficult to guess by what argu-ments he and other well meaning men, who, like him, followed the fashion of their age, quieted their consciences.   No casuist, however severe, has denied that it may be a duty to give what it is a crime to take.   It was infamous in Jeffreys to demand money for the lives of the unhappy prisoners whom he tried at Dorchester and Taunton.   But it was not infamous, nay, it was laudable, in the kinsmen and friends of a prisoner to contribute of their substance in order to make up a purse for Jeffreys.   The Sallee rover, who threatened to bastinado a Christian captive to death unless a ransom was forthcoming, was an odious ruffian.   But to ransom a Christian captive from a Sallee rover was, not merely an innocent, but a highly meritorious act.   It is improper in such cases to use the word corruption.   Those who receive the filthy lucre are corrupt already.   He who bribes them does not make them wicked: he finds them so; and he merely prevents their evil propensities from producing evil effects.   And might not the same plea be urged in defence of a minister who, when no other expedient would avail, paid greedy and lowminded members of parliament not to ruin their country?

It was by some such reasoning as this that the scruples of William were overcome.   Honest Burnet, with the uncourtly courage which dis-tinguished him, ventured to remonstrate with the King.   " Nobody," William answered, " hates bribery more than I.   But I have to do with a set of men who must be managed in this vile way or not at all. I must strain a point ; or the country is lost." [1]

It was necessary for the Lord President to have in the House of Commons an agent for the purchase of members ; and Lowther was both too awkward and too scrupulous to be such an agent. Sir John But a man in whom craft and profligacy were united in a Trevor high degree was without difficulty found.   This was the Master of the Rolls, Sir John Trevor, who had been Speaker in the single Parliament held by James.   High as Trevor had risen in the world, there were people who could still remember him a strange looking clerk in the Inner Temple.   Indeed, nobody who had ever seen him was likely

[1] Burnet, ii. 76.

to forget him.   For his grotesque features and his hideous squint were far beyond the reach of caricature.   His parts, which were quick and vigorous, had enabled him early to master the science of chicane. Gambling and betting were his amusements ; and out of·these amusements he contrived to extract much business in the way of his profession.   For his opinion on a question arising out of a wager or a game at chance had as much authority as a judgment of any court in Westminster Hall.   He soon rose to be one of the boon companions whom Jeffreys hugged in fits of maudlin friendship over the bottle at night, and cursed and reviled in court on the morrow.   Under such a teacher, Trevor rapidly became a proficient in that peculiar kind of rhetoric which had enlivened the trials of Baxter and of Alice Lisle.   Report indeed spoke of some scolding matches between the Chancellor and his friend, in which the disciple had been not less voluble and scurrilous than the master.   These contests, however, did not take place till the younger adventurer had attained riches and dignities such that he no longer stood in need of the patronage which had raised him.[1] Among High Churchmen Trevor, in spite of his notorious want of principle, had at this time a certain popularity, which he seems to have owed chiefly to their conviction that, however insincere he might be in general, his hatred of the dissenters was genuine and hearty.   There was little doubt that, in a House of Commons in which the Tories had a majority, he might easily, with the support of the Court, be chosen Speaker.   He was impatient to be again in his old post, which he well knew how to make one of the most lucrative in the kingdom ; and he willingly undertook that secret and shameful office for which Lowther was altogether unqualified.

Richard Hampden was appointed Chancellor of the Exchequer. This appointment was probably intended as a mark of royal gratitude for the moderation of his conduct, and for the attempts which he had made to curb the violence of his Whig friends, and especially of his son.

Godolphin voluntarily left the Treasury ; why, we are not informed. We can scarcely doubt that the dissolution and the result of the general election must have given him pleasure.   For his political opinions leaned towards Toryism ; and he had, in the late reign, done some things which, though not very heinous, stood in need of an indemnity.   It is probable that he did not think it compatible with his personal dignity to sit at the Board below Lowther, who was in rank his inferior.[2]

Godolphin retires

[1] Roger North's Life of Guildford.

[2] Till some years after this time the First Lord of the Treasury was always the man of highest rank at the Board.   Thus Monmouth, Delamere, and Godolphin took their places according to the order of precedence in which they stood as peers.

SIR JOHN TREVOR.

SIR JOHN TREVOR, MASTER OF THE ROLLS

From an engraving by W. Bond in the Sutherland Collection

A new Commission of Admiralty was issued. At the head of the naval administration was placed Thomas Herbert, Earl of Pembroke, a high born and high bred man, who had ranked among the Tories, who had voted for a Regency, and who had married the daughter of Sawyer. That Pembroke's Toryism, however, was not of a narrow and illiberal kind is sufficiently proved by the fact that, immediately after the Revolution, the Essay on the Human Understanding was dedicated to him by John Locke, in token of gratitude for kind offices done in evil times.[1]

Changes at the Admiralty

Nothing was omitted which could reconcile Torrington to this change. For, though he had been found an incapable administrator, he still stood so high in general estimation as a seaman that the government was unwilling to lose his services. He was assured that no slight was intended to him. He could not serve his country at once on the ocean and at Westminster; and it had been thought less difficult to supply his place in his office than on the deck of his flag ship. He was at first very angry, and actually laid down his commission: but some concessions were made to his pride: a pension of three thousand pounds a year and a grant of ten thousand acres of crown land in the Peterborough level were irresistible baits to his cupidity; and, in an evil hour for England, he consented to remain at the head of the naval force on which the safety of her coasts depended.[2]

While these changes were making in the offices round Whitehall, the Commissions of Lieutenancy all over the kingdom were revised. The Tories had, during twelve months, been complaining that their share in the government of the districts in which they lived bore no proportion to their number, to their wealth, and to the consideration which they enjoyed in society. They now regained with great delight their former position in their shires. The Whigs raised a cry that the King was foully betrayed, and that he had been induced by evil counsellors to put the sword into the hands of men who, as soon as a favourable opportunity offered, would turn the edge against himself. In a dialogue which was believed to have been written by the newly created Earl of Warrington, and which had a wide circulation at the time, but has long been forgotten, the Lord Lieutenant of a county was introduced expressing his apprehensions that the majority of his deputies were traitors at heart.[3] But nowhere was the

Changes in the Commissions of Lieutenancy

---

[1] The dedication, however, was thought too laudatory. "The only thing, Mr. Pope used to say, he could never forgive his philosophic master was the dedication to the Essay."—Ruffhead's Life of Pope.

[2] Van Citters to the States General, $\frac{\text{April 25}}{\text{May 5}}$. 1690; Narcissus Luttrell's Diary; Treasury Letter Book, Feb. 4. 16$\frac{89}{90}$.

[3] The Dialogue between a Lord Lieutenant and one of his Deputies will not be found in the

Honoratissimus Thomas Dominus Herbert Comes de Pembroke et Montgomery &c &c Classis Britannicæ et Hiberniæ summus Præfectus &c &c

H. Wissing pinx.   J. Smith fec.

THOMAS HERBERT, EIGHTH EARL OF PEMBROKE

From a mezzotint by J. Smith, after a painting by W. Wissing excitement produced by the new distribution of power so great as in the capital. By a Commission of Lieutenancy which had been issued immediately after the Revolution, the trainbands of London had been put under the command of stanch Whigs. Those powerful and opulent citizens whose names were omitted alleged that the list was filled with elders of Puritan congregations, with Shaftesbury's brisk boys, with Rye House plotters, and that it was scarcely possible to find, mingled with that multitude of fanatics and levellers, a single man sincerely attached to monarchy and to the Church. A new Commission now appeared framed by Caermarthen and Nottingham. They had taken counsel with Compton, the Bishop of the diocese; and Compton was not a very discreet adviser. He had originally been a High Churchman and a Tory. The severity with which he had been treated in the late reign had transformed him into a Latitudinarian and a rebel; and he had now, from jealousy of Tillotson, turned High Churchman and Tory again. The changes which were made by his recommendation raised a storm in the City. The Whigs complained that they were ungratefully proscribed by a government which owed its existence to them; that some of the best friends of King William had been dismissed with contumely to make room for some of his worst enemies, for men who were as unworthy of trust as any Irish Rapparee, for men who had delivered up to a tyrant the charter and the immemorial privileges of London, for men who had made themselves notorious by the cruelty with which they had enforced the penal laws against Protestant dissenters, nay, for men who had sate on those juries which had found Russell and Cornish guilty.[1] The discontent was so great that it seemed, during a short time, likely to cause pecuniary embarrassment to the State. The supplies voted by the late Parliament came in slowly. The wants of the public service were pressing. In such circumstances it was to the citizens of the capital that the government always looked for help; and the government of William had hitherto looked especially to those citizens who professed Whig opinions. Things were now changed. A few eminent Whigs, in their first anger, sullenly refused to advance money. Nay, one or two unexpectedly withdrew considerable sums from the Exchequer.[2] The financial

collection of Warrington's writings which was published in 1694, under the sanction, as it should seem, of his family.

[1] Van Citters to the States General, March $\frac{18}{28}$., April $\frac{4}{14}$. 1690; Narcissus Luttrell's Diary; Burnet, ii. 72.; The Triennial Mayor, or the Rapparees, a Poem, 1691. The poet says of one of the new civic functionaries:

> "Soon his pretence to conscience we can rout,
> And in a bloody jury find him out,
> Where noble Publius worried was with rogues."

[2] Treasury Minute Book, Feb. 5. 16$\frac{89}{90}$.

difficulties might have been serious, had not some wealthy Tories, who,
if Sacheverell's clause had become law, would have been excluded from

HENRY COMPTON, BISHOP OF LONDON

From a mezzotint by J. Simon, after a painting by J. Hargrave

all municipal honours, offered the Treasury a hundred thousand pounds
down, and promised to raise a still larger sum.[1]

[1] Van Citters, Feb. $\frac{11}{21}$., Mar. $\frac{14}{24}$., Mar. $\frac{18}{28}$. 1690.

While the City was thus agitated, came a day appointed by royal proclamation for a general fast. The reasons assigned for this solemn act of devotion were the lamentable state of Ireland and the approaching departure of the King. Prayers were offered up for the safety of His Majesty's person and for the success of his arms. The churches of London were crowded. The most eminent preachers of the capital, who were, with scarcely an exception, either moderate Tories or moderate Whigs, did their best to calm the public mind, and earnestly exhorted their flocks not to withhold, at this great conjuncture, a hearty support from the prince, with whose fate was bound up the fate of the whole nation. Burnet told a large congregation from the pulpit how the Greeks, when the Great Turk was preparing to besiege Constantinople, could not be persuaded to contribute any part of their wealth for the common defence, and how bitterly they repented of their avarice when they were compelled to deliver up to the victorious infidels the treasures which had been refused to the supplications of the last Christian emperor.[1]

The Whigs, however, as a party, did not stand in need of such an admonition. Grieved and angry as they were, they were perfectly
Temper of the Whigs sensible that on the stability of the throne of William depended all that they most highly prized. What some of them might, at this conjuncture, have been tempted to do if they could have found another leader, if, for example, their Protestant Duke, their King Monmouth, had still been living, may be doubted. But their only choice was between the Sovereign whom they had set up and the Sovereign whom they had pulled down. It would have been strange indeed if they had taken part with James in order to punish William, when the worst fault which they imputed to William was that he did not participate in the vindictive feeling with which they remembered the tyranny of James. Much as they disliked the Bill of Indemnity, they had not forgotten the Bloody Circuit. They therefore, even in their ill humour, continued true to their own King, and, while grumbling at him, were ready to stand by him against his adversary with their lives and fortunes.[2]

There were indeed exceptions : but they were very few ; and they were to be found almost exclusively in two classes, which, though widely differing from each other in social position, closely resembled each other in laxity of principle. All the Whigs who are known to have trafficked with Saint Germains, belonged, not to the main body of the party, but either to the head or to the tail. They were either patricians high in rank and office, or caitiffs who had long been em-

[1] Van Citters, March $\frac{14}{24}$. 1690. But he is mistaken as to the preacher. The sermon is extant. It was preached at Bow Church before the Court of Aldermen.

[2] Welwood's Mercurius Reformatus, Feb. 12. 1690.

ployed in the foulest drudgery of faction. To the former class belonged Shrewsbury. Of the latter class the most remarkable specimen was Robert Ferguson. From the day on which the Convention Parliament was dissolved, Shrewsbury began to waver in his allegiance: but that he had ever wavered was not, till long after, suspected by the public. That Ferguson had, a few months after the Revolution, become a furious Jacobite, was no secret to anybody, and ought not to have been matter of surprise to anybody. For his apostasy he could not plead even the miserable excuse that he had been neglected. The ignominious services which he had formerly rendered to his party as a spy, a raiser of riots, a dispenser of bribes, a writer of libels, a prompter of false witnesses, had been rewarded only too prodigally for the honour of the new government. That he should hold any high office was of course impossible. But a sinecure place of five hundred a year had been created for him in the department of the Excise. He now had what to him was opulence: but opulence did not satisfy him. For money indeed he had never scrupled to be guilty of fraud aggravated by hypocrisy: yet the love of money was not his strongest passion. Long habit had developed in him a moral disease from which people who have made political agitation their calling are seldom wholly free. He could not be quiet. Sedition, from being his business, had become his pleasure. It was as impossible for him to live without doing mischief as for an old dram drinker or an old opium eater to live without the daily dose of poison. The very discomforts and hazards of a lawless life had a strange attraction for him. He could no more be turned into a peaceable and loyal subject than the fox can be turned into a shepherd's dog, or than the kite can be taught the habits of the barn door fowl. The Red Indian prefers his hunting ground to cultivated fields and stately cities: the gipsy, sheltered by a commodious roof, and provided with meat in due season, still pines for the ragged tent on the moor and the chance meal of carrion; and even so Ferguson became weary of plenty and security, of his salary, his house, his table, and his coach, and longed to be again the president of societies into which none could enter without a password, the director of secret presses, the distributor of inflammatory pamphlets; to see the walls placarded with descriptions of his person and offers of reward for his apprehension; to have six or seven names, with a different wig and cloak for each, and to change his lodgings thrice a week at dead of night. His hostility was not to Popery or to Protestantism, to monarchical government or to republican government, to the House of Stuart or to the House of Nassau, but to whatever was at the time established.

By the Jacobites this new ally was eagerly welcomed. They were

(marginal note) Dealings of some Whigs with Saint Germains: Shrewsbury; Ferguson

at that moment busied with schemes in which the help of a veteran plotter was much needed. There had been a great stir among them from the day on which it had been announced that William had determined to take the command in Ireland; and they were all looking forward with impatient hope to his departure. He was not one of those princes against whom men lightly venture to set up a standard of rebellion. His courage, his sagacity, the secrecy of his counsels, the success which had generally crowned his enterprises, overawed the vulgar. Even his most acrimonious enemies feared him at least as much as they hated him. While he was at Kensington, ready to take horse at a moment's notice, malecontents who prized their heads and their estates were generally content to vent their hatred by drinking confusion to his hooked nose, and by squeezing with significant energy the orange which was his emblem. But their courage rose when they reflected that the sea would soon roll between him and our island. In the military and political calculations of that age, thirty leagues of water were as important as three hundred leagues now are. The winds and waves frequently interrupted all communication between England and Ireland. It sometimes happened that, during a fortnight or three weeks, not a word of intelligence from London reached Dublin. Twenty English counties might be up in arms long before any rumour that an insurrection was even apprehended could reach Ulster. Early in the spring, therefore, the leading malecontents assembled in London for the purpose of concerting an extensive plan of action, and corresponded assiduously both with France and with Ireland.

Hopes of the Jacobites

Such was the temper of the English factions when, on the twentieth of March, the new Parliament met. The first duty which the Commons had to perform was that of choosing a Speaker. Trevor was proposed by Lowther, was elected without opposition, and was presented and approved with the ordinary ceremonial. The King then made a speech in which he especially recommended to the consideration of the Houses two important subjects, the settling of the revenue and the granting of an amnesty. He represented strongly the necessity of despatch. Every day was precious, the season for action was approaching. " Let not us," he said, " be engaged in debates while our enemies are in the field." [1]

Meeting of the new Parliament

The first subject which the Commons took into consideration was the state of the revenue. A great part of the taxes had, since the accession of William and Mary, been collected under the authority of Acts passed for short terms, and it was now time to determine on a permanent arrangement. A list of the salaries and pensions for which provision was to be made was laid before the House;

Settlement of the revenue

[1] Commons' Journals, March 20, 21, 22. 16$\frac{89}{90}$.

Sꞅ Charles Sedley.

From an Original Picture at Knole, Kent.

SIR CHARLES SEDLEY

From a sketch in the Sutherland Collection, by Thomas Athow, of a painting at Knole and the amount of the sums thus expended called forth very just complaints from the independent members, among whom Sir Charles Sedley distinguished himself by his sarcastic pleasantry. A clever speech which he made against the placemen stole into print and was widely circulated : it has since been often republished ; and it proves, what his poems and plays might make us doubt, that his contemporaries were not mistaken in considering him as a man of parts and vivacity. Unfortunately the ill humour which the sight of the Civil List caused evaporated in jests and invectives without producing any reform.

The ordinary revenue by which the government had been supported before the Revolution had been partly hereditary, and had been partly drawn from taxes granted to each sovereign for life   The hereditary revenue had passed, with the crown, to William and Mary. It was derived from the rents of the royal domains, from fees, from fines, from wine licenses, from the first fruits and tenths of benefices, from the receipts of the Post Office, and from that part of the excise which had, immediately after the Restoration, been granted to Charles the Second and to his successors for ever in lieu of the feudal services due to our ancient kings. The income from all these sources was estimated at between four and five hundred thousand pounds.[1]

Those duties of excise and customs which had been granted to James for life had, at the close of his reign, yielded about nine hundred thousand pounds annually. William naturally wished to have this income on the same terms on which his uncle had enjoyed it ; and his ministers did their best to gratify his wishes. Lowther moved that the grant should be to the King and Queen for their joint and separate lives, and spoke repeatedly and earnestly in defence of this motion. He set forth William's claims to public gratitude and confidence ; the nation rescued from Popery and arbitrary power ; the Church delivered from persecution ; the constitution established on a firm basis. Would the Commons deal grudgingly with a prince who had done more for England than had ever been done for her by any of his predecessors in so short a time, with a prince who was now about to expose himself to hostile weapons and pestilential air in order to preserve the English colony in Ireland, with a prince who was prayed for in every corner of the world where a congregation of Protestants could meet for the worship of God?[2] But on this subject Lowther harangued in vain. Whigs and Tories were equally fixed in the opinion that the liberality of Parliaments had been the chief cause of the disasters of the last thirty years ; that to the liberality of the Parliament of 1660 was to be ascribed the misgovern-

---

[1] Commons' Journals, March 28. 1690, and March 1. and March 20. 168⅞.
[2] Grey's Debates, March 27. and 28. 1690.

ment of the Cabal, that to the liberality of the Parliament of 1685 was to be ascribed the Declaration of Indulgence, and that the Parliament of 1690 would be inexcusable if it did not profit by experience.   After much dispute a compromise was made.   That portion of the excise which had been settled for life on James, and which was estimated at three hundred thousand pounds a year, was settled on William and Mary for their joint and separate lives.   It was supposed that, with the hereditary revenue, and with three hundred thousand a year more from the excise, Their Majesties would have, independent of parliamentary control, between seven and eight hundred thousand a year.   Out of this income was to be defrayed the charge both of the royal household and of those civil offices of which a list had been laid before the House. This income was therefore called the Civil List.   The expenses of the royal household are now entirely separated from the expenses of civil government : but, by a whimsical perversion, the name of Civil List has remained attached to that portion of the revenue which is appropriated to the expenses of the royal household.   It is still more strange that several neighbouring nations should have thought this most unmeaning of all names worth borrowing.   Those duties of customs which had been settled for life on Charles and James successively, and which, in the year before the Revolution, had yielded six hundred thousand pounds, were granted to the Crown for a term of only four years.[1]

William was by no means well pleased with this arrangement.   He thought it unjust and ungrateful in a people whose liberties he had saved to bind him over to his good behaviour.   " The gentlemen of England," he said to Burnet, " trusted King James who was an enemy of their religion and of their laws ; and they will not trust me by whom their religion and their laws have been preserved."   Burnet answered very properly that there was no mark of personal confidence which His Majesty was not entitled to demand, but that this question was not a question of personal confidence.   The Estates of the Realm wished to establish a general principle.   They wished to set a precedent which might secure a remote posterity against evils such as the indiscreet liberality of former Parliaments had produced.   " From those evils Your Majesty has delivered this generation.   By accepting the gift of the Commons on the terms on which it is offered Your Majesty will be also a deliverer of future generations."   William was not convinced : but he had too much wisdom and self-command to give way to his ill humour ; and he accepted graciously what he could not but consider as ungraciously given.[2]

[1] Commons' Journals, Mar. 28. 1690. A very clear and exact account of the way in which the revenue was settled was sent by Van Citters to the States General, April $\frac{7}{17}$. 1690.

[2] Burnet, ii. 43.

The Civil List was charged with an annuity of twenty thousand pounds to the Princess of Denmark, in addition to an annuity of thirty thousand pounds which had been settled on her at the time of her marriage. This arrangement was the result of a compromise which had been effected with much difficulty and after many irritating disputes. The King and Queen had never, since the commencement of their reign, been on very good terms with their sister. That William should have been disliked by a woman who had just sense enough to perceive that his temper was sour and his manners repulsive, and who was utterly incapable of appreciating his higher qualities, is not extraordinary. But Mary was made to be loved. So lively and intelligent a woman could not indeed derive much pleasure from the society of Anne, who, when in good humour, was meekly stupid, and, when in bad humour, was sulkily stupid. Yet the Queen, whose kindness had endeared her to her humblest attendants, would hardly have made an enemy of one whom it was her duty and her interest to make a friend, had not an influence strangely potent and strangely malignant been incessantly at work to divide the Royal House against itself. The fondness of the Princess for Lady Marlborough was such as, in a superstitious age, would have been ascribed to some talisman or potion. Not only had the friends, in their confidential intercourse with each other, dropped all ceremony and all titles, and become plain Mrs. Morley and plain Mrs. Freeman ; but even Prince George, who cared as much for the dignity of his birth as he was capable of caring for anything but claret and calvered salmon, submitted to be Mr. Morley. The Countess boasted that she had selected the name of Freeman because it was peculiarly suited to the frankness and boldness of her character ; and, to do her justice, it was not by the ordinary arts of courtiers that she established and long maintained her despotic empire over the feeblest of minds. She had little of that tact which is the characteristic talent of her sex : she was far too violent to flatter or to dissemble : but, by a rare chance, she had fallen in with a nature on which dictation and contradiction acted as philtres. In this grotesque friendship all the loyalty, the patience, the selfdevotion, was on the side of the mistress. The whims, the haughty airs, the fits of ill temper, were on the side of the waiting woman.

Nothing is more curious than the relation in which the two ladies stood to Mr. Freeman, as they called Marlborough. In foreign countries people knew in general that Anne was governed by the Churchills. They knew also that the man who appeared to enjoy so large a share of her favour was not only a great soldier and politician, but also one of the finest gentlemen of his time, that his face and figure were eminently handsome, his temper at once bland and resolute, his manners at once

Provision
for the
Princess of
Denmark

SARAH JENNINGS, DUCHESS OF MARLBOROUGH, 1660-1744.

From the painting by M. Dahl, in the National Portrait Gallery.

engaging and noble.   Nothing could be more natural than that graces
and accomplishments like his should win a female heart.   On the
Continent therefore many persons imagined that he was Anne's favoured
lover ; and he was so described in contemporary French libels which
have long been forgotten.   In England this calumny never gained credit
even with the vulgar, and is nowhere to be found even in the most ribald
doggrel that was sung about our streets.   In truth the Princess seems
never to have been guilty of a thought inconsistent with her conjugal
vows.   To her, Marlborough, with all his genius and his valour, his
beauty and his grace, was nothing but the husband of her friend.   Direct
power over Her Royal Highness he had none.   He could influence her
only by the instrumentality of his wife ; and his wife was no passive
instrument.   Though it is impossible to discover, in anything that she
ever did, said, or wrote, any indication of superior understanding, her
fierce passions and strong will enabled her often to rule a husband who
was born to rule grave senates and mighty armies.   His courage, that
courage which the most perilous emergencies of war only made cooler
and more steady, failed him when he had to encounter his Sarah's ready
tears and voluble reproaches, the poutings of her lip and the tossings of
her head.   History exhibits to us few spectacles more remarkable than
that of a great and wise man, who, when he had contrived vast and profound schemes of policy, could carry them into effect only by inducing
one foolish woman, who was often unmanageable, to manage another
woman who was more foolish still.

   In one point the Earl and the Countess were perfectly agreed.   They
were equally bent on getting money; though, when it was got, he loved
to hoard it, and she was not unwilling to spend it.[1]   The favour of the
Princess they both regarded as a valuable estate.   In her father's reign
they had begun to grow rich by means of her bounty.   She was naturally
inclined to parsimony ; and even when she was on the throne, her equipages and tables were by no means sumptuous.[2]   It might have been
thought, therefore, that, while she was a subject, thirty thousand a year,
with a residence in the palace, would have been more than sufficient for
all her wants.   There were probably not in the kingdom two noblemen possessed of such an income.   But no income would satisfy the

---

[1] In a contemporary lampoon are these lines :

   " Oh, happy couple ! In their life
     There does appear no sign of strife ;
     They do agree so in the main,
     To sacrifice their souls for gain."

                                        The Female Nine, 1690.

[2] Swift mentions the deficiency of hospitality and magnificence in her household.   Journal to
Stella, August 8. 1711.

greediness of those who governed her. She repeatedly contracted debts which James repeatedly discharged, not without expressing much surprise and displeasure.

The Revolution opened to the Churchills a new and boundless prospect of gain. The whole conduct of their mistress at the great crisis had proved that she had no will, no judgment, no conscience, but theirs. To them she had sacrificed affections, prejudices, habits, interests. In obedience to them, she had joined in the conspiracy against her father : she had fled from Whitehall in the depth of winter, through ice and mire, to a hackney coach : she had taken refuge in the rebel camp : she had consented to yield her place in the order of succession to the Prince of Orange. They saw with pleasure that she, over whom they possessed such boundless influence, possessed no common influence over others. Scarcely had the Revolution been accomplished when many Tories, disliking both the King who had been driven out and the King who had come in, and doubting whether their religion had more to fear from Jesuits or from Latitudinarians, showed a strong disposition to rally round Anne. Nature had made her a bigot. Such was the constitution of her mind that to the religion of her nursery she could not but adhere, without examination and without doubt, till she was laid in her coffin. In the court of her father she had been deaf to all that could be urged in favour of transubstantiation and auricular confession. In the court of her brother in law she was equally deaf to all that could be urged in favour of a general union among Protestants. This slowness and obstinacy made her important. It was a great thing to be the only member of the Royal Family who regarded Papists and Presbyterians with impartial aversion. While a large party was disposed to make her an idol, she was regarded by her two artful servants merely as a puppet. They knew that she had it in her power to give serious annoyance to the government ; and they determined to use this power in order to extort money, nominally for her, but really for themselves. While Marlborough was commanding the English forces in the Low Countries, the execution of the plan was necessarily left to his wife ; and she acted, not as he would doubtless have acted, with prudence and temper, but, as is plain even from her own narrative, with odious violence and insolence. Indeed she had passions to gratify from which he was altogether free. He, though one of the most covetous, was one of the least acrimonious of mankind : but malignity was in her a stronger passion than avarice. She hated easily: she hated heartily; and she hated implacably. Among the objects of her hatred were all who were related to her mistress either on the paternal or on the maternal side. No person who had a natural interest in the Princess could observe without uneasiness the strange infatuation which made her the slave of an imperious and reckless termagant. This the Countess well knew. In her view the Royal Family and the family of Hyde, however they might differ as to other matters, were leagued against her ; and she detested them all, James and James's Queen, William and Mary, Clarendon and Rochester. Now was the time to wreak the accumulated spite of years. It was not enough to obtain a great, a regal, revenue for Anne. That revenue must be obtained by means which would wound and humble those whom the favourite abhorred. It must not be asked, it must not be accepted, as a mark of fraternal kindness, but demanded in hostile tones, and wrung by force from reluctant hands. No application was made to the King and Queen. But they learned with astonishment that Lady Marlborough was indefatigable in canvassing the Tory members of Parliament, that a Princess's party was forming, that the House of Commons would be moved to settle on Her Royal Highness a vast income independent of the Crown. Mary asked her sister what these proceedings meant. "I hear," said Anne, "that my friends have a mind to make me some settlement." It is said, that the Queen, greatly hurt by an expression which seemed to imply that she and her husband were not among her sister's friends, replied with unwonted sharpness, "Of what friends do you speak ? What friends have you except the King and me ?"[1] The subject was never again mentioned between the sisters. Mary was probably sensible that she had made a mistake in addressing herself to one who was merely a passive instrument in the hands of others. An attempt was made to open a negotiation with the Countess. After some inferior agents had expostulated with her in vain, Shrewsbury waited on her. It might have been expected that his intervention would have been successful : for, if the scandalous chronicle of those times could be trusted, he had stood high, too high, in her favour.[2] He was authorised by the King to promise that, if the Princess would desist from soliciting the members of the House of Commons to support her cause, the income of Her Royal Highness should be increased from thirty thousand pounds to fifty thousand. The Countess flatly rejected this offer. The King's word, she had the insolence to hint, was not a sufficient security. "I am confident," said Shrewsbury, "that His Majesty will strictly fulfil his engagements. If he breaks them I will not serve him an hour longer." "That may be very honourable in you," answered the pertinacious vixen : "but it will be very poor comfort to the Princess." Shrewsbury, after vainly attempting to move the servant, was at length admitted to an audience of the mistress. Anne, in language doubtless dictated by her friend Sarah, told him that the

---

[1] Duchess of Marlborough's Vindication. But the Duchess was so abandoned a liar that it is impossible to believe a word that she says, except when she accuses herself.

[2] See the Female Nine.

business had gone too far to be stopped, and must be left to the decision of the Commons.[1]

The truth was that the Princess's prompters hoped to obtain from Parliament a much larger sum than was offered by the King. Nothing less than seventy thousand a year would content them. But their cupidity overreached itself. The House of Commons showed a great disposition to gratify Her Royal Highness. But, when at length her too eager adherents ventured to name the sum which they wished to grant, the murmurs were loud. Seventy thousand a year at a time when the necessary expenses of the State were daily increasing, when the receipt of the customs was daily diminishing, when trade was low, when every gentleman, every merchant, was retrenching something from the charge of his table and his cellar! The general opinion was that the sum which the King was understood to be willing to give would be amply sufficient.[2] At last something was conceded on both sides. The Princess was forced to content herself with fifty thousand a year; and William agreed that this sum should be settled on her by Act of Parliament. She rewarded the services of Lady Marlborough with a pension of a thousand a year;[3] but this was in all probability a very small part of what the Churchills gained by the arrangement.

After these transactions the two royal sisters continued during many months to live on terms of civility and even of apparent friendship. But Mary, though she seems to have borne no malice to Anne, undoubtedly felt against Lady Marlborough as much resentment as a very gentle heart is capable of feeling. Marlborough had been out of England during a great part of the time which his wife had spent in canvassing among the Tories, and, though he had undoubtedly acted in concert with her, had acted, as usual, with temper and decorum. He therefore continued to receive from William many marks of favour which were unaccompanied by any indication of displeasure.

In the debates on the settling of the revenue, the distinction between Whigs and Tories does not appear to have been very clearly marked. In truth, if there was anything about which the two parties were agreed, it was the expediency of granting the customs to the Crown for a time not exceeding four years. But there were other questions which called forth the old animosity in all its strength. The Whigs were now a minority, but a minority formidable in numbers, and more formidable

---

[1] The Duchess of Marlborough's Vindication. With that habitual inaccuracy, which, even when she has no motive for lying, makes it necessary to read every word written or dictated by her with suspicion, she creates Shrewsbury a Duke, and represents herself as calling him "Your Grace." He was not made a Duke till 1694.

[2] Commons' Journals, December 17. and 18. 1689.

[3] Vindication of the Duchess of Marlborough.

in ability.   They carried on the parliamentary war, not less acrimoni-
ously than when they were a majority, but somewhat more artfully.
They brought forward several motions, such as no High Churchman
could well support, yet such as no servant of William and Mary could
well oppose.   The Tory who voted for those motions would run a great
risk of being pointed at as a turncoat by the sturdy Cavaliers of his
county.   The Tory who voted against those motions would run a great
risk of being frowned upon at Kensington.

It was apparently in pursuance of this policy that the Whigs laid on
the table of the House of Lords a bill declaring all the laws passed by
the late Parliament to be valid laws.   No sooner had this bill **Bill declar-**
been read than the controversy of the preceding spring was **ing the Acts
of the**
renewed.   The Whigs were joined on this occasion by almost **preceding
Parliament**
all those noblemen who were connected with the government. **valid**
The rigid Tories, with Nottingham at their head, professed themselves
willing to enact that every statute passed in 1689 should have the same
force that it would have had if it had been passed by a parliament convoked in a regular manner : but nothing would induce them to acknowledge that an assembly of lords and gentlemen, who had come together
without authority from the Great Seal, was constitutionally a Parliament.
Few questions seem to have excited stronger passions than the question,
practically altogether unimportant, whether the bill should or should not
be declaratory.   Nottingham, always upright and honourable, but a
bigot and a formalist, was on this subject singularly obstinate and
unreasonable.   In one debate he lost his temper, forgot the decorum
which in general he strictly observed, and narrowly escaped being committed to the custody of the Black Rod.[1]   After much wrangling, the
Whigs carried their point by a majority of seven.[2]   Many peers signed
a strong protest written by Nottingham.   In this protest the bill, which
was indeed open to verbal criticism, was contemptuously described as
being neither good English nor good sense.   The majority passed a
resolution that the protest should be expunged ; and against this resolution Nottingham and his followers again protested.[3]   The King was
displeased by the pertinacity of his Secretary of State ; so much displeased indeed that Nottingham declared his intention of resigning the
Seals : but the dispute was soon accommodated.   William was too wise
not to know the value of an honest man in a dishonest age.   The very
scrupulosity which made Nottingham a mutineer was a security that he
would never be a traitor.[4]

The Bill went down to the Lower House ; and it was fully expected
that the contest there would be long and fierce : but a single speech

[1] Van Citters, April $\frac{8}{18}$. 1690.   [2] Ibid. ; Luttrell's Diary.

[3] Lords' Journals, April 8. and 10. 1690 ; Burnet, ii. 41.   [4] Van Citters, $\frac{\text{April 25.}}{\text{May 5.}}$ 1690,

settled the question.　Somers, with a force and eloquence which surprised even an audience accustomed to hear him with pleasure, exposed the absurdity of the doctrine held by the High Tories.　" If the Convention,"—it was thus that he argued,—" was not a Parliament, how can we be a Parliament?　An Act of Elizabeth provides that no person shall sit or vote in this House till he has taken the old oath of supremacy. Not one of us has taken that oath.　Instead of it, we have all taken the new oath of supremacy which the late Parliament substituted for the old oath.　It is therefore a contradiction to say that the Acts of the late Parliament are not now valid, and yet to ask us to enact that they shall henceforth be valid.　For either they already are so, or we never can make them so."　This reasoning, which was in truth as unanswerable as that of Euclid, brought the debate to a speedy close.　The bill passed the Commons within forty eight hours after it had been read the first time.[1]

This was the only victory won by the Whigs during the whole session.　They complained loudly in the Lower House of the change

Debate on the changes in the Lieutenancy of London

which had been made in the military government of the city of London.　The Tories, conscious of their strength, and heated by resentment, not only refused to censure what had been done, but determined to express publicly and formally their gratitude to the King for having brought in so many churchmen and turned out so many schismatics.　An address of thanks was moved by Clarges, member for Westminster, who was known to be attached to Caermarthen.　" The alterations which have been made in the City," said Clarges, " show that His Majesty has a tender care of us.　I hope that he will make similar alterations in every county of the realm." The minority struggled hard.　" Will you thank the King," they said, " for putting the sword into the hands of his most dangerous enemies? Some of those whom he has been advised to entrust with military command have not yet been able to bring themselves to take the oath of allegiance to him.　Others were well known, in the evil days, as stanch jurymen, who were sure to find an Exclusionist guilty on any evidence or no evidence."　Nor did the Whig orators refrain from using those topics on which all factions are eloquent in the hour of distress, and which all factions are but too ready to treat lightly in the hour of prosperity.　" Let us not," they said, " pass a vote which conveys a reflection on a large body of our countrymen, good subjects, good Protestants.　The King ought to be the head of his whole people.　Let us not make him the head of a party."　This was excellent doctrine : but it scarcely became the lips of men who, a few weeks before, had opposed the Indemnity Bill and voted for the Sacheverell clause.　The

---

[1] Commons' Journals, April 8. and 9. 1690 ; Grey's Debates ; Burnet, ii. 42.　Van Citters, writing on the 8th, mentions that a great struggle in the Lower House was expected.

address was carried by a hundred and eighty five votes to a hundred and thirty six.[1]

As soon as the numbers had been announced, the minority, smarting from their defeat, brought forward a motion which caused no little embarrassment to the Tory placemen. The oath of allegiance,   **Abjuration** the Whigs said, was drawn in terms far too lax. It might   **Bill** exclude from public employment a few honest Jacobites who were generally too dull to be mischievous : but it was altogether inefficient as a means of binding the supple and slippery consciences of cunning priests, who, while affecting to hold the Jesuits in abhorrence, were proficients in that immoral casuistry which was the worst part of Jesuitism. Some grave divines had openly said, others had even dared to write, that they had sworn fealty to William in a sense altogether different from that in which they had sworn fealty to James. To James they had plighted the entire faith which a loyal subject owes to a rightful sovereign : but, when they promised to bear true allegiance to William, they meant only that they would not, whilst he was able to hang them for rebelling or conspiring against him, run any risk of being hanged. None could wonder that the precepts and example of the malecontent clergy should have corrupted the malecontent laity. When Prebendaries and Rectors were not ashamed to avow that they had equivocated in the very act of kissing the Gospels, it was hardly to be expected that attorneys and taxgatherers would be more scrupulous. The consequence was that every department swarmed with traitors ; that men who ate the King's bread, men who were entrusted with the duty of collecting and disbursing his revenues, of victualling his ships, of clothing his soldiers, of making his artillery ready for the field, were in the habit of calling him an usurper, and of drinking to his speedy downfall. Could any government be safe which was hated and betrayed by its own servants ? And was not the English government exposed to dangers which, even if all its servants were true, might well excite serious apprehensions ? A disputed succession, war with France, war in Scotland, war in Ireland, was not all this enough without treachery in every arsenal and in every custom house ? There must be an oath drawn in language too precise to be explained away, in language which no Jacobite could repeat without the consciousness that he was perjuring himself. Though the zealots of indefeasible hereditary right had in general no objection to swear allegiance to William, they would probably not choose to abjure James. On such grounds as these, an Abjuration Bill of extreme severity was brought into the House of Commons. It was proposed to enact that every person who held any office, civil, military, or spiritual, should, on pain of deprivation, solemnly abjure the

[1] Commons' Journals, April 24. 1690 ; Grey's Debates.

exiled King; that the oath of abjuration might be tendered by any justice of the peace to any subject of Their Majesties; and that, if it were refused, the recusant should be sent to prison, and should lie there as long as he continued obstinate.

The severity of this last provision was generally and most justly blamed. To turn every ignorant meddling magistrate into a state inquisitor, to insist that a plain man, who lived peaceably, who obeyed the laws, who paid his taxes, who had never held and who did not expect ever to hold any office, and who had never troubled his head about problems of political philosophy, should declare, under the sanction of an oath, a decided opinion on a point about which the most learned doctors of the age had written whole libraries of controversial books, and to send him to rot in a gaol if he could not bring himself to swear, would surely have been the height of tyranny. The clause, which required public functionaries, on pain of deprivation, to abjure the deposed King, was not open to the same objections. Yet even against this clause some weighty arguments were urged. A man, it was said, who has an honest heart and a sound understanding, is sufficiently bound by the present oath. Every such man, when he swears to be faithful and to bear true allegiance to King William, does, by necessary implication, abjure King James. There may doubtless be among the servants of the State, and even among the ministers of the Church, some persons who have no sense of honour or religion, and who are ready to forswear themselves for lucre. There may be others who have contracted the pernicious habit of quibbling away the most sacred obligations, and who have convinced themselves that they can innocently make, with a mental reservation, a promise which it would be sinful to make without such a reservation. Against these two classes of Jacobites it is true that the present test affords no security. But will the new test, will any test, be more efficacious? Will a person who has no conscience, or a person whose conscience can be set at rest by immoral sophistry, hesitate to repeat any phrase that you can dictate? The former will kiss the book without any scruple at all. The scruples of the latter will be very easily removed. He now swears allegiance to one King with a mental reservation. He will then abjure the other King with a mental reservation. Do not flatter yourselves that the ingenuity of lawgivers will ever devise an oath which the ingenuity of casuists will not evade. What indeed is the value of any oath in such a matter? Among the many lessons which the troubles of the last generation have left us none is more plain than this, that no form of words, however precise, no imprecation, however awful, ever saved, or ever will save, a government from destruction. Was not the Solemn League and Covenant burned by the common hangman amidst the huzzas of tens of thousands who had themselves subscribed it? Among the statesmen and warriors who bore the chief part in restoring Charles the Second, how many were there who had not repeatedly abjured him? Nay, is it not well known that some of those persons boastfully declared that, if they had not abjured him, they never could have restored him?

The debates were sharp; and the issue during a short time seemed doubtful: for some of the Tories who were in office were unwilling to give a vote which might be thought to indicate that they were lukewarm in the cause of the King whom they served. William, however, took care to let it be understood that he had no wish to impose a new test on his subjects. A few words from him decided the event of the conflict. The bill was rejected thirty six hours after it had been brought in by a hundred and ninety two votes to a hundred and sixty five.[1]

Even after this defeat the Whigs pertinaciously returned to the attack. Having failed in one House they renewed the battle in the other. Five days after the Abjuration Bill had been thrown out in the Commons, another Abjuration Bill, somewhat milder, but still very severe, was laid on the table of the Lords.[2] What was now proposed was that no person should sit in either House of Parliament or hold any office, civil, military, or judicial, without making a declaration that he would stand by William and Mary against James and James's adherents. Every male in the kingdom who had attained the age of sixteen was to make the same declaration before a certain day. If he failed to do so he was to pay double taxes and to be incapable of exercising the elective franchise.

On the day fixed for the second reading, the King came down to the House of Peers. He gave his assent in form to several laws, unrobed, took his seat on a chair of state which had been placed for him, and listened with much interest to the debate. To the general surprise, two noblemen who had been eminently zealous for the Revolution spoke against the proposed test. Lord Wharton, a Puritan who had fought for the Long Parliament, said, with amusing simplicity, that

[1] Commons' Journals, April 24, 25, and 26; Grey's Debates; Narcissus Luttrell's Diary. Narcissus is unusually angry. He calls the bill "a perfect trick of the fanatics to turn out the Bishops and most of the Church of England Clergy." In a Whig pasquinade entitled "A speech intended to have been spoken on the Triennial Bill, on Jan. 28." 169⅔, the King is said to have "browbeaten the Abjuration Bill."

[2] Lords' Journals, May 1. 1690. This Bill is among the Archives of the House of Lords. Burnet confounds it with the bill which the Commons had rejected in the preceding week. Ralph, who saw that Burnet had committed a blunder, but did not see what the blunder was, has, in trying to correct it, added several blunders of his own; and the Oxford editor of Burnet has been misled by Ralph.

he was a very old man, that he had lived through troubled times, that he had taken a great many oaths in his day, and that he was afraid that he had not kept them all. He prayed that the sin might not be laid to his charge; and he declared that he could not consent to lay any more snares for his own soul and for the souls of his neighbours. The Earl of Macclesfield, the captain of the English volunteers who had accompanied William from Helvoetsluys to Torbay, declared that he was much in the same case with Lord Wharton. Marlborough supported the bill. He wondered, he said, that it should be opposed by Macclesfield, who had borne so prominent a part in the Revolution. Macclesfield, irritated by the charge of inconsistency, retorted with terrible severity: "The noble Earl," he said, "exaggerates the share which I had in the deliverance of our country. I was ready, indeed, and always shall be ready, to venture my life in defence of her laws and liberties. But there are lengths to which, even for the sake of her laws and liberties, I could never go. I only rebelled against a bad King: there were those who did much more." Marlborough, though not easily discomposed, could not but feel the edge of this sarcasm: William looked displeased; and the aspect of the whole House was troubled and gloomy. It was resolved by fifty one votes to forty that the bill should be committed; and it was committed, but never reported. After many hard struggles between the Whigs headed by Shrewsbury and the Tories headed by Caermarthen, it was so much mutilated that it retained little more than its name, and did not seem to those who had introduced it to be worth any further contest.[1]

The discomfiture of the Whigs was completed by a communication from the King. Caermarthen appeared in the House of Lords bearing **Act of Grace** in his hand a parchment signed by William. It was an Act of Grace for political offences.

Between an Act of Grace originating with the Sovereign and an Act of Indemnity originating with the Estates of the Realm there are some remarkable distinctions. An Act of Indemnity passes through all the stages through which other laws pass, and may, during its progress, be amended by either House. An Act of Grace is received with peculiar marks of respect, is read only once by the Lords and once by the Commons, and must be either rejected altogether or accepted as it stands.[2] William had not ventured to submit such an Act to the preceding Parliament. But in the new Parliament he was certain of a majority. The minority gave no trouble. The stubborn spirit which

[1] Lords' Journals, May 2. and 3. 1690; Van Citters, May 2.; Narcissus Luttrell's Diary; Burnet, ii. 44.; and Lord Dartmouth's note. The changes made by the Committee may be seen on the bill in the Archives of the House of Lords.

[2] These distinctions were much discussed at the time. Van Citters, May $\frac{29}{30}$. 1690.

PHILIP, FOURTH LORD WHARTON

From the painting by Van Dyck in the Hermitage Gallery. St. Petersburg

had, during two sessions, obstructed the progress of the Bill of Indemnity had been at length broken by defeats and humiliations. Both
Houses stood up uncovered while the Act of Grace was read, and gave
their sanction to it without one dissentient voice.

There would not have been this unanimity had not a few great
criminals been excluded from the benefits of the amnesty. Foremost
among them stood the surviving members of the High Court of Justice
which had sate on Charles the First. With these ancient men were
joined the two nameless executioners who had done their office, with
masked faces, on the scaffold before the Banqueting House. None
knew who they were, or of what rank. It was probable that they had
been long dead. Yet it was thought necessary to declare that, if even
now, after the lapse of forty one years, they should be discovered, they
would still be liable to the punishment of their great crime. Perhaps it
would hardly have been thought necessary to mention these men, if the
animosities of the preceding generation had not been rekindled by the
recent appearance of Ludlow in England. About thirty of the agents
of the tyranny of James were left to the law. With these exceptions,
all political offences, committed before the day on which the royal signature was affixed to the Act, were covered with a general oblivion.[1]
Even the criminals who were by name excluded had little to fear.
Many of them were in foreign countries; and those who were in England
were well assured that, unless they committed some new fault, they
would not be molested.

The Act of Grace the nation owed to William alone; and it is one
of his noblest and purest titles to renown. From the commencement of
the civil troubles of the seventeenth century down to the Revolution,
every victory gained by either party had been followed by a sanguinary
proscription. When the Roundheads triumphed over the Cavaliers,
when the Cavaliers triumphed over the Roundheads, when the fable of
the Popish plot gave the ascendency to the Whigs, when the detection
of the Rye House Plot transferred the ascendency to the Tories, blood,
and more blood, and still more blood, had flowed. Every great explosion and every great recoil of public feeling had been accompanied by
severities which, at the time, the predominant faction loudly applauded,
but which, on a calm review, history and posterity have condemned.
No wise and humane man, whatever may be his political opinions, now
mentions without reprehension the death either of Laud or of Vane,
either of Stafford or of Russell. Of the alternate butcheries the last and
the worst is that which is inseparably associated with the names of
James and Jeffreys. But it assuredly would not have been the last,
perhaps it might not have been the worst, if William had not had the

_____
[1] Stat. 2 W. & M. sess. I. c. 10.

virtue and the firmness resolutely to withstand the importunity of his most zealous adherents. These men were bent on exacting a terrible retribution for all they had undergone during seven disastrous years. The scaffold of Sidney, the gibbet of Cornish, the stake at which Elizabeth Gaunt had perished in the flames for the crime of harbouring a fugitive, the porches of the Somersetshire churches surmounted by the skulls and quarters of murdered peasants, the holds of those Jamaica ships from which every day the carcass of some prisoner dead of thirst and foul air had been flung to the sharks, all these things were fresh in the memory of the party which the Revolution had made, for a time, dominant in the State. Some chiefs of that party had redeemed their necks by paying heavy ransom. Others had languished long in Newgate. Others had starved and shivered, winter after winter, in the garrets of Amsterdam. It was natural that in the day of their power and prosperity they should wish to inflict some part of what they had suffered. During a whole year they pursued their scheme of revenge. They succeeded in defeating Indemnity Bill after Indemnity Bill. Nothing stood between them and their victims, but William's immutable resolution that the glory of the great deliverance which he had wrought should not be sullied by cruelty. His clemency was peculiar to himself. It was not the clemency of an ostentatious man, or of a sentimental man, or of an easy tempered man. It was cold, unconciliating, inflexible. It produced no fine stage effects. It drew on him the savage invectives of those whose malevolent passions he refused to satisfy. It won for him no gratitude from those who owed to him fortune, liberty, and life. While the violent Whigs railed at his lenity, the agents of the fallen tyranny, as soon as they found themselves safe, instead of acknowledging their obligations to him, reproached him in insulting language with the mercy which he had extended to them. His Act of Grace, they said, had completely refuted his Declaration. Was it possible to believe that, if there had been any truth in the charges which he had brought against the late government, he would have granted impunity to the guilty? It was now acknowledged by himself, under his own hand, that the stories by which he and his friends had deluded the nation and driven away the royal family were mere calumnies devised to serve a turn. The turn had been served; and the accusations by which he had inflamed the public mind to madness were coolly withdrawn.[1] But none of these things moved him. He had done well. He had risked his popularity with men who had been his warmest admirers, in order to give repose and security to men by whom his name was never mentioned without a curse. Nor had he conferred a

---

[1] Roger North was one of the many malecontents who were never tired of harping on this string.

less benefit on those whom he had disappointed of their revenge than on those whom he had protected. If he had saved one faction from a proscription, he had saved the other from the reaction which such a proscription would inevitably have produced. If his people did not justly appreciate his policy, so much the worse for them. He had discharged his duty by them. He feared no obloquy ; and he wanted no thanks.

On the twentieth of May the Act of Grace was passed. The King then informed the Houses that his visit to Ireland could no longer be **The Parliament prorogued** delayed, that he had therefore determined to prorogue them, and that, unless some unexpected emergency made their advice and assistance necessary to him, he should not call them again from their homes till the next winter. " Then," he said, " I hope, by the blessing of God, we shall have a happy meeting."

The Parliament had passed an Act providing that, whenever he should go out of England, it should be lawful for Mary to administer the government of the kingdom in his name and her own. It was added that he should nevertheless, during his absence, retain all his authority. Some objections were made to this arrangement. Here, it was said, were two supreme powers in one State. A public functionary might receive diametrically opposite orders from the King and the Queen, and might not know which to obey. The objection was, beyond all doubt, speculatively just ; but there was such perfect confidence and affection between the royal pair that no practical inconvenience was to be apprehended.[1]

As far as Ireland was concerned, the prospects of William were much more cheering than they had been a few months earlier. The **Preparations for the first war** activity with which he had personally urged forward the preparations for the next campaign had produced an extraordinary effect. The nerves of the government were new strung. In every department of the military administration the influence of a vigorous mind was perceptible. Abundant supplies of food, clothing, and medicine, very different in quality from those which Shales had furnished, were sent across Saint George's Channel. A thousand baggage waggons had been made or collected with great expedition ; and, during some weeks, the road between London and Chester was covered with them. Great numbers of recruits were sent to fill the chasms which pestilence had made in the English ranks. Fresh regiments from Scotland, Cheshire, Lancashire, and Cumberland had landed in the Bay of Belfast. The uniforms and arms of the new comers clearly indicated the potent influence of the master's eye. With the British battalions were interspersed several hardy bands of German

[1] Stat. 2 W. & M. sess. 1. c. 6. ; Grey's Debates, April 29., May 1. 5. 6, 7. 1690.

and Scandinavian mercenaries. Before the end of May the English force in Ulster amounted to thirty thousand fighting men. A few more troops and an immense quantity of military stores were on board of a fleet which lay in the estuary of the Dee, and which was ready to weigh anchor as soon as the King was on board.[1]

James ought to have made an equally good use of the time during which his army had been in winter quarters. Strict discipline and regular drilling might, in the interval between November and May, have turned the athletic and enthusiastic peasants who were assembled under his standard into good soldiers. But the opportunity was lost. The Court of Dublin was, during that season of inaction, busied with dice and claret, love letters and challenges. The aspect of the capital was indeed not very brilliant. The whole number of coaches which could be mustered there, those of the King and of the French Legation included, did not amount to forty.[2] But though there was little splendour there was much dissoluteness. Grave Roman Catholics shook their heads and said that the Castle did not look like the palace of a King who gloried in being the champion of the Church.[3] The military administration was as deplorable as ever. The cavalry indeed was, by the exertions of some gallant officers, kept in a high state of efficiency. But a regiment of infantry differed in nothing but name from a large gang of Rapparees. Indeed a gang of Rapparees gave less annoyance to peaceable citizens, and more annoyance to the enemy, than a regiment of infantry. Avaux strongly represented, in a memorial which he delivered to James, the abuses which made the Irish foot a curse and a scandal to Ireland. Whole companies, said the ambassador, quit their colours on the line of march and wander to right and left pillaging and destroying : the soldier takes no care of his arms : the captain never troubles himself to ascertain whether the arms are in good order : the consequence is that one man in every three has lost his musket, and that another man in every three has a musket that will not go off. Avaux adjured the King to prohibit marauding, to give orders that the troops should be regularly exercised, and to punish every officer who suffered his men to neglect their weapons and accoutrements. If these things were done, His Majesty might hope to have, in the approaching spring, an army with which the enemy would be unable to contend. This was good advice : but James was so far from taking it that he would hardly listen to it with patience. Before he had heard

Administration of James at Dublin

---

[1] Story's Impartial History ; Narcissus Luttrell's Diary.   [2] Avaux, Jan. $\frac{15}{25}$. 1690.

[3] Macariæ Excidium. This most curious work has been recently edited with great care and diligence by Mr. O'Callaghan. I owe so much to his learning and industry that I most readily excuse the national partiality which sometimes, I cannot but think, perverts his judgment. When I quote the Macariæ Excidium, I always quote the Latin text. The English version is, I am convinced, merely a translation from the Latin, and a very careless and imperfect translation.

eight lines read he flew into a passion and accused the ambassador of exaggeration. "This paper, Sir," said Avaux, "is not written to be published. It is meant solely for Your Majesty's information ; and, in a paper meant solely for Your Majesty's information, flattery and disguise would be out of place : but I will not persist in reading what is so disagreeable." "Go on," said James very angrily; "I will hear the whole." He gradually became calmer, took the memorial, and promised to adopt some of the suggestions which it contained. But his promise was soon forgotten.[1]

His financial administration was of a piece with his military administration. His one fiscal resource was robbery, direct or indirect. Every Protestant who had remained in any part of the three southern provinces of Ireland was robbed directly, by the simple process of taking money out of his strong box, drink out of his cellars, fuel from his turf stack, and clothes from his wardrobe. He was robbed indirectly by a new issue of counters, smaller in size and baser in material than any which had yet borne the image and superscription of James. Even brass had begun to be scarce at Dublin ; and it was necessary to ask assistance from Lewis, who charitably bestowed on his ally an old cracked piece of cannon to be coined into crowns and shillings.[2]

But the French King had determined to send over succours of a very different kind. He proposed to take into his own service, and to form by the best discipline then known in the world, four Irish regiments. They were to be commanded by Macarthy, who had been severely wounded and taken prisoner at Newton Butler. His wounds had been healed ; and he had regained his liberty by violating his parole. This disgraceful breach of faith he had made more disgraceful by paltry tricks and sophistical excuses which would have become a Jesuit better than a gentleman and a soldier. Lewis was willing that the Irish regiments should be sent to him in rags and unarmed, and insisted only that the men should be stout, and that the officers should not be bankrupt traders and discarded lacqueys, but, if possible, men of good family who had seen service. In return for these troops, who were in number not quite four thousand, he undertook to send to Ireland between seven and eight thousand excellent French infantry, who were likely in a day of battle to be of more use than all the kernes of Leinster, Munster, and Connaught together.[3]

An auxiliary force sent from France to Ireland

[1] Avaux, Nov. $\frac{14}{24}$. 1689.

[2] Louvois writes to Avaux, $\frac{\text{Dec. 26.}}{\text{Jan. 5.}}$ 168$\frac{9}{10}$: "Comme le Roy a veu par vos lettres que le Roy d'Angleterre craignoit de manquer de cuivre pour faire de la monnoye, Sa Majesté a donné ordre que l'on mist sur le bastiment qui portera cette lettre une pièce de canon du calibre de deux qui est éventée, de laquelle ceux qui travaillent à la monnoye du Roy d'Angleterre pourront se servir pour continuer a faire de la monnoye."

[3] Louvois to Avaux, Nov. $\frac{1}{11}$. 1689. The force sent by Lewis to Ireland appears by the lists at the French War Office to have amounted to seven thousand two hundred and ninety one men

One great error he committed.   The army which he was sending to assist James, though small indeed when compared with the army of Flanders or with the army of the Rhine, was destined for a service on which the fate of Europe might depend, and ought therefore to have been commanded by a general of eminent abilities.   There was no want of such generals in the French service.   But James and his Queen begged hard for Lauzun, and carried this point against the strong representations of Avaux, against the advice of Louvois, and against the judgment of Lewis himself.

When Lauzun went to the cabinet of Louvois to receive instructions, the wise minister held language which showed how little confidence he felt in the vain and eccentric knight errant.   " Do not, for God's sake, suffer yourself to be hurried away by your desire for fighting.   Put all your glory in tiring the English out ; and, above all things, maintain strict discipline." [1]

Not only was the appointment of Lauzun in itself a bad appointment : but, in order that one man might fill a post for which he was unfit, it was necessary to remove two men from posts for which they were eminently fit.   Immoral and hardhearted as Rosen and Avaux were, Rosen was a skilful captain, and Avaux was a skilful politician. Though it is not probable that they would have been able to avert the doom of Ireland, it is probable that they might have been able to protract the contest ; and it was evidently for the interest of France that the contest should be protracted.   But it would have been an affront to the old general to put him under the orders of Lauzun ; and between the ambassador and Lauzun there was such an enmity that they could not be expected to act cordially together.   Both Rosen and Avaux, therefore, were, with many soothing assurances of royal approbation and favour, recalled to France.   They sailed from Cork early in the spring by the fleet which had conveyed Lauzun thither.[2]   Lauzun had no sooner landed than he found that, though he had been long expected, nothing had been prepared for his reception.   No lodgings had been provided for his men, no place of security for his stores, no horses, no carriages.[3]   His troops had to undergo the hardships of a long march through a desert before they arrived at Dublin.   At Dublin, indeed,

of all ranks.   At the French War Office is a letter from Marshal d'Estrées who saw the four Irish regiments soon after they had landed at Brest.   He describes them as " mal chaussés, mal vêtus, et n'ayant point d'uniforme dans leurs habits, si ce n'est qu'ils sont tous fort mauvais."   A very exact account of Macarthy's breach of parole will be found in Mr. O'Callaghan's History of the Irish Brigades.   I am sorry that a writer to whom I owe so much should try to vindicate conduct which, as described by himself, was in the highest degree dishonourable.

[1] Lauzun to Louvois, $\frac{May\ 28.}{June\ 7.}$ and June $\frac{18.}{28.}$. 1690, at the French War Office.

[2] See the later letters of Avaux.

[3] Avaux to Louvois, March $\frac{14.}{24.}$. 1690 ; Lauzun to Louvois, $\frac{March\ 23.}{April\ 2.}$

they found tolerable accommodation. They were billeted on Protestants, lived at free quarter, had plenty of bread, and threepence a day. Lauzun was appointed Commander in Chief of the Irish army, and took up his residence in the Castle.[1] His salary was the same with that of the Lord Lieutenant, eight thousand Jacobuses, equivalent to ten thousand pounds sterling, a year. This sum James offered to pay, not in the brass which bore his own effigy, but in French gold. But Lauzun, among whose faults avarice had no place, refused to fill his own coffers from an almost empty treasury.[2]

On him and on the Frenchmen who accompanied him the misery of the Irish people and the imbecility of the Irish administration produced an effect which they found it difficult to describe. Lauzun wrote to Louvois that the Court and the whole kingdom were in a state not to be imagined by a person who had always lived in happier countries. It was, he said, a chaos, such as he had read of in the book of Genesis. The whole business of all the public functionaries was to quarrel with each other, and to plunder the government and the people. After he had been about a month at the Castle, he declared that he would not go through such another month for all the world. His ablest officers confirmed his testimony.[3] One of them, indeed, was so unjust as to represent the people of Ireland, not merely as ignorant and idle, which they were, but as hopelessly stupid and unfeeling, which they assuredly were not. The English policy, he said, had so completely brutalised them that they could hardly be called human beings. They were insensible to praise and blame, to promises and threats. And yet it was pity of them : for they were physically the finest race of men in the world.[4]

By this time Schomberg had opened the campaign auspiciously. He had with little difficulty taken Charlemont, the last important fastness which the Irish occupied in Ulster. But the great work of reconquering the three southern provinces of the island he deferred till William should arrive. William meanwhile was busied in making arrangements for the government and defence of England during his absence. He well knew that the Jacobites were on the alert. They had not till very lately been an united and organised faction. There had been, to use Melfort's

---

[1] Story's Impartial History ; Lauzun to Louvois, May $\frac{2 0}{3 0}$. 1690.

[2] Lauzun to Louvois, $\frac{\text{May 28.}}{\text{June 7.}}$ 1690.

[3] Lauzun to Louvois, April $\frac{2}{1 2}$., May $\frac{1 0}{2 0}$. 1690. La Hoguette, who held the rank of Maréchal de Camp, wrote to Louvois to the same effect about the same time.

[4] "La politique des Anglois a été de tenir ces peuples cy comme des esclaves, et si bas qu'il ne leur estoit pas permis d'apprendre à lire et à écrire. Cela les a rendu si bestes qu'ils n'ont presque point d'humanité. Rien ne les esmeut. Ils sont peu sensibles à l'honneur ; et les menaces ne les estonnent point. L'interest même ne les peut engager au travail. Ce sont pourtant les gens du monde les mieux faits."—Desgrigny to Louvois, $\frac{\text{May 27.}}{\text{June 6.}}$ 1690.

PLAN OF CHARLEMONT

From George Story's Impartial History of the Wars of Ireland, 1693

phrase, numerous gangs, which were all in communication with James at Dublin Castle, or with Mary of Modena at Saint Germains, but which had no connection with each other and were unwilling to trust each other.[1] But since it had been known that the usurper was about to cross the sea, and that his sceptre would be left in a female hand, these gangs had been drawing close together, and had begun to form one extensive confederacy. Clarendon, who had refused the oaths, and Ailesbury, who had dishonestly taken them, were among the chief traitors. Dartmouth, though he had sworn allegiance to the sovereigns who were in possession, was one of their most active enemies, and undertook what may be called the maritime department of the plot. His mind was constantly occupied by schemes, disgraceful to an English seaman, for the destruction of the English fleets and arsenals. He was in close communication with some naval officers, who, though they served the new government, served it sullenly and with half a heart; and he flattered himself that by promising these men ample rewards, and by artfully inflaming the jealous animosity with which they regarded the Dutch flag, he should prevail on them to desert and to carry their ships into some French or Irish port.[2]

Plan of the English Jacobites; Clarendon, Ailesbury, Dartmouth

The conduct of Penn was scarcely less scandalous. He was a zealous and busy Jacobite; and his new way of life was even more unfavourable than his late way of life had been to moral purity. It was hardly possible to be at once a consistent Quaker and a courtier: but it was utterly impossible to be at once a consistent Quaker and a conspirator. It is melancholy to relate that Penn, while professing to consider even defensive war as sinful, did everything in his power to bring a foreign army into the heart of his own country. He wrote to inform James that the adherents of the Prince of Orange dreaded nothing so much as an appeal to the sword, and that, if England were now invaded from France or from Ireland, the number of Royalists would appear to be greater than ever. Avaux thought this letter so important, that he sent a translation of it to Lewis.[3] A good effect, the

Penn

[1] See Melfort's Letters to James written in October 1689. They are among the Nairne Papers, and were printed by Macpherson.

[2] Life of James, ii. 443. 450.; and Trials of Ashton and Preston.

[3] Avaux wrote thus to Lewis on the 5th of June 1689: "Il nous est venu des nouvelles assez considérables d'Angleterre et d'Escosse. Je me donne l'honneur d'en envoyer des mémoires à vostre Majesté, tels que je les ay receus du Roy de la Grande Bretagne. Le commencement des nouvelles dattées d'Angleterre est la copie d'une lettre de M. Pen, que j'ay veue en original." The Mémoire des Nouvelles d'Angleterre et d'Escosse, which was sent with this despatch, begins with the following sentences, which must therefore have been part of Penn's letter: " Le Prince d'Orange commence d'estre fort dégoutté de l'humeur des Anglois; et la face des choses change bien viste, selon la nature des insulaires; et sa santé est fort mauvaise. Il y a un nuage qui commence à se former au nord des deux royaumes, où le Roy a beaucoup d'amis, ce qui donne

shrewd ambassador wrote, had been produced, by this and similar communications, on the mind of King James.   His Majesty was at last
convinced that he could recover his dominions only sword in hand.   It
is a curious fact that it should have been reserved for the great preacher
of peace to produce this conviction in the mind of the old tyrant.[1]
Penn's proceedings had not escaped the observation of the government.
Warrants had been out against him ; and he had been taken into
custody ; but the evidence against him had not been such as would
support a charge of high treason : he had, as, with all his faults, he
deserved to have, many friends in every party : he therefore soon
regained his liberty, and returned to his plots.[2]

But the chief conspirator was Richard Graham, Viscount Preston,
who had, in the late reign, been Secretary of State.   Though a peer in
Scotland, he was only a baronet in England.   He had, indeed,   Preston
received from Saint Germains an English patent of nobility,
but the patent bore a date posterior to that flight which the Convention
had pronounced an abdication.   The Lords had, therefore, not only
refused to admit him to a share of their privileges, but had sent him to
prison for presuming to call himself one of their order.   He had, however, by humbling himself, and by withdrawing his claim, obtained his
liberty.[3]   Though the submissive language which he had condescended
to use on this occasion did not indicate a spirit prepared for martyrdom,
he was regarded by his party, and by the world in general, as a man of
courage and honour.   He still retained the seals of his office, and was
still considered by the adherents of indefeasible hereditary right as the
real Secretary of State.   He was in high favour with Lewis, at whose
court he had formerly resided, and had, since the Revolution, been
entrusted by the French government with considerable sums of money
for political purposes.[4]

While Preston was consulting in the capital with the other heads of
the faction, the rustic Jacobites were laying in arms, holding musters,

beaucoup d'inquiétude aux principaux amis du Prince d'Orange, qui, estant riches, commencent
à estre persuadez que ce sera l'espée qui décidera de leur sort, ce qu'ils ont tant taché d'éviter.
Ils appréhendent une invasion d'Irlande et de France ; et en ce cas le Roy aura plus d'amis que
jamais."

[1] " Le bon effet, Sire, que ces lettres d'Escosse et d'Angleterre ont produit, est qu'elles ont
enfin persuadé le Roy d'Angleterre qu'il ne recouvrera ses estats que les armes à la main ; et ce
n'est pas peu de l'en avoir convaincu."

[2] Van Citters to the States General, March $\frac{1}{11}$. 1689.   Van Citters calls Penn " den bekenden
Archquaker."

[3] See his trial in the Collection of State Trials, and the Lords' Journals of Nov. 11, 12. and
27. 1689.

[4] One remittance of two thousand pistoles is mentioned in a letter of Croissy to Avaux, Feb.
$\frac{16}{24}$. 1689.   James, in a letter dated Jan. 26. 1689, directs Preston to consider himself as still
Secretary, notwithstanding Melfort's appointment.

and forming themselves into companies, troops, and regiments.   There
were alarming symptoms in Worcestershire.   In Lancashire many gentlemen had received commissions signed by James, called themselves
colonels and captains, and made out long lists of noncommissioned
officers and privates.   Letters from Yorkshire brought news that large
bodies of men, who seemed to have met for no good purpose, had been
seen on the moors near Knaresborough.   Letters from Newcastle gave
an account of a great match at football which had been played in
Northumberland, and was suspected to have been a pretext for a gathering of the disaffected.   In the crowd, it was said, were a hundred
and fifty horsemen well mounted and armed, of whom many were
Papists.[1]

Meantime packets of letters full of treason were constantly passing
and repassing between Kent and Picardy, and between Wales and
Ireland.   Some of the messengers were honest fanatics : but others
were mere mercenaries, and trafficked in the secrets of which they were
the bearers.

Of these double traitors the most remarkable was William Fuller.
This man has himself told us that, when he was very young, he fell in
The
Jacobites with a pamphlet which contained an account of the flagitious
betrayed by life and horrible death of Dangerfield.   The boy's imagination
Fuller was set on fire : he devoured the book : he almost got it by
heart ; and he was soon seized, and ever after haunted, by a strange
presentiment that his fate would resemble that of the wretched adventurer whose history he had so eagerly read.[2]   It might have been
supposed that the prospect of dying in Newgate, with a back flayed and
an eye knocked out, would not have seemed very attractive.   But
experience proves that there are some distempered minds for which
notoriety, even when accompanied with pain and shame, has an irresistible fascination.   Animated by this loathsome ambition, Fuller equalled,
and perhaps surpassed, his model.   He was bred a Roman Catholic,
and was page to Lady Melfort, when Lady Melfort shone at Whitehall
as one of the loveliest women in the train of Mary of Modena.   After
the Revolution, he followed his mistress to France, was repeatedly
employed in delicate and perilous commissions, and was thought at
Saint Germains to be a devoted servant of the House of Stuart.   In

---

[1] Narcissus Luttrell's Diary ; Commons' Journals, May 14, 15. 20. 1690 ; Kingston's True
History, 1697.

[2] The Whole Life of Mr. William Fuller, being an impartial Account of his Birth, Education,
Relations and Introduction into the service of the late King James and his Queen, together with
a True Discovery of the Intrigues for which he lies now confined ; as also of the Persons that
employed and assisted him therein, with his Hearty Repentance for the Misdemeanours he did
in the late Reign, and all others whom he hath injured ; impartially writ by Himself during his
Confinement in the Queen's Bench, 1703.   Of course I shall use this narrative with caution.

truth, however, he had, in the course of one of his expeditions to London, sold himself to the new government, and had abjured the faith in which he had been brought up. The honour, if it is to be so called, of

From an engraving in the British Museum

turning him from a worthless Papist into a worthless Protestant he ascribed, with characteristic impudence, to the lucid reasoning and blameless life of Tillotson.

In the spring of 1690, Mary of Modena wished to send to her correspondents in London some highly important despatches. As these despatches were too bulky to be concealed in the clothes of a single messenger, it was necessary to employ two confidential persons. Fuller was one. The other was a zealous young Jacobite named Crone. Before they set out, they received full instructions from the Queen herself. Not a scrap of paper was to be detected about them by an ordinary search : but their buttons contained letters written in invisible ink.

The pair proceeded to Calais. The governor of that town furnished them with a boat, which, under cover of the night, set them on the low marshy coast of Kent, near the lighthouse of Dungeness. They walked to a farmhouse, procured horses, and took different roads to London. Fuller hastened to the palace at Kensington, and delivered the documents with which he was charged into the King's hand. The first letter which William unrolled seemed to contain only florid compliments : but a pan of charcoal was lighted : a liquor well known to the diplomatists of that age was applied to the paper : an unsavoury steam filled the closet ; and lines full of grave meaning began to appear.

The first thing to be done was to secure Crone. He had unfortunately had time to deliver his letters before he was caught : but a snare was laid for him into which he easily fell. In truth the sincere Jacobites were generally wretched plotters. There was among them an unusually large proportion of sots, braggarts, and babblers ; and Crone was one of these. Had he been wise, he would have shunned places of public resort, kept strict guard over his tongue, and stinted himself to one bottle at a meal. He was found by the messengers of the government at a tavern table in Gracechurch Street, swallowing bumpers to the health of King James, and ranting about the coming restoration, the French fleet, and the thousands of honest Englishmen who were awaiting the signal to rise in arms for their rightful Sovereign. He was carried to the Secretary's office at Whitehall. He at first seemed to be confident and at his ease : but when, among the bystanders, Fuller appeared at liberty, and in a fashionable garb, with a sword, the prisoner's courage fell; and he was scarcely able to articulate.[1]

Crone arrested

The news that Fuller had turned king's evidence, that Crone had been arrested, and that important letters from Saint Germains were in the hands of William, flew fast through London, and spread dismay among all who were conscious of guilt.[2] It was true that the testimony of one witness, even if that witness had been more respectable than

[1] Fuller's Life of himself.
[2] Clarendon's Diary, March 6. 1690 ; Narcissus Luttrell's Diary.

Fuller, was not legally sufficient to convict any person of high treason. But Fuller had so managed matters that several witnesses could be produced to corroborate his evidence against Crone; and, if Crone, under the strong terror of death, should imitate Fuller's example, the heads of all the chiefs of the conspiracy would be at the mercy of the government. The spirits of the Jacobites rose, however, when it was known that Crone, though repeatedly interrogated by those who had him in their power, and though assured that nothing but a frank confession could save his life, had resolutely continued silent. What effect a verdict of Guilty and the near prospect of the gallows might produce on him remained to be seen. His accomplices were by no means willing that his fortitude should be tried by so severe a test. They therefore employed numerous artifices, legal and illegal, to avert a conviction. A woman named Clifford, with whom he had lodged, and who was one of the most active and cunning agents of the Jacobite faction, was entrusted with the duty of keeping him steady to the cause, and of rendering to him services from which scrupulous or timid agents might have shrunk. When the dreaded day came, Fuller was too ill to appear in the witness box, and the trial was consequently postponed. He asserted that his malady was not natural, that a noxious drug had been administered to him in a dish of porridge, that his nails were discoloured, that his hair came off, and that able physicians pronounced him poisoned. But such stories, even when they rest on authority much better than his, ought to be received with very great distrust.

While Crone was awaiting his trial, another agent of the Court of Saint Germains, named Tempest, was seized on the road between Dover and London, and was found to be the bearer of numerous letters addressed to malecontents in England.[1] Every day it became more plain that the State was surrounded by dangers; and yet it was absolutely necessary that, at this conjuncture, the Chief of the State should quit his post.

William, with painful anxiety, such as he alone was able to conceal under an appearance of stoical serenity, prepared to take his departure. Mary was in agonies of grief; and her distress affected him Difficulties more than was imagined by those who judged of his heart by of William his demeanour.[2] He knew too that he was about to leave her surrounded by difficulties with which her habits had not qualified her to contend. She would be in constant need of wise and upright counsel; and where was such counsel to be found? There were indeed among his servants many able men and a few virtuous men. But, even when he was present, their political and personal animosities had too often

[1] Clarendon's Diary, May 10. 1690.
[2] He wrote to Portland, "Je plains la povre reine, qui est en des terribles afflictions."

made both their abilities and their virtues useless to him.   What chance
was there that the gentle Mary would be able to restrain that party
spirit and that emulation which had been but very imperfectly kept in
order by her resolute and politic husband?   If the interior cabinet
which was to assist the Queen were composed exclusively either of
Whigs or of Tories, half the nation would be disgusted.   Yet, if Whigs
and Tories were mixed, it was certain that there would be constant
dissension.   Such was William's situation that he had only a choice of
evils.

All these difficulties were increased by the conduct of Shrewsbury.
The character of this man is a curious study.   He seemed to be the
Conduct of petted favourite both of nature and of fortune.   Illustrious
Shrewsbury birth, exalted rank, ample possessions, fine parts, extensive
acquirements, an agreeable person, manners singularly graceful and
engaging, combined to make him an object of admiration and envy.
But, with all these advantages, he had some moral and intellectual
peculiarities which made him a torment to himself and to all connected
with him.   His conduct at the time of the Revolution had given the
world a high opinion, not merely of his patriotism, but of his courage,
energy, and decision.   It should seem, however, that youthful enthusiasm
and the exhilaration produced by public sympathy and applause had, on
that occasion, raised him above himself.   Scarcely any other part of
his life was of a piece with that splendid commencement.   He had
hardly become Secretary of State when it appeared that his nerves
were too weak for such a post.   The daily toil, the heavy responsibility,
the failures, the mortifications, the obloquy, which are inseparable from
power, broke his spirit, soured his temper, and impaired his health.   To
such natures as his the sustaining power of high religious principle seems
to be peculiarly necessary ; and unfortunately Shrewsbury had, in the
act of shaking off the yoke of that superstition in which he had been
brought up, liberated himself also from more salutary bands which might
perhaps have braced his too delicately constituted mind into steadfastness and uprightness.   Destitute of such support, he was, with great
abilities, a weak man, and, though endowed with many amiable and
attractive qualities, could not be called an honest man.   For his own
happiness, he should either have been much better or much worse.   As
it was, he never knew either that noble peace of mind which is the
reward of rectitude, or that abject peace of mind which springs from
impudence and insensibility.   Few people who have had so little
power to resist temptation have suffered so cruelly from remorse and
shame.

To a man of this temper the situation of a minister of state during
the year which followed the Revolution must have been constant torture.

The difficulties by which the government was beset on all sides, the malignity of its enemies, the unreasonableness of its friends, the virulence with which the hostile factions fell on each other and on every mediator who attempted to part them, might indeed have discouraged a more resolute spirit. Before Shrewsbury had been six months in office, he had completely lost heart and head. He began to address to William letters which it is difficult to imagine that a prince so strongminded can have read without mingled compassion and contempt. " I am sensible," —such was the constant burden of these epistles,—" that I am unfit for my place. I cannot exert myself. I am not the same man that I was half a year ago. My health is giving way. My mind is on the rack. My memory is failing. Nothing but quiet and retirement can restore me." William returned friendly and soothing answers ; and for a time these answers calmed the troubled mind of his minister.[1] But at length the dissolution, the general election, the change in the Commissions of Peace and Lieutenancy, and finally the debates on the two Abjuration Bills, threw Shrewsbury into a state bordering on distraction. He was angry with the Whigs for using the King ill, and still more angry with the King for showing favour to the Tories. At what moment and by what influence the unhappy man was induced to commit a treason, the consciousness of which threw a dark shade over all his remaining years, is not accurately known. But it is highly probable that his mother, who, though the most abandoned of women, had great power over him, took a fatal advantage of some unguarded hour, when he was irritated by finding his advice slighted, and that of Danby and Nottingham preferred. She was still a member of that Church which her son had quitted, and may have thought that, by reclaiming him from rebellion, she might make some atonement for the violation of her marriage vow and the murder of her lord.[2] What is certain is that, before the end of the spring of 1690, Shrewsbury had offered his services to James, and that James had accepted them. One proof of the sincerity of the convert was demanded. He must resign the seals which he had taken from the hand of the usurper.[3] It is probable that Shrewsbury had scarcely committed his fault when he began to repent of it. But he had not strength of mind to stop short in the path of evil. Loathing his

---

[1] See the Letters of Shrewsbury in Coxe's Correspondence, Part I. chap. i.

[2] That Lady Shrewsbury was a Jacobite, and did her best to make her son so, is certain from Lloyd's Paper of May 1694, which is among the Nairne MSS., and was printed by Macpherson.

[3] This is proved by a few words in a paper which James, in November 1692, laid before the French government. " Il y a," says he, " le Comte de Shrusbery, qui, étant Secrétaire d'Etat du Prince d'Orange, s'est défait de sa charge par mon ordre." One copy of this most valuable paper is in the Archives of the French Foreign Office. Another is among the Nairne MSS. in the Bodleian Library. A translation into English will be found in Macpherson's collection.

own baseness, dreading a detection which must be fatal to his honour, afraid to go forward, afraid to go back, he underwent tortures of which it is impossible to think without commiseration.   The true cause of his distress was as yet a profound secret : but his mental struggles and changes of purpose were generally known, and furnished the town, during some weeks, with topics of conversation.   One night, when he was actually setting out in a state of great excitement for the palace, with the seals in his hand, he was induced by Burnet to defer his resignation for a few hours.   Some days later, the eloquence of Tillotson was employed for the same purpose.[1]   Three or four times the Earl laid the ensigns of his office on the table of the royal closet, and was three or four times induced, by the kind expostulations of the master whom he was conscious of having wronged, to take them up and carry them away.   Thus the resignation was deferred till the eve of the King's departure.   By that time agitation had thrown Shrewsbury into a low fever.   Bentinck, who made a last effort to persuade him to retain office, found him in bed and too ill for conversation.[2]   The resignation so often tendered was at length accepted ; and during some months Nottingham was the only Secretary of State.

It was no small addition to William's troubles that, at such a moment, his government should be weakened by this defection.   He **The Council of Nine** tried, however, to do his best with the materials which remained to him, and finally selected nine privy councillors, by whose advice he enjoined Mary to be guided.   Four of these, Devonshire, Dorset, Monmouth, and Edward Russell, were Whigs.   The other five, Caermarthen, Pembroke, Nottingham, Marlborough, and Lowther, were Tories.[3]

William ordered the Nine to attend him at the office of the Secretary of State.   When they were assembled, he came leading in the Queen, desired them to be seated, and addressed to them a few earnest and weighty words.   "She wants experience," he said : "but I hope that, by choosing you to be her counsellors, I have supplied that defect. I put my kingdom into your hands.   Nothing foreign or domestic shall be kept secret from you.   I implore you to be diligent and to be united."[4] In private he told his wife what he thought of the characters of the

---

[1] Burnet, ii. 45.   [2] Shrewsbury to Somers, Sept. 22. 1697.

[3] Among the State Poems (vol. ii. p. 211.) will be found a piece which some ignorant editor has entitled, "A Satyr written when the K—— went to Flanders and left nine Lords Justices." I have a manuscript copy of this satire, evidently contemporary, and bearing the date 1690.   It is indeed evident at a glance that the nine persons satirised are the nine members of the interior council which William appointed to assist Mary when he went to Ireland.   Some of them never were Lords Justices.

[4] From a narrative written by Lowther, which is among the Mackintosh MSS.

Serenissima Maria D. G. Angl. Scot. Franz. et Hib. Regina.

QUEEN MARY II

From a mezzotint by J. Faber, after a painting by Sir G. Kneller

Nine ; and it should seem, from her letters to him, that there were few of the number for whom he expressed any high esteem.   Marlborough was to be her guide in military affairs, and was to command the troops in England.   Russell, who was Admiral of the Blue, and had been rewarded for the service which he had done at the time of the Revolution with the lucrative place of Treasurer of the Navy, was well fitted to be her adviser on all questions relating to the fleet.   But Caermarthen was designated as the person on whom, in case of any difference of opinion in the council, she ought chiefly to rely.   Caermarthen's sagacity and experience were unquestionable : his principles, indeed, were lax : but, if there was any person in existence to whom he was likely to be true, that person was Mary.   He had long been in a peculiar manner her friend and servant: he had gained a high place in her favour by bringing about her marriage ; and he had, in the Convention, carried his zeal for her interests to a length which she had herself blamed as excessive. There was, therefore, every reason to hope that he would serve her at this critical conjuncture with sincere good will.[1]

One of her nearest kinsmen, on the other hand, was one of her bitterest enemies.   The evidence which was in the possession of the **Conduct of** government proved beyond dispute that Clarendon was deeply **Clarendon** concerned in the Jacobite schemes of insurrection.   But the Queen was most unwilling that her kindred should be harshly treated ; and William, remembering through what ties she had broken, and what reproaches she had incurred, for his sake, readily gave her uncle's life and liberty to her intercession.   But, before the King set out for Ireland, he spoke seriously to Rochester.   " Your brother has been plotting against me.   I am sure of it.   I have the proofs under his own hand. I was urged to leave him out of the Act of Grace : but I would not do what would have given so much pain to the Queen.   For her sake I forgive the past : but my Lord Clarendon will do well to be cautious for the future.   If not, he will find that these are no jesting matters." Rochester communicated the admonition to Clarendon.   Clarendon, who was in constant correspondence with Dublin and Saint Germains, protested that his only wish was to be quiet, and that, though he felt a scruple about the oaths, the existing government had not a more obedient subject than he purposed to be.[2]

Among the letters which the government had intercepted was one from James to Penn.   That letter, indeed, was not legal evidence to **Penn held** prove that the person to whom it was addressed had been **to bail** guilty of high treason : but it raised suspicions which are now known to have been well founded.   Penn was brought before the

---

[1] See Mary's Letters to William, published by Dalrymple.
[2] Clarendon's Diary, May 30. 1690.

Privy Council, and interrogated. He said very truly that he could not prevent people from writing to him, and that he was not accountable for what they might write to him. He acknowledged that he was bound to the late King by ties of gratitude and affection which no change of fortune could dissolve. " I should be glad to do him any service in his private affairs : but I owe a sacred duty to my country ; and therefore I was never so wicked as even to think of endeavouring to bring him back." This was a falsehood ; and William was probably aware that it was so. He was unwilling however to deal harshly with a man who had many titles to respect, and who was not likely to be a very formidable plotter. He therefore declared himself satisfied, and proposed to discharge the prisoner. Some of the Privy Councillors, however, remonstrated ; and Penn was required to give bail.[1]

On the day before William's departure, he called Burnet into his closet, and, in firm but mournful language, spoke of the dangers which on every side menaced the realm, of the fury of the contending factions, and of the evil spirit which seemed to possess too many of the clergy. " But my trust is in God. I will go through with my work or perish in it. Only I cannot help feeling for the poor Queen ; " and twice he repeated with unwonted tenderness, " the poor Queen." " If you love me," he added, " wait on her often, and give her what help you can. As for me, but for one thing, I should enjoy the prospect of being on horseback and under canvass again. For I am sure that I am fitter to direct a campaign than to manage your Houses of Lords and Commons. But, though I know that I am in the path of duty, it is hard on my wife that her father and I must be opposed to each other in the field. God send that no harm may happen to him. Let me have your prayers, Doctor." Burnet retired greatly moved, and doubtless put up, with no common fervour, those prayers for which his master had asked.[2]

Interview between William and Burnet

On the following day, the fourth of June, the King set out for Ireland. Prince George had offered his services, had equipped himself at great charge, and fully expected to be complimented with a seat in the royal coach. But William, who promised himself little pleasure or advantage from His Royal Highness's conversation, and who seldom stood on ceremony, took Portland for a travelling companion, and never once, during the whole of that eventful campaign, seemed to be aware of the Prince's existence.[3] George, if left to himself, would hardly have noticed the affront. But, though he was too dull to feel, his wife felt for him ; and her resentment was studiously kept alive by mischiefmakers of no common dexterity. On

William sets out for Ireland

[1] Gerard Croese.   [2] Burnet, ii. 46.
[3] The Duchess of Marlborough's Vindication.

this, as on many other occasions, the infirmities of William's temper proved seriously detrimental to the great interests of which he was the guardian. His reign would have been far more prosperous if, with his own courage, capacity, and elevation of mind, he had had a little of the easy good humour and politeness of his uncle Charles.

In four days the King arrived at Chester, where a fleet of transports was awaiting the signal for sailing. He embarked on the eleventh of June, and was convoyed across Saint George's Channel by a squadron of men of war under the command of Sir Cloudesley Shovel.[1]

The month which followed William's departure from London was one of the most eventful and anxious months in the whole history of England. A few hours after he had set out, Crone was brought to the bar of the Old Bailey. A great array of judges was on the Bench. Fuller had recovered sufficiently to make his appearance in court ; and the trial proceeded. The Jacobites had been indefatigable in their efforts to ascertain the political opinions of the persons whose names were on the jury list. So many were challenged that there was some difficulty in making up the number of twelve ; and among the twelve was one on whom the malecontents thought that they could depend. Nor were they altogether mistaken; for this man held out against his eleven companions all night and half the next day; and he would probably have starved them into submission had not Mrs. Clifford, who was in league with him, been caught throwing sweetmeats to him through the window. His supplies having been cut off, he yielded ; and a verdict of Guilty, which, it was said, cost two of the jurymen their lives, was returned. A motion in arrest of judgment was instantly made, on the ground that a Latin word endorsed on the back of the indictment was incorrectly spelt. The objection was undoubtedly frivolous. Jeffreys would have at once overruled it with a torrent of curses, and would have proceeded to the most agreeable part of his duty, that of describing to the prisoner the whole process of half hanging, disembowelling, mutilating, and quartering. But Holt and his brethren remembered that they were now for the first time since the Revolution trying a culprit on a charge of high treason. It was therefore desirable to show, in a manner not to be misunderstood, that a new era had commenced, and that the tribunals would in future rather err on the side of humanity than imitate the cruel haste and levity with which Cornish had, when pleading for his life, been silenced by servile judges. The passing of the sentence was therefore deferred : a day was appointed for considering the point raised by Crone; and counsel were assigned to argue in his behalf.

Trial of Crone

---

[1] London Gazettes, June 5. 12. 16. 1690 ; Hop to the States General from Chester, June $\frac{9}{19}$. Hop attended William to Ireland as envoy from the States.

"This would not have been done, Mr. Crone," said the Lord Chief Justice significantly, "in either of the last two reigns." After a full

ANNE HILARION DE COTENTIN, COUNT DE TOURVILLE

From an engraving by S. Gantrel, after a painting by M. Menard

hearing, the Bench unanimously pronounced the error to be immaterial; and the prisoner was condemned to death. He owned that his trial had been fair, thanked the judges for their patience, and besought them to intercede for him with the Queen.[1]

He was soon informed that his fate was in his own hands. The government was willing to spare him if he would earn his pardon by a full confession. The struggle in his mind was terrible and doubtful. At one time Mrs. Clifford, who had access to his cell, reported to the Jacobite chiefs that he was in a great agony. He could not die, he said : he was too young to be a martyr.[2] The next morning she found him cheerful and resolute.[3] He held out till the eve of the day fixed for his execution. Then he sent to ask for an interview with the Secretary of State. Nottingham went to Newgate : but, before he arrived, Crone had changed his mind and was determined to say nothing. "Then," said Nottingham, "I shall see you no more ; for tomorrow will assuredly be your last day." But after Nottingham had departed, Monmouth repaired to the gaol, and flattered himself that he had shaken the prisoner's resolution. At a very late hour that night came a respite for a week.[4] The week however passed away without any disclosure : the gallows and quartering block were ready at Tyburn : the sledge and axe were at the door of Newgate : the crowd was thick all up Holborn Hill and along the Oxford Road ; when a messenger brought another respite, and Crone, instead of being dragged to the place of execution, was conducted to the Council chamber at Whitehall. His fortitude had been at last overcome by the near prospect of death ; and on this occasion he gave important information.[5]

Such information as he had it in his power to give was indeed at that moment much needed. Both an invasion and an insurrection were hourly expected.[6] Scarcely had William set out from London when a great French fleet commanded by the Count of Tourville left the port of Brest and entered the British Channel. Tourville was the ablest maritime commander that his country then possessed. He had studied every part of his profession. It was said of him that he was competent to fill any place on shipboard from that of carpenter up to that of admiral. It was said of him, also, that to the dauntless courage of a seaman he united the suavity and urbanity of an accomplished gentleman.[7] He now stood over to the English shore, and approached it so near that his

Danger of invasion and insurrection. Tourville's fleet in the Channel

[1] Clarendon's Diary, June 7. and 12. 1690 ; Narcissus Luttrell's Diary ; Baden, the Dutch Secretary of Legation, to Van Citters, June $\frac{16}{26}$.; Fuller's Life of himself ; Welwood's Mercurius Reformatus, June 11. 1690.

[2] Clarendon's Diary, June 8. 1690.   [3] Ibid. June 10.

[4] Baden to Van Citters, June $\frac{26}{36}$. 1690 ; Clarendon's Diary, June 19. ; Luttrell's Diary.

[5] Clarendon's Diary, June 25.   [6] Luttrell's Diary.   [7] Memoirs of Saint Simon.

ships could be plainly descried from the ramparts of Plymouth. From Plymouth he proceeded slowly along the coast of Devonshire and

ADMIRAL CORNELIS EVERTSEN

From a painting by N. Maes in the Rijks Museum at Amsterdam

Dorsetshire. There was great reason to apprehend that his movements had been concerted with the English malecontents.[1]

The Queen and her Council hastened to take measures for the

[1] London Gazette, June 26. 1690; Baden to Van Citters, $\frac{\text{June 24.}}{\text{July 4.}}$

defence of the country against both foreign and domestic enemies.
Torrington took the command of the English fleet which lay in the
Downs, and sailed to Saint Helen's.   He was there joined by a Dutch
squadron under the command of Evertsen.   It seemed that the cliffs of
the Isle of Wight would witness one of the greatest naval conflicts
recorded in history.   A hundred and fifty ships of the line could be
counted at once from the watchtower of Saint Catharine.   On the east
of the huge precipice of Black Gang Chine, and in full view of the
richly wooded rocks of Saint Lawrence and Ventnor, were collected the
maritime forces of England and Holland.   On the west, stretching to
that white cape where the waves roar among the Needles, lay the armament of France.

It was on the twenty-sixth of June, less than a fortnight after
William had sailed for Ireland, that the hostile fleets took up these
Arrests of positions.   A few hours earlier, there had been an im-
suspected portant and anxious sitting of the Privy Council at White-
persons hall.   The malecontents who were leagued with France were
alert and full of hope.   Mary had remarked, while taking her airing,
that Hyde Park was swarming with them.   The whole board was of
opinion that it was necessary to arrest some persons of whose guilt
the government had proofs.   When Clarendon was named, something
was said in his behalf by his friend and relation, Sir Henry Capel.
The other councillors stared, but remained silent.   It was no pleasant
task to accuse the Queen's kinsman in the Queen's presence.   Mary
had scarcely ever opened her lips at Council : but now, being possessed
of clear proofs of her uncle's treason in his own handwriting, and
knowing that respect for her prevented her advisers from proposing
what the public safety required, she broke silence.   "Sir Henry," she
said, "I know, and everybody here knows as well as I, that there is
too much against my Lord Clarendon to leave him out."   The warrant
was drawn up ; and Capel signed it with the rest.   "I am more sorry
for Lord Clarendon," Mary wrote to her husband, "than, may be, will
be believed."   That evening Clarendon, and several other noted Jacobites, were lodged in the Tower.[1]

When the Privy Council had risen, the Queen and the interior
Council of Nine had to consider a question of the gravest importance.
Torrington What orders were to be sent to Torrington ?   The safety of
ordered to the State might depend on his judgment and presence of
give battle
to Tourville mind ; and some of Mary's advisers apprehended that he
would not be found equal to the occasion.   Their anxiety increased
when news came that he had abandoned the coast of the Isle of
Wight to the French, and was retreating before them towards the Straits

[1] Mary to William, June 26. 1690 ; Clarendon's Diary of the same date ; Luttrell's Diary.

WMR.

Right Trusty & right wel-beloved Cousin & Councellor
We greet you well: We have heard yᵉ letter dated June
26ᵗʰ to our Secretary of State & doe not doubt of yᵉ Skill
& Conduct in this important Conjuncture to take all
opportunities of advantage against the Enemy: But We
apprehend yᵉ Consequences of your retireing to yᵉ Gunfleet
to be so fatall yᵗ We choose rather yᵗ you should upon
any advantage of yᵉ Wind give battle to yᵉ Enemy then
retreat farther then is necessary to gett an advantage upon
yᵉ Enemy. But in case you find it necessary to goe to
yᵉ Westward of yᵉ French fleet in order to yᵉ better ioyning
wᵗʰ you our Ships from Plimouth or any others coming from
yᵉ Westward. We leave it to your discretion So as you
by no meanes ever loose sight of yᵉ French fleet; whereby
they may have opportunities of making attempts upon the
shoar or in yᵉ Rivers of Medway or Thames Or gett away
wᵗʰout Fighting. And so We bid you heartily Farewill.
Given at Our Court at Whitehall this 29ᵃᵉ day of
June 1690 In the Second year of Our Reigne.

To our Right Trusty and
Right wel-beloved Cousin &
Councellour Arthur Earl of
Torrington &c.

By Her Maᵗⁱᵉˢ Command

Nottingham

REDUCED FACSIMILE OF THE ORDERS SENT TO THE EARL OF TORRINGTON
ON 29 JUNE, 1690

From the British Museum. (Egerton MS. 2621, f. 91)

H.E. IV

X

of Dover.   The sagacious Caermarthen and the enterprising Monmouth agreed in blaming these cautious tactics.   It was true that Torrington had not so many vessels as Tourville : but Caermarthen thought that, at such a time, it was advisable to fight, although against odds ; and Monmouth was, through life, for fighting at all times and against all odds.   Russell, who was indisputably one of the best seamen of the age, held that the disparity of numbers was not such as ought to cause any uneasiness to an officer who commanded English and Dutch sailors. He therefore proposed to send to the Admiral a reprimand couched in terms so severe that the Queen did not like to sign it.   The language was much softened : but, in the main, Russell's advice was followed. Torrington was positively ordered to retreat no further, and to give battle immediately.   Devonshire, however, was still unsatisfied.   " It is my duty, Madam," he said, " to tell Your Majesty exactly what I think on a matter of this importance ; and I think that my Lord Torrington is not a man to be trusted with the fate of three kingdoms."   Devonshire was right : but his colleagues were unanimously of opinion that to supersede a commander in sight of the enemy, and on the eve of a general action, would be a course full of danger ; and it is difficult to say that they were wrong.   " You must either," said Russell, " leave him where he is, or send for him as a prisoner."   Several expedients were suggested.   Caermarthen proposed that Russell should be sent to assist Torrington.   Monmouth passionately implored permission to join the fleet in any capacity, as a captain, or as a volunteer.   " Only let me be once on board ; and I pledge my life that there shall be a battle." After much discussion and hesitation, it was resolved that both Russell and Monmouth should go down to the coast.[1]   They set out, but too late.   The despatch which ordered Torrington to fight had preceded them.   It reached him when he was off Beachy Head.   He read it, and was in a great strait.   Not to give battle was to be guilty of direct disobedience.   To give battle was, in his judgment, to incur serious risk of defeat.   He probably suspected,—for he was of a captious and jealous temper,—that the instructions which placed him in so painful a dilemma had been framed by enemies and rivals with a design unfriendly to his fortune and his fame.   He was exasperated by the thought that he was ordered about and overruled by Russell, who, though his inferior in professional rank, exercised, as one of the Council of Nine, a supreme control over all the departments of the public service.   There seems to be no sufficient ground for charging Torrington with disaffection.   Still less can it be suspected that an officer, whose whole life had been passed in confronting danger, and who had always borne himself bravely, wanted the personal courage which hundreds of sailors on board of

[1] Mary to William, June 28. and July 2. 1690.

PLAN OF THE BATTLE OF BEACHY HEAD

From an engraving in the Sutherland Collection

every ship under his command possessed. But there is a higher courage of which Torrington was wholly destitute. He shrank from all responsibility, from the responsibility of fighting, and from the responsibility of not fighting ; and he succeeded in finding out a middle way which united all the inconveniences which he wished to avoid. He would conform to the letter of his instructions : yet he would not put everything to hazard. Some of his ships should skirmish with the enemy : but the great body of his fleet should not be risked. It was evident that the vessels which engaged the French would be placed in a most dangerous situation, and would suffer much loss ; and there is but too good reason to believe that Torrington was base enough to lay his plans in such a manner that the danger and loss might fall almost exclusively to the share of the Dutch. He bore them no love ; and in England they were so unpopular that the destruction of their whole squadron was likely to cause fewer murmurs than the capture of one of our own frigates.

It was on the twenty-ninth of June that the Admiral received the order to fight. The next day, at four in the morning, he bore down on the French fleet, and formed his vessels in order of battle.

Battle of Beachy Head

He had not sixty sail of the line, and the French had at least eighty ; but his ships were more strongly manned than those of the enemy. He placed the Dutch in the van and gave them the signal to engage. That signal was promptly obeyed. Evertsen and his countrymen fought with a courage to which both their English allies and their French enemies, in spite of national prejudices, did full justice. In none of Van Tromp's or De Ruyter's battles had the honour of the Batavian flag been more gallantly upheld. During many hours the van maintained the unequal contest with very little assistance from any other part of the fleet. At length the Dutch Admiral drew off, leaving one shattered and dismasted hull to the enemy. His second in command and several officers of high rank had fallen. To keep the sea against the French after this disastrous and ignominious action was impossible. The Dutch ships which had come out of the fight were in lamentable condition. Torrington ordered some of them to be destroyed : the rest he took in tow : he then fled along the coast of Kent, and sought a refuge in the Thames. As soon as he was in the river, he ordered all the buoys to be pulled up, and thus made the navigation so dangerous, that the pursuers could not venture to follow him.[1]

[1] Report of the Commissioners of the Admiralty to the Queen, dated Sheerness, July 18. 1690 ; Evidence of Captains Cornwall, Jones, Martin and Hubbard, and of Vice Admiral Delaval ; Burnet ii. 52., and Speaker Onslow's Note ; Mémoires du Maréchal de Tourville ; Memoirs of Transactions at Sea by Josiah Burchett, Esq., Secretary to the Admiralty, 1703 ; London Gazette, July 3.; Historical and Political Mercury for July 1690; Mary to William, July 2.; Torrington to Caermarthen, July 1. The account of the battle in the Paris Gazette of July 15. 1690 is not to be read without shame : " On a sçeu que les Hollandois s'estoient très bien battus, et qu'ils

It was, however, thought by many, and especially by the French ministers, that, if Tourville had been more enterprising, the allied fleet might have been destroyed.   He seems to have borne, in one respect, too much resemblance to his vanquished opponent.   Though a brave man, he was a timid commander.   His life he exposed with careless gaiety : but it was said that he was nervously anxious and pusillani- mously cautious when his professional reputation was in danger.   He was so much annoyed by these censures that he soon became, unfortun- ately for his country, bold even to temerity.[1]

There has scarcely ever been so sad a day in London as that on which the news of the Battle of Beachy Head arrived.   The shame was insupportable : the peril was imminent.   What if the vic-   **Alarm in** torious enemy should do what De Ruyter had done ?   What   **London** if the dockyards of Chatham should again be destroyed ?   What if the Tower itself should be bombarded ?   What if the vast wood of masts and yardarms below London Bridge should be in a blaze ?   Nor was this all.   Evil tidings had just arrived from the Low Countries.   The allied forces under Waldeck had, in the neighbourhood of Fleurus, encountered the French commanded by the Duke of Luxem-   **Battle of** burg.   The day had been long and fiercely disputed.   At   **Fleurus** length the skill of the French general and the impetuous valour of the French cavalry had prevailed.[2]   Thus at the same moment the army of Lewis was victorious in Flanders, and his navy was in undisputed possession of the Channel.   Marshal Humieres with a considerable force lay not far from the Straits of Dover.   It had been given out that he was about to join Luxemburg.   But the information which the English government received from able military men in the Netherlands and from spies who mixed with the Jacobites, and which to so great a master of the art of war as Marlborough seemed to deserve serious attention, was that the army of Humieres would instantly march to Dunkirk and would there be taken on board of the fleet of Tourville.[3] Between the coast of Artois and the Nore not a single ship bearing the red cross of Saint George could venture to show herself.   The embarka- tion would be the business of a few hours.   A few hours more might suffice for the voyage.   At any moment London might be appalled by the news that twenty thousand French veterans were in Kent.   It was

s'estoient comportez en cette occasion en braves gens, mais que les Anglois n'en avoient pas agi de même."   In the French official relation of the battle off Cape Bevézier,—an odd corruption of Pevensey,—are some passages to the same effect : " Les Hollandois combattirent avec beaucoup de courage et de fermeté ; mais ils ne furent pas bien secondez par les Anglois."   " Les Anglois se distinguèrent des vaisseaux de Hollande par le peu de valeur qu'ils montrèrent dans le combat."

[1] Life of James, ii. 409.; Burnet, ii. 5.

[2] London Gazette, June 30. 1690 ; Historical and Political Mercury for July 1690.

[3] Nottingham to William, July 15. 1690.

notorious that, in every part of the kingdom, the Jacobites had been, during some months, making preparations for a rising. All the regular troops who could be assembled for the defence of the island did not amount to more than ten thousand men. It may be doubted whether our country has ever passed through a more alarming crisis than that of the first week of July 1690.

But the evil brought with it its own remedy. Those little knew England who imagined that she could be in danger at once of rebellion **Spirit of the nation** and invasion : for in truth the danger of invasion was the best security against the danger of rebellion. The cause of James was the cause of France ; and, though to superficial observers the French alliance seemed to be his chief support, it really was the obstacle which made his restoration impossible. In the patriotism, the too often unamiable and unsocial patriotism of our forefathers, lay the secret at once of William's weakness and of his strength. They were jealous of his love for Holland : but they cordially sympathised with his hatred of Lewis. To their strong sentiment of nationality are to be ascribed almost all those petty annoyances which made the throne of the Deliverer, from his accession to his death, so uneasy a seat. But to the same sentiment it is to be ascribed that his throne, constantly menaced and frequently shaken, was never subverted. For, much as his people detested his foreign favourites, they detested his foreign adversaries still more. The Dutch were Protestants : the French were Papists. The Dutch were regarded as selfseeking, grasping, overreaching allies : the French were mortal enemies. The worst that could be apprehended from the Dutch was that they might obtain too large a share of the patronage of the Crown, that they might throw on us too large a part of the burdens of the war, that they might obtain commercial advantages at our expense. But the French would conquer us : the French would enslave us : the French would inflict on us calamities such as those which had turned the fair fields and cities of the Palatinate into a desert. The hopgrounds of Kent would be as the vineyards of the Neckar. The High Street of Oxford and the close of Salisbury would be piled with ruins such as those which covered the spots where the palaces and churches of Heidelberg and Manheim had once stood. The parsonage overshadowed by the old steeple, the farmhouse peeping from among beehives and appleblossoms, the manorial hall embosomed in elms, would be given up to a soldiery which knew not what it was to pity old men, or delicate women, or sucking children. The words, "The French are coming," like a spell, quelled at once all murmurs about taxes and abuses, about William's ungracious manners and Portland's lucrative places, and raised a spirit as high and unconquerable as had pervaded, a hundred years before, the ranks which Elizabeth reviewed

LOUIS DE CREVANT D'HUMIÈRES, MARSHAL OF FRANCE

From an engraving by J. Lubin, after a painting by F. Voet

at Tilbury. Had the army of Humieres landed, it would assuredly have been withstood by every male capable of bearing arms. Not only the muskets and pikes but the scythes and pitchforks would have beer too few for the hundreds of thousands who, forgetting all distinction of sect or faction, would have risen up like one man to defend the English soil.

The immediate effect therefore of the disasters in the Channel and in Flanders was to unite for a moment the great body of the people. The national antipathy to the Dutch seemed to be suspended. Their gallant conduct in the fight off Beachy Head was loudly applauded. The inaction of Torrington was loudly condemned. London set the example of concert and of exertion. The irritation produced by the late election at once subsided. All distinctions of party disappeared. The Lord Mayor was summoned to attend the Queen. She requested him to ascertain as soon as possible what the capital would undertake to do if the enemy should venture to make a descent. He called together the representatives of the wards, conferred with them, and returned to Whitehall to report that they had unanimously bound themselves to stand by the government with life and fortune; that a hundred thousand pounds were ready to be paid into the Exchequer; that ten thousand Londoners, well armed and appointed, were prepared to march at an hour's notice; and that an additional force, consisting of six regiments of foot, a strong regiment of horse, and a thousand dragoons, should be instantly raised without costing the Crown a farthing. Of Her Majesty the City had nothing to ask, but that she would be pleased to set over these troops officers in whom she could confide. The same spirit was shown in every part of the country. Though in the southern counties the harvest was at hand, the rustics repaired with unusual cheerfulness to the musters of the militia. The Jacobite country gentlemen, who had, during several months, been laying in swords and carbines for the insurrection which was to take place as soon as William was gone and as help arrived from France, now that William was gone, now that a French invasion was hourly expected, burned their commissions signed by James, and hid their arms behind wainscots or in haystacks. The malecontents in the towns were insulted wherever they appeared, and were forced to shut themselves up in their houses from the exasperated populace.[1]

Nothing is more interesting to those who love to study the intricacies of the human heart than the effect which the public danger produced on
Conduct of Shrewsbury Shrewsbury. For a moment he was again the Shrewsbury of 1688. His nature, lamentably unstable, was not ignoble; and the thought, that, by standing foremost in the defence of his country

[1] Burnet, ii. 53, 54.; Narcissus Luttrell's Diary, July 7. 11. 1690; London Gazette, July 14. 1690.

FRENCH MEDALS COMMEMORATING THE BATTLES OF BEACHY HEAD AND FLEURUS at so perilous a crisis, he might repair his great fault and regain his own esteem, gave new energy to his body and his mind.　He had retired to Epsom, in the hope that repose and pure air would produce a salutary effect on his shattered frame and wounded spirit.　But, a few hours after the news of the Battle of Beachy Head had arrived, he was at Whitehall, and had offered his purse and sword to the Queen.　It had been in contemplation to put the fleet under the command of some great nobleman with two experienced naval officers to advise him. Shrewsbury begged that, if such an arrangement were made, he might be appointed.　It concerned, he said, the interest and the honour of every man in the kingdom not to let the enemy ride victorious in the Channel; and he would gladly risk his life to retrieve the lost fame of the English flag.[1]

His offer was not accepted.　Indeed, the plan of dividing the naval command between a man of quality who did not know the points of the compass, and two weatherbeaten old seamen who had risen from being cabin boys to be Admirals, was very wisely laid aside.　Active exertions were made to prepare the allied squadrons for service.　Nothing was omitted which could assuage the natural resentment of the Dutch.　The Queen sent a Privy Councillor, charged with a special mission to the States General.　He was the bearer of a letter to them in which she extolled the valour of Evertsen's gallant squadron.　She assured them that their ships should be repaired in the English dockyards, and that the wounded Dutchmen should be as carefully tended as wounded Englishmen.　It was announced that a strict inquiry would be instituted into the causes of the late disaster ; and Torrington, who indeed could not at that moment have appeared in public without risk of being torn in pieces, was sent to the Tower.[2]

During the three days which followed the arrival of the disastrous tidings from Beachy Head the aspect of London was gloomy and agitated.　But on the fourth day all was changed.　Bells were pealing : flags were flying : candles were arranged in the windows for an illumination : men were eagerly shaking hands with each other in the streets. A courier had that morning arrived at Whitehall with great news from Ireland.

[1] Mary to William, July 3. 10. 1690 ; Shrewsbury to Caermarthen, July 15.

[2] Mary to the States General, July 12. ; Burchett's Memoirs ; An important Account of some remarkable Passages in the Life of Arthur, Earl of Torrington, 1691.

SIR RICHARD HADDOCK

From an engraving by W. Faithorne, after a painting by J. Closterman

CHAPTER XVI

WILLIAM had been, during the whole spring, impatiently expected in Ulster. The Protestant settlements along the coast of that province

William lands at Carrick- fergus and proceeds to Belfast

had, in the course of the month of May, been repeatedly agitated by false reports of his arrival. It was not, however, till the afternoon of the fourteenth of June that he landed at Carrickfergus. The inhabitants of the town crowded the main street and greeted him with loud acclamations : but they caught only a glimpse of him. As soon as he was on dry ground he mounted and set off for Belfast. On the road he was met by Schomberg. The meeting took place close to a white house, the only human dwelling then visible, in the space of many miles, on the dreary strand of the estuary of the Laggan. A village and a cotton mill now rise where the white house then stood alone ; and all the shore is adorned by a gay succession of country houses, shrubberies, and flower beds. Belfast has become one of the greatest and most flourishing seats of industry in the British isles. A busy population of a hundred thousand souls is collected there. The duties annually paid at the Custom House exceed the duties annually paid at the Custom House of London in the most prosperous years of the reign of Charles the Second. Other Irish towns may present more picturesque forms to the eye. But Belfast is the only large Irish town in which the traveller is not disgusted by the loath- some aspect and odour of long lines of human dens far inferior in comfort and cleanliness to the dwellings which, in happier countries, are provided for cattle. No other large Irish town is so well cleaned, so well paved, so brilliantly lighted. The place of domes and spires is supplied by edifices, less pleasing to the taste, but not less indicative of prosperity, huge factories, towering many stories above the chimneys of the houses, and resounding with the roar of machinery. The Belfast which William entered was a small English settlement of about three hundred houses, commanded by a castle which has long disappeared, the seat of the noble family of Chichester. In this mansion, which is said to have borne some resemblance to the palace of Whitehall, and which was celebrated for its terraces and orchards stretching down to the river side, preparations had been made for the King's reception. He was welcomed at the North Gate by the magistrates and burgesses in their robes of office. The multitude pressed on his carriage with shouts of " God save the Protestant King." For the town was one of the strong-holds of the Reformed Faith; and, when, two generations later, the inhabitants were, for the first time, numbered, it was found that the Roman Catholics were not more than one in fifteen.[1]

The night came: but the Protestant counties were awake and up. A royal salute had been fired from the castle of Belfast. It had been echoed and reechoed by guns which Schomberg had placed at wide intervals for the purpose of conveying signals from post to post. Wher-ever the peal was heard, it was known that King William was come. Before midnight all the heights of Antrim and Down were blazing with bonfires. The light was seen across the bays of Carlingford and Dun-dalk, and gave notice to the outposts of the enemy that the decisive hour was at hand. Within forty eight hours after William had landed, James set out from Dublin for the Irish camp, which was pitched near the northern frontier of Leinster.[2]

In Dublin the agitation was fearful. None could doubt that the decisive crisis was approaching; and the agony of suspense stimu-lated to the highest point the passions of both the hostile castes. The majority could easily detect, in the looks and State of Dublin tones of the oppressed minority, signs which indicated the hope of a speedy deliverance and of a terrible revenge. Simon Luttrell, to whom the care of the capital was entrusted, hastened to take such pre-cautions as fear and hatred dictated. A proclamation appeared, enjoin-ing all Protestants to remain in their houses from nightfall to dawn, and prohibiting them, on pain of death, from assembling in any place or for any purpose to the number of more than five. No indulgence was granted even to those divines of the Established Church who had never ceased to teach the doctrine of nonresistance. Doctor William King, who had, after long holding out, lately begun to waver in his political creed, was committed to custody. There was no gaol large enough to hold one half of those whom the governor suspected of evil

---

[1] London Gazette, June 19. 1690; History of the Wars in Ireland by an Officer in the Royal Army, 1690; Villare Hibernicum, 1690; Story's Impartial History, 1691; Historical Collections relating to the town of Belfast, 1817. This work contains curious extracts from MSS. of the seventeenth century. In the British Museum is a map of Belfast made in 1685, so exact that the houses may be counted.

[2] Lauzun to Louvois, June $\frac{18}{28}$. The messenger who brought the news to Lauzun had heard the guns and seen the bonfires. History of the Wars in Ireland by an Officer of the Royal Army, 1690; Life of James, ii. 392., Orig. Mem.; Burnet, ii. 47. Burnet is strangely mistaken when he says that William had been six days in Ireland before his arrival was known to James.

Sea banck

The New Catt River

A Bridg 2794 feet in length

A Scale Containing one Thousand feet

Belfast River

South

Laggan River

A place to Recive Soldiers

Strand dry at low water

PLAN OF BELFAST IN 1685,

From the

BY THOMAS PHILLIPS

British Museum

designs. The College and several parish churches were used as prisons; and into those buildings men accused of no crime but their religion were crowded in such numbers that they could hardly breathe.[1]

The two rival princes meanwhile were busied in collecting their forces. Loughbrickland was the place appointed by William for the rendezvous of the scattered divisions of his army. While his troops were assembling, he exerted himself indefatigably to improve their discipline and to provide for their subsistence. He had brought from England two hundred thousand pounds in money, and a great quantity of ammunition and provisions. Pillaging was prohibited under severe penalties. At the same time supplies were liberally dispensed; and all the paymasters of regiments were directed to send in their accounts without delay, in order that there might be no arrears.[2] Thomas Coningsby, Member of Parliament for Leominster, a busy and unscrupulous Whig, accompanied the King, and acted as Paymaster General. It deserves to be mentioned that William, at this time, authorised the Collector of Customs at Belfast to pay every year twelve hundred pounds into the hands of some of the principal dissenting ministers of Down and Antrim, who were to be trustees for their brethren. The King declared that he bestowed this sum on the nonconformist divines, partly as a reward for their eminent loyalty to him, and partly as a compensation for their recent losses. Such was the origin of that donation which is still annually bestowed by the government on the Presbyterian clergy of Ulster.[3]

William was all himself again. His spirits, depressed by eighteen months passed in dull state, amidst factions and intrigues which he but half understood, rose high as soon as he was surrounded by tents and standards.[4] It was strange to see how rapidly this man, so unpopular at Westminster, obtained a complete mastery over the hearts of his brethren in arms. They observed with delight that, infirm as he was, he took his share of every hardship which they underwent; that he thought more of their comfort than of his own; that he sharply reprimanded some officers, who were so anxious to procure luxuries for his table as to forget the wants of the common soldiers; that he never once, from the day on which he took the field, lodged in a house, but, even in the neighbourhood of cities and palaces, slept in his small

(marginal note:) William's military arrangements

[1] A True and Perfect Journal of the Affairs of Ireland by a Person of Quality, 1690; King, iii. 18. Luttrell's proclamation will be found in King's Appendix.

[2] Villare Hibernicum, 1690.

[3] The order addressed to the Collector of Customs will be found in Dr. Reid's History of the Presbyterian Church in Ireland.

[4] "La gayeté peinte sur son visage," says Dumont, who saw him at Belfast, "nous fit tout espérer pour les heureux succès de la campagne."

travelling hut of wood ; that no solicitations could induce him, on a hot day and in a high wind, to move out of the choking cloud of dust, which overhung the line of march, and which severely tried lungs less delicate than his. Every man under his command became familiar with his looks and with his voice ; for there was not a regiment which he did not inspect with minute attention. His pleasant looks and sayings were long remembered. One brave soldier has recorded in his journal the kind and courteous manner in which a basket of the first cherries of the year was accepted from him by the King, and the sprightliness with which His Majesty conversed at supper with those who stood round the table.[1]

On the twenty-fourth of June, the tenth day after William's landing, he marched southward from Loughbrickland with all his forces. He was fully determined to take the first opportunity of fighting. Schomberg and several other officers recommended caution and delay. But the King answered that he had not come to Ireland to let the grass grow under his feet. The event seems to prove that he judged rightly as a general. That he judged rightly as a statesman cannot be doubted. He knew that the English nation was discontented with the way in which the war had hitherto been conducted, that nothing but rapid and splendid success could revive the enthusiasm of his friends and quell the spirit of his enemies, and that a defeat could scarcely be more injurious to his fame and to his interests than a languid and indecisive campaign.

William marches southward

The country through which he advanced had, during eighteen months, been fearfully wasted both by soldiers and by Rapparees. The cattle had been slaughtered : the plantations had been cut down : the fences and houses were in ruins. Not a human being was to be found near the road, except a few naked and meagre wretches who had no food but the husks of oats, and who were seen picking those husks, like chickens, from amidst dust and cinders.[2] Yet, even under such disadvantages, the natural fertility of the country, the rich green of the earth, the bays and rivers so admirably fitted for trade, could not but strike the King's observant eye. Perhaps he thought how different an aspect that unhappy region would have presented if it had been blessed with such a government and such a religion as had made his native Holland the wonder of the world ; how endless a succession of pleasure houses, tulip gardens, and dairy farms would have lined the road from Lisburn to Belfast ; how many hundreds of barges would have been constantly passing up and down the Laggan ; what a forest of masts would have bristled in the desolate port of Newry ; and what

[1] Story's Impartial Account ; MS. Journal of Colonel Bellingham ; The Royal Diary.
[2] Story's Impartial Account.

H.E. IV   Y

vast warehouses and stately mansions would have covered the space occupied by the noisome alleys of Dundalk. "The country," he was heard to say, "is worth fighting for."

The original intention of James seems to have been to try the chances of a pitched field on the border between Leinster and Ulster. **The Irish army retreats** But this design was abandoned, in consequence, apparently, of the representations of Lauzun, who, though very little disposed and very little qualified to conduct a campaign on the Fabian system, had the admonitions of Louvois still in his ears.[1] James, though resolved not to give up Dublin without a battle, consented to retreat till he should reach some spot where he might have the vantage of ground. When therefore William's advanced guard reached Dundalk, nothing was to be seen of the Irish army, except a great cloud of dust which was slowly rolling southwards towards Ardee. The English halted one night near the ground on which Schomberg's camp had been pitched in the preceding year; and many sad recollections were awakened by the sight of that dreary marsh, the sepulchre of thousands of brave men.[2]

Still William continued to push forward, and still the Irish receded before him, till, on the morning of Monday, the thirtieth of June, his army, marching in three columns, reached the summit of a rising ground near the southern frontier of the county of Louth. Beneath lay a valley, now so rich and so cheerful that the Englishman who gazes on it may imagine himself to be in one of the most highly favoured parts of his own highly favoured country. Fields of wheat, woodlands, meadows bright with daisies and clover, slope gently down to the edge of the Boyne. That bright and tranquil stream, the boundary of Louth and Meath, having flowed many miles between green banks crowned by modern palaces, and by the ruined keeps of old Norman barons of the pale, is here about to mingle with the sea. Five miles to the west of the place from which William looked down on the river, now stands, on a verdant bank, amidst noble woods, Slane Castle, the mansion of the Marquess of Conyngham. Two miles to the east, a cloud of smoke from factories and steam vessels overhangs the busy town and port of Drogheda. On the Meath side of the Boyne, the ground, still all corn, grass, flowers, and foliage, rises with a gentle swell to an eminence surmounted by a conspicuous tuft of ash trees which overshades the ruined church and desolate graveyard of Dunore.[3]

---

[1] Lauzun to Louvois, $\frac{\text{June 23.}}{\text{July 3.}}$ 1690 ; Life of James, ii. 393., Orig. Mem.

[2] Story's Impartial Account ; Dumont MS.

[3] Much interesting information respecting the field of battle and the surrounding country will be found in Mr. Wilde's pleasing volume entitled "The Beauties of the Boyne and Blackwater."

MAP ILLUSTRATING THE CAMPAIGN OF WILLIAM III IN IRELAND

In the seventeenth century the landscape presented a very different aspect. The traces of art and industry were few. Scarcely a vessel was on the river except those rude coracles of wickerwork covered with the skins of horses, in which the Celtic peasantry fished for trout and salmon. Drogheda, now peopled by twenty thousand industrious inhabitants, was a small knot of narrow, crooked, and filthy lanes, encircled by a ditch and a mound. The houses were built of wood with high gables and projecting upper stories. Without the walls of the town, scarcely a dwelling was to be seen except at a place called Oldbridge. At Oldbridge the river was fordable; and on the south of the ford were a few mud cabins, and a single house built of more solid materials.

When William caught sight of the valley of the Boyne, he could not suppress an exclamation and gesture of delight. He had been

The Irish make a stand at the Boyne apprehensive that the enemy would avoid a decisive action, and would protract the war till the autumnal rains should return with pestilence in their train. He was now at ease. It was plain that the contest would be sharp and short. The pavilion of James was pitched on the eminence of Donore. The flags of the House of Stuart and of the House of Bourbon waved together in defiance on the walls of Drogheda. All the southern bank of the river was lined by the camp and batteries of the hostile army. Thousands of armed men were moving about among the tents; and every one, horse soldier or foot soldier, French or Irish, had a white badge in his hat. That colour had been chosen in compliment to the House of Bourbon. " I am glad to see you, gentlemen," said the King, as his keen eye surveyed the Irish lines. " If you escape me now the fault will be mine." [1]

Each of the contending princes had some advantages over his rival. James, standing on the defensive behind entrenchments, with a river

The army of James before him, had the stronger position [2] : but his troops were inferior both in number and in quality to those which were opposed to him. He probably had thirty thousand men. About a third part of this force consisted of excellent French infantry and excellent Irish cavalry. But the rest of his army was the scoff of all Europe. The Irish dragoons were bad ; the Irish foot worse. It was said that their ordinary way of fighting was to discharge their pieces

---

[1] Memorandum in the handwriting of Alexander, Earl of Marchmont. He derived his information from Lord Selkirk, who was in William's army.

[2] James says (Life, ii. 393., Orig. Mem.) that the country afforded no better position. King, in a thanksgiving sermon which he preached at Dublin after the close of the campaign, told his hearers that " the advantage of the post of the Irish was, by all intelligent men, reckoned above three to one." See King's Thanksgiving Sermon, preached on Nov. 16. 1690, before the Lords Justices. This is, no doubt, an absurd exaggeration. But M. de la Hoguette, one of the principal French officers who was present at the battle of the Boyne, informed Louvois that the Irish army occupied a good defensive position. Letter of La Hoguette from Limerick, $\frac{\text{July 31.}}{\text{Aug. 10.}}$ 1690.

PLAN OF THE BATTLE OF THE BOYNE

From George Story's Impartial History of the Wars of Ireland, 1693

once, and then to run away bawling " Quarter " and " Murder." Their
inefficiency was, in that age, commonly imputed, both by their enemies
and by their allies, to natural poltroonery. How little ground there
was for such an imputation has since been signally proved by many
brave achievements in every part of the globe. It ought indeed, even
in the seventeenth century, to have occurred to reasonable men, that a
race which furnished some of the best horse soldiers in the world, would
certainly, with judicious training, furnish good foot soldiers. But the
Irish foot soldiers had not merely not been well trained : they had been
elaborately ill trained. The greatest of our generals repeatedly and
emphatically declared that even the admirable army which fought its
way, under his command, from Torres Vedras to Toulouse, would, if he
had suffered it to contract habits of pillage, have become, in a few
weeks, unfit for all military purposes. What then was likely to be the
character of troops who, from the day on which they enlisted, were not
merely permitted, but invited, to supply the deficiencies of pay by
marauding ? They were, as might have been expected, a mere mob,
furious indeed, and clamorous in their zeal for the cause which they
had espoused, but incapable of opposing a steadfast resistance to a well
ordered force. In truth, all that the discipline, if it is to be so called,
of James's army had done for the Celtic kerne had been to debase and
enervate him. After eighteen months of nominal soldiership, he was
positively farther from being a soldier than on the day on which he
quitted his hovel for the camp.

William had under his command near thirty six thousand men, born in
many lands, and speaking many tongues. Scarcely one Protestant Church,
The army
of William
scarcely one Protestant nation, was unrepresented in the army
which a strange series of events had brought to fight for the
Protestant religion in the remotest island of the west. About half the
troops were natives of England. Ormond was there with the Life
Guards, and Oxford with the Blues. Sir John Lanier, an officer who
had acquired military experience on the Continent, and whose prudence
was held in high esteem, was at the head of the Queen's regiment of
horse, now the First Dragoon Guards. There were Beaumont's foot,
who had, in defiance of the mandate of James, refused to admit Irish
Papists among them, and Hastings's foot, who had, on the disastrous day
of Killiecrankie, maintained the military reputation of the Saxon race.
There were the two Tangier battalions, hitherto known only by deeds
of violence and rapine, but destined to begin on the following morning
a long career of glory. Two fine English regiments, which had been in
the service of the States General, and had often looked death in the face
under William's leading, followed him in this campaign, not only as their
general, but as their native King. They now rank as the fifth and

sixth of the line. The former was led by an officer who had no skill in the higher parts of military science, but whom the whole army allowed to be the bravest of all the brave, John Cutts. The Scotch footguards marched under the command of their countryman James Douglas. Conspicuous among the Dutch troops were Portland's and Ginkell's Horse, and Solmes's Blue regiment, consisting of two thousand of the finest infantry in Europe. Germany had sent to the field some warriors sprung from her noblest houses. Prince George of Hesse Darmstadt, a gallant youth, who was serving his apprenticeship in the military art, rode near the King. A strong brigade of Danish mercenaries was commanded by Duke Charles Frederic of Wurtemberg. It was reported that of all the soldiers of William these were most dreaded by the Irish. For centuries of Saxon domination had not effaced the recollection of the violence and cruelty of the Scandinavian sea kings ; and an ancient prophecy that the Danes would one day destroy the children of the soil was still repeated with superstitious horror.[1] Among the foreign auxiliaries were a Brandenburg regiment and a Finland regiment. But in that great array, so variously composed, were two bodies of men animated by a spirit peculiarly fierce and implacable, the Huguenots of France thirsting for the blood of the French, and the Englishry of Ireland impatient to trample down the Irish. The ranks of the refugees had been effectually purged of spies and traitors, and were now made up of men such as had contended in the preceding century against the power of the House of Valois and the genius of the House of Lorraine. All the boldest spirits of the unconquerable colony had repaired to William's camp. Mitchelburne was there with the stubborn defenders of Londonderry, and Wolseley with the warriors who had raised the unanimous shout of "Advance" on the day of Newton Butler. Sir Albert Conyngham, the ancestor of the noble family whose seat now overlooks the field of battle, had brought from the neighbourhood of Lough Erne a regiment of dragoons which still glories in the name of Enniskillen, and which has proved on the shores of the Euxine that it has not degenerated since the day of the Boyne.[2]

    Walker, notwithstanding his advanced age and his peaceful profession, accompanied the men of Londonderry, and tried to animate their zeal by exhortation and by example. He was now a great prelate. Ezekiel Hopkins had taken refuge from Popish persecutors and Presbyterian rebels in the city of London, had brought himself to swear allegiance to the government, had obtained a cure, and had died in the performance of the humble duties

Walker, now Bishop of Derry, accompanies the army

[1] Luttrell's Diary, March 1690.

[2] See the Historical records of the Regiments of the British army, and Story's list of the army of William as it passed in review at Finglass, a week after the battle.

of a parish priest.[1]   William, on his march through Louth, learned that
the rich see of Derry was at his disposal.   He instantly made choice of
Walker to be the new Bishop.   The brave old man, during the few hours
of life which remained to him, was overwhelmed with salutations and
congratulations.   Unhappily he had, during the siege in which he had
so highly distinguished himself, contracted a passion for war ; and he
easily persuaded himself that, in indulging this passion, he was discharging a duty to his country and his religion.   He ought to have
remembered that the peculiar circumstances which had justified him in
becoming a combatant had ceased to exist, and that, in a disciplined
army led by generals of long experience and great fame, a fighting
divine was likely to give less help than scandal.   The Bishop elect was
determined to be wherever danger was ; and the way in which he
exposed himself excited the extreme disgust of his royal patron, who
hated a meddler almost as much as a coward.   A soldier who ran
away from a battle and a gownsman who pushed himself into a battle
were the two objects which most strongly excited William's spleen.

It was still early in the day.   The King rode slowly along the
northern bank of the river, and closely examined the position of the
William Irish, from whom he was sometimes separated by an interval
reconnoitres of little more than two hundred feet.   He was accompanied
the Irish
position by Schomberg, Ormond, Sidney, Solmes, Prince George of
Hesse, Coningsby, and others.   " Their army is but small ; " said one of
the Dutch officers.   Indeed it did not appear to consist of more than
sixteen thousand men.   But it was well known, from the reports brought
by deserters, that many regiments were concealed from view by the
undulations of the ground.   " They may be stronger than they look,"
said William ; " but, weak or strong, I will soon know all about them." [2]

At length he alighted at a spot nearly opposite to Oldbridge, sate
down on the turf to rest himself, and called for breakfast.   The sumpter
horses were unloaded : the canteens were opened ; and a tablecloth
was spread on the grass.   The place is marked by an obelisk, built
while many veterans who could well remember the events of that day
were still living.

While William was at his repast, a group of horsemen appeared
close to the water on the opposite shore.   Among them his attendants
William is could discern some who had once been conspicuous at reviews
wounded in Hyde Park and at balls in the gallery of Whitehall, the
youthful Berwick, the small, fairhaired Lauzun, Tyrconnel, once admired

---

[1] See his Funeral Sermon preached at the church of Saint Mary Aldermary on the 24th of
June 1690.

[2] Story's Impartial History ; History of the Wars in Ireland by an Officer of the Royal Army ;
Hop to the States General, $\frac{\text{June 30.}}{\text{July 10.}}$ 1690.

by maids of honour as the model of manly vigour and beauty, but now bent down by years and crippled by gout, and, overtopping all, the stately head of Sarsfield.

VIEW OF THE OBELISK ERECTED AT THE BOYNE IN 1736

From a mezzotint by Brookes and Croft, after a painting by Tudor

    The chiefs of the Irish army soon discovered that the person who, surrounded by a splendid circle, was breakfasting on the opposite bank, was the Prince of Orange. They sent for artillery. Two field pieces, screened from view by a troop of cavalry, were brought down almost to the brink of the river, and placed behind a hedge. William, who had just risen from his meal, and was again in the saddle, was the mark of both guns. The first shot struck one of the holsters of Prince George of Hesse, and brought his horse to the ground. "Ah!" cried the King; "the poor Prince is killed." As the words passed his lips, he was himself hit by a second ball, a sixpounder. It merely tore his coat, grazed his shoulder, and drew two or three ounces of blood. Both armies saw that the shot had taken effect; for the King sank down for a moment on his horse's neck. A yell of exultation rose from the Irish camp. The English and their allies were in dismay. Solmes flung himself prostrate on the earth, and burst into tears. But William's deportment soon reassured his friends. "There is no harm done," he said: "but the bullet came quite near enough." Coningsby put his handkerchief to the wound: a surgeon was sent for: a plaster was applied; and the King, as soon as the dressing was finished, rode round all the posts of his army amidst loud acclamations. Such was the energy of his spirit that, in spite of his feeble health, in spite of his recent hurt, he was that day nineteen hours on horseback.[1]

A cannonade was kept up on both sides till the evening. William observed with especial attention the effect produced by the Irish shots on the English regiments which had never been in action, and declared himself satisfied with the result. "All is right," he said: "they stand fire well." Long after sunset he made a final inspection of his forces by torchlight, and gave orders that everything should be ready for forcing a passage across the river on the morrow. Every soldier was to put a green bough in his hat. The baggage and great coats were to be left under a guard. The word was Westminster.

The King's resolution to attack the Irish was not approved by all his lieutenants. Schomberg, in particular, pronounced the experiment too hazardous, and, when his opinion was overruled, retired to his tent in no very good humour. When the order of battle was delivered to him, he muttered that he had been more used to give such orders than to receive them. For this little fit of sullenness, very pardonable in a general who had won great victories when his master was still a child, the brave veteran made, on the following morning, a noble atonement.

The first of July dawned, a day which has never since returned without exciting strong emotions of very different kinds in the two **Battle of** populations which divide Ireland. The sun rose bright and **the Boyne** cloudless. Soon after four both armies were in motion. William ordered his right wing, under the command of Meinhart

[1] London Gazette, July 7. 1690; Story's Impartial History; History of the Wars in Ireland by an Officer of the Royal Army; Narcissus Luttrell's Diary; Lord Marchmont's Memorandum; Burnet, ii. 50. and Thanksgiving Sermon; Dumont MS.

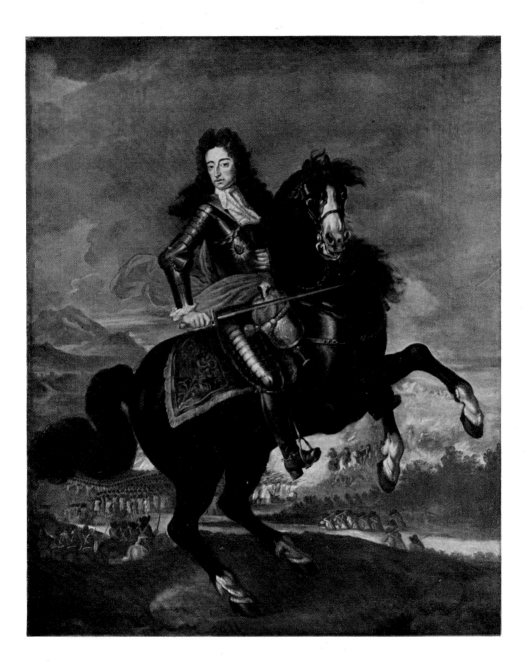

WILLIAM III., 1650-1702, AT THE BATTLE OF THE BOYNE.
From the painting by Jan Wyck, in the National Portrait Gallery.

Schomberg, one of the Duke's sons, to march to the bridge of Slane, some miles up the river, to cross there, and to turn the left flank of the Irish army. Meinhart Schomberg was assisted by Portland and Douglas. James, anticipating some such design, had already sent to the bridge a regiment of dragoons, commanded by Sir Neil O'Neil. O'Neil behaved himself like a brave gentleman : but he soon received a mortal wound ; his men fled ; and the English right wing passed the river.

This move made Lauzun uneasy. What if the English right wing should get into the rear of the army of James? About four miles south of the Boyne was a place called Duleek, where the road to

MEDAL REPRESENTING WILLIAM III AT THE BATTLE OF THE BOYNE

Dublin was so narrow, that two cars could not pass each other, and where on both sides of the road lay a morass which afforded no firm footing. If Meinhart Schomberg should occupy this spot, it would be impossible for the Irish to retreat. They must either conquer, or be cut off to a man. Disturbed by this apprehension, the French general marched with his countrymen and with Sarsfield's horse in the direction of Slane Bridge. Thus the fords near Oldbridge were left to be defended by the Irish alone.

It was now near ten o'clock. William put himself at the head of his left wing, which was composed exclusively of cavalry, and prepared to pass the river not far above Drogheda. The centre of his army, which consisted almost exclusively of foot, was entrusted to the command of Schomberg, and was marshalled opposite to Oldbridge. At Oldbridge had been collected the whole Irish army, foot, dragoons, and horse, Sarsfield's regiment alone excepted. The Meath bank bristled with pikes and bayonets.   A fortification had been made by French engineers out of the hedges and buildings ; and a breastwork had been thrown up close to the water side.[1]   Tyrconnel was there; and under him were Richard Hamilton and Antrim.

Schomberg gave the word.   Solmes's Blues were the first to move. They marched gallantly, with drums beating, to the brink of the Boyne. Then the drums stopped ; and the men, ten abreast, descended into the water.   Next plunged Londonderry and Enniskillen.   A little to the left of Londonderry and Enniskillen, Caillemot crossed, at the head of a long column of French refugees.   A little to the left of Caillemot and his refugees, the main body of the English infantry struggled through the river, up to their armpits in water.   Still further down the stream the Danes found another ford.   In a few minutes the Boyne, for a quarter of a mile, was alive with muskets and green boughs.

It was not till the assailants had reached the middle of the channel that they became aware of the whole difficulty and danger of the service in which they were engaged.   They had as yet seen little more than half the hostile army.   Now whole regiments of foot and horse seemed to start out of the earth.   A wild shout of defiance rose from the whole shore : during one moment the event seemed doubtful : but the Protestants pressed resolutely forward ; and in another moment the whole Irish line gave way.   Tyrconnel looked on in helpless despair. He did not want personal courage : but his military skill was so small that he hardly ever reviewed his regiment in the Phœnix Park without committing some blunder ; and to rally the ranks which were breaking all round him was no task for a general who had survived the energy of his body and of his mind, and yet had still the rudiments of his profession to learn.   Several of his best officers fell while vainly endeavouring to prevail on their soldiers to look the Dutch Blues in the face. Richard Hamilton ordered a body of foot to fall on the French refugees, who were still deep in water.   He led the way, and, accompanied by some courageous gentlemen, advanced, sword in hand, into the river. But neither his commands nor his example could infuse valour into that mob of cowstealers.   He was left almost alone, and retired from the bank in despair.   Further down the river, Antrim's division ran like sheep at the approach of the English column.   Whole regiments flung away arms, colours, and cloaks, and scampered off to the hills without striking a blow or firing a shot.[2]

[1] La Hoguette to Louvois, $\frac{\text{July 31.}}{\text{Aug. 10.}}$ 1690.

[2] That I have done no injustice to the Irish infantry and dragoons will appear from the accounts which the French officers who were at the Boyne sent to their government and their families.   La Hoguette, writing hastily to Louvois on the $\frac{14}{4}$th of July, says : "Je vous diray seulement, Monseigneur, que nous n'avons pas esté battus, mais que les ennemys ont chassés

It required many years and many heroic exploits to take away the reproach which that ignominious rout left on the Irish name. Yet, even before the day closed, it was abundantly proved that the reproach was unjust. Richard Hamilton put himself at the head of the cavalry, and, under his command, they made a gallant, though an unsuccessful attempt to retrieve the day. They maintained a desperate fight in the bed of the river with Solmes's Blues. They drove the Danish brigade back into the stream. They fell impetuously on the Huguenot regiments, which, not being provided with pikes, then ordinarily used by foot to repel horse, began to give ground. Caillemot, while encouraging his fellow exiles, received a mortal wound in the thigh. Four of his men carried him back across the ford to his tent. As he passed, he continued to urge forward the rear ranks which were still up to the breast in the water. "On ; on ; my lads ! To glory! To glory." Schomberg, who had remained on the northern bank, and who had thence watched the progress of his troops with the eye of a general, now thought that the emergency required from him the personal exertion of a soldier. Those who stood about him besought him in vain to put on his cuirass. Without defensive armour he rode through the river, and rallied the refugees whom the fall of Caillemot had dismayed. "Come on," he cried in French, pointing to the Popish squadrons : "come on, gentlemen : there are your persecutors." Those were his last words. As he spoke, a band of Irish horsemen rushed upon him and encircled him for a moment. When they retired, he was on the ground. His friends raised him : but he was already a corpse. Two sabre wounds were on his head ; and a bullet from a carbine was lodged in his neck. Almost at the same

---

devant eux les trouppes Irlandoises comme des moutons, sans avoir essayé un seul coup de mousquet."

Writing some weeks later more fully from Limerick, he says, "J'en meurs de honte." He admits that it would have been no easy matter to win the battle, at best. "Mais il est vray aussi," he adds, "que les Irlandois ne firent pas la moindre resistance, et plièrent sans tirer un seul coup." Zurlauben, Colonel of one of the finest regiments in the French service, wrote to the same effect, but did justice to the courage of the Irish horse, whom La Hoguette does not mention.

There is at the French War Office a letter hastily scrawled by Boisseleau, Lauzun's second in command, to his wife after the battle. He wrote thus : "Je me porte bien, ma chère feme. Ne t'inquieste pas de moy. Nos Irlandois n'ont rien fait qui vaille. Ils ont tous laché le piè."

Desgrigny, writing on the $\frac{10}{20}$th of July, assigns several reasons for the defeat. "La première et la plus forte est la fuite des Irlandois qui sont en vérité des gens sur lesquels il ne faut pas compter du tout." In the same letter he says : "Il n'est pas naturel de croire qu'une armée de vingt cinq mille hommes qui paroissoit de la meilleure volonté du monde, et qui à la veue des ennemis faisoit des cris de joye, dût être entièrement défaite sans avoir tiré l'épée et un seul coup de mousquet. Il y a eu tel regiment tout entier qui a laissé ses habits, ses armes, et ses drapeaux sur le champ de bataille, et a gagné les montagnes avec ses officiers."

I looked in vain for the despatch in which Lauzun must have given Louvois a detailed account of the battle.

moment Walker, while exhorting the colonists of Ulster to play the men, was shot dead.   During near half an hour the battle continued to rage along the southern shore of the river.   All was smoke, dust, and din.   Old soldiers were heard to say that they had seldom seen sharper work in the Low Countries.   But, just at this conjuncture, William came up with the left wing.   He had found much difficulty in crossing.   The tide was running fast.   His charger had been forced to swim, and had been almost lost in the mud.   As soon as the King was on firm ground he took his sword in his left hand,—for his right arm was stiff with his wound and his bandage,—and led his men to the place where the fight was the hottest.   His arrival decided the fate of the day.   Yet the Irish horse retired fighting obstinately.   It was long remembered among the Protestants of Ulster that, in the midst of the tumult, William rode to the head of the Enniskilleners.   "What will you do for me?" he cried. He was not immediately recognised; and one trooper, taking him for an enemy, was about to fire.   William gently put aside the carbine. "What," said he, "do you not know your friends?"   "It is His Majesty;" said the Colonel.   The ranks of sturdy Protestant yeomen set up a shout of joy.   "Gentlemen," said William, "you shall be my guards to day.   I have heard much of you.   Let me see something of you."   One of the most remarkable peculiarities of this man, ordinarily so saturnine and reserved, was that danger acted on him like wine, opened his heart, loosened his tongue, and took away all appearance of constraint from his manner.   On this memorable day he was seen wherever the peril was greatest.   One ball struck the cap of his pistol : another carried off the heel of his jackboot : but his lieutenants in vain implored him to retire to some station from which he could give his orders without exposing a life so valuable to Europe.   His troops, animated by his example, gained ground fast.   The Irish cavalry made their last stand at a house called Plottin Castle, about a mile and a half south of Oldbridge.   There the Enniskilleners were repelled with the loss of fifty men, and were hotly pursued, till William rallied them and turned the chase back.   In this encounter Richard Hamilton, who had done all that could be done by valour to retrieve a reputation forfeited by perfidy,[1] was severely wounded, taken prisoner, and instantly brought, through the smoke and over the carnage, before the prince whom he had foully wronged.   On no occasion did the character of William show itself in a more striking manner.   "Is this business over?" he said ; "or will your horse make more fight?"   "On my honour, Sir," answered Hamilton, "I believe that they will."   "Your honour!" muttered William ; "your honour!"   That half suppressed exclamation was the

---

[1] Lauzun wrote to Seignelay, July $\frac{18}{28}$. 1690, "Richard Amilton a été fait prisonnier, faisant fort bein son devoir."

only revenge which he condescended to take for an injury for which many sovereigns, far more affable and gracious in their ordinary deportment, would have exacted a terrible retribution. Then, restraining himself, he ordered his own surgeon to look to the hurts of the captive.[1]

And now the battle was over. Hamilton was mistaken in thinking that his horse would continue to fight. Whole troops had been cut to pieces. One fine regiment had only thirty unwounded men left. It was enough that these gallant soldiers had disputed the field till they were left without support, or hope, or guidance, till their bravest leader was a captive, and till their King had fled.

MEDAL COMMEMORATING THE DUKE OF SCHOMBERG

(The head resembles Ginkell rather than Schomberg)

Whether James had owed his early reputation for valour to accident and flattery, or whether, as he advanced in life, his character underwent a change, may be doubted. But it is certain that, in his youth, he was generally believed to possess, not merely that average measure of fortitude which qualifies a soldier to go through a campaign without disgrace, but that high and serene intrepidity which

Flight of James

[1] My chief materials for the history of this battle are Story's Impartial Account and Continuation ; the History of the War in Ireland by an Officer of the Royal Army ; the despatches in the French War Office ; the Life of James, Orig. Mem. ; Burnet, ii. 50. 60. ; Narcissus Luttrell's Diary ; the London Gazette of July 10. 1690 ; the Despatches of Hop and Baden ; a narrative probably drawn up by Portland, which William sent to the States General ; Portland's private letter to Melville ; Captain Richardson's Narrative and map of the battle ; the Dumont MS., and the Bellingham MS. I have also seen an account of the battle in a Diary kept in bad Latin and in an almost undecipherable hand by one of the beaten army who seems to have been a hedge schoolmaster turned Captain. This Diary was kindly lent to me by Mr. Walker, to whom it belongs. The writer relates the misfortunes of his country in a style of which a short specimen may suffice : " 1 July, 1690. O diem illum infandum, cum inimici potiti sunt pass apud Oldbridge et nos circumdederunt et fregerunt prope Plottin. Hinc omnes fugimus Dublin versus. Ego mecum tuli Cap Moore et Georgium Ogle, et venimus hac nocte Dub. "

is the virtue of great commanders.[1]　It is equally certain that, in his
later years, he repeatedly, at conjunctures such as have often inspired
timorous and delicate women with heroic courage, showed a pusillanimous
anxiety about his personal safety.　Of the most powerful motives which
can induce human beings to encounter peril, none was wanting to him
on the day of the Boyne.　The eyes of contending nations and churches,
of friends devoted to his cause and of enemies eager to witness his
humiliation, were fixed upon him.　He had, in his own opinion, sacred
rights to maintain and cruel wrongs to revenge.　He was a King come
to fight for three kingdoms.　He was a father come to fight for the
birthright of his child.　He was a zealous Roman Catholic, come to
fight in the holiest of crusades.　If all this was not enough, he saw,
from the secure position which he occupied on the height of Donore, a
sight which, it might have been thought, would have roused the most
torpid of mankind to emulation.　He saw his rival, weak, sickly, wounded,
swimming the river, struggling through the mud, leading the charge,
stopping the flight, grasping the sword with the left hand, managing
the bridle with a bandaged arm.　But none of these things moved that
sluggish and ignoble nature.　He watched, from a safe distance, the
beginning of the battle on which his fate and the fate of his race
depended.　When it became clear that the day was going against
Ireland, he was seized with an apprehension that his flight might be
intercepted, and galloped towards Dublin.　He was escorted by a body-
guard under the command of Sarsfield, who had, on that day, had no
opportunity of displaying the skill and courage which his enemies
allowed that he possessed.[2]　The French auxiliaries, who had been
employed the whole morning in keeping William's right wing in check,
covered the flight of the beaten army.　They were indeed in some
danger of being broken and swept away by the torrent of runaways,
all pressing to get first to the pass of Duleek, and were forced to fire
repeatedly on these despicable allies.[3]　The retreat was, however, effected

---

[1] See Pepys's Diary, June 4. 1664.　"He tells me above all of the Duke of York, that he is
more himself, and more of judgment is at hand in him, in the middle of a desperate service than
at other times."　Clarendon repeatedly says the same.　Swift wrote on the margin of his copy of
Clarendon, in one place, "How old was he (James) when he turned Papist and a coward?" — in
another, "He proved a cowardly Popish king."

[2] The Père Orléans mentions that Sarsfield accompanied James.　The battle of the Boyne had
scarcely been fought when it was made the subject of a drama, the Royal Flight, or the Conquest
of Ireland, a Farce, 1690.　Nothing more execrable was ever written, even for Bartholomew
Fair.　But it deserves to be remarked that, in this wretched piece, though the Irish generally
are represented as poltroons, an exception is made in favour of Sarsfield.　"This fellow," says
James, aside, "will make me valiant, I think, in spite of my teeth."　"Curse of my stars!" says
Sarsfield, after the battle.　"That I must be detached!　I would have wrested victory out of
heretic Fortune's hands."

[3] Both La Hoguette and Zurlauben informed their government that it had been necessary to
fire on the Irish fugitives, who would otherwise have thrown the French ranks into confusion.

with less loss than might have been expected. For even the admirers of William owned that he did not show in the pursuit the energy which even his detractors acknowledged that he had shown in the battle. Perhaps his physical infirmities, his hurt, and the fatigue which he had undergone, had made him incapable of bodily or mental exertion. Of the last forty hours he had passed thirty five on horseback. Schomberg, who might have supplied his place, was no more. It was said in the camp that the King could not do everything, and that what was not done by him was not done at all.

The slaughter had been less than on any battle field of equal importance and celebrity. Of the Irish only about fifteen hundred

MEDALS REPRESENTING WILLIAM III AND JAMES II

had fallen : but they were almost all cavalry, the flower of the army, brave and well disciplined men, whose place could not easily be supplied. William gave strict orders that there should be no unnecessary bloodshed, and enforced those orders by an act of laudable severity. One of his soldiers, after the fight was over, butchered three defenceless Irishmen who asked for quarter. The King ordered the murderer to be hanged on the spot.[1]

Loss of the two armies

The loss of the conquerors did not exceed five hundred men : but among them was the first captain in Europe. To his corpse every honour was paid. The only cemetery in which so illustrious a warrior, slain in arms for the liberties and religion of England, could properly be laid was that venerable Abbey, hallowed by the dust of many generations of princes, heroes, and poets. It was announced that the brave veteran would have a public funeral at Westminster. In the mean time his corpse was embalmed with such skill as could be found in the camp, and was deposited in a leaden coffin.[2]

[1] Baden to Van Citters, July ⁸⁄₁₈. 1690.   [2] New and Perfect Journal, 1690 ; Luttrell's Diary.

Walker was treated less respectfully. William thought him a busy-body who had been properly punished for running into danger without any call of duty, and expressed that feeling, with characteristic bluntness, on the field of battle. "Sir," said an attendant, "the Bishop of Derry has been killed by a shot at the ford." "What took him there?" growled the King.

The victorious army advanced that day to Duleek, and passed the warm summer night there under the open sky. The tents and the bag-gage waggons were still on the north of the river. William's coach had been brought over; and he slept in it surrounded by his soldiers. On the following day, Drogheda surrendered without a blow, and the garrison, thirteen hundred strong, marched out unarmed.[1]

Fall of Drogheda

Meanwhile Dublin had been in violent commotion. On the thirtieth of June it was known that the armies were face to face with the Boyne between them, and that a battle was almost inevitable. The news that William had been wounded came that evening. The first report was that the wound was mortal. It was believed, and confidently repeated, that the usurper was no more; and, before the truth was known, couriers started bearing the glad tidings of his death to the French ships which lay in the ports of Munster. From daybreak on the first of July the streets of Dublin were filled with persons eagerly asking and telling news. A thousand wild rumours wandered to and fro among the crowd. A fleet of men of war under the white flag had been seen from the hill of Howth. An army commanded by a Marshal of France had landed in Kent. There had been hard fighting at the Boyne: but the Irish had won the day: the English right wing had been routed: the Prince of Orange was a prisoner. While the Roman Catholics heard and repeated these stories in all the places of public resort, the few Protestants who were still out of prison, afraid of being torn to pieces, shut themselves up in their inner chambers. But, towards five in the afternoon, a few runaways on tired horses came straggling in with evil tidings. By six it was known that all was lost. Soon after sunset, James, escorted by two hundred cavalry, rode into the Castle. At the threshold he was met by the wife of Tyrconnel, once the gay and beautiful Fanny Jennings, the loveliest coquette in the brilliant Whitehall of the Restoration. To her the vanquished King had to announce the ruin of her fortunes and of his own. And now the tide of fugitives came in fast. Till midnight all the northern avenues of the capital were choked by trains of cars and by bands of dragoons, spent with running and riding, and begrimed with dust. Some had lost their fire arms, and some their swords. Some were disfigured by recent

State of Dublin

[1] Story; London Gazette, July 10. 1690.

922.

THE Proteſtant Triumph:

OR,

The ſignal Victory of K. *William* over the *French* and *Iriſh*, Chaſing them from Hill to Hill, taking their Arms and Ammunition alſo; the Surrender of *Drogheda*, and the King's entring the City of *Dublin*; to the unſpeakable Joy and Satisfaction of all True Proteſtants.

This Victory was obtain'd on Tueſday the Firſt of July 1690.

To the Tune of *The Winning lover.*

Licenſed according to Order.

Brave Boys, let Bells now ſweetly ring,
and ſounding Vowels go freely roun',
with Healths to our moſt gracious King,
who is this day with Triumph Crown'd:
A Fig for all our Romiſh Foes,
K. William Conquers where he goes.

The Trumpets ſounded Victory,
and rattling Vvarlike Drums do beat;
Vve laugh'd to ſee the Tories flee,
in what Confuſion they retreat,
While we purſu'd with hardy Blows,
K. William Conquers where he goes.

The French and Tory brethren ſat,
as ſoon as ever we drew near,
and did their Paſſion ſoon forſake,
being glad to run away for fear:
They knew they could not us oppoſe,
K. William Conquers where he goes.

To Ardee firſt we march'd with ſpeed,
where many Thouſand Tories lay,
who being then the Iriſh breed,
they ran to wreck and run away:
K. William he ſuch Courage ſhows,
Which Conquers all where e'er he goes.

Our right renowned King reply'd,
Fear not, my valiant warlike Boys,
For we ſhall ſoon ſubdue the Pride
of both the French and the Dear-joys:
Thus did he Chaſe his flying Foes,
and Conquers all where e'er he goes.

King William Marching in the Head,
whoſe Trumpets did moſt ſweetly ſound,
And all our flying Colours ſpread,
which fight did all our Foes confound:
K. VVilliam's Courage ſcares his Foes,
He Conquers all where e'er he goes.

At length we had a bloody Fray,
our Guns like Thunder then did roar,
K. Vvilliam he did win the Day,
and laid the French in reaking Gore:
His Courage ſcares his mighty Foes,
He conquers all where e'er he goes.

Soto while the fight we did maintain,
we made the Tory Rebells rue;
Lord Carlingford be being ſlain,
and many Great Commanders too:
K. VVilliam's Courage daunts his Foes,
He Conquers all where e'er he goes.

Stout Colonel Parker, with his Teagues,
likewiſe lay bleeding on the Ground,
VVe ſcorn'd to term for their late Intrigues;
while our King is with Trophies Crown'd:
To Dublin Gates he chas'd his Foes,
He Conquers all where e'er he goes.

The King be ſent to Drogheda,
to field before it was too late;
Or elſe his roaring Guns be'd play,
with that they did ſurrender Graft;
Now they could not him oppoſe,
VVho Conquers all where e'er he goes.

Late James he quitted Dublin ſtreight,
And great King William did march in,
'Tis joyfull Tydings to relate,
how he do's Fame and Honour win:
His Courage ſcares the mighty Foes,
He Conquers, &c.

Poor Proteſtants be old free,
which in cloſe Priſons long both lain,
They all enjoy their Liberty,
under K. VVilliam who do's Reign
In ſight of all inſulting Foes,
He Conquers all where e'er he goes.

Printed for P. Brookſby, J. Deacon, J. Blare, J. Back.

THE PROTESTANT TRIUMPH

From the Pepysian Collection of Ballads

wounds.   At two in the morning Dublin was still : but, before the early dawn of midsummer, the sleepers were roused by the peal of trumpets ; and the horse, who had, on the preceding day, so well supported the honour of their country, came pouring through the streets, with ranks fearfully thinned, yet preserving, even in that extremity, some show of military order.   Two hours later Lauzun's drums were heard ; and the French regiments, in unbroken array, marched into the city.[1]   Many thought that, with such a force, a stand might still be made.   But, before six o'clock, the Lord Mayor and some of the principal Roman Catholic citizens were summoned in haste to the Castle.   James took leave of them with a speech which did him little honour.   He had often, he said, been warned that Irishmen, however well they might look, would never acquit themselves well on a field of battle ; and he had now found that the warning was but too true.   He had been so unfortunate as to see himself in less than two years abandoned by two armies.   His English troops had not wanted courage : but they had wanted loyalty.   His Irish troops were, no doubt, attached to his cause, which was their own.   But, as soon as they were brought front to front with an enemy, they ran away.   The loss indeed had been little.   More shame for those who had fled with so little loss.   " I will never command an Irish army again.   I must shift for myself ; and so must you."   After thus reviling his soldiers for being the rabble which his own mismanagement had made them, and for following the example of cowardice which he had himself set them, he uttered a few words more worthy of a King.   He knew, he said, that some of his adherents had declared that they would burn Dublin down rather than suffer it to fall into the hands of the English. Such an act would disgrace him in the eyes of all mankind : for nobody would believe that his friends would venture so far without his sanction. Such an act would also draw on those who committed it severities which otherwise they had no cause to apprehend : for inhumanity to vanquished enemies was not among the faults of the Prince of Orange. For these reasons James charged his hearers on their allegiance neither to sack nor to destroy the city.[2]   He then took his departure, crossed the Wicklow hills with all speed, and never stopped till he was fifty

James flies   miles from Dublin.   Scarcely had he alighted to take some
to France   refreshment when he was scared by an absurd report that the pursuers were close upon him.   He started again, rode hard all night, and gave orders that the bridges should be pulled down behind him. At sunrise on the third of July he reached the harbour of Waterford.

[1] True and Perfect Journal ; Villare Hibernicum ; Story's Impartial History.

[2] Story ; True and Perfect Journal ; London Gazette, July 10. 1690 ; Burnet, ii. 51.; Leslie's Answer to King.

Thence he went by sea to Kinsale, where he embarked on board of a French frigate, and sailed for Brest.[1]

After his departure the confusion in Dublin increased hourly. During the whole of the day which followed the battle, flying foot soldiers, weary and soiled with travel, were constantly coming in. Roman Catholic citizens, with their wives, their families and their household stuff, were constantly going out. In some parts of the capital there was still an appearance of martial order and preparedness. Guards were posted at the gates : the Castle was occupied by a strong body of troops ; and it was generally supposed that the enemy would not be admitted without a struggle. Indeed some swaggerers, who had, a few hours before, run from the breastwork at Oldbridge without drawing a trigger, now swore that they would lay the town in ashes rather than leave it to the Prince of Orange. But towards the evening Tyrconnel and Lauzun collected all their forces, and marched out of the city by the road leading to that vast sheepwalk which extends over the table land of Kildare. Instantly the face of things in Dublin was changed. The Protestants everywhere came forth from their hidingplaces. Some of them entered the houses of their persecutors and demanded arms. The doors of the prisons were opened. The Bishops of Meath and Limerick, Doctor King, and others, who had long held the doctrine of passive obedience, but who had at length been converted by oppression into moderate Whigs, formed themselves into a provisional government, and sent a messenger to William's camp, with the news that Dublin was prepared to welcome him. At eight that evening a troop of English dragoons arrived. They were met by the whole Protestant population on College Green, where the statue of the deliverer now stands. Hundreds embraced the soldiers, hung fondly about the necks of the horses, and ran wildly about, shaking hands with each other. On the morrow a large body of cavalry arrived ; and soon from every side came news of the effects which the victory of the Boyne had produced. James had quitted the island. Wexford had declared for King William. Within twenty five miles of the capital there was not a Papist in arms. Almost all the baggage and stores of the defeated army had been seized by the conquerors. The Enniskilleners had taken not less than three hundred cars, and had found among the booty ten thousand pounds in money, much plate, many valuable trinkets, and all the rich camp equipage of Tyrconnel and Lauzun.[2]

Dublin evacuated by the French and Irish troops

[1] Life of James, ii. 404., Orig. Mem.; Monthly Mercury for August, 1690.

[2] True and Perfect Journal ; London Gazette, July 10. and 14. 1690 ; Narcissus Luttrell's Diary. In the Life of James Bonnell, Accountant General of Ireland (1703), is a remarkable religious meditation, from which I will quote a short passage. "How did we see the

William fixed his headquarters at Finglass, about two miles from Dublin. Thence, on the morning of Sunday, the sixth of July, he rode in great state to the cathedral, and there, with the crown on his head, returned public thanks to God in the choir which is now hung with the banners of the Knights of Saint Patrick. There the remains of Schomberg were deposited, as it was then thought, only for a time; and there they still remain. Doctor King preached, with all the fervour of a neophyte, on the great deliverance which God had wrought for the Church. The Protestant magistrates of the city appeared again, after a long interval, in the pomp of office. William could not be persuaded to repose himself at the Castle, but in the evening returned to his camp, and slept there in his wooden cabin.[1]

Entry of William into Dublin

The fame of these great events flew fast, and excited strong emotions all over Europe. The news of William's wound everywhere preceded by a few hours the news of his victory. Paris was roused at dead of night by the arrival of a courier who brought the joyful intelligence that the heretic, the parricide, the mortal enemy of the greatness of France, had been struck dead by a cannon ball in the sight of the two armies. The commissaries of police ran about the city, knocked at the doors, and called the people up to illuminate. In an hour streets, quays, and bridges were in a blaze: drums were beating and trumpets sounding: the bells of Notre Dame were ringing: peals of cannon were resounding from the batteries of the Bastille. Tables were set out in the streets; and wine was served to all who passed. A Prince of Orange, made of straw, was trailed through the mud, and at last committed to the flames. He was attended by a hideous effigy of the devil, carrying a scroll, on which was written, " I have been waiting for thee these two years." The shops of several Huguenots, who had been dragooned into calling themselves Catholics, but who were suspected of being still heretics at heart, were sacked by the rabble. It was hardly safe to question the truth of the report which had been so eagerly welcomed by the multitude. Soon, however, some coolheaded people ventured to remark that the fact of the tyrant's death was not quite so certain as

Effect produced in France by the news from Ireland

Protestants on the great day of our Revolution, Thursday the third of July, a day ever to be remembered by us with the greatest thankfulness, congratulate and embrace one another as they met, like persons alive from the dead, like brothers and sisters meeting after a long absence, and going about from house to house to give each other joy of God's great mercy, enquiring of one another how they past the late days of distress and terror, what apprehensions they had, what fears or dangers they were under; those that were prisoners, how they got their liberty, how they were treated, and what, from time to time, they thought of things."

[1] London Gazette, July 14. 1690; Story; True and Perfect Journal; Dumont MS. Dumont is the only person who mentions the crown. As he was present, he could not be mistaken. It was probably the crown which James had been in the habit of wearing when he appeared on the throne at the King's Inns.

might be wished. Then arose a vehement controversy about the effect of such wounds : for the vulgar notion was that no person struck by a cannon ball on the shoulder could recover. The disputants appealed to medical authority; and the doors of the great surgeons and physicians

A FRENCH CARICATURE REPRESENTING THE FUNERAL OF WILLIAM III

Number 1242 in the British Museum Catalogue of Satirical Prints

were thronged, it was jocosely said, as if there had been a pestilence in Paris. The question was soon settled by a letter from James, which announced his defeat and his arrival at Brest.[1]

[1] Monthly Mercury for August 1690; Burnet, ii. 50.; Dangeau, Aug. 2. 1690, and Saint Simon's note; The Follies of France, or a true Relation of the extravagant Rejoicings, &c., dated Paris, Aug. 8. 1690.

At Rome the news from Ireland produced a sensation of a very different kind. There too the report of William's death was, during a short time, credited. At the French embassy all was joy and triumph : but the Ambassadors of the House of Austria were in despair ; and the aspect of the Pontifical Court by no means indicated exultation.[1] Melfort, in a transport of joy, sate down to write a letter of congratulation to Mary of Modena. That letter is still extant, and would alone suffice to explain why he was the favourite of James. Herod,—so William was designated, —was gone. There must be a restoration ; and that restoration ought to be followed by a terrible revenge and by the establishment of despotism. The power of the purse must be taken away from the Commons. Political offenders must be tried, not by juries, but by judges on whom the Crown could depend. The Habeas Corpus Act must be rescinded. The authors of the Revolution must be punished with merciless severity. " If," the cruel apostate wrote, " if the King is forced to pardon, let it be as few rogues as he can." [2] After the lapse of some anxious hours, a messenger bearing later and more authentic intelligence alighted at the palace occupied by the representative of the Catholic King. In a moment all was changed. The enemies of France,—and all the population, except Frenchmen and British Jacobites, were her enemies,—eagerly felicitated one another. All the clerks of the Spanish legation were too few to make transcripts of the despatches for the Cardinals and Bishops who were impatient to know the details of the victory. The first copy was sent to the Pope, and was doubtless welcome to him.[3]

The good news from Ireland reached London at a moment when good news was needed. The English flag had been disgraced in the English seas. A foreign enemy threatened the coast. Traitors were at work within the realm. Mary had exerted herself beyond her strength. Her gentle nature was unequal to the cruel anxieties of her position ; and she complained that she could scarcely snatch a moment from business to calm herself by prayer. Her distress rose to the highest point when she learned that the camps of her father and her husband were pitched near to each

Effect produced at Rome by the news from Ireland

Effect produced in London by the news from Ireland

---

[1] " Me tiene," the Marquis of Cogolludo, Spanish minister at Rome, says of this report, " en sumo cuidado y desconsuelo, pues esta seria la ultima ruina de la causa comun."—Cogolludo to Ronquillo, Rome, Aug. 2. 1690.

[2] Original Letters published by Sir Henry Ellis.

[3] " Del sucesso de Irlanda doy a v. Exca la enorabuena, y le aseguro no ha bastado casi la gente que tengo en la Secretaria para repartir copias dello, pues le he embiado a todo el lugar, y la primera al Papa."—Cogolludo to Ronquillo, postscript to the letter of Aug. 2. Cogolludo, of course, uses the new style. The tidings of the battle, therefore, had been three weeks in getting to Rome.

A DUTCH CARICATURE REPRESENTING THE DEATH-BED OF LEWIS XIV

Number 1245 in the British Museum Catalogue of Satirical Prints

other, and that tidings of a battle might be hourly expected. She stole time for a visit to Kensington, and had three hours of quiet in the garden, then a rural solitude.[1] But the recollection of days passed there with him whom she might never see again overpowered her. " The place," she wrote to him, " made me think how happy I was there when I had your dear company. But now I will say no more ; for I shall hurt my own eyes, which I want now more than ever. Adieu. Think of me and love me as much as I shall you, whom I love more than my life." [2]

Early on the morning after these tender lines had been despatched, Whitehall was roused by the arrival of a post from Ireland. Nottingham was called out of bed. The Queen, who was just going to the chapel where she daily attended divine service, was informed that William had been wounded. She had wept much : but till that moment she had wept alone, and had constrained herself to show a cheerful countenance to her Court and Council. But when Nottingham put her husband's letter into her hands, she burst into tears. She was still trembling with the violence of her emotions, and had scarcely finished a letter to William in which she poured out her love, her fears, and her thankfulness, with the sweet natural eloquence of her sex, when another messenger arrived with the news that the English army had forced a passage across the Boyne, that the Irish were flying in confusion, and that the King was well. Yet she was visibly uneasy till Nottingham had assured her that James was safe. The grave Secretary, who seems to have really esteemed and loved her, afterwards described with much feeling that struggle of filial duty with conjugal affection. On the same day she wrote to adjure her husband to see that no harm befell her father. " I know," she said. " I need not beg you to let him be taken care of : for I am confident you will for your own sake : yet add that to all your kindness ; and, for my sake, let people know you would have no hurt happen to his person." [3] This solicitude, though amiable, was superfluous. Her father was perfectly competent to take care of himself. He had never, during the battle, run the smallest risk of hurt ; and, while his daughter was shuddering at the dangers to which she fancied that he was exposed in Ireland, he was half way on his voyage to France.

It chanced that the glad tidings arrived at Whitehall on the day to which the Parliament stood prorogued. The Speaker and several members of the House of Commons who were in London met, according to form, at ten in the morning, and were summoned by Black Rod to the bar of the Peers. The Parliament was then again prorogued by

---

[1] Evelyn (Feb. 25. 16$\frac{89}{90}$) calls it "a sweet villa."   [2] Mary to William, July 5. 1690.
[3] Mary to William, July 6. and 7. 1690 ; Burnet, ii. 55.

De onverwagte Tijding uyt Yerlandt, aen den
Koninck van Vranckrijck,

1. De Koningh van Vranckrijk van onftelte-
tenis te bed leggende, vande ongewenfte
tijdinge vande flag van de Koningh Jacobus fijn
Confrater, en daer foo veel Franfen in doot ge-
bleven fijn, daarom fal hy geklefteert worde.

2. Van de Sultan als Doctoor gekleedt fal hem
klefteeren.

3. De Duyvel mede in Doctoors kleeding is
hem mede hulpfaam om de hand te bieden, roept
daarom noch een onder-aertfe Doctoor by hem,
die mede heel verbaeft fiet.

4. Een Turkfe Doctoor, die hem naeft aen 't
hert leyt, vragende hem of hy iets wilde ordon-
nere voor fijn vrint, dat hy op hem mocht vaft
gaen, want dat hy niet garen hadde, dat hy in
fchielijkheyt van de werelt foude fcheyde.

5. De Portugefen Doctoor heeft mede wat
klaer gemaakt om hem te falveren.

6. De Yerfen Doctoor voelt hem de pols, en
befiet de pis of 'er iets mogt haperen.

7. Pater Petrus in Doctors kleeren, heeft den
brief in de handt, waar uyt de Koning de altera-
fy op een nieu overkomt.

8. De Konings oude Doctoor van 't Hof.

9. Hoffe Paep Doctoor.

10. Hoffe Paep Doctoor, de krijgende laefte
brief, en refoneren daer uyt dat Koning William doot is, tot verlichting van hare Koningh
Louwies droef heyt.

11. Och helaes hier komt Jacobus op het laeft
en is de Boode tot vermeerdering van fijn pijn,
om dat hy quade tijding brengt, is hy verminckt
en fpringt op krukke.

12. Sijn Leeger volgt hem kort op de hielen al
mank en hanckent naer huys, en droevig afge-
fmeerdt.

13. De twee Duyvels verfchijne op 't laeftsten
of hem den een te fwack kende, om malkan-
der hem te helpen verbedden naar een andere
plaets.

A DUTCH CARICATURE REPRESENTING LEWIS XIV RECEIVING THE
NEWS FROM IRELAND

Number 1246 in the British Museum Catalogue of Satirical Prints

commission. As soon as this ceremony had been performed, the Chancellor of the Exchequer put into the hands of the Clerk the despatch which had just arrived from Ireland, and the Clerk read it with a loud voice to the Lords and gentlemen present.[1] The good news spread rapidly from Westminster Hall to all the coffeehouses, and was received with transports of joy. For those Englishmen who wished to see an English army beaten and an English colony extirpated by the French and Irish were a minority even of the Jacobite party.

On the ninth day after the battle of the Boyne James landed at Brest, with an excellent appetite, in high spirits, and in a talkative humour.

James arrives in France: his reception there He told the history of his defeat to everybody who would listen to him. But French officers who understood war, and who compared his story with other accounts, pronounced that, though His Majesty had witnessed the battle, he knew nothing about it, except that his army had been routed.[2] From Brest he proceeded to Saint Germains, where, a few hours after his arrival, he was visited by Lewis. The French King had too much delicacy and generosity to utter a word which could sound like reproach. Nothing, he declared, that could conduce to the comfort of the royal family of England should be wanting, as far as his power extended. But he was by no means disposed to listen to the political and military projects of his unlucky guest. James recommended an immediate descent on England. That kingdom, he said, had been drained of troops by the demands of Ireland. The seven or eight thousand regular soldiers who were left would be unable to withstand a great French army. The people were ashamed of their error and impatient to repair it. As soon as their rightful King showed himself, they would rally round him in multitudes.[3] Lewis was too polite and goodnatured to express what he must have felt. He contented himself with answering coldly that he could not decide upon any plan about the British islands till he had heard from his generals in Ireland. James was importunate, and seemed to think himself ill used, because, a fortnight after he had run away from one army, he was not entrusted with another. Lewis was not to be provoked

---

[1] Baden to Van Citters, July $\frac{8}{18}$. 1690.

[2] See two letters annexed to the Memoirs of the Intendant Foucault, and printed in the work of M. de Sirtema de Grovestins. In the archives of the War Office at Paris is a letter written from Brest by the Count of Bouridal on July $\frac{11}{21}$. 1690. The Count says : " Par la relation du combat que j'ay entendu faire au Roy d'Angleterre et à plusieurs de sa suite en particulier, il ne me paroit pas qu'il soit bien informé de tout ce qui s'est passé dans cette action, et qu'il ne sçait que la déroute de ses troupes."

[3] It was not only on this occasion that James held this language. From one of the letters quoted in the last note it appears that on his road from Brest to Paris he told everybody that the English were impatiently expecting him. " Ce pauvre prince croit que ses sujets l'aiment encore."

Le Roy

LEWIS XIV

From an engraving by N. Habert in the Sutherland Collection

into uttering an unkind or uncourteous word : but he was resolute; and, in order to avoid solicitations which gave him pain, he pretended to be unwell.   During some time, whenever James came to Versailles, he was respectfully informed that His Most Christian Majesty was not equal to the transaction of business.   The highspirited and quickwitted nobles who daily crowded the antechambers could not help sneering while they bowed low to the royal visitor, whose poltroonery and stupidity had a second time made him an exile and a mendicant.   They even whispered their sarcasms loud enough to call up the haughty blood of Este in the cheeks of Mary of Modena.   But her husband stood among the scoffers serene and well pleased with himself.   Contempt, says the fine Indian proverb, pierces through the shell of the tortoise : but the insensibility of James was proof even against contempt.[1]

While he was enduring with ignominious fortitude the polite scorn of the French aristocracy, and doing his best to weary out his benefactor's **Tourville attempts a descent on England** patience and good breeding by repeating that this was the very moment for an invasion of England, and that the whole island was impatiently expecting its foreign deliverers, events were passing which signally proved how little the banished oppressor understood the character of his countrymen.

Tourville had, since the battle of Beachy Head, ranged the Channel unopposed.   On the twenty-first of July his masts were seen from the rocks of Portland.   On the twenty-second he anchored in the harbour of Torbay, under the same heights which had, not many months before, sheltered the armament of William.   The French fleet, which now had a considerable number of troops on board, consisted of a hundred and eleven sail.   The galleys, which formed a large part of this force, resembled rather those ships with which Alcibiades and Lysander disputed the sovereignty of the Ægean than those which contended at the Nile and at Trafalgar.   The galley was very long and very narrow, the deck not more than two feet from the water edge.   Each galley was propelled by fifty or sixty huge oars, and each oar was tugged by five or six slaves.   The full complement of slaves to a vessel was three hundred and thirty six ; the full complement of officers and soldiers a hundred and fifty.   Of the unhappy rowers some were criminals who had been justly condemned to a life of hardship and danger : a few had been guilty only of adhering obstinately to the Huguenot worship : the great majority were purchased bondsmen, generally Turks and Moors. They were of course always forming plans for massacring their tyrants and escaping from servitude, and could be kept in order only by constant stripes, and by the frequent infliction of death in horrible forms. An Englishman, who happened to fall in with about twelve hundred of

---

[1] Life of James, ii. 411, 412.; Burnet, ii. 57., and Dartmouth's note.

these most miserable and most desperate of human beings on their road from Marseilles to join Tourville's squadron, heard them vowing that, if they came near a man of war bearing the cross of Saint George, they would never again see a French dockyard.[1]

In the Mediterranean Sea galleys were in ordinary use : but none had ever before been tossed on the stormy ocean which roars round our island. The flatterers of Lewis said that the appearance of such a squadron on the Atlantic was one of those wonders which were reserved for his reign ; and a medal was struck at Paris to commemorate this bold experiment in maritime war.[2] English sailors, with more reason, predicted that the first gale would send the whole of his fairweather armament to the bottom of the Channel. Indeed the galley, like the ancient trireme, generally kept close to the shore, and ventured out of sight of land only when the water was unruffled and the sky serene. But the qualities which made this sort of ship unfit to brave tempests and billows made it peculiarly fit for the purpose of landing soldiers. Tourville determined to try what effect would be produced by a disembarkation. The English Jacobites who had taken refuge in France were all confident that the whole population of the island was ready to rally round an invading army ; and he probably gave them credit for understanding the temper of their countrymen.

Never was there a greater error. Indeed the French admiral is said by tradition to have received, while he was still out at sea, a lesson which might have taught him not to rely on the assurances of exiles. He picked up a fishing boat, and interrogated the owner, a plain Sussex man, about the sentiments of the nation. " Are you," Tourville asked, " for King James ? " " I do not know much about such matters," answered the fisherman. " I have nothing to say against King James. He is a very worthy gentleman, I believe. God bless him ! " " A good fellow ! " said Tourville : " then I am sure you will have no objection to take service with us." " What ! " cried the prisoner ; " go with the French to fight against the English ! Your honour must excuse me. I could not do it to save my life." [3] This poor fisherman, whether he was a real or an imaginary person, spoke the sense of the nation. The beacon on the ridge overlooking Teignmouth was kindled : the High Tor and Causland made answer ; and soon all the hill tops of the West

---

[1] See the articles Galère and Galérien, in the Encyclopédie, with the plates; A True Relation of the Cruelties and Barbarities of the French upon the English Prisoners of War, by R. Hutton, licensed June 27. 1690.

[2] See the Collection of Medals of Lewis the Fourteenth.

[3] This anecdote, true or false, was current at the time, or soon after. In 1745 it was mentioned as a story which old people had heard in their youth. It is quoted in the Gentleman's Magazine of that year from another periodical work.

were on fire. Messengers were riding hard all night from Deputy Lieutenant to Deputy Lieutenant. Early the next morning, without chief, without summons, five hundred gentlemen and yeomen, armed and mounted, had assembled on the summit of Haldon Hill. In twenty four hours all Devonshire was up. Every road in the county from sea to sea was covered by multitudes of fighting men, all with their faces set towards Torbay. The lords of a hundred manors, proud of their long pedigrees and old coats of arms, took the field at the head of their tenantry, Drakes, Prideauxes, and Rolles, Fowell of Fowelscombe and Fulford of Fulford, Sir Bourchier Wrey of Tawstock Park and Sir William Courtenay of Powderham Castle. Letters written by several of the Deputy Lieutenants who were most active during this anxious week are still preserved. All these letters agree in extolling the courage and enthusiasm of the people. But all agree also in expressing the most painful solicitude as to the result of an encounter between a raw militia and veterans who had served under Turenne and Luxemburg; and all call for the help of regular troops, in language very unlike that which, when the pressure of danger was not felt, country gentlemen were then in the habit of using about standing armies.

Tourville, finding that the whole population was united as one man against him, contented himself with sending his galleys to ravage

Teign-mouth destroyed

Teignmouth, an unfortified market town which had given no provocation and could make no defence. A short cannonade put the inhabitants to flight. Seventeen hundred men landed and marched into the deserted streets. More than a hundred houses were burned to the ground. The cattle were slaughtered. The barks and fishing smacks which lay in the river were destroyed. Two parish churches were sacked, the Bibles and Prayerbooks torn and scattered about the roads, the pulpits and communion tables demolished. By this time sixteen or seventeen thousand Devonshire men had encamped close to the shore; and all the neighbouring counties had risen. The tin mines of Cornwall had sent forth a great multitude of rude and hardy men mortally hostile to Popery. Ten thousand of them had just signed an address to the Queen, in which they had promised to stand by her against every enemy; and they now kept their word.[1] In truth, the whole nation was stirred. Two and twenty troops of cavalry, furnished by Suffolk, Essex, Hertfordshire and Buckinghamshire, were reviewed by Mary at Hounslow, and were complimented by Marlborough on their martial appearance. The militia of Kent and Surrey encamped on Blackheath.[2] Van Citters informed the States General that all England was up in arms, on foot or on horse-

[1] London Gazette, July 7. 1690.   [2] Narcissus Luttrell's Diary.

back, that the disastrous event of the battle of Beachy Head had not cowed, but exasperated the people, and that every company of soldiers

From the Roxburghe Ballads

which he passed on the road was shouting with one voice, " God bless King William and Queen Mary."[1]

---

[1] I give this interesting passage in Van Citters's own words. " Door geheel het ryk alles te voet en te paarde in de wapenen op was ; en't gene een seer groote gerustheyt gaf was dat alle

Charles Granville, Lord Lansdowne, eldest son of the Earl of Bath, came with some troops from the garrison of Plymouth to take the command of the tumultuary army which had assembled round the basin of Torbay. Lansdowne was no novice. He had served several hard campaigns against the common enemy of Christendom, and had been created a Count of the Roman Empire in reward of the valour which he had displayed on that memorable day, sung by Filicaja and by Waller, when the infidels retired from the walls of Vienna. He made preparations for action; but the French did not choose to attack him, and were indeed impatient to depart. They found some difficulty in getting away. One day the wind was adverse to the sailing vessels. Another day the water was too rough for the galleys. At length the fleet stood out to sea. As the line of ships turned the lofty cape which overlooks Torquay, an incident happened which, though slight in itself, greatly interested the thousands who lined the coast. Two wretched slaves disengaged themselves from an oar, and sprang overboard. One of them perished. The other, after struggling more than an hour in the water, came safe to English ground, and was cordially welcomed by a population to which the discipline of the galleys was a thing strange and shocking. He proved to be a Turk, and was humanely sent back to his own country.

A pompous description of the expedition appeared in the Paris Gazette. But in truth Tourville's exploits had been inglorious, and yet less inglorious than impolitic. The injury which he had done bore no proportion to the resentment which he had roused. Hitherto the Jacobites had tried to persuade the nation that the French would come as friends and deliverers, would observe strict discipline, would respect the temples and the ceremonies of the established religion, and would depart as soon as the Dutch oppressors had been expelled and the ancient constitution of the realm restored. The short visit of Tourville to our coast had shown how little reason there was to expect such moderation from the soldiers of Lewis. They had been in our island only a few hours, and had occupied only a few acres. But within a few hours and a few acres had been exhibited in miniature the devastation of the Palatinate. What had happened was communicated to the whole kingdom far more rapidly than by gazettes or newsletters. A brief for the relief of the people of Teignmouth was read in all the ten thousand parish churches of the land. No congregation could hear without emotion that the Popish marauders

Excitement of the English nation against the French

en een yder even seer tegen de Franse door de laatste voorgevallen bataille verbittert en geanimeert waren. Gelyk door de troupes, dewelke ik op de weg alomme gepasseert ben, niet anders heb konnen hooren als een eenpaarig en generaal geluydt van God bless King William en Queen Mary." $\frac{\text{July 25.}}{\text{Aug. 4.}}$ 1690.

THE ATTACK ON TEIGNMOUTH

From a drawing by R. Chasse in the Cabinet des Estampes

had made desolate the habitations of quiet fishermen and peasants, had outraged the altars of God, had torn to pieces the Gospels and the Liturgy. A street, built out of the contributions of the charitable, on the site of the dwellings which the invaders had destroyed, still retains the name of French Street.[1]

The outcry against those who were, with good reason, suspected of having invited the enemy to make a descent on our shores was vehement and general, and was swollen by many voices which had recently been loud in clamour against the government of William. The question had ceased to be a question between two dynasties, and had become a question between England and France. So strong was the national sentiment that nonjurors and Papists shared or affected to share it. Dryden, not long after the burning of Teignmouth, laid a play at the feet of Halifax, with a dedication eminently ingenious, artful, and eloquent. The dramatist congratulated his patron on having taken shelter in a calm haven from the storms of public life, and, with great force and beauty of diction, magnified the felicity of the statesman who exchanges the bustle of office and the fame of oratory for philosophic studies and domestic endearments. England could not complain that she was defrauded of the service to which she had a right. Even the severe discipline of ancient Rome permitted a soldier, after many campaigns, to claim his dismission ; and Halifax had surely done enough for his country to be entitled to the same privilege. But the poet added that there was one case in which the Roman veteran, even after his discharge, was required to resume his shield and his pilum ; and that one case was a Gallic invasion. That a writer who had purchased the smiles of James by apostasy, who had been driven in disgrace from the court of William, and who had a deeper interest in the restoration of the exiled House than any man who made letters his calling, should have used such language as this, is a fact which may convince us that the determination never to be subjugated by foreigners was fixed in the hearts of the people.[2]

---

[1] As to this expedition I have consulted the London Gazettes of July 24. 28. 31., Aug. 4. 1690 ; Narcissus Luttrell's Diary ; Welwood's Mercurius Reformatus, Sept. 5. ; the Gazette de Paris ; a letter from Mr. Duke, a Deputy Lieutenant of Devonshire, to Hampden, dated July 25.; a letter from Mr. Fulford of Fulford to Lord Nottingham, dated July 26. ; a letter of the same date from the Deputy Lieutenants of Devonshire to the Earl of Bath ; a letter of the same date from Lord Lansdowne to the Earl of Bath. These four letters are among the MSS. of the Royal Irish Academy. Mr. Jordan of Teignmouth has kindly sent me a copy of the brief, which has enabled me to correct some errors of detail into which I had been led by documents less authentic. Dangeau inserted in his Journal, August 16., a series of extravagant lies. Tourville had routed the militia, taken their cannon and colours, burned men of war, captured richly laden merchantships, and was going to destroy Plymouth. This is a fair specimen of Dangeau's English news. Indeed he complains that it was hardly possible to get at true information about England.

[2] Dedication of Arthur.

There was indeed a Jacobite literature in which no trace of this patriotic spirit can be detected, a literature the remains of which prove that there were Englishmen perfectly willing to see the Eng- The Jaco-lish flag dishonoured, the English soil invaded, the English bite Press capital sacked, the English crown worn by a vassal of Lewis, if only they might avenge themselves on their enemies, and especially on William, whom they hated with a hatred half frightful, half ludicrous. But this literature was altogether a work of darkness. The law by which the Parliament of James had subjected the press to the control of censors was still in force; and, though the officers whose business it was to prevent the infraction of that law were not extreme to mark every irregularity committed by a bookseller who understood the art of conveying a guinea in a squeeze of the hand, they could not wink at the open vending of unlicensed pamphlets filled with ribald insults to the Sovereign, and with direct instigations to rebellion. But there had long lurked in the garrets of London a class of printers who worked steadily at their calling with precautions resembling those employed by coiners and forgers. Women were on the watch to give the alarm by their screams if an officer appeared near the workshop. The press was immediately pushed into a closet behind the bed: the types were flung into the coalhole, and covered with cinders: the compositor disappeared through a trapdoor in the roof, and made off over the tiles of the neighbouring houses. In these dens were manufac-tured treasonable works of all classes and sizes, from halfpenny broad-sides of doggrel verse up to massy quartos filled with Hebrew quotations. It was not safe to exhibit such publications openly on a counter. They were sold only by trusty agents, and in secret places. Some tracts, which were thought likely to produce a great effect, were given away in immense numbers at the expense of wealthy Jacobites. Sometimes a paper was thrust under a door, sometimes dropped on the table of a coffeehouse. One day a thousand copies of a scurrilous pamphlet went out by the postbags. On another day, when the shopkeepers rose early to take down their shutters, they found the whole of Fleet Street and the Strand white with seditious handbills.[1]

Of the numerous performances which were ushered into the world by such shifts as these, none produced a greater sensation The Jaco-than a little book which purported to be a form of prayer and bite Form of Prayer and humiliation for the use of the persecuted Church. It was im- Humiliation possible to doubt that a considerable sum had been expended on this

---

[1] See the accounts of Anderton's Trial, 1693; the Postman of March 12. 169⅚; the Flying Post of March 7. 1700; Some Discourses upon Dr. Burnet and Dr. Tillotson, by Hickes, 1695. The appendix to these Discourses contains a curious account of the inquisition into printing offices under the Licensing Act.

work.　Ten thousand copies were, by various means, scattered over the kingdom.　No more mendacious, more malignant, or more impious lampoon was ever penned.　Though the government had as yet treated its enemies with a lenity unprecedented in the history of our country, though not a single person had, since the Revolution, suffered death for any political offence, the authors of this liturgy were not ashamed to pray that God would assuage their enemy's insatiable thirst for blood, or would, if any more of them were to be brought through the Red Sea to the Land of Promise, prepare them for the passage.[1]　They complained that the Church of England, once the perfection of beauty, had become a scorn and derision, a heap of ruins, a vineyard of wild grapes; that her services had ceased to deserve the name of public worship; that the bread and wine which she dispensed had no longer any sacramental virtue; that her priests, in the act of swearing fealty to the usurper, had lost the sacred character which had been conferred on them by their ordination.[2]　James was profanely described as the stone which foolish builders had rejected; and a fervent petition was put up that Providence would again make him the head of the corner.　The blessings which were called down on our country were of a singular description.　There was something very like a prayer for another Bloody Circuit; "Give the King the necks of his enemies:" there was something very like a prayer for a French invasion; "Raise him up friends abroad;" and there was a more mysterious prayer, the best comment on which was afterwards furnished by the Assassination Plot; "Do some great thing for him, which we in particular know not how to pray for."[3]

　　This liturgy was composed, circulated, and read, it is said, in some congregations of Jacobite schismatics, before William set out for Ireland, **Clamour against the nonjuring Bishops** but did not attract general notice till the appearance of a foreign armament on our coast had roused the national spirit. Then rose a roar of indignation against the Englishmen who had dared, under the hypocritical pretence of devotion, to imprecate curses on England.　The deprived Prelates were suspected, and not without some show of reason.　For the nonjurors were, to a man, zealous Episcopalians.　Their doctrine was that, in ecclesiastical matters of grave moment, nothing could be well done without the sanction of

---

[1] This was the ordinary cant of the Jacobites.　A Whig writer had justly said in the preceding year, " They scurrilously call our David a man of blood, though, to this day, he has not suffered a drop to be spilt."—Mephibosheth and Ziba, licensed Aug. 30. 1689.

[2] " Restore unto us again the publick worship of thy name, the reverent administration of thy sacraments.　Raise up the former government both in church and state, that we may be no longer without King, without priest, without God in the world."

[3] A Form of Prayer and Humiliation for God's Blessing upon His Majesty and his Dominions, and for Removing and Averting of God's Judgments from this Church and State, 1690.

the Bishop. And could it be believed that any who held this doctrine would compose a service, print it, circulate it, and actually use it in public worship, without the approbation of Sancroft, whom the whole party revered, not only as the true Primate of all England, but also as a Saint and a Confessor? It was known that the Prelates who had refused the oaths had lately held several consultations at Lambeth. The subject of those consultations, it was now said, might easily be guessed. The holy fathers had been engaged in framing prayers for the destruction of the Protestant colony in Ireland, for the defeat of the English fleet in the Channel, and for the speedy arrival of a French army in Kent. The extreme section of the Whig party pressed this accusation with vindictive eagerness. This then, said those implacable politicians, was the fruit of King William's merciful policy. Never had he committed a greater error than when he had conceived the hope that the hearts of the clergy were to be won by clemency and moderation. He had not chosen to give credit to men who had learned by a long and bitter experience that no kindness will tame the sullen ferocity of a priesthood. He had stroked and pampered when he should have tried the effect of chains and hunger. He had hazarded the good will of his best friends by protecting his worst enemies. Those Bishops who had publicly refused to acknowledge him as their Sovereign, and who, by that refusal, had forfeited their dignities and revenues, still continued to live unmolested in palaces which ought to be occupied by better men. And for his indulgence, an indulgence unexampled in the history of revolutions, what return had been made? Even this, that the men, whom he had, with so much tenderness, screened from just punishment, had the insolence to describe him in their prayers as a persecutor defiled with the blood of the righteous; that they asked for grace to endure with fortitude his sanguinary tyranny; that they cried to heaven for a foreign fleet and army to deliver them from his yoke; nay, that they hinted at a wish so odious that even they had not the front to speak it plainly. One writer, in a pamphlet which produced a great sensation, expressed his wonder that the people had not, when Tourville was riding victorious in the Channel, Dewitted the nonjuring Prelates. Excited as the public mind then was, there was some danger that this suggestion might bring a furious mob to Lambeth. At Norwich indeed the people actually rose, attacked the palace which the Bishop was still suffered to occupy, and would have pulled it down but for the timely arrival of the trainbands.[1] The government very properly instituted criminal proceedings against the publisher of the work which had produced this alarming breach of the peace.[2] The deprived

[1] Letter of Lloyd, Bishop of Norwich, to Sancroft, in the Tanner MSS.
[2] Luttrell's Diary.

Prelates meanwhile put forth a defence of their conduct. In this document they declared, with all solemnity, and as in the presence of God, that they had no hand in the new liturgy, that they knew not who had framed it, that they had never used it, that they had never held any correspondence directly or indirectly with the French court, that they were engaged in no plot against the existing government, and that they would willingly shed their blood rather than see England subjugated by a foreign prince, who had, in his own kingdom, cruelly persecuted their Protestant brethren. As to the writer who had marked them out to the public vengeance by a fearful word, but too well understood, they commended him to the Divine mercy, and heartily prayed that his great sin might be forgiven him. Most of those who signed this paper did so doubtless with sincerity : but there is good reason to believe that one at least of the subscribers added to the crime of betraying his country the crime of calling his God to witness a falsehood.[1]

The events which were passing in the Channel and on the Continent compelled William to make repeated changes in his plans. During the

Military operations in Ireland : Waterford taken

week which followed his triumphal entry into Dublin, messengers charged with evil tidings arrived from England in rapid succession. First came the account of Waldeck's defeat at Fleurus. The King was much disturbed. All the pleasure, he said, which his own victory had given him was at an end. Yet, with that generosity which was hidden under his austere aspect, he sate down, even in the moment of his first vexation, to write a kind and encouraging letter to the unfortunate general.[2] Three days later came intelligence more alarming still. The allied fleet had been ignominiously beaten. The sea from the Downs to the Land's End was in possession of the enemy. The next post might bring news that Kent was invaded. A French squadron might appear in Saint George's Channel, and might without difficulty burn all the transports which lay at anchor in the Bay of Dublin. William determined to return to England : but he wished to obtain, before he went, the command of a safe haven on the eastern coast of Ireland. Waterford was the best place suited to his purpose ;

[1] A Modest Inquiry into the Causes of the present Disasters in England, and who they are that brought the French into the English Channel described, 1690 ; Reflections upon a Form of Prayer lately set out for the Jacobites, 1690 ; A Midnight Touch at an Unlicensed Pamphlet, 1690. The paper signed by the nonjuring Bishops has often been reprinted.

Since the first edition of this part of my work appeared I have learned that the Jacobite Form of Prayer which produced so much excitement and controversy in 1690 was, to a great extent, copied from a Form of Prayer which had been composed and clandestinely printed, soon after the battle of Worcester, for the use of the Royalists. This curious fact, which seems to have been quite unknown both to the accused Bishops and to their accusers, was discovered by Mr. Lathbury, after the publication of his History of the Nonjurors, and was, in the most obliging manner, communicated by him to me.

[2] William to Heinsius, July $\frac{4}{14}$. 1690.

CASTLE OF KILKENNY.
FROM THE COLLEGE MEADOW.

Drawn by Robertson.   Engraved by W. Taylor.

VIEW OF KILKENNY CASTLE

From an engraving by W. Taylor in the British Museum

and towards Waterford he immediately proceeded.   Clonmel and Kil-kenny were abandoned by the Irish troops as soon as it was known that he was approaching.   At Kilkenny he was entertained, on the nine-teenth of July, by the Duke of Ormond, in the ancient castle of the Butlers, which had not long before been occupied by Lauzun, and which therefore, in the midst of the general devastation, still had tables and chairs, hangings on the walls, and claret in the cellars.   On the twenty-first, two regiments which garrisoned Waterford consented to march out after a faint show of resistance : a few hours later the fort of Duncannon, which, towering on a rocky promontory, commanded the entrance of the harbour, surrendered ; and William was master of the whole of that secure and spacious basin which is formed by the united waters of the Suir, the Nore, and the Barrow.   He then announced his intention of instantly returning to England, and, having declared Count Solmes Commander in Chief of the army of Ireland, set out for Dublin.[1]

But good news met him on the road.   Tourville had appeared on the coast of Devonshire, had put some troops on shore, and had sacked Teignmouth : but the only effect of this insult had been to raise the whole population of the western counties in arms against the invaders. The enemy had departed, after doing just mischief enough to make the cause of James as odious for a time to Tories as to Whigs.   William therefore again changed his plans, and hastened back to his army, which, during his absence, had moved westward, and which he rejoined in the neighbourhood of Cashel.[2]

About this time he received from Mary a letter requesting him to decide an important question on which the Council of Nine was divided. Marlborough was of opinion that all danger of invasion was over for that year.   The sea, he said, was open : for the French ships had returned into port, and were refitting.   Now was the time to send an English fleet, with five thousand troops on board, to the southern extremity of Ireland.   Such a force might easily reduce Cork and Kinsale, two of the most important strongholds still occupied by the forces of James.   Marlborough was strenuously supported by Notting-ham, and as strenuously opposed by the other members of the interior council with Caermarthen at their head.   The Queen referred the matter to her husband.   He highly approved of the plan, and gave orders that it should be executed by the General who had formed it. Caermarthen submitted, though with a bad grace, and with some mur-murs at the extraordinary partiality of His Majesty for Marlborough.[3]

[1] Story ; London Gazette, Aug. 4. 1690 ; Dumont MS.

[2] Story ; William to Heinsius, $\frac{\text{July 31.}}{\text{Aug. 10.}}$ 1690 ; London Gazette, Aug. 11.

[3] Mary to William, Aug. $\frac{7}{17}$. $\frac{\text{Aug. 22.}}{\text{Sept. 1.}}$ $\frac{\text{Aug. 26.}}{\text{Sept. 5.}}$ 1690.

William meanwhile was advancing towards Limerick. In that city the army which he had put to rout at the Boyne had taken refuge, discomfited, indeed, and disgraced, but very little diminished. He would not have had the trouble of besieging the place, if the advice of Lauzun and of Lauzun's countrymen had been followed. They laughed at the thought of defending such fortifications, and indeed would not admit that the name of fortifications could properly be given to heaps of dirt, which certainly bore little resemblance to the works of Valenciennes and Philipsburg. "It is unnecessary," said Lauzun, with an oath, "for the English to bring cannon against such a place as this. What you call your ramparts might be battered down with roasted apples." He therefore gave his voice for evacuating Limerick, and declared that, at all events, he was determined not to throw away, in a hopeless resistance, the lives of the brave men who had been entrusted to his care by his master.[1] The truth is, that the judgment of the brilliant and adventurous Frenchman was biassed by his inclinations. He and his companions were sick of Ireland. They were ready to face death with courage, nay, with gaiety, on a field of battle. But the dull, squalid, barbarous life, which they had now been leading during several months, was more than they could bear. They were as much out of the pale of the civilised world as if they had been banished to Dahomey or Spitzbergen. The climate affected their health and spirits. In that unhappy country, wasted by years of predatory war, hospitality could offer little more than a couch of straw, a trencher of meat half raw and half burned, and a draught of sour milk. A crust of bread, a pint of wine, could hardly be purchased for money. A year of such hardships seemed a century to men who had always been accustomed to carry with them to the camp the luxuries of Paris, soft bedding, rich tapestry, sideboards of plate, hampers of Champagne, opera dancers, cooks, and musicians. Better to be a prisoner in the Bastille, better to be a recluse at La Trappe, than to be generalissimo of the half naked savages who burrowed in the dreary swamps of Munster. Any plea was welcome which would serve as an excuse for returning from that miserable exile to the land of cornfields and vineyards, of gilded coaches and laced cravats, of ballrooms and theatres.[2]

The Irish army collected at Limerick

Lauzun pronounces that the place cannot be defended

---

[1] Macariæ Excidium; Mac Geoghegan; Life of James ii. 420.; London Gazette, Aug. 14. 1690.

[2] The impatience of Lauzun and his countrymen to get away from Ireland is mentioned in a letter of Oct. 21. 1690, quoted in the Memoirs of James, ii. 421. "Asimo," says Colonel Kelly, the author of the Macariæ Excidium, "diuturnam absentiam tam ægre molesteque ferebat ut bellum in Cypro protrahi continuarique ipso ei auditu acerbissimum esset. Nec incredibile est ducum in illius exercitu nonnullos, potissimum qui patrii cœli dulcedinem impatientius suspirabant, sibi persuasisse desperatas Cypri res nulla humana ope defendi sustentarique posse." Asimo is Lauzun, and Cyprus Ireland.

Very different was the feeling of the children of the soil. The island, which to French courtiers was a disconsolate place of banish-

The Irish insist on defending Limerick ment, was the Irishman's home. There were collected all the objects of his love and of his ambition; and there he hoped that his dust would one day mingle with the dust of his fathers. To him even the heaven dark with the vapours of the ocean, the wildernesses of black rushes and stagnant water, the mud cabins where the peasants and the swine shared their meal of roots, had a charm which was wanting to the sunny skies, the cultured fields, and the stately mansions of the Seine. He could imagine no fairer spot than his country, if only his country could be freed from the tyranny of the Saxons; and all hope that his country would be freed from the tyranny of the Saxons must be abandoned if Limerick were surrendered.

The conduct of the Irish during the last two months had sunk their military reputation to the lowest point. They had, with the exception of some gallant regiments of cavalry, fled disgracefully at the Boyne, and had thus incurred the bitter contempt both of their enemies and of their allies. The English who were at Saint Germains never spoke of the Irish but as a people of dastards and traitors.[1] The French were so much exasperated against the unfortunate nation, that Irish merchants, who had been many years settled at Paris and Bordeaux, durst not walk the streets for fear of being insulted by the populace.[2] So strong was the prejudice, that absurd stories were invented to explain the intrepidity with which the horse had fought. It was said that the troopers were not men of Celtic blood, but descendants of the old English of the pale.[3] It was also said that they had been intoxicated with brandy just before the battle.[4] Yet nothing can be more certain than that they must have been generally of Irish race; nor did the steady valour which they displayed in a long and almost hopeless conflict against great odds bear any resemblance to the fury of a coward maddened by strong drink into momentary hardihood. Even in the infantry, undisciplined and disorganised as it was, there was much spirit, though little firmness. Fits of enthusiasm and fits of faintheartedness succeeded each other. The same battalion, which at one time threw away its arms in a panic and

[1] " Pauci illi ex Cilicibus aulicis, qui cum regina in Syria commorante remanserant, . . . non cessabant universam nationem fœde traducere, et ingestis insuper convitiis lacerare, pavidos et malefidos proditores ac mortalium consceleratissimos publice appellando."—Macariæ Excidium. The Cilicians are the English. Syria is France.

[2] " Tanta infamia tam operoso artificio et subtili commento in vulgus sparsa, tam constantibus de Cypriorum perfidia atque opprobrio rumoribus, totam, qua lata est, Syriam ita pervasit, ut mercatores Cyprii, . . . propter inustum genti dedecus, intra domorum septa clausi nunquam prodire auderent; tanto eorum odio populus in universum exarserat."—Macariæ Excidium.

[3] I have seen this assertion in a contemporary pamphlet of which I cannot recollect the title.

[4] Story; Dumont MS.

shrieked for quarter, would on another occasion fight valiantly. On the day of the Boyne the courage of the ill trained and ill commanded kernes had ebbed to the lowest point. When they had rallied at Limerick, their blood was up. Patriotism, fanaticism, shame, revenge, despair, had raised them above themselves. With one voice officers and men insisted that the city should be defended to the last. At the head of those who were for resisting was the brave Sarsfield ; and his exhortations diffused through all ranks a spirit resembling his own. To save his country was beyond his power. All that he could do was to prolong her last agony through one bloody and disastrous year.[1]

Tyrconnel was altogether incompetent to decide the question on which the French and the Irish differed. The only military qualities that he had ever possessed were personal bravery and skill in the use of the sword. These qualities had once enabled him to frighten away rivals from the doors of his mistresses, and to play the Hector at cockpits and hazard tables. *Tyrconnel is against defending Limerick* But more was necessary to enable him to form an opinion as to the possibility of defending Limerick. He would probably, had his temper been as hot as in the days when he diced with Grammont and threatened to cut the old Duke of Ormond's throat, have voted for running any risk however desperate. But age, pain, and sickness had left little of the ranting, bullying, fighting Dick Talbot of the Restoration. He had sunk into deep despondency. He was incapable of strenuous exertion. The French officers pronounced him utterly ignorant of the art of war. They had observed that at the Boyne he had seemed to be stupified, unable to give directions himself, unable even to make up his mind about the suggestions which were offered by others.[2] The disasters which had since followed one another in rapid succession were not likely to restore the tone of a mind so pitiably unnerved. His wife was already in France with the little which remained of his once ample fortune : his own wish was to follow her thither ; his voice was therefore given for abandoning the city.

At last a compromise was made. Lauzun and Tyrconnel, with the French troops, retired to Galway. The great body of the native army,

---

[1] Macariæ Excidium. Boisseleau remarked the ebb and flow of courage among the Irish. I have quoted one of his letters to his wife. It is but just to quote another. "Nos Irlandois n'avoient jamais vu le feu ; et cela les a surpris. Presentement, ils sont si fâchés de n'avoir pas fait leur devoir que je suis bien persuadé qu'ils feront mieux pour l'avenir."

[2] La Hoguette, writing to Louvois from Limerick, $\frac{\text{July 31.}}{\text{Aug. 10.}}$ 1690, says of Tyrconnel: "Il a d'ailleurs trop peu de connoissance des choses de notre metier. Il a perdu absolument la confiance des officiers du pays, surtout depuis le jour de notre déroute; et, en effet, Monseigneur, je me crois obligé de vous dire que dès le moment où les ennemis parurent sur le bord de la rivière le premier jour, et dans toute la journée du lendemain, il parut à tout le monde dans une si grande léthargie qu'il étoit incapable de prendre aucun parti, quelque chose qu'on lui proposât."

about twenty thousand strong, remained at Limerick. The chief command there was entrusted to Boisseleau, who understood the character of the Irish better, and consequently judged them more favourably, than any of his countrymen. In general, the French captains spoke of their unfortunate allies with boundless contempt and abhorrence, and thus made themselves as hateful as the English.[1]

Limerick defended by the Irish alone

Lauzun and Tyrconnel had scarcely departed when the advanced guard of William's army came in sight. Soon the King himself, accompanied by Auverquerque and Ginkell, and escorted by three hundred horse, rode forward to examine the fortifications. The city, then the second in Ireland, though less altered since that time than most large cities in the British isles, has undergone a great change. The new town did not then exist. The ground now covered by those smooth and broad pavements, those neat gardens, those stately shops flaming with red brick, and gay with shawls and china, was then an open meadow lying without the walls. The city consisted of two parts, which had been designated during several centuries as the English and the Irish town. The English town stands on an island surrounded by the Shannon, and consists of a knot of antique houses with gable ends, crowding thick round a venerable cathedral. The aspect of the streets is such that a traveller who wanders through them may easily fancy himself in Normandy or Flanders. Not far from the cathedral, an ancient castle overgrown with weeds and ivy looks down on the river. A narrow and rapid stream, over which, in 1690, there was only a single bridge, divides the English town from the quarter anciently occupied by the hovels of the native population. The view from the top of the cathedral now extends many miles over a level expanse of rich mould, through which the greatest of Irish rivers winds between artificial banks. But in the seventeenth century those banks had not been constructed; and that wide plain, of which the grass, verdant even beyond the verdure of Munster, now feeds some of the finest cattle in Europe, was then almost always a marsh and often a lake.[2]

When it was known that the French troops had quitted Limerick, and that the Irish only remained, the general expectation in the English camp was that the city would be an easy conquest.[3] Nor was that expectation unreasonable: for even Sarsfield desponded. One

---

[1] Desgrigny says of the Irish: " Ils sont toujours prêts de nous égorger par l'antipathie qu'ils ont pour nous. C'est la nation du monde la plus brutale, et qui a le moins d'humanité." Aug. $\frac{12}{22}$. 1690.

[2] Story; Account of the Cities in Ireland that are still possessed by the Forces of King James, 1690. There are some curious old maps of Limerick in the British Museum.

[3] Story; Dumont MS.

chance, in his opinion, there still was.   William had brought with him
none but small guns.   Several large pieces of ordnance, a great quantity

From George Story's Impartial History of the Wars of Ireland, 1693

of provisions and ammunition, and a bridge of tin boats, which in the
watery plain of the Shannon was frequently needed, were slowly following from Cashel.   If the guns and gunpowder could be intercepted and
destroyed, there might be some hope.   If not, all was lost ; and the

best thing that a brave and highspirited Irish gentleman could do was to forget the country which he had in vain tried to defend, and to seek in some foreign land a home or a grave.

A few hours, therefore, after the English tents had been pitched before Limerick, Sarsfield set forth, under cover of the night, with a strong body of horse and dragoons. He took the road to Killaloe, and crossed the Shannon there. During the day he lurked with his band in a wild mountain tract named from the silver mines which it contains. Those mines had many years before been worked by English proprietors, with the help of engineers and labourers imported from the Continent. But, in the rebellion of 1641, the aboriginal population had destroyed the works and massacred the workmen; nor had the devastation then committed been since repaired. In this desolate region Sarsfield found no lack of scouts or of guides: for all the peasantry of Munster were zealous on his side. He learned in the evening that the detachment which guarded the English artillery had halted for the night, seven miles from William's camp, on a pleasant carpet of green turf, and under the ruined walls of an old castle; that officers and men seemed to think themselves perfectly secure; that the beasts had been turned loose to graze, and that even the sentinels were dozing. When it was dark the Irish horsemen quitted their hidingplace, and were conducted by the people of the country to the spot where the escort lay sleeping round the guns. The surprise was complete. Some of the English sprang to their arms and made an attempt to resist, but in vain. About sixty fell. One only was taken alive. The rest fled. The victorious Irish made a huge pile of waggons and pieces of cannon. Every gun was stuffed with powder, and fixed with its mouth in the ground; and the whole mass was blown up. The solitary prisoner, a lieutenant, was treated with great civility by Sarsfield. "If I had failed in this attempt," said the gallant Irishman, "I should have been off to France." [1]

Sarsfield surprises the English artillery

Intelligence had been carried to William's headquarters that Sarsfield had stolen out of Limerick and was ranging the country. The King guessed the design of his brave enemy, and sent five hundred horse to protect the guns. Unhappily there was some delay, which the English, always disposed to believe the worst of the Dutch courtiers, attributed to the negligence or perverseness of Portland. At one in the morning the detachment set out, but had scarcely left the camp when a blaze like lightning and a crash like thunder announced to the wide plain of the Shannon that all was over. [2]

Sarsfield had long been the favourite of his countrymen; and this most seasonable exploit, judiciously planned and vigorously executed,

[1] Story; James, ii. 416.; Burnet, ii. 58.; Dumont MS.　　[2] Story; Dumont MS.

raised him still higher in their estimation. Their spirits rose ; and the besiegers began to lose heart. William did his best to repair his loss. Two of the guns which had been blown up were found to be still serviceable. Two more were sent for from Waterford. Batteries were constructed of small field pieces, which, though they might have been useless against one of the fortresses of Hainault or Brabant, made some impression on the feeble defences of Limerick. Several outworks were carried by storm ; and a breach in the rampart of the city began to appear.

During these operations, the English army was astonished and amused by an incident, which produced indeed no very important consequences, but which illustrates in the most striking manner **Arrival of** the real nature of Irish Jacobitism. In the first rank of **Baldearg O'Donnel** those great Celtic houses, which, down to the close of the **at Limerick** reign of Elizabeth, bore rule in Ulster, were the O'Donnels. The head of that house had yielded to the skill and energy of Mountjoy, had kissed the hand of James the First, and had consented to exchange the rude independence of a petty prince for an eminently honourable place among British subjects. During a short time the vanquished chief held the rank of an Earl, and was the landlord of an immense domain of which he had once been the sovereign. But soon he began to suspect the government of plotting against him, and, in revenge or in self-defence, plotted against the government. His schemes failed : he fled to the Continent : his title and his estates were forfeited ; and an Anglosaxon colony was planted in the territory which he had governed. He meanwhile took refuge at the court of Spain. Between that court and the aboriginal Irish there had, during the long contest between Philip and Elizabeth, been a close connection. The exiled chieftain was welcomed at Madrid as a good Catholic flying from heretical persecutors. His illustrious descent and princely dignity, which to the English were subjects of ridicule, secured to him the respect of the Castilian grandees. His honours were inherited by a succession of banished men who lived and died far from the land where the memory of their family was fondly cherished by a rude peasantry, and was kept fresh by the songs of minstrels and the tales of begging friars. At length, in the eighty-third year of the exile of this ancient dynasty, it was known over all Europe that the Irish were again in arms for their independence. Baldearg O'Donnel, who called himself the O'Donnel, a title far prouder, in the estimation of his race, than any marquisate or dukedom, had been bred in Spain, and was in the service of the Spanish government. He requested the permission of that government to repair to Ireland ; but the House of Austria was now closely leagued with England ; and the permission was refused. The

O'Donnel made his escape, and by a circuitous route, in the course of which he visited Turkey, arrived at Kinsale a few days after James had sailed thence for France. The effect produced on the native population by the arrival of this solitary wanderer was marvellous. Since Ulster had been reconquered by the Englishry, great multitudes of the Irish inhabitants of that province had migrated southward, and were now leading a vagrant life in Connaught and Munster. These men, accustomed from their infancy to hear of the good old times, when the O'Donnel, solemnly inaugurated on the rock of Kilmacrenan by the successor of Saint Columb, governed the mountains of Donegal in defiance of the strangers of the pale, flocked to the standard of the restored exile. He was soon at the head of seven or eight thousand Rapparees, or, to use the name peculiar to Ulster, Creaghts; and his followers adhered to him with a loyalty very different from the languid sentiment which the Saxon James had been able to inspire. Priests and even Bishops swelled the train of the adventurer. He was so much elated by his reception that he sent agents to France, who assured the ministers of Lewis that the O'Donnel would, if furnished with arms and ammunition, bring into the field thirty thousand Celts from Ulster, and that the Celts of Ulster would be found far superior in every military quality to those of Leinster, Munster, and Connaught. No expression used by Baldearg indicated that he considered himself as a subject. His notion evidently was that the House of O'Donnel was as truly and as indefeasibly royal as the House of Stuart; and not a few of his countrymen were of the same mind. He made a pompous entrance into Limerick; and his appearance there raised the hopes of the garrison to a strange pitch. Numerous prophecies were recollected or invented. An O'Donnel with a red mark was to be the deliverer of his country; and Baldearg meant a red mark. An O'Donnel was to gain a great battle over the English near Limerick; and at Limerick the O'Donnel and the English were now brought face to face.[1]

While these predictions were eagerly repeated by the defenders of the city, evil presages, grounded, not on barbarous oracles, but on grave military reasons, began to disturb William and his most experienced officers. The blow struck by Sarsfield had told: the artillery had been long in doing its work: that work was even now very imperfectly done: the stock of powder had begun to run low: the autumnal rain had begun to fall. The soldiers in the trenches

The besiegers suffer from the rains

[1] See the account of the O'Donnels in Sir William Betham's Irish Antiquarian Researches. It is strange that he makes no mention of Baldearg, whose appearance in Ireland is the most extraordinary event in the whole history of the race. See also Story's Impartial History; Macariæ Excidium, and Mr. O'Callaghan's note; Life of James, ii. 434.; the Letter of O'Donnel to Avaux, and the Memorial entitled, "Mémoire donnée par un homme du Comte O'Donnel à M. D'Avaux."

were up to their knees in mire.   No precaution was neglected : but, though drains were dug to carry off the water, and though pewter basins of usquebaugh and brandy blazed all night in the tents, cases of fever had already occurred ; and it might well be apprehended that, if the army remained but a few days longer on that swampy soil, there would be a pestilence more terrible than that which had raged twelve months before under the walls of Dundalk.[1]   A council of war was held.   It was determined to make one great effort, and, if that effort failed, to raise the siege.

On the twenty-seventh of August, at three in the afternoon, the signal was given.   Five hundred grenadiers rushed from the English

MEDAL COMMEMORATING THE SUBJUGATION OF IRELAND BY WILLIAM III

trenches to the counterscarp, fired their pieces, and threw their grenades. The Irish fled into the town, and were followed by the assailants, who, in the excitement of victory, did not wait for orders.   Then **Unsuccessful assault on Limerick.** began a terrible street fight.   The Irish, as soon as they had recovered from their surprise, stood resolutely to their **The siege raised** arms ; and the English grenadiers, overwhelmed by num- bers, were, with great loss, driven back to the counterscarp.   There the struggle was long and desperate.   When indeed was the Roman Catholic Celt to fight if he did not fight on that day ?   The very women of Limerick mingled in the combat, stood firmly under the hottest fire, and flung stones and broken bottles at the enemy.   In the moment when the conflict was fiercest a mine exploded, and hurled a fine

[1] The reader will remember Corporal Trim's explanation of radical heat and radical moisture. Sterne is an authority not to be despised on these subjects.   His boyhood was passed in barracks: he was constantly listening to the talk of old soldiers who had served under King William, and has used their stories like a man of true genius.

German battalion into the air. During four hours the carnage and uproar continued. The thick cloud which rose from the breach streamed out on the wind for many miles, and disappeared behind the hills of Clare. Late in the evening the besiegers retired slowly and sullenly to their camp. Their hope was that a second attack would be made on the morrow ; and the soldiers vowed to have the town or die. But the powder was now almost exhausted : the rain fell in torrents : the gloomy masses of cloud which came up from the south west threatened a havoc more terrible than that of the sword ; and there was reason to fear that the roads, which were already deep in mud, would soon be in such a state that no wheeled carriage could be dragged through them. The King determined to raise the siege, and to move his troops to a healthier region. He had in truth staid long enough : for it was with great difficulty that his guns and waggons were tugged away by long teams of oxen.[1]

The history of the first siege of Limerick bears, in some respects, a remarkable analogy to the history of the siege of Londonderry. The southern city was, like the northern city, the last asylum of a Church and of a nation. Both places were crowded by fugitives from all parts of Ireland. Both places appeared to men who had made a regular study of the art of war incapable of resisting an enemy. Both were, in the moment of extreme danger, abandoned by those commanders who should have defended them. Lauzun and Tyrconnel deserted Limerick as Cunningham and Lundy had deserted Londonderry. In both cases, religious and patriotic enthusiasm struggled unassisted against great odds ; and, in both cases, religious and patriotic enthusiasm did what veteran warriors had pronounced it absurd to attempt.

It was with no pleasurable emotions that Lauzun and Tyrconnel learned at Galway the fortunate issue of the conflict in which they had **Tyrconnel and Lauzun go to France** refused to take a part. They were weary of Ireland : they were apprehensive that their conduct might be unfavourably represented in France : they therefore determined to be beforehand with their accusers, and took ship together for the Continent.

Tyrconnel, before he departed, delegated his civil authority to one council, and his military authority to another. The young Duke of Berwick was declared Commander in Chief : but this dignity was merely nominal.

---

[1] Story ; William to Waldeck, Sept. 22. 1690 ; London Gazette, Sept. 4. Berwick asserts that when the siege was raised not a drop of rain had fallen during a month, that none fell during the following three weeks, and that William pretended that the weather was wet merely to hide the shame of his defeat. Story, who was on the spot, says, " It was cloudy all about, and rained very fast, so that every body began to dread the consequences of it ; " and again, " The rain which had already fallen had softened the ways. . . . This was one main reason for raising the siege : for, if we had not, granting the weather to continue bad, we must either have taken the town, or of necessity have lost our cannon." Dumont, another eyewitness, says that before the siege was raised the rains had been most violent ; that the Shannon was swollen ; that the earth was soaked ; that the horses could not keep their feet.

The Royal Salutation,

OR,

The Courtly Greeting between K. *William* and Qu. *Mary* at his Return from the Wars in *Ireland* to his Royal Pallace.

Licensed according to Order.

Tune is, *I often for my* Jenny *ftrove.*

Queen.

W Hen Noble King VVilliam of renown
came from the Warp and bloody Scene,
Rioing in triumph to the Town,
for to embrace his Gracious Queen,
He was greatly then rejoyc'd,
Loves, and all the Princely train.
This is a bleſſing, I'm poſſeſſing,
for to ſee my Lord again.

The Iriſh Rebels felt thy Rage,
whoſe Remnants did not dare;
Unable thy wars to ingage,
Or fraught with thy Boys dib age:

When this joyful News arrived,
Proteſtants ridge d amain;
And now a bleſſing, I'm poſſeſſing,
to embrace thee once again.

King.

Said he, My noble Army too,
we'r bath d in the inſulting foe;
But fought like noble Hearts of Gold,
true Engliſh Courage they did ſhow:
Falling on like men undaunted,
Charging through the Front and Rear;
Still as we fir'd, they retir'd,
thus the coaſt we ſoon did clear—

The River Boyne we then did wade,
having paſſed the other Shore:
The Rebells then we ſpatoling ſaid,
they never found us like before:
Horſe and Foot did boldly venture,
being ſtrangers unto fear:
Still as we fir'd, they retir'd,
thus our foes we ſoon did clear.

Queen.

My Royal Lord, repl'y the Queen,
thou waſt expos'd to Dangers great,
Where mought Hur fire and Smoak was ſeen
yet Providence on thee did wait:
And preſerv'd thy life in Battel,
where great numbers did lye ſlain:
This is my bleſſing, I'm poſſeſſing,
of my deareſt Lord again.

King.

Although my Army won the Day,
and foes on us their backs they turn'd;
Yet warlike Schomberg in the Fray
was ſlain, for whom I'm much concern'd:

O that brave Couragious Hero
likewiſe Valiant VValker too:
Though they expir'd, when they fir'd,
France ſhall one Day for it rue.

Queen.

Alas! that ſad ſurpriſing News
did grieve each loyal Subject here:
And did their ſenſes ſo annoy,
none could forbear to ſhed a tear:
Many have the couragious Souldiers
near the River Boyne was ſlain:
Yet this great bleſſing, I'm poſſeſſing,
to enjoy my Lord again.

Caſt by thy weary Armour bright,
receive thy Scepter, Crown and Ball:
Whilſt Lords and Ladies take delight,
thou being King and Lord of all:
Thou on Englands Throne art ſeated,
Subjects with a happy Reign,
This is a bleſſing, I'm poſſeſſing,
to embrace my Lord again.

printed by and for *F. Millet*, at the *Angel* in *Little-Britain* : Where Countrey
Chapmen may be furniſh'd with all ſorts of New and Old ſmall Books and
Ballads at reaſonable rates.

THE ROYAL SALUTATION

From the Pepysian Collection of Ballads

Sarsfield, undoubtedly the first of Irish soldiers, was placed last in the list of the councillors to whom the conduct of the war was entrusted ; and some believed that he would not have been in the list at all, had not the Viceroy feared that the omission of so popular a name might produce a mutiny.

William meanwhile proceeded to Waterford, and sailed thence for England. Before he embarked, he entrusted the government of Ireland to three Lords Justices. Henry Sidney, now Viscount Sidney, stood first in the commission ; and with him were joined Coningsby and Sir Charles Porter. Porter had formerly held the Great Seal of the kingdom, had, merely because he was a Protestant, been deprived of it by James, and had now received it again from the hand of William.

William returns to England

On the sixth of September the King, after a voyage of twenty four hours, landed at Bristol. Thence he travelled to London, stopping by the road at the mansions of some great lords ; and it was remarked that all those who were thus honoured were Tories. He was entertained one day at Badminton by the Duke of Beaufort, who was supposed to have brought himself with great difficulty to take the oaths, and on a subsequent day at a large house near Marlborough, which, in our own time, before the great revolution produced by railways, was renowned as one of the best inns in England, but which, in the seventeenth century, was a seat of the Duke of Somerset. William was everywhere received with marks of respect and joy. His campaign indeed had not ended quite so prosperously as it had begun : but on the whole his success had been great beyond expectation, and had fully vindicated the wisdom of his resolution to command his army in person. The sack of Teignmouth too was fresh in the minds of Englishmen, and had for a time reconciled all but the most fanatical Jacobites to each other and to the throne. The magistracy and clergy of the capital repaired to Kensington with thanks and congratulations. The people rang bells and kindled bonfires. For the Pope, whom good Protestants had been accustomed to immolate, the French King was on this occasion substituted, probably by way of retaliation for the insults which had been offered to the effigy of William by the Parisian populace. A waxen figure, which was doubtless a hideous caricature of the most graceful and majestic of princes, was dragged about Westminster in a chariot. Above was inscribed, in large letters, " Lewis the greatest tyrant of fourteen." After the procession, the image was committed to the flames, amidst loud huzzas, in the middle of Covent Garden.[1]

Reception of William in England

When William arrived in London, the expedition destined for Cork was ready to sail from Portsmouth ; and Marlborough had been some

[1] London Gazette, September 11. 1690 ; Narcissus Luttrell's Diary. I have seen a contemporary engraving of Covent Garden as it appeared on this night.

A VIEW OF THE FIREWORKS IN COVENT GARDEN

From a mezzotint by B. Lens in the British Museum

time on board waiting for a fair wind. He was accompanied by Grafton. This young man had been, immediately after the departure of **Expedition to the South of Ireland** James, and while the throne was still vacant, named by William Colonel of the First Regiment of Foot Guards. The Revolution had scarcely been consummated, when signs of disaffection began to appear in that regiment, the most important, both because of its peculiar duties and because of its numerical strength, of all the regiments in the army. It was thought that the Colonel had not put this bad spirit down with a sufficiently firm hand. He was known not to be perfectly satisfied with the new arrangement : he had voted for a Regency ; and it was rumoured, perhaps without reason, that he had dealings with Saint Germains. The honourable and lucrative command to which he had just been appointed was taken from him.[1] Though severely mortified, he behaved like a man of sense and spirit. Bent on proving that he had been wrongfully suspected, and animated by an honourable ambition to distinguish himself in his profession, he obtained permission to serve as a volunteer under Marlborough in Ireland.

At length, on the eighteenth of September, the wind changed. The fleet stood out to sea, and, on the twenty-first, appeared before the harbour of Cork. The troops landed, and were speedily joined by the Duke of Wurtemberg, with several regiments, Dutch, Danish, and French, detached from the army which had lately besieged Limerick. The Duke immediately put forward a claim which, if the English general had not been a man of excellent judgment and temper, might have been fatal to the expedition. His Highness contended that, as a prince of a sovereign house, he was entitled to command in chief. Marlborough calmly and politely showed that the pretence was unreasonable. A dispute followed, in which it is said that the German behaved with rudeness, and the Englishman with that gentle firmness to which, more perhaps than even to his great abilities, he owed his success in life. At length a Huguenot officer suggested a compromise. Marlborough consented to waive part of his rights, and to allow precedence to the Duke on the alternate days. The first morning on which Marlborough had the command, he gave the word " Wurtemberg." The Duke's heart was won by this compliment ; and on the next day he gave the word " Marlborough."

But, whoever might give the word, genius asserted its indefeasible superiority. Marlborough was on every day the real general. Cork **Marlborough takes Cork** was vigorously attacked. Outwork after outwork was rapidly carried. In forty eight hours all was over. The traces of the short struggle may still be seen. The old fort, where the Irish made the hardest fight, lies in ruins. The Doric Cathedral,

[1] Van Citters to the States General, March 18/28. 1689.

PLAN OF CORK

From George Story's Impartial History of the Wars of Ireland, 1693

so ungracefully joined to the ancient tower, stands on the site of a Gothic edifice which was shattered by the English cannon. In the neighbouring churchyard is still shown the spot where stood, during many ages, one of those round towers which have perplexed antiquaries. This venerable monument shared the fate of the neighbouring church. On another spot, which is now called the Mall, and is lined by the stately houses of banking companies, railway companies, and insurance companies, but which was then a bog known by the name of the Rape Marsh, four English regiments, up to the shoulders in water, advanced gallantly to the assault. Grafton, ever foremost in danger, while struggling through the quagmire, was struck by a shot from the ramparts, and was carried back dying. The place where he fell, then about a hundred yards without the City, but now situated in the very centre of business and population, is still called Grafton Street. The assailants had made their way through the swamp, and the close fighting was just about to begin, when a parley was beaten. Articles of capitulation were speedily adjusted. The garrison, between four and five thousand fighting men, became prisoners. Marlborough promised to intercede with the King both for them and for the inhabitants, and to prevent outrage and spoliation. His troops he succeeded in restraining : but crowds of sailors and camp followers came into the city through the breach ; and the houses of many Roman Catholics were sacked before order was restored.

No commander has ever understood better than Marlborough how to improve a victory. A few hours after Cork had fallen, his cavalry were on the road to Kinsale. A trumpeter was sent to summon the place. The Irish threatened to hang him for bringing such a message, set fire to the town, and retired into two forts called the Old and the New. The English horse arrived just in time to extinguish the flames. Marlborough speedily followed with his infantry. The Old Fort was scaled ; and four hundred and fifty men who defended it were killed or taken. The New Fort it was necessary to attack in a more methodical way. Batteries were planted : trenches were opened : mines were sprung : in a few days the besiegers were masters of the counterscarp; and all was ready for storming, when the governor offered to capitulate. The garrison, twelve hundred strong, was suffered to retire to Limerick ; but the conquerors took possession of the stores, which were of considerable value. Of all the Irish ports Kinsale was the best situated for intercourse with France. Here, therefore, was a plenty unknown in any other part of Munster. At Limerick bread and wine were luxuries which generals and privy councillors were not always able to procure. But in the New Fort of Kinsale Marlborough found a thousand barrels of wheat and eighty pipes of claret.

Marl-borough takes Kinsale

PLAN OF KINSALE

From George Story's Impartial History of the Wars of Ireland, 1693

His success had been complete and rapid ; and indeed, had it not been rapid, it would not have been complete.   His campaign, short as it was, had been long enough to allow time for the deadly work which, in that age, the moist earth and air of Ireland seldom failed, in the autumnal season, to perform on English soldiers.   The malady which had thinned the ranks of Schomberg's army at Dundalk, and which had compelled William to make a hasty retreat from the estuary of the Shannon, had begun to appear at Kinsale.   Quick and vigorous as Marlborough's operations were, he lost a much greater number of men by disease than by the fire of the enemy.   He presented himself at Kensington only five weeks after he had sailed from Portsmouth, and was most graciously received.   " No officer living," said William, " who has seen so little service as my Lord Marlborough, is so fit for great commands." [1]

In Scotland, as in Ireland, the aspect of things had, during this memorable summer, changed greatly for the better.   That club of dis-

Affairs of Scotland   contented Whigs which had, in the preceding year, ruled the Parliament, browbeaten the ministers, refused the supplies, and stopped the signet, had sunk under general contempt, and had at length ceased to exist.   There was harmony between the Sovereign and the Estates ; and the long contest between two forms of ecclesiastical government had been terminated in the only way compatible with the peace and prosperity of the country.

This happy turn in affairs is to be chiefly ascribed to the errors of the perfidious, turbulent and revengeful Montgomery.   Some weeks

Intrigues of Mont- gomery with the Jacobites   after the close of that session during which he had exercised a boundless authority over the Scottish Parliament, he went to London with his two principal confederates, the Earl of Annandale and the Lord Ross.   The three had an audience of William, and presented to him a manifesto setting forth what they demanded for the public.   They would very soon have changed their tone if he would have granted what they demanded for themselves. But he resented their conduct deeply, and was determined not to pay them for annoying him.   The reception which he gave them convinced them that they had no favour to expect.   Montgomery's passions were fierce : his wants were pressing : he was miserably poor ; and, if he could not speedily force himself into a lucrative office, he would be in danger of rotting in a gaol.   Since his services were not likely to be bought by William, they must be offered to · James.   A broker was easily found.   Montgomery was an old acquaintance of Ferguson.   The two traitors soon understood each other.   They were kindred spirits,

[1] As to Marlborough's expedition, see Story's Impartial History ; the Life of James, ii. 419, 420.; London Gazette, Oct. 6. 13. 16. 27. 30. 1690 ; Monthly Mercury for Nov. 1690 ; History of King William, 1702 ; Burnet, ii. 60.; the Life of Joseph Pike, a Quaker of Cork.

differing widely in intellectual power, but equally vain, restless, false, and malevolent.   Montgomery was introduced to Neville Payne, one of the most adroit and resolute agents of the exiled family.   Payne had been long well known about town as a dabbler in poetry and politics. He had been an intimate friend of the indiscreet and unfortunate Coleman, and had been committed to Newgate as an accomplice in the Popish plot.   His moral character had not stood high : but he soon had an opportunity of proving that he possessed courage and fidelity worthy of a better cause than that of James, and of a better associate than Montgomery.

The negotiation speedily ended in a treaty of alliance.   Payne confidently promised Montgomery, not merely pardon, but riches, power, and dignity.   Montgomery as confidently undertook to induce the Parliament of Scotland to recall the rightful King.   Ross and Annandale readily agreed to whatever their able and active colleague proposed. An adventurer, who was sometimes called Simpson and sometimes Jones, who was perfectly willing to serve or to betray any government for hire, and who received wages at once from Portland and from Neville Payne, undertook to carry the offers of the Club to James. Montgomery and his two noble accomplices returned to Edinburgh, and there proceeded to form a coalition with their old enemies, the defenders of prelacy and of arbitrary power.[1]

The two extreme Scottish factions, one hostile to all liberty, the other impatient of all government, flattered themselves during a short time with hopes that the civil war would break out in the **War in the** Highlands with redoubled fury.   But those hopes were dis- **Highlands** appointed.   In the spring of 1690 an officer named Buchan arrived in Lochaber from Ireland.   He bore a commission which appointed him general in chief of all the forces which were in arms for King James throughout the kingdom of Scotland.   Cannon, who had, since the death of Dundee, held the first post, and had proved himself unfit for it, became second in command.   Little however was gained by the change.   It was no easy matter to induce the Gaelic princes to renew the war.   Indeed, but for the influence and eloquence of Lochiel, not a sword would have been drawn in the cause of the House of Stuart.   He, with some difficulty, persuaded the chieftains, who had, in the preceding year, fought at Killiecrankie, to come to a resolution that, before the end of the summer, they would muster all their followers and march into the Lowlands.   In the mean time twelve hundred mountaineers of different tribes were placed under the orders of Buchan, who undertook, with this force, to keep the English garrisons in constant alarm

[1] Balcarras ; Annandale's Confession in the Leven and Melville Papers ; Burnet, ii. 35. As to Payne, see the Second Modest Inquiry into the Cause of the present Disasters, 1690.

by feints and incursions, till the season for more important operations should arrive. He accordingly marched into Strathspey. But all his plans were speedily disconcerted by the boldness and dexterity of Sir Thomas Livingstone, who held Inverness for King William. Livingstone, guided and assisted by the Grants, who were firmly attached to the new government, came, with a strong body of cavalry and dragoons, by forced marches and through arduous defiles, to the place where the Jacobites had taken up their quarters. He reached the camp fires at dead of night. The first alarm was given by the rush of the horses over the terrified sentinels into the midst of the crowd of Celts who lay sleeping in their plaids. Buchan escaped bareheaded and without his sword. Cannon ran away in his shirt. The conquerors lost not a man. Four hundred Highlanders were killed or taken. The rest fled to their hills and mists.[1]

This event put an end to all thoughts of civil war. The gathering which had been planned for the summer never took place. Lochiel, even if he had been willing, was not able to sustain any longer the falling cause. He had been laid on his bed by a mishap which would alone suffice to show how little could be effected by a confederacy of the petty kings of the mountains. At a consultation of the Jacobite leaders, a gentleman from the Lowlands spoke with severity of those sycophants who had changed their religion to curry favour with King James. Glengarry was one of those people who think it dignified to suppose that everybody is always insulting them. He took it into his head that some allusion to himself was meant. " I am as good a Protestant as you ; " he cried, and added a word not to be patiently borne by a man of spirit. In a moment both swords were out. Lochiel thrust himself between the combatants, and, while forcing them asunder, received a wound which was at first believed to be mortal.[2]

So effectually had the spirit of the disaffected clans been cowed that Mackay marched unresisted from Perth into Lochaber, fixed his

Fort William built

headquarters at Inverlochy, and proceeded to execute his favourite design of erecting at that place a fortress which might overawe the mutinous Camerons and Macdonalds. In a few days the walls were raised : the ditches were sunk : the palisades were fixed : demiculverins from a ship of war were ranged along the parapets ; and the general departed, leaving an officer named Hill in command of a sufficient garrison. Within the defences there was no want of oatmeal, red herrings, and beef ; and there was rather a superabundance of brandy. The new stronghold, which, hastily and rudely

---

[1] Balcarras ; Mackay's Memoirs ; History of the late Revolution in Scotland, 1690 ; Livingstone's Report, dated May 1. ; London Gazette, May 12. 1690.

[2] History of the late Revolution in Scotland, 1690.

South West View of Fort William & Inver Lochy-Fort / The Wall with the old Fort William & Inver Lochy or Castle.
London. Printed for Rob.t Sayer opposite Fetter lane Fleet Street. & the Written without Aldgate.

VIEW OF FORT WILLIAM

From an engraving published by Robert Sayer

as it had been constructed, seemed doubtless to the people of the neigh-bourhood the most stupendous work that power and science united had ever produced, was named Fort William in honour of the King.[1]

By this time the Scottish Parliament had reassembled at Edinburgh. William had found it no easy matter to decide what course should be

Meeting of the Scottish Parliament

taken with that capricious and unruly body. The English Commons had sometimes put him out of temper. Yet they had granted him millions, and had never asked from him such concessions as had been imperiously demanded by the Scottish legislature, which could give him little and had given him nothing. The English statesmen with whom he had to deal did not generally stand or deserve to stand high in his esteem. Yet few of them were so utterly false and shameless as the leading Scottish politicians. Hamilton was, in morality and honour, rather above than below his fellows ; and even Hamilton was fickle, false, and greedy. " I wish to heaven," William was once provoked into exclaiming, " that Scotland were a thousand miles off, and that the Duke of Hamilton were King of it. Then I should be rid of them both."

After much deliberation, William determined to send Melville down to Edinburgh as Lord High Commissioner. Melville was not a great

Melville Lord High Commis- sioner

statesman : he was not a great orator : he did not look or move like the representative of royalty : his character was not of more than standard purity; and the standard of purity among Scottish senators was not high : but he was by no means deficient in prudence or temper ; and he succeeded, on the whole, better than a man of much higher qualities might have done.

During the first days of the Session, the friends of the government desponded, and the chiefs of the opposition were sanguine. Mont-

The govern- ment obtains a majority

gomery's head, though by no means a weak one, had been turned by the triumphs of the preceding year. He believed that his intrigues and his rhetoric had completely subjugated the Estates. It seemed to him impossible that, having exercised a boundless empire in the Parliament House when the Jacobites were absent, he should be defeated when they were present, and ready to support whatever he proposed. He had not indeed found it easy to prevail on them to attend : for they could not take their seats without taking the oaths. A few of them had some slight scruple of con-science about forswearing themselves ; and many, who did not know what a scruple of conscience meant, were apprehensive that they might offend

---

[1] Mackay's Memoirs and Letters to Hamilton of June 20. and 24. 1690 ; Colonel Hill to Melville, July 10. 26. ; London Gazette, July 17. 21. As to Inverlochy, see among the Culloden papers, a Plan for preserving the Peace of the Highlands, drawn up, at this time, by the father of President Forbes.

the rightful King by vowing fealty to the actual King.   Some Lords, however, who were supposed to be in the confidence of James, asserted that, to their knowledge, he wished his friends to perjure themselves; and this assertion induced most of the Jacobites, with Balcarras at their head, to be guilty of perfidy aggravated by impiety.[1]

It soon appeared, however, that Montgomery's faction, even with this reinforcement, was no longer a majority of the legislature.   For every supporter that he had gained he had lost two.   He had committed an error which has more than once, in British history, been fatal to great parliamentary leaders.   He had imagined that, as soon as he chose to coalesce with those to whom he had recently been opposed, all his followers would imitate his example.   He soon found that it was much easier to inflame animosities than to appease them.   The great body of Whigs and Presbyterians shrank from the fellowship of the Jacobites. Some waverers were purchased by the government; nor was the purchase expensive; for a sum which would hardly be missed in the English treasury was immense in the estimation of the needy barons of the North.[2]   Thus the scale was turned; and, in the Scottish Parliaments of that age, the turn of the scale was everything : the tendency of majorities was almost always to increase, the tendency of minorities to diminish.

The first question on which a vote was taken related to the election for a borough.   The ministers carried their point by six voices.[3]   In an instant everything was changed : the spell was broken : the Club, from being a bugbear, became a laughingstock : the timid and the venal passed over in crowds from the weaker to the stronger side.   It was in vain that the opposition attempted to revive the disputes of the preceding year.   The King had wisely authorised Melville to give up the Committee of Articles.   The Estates, on the other hand, showed no disposition to pass another Act of Incapacitation, to censure the government for opening the Courts of Justice, or to question the right of the Sovereign to name the Judges.   An extraordinary supply was voted, small, according to the notions of English financiers, but large for the means of Scotland.   The sum granted was a hundred and sixty two thousand pounds sterling, to be raised in the course of four years.[4]

The Jacobites, who found that they had forsworn themselves to no purpose, sate, bowed down by shame and writhing with vexation, while Montgomery, who had deceived himself and them, and who, in his rage, had utterly lost, not indeed his parts and his fluency, but all decorum and selfcommand, scolded like a waterman on the Thames,

[1] Balcarras.

[2] See the instructions to the Lord High Commissioner in the Leven and Melville Papers.

[3] Balcarras.   [4] Act. Parl. June 7. 1690.

H.E. IV   2 C

and was answered with equal asperity and even more than equal ability by Sir John Dalrymple.[1]

The most important Acts of this Session were those which fixed the ecclesiastical constitution of Scotland.   By the Claim of Right it had been declared that the authority of Bishops was an insupportable grievance ; and William, by accepting the Crown, had bound himself not to uphold an institution condemned by the very instrument on which his title to the Crown depended. But the Claim of Right had not defined the form of Church government which was to be substituted for episcopacy ; and, during the stormy Session held in the summer of 1689, the violence of the Club had made legislation impossible. During many months therefore everything had been in confusion.   One polity had been pulled down ; and no other polity had been set up.   In the Western Lowlands, the beneficed clergy had been so effectually rabbled, that scarcely one of them had remained at his post. In Berwickshire, the three Lothians and Stirlingshire, most of the curates had been removed by the Privy Council for not obeying that vote of the Convention which had directed all ministers of parishes, on pain of deprivation, to proclaim William and Mary King and Queen of Scotland.   Thus, throughout a great part of the realm, there was no public worship, except what was performed by Presbyterian divines, who sometimes officiated in tents, and sometimes, without any legal right, took possession of the churches. But there were large districts, especially on the north of the Tay, where the people had no strong feeling against episcopacy ; and there were many priests who were not disposed to lose their manses and stipends for the sake of King James.   Hundreds of the old curates, therefore, having been neither hunted by the populace nor deposed by the Council, still continued to exercise their spiritual functions.   Every minister was, during this time of transition, free to conduct the service and to administer the sacraments as he thought fit.   There was no controlling authority.   The legislature had taken away the jurisdiction of Bishops, and had not established the jurisdiction of Synods.[2]

To put an end to this anarchy was one of the first duties of the Parliament.   Melville had, with the powerful assistance of Carstairs, obtained from the King, in spite of the remonstrances of English statesmen and divines, authority to assent to such ecclesiastical arrangements as might satisfy the Scottish nation.   One of the first laws which the Lord Commissioner touched with the sceptre repealed the Act of Supremacy.   He next gave the royal assent to a law enacting that the Presbyterian divines who had been pastors of parishes in the days

Ecclesiastical legislation

---

[1] Balcarras.

[2] Faithful Contendings Displayed ; Case of the present Afflicted Episcopal Clergy in Scotland, 1690.

of the Covenant, and had, after the Restoration, been ejected for refusing to acknowledge episcopal authority, should be restored. The
number of those pastors had originally been about three hundred and
fifty : but not more than sixty were still living.[1]

The Estates then proceeded to fix the national creed. The Confession of Faith drawn up by the Assembly of Divines at Westminster,
the Longer and Shorter Catechism, and the Directory, were considered
by every good Presbyterian as the standards of orthodoxy ; and it was
hoped that the legislature would recognise them as such.[2]   This hope,
however, was in part disappointed. The Confession was read at length,
amidst much yawning, and adopted without alteration. But, when it
was proposed that the Catechisms and the Directory should be taken
into consideration, the ill humour of the audience broke forth into
murmurs. For that love of long sermons which was strong in the Scottish
commonalty was not shared by the Scottish aristocracy. The Parliament had already been listening during three hours to dry theology,
and was not inclined to hear anything more about original sin and
election. The Duke of Hamilton said that the Estates had already
done all that was essential. They had given their sanction to a digest
of the great principles of Christianity. The rest might well be left to
the Church. The weary majority eagerly assented, in spite of the
muttering of some zealous Presbyterian ministers who had been admitted
to hear the debate, and who could sometimes hardly restrain themselves
from taking part in it.[3]

The memorable law which fixed the ecclesiastical constitution of
Scotland was brought in by the Earl of Sutherland. By this law the
synodical polity was reestablished. The rule of the Church was
entrusted to the sixty ejected ministers who had just been restored, and
to such other persons, whether ministers or elders, as the Sixty should
think fit to admit to a participation of power. The Sixty and their
nominees were authorised to visit all the parishes in the kingdom, and
to turn out all ministers who were deficient in abilities, scandalous in
morals, or unsound in faith. Those parishes which had, during the
interregnum, been deserted by their pastors, or, in plain words, those
parishes of which the pastors had been rabbled, were declared vacant.[4]

To the clause which reestablished synodical government no serious
opposition appears to have been made. But three days were spent in

[1] Act Parl. April 25. 1690.

[2] See the Humble Address of the Presbyterian Ministers and Professors of the Church of
Scotland to His Grace His Majesty's High Commissioner and to the Right Honourable the
Estates of Parliament.

[3] See the Account of the late Establishment of Presbyterian Government by the Parliament of
Scotland, Anno 1690. This is an Episcopalian narrative. Act. Parl. May 26. 1690.

[4] Act Parl. June 7. 1690.

discussing the question whether the Sovereign should have power to convoke and to dissolve ecclesiastical assemblies ; and the point was at last left in dangerous ambiguity. Some other clauses were long and vehemently debated. It was said that the immense power given to the Sixty was incompatible with the fundamental principle of the polity which the Estates were about to set up. That principle was that all presbyters were equal, and that there ought to be no order of ministers of religion superior to the order of presbyters. What did it matter whether the Sixty were called prelates or not, if they were to lord it with more than prelatical authority over God's heritage ? To the argument that the proposed arrangement was, in the very peculiar circumstances of the Church, the most convenient that could be made, the objectors replied that such reasoning might suit the mouth of an Erastian, but that all orthodox Presbyterians held the parity of ministers to be ordained by Christ, and that, where Christ had spoken, Christians were not at liberty to consider what was convenient.[1]

With much greater warmth and much stronger reason, the minority attacked the clause which sanctioned the lawless acts of the Western fanatics. Surely, it was said, a rabbled curate might well be left to the severe scrutiny of the sixty Inquisitors. If he was deficient in parts or learning, if he was loose in life, if he was heterodox in doctrine, those stern judges would not fail to detect and to depose him. They would probably think a game at bowls, a prayer borrowed from the English Liturgy, or a sermon in which the slightest taint of Arminianism could be discovered, a sufficient reason for pronouncing his benefice vacant. Was it not monstrous, after constituting a tribunal from which he could scarcely hope for bare justice, to condemn him without allowing him to appear even before that tribunal, to condemn him without a trial, to condemn him without an accusation ? Did ever any grave senate, since the beginning of the world, treat a man as a criminal merely because he had been robbed, pelted, hustled, dragged through snow and mire, and threatened with death if he returned to the house which was his by law ? The Duke of Hamilton, glad to have so good an opportunity of attacking the new Lord Commissioner, spoke with great vehemence against this odious clause. We are told that no attempt was made to answer him ; and, though those who tell us so were zealous Episcopalians, we may believe their report : for what answer was it possible to return ? Melville, on whom the chief responsibility lay, sate on the throne in profound silence through the whole of this tempestuous debate. It is probable that his conduct was determined by considerations which prudence and shame prevented him from

[1] An Historical Relation of the late Presbyterian General Assembly in a Letter from a Person in Edinburgh to his Friend in London. London licensed April 20. 1691.

explaining. The state of the southwestern shires was such that it would have been impossible to put the rabbled ministers in possession of their dwellings and churches without employing a military force, without garrisoning every manse, without placing guards round every pulpit, and without handing over some ferocious enthusiasts to the Provost Marshal ; and it would be no easy task for the government to keep down by the sword at once the Jacobites of the Highlands and the Covenanters of the Lowlands. The majority, having, for reasons which could not well be produced, made up their minds, became clamorous for the question. " No more debate," was the cry : " We have heard enough : a vote ! a vote ! " The question was put according to the Scottish form, " Approve or not approve the article ? " Hamilton insisted that the question should be, "Approve or not approve the rabbling ? " After much altercation, he was overruled, and the clause passed. Only fifteen or sixteen members voted with him. He warmly and loudly exclaimed, amidst much angry interruption, that he was sorry to see a Scottish Parliament disgrace itself by such iniquity. He then left the house with several of his friends. It is impossible not to sympathise with the indignation which he expressed. Yet we ought to remember that it is the nature of injustice to generate injustice. There are wrongs which it is almost impossible to repair without committing other wrongs ; and such a wrong had been done to the people of Scotland in the preceding generation. It was because the Parliament of the Restoration had legislated in insolent defiance of the sense of the nation that the Parliament of the Revolution had to abase itself before the mob.

When Hamilton and his adherents had retired, one of the preachers who had been admitted to the hall called out to the members who were near him ; " Fie ! Fie ! Do not lose time. Make haste, and get all over before he comes back." This advice was taken. Four or five sturdy Prelatists staid to give a last vote against Presbytery. Four or five equally sturdy Covenanters staid to mark their dislike of what seemed to them a compromise between the Lord and Baal. But the Act was passed by an overwhelming majority.[1]

Two supplementary Acts speedily followed. One of them, now happily repealed, required every office-bearer in every University of Scotland to sign the Confession of Faith and to give in his adhesion to the new form of Church government.[2] The other, long ago most unhappily repealed, settled the important and delicate question of patronage. Knox had, in the First Book of Discipline, asserted the right of every Christian

---

[1] Account of the late Establishment of the Presbyterian Government by the Parliament of Scotland, 1690.

[2] Act. Parl. July 4. 1690.

congregation to choose its own pastor. Melville had not, in the Second Book of Discipline, gone quite so far : but he had declared that no pastor could lawfully be forced on an unwilling congregation. Patronage had been abolished by a Covenanted Parliament in 1649, and restored by a Royalist Parliament in 1661. What ought to be done in 1690 it was no easy matter to decide. Scarcely any question seems to have caused so much anxiety to William. He had, in his private instructions, given the Lord Commissioner authority to assent to the abolition of patronage, if nothing else would satisfy the Estates. But this authority was most unwillingly given ; and the King hoped that it would not be used. " It is," he said, " the taking of men's property." Melville succeeded in effecting a compromise. Patronage was abolished : but it was enacted that every patron should receive six hundred marks Scots, equivalent to about thirty five pounds sterling, as a compensation for his rights. The sum seems ludicrously small. Yet, when the nature of the property and the poverty of the country are considered, it may be doubted whether a patron would have made much more by going into the market. The largest sum that any member ventured to suggest was nine hundred marks, little more than fifty pounds sterling. The right of proposing a minister was given to a parochial council consisting of the Protestant landowners and the elders. The congregation might object to the person proposed ; and the Presbytery was to judge of the objections. This arrangement did not give to the people all the power to which even the Second Book of Discipline had declared that they were entitled. But the odious name of patronage was taken away : it was probably thought that the elders and landowners of a parish would seldom persist in nominating a person to whom the majority of the congregation had strong objections ; and indeed it does not appear that, while the Act of 1690 continued in force, the peace of the Church was ever broken by disputes such as produced the schisms of 1732, of 1756, and of 1843.[1]

Montgomery had done all in his power to prevent the Estates from settling the ecclesiastical polity of the realm. He had incited the zealous Covenanters to demand what he knew that the government would never grant. He had protested against all Erastianism, against all compromise. Dutch Presbyterianism, he said, would not do for Scotland. She must have again the system of 1649. That system was deduced from the Word of God : it was the most powerful check that had ever been devised on the tyranny of wicked kings ; and it ought to be restored without addition or diminution. His Jacobite allies could not conceal their disgust and mortification at hearing him hold such language, and were by no means satisfied

The coalition between the Club and the Jacobites dissolved

---

[1] Act. Parl. July 19. 1690 ; Lockhart to Melville, April 29. 1690.

with the explanations which he gave them in private. While they were wrangling with him on this subject, a messenger arrived at Edinburgh with important despatches from James and from Mary of Modena. These despatches had been written in the confident expectation that the large promises of Montgomery would be fulfilled, and that the Scottish Estates would, under his dexterous management, declare for the rightful Sovereign against the Usurper. James was so grateful for the unexpected support of his old enemies that he entirely forgot the services and disregarded the feelings of his old friends. The three chiefs of the Club, rebels and Puritans as they were, had become his favourites. Annandale was to be a Marquess, Governor of Edinburgh Castle, and Lord High Commissioner. Montgomery was to be Earl of Ayr and Secretary of State. Ross was to be an Earl and to command the guards. James Stewart, the most unprincipled of lawyers, who had been deeply concerned in Argyle's insurrection, who had changed sides and supported the dispensing power, who had then changed sides a second time and concurred in the Revolution, and who had now changed sides a third time and was scheming to bring about a Restoration, was to be Lord Advocate. The Privy Council, the Court of Session, the army, were to be filled with Whigs. A Council of Five was appointed, which all loyal subjects were to obey ; and in this Council Annandale, Ross, and Montgomery formed the majority. Mary of Modena informed Montgomery that five thousand pounds sterling had been remitted to his order, and that five thousand more would soon follow. It was impossible that Balcarras and those who had acted with him should not bitterly resent the manner in which they were treated. Their names were not even mentioned. All that they had done and suffered seemed to have faded from their master's mind. He had now given them fair notice that, if they should, at the hazard of their lands and lives, succeed in restoring him, all that he had to give would be given to those who had deposed him. They too, when they read his letters, knew, what he did not know when the letters were written, that he had been duped by the confident boasts and promises of the apostate Whigs. He, when he despatched his messengers, imagined that the Club was omnipotent at Edinburgh ; and, before the messengers reached Edinburgh, the Club had become a mere byword of contempt. The Tory Jacobites easily found pretexts for refusing to obey the Presbyterian Jacobites to whom the banished King had delegated his authority. They complained that Montgomery had not shown them all the despatches which he had received. They affected to suspect that he had tampered with the seals. He called God Almighty to witness that the suspicion was unfounded. But oaths were very naturally regarded as insufficient guarantees by men who had just been swearing allegiance to a King against whom they

were conspiring.   There was a violent outbreak of passion on both
sides : the coalition was dissolved : the papers were flung into the fire ;
and, in a few days, the infamous triumvirs who had been, in the short
space of a year, violent Williamites and violent Jacobites, became Williamites again, and attempted to make their peace with the government
by accusing each other.[1]

Ross was the first who turned informer.   After the fashion of the
school in which he had been bred, he committed this base action with all
The chiefs the forms of sanctity.   He pretended to be greatly troubled
of the
Club betray in mind, sent for a celebrated Presbyterian minister named
each other Dunlop, and bemoaned himself piteously : "There is a load on
my conscience : there is a secret which I know that I ought to disclose :
but I cannot bring myself to do it."   Dunlop prayed long and fervently :
Ross groaned and wept : at last it seemed that heaven had been stormed
by the violence of supplication : the truth came out, and many lies with
it.   The divine and the penitent then returned thanks together.   Dunlop
went with the news to Melville.   Ross set off for England to make his
peace at court, and performed his journey in safety, though some of his
accomplices, who had heard of his repentance, but had been little edified
by it, had laid plans for cutting his throat by the way.   At London he
protested, on his honour, and on the word of a gentleman, that he had
been drawn in, that he had always disliked the plot, and that Montgomery and Ferguson were the real criminals.[2]

Dunlop was, in the meantime, magnifying, wherever he went, the
divine goodness which had, by so humble an instrument as himself,
brought a noble person back to the right path.   Montgomery no sooner
heard of this wonderful work of grace than he too began to experience
compunction.   He went to Melville, made a confession not exactly
coinciding with Ross's, and obtained a pass for England.   William was
then in Ireland ; and Mary was governing in his stead.   At her feet
Montgomery threw himself.   He tried to move her pity by speaking of
his broken fortunes, and to ingratiate himself with her by praising her
sweet and affable manners.   He gave up to her the names of his fellow
plotters.   He vowed to dedicate his whole life to her service, if she
would obtain for him some place which might enable him to subsist
with decency.   She was so much touched by his supplications and
flatteries that she recommended him to her husband's favour : but the
just distrust and abhorrence with which William regarded Montgomery
were not to be overcome.[3]

[1] Balcarras ; Confession of Annandale in the Leven and Melville papers.

[2] Balcarras ; Notes of Ross's Confession in the Leven and Melville Papers.

[3] Balcarras ; Mary's account of her interview with Montgomery, printed among the Leven
and Melville Papers.

Before the traitor had been admitted to Mary's presence, he had obtained a promise that he should be allowed to depart in safety. The

WILLIAM JOHNSTONE, MARQUIS OF ANNANDALE
From a mezzotint by J. Smith, after a painting by Sir G. Kneller

promise was kept. During some months, he lay hid in London, and contrived to carry on a negotiation with the government. He offered to be a witness against his accomplices on condition of having a good place. William would bid no higher than a pardon. At length the communications were broken off. Montgomery retired for a time to France. He soon returned to London and passed the miserable remnant of his life in forming plots which came to nothing, and in writing libels which are distinguished by the grace and vigour of their style from most of the productions of the Jacobite press.[1]

Annandale, when he learned that his two accomplices had turned approvers, retired to Bath, and pretended to drink the waters. Thence he was soon brought up to London by a warrant. He acknowledged that he had been seduced into treason : but he declared that he had only said Amen to the plans of others, and that his childlike simplicity had been imposed on by Montgomery, that worst, that falsest, that most unquiet of human beings. The noble penitent then proceeded to make atonement for his own crime by criminating other people, English and Scotch, Whig and Tory, guilty and innocent. Some he accused on his own knowledge, and some on mere hearsay. Among those whom he accused on his own knowledge was Neville Payne, who had not, it should seem, been mentioned either by Ross or by Montgomery.[2]

Payne, pursued by messengers and warrants, was so ill advised as to take refuge in Scotland. Had he remained in England he would have been safe : for, though the moral proofs of his guilt were complete, there was not such legal evidence as would have satisfied a jury that he had committed high treason : he could not be subjected to torture in order to force him to furnish evidence against himself; nor could he be long confined without being brought to trial. But the moment that he passed the border he was at the mercy of the government of which he was the deadly foe. The Claim of Right had recognised torture as, in cases like his, a legitimate mode of obtaining information ; and no Habeas Corpus Act secured him against a long detention. The unhappy man was arrested, carried to Edinburgh, and brought before the Privy Council. The general notion was, that he was a knave and a coward, and that the first sight of the boots and thumbscrews would bring out all the guilty secrets with which he had been entrusted. But Payne had a far braver spirit than those highborn plotters with whom it was his misfortune to have been connected. Twice he was subjected to frightful torments ; but not a word inculpating himself or any other person could be wrung out of him. Some councillors left the board in horror. But the pious Crawford presided. He was not much troubled with the weakness of compassion where an Amalekite was concerned, and forced

---

[1] Compare Balcarras with Burnet, ii. 62. The pamphlet entitled Great Britain's Just Complaint is a good specimen of Montgomery's manner.

[2] Balcarras ; Annandale's Confession.

the executioner to hammer in wedge after wedge between the knees of the prisoner till the pain was as great as the human frame can sustain without dissolution. Payne was then carried to the Castle of Edinburgh, where he long remained, utterly forgotten, as he touchingly complained, by those for whose sake he had endured more than the bitterness of death. Yet no ingratitude could damp the ardour of his fanatical loyalty ; and he continued, year after year, in his cell, to plan insurrections and invasions.[1]

Before Payne's arrest the Estates had been adjourned after a Session as important as any that had ever been held in Scotland. The nation generally acquiesced in the new ecclesiastical constitution. *General acquiescence in the new ecclesiastical polity* The indifferent, a large portion of every society, were glad that the anarchy was over, and conformed to the Presbyterian Church as they had conformed to the Episcopal Church. To the moderate Presbyterians the settlement which had been made was on the whole satisfactory. Most of the strict Presbyterians brought themselves to accept it under protest, as a large instalment of what was due. They missed indeed what they considered as the perfect beauty and symmetry of that Church which had, forty years before, been the glory of Scotland. But, though the second temple was not equal to the first, the chosen people might well rejoice to think that they were, after a long captivity in Babylon, suffered to rebuild, though imperfectly, the House of God on the old foundations ; nor could it misbecome them to feel for the latitudinarian William a grateful affection such as the restored Jews had felt for the heathen Cyrus.

There were however two parties which regarded the settlement of 1690 with implacable detestation. Those Scotchmen who were Episcopalians on conviction and with fervour appear to have *Complaints of the Episcopalians* been few : but among them were some persons superior, not perhaps in natural parts, but in learning, in taste, and in the art of composition, to the theologians of the sect which had now become dominant. It might not have been safe for the ejected Curates and Professors to give vent in their own country to the anger which they felt. But the English press was open to them ; and they were sure of the approbation of a large part of the English people. During several years they continued to torment their enemies and to amuse the public with a succession of ingenious and spirited pamphlets. In some of these works the hardships suffered by the rabbled priests of the western shires are set forth with a skill which irresistibly moves pity and indignation. In others, the cruelty with which the Covenanters had been treated during the reigns of the last two kings of the House of Stuart

---

[1] Burnet, ii. 62. ; Lockhart to Melville, Aug. 30. 1690 ; and Crawford to Melville, Dec. 11. 1690, in the Leven and Melville Papers ; Neville Payne's letter of Dec. 3. 1692, printed in 1693.

is extenuated by every artifice of sophistry. There is much joking on the bad Latin which some Presbyterian teachers had uttered while seated in academic chairs lately occupied by great scholars. Much was said about the ignorant contempt which the victorious barbarians professed for science and literature. They were accused of anathematising the modern systems of natural philosophy as damnable heresies, of condemning geometry as a souldestroying pursuit, of discouraging even the study of those tongues in which the sacred books were written. Learning, it was said, would soon be extinct in Scotland. The Universities, under their new rulers, were languishing and must soon perish. The booksellers had been half ruined : they found that the whole profit of their business would not pay the rent of their shops, and were preparing to emigrate to some country where letters were held in esteem by those whose office was to instruct the public. Among the ministers of religion no purchaser of books was left. The Episcopalian divine was glad to sell for a morsel of bread whatever part of his library had not been torn to pieces or burned by the Christmas mobs ; and the only library of a Presbyterian divine consisted of an explanation of the Apocalypse and a commentary on the Song of Songs.[1] The pulpit oratory of the triumphant party was an inexhaustible subject of mirth. One little volume, entitled the Scotch Presbyterian Eloquence Displayed, had an immense success in the South among both High Churchmen and scoffers, and is not yet quite forgotten. It was indeed a book well fitted to lie on the hall table of a Squire whose religion consisted in hating extemporaneous prayer and nasal psalmody. On a rainy day, when it was impossible to hunt or shoot, neither the card table nor the backgammon board would have been, in the intervals of the flagon and the pasty, so agreeable a resource. Nowhere else, perhaps, can be found, in so small a compass, so large a collection of ludicrous quotations and anecdotes. Some grave men, however, who bore no love to the Calvinistic doctrine or discipline, shook their heads over this lively jest book, and hinted their opinion that the writer, while holding up to derision the absurd rhetoric by which coarseminded and ignorant men tried to illustrate dark questions of theology and to excite devotional feeling among the populace, had sometimes forgotten the reverence due to sacred things. The effect which tracts of this sort produced on the public mind of England could not be fully discerned while England and Scotland were independent of each other, but manifested itself, very soon after the union of the kingdoms, in a way which we still have reason, and which our posterity will probably long have reason, to lament.

[1] Historical Relation of the late Presbyterian General Assembly, 1691 ; The Presbyterian Inquisition as it was lately practised against the Professors of the College of Edinburgh, 1691.

The extreme Presbyterians were as much out of humour as the extreme Prelatists, and were as little inclined as the extreme Prelatists to take the oath of allegiance to William and Mary. Indeed, though the Jacobite nonjuror and the Cameronian nonjuror were diametrically opposed to each other in opinion, though they regarded each other with mortal aversion, though neither of them would have had any scruple about persecuting the other, they had much in common. They were perhaps the two most remarkable specimens that the world could show of perverse absurdity. Each of them considered his darling form of ecclesiastical polity, not as a means, but as an end, as the one thing needful, as the quintessence of the Christian religion. Each of them childishly fancied that he had found a theory of civil government in his Bible. Neither shrank from the frightful consequences to which his theory led. To all objections both had one answer,—Thus saith the Lord. Both agreed in boasting that the arguments which to atheistical politicians seemed irrefragable presented no difficulty to the Saint. It might be perfectly true that, by relaxing the rigour of his principles, he might save his country from slavery, anarchy, universal ruin. But his business was not to save his country, but to save his soul. He obeyed the commands of God, and left the event to God. One of the two fanatical sects held that, to the end of time, the nation would be bound to obey the heir of the Stuarts : the other held that, to the end of time, the nation would be bound by the Solemn League and Covenant ; and thus both agreed in regarding the new Sovereigns as usurpers.

The Presbyterian nonjurors have scarcely been heard of out of Scotland ; and perhaps it may not now be generally known, even in Scotland, that they still continue to form a distinct class. They maintained that their country was under a precontract to the Most High, and could never, while the world lasted, enter into any engagement inconsistent with that precontract. An Erastian, a latitudinarian, a man who knelt to receive the bread and wine from the hands of bishops, and who bore, though not very patiently, to hear anthems chaunted by choristers in white vestments, could not be King of a covenanted kingdom. William had moreover forfeited all claim to the crown by committing that sin for which, in the old time, a dynasty preternaturally appointed had been preternaturally deposed. He had connived at the escape of his father in law, that idolater, that murderer, that man of Belial, who ought to have been hewn in pieces before the Lord, like Agag. Nay, the crime of William had exceeded that of Saul. Saul had spared only one Amalekite, and had smitten the rest. What Amalekite had William smitten ? The pure Church had been twenty eight years under persecution. Her children had been

The Presbyterian nonjurors

imprisoned, transported, branded, shot, hanged, drowned, tortured. And yet he who called himself her deliverer had not suffered her to see her desire upon her enemies.[1] The bloody Claverhouse had been graciously received at Saint James's. The bloody Mackenzie had found a secure and luxurious retreat among the malignants of Oxford. The younger Dalrymple who had prosecuted the Saints, the elder Dalrymple who had sate in judgment on the Saints, were great and powerful. It was said, by careless Gallios, that there was no choice but between William and James, and that it was wisdom to choose the less of two evils. Such was indeed the wisdom of this world. But the wisdom which was from above taught us that of two things, both of which were evil in the sight of God, we should choose neither. As soon as James was restored, it would be a duty to disown and withstand him. The present duty was to disown and withstand his son in law. Nothing must be said, nothing must be done, that could be construed into a recognition of the authority of the man from Holland. The godly must pay no duties to him, must hold no offices under him, must receive no wages from him, must sign no instruments in which he was styled King. Anne succeeded William; and Anne was designated, by those who called themselves the Reformed Presbytery, and the remnant of the true Church, as the pretended Queen, the wicked woman, the Jezebel. George the First succeeded Anne; and George the First was the pretended King, the German Beast.[2] George the Second succeeded George the First: George the Second too was a pretended King; and he was accused of having outdone the wickedness of his wicked predecessors by passing a law in defiance of that divine law which ordains that no witch shall be suffered to live.[3] George the Third

---

[1] One of the most curious of the many curious papers written by the Covenanters of that generation is entitled, " Nathaniel, or the Dying Testimony of John Matthieson in Closeburn." Matthieson did not die till 1709, but his Testimony was written some years earlier, when he was in expectation of death. "And now," he says, "I, as a dying man, would in a few words tell you that are to live behind me my thoughts as to the times. When I saw, or rather heard, the Prince and Princess of Orange being set up as they were, and his pardoning all the murderers of the saints, and receiving all the bloody beasts, soldiers, and others, all these officers of their state and army, and all the bloody counsellors, civil and ecclesiastic, and his letting slip that son of Belial, his father in law, who, both by all the laws of God and man, ought to have died, I knew he would do no good to the cause and work of God."

[2] See the Dying Testimony of Mr. Robert Smith, Student of Divinity, who lived in Douglas Town, in the Shire of Clydesdale, who died about two o'clock in the Sabbath morning, Dec. 13. 1724, aged 58 years; and the Dying Testimony of William Wilson, sometime Schoolmaster of Park in the Parish of Douglas, aged 68, who died May 7. 1757.

[3] See the Dying Testimony of William Wilson, mentioned in the last note. It ought to be remarked that, on the subject of witchcraft, the Divines of the Associate Presbytery were as absurd as this poor crazy Dominie. See their Act, Declaration, and Testimony, published in 1773 by Adam Gib.

succeeded George the Second ; and still these men continued, with unabated steadfastness, though in language less ferocious than before, to disclaim all allegiance to an uncovenanted Sovereign.[1] At length this schismatical body was subdivided by a new schism. The majority of the Reformed Presbyterians, though they still refused to swear fealty to the Sovereign or to hold office under him, thought themselves justified in praying for him, in paying tribute to him, and in accepting his protection. But there was a minority which would hear of no compromise. So late as the year 1806, a few persons were still bearing their public testimony against the sin of owning an Antichristian government by paying taxes, by taking out excise licenses, or by labouring on public works.[2] The number of these zealots went on diminishing till at length they were so thinly scattered over Scotland that they were nowhere numerous enough to have a meeting house, and were known by the name of the Nonhearers. They, however, still assembled and prayed in private dwellings, and still persisted in considering themselves as the chosen generation, the royal priesthood, the holy nation, the peculiar people, which, amidst the common degeneracy, alone preserved the faith of a better age. It is by no means improbable that this superstition, the most irrational and the most unsocial into which Protestant Christianity has ever been corrupted by human prejudices and passions, may still linger in a few obscure farmhouses.

[1] In the year 1791, Thomas Henderson of Paisley wrote, in defence of the Reformed Presbytery, against a writer who had charged them with "disowning the present excellent sovereign as the lawful King of Great Britain." "The Reformed Presbytery and their connections," says Mr. Henderson, "have not been much accustomed to give flattering titles to princes." . . . . . . "However, they entertain no resentment against the person of the present occupant, nor any of the good qualities which he possesses. They sincerely wish that he were more excellent than external royalty can make him, that he were adorned with the image of Christ," &c., &c., &c. "But they can by no means acknowledge him, nor any of the episcopal persuasion, to be a lawful king over these covenanted lands."

[2] An enthusiast, named George Calderwood, in his preface to a Collection of Dying Testimonies, published in 1806, accuses the Reformed Presbytery of scandalous compliances. "As for the Reformed Presbytery," he says, "though they profess to own the martyrs' testimony in hairs and hoofs, yet they have now adopted so many new distinctions, and given up their old ones, that they have made it so evident that it is neither the martyrs' testimony nor yet the one that that Presbytery adopted at first that they are now maintaining. When the Reformed Presbytery was in its infancy, and had some appearance of honesty and faithfulness among them, they were blamed by all the other parties for using of distinctions that no man could justify, i.e. they would not admit into their communion those that paid the land tax or subscribed tacks to do so ; but now they can admit into their communions both rulers and members who voluntarily pay all taxes and subscribe tacks." . . . . "It shall be only referred to government's books, since the commencement of the French war, how many of their own members have accepted of places of trust, to be at government's call, such as bearers of arms, driving of cattle, stopping of ways, &c.; and what is all their license for trading by sea or land but a serving under government?" The doctrines of those more moderate nonjurors who call themselves the Reformed Presbyterian Church have been recently set forth in a Prize Catechism by the Reverend Thomas Martin.

The King was but half satisfied with the manner in which the ecclesiastical polity of Scotland had been settled. He thought that the Episcopalians had been hardly used ; and he apprehended that they might be still more hardly used when the new system was fully organised. He had been very desirous that the Act which established the Presbyterian Church should be accompanied by an Act allowing persons who were not members of that Church to hold their own religious assemblies freely ; and he had particularly directed Melville to look to this.[1] But some popular preachers harangued so vehemently at Edinburgh against liberty of conscience, which they called the mystery of iniquity, that Melville did not venture to obey his master's instructions. A draught of a Toleration Act was offered to the Parliament by a private member, but was coldly received and suffered to drop.[2]

William dissatisfied with the ecclesiastical arrangements in Scotland

William, however, was fully determined to prevent the dominant sect from indulging in the luxury of persecution ; and he took an early opportunity of announcing his determination. The first General Assembly of the newly established Church met soon after his return from Ireland. It was necessary that he should appoint a Commissioner and send a letter. Some zealous Presbyterians hoped that Crawford would be the Commissioner; and the ministers of Edinburgh drew up a paper in which they very intelligibly hinted that this was their wish. William, however, selected Lord Carmichael, a nobleman distinguished by good sense, humanity, and moderation.[3] The royal letter to the Assembly was eminently wise in substance and impressive in language. "We expect," the King wrote, "that your management shall be such that we may have no reason to repent of what we have done. We never could be of the mind that violence was suited to the advancing of true religion ; nor do we intend that our authority shall ever be a tool to the irregular passions of any party. Moderation is what religion enjoins, what neighbouring Churches expect from you, and what we recommend to you." The Sixty and their associates would probably have been glad to reply in language resembling that which, as some of them could well remember, had been held by the clergy to Charles the Second during his residence in Scotland. But they had just been informed that there was in England a strong feeling in favour of the rabbled curates, and that it would, at such a conjuncture, be madness in the body which represented the

Meeting of the General Assembly of the Church of Scotland

---

[1] The King to Melville, May 22. 1690, in the Leven and Melville Papers.

[2] Account of the Establishment of Presbyterian Government.

[3] Carmichael's good qualities are fully admitted by the Episcopalians. See the Historical Relation of the late Presbyterian General Assembly and the Presbyterian Inquisition.

Presbyterian Church to quarrel with the King.[1]　The Assembly therefore returned a grateful and respectful answer to the royal letter, and assured His Majesty that they had suffered too much from oppression ever to be oppressors.[2]

Meanwhile the troops all over the Continent were going into winter quarters.　The campaign had everywhere been indecisive.　The victory gained by Luxemburg at Fleurus had produced no important effect.　On the Upper Rhine great armies had eyed each other, month after month, without exchanging a blow.　In Catalonia a few small forts had been taken. State of affairs on the Continent　In the east of Europe the Turks had been successful on some points, the Christians on other points ; and the termination of the contest seemed to be as remote as ever.　The coalition had in the course of the year lost one valuable member, and gained another.　The Duke of Lorraine, the ablest captain in the Imperial service, was no more.　He had died, as he had lived, an exile and a wanderer, and had bequeathed to his children nothing but his name and his rights.　It was popularly said that the confederacy could better have spared thirty thousand soldiers than such a general. But scarcely had the allied Courts gone into mourning for him when they were consoled by learning that another prince, superior to him in power, and not inferior to him in capacity or courage, had joined the league against France.

This was Victor Amadeus, Duke of Savoy.　He was a young man : but he was already versed in those arts for which the statesmen of Italy had, ever since the thirteenth century, been celebrated, those arts by which Castruccio Castracani and Francis Sforza rose to greatness, and which Machiavel reduced to a system.　No The Duke of Savoy joins the coalition sovereign in modern Europe has, with so small a principality, exercised so great an influence during so long a period.　He had for a time submitted, with a show of cheerfulness, but with secret reluctance and resentment, to the French ascendency.　When the war broke out, he professed neutrality, but entered into private negotiations with the House of Austria.　He would probably have continued to dissemble till he found some opportunity of striking an unexpected blow, had not his crafty schemes been disconcerted by the decision and vigour of Lewis. A French army commanded by Catinat, an officer of great skill and

---

[1] See, in the Leven and Melville Papers, Melville's Letters written from London at this time to Crawford, Rule, Williamson, and other vehement Presbyterians.　He says : "The clergy that were putt out, and come up, make a great clamour : many here encourage and rejoyce at it. . . . .　There is nothing now but the greatest sobrietie and moderation imaginable to be used, unless we will hazard the overturning of all : and take this as earnest, and not as imaginations and fears only."

[2] Principal Acts of the General Assembly of the Church of Scotland held in and begun at Edinburgh the 16th day of October, 1690 ; Edinburgh, 1691.

valour, marched into Piedmont.   The Duke was informed that his conduct had excited suspicions which he could remove only by admitting
foreign garrisons into Turin and Vercelli.   He found that he must
be either the slave or the open enemy of his powerful and imperious
neighbour.   His choice was soon made; and a war began which, during
seven years, found employment for some of the best generals and best
troops of Lewis.   An Envoy Extraordinary from Savoy went to the
Hague, proceeded thence to London, presented his credentials in the
Banqueting House, and addressed to William a speech which was
speedily translated into many languages and read in every part of
Europe.   The orator congratulated the King on the success of that
great enterprise which had restored England to her ancient place among
the nations, and had broken the chains of Europe.   "That my master,"
he said, "can now at length venture to express feelings which have been
long concealed in the recesses of his heart is part of the debt which he
owes to Your Majesty.   You have inspired him with the hope of freedom after so many years of bondage." [1]

   It had been determined that, during the approaching winter, a Congress of all the powers hostile to France should be held at the Hague.
William was impatient to proceed thither.   But it was necessary that
he should first hold a Session of Parliament.   Early in October the
Houses reassembled at Westminster.   The members had generally
come up in good humour.   Those Tories whom it was possible to conciliate had been conciliated by the Act of Grace, and by the large share
which they had obtained of the favours of the Crown.   Those Whigs
who were capable of learning had learned much from the lesson which
William had given them, and had ceased to expect that he would
descend from the rank of a King to that of a party leader.   Both
Whigs and Tories had, with few exceptions, been alarmed by the prospect of a French invasion, and cheered by the news of the victory of
the Boyne.   The Sovereign who had shed his blood for their nation
and their religion stood at this moment higher in public estimation
than at any time since his accession.   His speech from the throne
called forth the loud acclamations of Lords and Commons. [2]   Thanks
were unanimously voted by both Houses to the King for his achievements in Ireland, and to the Queen for the prudence with which she
had, during his absence, governed England. [3]   Thus commenced a
Session distinguished among the Sessions of that reign by harmony
and tranquillity.   No report of the debates has been preserved, unless
a long forgotten lampoon, in which some of the speeches made on the

[1] Monthly Mercuries ; London Gazettes of November 3. and 6. 1690.
[2] Van Citters to the States General, Oct. $\frac{3}{13}$. 1690.
[3] Lords' Journals, Oct. 6. 1690 ; Commons' Journals, October 8.

VICTOR AMADEUS, DUKE OF SAVOY

From an engraving by A. Moetjens in the Sutherland Collection

first day are burlesqued in doggrel rhymes, may be called a report.[1]
The time of the Commons appears to have been chiefly occupied in
discussing questions arising out of the elections of the preceding spring.

Supplies voted The supplies necessary for the war, though large, were granted
with alacrity. The number of regular troops for the next year
was fixed at seventy thousand, of whom twelve thousand were to be
horse or dragoons. The charge of this army, the greatest that England
had ever maintained, amounted to about two million three hundred
thousand pounds; the charge of the navy to about eighteen hundred
thousand pounds. The charge of the ordnance was included in these
sums, and was roughly estimated at one eighth of the naval and one
fifth of the military expenditure.[2] The whole of the extraordinary aid
granted to the King exceeded four millions.

The Commons justly thought that the extraordinary liberality with
which they had provided for the public service entitled them to demand
extraordinary securities against waste and peculation. A bill was brought
in empowering nine Commissioners to examine and state the public
accounts. The nine were named in the bill, and were all members of
the Lower House. The Lords agreed to the bill without amendments;
and the King gave his assent.[3]

The debates on the Ways and Means occupied a considerable part
of the Session. It was resolved that sixteen hundred and fifty thousand
Ways and Means pounds should be raised by a direct monthly assessment on
land. The excise duties on ale and beer were doubled; and
the import duties on raw silk, linen, timber, glass, and other articles,
were increased.[4] Thus far there was little difference of opinion. But
soon the smooth course of business was disturbed by a proposition
which was much more popular than just or humane. Taxes of unprecedented severity had been imposed; and yet it might well be doubted
whether these taxes would be sufficient. Why, it was asked, should
not the cost of the Irish war be borne by the Irish insurgents? How
those insurgents had acted in their mock Parliament all the world
knew; and nothing could be more reasonable than to mete to them
from their own measure. They ought to be treated as they had treated
the Saxon colony. Every acre which the Act of Settlement had left
them ought to be seized by the state for the purpose of defraying that
expense which their turbulence and perverseness had made necessary.
It is not strange that a plan, which at once gratified national animosity,

[1] I am not aware that this lampoon has ever been printed. I have seen it only in two contemporary manuscripts. It is entitled The Opening of the Session, 1690.

[2] Commons' Journals, Oct. 9, 10. 13, 14. 1690.

[3] Commons' Journals of December, 1690, particularly of Dec. 26.; Stat. 2 W. & M. sess. 2. c. 11.

[4] Stat. 2 W. & M. sess. 2. c. 1. 3, 4.

The most Serene Prince Eugene of Savoy, Knight of the Order of
the Golden Fleece Privy Councellour to his Imperial Majesty President
of the Council of War, and Generalissimo of all his Forces in Italy &c.

D. Richter pinx   J Smith fec   Sold by I Smith at ý Lyon & Crown in Russel-Street Covent Garden

PRINCE EUGENE OF SAVOY

From a mezzotint by J. Smith, after a painting by D. Richter and held out the hope of pecuniary relief, should have been welcomed with eager delight. A bill was brought in which bore but too much resemblance to some of the laws passed by the Jacobite legislators of Dublin. By this bill it was provided that the property of every person who had been in rebellion against the King and Queen since the day on which they were proclaimed should be confiscated, and that the proceeds should be applied to the support of the war. An exception was made in favour of such Protestants as had merely submitted to superior force : but to Papists no indulgence was shown. The royal prerogative of clemency was limited. The King might indeed, if such were his pleasure, spare the lives of his vanquished enemies : but he was not to be permitted to save any part of their estates from the general doom. He was not to have it in his power to grant a capitulation which should secure to Irish Roman Catholics the enjoyment of their hereditary lands. Nay, he was not to be allowed to keep faith with persons whom he had already received to mercy, who had kissed his hand, and had heard from his lips the promise of protection. An attempt was made to insert a proviso in favour of Lord Dover. Dover, who, with all his faults, was not without some English feelings, had, by defending the interests of his native country at Dublin, made himself odious to both the Irish and the French. After the battle of the Boyne his situation was deplorable. Neither at Limerick nor at Saint Germains could he hope to be welcomed. In his despair, he threw himself at William's feet, promised to live peaceably, and was graciously assured that he had nothing to fear. Though the royal word seemed to be pledged to this unfortunate man, the Commons resolved, by a hundred and nineteen votes to a hundred and twelve, that his property should not be exempted from the general confiscation.

The bill went up to the Peers : but the Peers were not inclined to pass it without considerable amendments ; and such amendments there was not time to make. Numerous heirs at law, reversioners, and creditors implored the Upper House to introduce such provisoes as might secure the innocent against all danger of being involved in the punishment of the guilty. Some petitioners asked to be heard by counsel. The King had made all his arrangements for a voyage to the Hague ; and the day beyond which he could not postpone his departure drew near. The bill was therefore, happily for the honour of English legislation, consigned to that dark repository in which the abortive statutes of many generations sleep a sleep rarely disturbed by the historian or the antiquary.[1]

---

[1] Burnet, ii. 67. See the Journals of both Houses, particularly the Commons' Journals of the 19th of December and the Lords' Journals of the 30th of December and the 1st of January. The bill itself will be found in the archives of the House of Lords.

Another question, which slightly, and but slightly, discomposed the tranquillity of this short session, arose out of the disastrous and disgraceful battle of Beachy Head.   Torrington had, immediately Proceedings against Torrington after that battle, been sent to the Tower, and had ever since remained there.   A technical difficulty had arisen about the mode of bringing him to trial.   There was no Lord High Admiral ; and whether the Commissioners of the Admiralty were competent to execute martial law was a point which to some jurists appeared not perfectly clear.   The majority of the Judges held that the Commissioners were competent : but, for the purpose of removing all doubt, a bill was brought into the Upper House ; and to this bill several Lords offered an opposition which seems to have been most unreasonable.   The proposed law, they said, was a retrospective penal law, and therefore objectionable.   If they used this argument in good faith, they were ignorant of the very rudiments of the science of legislation.   To make a law for punishing that which, at the time when it was done, was not punishable, is contrary to all sound principle.   But a law which merely alters the criminal procedure may with perfect propriety be made applicable to past as well as to future offences.   It would have been the grossest injustice to give a retrospective operation to the law which made slavetrading felony.   But there was not the smallest injustice in enacting that the Central Criminal Court should try felonies committed long before that Court was in being.   In Torrington's case the substantive law continued to be what it had always been.   The definition of the crime, the amount of the penalty, remained unaltered.   The only change was in the form of procedure ; and that change the legislature was perfectly justified in making retrospectively.   It is indeed hardly possible to believe that some of those who opposed the bill were duped by the fallacy of which they condescended to make use.   The truth probably is that the feeling of caste was strong among the Lords.   That one of themselves should be tried for his life by a court composed of plebeians seemed to them a degradation of their whole order.   If their noble brother had offended, articles of impeachment ought to be exhibited against him : Westminster Hall ought to be fitted up : his peers ought to meet in their robes, and to give in their verdict on their honour : a Lord High Steward ought to pronounce the sentence, and to break the staff.   There was an end of privilege if an Earl was to be doomed to death by tarpaulins seated round a table in the cabin of a ship.   These feelings had so much influence that the bill passed the Upper House by a majority of only two.[1]   In the Lower House, where

[1] Lords' Journals, Oct. 30. 1690. The numbers are never given in the Lords' Journals. That the majority was only two is asserted by Ralph, who had, I suppose, some authority which I have not been able to find.

the dignities and immunities of the nobility were regarded with no friendly feeling, there was little difference of opinion. Torrington requested to be heard at the bar, and spoke there at great length, but weakly and confusedly. He boasted of his services, of his sacrifices, and of his wounds. He abused the Dutch, the Board of Admiralty, and the Secretary of State. The bill, however, went through all its stages without a division.[1]

Early in December Torrington was sent under a guard down the river to Sheerness. There the Court Martial met on board of a frigate named the Kent. The investigation lasted three days ; and **Torrington's trial and acquittal** during those days the ferment was great in London. Nothing was heard of on the exchange, in the coffeehouses, nay even at the church doors, but Torrington. Parties ran high : wagers to an immense amount were depending : rumours were hourly arriving by land and water ; and every rumour was exaggerated and distorted by the way. From the day on which the news of the ignominious battle arrived, down to the very eve of the trial, public opinion had been very unfavourable to the prisoner. His name, we are told by contemporary pamphleteers, was hardly ever mentioned without a curse. But, when the crisis of his fate drew nigh, there was, as in our country there often is, a reaction. All his merits, his courage, his good nature, his firm adherence to the Protestant religion in the evil times, were remembered. It was impossible to deny that he was sunk in sloth and luxury, that he neglected the most important business for his pleasures, and that he could not say No to a boon companion or to a mistress : but for these faults excuses and soft names were found. His friends used without scruple all the arts which could raise a national feeling in his favour ; and these arts were powerfully assisted by the intelligence that the hatred which was felt towards him in Holland had vented itself in indignities to some of his countrymen. The cry was that a bold, jolly, freehanded English gentleman, of whom the worst that could be said was that he liked wine and women, was to be shot in order to gratify the spite of the Dutch. What passed at the trial tended to confirm the populace in this notion. Most of the witnesses against the prisoner were Dutch officers. The Dutch rear admiral, who took on himself the part of prosecutor, forgot himself so far as to accuse the judges of partiality. When at length, on the evening of the third day, Torrington was pronounced not guilty, many who had recently clamoured for his blood seemed to be well pleased with his acquittal. He returned to London free, and with his sword by his side. As his yacht went up the Thames, every ship which he passed saluted him. He took his seat

---

[1] Van Citters to the States General, Nov. $\frac{14}{24}$. 1690. The Earl of Torrington's speech to the House of Commons, 1710.

in the House of Lords, and even ventured to present himself at court. But most of the peers looked coldly on him : William would not see him, and ordered him to be dismissed from the service.[1]

THE EARL OF TORRINGTON

From a Dutch mezzotint in the Sutherland Collection

There was another subject about which no vote was passed by either of the Houses, but about which there is reason to believe that

[1] Burnet, ii. 67, 68. ; Van Citters to the States General, $\frac{Nov. 20.}{Dec. 1.}$ Dec. $\frac{0}{19}$. $\frac{12}{23}$. $\frac{16}{28}$. 1690 ; An impartial Account of some remarkable Passages in the Life of Arthur, Earl of Torrington,

some acrimonious discussion took place in both. The Whigs, though much less violent than in the preceding year, could not patiently see **Animosity of the Whigs against Caermarthen** Caermarthen as nearly prime minister as any English subject could be under a prince of William's character. Though no man had taken a more prominent part in the Revolution than the Lord President, though no man had more to fear from a counterrevolution, his old enemies would not believe that he had from his heart renounced those arbitrary doctrines for which he had once been zealous, or that he could bear true allegiance to a government sprung from resistance. Through the last six months of 1690 he was mercilessly lampooned. Sometimes he was King Thomas, and sometimes Tom the Tyrant.[1] William was adjured not to go to the Continent leaving his worst enemy close to the ear of the Queen. Halifax, who had, in the preceding year, been ungenerously and ungratefully persecuted by the Whigs, was now mentioned by them with respect and regret: for he was the enemy of their enemy.[2] The face, the figure, the bodily infirmities of Caermarthen were ridiculed.[3] Those dealings with the French Court in which, twelve years before, he had, rather by his misfortune than by his fault, been implicated, were represented in the most odious colours. He was reproached with his impeachment and his imprisonment. Once, it was said, he had escaped: but vengeance might still overtake him; and London might enjoy the long deferred pleasure of seeing the old traitor flung off the ladder in

together with some modest Remarks on the Trial and Acquitment, 1691 ; Reasons for the Trial of the Earl of Torrington by Impeachment, 1690 ; The Parable of the Bearbaiting, 1690 ; The Earl of Torrington's Speech to the House of Commons, 1710. That Torrington was coldly received by the peers I learned from an Article in the Noticias Ordinarias of February 6. 1691, Madrid.

[1] In one Whig lampoon of this year are these lines :
> "David, we thought, succeeded Saul,
> When William rose on James's fall ;
> But now King Thomas governs all."

In another are these lines :
> "When Charles did seem to fill the throne,
> This tyrant Tom made England groan."

A third says :
> "Yorkshire Tom was rais'd to honour,
> For what cause no creature knew ;
> He was false to the royal donor,
> And will be the same to you."

[2] A Whig poet compares the two Marquesses, as they were often called, and gives George the preference over Thomas :
> "If a Marquess needs must steer us,
> Take a better in his stead,
> Who will in your absence cheer us,
> And has far a wiser head."

[3] "A thin, illnatured ghost that haunts the King."

the blue riband which he disgraced. All the members of his family, wife, son, daughters, were assailed with savage invective and contemptuous sarcasm.[1] All who were supposed to be closely connected with him by political ties came in for a portion of this abuse ; and none had so large a portion as Lowther. The feeling indicated by these satires was strong among the Whigs in Parliament. Several of them deliberated on a plan of attack, and were in hopes that they should be able to raise such a storm as would make it impossible for Caermarthen to remain at the head of affairs. It should seem that, at this time, his influence in the royal closet was not quite what it had been. Godolphin, whom he did not love, and could not control, but whose financial skill had been greatly missed during the summer, was brought back to the Treasury, and made First Commissioner. Lowther, who was the Lord President's own man, still sate at the board, but no longer presided there. It is true that there was not then such a difference as there now is between the First Lord and his colleagues. Still the change was important and significant. Marlborough, whom Caermarthen disliked, was, in military affairs, not less trusted than Godolphin in financial affairs. The seals which Shrewsbury had resigned in the summer had ever since been lying in William's secret drawer. The Lord President probably expected that he should be consulted before they were given away ; but he was disappointed. Sidney was sent for from Ireland : and the seals were delivered to him. The first intimation which the Lord President received of this important appointment was not made in a manner likely to sooth his feelings. " Did you meet the new Secretary of State going out ? " said William. " No, Sir," answered the Lord President ; " I met nobody but my Lord Sidney." " He is the new Secretary," said William. " He will do till I find a fit man ; and he will be quite willing to resign as soon as I find a fit man. Any other person that I could put in would think himself ill used if I were to put him out." If William had said all that was in his mind, he would probably have added that Sidney, though not a great orator or statesman, was one of the very few English politicians who could be as entirely trusted as Bentinck or Zulestein. Caermarthen listened with a bitter smile. It was new, he afterwards said, to see a nobleman placed in the Secretary's office, as a footman was placed in a box at the theatre, merely in order to keep a seat till his betters came.[2] But this jest was a cover for serious mortification and alarm. The situation of the prime minister was unpleasant and

---

[1] " Let him with his blue riband be
    Tied close up to the gallows tree ;
    For my lady a cart ; and I'd contrive it,
    Her dancing son and heir should drive it."

[2] See Lord Dartmouth's Note on Burnet, ii. 5.

even perilous ; and the duration of his power would probably have been short, had not fortune, just at this moment, enabled him to confound his adversaries by rendering a great service to the state.[1]

The Jacobites had seemed in August to be completely crushed. The victory of the Boyne, and the irresistible explosion of patriotic feeling produced by the appearance of Tourville's fleet on the coast of Devonshire, had cowed the boldest champions of hereditary right. Most of the chief plotters had passed some weeks in confinement or in concealment. But, widely as the ramifications of the conspiracy had extended, only one traitor had suffered the punishment of his crime. This was a man named Godfrey Cross, who kept an inn on the beach near Rye, and who, when the French fleet was on the coast of Sussex, had given information to Tourville. When it appeared that this solitary example was thought sufficient, when the danger of invasion was over, when the popular enthusiasm excited by that danger had subsided, when the lenity of the government had permitted some conspirators to leave their prisons and had encouraged others to venture out of their hidingplaces, the faction which had been prostrated and stunned began to give signs of returning animation. The old traitors again mustered at the old haunts, exchanged significant looks and eager whispers, and drew from their pockets libels on the Court of Kensington, and letters in milk and lemon juice from the Court of Saint Germains. Preston, Dartmouth, Clarendon, Penn, were among the most busy. With them was leagued the nonjuring Bishop of Ely, who was still permitted by the government to reside in the palace, now no longer his own, and who had, but a short time before, called heaven to witness that he detested the thought of inviting foreigners to invade England. One good opportunity had been lost : but another was at hand, and must not be suffered to escape. The usurper would soon be again out of England. The administration would soon be again confided to a weak woman and a divided council. The year which was closing had certainly been unlucky ; but that which was about to commence might be more auspicious.

In December a meeting of the leading Jacobites was held.[2] The sense of the assembly, which consisted exclusively of Protestants, was

A Jacobite plot

---

[1] As to the designs of the Whigs against Caermarthen, see Burnet, ii. 68, 69., and a very significant protest in the Lords' Journals, October 30. 1690. As to the relations between Caermarthen and Godolphin, see Godolphin's letter to William dated March 20. 1691, in Dalrymple.

[2] My account of this conspiracy is chiefly taken from the evidence, oral and documentary, which was produced on the trial of the conspirators. See also Burnet, ii. 69, 70., the Appendix to Dalrymple's Memoirs, Part II. Book vi., and the Life of James, ii. 441. Narcissus Luttrell remarks that no Roman Catholic appeared to have been admitted to the consultations of the conspirators.

that something ought to be attempted, but that the difficulties were great. None ventured to recommend that James should come over unaccompanied by regular troops. Yet all, taught by the experience Meeting of the leading conspirators of the preceding summer, dreaded the effect which might be produced by the sight of French uniforms and standards on English ground. A paper was drawn up which would, it was hoped,

HENRY SIDNEY, FIRST EARL OF ROMNEY

From a drawing by G. P. Harding of a painting in the possession of Lord De Lisle

convince both James and Lewis that a restoration could not be effected without the cordial concurrence of the nation. France,—such was the substance of this remarkable document,—might possibly make the island a heap of ruins, but never a subject province. It was hardly possible for any person, who had not had an opportunity of observing the temper of the public mind, to imagine the savage and dogged determination with which men of all classes, sects, and factions, were prepared to resist any foreign potentate who should attempt to conquer the kingdom by force of arms. Nor could England be governed as a Roman Catholic country. There were five millions of Protestants in the realm : there were not a hundred thousand Papists : that such a minority should keep down such a majority was physically impossible ; and to physical impossibility all other considerations must give way. James would therefore do well to take without delay such measures as might indicate his resolution to protect the established religion. Unhappily every letter which arrived from France contained something tending to irritate feelings which it was most desirable to sooth. Stories were everywhere current of slights offered at Saint Germains to Protestants who had given the highest proof of loyalty by following into banishment a master zealous for a faith which was not their own. The edicts which had been issued against the Huguenots might perhaps have been justified by the anarchical opinions and practices of those sectaries : but it was the height of injustice and of inhospitality to put those edicts in force against men who had been driven from their country solely on account of their attachment to a Roman Catholic King. Surely sons of the Anglican Church, who had, in obedience to her teaching, sacrificed all that they most prized on earth to the royal cause, ought not to be any longer interdicted from assembling in some modest edifice to celebrate her rites and to receive her consolations. An announcement that Lewis had, at the request of James, permitted the English exiles to worship God according to their national forms would be the best prelude to the great attempt. That attempt ought to be made early in the spring. A French force must undoubtedly accompany His Majesty. But he must declare that he brought that force only for the defence of his person and for the protection of his loving subjects, and that, as soon as the foreign oppressors had been expelled, the foreign deliverers should be dismissed. He must also promise to govern according to law, and must refer all the points which had been in dispute between him and his people to the decision of a Parliament.

It was determined that Preston should carry to Saint Germains the resolutions and suggestions of the conspirators. John Ashton, a person who had been clerk of the closet to Mary of Modena when she was on the throne, and who was entirely devoted to the interests of the exiled family, undertook to procure the means of conveyance, and for this purpose engaged the cooperation of a hotheaded young Jacobite named Elliot, who only knew in general that a service of some hazard was to be rendered to the good cause.

The conspirators determine to send Preston to Saint Germains

JOHN ASHTON

From an engraving in the Sutherland Collection, after a painting by J. Riley

It was easy to find in the port of London a vessel the owner of which was not scrupulous about the use for which it might be wanted. Ashton and Elliot were introduced to the master of a smack named the James and Elizabeth. The Jacobite agents pretended to be smugglers, and talked of the thousands of pounds which might be got by a single lucky trip to France and back again. A bargain was struck: a sixpence was broken ; and all the arrangements were made for the voyage.

Preston was charged by his friends with a packet containing several important papers. Among these was a list of the English fleet furnished by Dartmouth, who was in communication with some of his old companions in arms, a minute of the resolutions which had been adopted at the meeting of the conspirators, and the heads of a Declaration which it was thought desirable that James should publish at the moment of his landing. There were also six or seven letters from persons of note in the Jacobite party. Most of these letters were parables, but parables which it was not difficult to unriddle. One plotter used the cant of the law. There was hope that Mr. Jackson would soon recover his estate. The new landlord was a hard man, and had set the freeholders against him. A little matter would redeem the whole property. The opinions of the best counsel were in Mr. Jackson's favour. All that was necessary was that he should himself appear in Westminster Hall. The final hearing ought to be before the close of Easter Term. Other writers affected the style of the Royal Exchange. There was great demand for a cargo of the right sort. There was reason to hope that the old firm would soon form profitable connections with houses with which it had hitherto had no dealings. This was evidently an allusion to the discontented Whigs. But, it was added, the shipments must not be delayed. Nothing was so dangerous as to overstay the market. If the expected goods did not arrive by the tenth of March, the whole profit of the year would be lost. As to details, entire reliance might be placed on the excellent factor who was going over. Clarendon assumed the character of a matchmaker. There was great hope that the business which he had been negotiating would be brought to bear, and that the marriage portion would be well secured. " Your relations," he wrote, in allusion to his recent confinement, " have been very hard on me this last summer. Yet, as soon as I could go safely abroad, I pursued the business." Catharine Sedley entrusted Preston with a letter in which, without allegory or circumlocution, she complained that her lover had left her a daughter to support, and begged very hard for money. But the two most important despatches were from Bishop Turner. They were directed to Mr. and Mrs. Redding : but the language was such as it would be thought abject in any gentleman to hold except to royalty.

Papers entrusted to Preston

The Bishop assured Their Majesties that he was devoted to their cause, that he earnestly wished for a great occasion to prove his zeal, and that he would no more swerve from his duty to them than renounce his hope of heaven. He added, in phraseology metaphorical indeed, but perfectly intelligible, that he was the mouthpiece of several of the nonjuring prelates, and especially of Sancroft. " Sir, I speak in the plural,"—these are the words of the letter to James,—" because I write my elder brother's sentiments as well as my own, and the rest of our family." The letter to Mary of Modena is to the same effect. " I say this in behalf of my elder brother, and the rest of my nearest relations, as well as from myself." [1]

All the letters with which Preston was charged referred the Court of Saint Germains to him for fuller information. He carried with him minutes in his own handwriting of the subjects on which he was to converse with his master and with the ministers of Lewis. These minutes, though concise and desultory, can for the most part be interpreted without difficulty. The vulnerable points of the coast are mentioned. Gosport is defended only by palisades. The garrison of Portsmouth is small. The French fleet ought to be out in April, and to fight before the Dutch are in the Channel. There is a memorandum which proves that Preston had been charged,—by whom it is easy to guess,—with a commission relating to Pennsylvania; and there are a few broken words clearly importing that some at least of the nonjuring bishops, when they declared, before God, that they abhorred the thought of inviting the French over, were dissembling.[2]

Everything was now ready for Preston's departure. But the owner of the James and Elizabeth had conceived a suspicion that the expedition for which his smack had been hired was rather of a political than of a commercial nature. It occurred to him that more might be made by informing against his passengers than by carrying them safely. Intelligence of what was passing was conveyed to the Lord President. No intelligence could be more welcome to him. He was delighted to find that it was in his

Information of the plot given to Caermarthen

---

[1] The genuineness of these letters was once contested on very frivolous grounds. But the letter of Turner to Sancroft, which is among the Tanner papers in the Bodleian Library, and which will be found in the Life of Ken by a Layman, must convince the most incredulous.

[2] The memorandum relating to Pennsylvania ought to be quoted together with the two sentences which precede it. " A commission given to me from Mr. P.—Fr. Fl. hinder Eng. and D. from joining—two vessels of 150*l.* price for Pensilvania for 13 or 14 months." I have little doubt that the first and third of these sentences are parts of one memorandum, and that the words which evidently relate to the fleets were jotted down at a different time in the place left vacant between two lines. The words relating to the Bishops are these : " The Modest Inquiry —The Bishops' Answer—Not the chilling of them—But the satisfying of friends." The Modest Inquiry was the pamphlet which hinted at Dewitting.

power to give a signal proof of his attachment to the government which his enemies had accused him of betraying. He took his measures with his usual energy and dexterity. His eldest son, the Earl of Danby, a bold, volatile, and somewhat eccentric young man, was fond of the sea, lived much among sailors, and was the proprietor of a small yacht of marvellous speed. This vessel, well manned, was placed under the command of a trusty officer named Billop, and was sent down the river, as if for the purpose of pressing mariners.

At dead of night, the last night of the year 1690, Preston, Ashton, and Elliot went on board of their smack near the Tower. They were in

Arrest of
Preston and
his com-
panions

great dread lest they should be stopped and searched, either by a frigate which lay off Woolwich, or by the guard posted at the blockhouse of Gravesend. But, when they had passed both frigate and blockhouse without being challenged, their spirits rose : their appetites became keen : they unpacked a hamper well stored with roast beef, mince pies, and bottles of wine, and were just sitting down to their Christmas cheer, when the alarm was given that a swift vessel from Tilbury was flying through the water after them. They had scarcely time to hide themselves in a dark hole among the gravel which was the ballast of their smack, when the chase was over, and Billop, at the head of an armed party, came on board. The hatches were taken up : the conspirators were arrested ; and their clothes were strictly examined. Preston, in his agitation, had dropped on the gravel his official seal and the packet of which he was the bearer. The seal was discovered where it had fallen. Ashton, aware of the importance of the papers, snatched them up and tried to conceal them : but they were soon found in his bosom.

The prisoners then tried to cajole or to corrupt Billop. They called for wine, pledged him, praised his gentlemanlike demeanour, and assured him that if he would accompany them, nay, if he would only let that little roll of paper fall overboard into the Thames, his fortune would be made. The tide of affairs, they said, was on the turn : things could not go on for ever as they had gone on of late; and it was in the captain's power to be as great and as rich as he could desire. Billop, though courteous, was inflexible. The conspirators became sensible that their necks were in imminent danger. The emergency brought out strongly the true characters of all the three, characters which, but for such an emergency, might have remained for ever unknown. Preston had always been reputed a highspirited and gallant gentleman : but the near prospect of a dungeon and a gallows altogether unmanned him. Elliot stormed and blasphemed, vowed that, if he ever got free, he would be revenged, and, with horrible imprecations, called on the thunder to strike the yacht, and on London

Bridge to fall in and crush her.   Ashton alone behaved with manly firmness.

Late in the evening the yacht reached Whitehall Stairs ; and the prisoners, strongly guarded, were conducted to the Secretary's office. The papers which had been found in Ashton's bosom were inspected that night by Nottingham and Caermarthen, and were, on the following morning, put by Caermarthen into the hands of the King.

Soon it was known all over London that a plot had been detected, that the messengers whom the adherents of James had sent to solicit the help of an invading army from France had been arrested by the agents of the vigilant and energetic Lord President, and that documentary evidence, which might affect the lives of some great men, was in the possession of the government.   The Jacobites were terrorstricken: the clamour of the Whigs against Caermarthen was suddenly hushed ; and the Session ended in perfect harmony.   On the fifth of January the King thanked the Houses for their support, and assured them that he would not grant away any forfeited property in Ireland till they should reassemble.   He alluded to the plot which had just been discovered, and expressed a hope that the friends of England would not, at such a moment, be less active or less firmly united than her enemies.   He then signified his pleasure that the Parliament should adjourn.   On the following day he set out, attended by a splendid train of nobles, for the Congress at the Hague.[1]

[1] Lords' and Commons' Journals, Jan. 5. 169⁰/₁ ; London Gazette, Jan. 8.

CHAPTER XVII

On the eighteenth of January 1691, the King, having been detained some days by adverse winds, went on board at Gravesend. Four
yachts had been fitted up for him and for his retinue. Among his attendants were Norfolk, Ormond, Devonshire, Dorset, Portland, Monmouth, Zulestein, and the Bishop of London. Two distinguished admirals, Cloudesley Shovel and George Rooke, commanded the men of war which formed the convoy. The passage was tedious and disagreeable. During many hours the fleet was becalmed off the Godwin Sands ; and it was not till the fifth day that the soundings proved the coast of Holland to be near. The sea fog was so thick that no land could be seen ; and it was not thought safe for the ships to proceed further in the darkness. William, tired out by the voyage, and impatient to be once more in his beloved country, determined to land in an open boat. The noblemen who were in his train tried to dissuade him from risking so valuable a life : but, when they found that his mind was made up, they insisted on sharing the danger. That danger proved more serious than they had expected. It had been supposed that in an hour the party would be on shore. But great masses of floating ice impeded the progress of the skiff : the night came on : the fog grew thicker : the waves broke over the King and the courtiers. Once the keel struck on a sand bank, and was with great difficulty got off. The hardiest mariners showed some signs of uneasiness. But William, through the whole night, was as composed as if he had been in the drawingroom at Kensington. " For shame," he said to one of the dismayed sailors : " are you afraid to die in my company ? " A bold Dutch seaman ventured to spring out, and, with great difficulty, swam and scrambled through breakers, ice, and mud, to firm ground. Here he discharged a musket and lighted a fire as a signal that he was safe. None of his fellow passengers, however, thought it prudent to follow his example. They lay tossing in sight of the flame which he had kindled, till the first pale light of a January morning showed them that they were close to the island of Goree.

The King and his Lords, stiff with cold and covered with icicles, gladly landed to warm and rest themselves.[1]

After reposing some hours in the hut of a peasant, William proceeded to the Hague. He was impatiently expected there : for, though the fleet which brought him was not visible from the shore, the royal salutes had been heard through the mist, and had apprised the whole coast of his arrival. Thousands had assembled at Honslaerdyk to welcome him with applause which came from their hearts and which went to his heart. That was one of the few white days of a life, beneficent indeed and glorious, but far from happy. After more than two years passed in a strange land, the exile had again set foot on his native soil. He heard again the language of his nursery. He saw again the scenery

MEDAL REPRESENTING THE LANDING OF WILLIAM IN HOLLAND

and the architecture which were inseparably associated in his mind with the recollections of childhood and the sacred feeling of home ; the dreary mounds of sand, shells, and weeds, on which the waves of the German Ocean broke ; the interminable meadows intersected by trenches ; the straight canals ; the villas bright with paint, and adorned with quaint images and inscriptions. He had lived during many weary months among a people who did not love him, who did not understand him, who could never forget that he was a foreigner. Those Englishmen who served him most faithfully served him without enthusiasm, without personal attachment, and merely from a sense of public duty. In their hearts they were sorry that they had no choice but between an English tyrant and a Dutch deliverer. All was now changed. William was among a population by which he was adored, as Elizabeth had been adored when she rode through her army at Tilbury, as Charles the

[1] Relation de la Voyage de Sa Majesté Britannique en Hollande, enrichie de planches très curieuses, 1692 ; Wagenaar ; London Gazette, Jan. 29. 169\frac{0}{1} ; Burnet, ii. 71.

Second had been adored when he landed at Dover. It is true that the old enemies of the House of Orange had not been inactive during the absence of the Stadtholder. There had been, not indeed clamours, but mutterings against him. He had, it was said, neglected his native land for his new kingdom. Whenever the dignity of the English flag, whenever the prosperity of the English trade was concerned, he forgot that he was a Hollander. But, as soon as his well remembered face was again seen, all jealousy, all coldness, was at an end. There was not a boor, not a fisherman, not an artisan, in the crowds which lined the road from Honslaerdyk to the Hague, whose heart did not swell with pride at the thought that the first minister of Holland had become a great King, had freed the English, and had conquered the Irish. It would have been madness in William to travel from Hampton Court to Westminster without a guard : but in his own land he needed no swords or carbines to defend him. " Do not keep the people off ; " he cried : " let them come close to me : they are all my good friends." He soon

William's entrance into the Hague

learned that sumptuous preparations were making for his entrance into the Hague. At first he murmured and objected. He detested, he said, noise and display. The necessary cost of the war was quite heavy enough. He hoped that his kind fellow townsmen would consider him as a neighbour, born and bred among them, and would not pay him so bad a compliment as to treat him ceremoniously. But all his expostulations were vain. The Hollanders, simple and parsimonious as their ordinary habits were, had set their hearts on giving their illustrious countryman a reception suited to his dignity and to his merit ; and he found it necessary to yield. On the day of his triumph the concourse was immense. All the wheeled carriages and horses of the province were too few for the multitudes that flocked to the show. Many thousands came sliding or skating along the frozen canals from Amsterdam, Rotterdam, Leyden, Haarlem, Delft. At ten in the morning of the twenty-sixth of January, the great bell of the Town House gave the signal. Sixteen hundred substantial burghers, well armed, and clad in the finest dresses which were to be found in the recesses of their wardrobes, kept order in the crowded streets. Balconies and scaffolds, embowered in evergreens and hung with tapestry, hid the windows. The royal coach, escorted by an army of halberdiers and running footmen, and followed by a long train of splendid equipages, passed under numerous arches rich with carving and painting, amidst incessant shouts of " Long live the King our Stadtholder." The front of the Town House and the whole circuit of the marketplace were in a blaze with brilliant colours. Civic crowns, trophies, emblems of arts, of sciences, of commerce, and of agriculture, appeared everywhere. In one place William saw portrayed the glorious

cations of his ancestors.   There was the silent prince, the founder of
the Batavian commonwealth, passing the Meuse with his warriors.
There was the more impetuous Maurice leading the charge at Nieuport.
A little further on, the hero might retrace the eventful story of his own

DINHALING VAN SYN KONINCKLYKE MAYESTEYT VAN GROOT
BRITTANIE WILLEM DE III BINNEN s'GRAVENHAGE OP DEN 5 FEBRUARY AN 1691

THE ENTRANCE OF WILLIAM III INTO THE HAGUE

From an engraving by I. Tangena

life.   He was a child at his widowed mother's knee.   He was at the
altar with Mary's hand in his.   He was landing at Torbay.   He was
swimming through the Boyne.   There, too, was a boat amidst the ice
and the breakers ; and above it was most appropriately inscribed, in
the majestic language of Rome, the saying of the great Roman, " What
dost thou fear ?   Thou hast Cæsar on board."   The task of furnishing

the Latin mottoes had been entrusted to two men, who, till Bentley appeared, held the highest place among the classical scholars of that age. Spanheim, whose knowledge of the Roman medals was unrivalled, imitated, not unsuccessfully, the noble conciseness of those ancient legends which he had assiduously studied ; and he was assisted by Grævius, who then filled a chair at Utrecht, and whose just reputation had drawn to that University multitudes of students from every part of Protestant Europe.[1] When the night came, fireworks were exhibited on the great tank which washes the walls of the palace of the Federation. That tank was now as hard as marble ; and the Dutch boasted that nothing had ever been seen, even on the terrace of Versailles, more

MEDALS COMMEMORATING WILLIAM'S RECEPTION AND VOYAGE

brilliant than the effect produced by the innumerable cascades of flame which were reflected in the smooth mirror of ice.[2] The English Lords congratulated their master on his immense popularity. " Yes," said he : " but I am not the favourite. The shouting was nothing to what it would have been if Mary had been with me."

A few hours after the triumphal entry, the King attended a sitting of the States General. His last appearance among them had been on the day on which he embarked for England. He had then, amidst the broken words and loud weeping of those grave Senators, thanked them for the kindness with which they had watched over his childhood,

[1] The names of these two great scholars are associated in a very interesting letter of Bentley to Grævius, dated April 29. 1698. " Sciunt omnes qui me norunt, et si vitam mihi Deus O. M. prorogaverit, scient etiam posteri, ut te et τὸν πάνυ Spanhemium, geminos hujus ævi Dioscuros, lucida literarum sidera, semper prædicaverim, semper veneratus sim."

[2] Relation de la Voyage de Sa Majesté Britannique en Hollande, 1692 ; London Gazette, Feb. 2. 169$\frac{0}{1}$; Le Triomphe Royal où l'on voit descrits les Arcs de Triomphe, Pyramides, Tableaux et Devises au Nombre de 65, erigez à la Haye à l'honneur de Guillaume Trois, 1692 ; Le Carnaval de la Haye, 1691. This last work is a savage pasquinade on William.

Ezechiel Spanhemius Liber Baro Seren.ᵐᵘ ac Potent.ᵐⁱ Borussorum Regis Friderici Minister Status, et nuper ad Seren.ᵘᵐ ac Potent.ᵘᵐ Magnæ Britanniæ Regem Gulielmum III. Nunc ad Seren.ᵃᵐ ac Potent.ᵃᵐ Reginam Annam Legatus Extraordinar.ᵘˢ Ano. Dmi. MDCCVII

B. Arlaud pinx. ad vivum.   *J. Simon.*

EZECHIEL SPANHEIM

From a mezzotint by J. Simon, after a painting by B. Artaud

trained his mind in youth, and supported his authority in his riper years ; and he had solemnly commended his beloved wife to their care. He now came back among them the King of three kingdoms, the head of the greatest coalition that Europe had seen since the League of Cambray ; and nothing was heard in the hall but applause and congratulations.[1]

By this time the streets of the Hague were overflowing with the equipages and retinues of princes and ambassadors who came flocking to the great Congress. First appeared the ambitious and ostentatious Frederic, Elector of Brandenburg, who, a few years later, took the title of King of Prussia. Then arrived the young Elector of Bavaria, the Regent of Wurtemberg, the Landgraves of Hesse Cassel and Hesse Darmstadt, and a long train of sovereign princes, sprung from the illustrious houses of Brunswick, of Saxony, of Holstein, and of Nassau. The Marquess of Gastanaga, Governor of the Spanish Netherlands, repaired to the assembly from the viceregal Court of Brussels. Extraordinary ministers had been sent by the Emperor, by the Kings of Spain, Poland, Denmark, and Sweden, and by the Duke of Savoy. There was scarcely room in the town and the neighbourhood for the English Lords and gentlemen and the German Counts and Barons whom curiosity or official duty had brought to the place of meeting. The grave capital of the most thrifty and industrious of nations was as gay as Venice in the Carnival. The walks cut among those noble limes and elms in which the villa of the Princes of Orange is embosomed were gay with the plumes, the stars, the flowing wigs, the embroidered coats, and the gold hilted swords of gallants from London, Berlin, and Vienna. With the nobles were mingled sharpers not less gorgeously attired than they. At night the hazard tables were thronged ; and the theatre was filled to the roof. Princely banquets followed one another in rapid succession. The meats were served in gold ; and, according to that old Teutonic fashion with which Shakspeare had made his countrymen familiar, as often as any of the great princes proposed a health, the kettle drums and trumpets sounded. Some English Lords, particularly Devonshire, gave entertainments which vied with those of Sovereigns. It was remarked that the German potentates, though generally disposed to be litigious and punctilious about etiquette, associated, on this occasion, in an unceremonious manner, and seemed to have forgotten their passion for heraldic controversy. The taste for wine, which was then characteristic of their nation, they had not

Congress at the Hague (marginal note)

---

[1] London Gazette, Feb. 5. 169⁰/₁ ; His Majesty's Speech to the Assembly of the States General of the United Provinces at the Hague, the 7th of February N.S., together with the Answer of their High and Mighty Lordships, as both are extracted out of the Register of the Resolutions of the States General, 1691.

FREDERIC, ELECTOR OF BRANDENBURG

From a mezzotint by G. Valck

forgotten. At the table of the Elector of Brandenburg much mirth was caused by the gravity of the statesmen of Holland, who, sober themselves, confuted out of Grotius and Puffendorf the nonsense stuttered by the tipsy nobles of the Empire. One of those nobles swallowed so many bumpers that he tumbled into the turf fire, and was not pulled out till his fine velvet suit had been burned.[1]

In the midst of all this revelry, business was not neglected. A formal meeting of the Congress was held at which William presided. In a short and dignified speech, which was speedily circulated throughout Europe, he set forth the necessity of firm union and strenuous exertion. The profound respect with which he was heard by that splendid assembly caused bitter mortification to his enemies both in England and in France. The German potentates were bitterly reviled for yielding precedence to an upstart. Indeed the most illustrious among them paid to him such marks of deference as they would scarcely have deigned to pay to the Imperial Majesty, mingled with the crowd in his antechamber, and at his table behaved as respectfully as any English lord in waiting. In one caricature the allied princes were represented as muzzled bears, some with crowns, some with caps of state. William had them all in a chain, and was teaching them to dance. In another caricature, he appeared taking his ease in an arm chair, with his feet on a cushion, and his hat on his head, while the Electors of Brandenburg and Bavaria, uncovered, occupied small stools on the right and left : the crowd of Landgraves and Sovereign dukes stood at humble distance ; and Gastanaga, the unworthy successor of Alva, awaited the orders of the heretic tyrant on bended knee.[2]

It was soon announced by authority that, before the beginning of summer, two hundred and twenty thousand men would be in the field against France.[3] The contingent which each of the allied powers was to furnish was made known. Matters about which it would have been inexpedient to put forth any declaration were privately discussed by the King of England with his allies. On this occasion, as on every other important occasion during his reign, he was his own minister for foreign affairs. It was necessary for the sake of form that he should be attended by a Secretary of State ; and Nottingham had therefore followed him to Holland. But Nottingham, though, in matters relating to the internal government of England, he enjoyed a large share of his master's con-

---

[1] Relation de la Voyage de Sa Majesté Britannique en Hollande ; Burnet, ii. 72.; London Gazette, Feb. 12. 19. 23. 169¾ ; Mémoires du Comte de Dohna ; William Fuller's Memoirs.

[2] Wagenaar, lxii.; Le Carnaval de la Haye, Mars 1691 ; Le Tabouret des Electeurs, April 1691 ; Cérémonial de ce qui s'est passé à la Haye entre le Roi Guillaume et les Electeurs de Bavière et de Brandebourg. This last tract is a MS. presented to the British Museum by George IV.

[3] London Gazette, Feb. 23. 169¾.

fidence, knew little more about the business of the Congress than what he saw in the Gazettes.

MEDALS COMMEMORATING THE CONGRESS AT THE HAGUE

This mode of transacting business would now be thought most unconstitutional; and many writers, applying the standard of their own age to the transactions of a former age, have severely blamed William

for acting without the advice of his ministers, and his ministers for submitting to be kept in ignorance of transactions which deeply concerned
**William
his own
minister
for foreign
affairs** the honour of the Crown and the welfare of the nation.   Yet
surely the presumption is that what the most honest and
honourable men of both parties, Nottingham, for example,
among the Tories, and Somers among the Whigs, not only
did, but avowed, cannot have been altogether inexcusable ; and a very
sufficient excuse will without difficulty be found.

The doctrine that the Sovereign is not responsible is doubtless as
old as any part of our constitution.   The doctrine that his ministers are
responsible is also of immemorial antiquity.   The doctrine that, where
there is no responsibility, there can be no trustworthy security against
maladministration, is one which, in our age and country, few people will
be inclined to dispute.   From these three propositions it plainly follows
that the administration is likely to be best conducted when the Sovereign
performs no public act without the concurrence and instrumentality of a
minister.   This argument is perfectly sound.   But we must remember
that arguments are constructed in one way, and governments in another.
In . logic, none but an idiot admits the premises and denies the legitimate conclusion.   But, in practice, we see that great and enlightened
communities often persist, generation after generation, in asserting principles, and refusing to act upon those principles.   It may be doubted
whether any real polity that ever existed has exactly corresponded to
the pure idea of that polity.   According to the pure idea of constitutional royalty, the prince reigns, and does not govern ; and constitutional royalty, as it now exists in England, comes nearer than in any
other country to the pure idea.   Yet it would be a great error to
imagine, even now, that our princes merely reign and never govern.
In the seventeenth century, both Whigs and Tories thought it, not only
the right, but the duty, of the first magistrate to govern.   All parties
agreed in blaming Charles the Second for not being his own Prime
Minister : all parties agreed in praising James for being his own Lord
High Admiral; and all parties thought it natural and reasonable that
William should be his own Foreign Secretary.

It may be observed that the ablest and best informed of those who
have censured the manner in which the negotiations of that time were
conducted are scarcely consistent with themselves.   For, while they
blame William for being his own Ambassador Plenipotentiary at the
Hague, they praise him for being his own Commander in Chief in
Ireland.   Yet where is the distinction in principle between the two
cases ?   Surely every reason which can be brought to prove that he
violated the constitution, when, by his own sole authority, he made
compacts with the Emperor and the Elector of Brandenburg, will

equally prove that he violated the constitution, when, by his own sole authority, he ordered one column to plunge into the water at Oldbridge and another to cross the bridge of Slane. If the constitution gave him the command of the forces of the State, the constitution gave him also the direction of the foreign relations of the State. On what principle then can it be maintained that he was at liberty to exercise the former power without consulting anybody, but that he was bound to exercise the latter power in conformity with the advice of a minister? Will it be said that an error in diplomacy is likely to be more injurious to the country than an error in strategy? Surely not. It is hardly conceivable that any blunder which William might have made at the Hague could have been more injurious to the public interests than a defeat at the Boyne. Or will it be said that there was greater reason for placing confidence in his military than in his diplomatic skill? Surely not. In war he showed some great moral and intellectual qualities: but, as a tactician, he did not rank high; and of his many campaigns only two were decidedly successful. In the talents of a negotiator, on the other hand, he has never been surpassed. Of the interests and the tempers of the continental courts he knew more than all his Privy Council together. Some of his ministers were doubtless men of great ability, excellent orators in the House of Lords, and versed in our insular politics. But, in the deliberations of the Congress, Caermarthen and Nottingham would have been found as far inferior to him as he would have been found inferior to them in a parliamentary debate on a question purely English. The coalition against France was his work. He alone had joined together the parts of that great whole; and he alone could keep them together. If he had trusted that vast and complicated machine in the hands of any of his subjects, it would instantly have fallen to pieces.

Some things indeed were to be done which none of his subjects would have ventured to do. Pope Alexander was really, though not in name, one of the allies: it was of the highest importance to have him for a friend: and yet such was the temper of the English nation that an English minister might well shrink from having any dealings, direct or indirect, with the Vatican. The Secretaries of State were glad to leave in the hands of their master a matter so delicate and so full of risk, and to be able to protest with truth that not a line to which the most intolerant Protestant could object had ever gone out of their offices.

It must not be supposed however that William ever forgot that his especial, his hereditary, mission was to protect the Reformed Faith. His influence with Roman Catholic princes was constantly and strenuously exerted for the benefit of their Protestant subjects. In the spring of 1691, the Waldensian shepherds, long and cruelly persecuted, and weary of their lives, were

William obtains a toleration for the Waldenses

surprised by glad tidings. Those who had been in prison for heresy returned to their homes. Children, who had been taken from their parents to be educated by priests, were sent back. Congregations, which had hitherto met only by stealth and with extreme peril, now worshipped God without molestation in the face of day. Those simple mountaineers probably never knew that their fate had been a subject of discussion at the Hague, and that they owed the happiness of their firesides and the security of their humble temples to the ascendency which William exercised over the Duke of Savoy.[1]

No coalition of which history has preserved the memory has had an abler chief than William. But even William often contended in vain

Vices inherent in the nature of coalitions

against those vices which are inherent in the nature of all coalitions. No undertaking which requires the hearty and long continued cooperation of many independent states is likely to prosper. Jealousies inevitably spring up. Disputes engender disputes. Every confederate is tempted to throw on others some part of the burden which he ought himself to bear. Scarcely one honestly furnishes the promised contingent. Scarcely one exactly observes the appointed day. But perhaps no coalition that ever existed was in such constant danger of dissolution as the coalition which William had with infinite difficulty formed. The long list of potentates, who met in person or by their representatives at the Hague, looked well in the Gazettes. The crowd of princely equipages, attended by many-coloured guards and lacqueys, looked well among the lime trees of the Voorhout. But the very circumstances which made the Congress more splendid than other congresses made the league weaker than other leagues. The more numerous the allies, the more numerous were the dangers which threatened the alliance. It was impossible that twenty governments, divided by quarrels about precedence, quarrels about territory, quarrels about trade, quarrels about religion, could long act together in perfect harmony. That they acted together during several years in imperfect harmony is to be ascribed to the wisdom, patience, and firmness of William.

The situation of his great enemy was very different. The resources of the French monarchy, though certainly not equal to those of England, Holland, the House of Austria, and the empire of Germany united, were yet very formidable: they were all collected in a central position; and they were all under the absolute direction of a single mind. Lewis could do with two words what William could hardly bring about by two months of negotiation at Berlin, Munich, Brussels, Turin, and Vienna. Thus France was found equal in effective strength to all the

---

[1] The secret article by which the Duke of Savoy bound himself to grant toleration to the Waldenses is in Dumont's collection. It was signed Feb. 8. 1691.

Vicit Inaccessis consisas Rupibus. Arces,
Miraris! per Rhenum hic sibi fecit iter.

Santolius Victorinus

LEWIS XIV

From an engraving by G. Edelinck of a painting by J. de la Haye states which were combined against her. For in the political, as in the natural world, there may be an equality of momentum between unequal bodies, when the body which is inferior in weight is superior in velocity.

This was soon signally proved. In March the princes and ambassadors who had been assembled at the Hague separated : and scarcely had they separated when all their plans were disconcerted by a bold and skilful move of the enemy.

Lewis was sensible that the meeting of the Congress was likely to produce a great effect on the public mind of Europe. That effect **Siege and** he determined to counteract by striking a sudden and terrible **fall of Mons** blow. While his enemies were settling how many troops each of them should furnish, he ordered numerous divisions of his army to march from widely distant points towards Mons, one of the most important, if not the most important, of the fortresses which protected the Spanish Netherlands. His purpose was discovered only when it was all but accomplished. William, who had retired for a few days to Loo, learned, with surprise and extreme vexation, that cavalry, infantry, artillery, bridges of boats, were fast approaching the fated city by many converging routes. A hundred thousand men had been brought together. All the implements of war had been largely provided by Louvois, the first of living administrators. The command was entrusted to Luxemburg, the first of living generals. The scientific operations were directed by Vauban, the first of living engineers. That nothing might be wanting which could kindle emulation through all the ranks of a gallant and loyal army, the magnificent King himself had set out from Versailles for the camp. Yet William had still some faint hope that it might be possible to raise the siege. He flew to the Hague, put all the forces of the States General in motion, and sent pressing messages to the German Princes. Within three weeks after he had received the first hint of the danger, he was in the neighbourhood of the besieged city, at the head of near fifty thousand troops of different nations. To attack a superior force commanded by such a captain as Luxemburg was a bold, almost a desperate enterprise. Yet William was so sensible that the loss of Mons would be an almost irreparable disaster and disgrace that he made up his mind to run the hazard. He was convinced that the event of the siege would determine the policy of the Courts of Stockholm and Copenhagen. Those Courts had lately seemed inclined to join the coalition. If Mons fell, they would certainly remain neutral ; and they might possibly become hostile. "The risk," he wrote to Heinsius, "is great : yet I am not without hope. I will do what can be done. The issue is in the hands of God." On the very day on which this letter was written Mons fell. The siege had been vigorously pressed.

Lewis himself, though suffering from the gout, had set the example of strenuous exertion. His household troops, the finest body of soldiers in Europe, had, under his eye, surpassed themselves. The young nobles

LEWIS XIV IN THE TRENCHES BEFORE MONS

From an engraving in the Cabinet des Estampes

of his court had tried to attract his notice by exposing themselves to the hottest fire with the same gay alacrity with which they were wont to exhibit their graceful figures at his balls. His wounded soldiers were charmed by the benignant courtesy with which he walked among their pallets, assisted while wounds were dressed by the hospital surgeons, and breakfasted on a porringer of the hospital broth.　While all was obedience and enthusiasm among the besiegers, all was disunion and dismay among the besieged.　The duty of the French lines was so well performed that no messenger sent by William was able to cross them.　The garrison did not know that relief was close at hand.　The burghers were appalled by the prospect of those horrible calamities which befall cities taken by storm.　Showers of shells and redhot bullets were falling in the streets.　The town was on fire in ten places at once.　The peaceful inhabitants derived an unwonted courage from the excess of their fear, and rose on the soldiers.　Thenceforth resistance was impossible ; and a capitulation was concluded.　The armies then retired into quarters.　Military operations were suspended during some weeks : Lewis returned in triumph to Versailles ; and William paid a short visit to England, where his presence was much needed.[1]

He found the ministers still employed in tracing out the ramifications of the plot which had been discovered just before his departure.

William returns to England　Early in January, Preston, Ashton, and Elliot had been arraigned at the Old Bailey.　They claimed the right of severing in their challenges.　It was therefore necessary to try them separately.　The audience was numerous and splendid. Many peers were present.　The Lord President and the two Secretaries

Trials of Preston and Ashton　of State attended in order to prove that the papers produced in Court were the same which Billop had brought to Whitehall.　A considerable number of Judges appeared on the bench ; and Holt presided.　A full report of the proceedings has come down to us, and well deserves to be attentively studied, and to be compared with the reports of other trials which had not long before taken place under the same roof.　The whole spirit of the tribunal had undergone in a few months a change so complete that it might seem to have been the work of ages.　Twelve years earlier, unhappy Roman Catholics, accused of wickedness which had never entered into their thoughts, had stood in that dock.　The witnesses for the Crown had repeated their hideous fictions amidst the applauding hums of the audience.　The judges had shared, or had pretended to share, the stupid credulity and the savage passions of the populace, had exchanged smiles and compliments with the perjured informers, had roared down

---

[1] London Gazette from March 26. to April 13. 1691 ; Monthly Mercuries of March and April ; William's Letters to Heinsius of March 18. and 29., April 7. 9. ; Dangeau's Memoirs ; the Siege of Mons, a tragi-comedy, 1691.　In this drama the clergy, who are in the interest of France, persuade the burghers to deliver up the town.　This treason calls forth an indignant exclamation :

"Oh priestcraft, shopcraft, how do ye effeminate
The minds of men !"

MEDALS COMMEMORATING THE CAPTURE OF MONS BY LEWIS XIV

the arguments feebly stammered forth by the prisoners, and had not been ashamed, in passing the sentence of death, to make ribald jests on purgatory and the mass.　As soon as the butchery of Papists was over, the butchery of Whigs had commenced ; and the judges had applied themselves to their new work with even more than their old barbarity. To these scandals the Revolution had put an end.　Whoever, after perusing the trials of Ireland and Pickering, of Grove and Berry, of Sidney, Cornish, and Alice Lisle, turns to the trials of Preston and Ashton, will be astonished by the contrast.　The Solicitor General, Somers, conducted the prosecutions with a moderation and humanity of which his predecessors had left him no example.　" I did never think," he said, " that it was the part of any who were of counsel for the King in cases of this nature to aggravate the crime of the prisoners, or to put false colours on the evidence." [1]　Holt's conduct was faultless. Pollexfen, an older man than Holt or Somers, retained a little,—and a little was too much,—of the tone of that bad school in which he had been bred.　But, though he once or twice forgot the austere decorum of his place, he cannot be accused of any violation of substantial justice. The prisoners themselves seem to have been surprised by the fairness and gentleness with which they were treated.　" I would not mislead the jury, I'll assure you," said Holt to Preston, " nor do Your Lordship any manner of injury in the world."　" No, my Lord ; " said Preston ; " I see it well enough that Your Lordship would not."　" Whatever my fate may be," said Ashton, " I cannot but own that I have had a fair trial for my life."

　　The culprits gained nothing by the moderation of the Solicitor General or by the impartiality of the Court : for the evidence was irresistible.　The meaning of the papers seized by Billop was so plain that the dullest juryman could not misunderstand it.　Of those papers part was fully proved to be in Preston's handwriting.　Part was in Ashton's handwriting : but this the counsel for the prosecution had not the means of proving.　They therefore rested the case against Ashton on the indisputable facts that the treasonable packet had been found in his bosom, and that he had used language which was quite unintelligible except on the supposition that he had a guilty knowledge of the contents.[2]

　　　[1] Trial of Preston in the Collection of State Trials.　A person who was present gives the following account of Somers's opening speech : " In the opening the evidence, there was no affected exaggeration of matters, nor ostentation of a putid eloquence, one after another, as in former trials, like so many geese cackling in a row.　Here was nothing besides fair matter of fact, or natural and just reflections from thence arising."　The pamphlet from which I quote these words is entitled, An Account of the late horrid Conspiracy, by a Person who was present at the Trials, 1691.

　　　[2] State Trials.

Behold his *Grave* and *Venerable Face*,
Who did the *ROYAL Seat of Justice Grace*;
Profoundly *Learn'd* in the *Misterious Laws*,
Quick and *Discerning* in the *Knotty'st Cause*;
The *Prisner's Counsel* and the *Pauper's Friend*,
Wise in his *Conduct Upright* to his *End*;
The *Orphans Father* and the *Widow's Spouse*;
Whose *Anger* never reach'd beyond his *Brows*;
Warm without *Passion*, *JUST*, but not *Severe*,
Of *Mercy* full, tho' in his *Looks Austere*.
Envy her Self, her *Malice* must *Suspend*,
To praise the *Lawyer* and the *Judge Commend*;
A second *HALES* may both in *Glory Join*,
And like the *Heavenly Twins* together *Shine*.

The R.t Hon.ble S.r Iohn Holt Kn.t LORD CHIEF JUSTICE of her Maj.ties Court
of QUEENS BENCH & one of y.e L.ds of her M.ties most Hon.ble Privy Councel

CHIEF-JUSTICE SIR JOHN HOLT

From an engraving in the Sutherland Collection

Both Preston and Ashton were convicted and sentenced to death. Ashton was speedily executed. He might have saved his life by **Execution of Ashton** making disclosures. But, though he declared that, if he were spared, he would always be a faithful subject of Their Majesties, he was fully resolved not to give up the names of his accomplices. In this resolution he was encouraged by the nonjuring divines who attended him in his cell. It was probably by their influence that he was induced to deliver to the Sheriffs on the scaffold a declaration which he had transcribed and signed, but had not, it is to be hoped, composed or attentively considered. In this paper he was made to complain of the unfairness of a trial which he had himself in public acknowledged to have been eminently fair. He was also made to aver, on the word of a dying man, that he knew nothing of the papers which had been found upon him. Unfortunately his declaration, when inspected, proved to be in the same handwriting with one of the most important of those papers. He died with manly fortitude.[1]

Elliot was not brought to trial. The evidence against him was not quite so clear as that on which his associates had been convicted ; and **Preston's irresolution and confessions** he was not worth the anger of the ruling powers. The fate of Preston was long in suspense. The Jacobites affected to be confident that the government would not dare to shed his blood. He was, they said, a favourite at Versailles, and his death would be followed by a terrible retaliation. They scattered about the streets of London papers in which it was asserted that, if any harm befell him, Mountjoy, and all the other Englishmen of quality who were prisoners in France, would be broken on the wheel.[2] These absurd threats would not have deferred the execution one day. But those who had Preston in their power were not unwilling to spare him on certain conditions. He was privy to all the counsels of the disaffected party, and could furnish information of the highest value. He was informed that his fate depended on himself. The struggle was long and severe. Pride, conscience, party spirit, were on one side ; the intense love of life on the other. He went during a time irresolutely to and fro. He listened to his brother Jacobites ; and his courage rose. He listened to the agents of the government ; and his heart sank within him. In an evening, when he had dined and drunk his claret, he feared nothing. He would die like a man, rather than save his neck by an act of baseness. But his temper was very different when he woke the next

---

[1] Paper delivered by Mr. Ashton, at his execution, to Sir Francis Child, Sheriff of London ; Answer to the Paper delivered by Mr. Ashton. The Answer was written by Dr. Edward Fowler, afterwards Bishop of Gloucester. Burnet, ii. 70. ; Letter from Bishop Lloyd to Dodwell, in the second volume of Gutch's Collectanea Curiosa.

[2] Narcissus Luttrell's Diary.

RICHARD GRAHAM, VISCOUNT PRESTON, 1648-1695.

From the painting in the National Portrait Gallery. (Artist unknown.)

morning, when the courage which he had drawn from wine and company had evaporated, when he was alone with the iron grates and stone walls, and when the thought of the block, the axe, and the sawdust rose in his mind.   During some time he regularly wrote a confession every forenoon, when he was sober, and burned it every night when he was merry.[1] His nonjuring friends formed a plan for bringing Sancroft to visit the Tower, in the hope, doubtless, that the exhortations of so great a prelate and so great a saint would confirm the wavering virtue of the prisoner.[2] Whether this plan would have been successful may be doubted : it was not carried into effect : the fatal hour drew near ; and the fortitude of Preston gave way.   He confessed his guilt, and named Clarendon, Dartmouth, the Bishop of Ely, and William Penn, as his accomplices.   He added a long list of persons against whom he could not himself give evidence, but who, if he could trust to Penn's assurances, were friendly to King James.   Among these persons were Devonshire and Dorset.[3]   There is not the slightest reason to believe that either of these great noblemen ever had any dealings, direct or indirect, with Saint Germains.   It is not, however, necessary to accuse Penn of deliberate falsehood.   He was credulous and garrulous.   The Lord Steward and the Lord Chamberlain had shared in the vexation with which their party had observed the leaning of William towards the Tories ; and they had probably expressed that vexation unguardedly.   So weak a man as Penn, wishing to find Jacobites everywhere, and prone to believe whatever he wished, might easily put an erroneous construction on invectives such as the haughty and irritable Devonshire was but too ready to utter, and on sarcasms such as, in moments of spleen, dropped but too easily from the lips of the keenwitted Dorset.   Caermarthen, a Tory, and a Tory who had been mercilessly persecuted by the Whigs, was disposed to make the most of this idle hearsay.   But he received no encouragement from his master, who, of all the great politicians mentioned in history, was the least prone to suspicion.   When William returned to England, Preston was brought before him, and was commanded to repeat the confession which had already been made to the ministers.   The King stood behind the Lord President's chair and listened gravely while Clarendon, Dartmouth, Turner, and Penn were named.   But as soon as the prisoner, passing from what he could himself testify, began to repeat the stories which Penn had told him, William touched Caermarthen on the shoulder, and said, " My Lord, we have had too much of this." [4]   The King's judicious magnanimity had its

[1] Narcissus Luttrell's Diary ; Burnet, ii. 71.

[2] Letter of Collier and Cook to Sancroft among the Tanner MSS.

[3] Caermarthen to William, February 3. 169$\frac{0}{1}$; Life of James, ii. 443.

[4] That this account of what passed is true in substance is sufficiently proved by the Life of

proper reward. Devonshire and Dorset became from that day more
zealous than ever in the cause of the master who, in spite of calumny,
for which their own indiscretion had perhaps furnished some ground,
had continued to repose confidence in their loyalty.[1]

Even those who were undoubtedly criminal were generally treated
with great lenity. Clarendon lay in the Tower about six months.

Lenity shown to the conspirators His guilt was fully established ; and a party among the
Whigs called loudly and importunately for his head. But he
was saved by the pathetic entreaties of his brother Rochester,
by the good offices of the humane and generous Burnet, and by Mary's
respect for the memory of her mother. The prisoner's confinement was
not strict. He was allowed to entertain his friends at dinner. When
at length his health began to suffer from restraint, he was permitted to
go into the country under the care of a warder : the warder was soon
removed ; and Clarendon was informed that, while he led a quiet rural
life, he should not be molested.[2]

The treason of Dartmouth was of no common dye. He was an
English seaman, and he had laid a plan for betraying Portsmouth to the

Dartmouth French, and had offered to take the command of a French
squadron against his country. It was a serious aggravation
of his guilt that he had been one of the very first persons who took the
oaths to William and Mary. He was arrested and brought to the
Council Chamber. A narrative of what passed there, written by himself,
has been preserved. In that narrative he admits that he was treated
with great courtesy and delicacy. He vehemently asserted his innocence.
He declared that he had never corresponded with Saint Germains, that
he was no favourite there, and that Mary of Modena in particular owed
him a grudge. " My Lords," he said, " I am an Englishman. I always,
when the interest of the House of Bourbon was strongest here, shunned
the French, both men and women. I would lose the last drop of my
blood rather than see Portsmouth in the power of foreigners. I am not
such a fool as to think that King Lewis will conquer us merely for the
benefit of King James. I am certain that nothing can be truly imputed
to me beyond some foolish talk over a bottle." His protestations seem
to have produced some effect ; for he was at first permitted to remain

James, ii. 443. I have taken one or two slight circumstances from Dalrymple, who, I believe,
took them from papers, now irrecoverably lost, which he had seen in the Scotch College at Paris.

[1] The wisdom of William's "seeming clemency" is admitted in the Life of James, ii. 443.
The Prince of Orange's method, it is acknowledged, "succeeded so well that, whatever sentiments those Lords which Mr. Penn had named might have had at that time, they proved in effect
most bitter enemies to His Majesty's cause afterwards." It ought to be observed that this part
of the Life of James was revised and corrected by his son.

[2] See his Diary ; Evelyn's Diary, Mar. 25., April 22., July 11. 1691 ; Burnet, ii. 71. ; Letters
of Rochester to Burnet, March 21. and April 2. 1691.

in the gentle custody of the Black Rod.   On further enquiry, however, it was determined to send him to the Tower.   After a confinement of a few weeks he died of apoplexy : but he lived long enough to complete his disgrace by offering his sword to the new government, and by expressing in fervent language his hope that he might, by the goodness of God and of Their Majesties, have an opportunity of showing how much he hated the French.[1]

Turner ran no serious risk : for the government was most unwilling to send to the scaffold one of the Seven who had signed the memorable petition.   A warrant was however issued for his apprehension ;   Turner and his friends had little hope that he would long remain undiscovered : for his nose was such as none who had seen it could forget ; and it was to little purpose that he put on a flowing wig, and that he suffered his beard to grow.   The pursuit was probably not very hot : for, after skulking a few weeks in England, he succeeded in crossing the Channel, and passed some time in France.[2]

A warrant was issued against Penn ; and he narrowly escaped the messengers.   It chanced that, on the day on which they were sent in search of him, he was attending a remarkable ceremony at   Penn some distance from his home.   An event had taken place which a historian, whose object is to record the real life of a nation, ought not to pass unnoticed.   While London was agitated by the news that a plot had been discovered, George Fox, the founder of the sect of Quakers, died.

More than forty years had elapsed since Fox had begun to see visions and to cast out devils.[3]   He was then a youth of pure morals and grave deportment, with a perverse temper, with the   Death of education of a labouring man, and with an intellect in the   George most unhappy of all states, that is to say, too much disordered   Fox : his character for liberty, and not sufficiently disordered for Bedlam.   The circumstances in which he was placed were such as could scarcely fail to bring out in the strongest form the constitutional diseases of his mind.   At the time when his faculties were ripening, Episcopalians, Presbyterians,

---

[1] Life of James, ii. 443. 450. ; Legge Papers in the Mackintosh Collection.

[2] Burnet, ii. 71. ; Evelyn's Diary, Jan. 4. and 18. 169⁰⁄₁ ; Letter from Turner to Sancroft, Jan. 19. 169⁰⁄₁ ; Letter from Sancroft to Lloyd of Norwich, April 2. 1692.   These two letters are among the Tanner MSS. in the Bodleian Library, and are printed in the Life of Ken by a Layman.   Turner's escape to France is mentioned in Narcissus Luttrell's Diary for February 1690.   See also a Dialogue between the Bishop of Ely and his Conscience, 16th February 169⁰⁄₁.   The dialogue is interrupted by the sound of trumpets.   The Bishop hears himself proclaimed a traitor, and cries out,
"Come, brother Pen, 'tis time we both were gone."

[3] For a specimen of his visions, see his Journal, page 13. ; for his casting out of devils, page 26.   I quote the folio edition of 1765.

Independents, Baptists, were striving for mastery, and were, in every corner of the realm, refuting and reviling each other.   He wandered from congregation to congregation : he heard priests harangue against Puritans : he heard Puritans harangue against priests : and he in vain applied for spiritual direction and consolation to doctors of both parties. One jolly old clergyman of the Anglican communion told him to smoke tobacco and sing psalms : another counselled him to go and lose some blood.[1]   From these advisers the young enquirer turned in disgust to the Dissenters, and found them also blind guides.[2]   After some time he came to the conclusion that no human being was competent to instruct him in divine things, and that the truth had been communicated to him by direct inspiration from heaven.   He argued that, as the division of languages began at Babel, and as the persecutors of Christ put on the cross an inscription in Latin, Greek, and Hebrew, the knowledge of languages, and more especially of Latin, Greek, and Hebrew, must be useless to a Christian Minister.[3]   Indeed, he was so far from knowing many languages that he knew none ; nor can the most corrupt passage in Hebrew be more unintelligible to the unlearned than his English often is to the most acute and attentive reader.[4]   One of the

---

[1] Journal, page 4.   [2] Ibid. page 7.

[3] " What they know, they know naturally, who turn from the command and err from the spirit, whose fruit withers, who saith that Hebrew, Greek, and Latine is the original : before Babell was, the earth was of one language ; and Nimrod, the cunning hunter, before the Lord, which came out of cursed Ham's stock, the original and builder of Babell, whom God confounded with many languages, and this they say is the original who erred from the spirit and command ; and Pilate had his original Hebrew, Greek, and Latine, which crucified Christ and set over him." —A message from the Lord to the Parliament of England, by G. Fox, 1654.   The same argument will be found in the Journal, but has been put by the editor into a little better English.   " Dost thou think to make ministers of Christ by these natural confused languages which sprung from Babell, are admired in Babylon, and set atop of Christ, the Life, by a persecutor ? "—Page 64.

[4] His Journal, before it was published, was revised by men of more sense and knowledge than himself, and therefore, absurd as it is, gives no notion of his genuine style.   The following is a fair specimen.   It is the exordium of one of his manifestoes.   " Them which the world who are without the fear of God calls Quakers in scorn do deny all opinions, and they do deny all conceivings, and they do deny all sects, and they do deny all imaginations, and notions, and judgments which riseth out of the will and the thoughts, and do deny witchcraft and all oaths, and the world and the works of it, and their worships and their customs with the light, and do deny false ways and false worships, seducers and deceivers which are now seen to be in the world with the light, and with it they are condemned, which light leadeth to peace and life from death, which now thousands do witness the new teacher Christ, him by whom the world was made, who raigns among the children of light, and with the spirit and power of the living God, doth let them see and know the chaff from the wheat, and doth see that which must be shaken with that which cannot be shaken or moved, what gives to see that which is shaken and moved, such as live in the notions, opinions, conceivings, and thoughts, and fancies, these be all shaken and comes to be on heaps, which they who witness those things before mentioned shaken and removed walks in peace not seen and discerned by them who walks in those things unremoved and not shaken." —A Warning to the World that are Groping in the Dark, by G. Fox, 1655.

GEORGE FOX

From a painting in Swarthmore College, Pennsylvania

precious truths which were divinely revealed to this new apostle was, that it was falsehood and adulation to use the second person plural instead of the second person singular. Another was, that to talk of the month of March was to worship the bloodthirsty god Mars, and that to talk of Monday was to pay idolatrous homage to the moon. To say Good morning or Good evening was highly reprehensible; for those phrases evidently imported that God had made bad days and bad nights.[1] A Christian was bound to face death itself rather than touch his hat to the greatest of mankind. When Fox was challenged to produce any Scriptural authority for this dogma, he cited the passage in which it is written that Shadrach, Meshach, and Abednego were thrown into the fiery furnace with their hats on; and, if his own narrative may be trusted, the Chief Justice of England was altogether unable to answer this argument except by crying out, "Take him away, gaoler."[2] Fox insisted much on the not less weighty argument that the Turks never show their bare heads to their superiors; and he asked, with great animation, whether those who bore the noble name of Christians ought not to surpass Turks in virtue.[3] Bowing he strictly prohibited, and, indeed, seemed to consider it as the effect of Satanical influence; for, as he observed, the woman in the Gospel, while she had a spirit of infirmity, was bowed together, and ceased to bow as soon as Divine power had liberated her from the tyranny of the Evil One.[4] His expositions of the sacred writings were of a very peculiar kind. Passages, which had been, in the apprehension of all the readers of the Gospels during sixteen centuries, figurative, he construed literally. Passages, which no human being before him had ever understood in any other than a literal sense, he construed figuratively. Thus, from those rhetorical expressions in which the duty of patience under injuries is enjoined he deduced the doctrine that selfdefence against pirates and assassins is unlawful. On the other hand, the plain commands to baptise with water, and to partake of bread and wine in commemoration of the redemption of mankind, he pronounced to be allegorical. He long wandered from place to place, teaching this strange theology, shaking like an aspen leaf in his paroxysms of fanatical excitement, forcing his way into churches, which he nicknamed steeple houses, interrupting prayers and sermons with clamour and scurrility,[5] and pestering rectors and justices with epistles much resembling burlesques of those sublime odes in which the Hebrew prophets foretold the calamities of

---

[1] See the piece entitled, Concerning Good morrow and Good even, the World's customs but by the Light which into the World is come by it made manifest to all who be in the Darkness, by G. Fox, 1657.

[2] Journal, page 166.   [3] Epistle from Harlingen, 11th of 6th month, 1677.

[4] Of Bowings, by G. Fox, 1657.   [5] See, for example, the Journal, pages 24. 26. and 51.

Babylon and Tyre.[1] He soon acquired great notoriety by these feats.
His strange face, his strange chant, his immovable hat, and his leather
breeches were known all over the country ; and he boasts that, as soon
as the rumour was heard, " The Man in Leather Breeches is coming,"
terror seized hypocritical professors, and hireling priests made haste to
get out of his way.[2] He was repeatedly imprisoned and set in the
stocks, sometimes justly, for disturbing the public worship of congregations, and sometimes unjustly, for merely talking nonsense.   He soon
gathered round him a body of disciples, some of whom went beyond
himself in absurdity.   He has told us that one of his friends walked
naked through Skipton declaring the truth,[3] and that another was
divinely moved to go naked during several years to marketplaces, and
to the houses of gentlemen and clergymen.[4] Fox complains bitterly
that these pious acts, prompted by the Holy Spirit, were requited by
an untoward generation with hooting, pelting, coachwhipping, and horse-
whipping.   But, though he applauded the zeal of the sufferers, he did
not go quite to their lengths.   He sometimes, indeed, was impelled to
strip himself partially.   Thus he pulled off his shoes and walked barefoot through Lichfield, crying, " Woe to the bloody city."[5] But it
does not appear that he ever thought it his duty to exhibit himself
before the public without that decent garment from which his popular
appellation was derived.

If we form our judgment of George Fox simply by looking at his
own actions and writings, we shall see no reason for placing him, morally
or intellectually, above Ludowick Muggleton or Joanna Southcote.
But it would be most unjust to rank the sect which regards him as its
founder with the Muggletonians or the Southcotians.   It chanced that
among the thousands whom his enthusiasm infected were a few persons
whose abilities and attainments were of a very different order from his
own.   Robert Barclay was a man of considerable parts and learning.
William Penn, though inferior to Barclay in both natural and acquired
abilities, was a gentleman and a scholar.   That such men should have
become the followers of George Fox ought not to astonish any person
who remembers what quick, vigorous, and highly cultivated intellects
were in our own time duped by the unknown tongues.   The truth is
that no powers of mind constitute a security against errors of this
description.   Touching God and His ways with man, the highest human
faculties can discover little more than the meanest.   In theology, the

---

[1] See, for example, the Epistle to Sawrey, a justice of the peace, in the Journal, page 86. ; the
Epistle to William Lampitt, a clergyman, which begins, " The word of the Lord to thee, oh
Lampitt," page 88. ; and the Epistle to another clergyman whom he calls Priest Tatham, page 92.

[2] Journal, page 55.   [3] Ibid. page 300.
[4] Ibid. page 323.   [5] Ibid. page 48.

interval is small indeed between Aristotle and a child, between Archimedes and a naked savage. It is not strange, therefore, that wise men, weary of investigation, tormented by uncertainty, longing to believe something, and yet seeing objections to everything, should submit themselves absolutely to teachers who, with firm and undoubting faith, lay claim to a supernatural commission. Thus we frequently see inquisitive and restless spirits take refuge from their own scepticism in the bosom of a church which pretends to infallibility, and, after questioning the existence of a Deity, bring themselves to worship a wafer. And thus it was that Fox made some converts to whom he was immeasurably inferior in everything except the energy of his convictions. By these converts his rude doctrines were polished into a form somewhat less shocking to good sense and good taste. No proposition which he had laid down was retracted. No indecent or ridiculous act which he had done or approved was condemned : but what was most grossly absurd in his theories and practices was softened down, or at least not obtruded on the public : whatever could be made to appear specious was set in the fairest light : his gibberish was translated into English : meanings which he would have been quite unable to comprehend were put on his phrases ; and his system, so much improved that he would not have known it again, was defended by numerous citations from Pagan philosophers and Christian fathers whose names he had never heard.[1] Still, however, those who had remodelled his theology continued to profess, and doubtless to feel, profound reverence for him; and his crazy epistles were to the last received and read with respect in Quaker meetings all over the country. His death produced a sensation which was not confined to his own disciples. On the morning of the funeral a great multitude assembled round the meeting house in Gracechurch Street. Thence the corpse was borne to the burial ground of the sect near Bunhill Fields. Several orators addressed the crowd which filled the cemetery. Penn was conspicuous among those disciples who committed the venerable corpse to the earth. The ceremony had scarcely been

---

[1] " Especially of late," says Leslie, the keenest of all the enemies of the sect, " some of them have made nearer advances towards Christianity than ever before; and among them the ingenious Mr. Penn has of late refined some of their gross notions, and brought them into some form, and has made them speak sense and English, of both which George Fox, their first and great apostle, was totally ignorant. . . . . They endeavour all they can to make it appear that their doctrine was uniform from the beginning, and that there has been no alteration ; and therefore they take upon them to defend all the writings of George Fox, and others of the first Quakers, and turn and wind them to make them (but it is impossible) agree with what they teach now at this day." (The Snake in the Grass, 3rd ed. 1698. Introduction.) Leslie was always more civil to his brother Jacobite Penn than to any other Quaker. Penn himself says of his master, " As abruptly and brokenly as sometimes his sentences would fall from him about divine things, it is well known they were often as texts to many fairer declarations." That is to say, George Fox talked nonsense, and some of his friends paraphrased it into sense.

finished when he learned that warrants were out against him. He instantly took flight, and remained many months concealed from the public eye.[1]

A short time after his disappearance, Sidney received from him a strange communication. Penn begged for an interview, but insisted on a promise that he should be suffered to return unmolested to his hidingplace. Sidney obtained the royal permission to make an appointment on these terms. Penn came to the rendezvous, and spoke at length in his own defence. He declared that   *Interview between Penn and Sidney*

WILLIAM PENN

From a portrait carved in ivory by Silvanus Beavan in the possession of Mrs. Alfred Waterhouse

he was a faithful subject of King William and Queen Mary, and that, if he knew of any design against them, he would discover it. Departing

---

[1] In the life of Penn which is prefixed to his works, we are told that the warrants were issued on the 16th of January 169$\frac{0}{1}$, in consequence of an accusation backed by the oath of William Fuller, who is truly designated as a wretch, a cheat, and an impostor ; and this story is repeated by Mr. Clarkson. It is, however, certainly false. Caermarthen, writing to William on the 3rd of February, says that there was then only one witness against Penn, and that Preston was that one witness. It is therefore evident that Fuller was not the informer on whose oath the warrant against Penn was issued. In fact Fuller appears, from his Life of Himself, to have been then at the Hague ; nor is there any reason to believe that he ever pretended to know anything about Preston's plot. When Nottingham wrote to William on the 26th of June, a second witness against Penn had come forward.

from his Yea and Nay, he protested, as in the presence of God, that he knew of no plot, and that he did not believe that there was any plot, unless the ambitious projects of the French government might be called plots. Sidney, amazed probably by hearing a person, who had such an abhorrence of lies that he would not use the common forms of civility, and such an abhorrence of oaths that he would not kiss the book in a court of justice, tell something very like a lie, and confirm it by something very like an oath, asked how, if there were really no plot, the letters and minutes which had been found on Ashton were to be explained. This question Penn evaded. " If," he said, " I could only see the King, I would confess everything to him freely. I would tell him much that it would be important for him to know. It is only in that way that I can be of service to him. A witness for the Crown I cannot be : for my conscience will not suffer me to be sworn." He assured Sidney that the most formidable enemies of the government were the discontented Whigs. " The Jacobites are not dangerous. There is not a man among them who has common understanding. Some persons who came over from Holland with the King are much more to be dreaded." It does not appear that Penn mentioned any names. He was suffered to depart in safety. No active search was made for him. He lay hid in London during some months, and then stole down to the coast of Sussex and made his escape to France. After about three years of wandering and lurking he, by the mediation of some eminent men, who overlooked his faults for the sake of his good qualities, made his peace with the government, and again ventured to resume his ministrations. The return which he made for the lenity with which he had been treated does not much raise his character. Scarcely had he again begun to harangue in public about the unlawfulness of war, when he sent a message earnestly exhorting James to make an immediate descent on England with thirty thousand men.[1]

Some months passed before the fate of Preston was decided. After several respites, the government, convinced that, though he had told much, he could tell more, fixed a day for his execution, and ordered

---

[1] Sidney to William, Feb. 27. 169$\frac{0}{1}$. The letter is in Dalrymple's Appendix, Part II. book vi. Narcissus Luttrell, in his Diary for September 1691, mentions Penn's escape from Shoreham to France. On the 5th of December 1693 Narcissus made the following entry : ''William Penn the Quaker, having for some time absconded, and having compromised the matters against him, appears now in public, and, on Friday last, held forth at the Bull and Mouth, in Saint Martin's.'' On December $\frac{18}{28}$. 1693 was drawn up at Saint Germains, under Melfort's direction, a paper containing a passage of which the following is a translation : '' Mr. Penn says that Your Majesty has had several occasions, but never any so favourable as the present ; and he hopes that Your Majesty will be earnest with the most Christian King not to neglect it : that a descent with thirty thousand men will not only reestablish Your Majesty, but according to all appearance break the league.'' This paper is among the Nairne MSS., and was translated by Macpherson.

the sheriffs to have the machinery of death in readiness.[1]　But he was again respited, and, after a delay of some weeks, obtained a pardon, which, however, extended only to his life, and left his property　Preston subject to all the consequences of his attainder.　As soon　pardoned as he was set at liberty he gave new cause of offence and suspicion, and was again arrested, examined, and sent to prison.[2]　At length he was permitted to retire, pursued by the hisses and curses of both parties, to a lonely manor house in the North Riding of Yorkshire.　There, at least, he had not to endure the scornful looks of old associates who had once thought him a man of dauntless courage and spotless honour, but who now pronounced that he was at best a meanspirited coward, and hinted their suspicions that he had been from the beginning a spy and a trepan.[3]　He employed the short and sad remains of his life in turning the Consolation of Boethius into English.　The translation was published after the translator's death.　It is remarkable chiefly on account of some very unsuccessful attempts to enrich our versification with new metres, and on account of the allusions with which the preface is filled.　Under a thin veil of figurative language, Preston exhibited to the public compassion or contempt his own blighted fame and broken heart.　He complained that the tribunal which had sentenced him to death had dealt with him more leniently than his former friends, and that many, who had never been tried by temptations like his, had very cheaply earned a reputation for courage by sneering at his poltroonery, and by bidding defiance at a distance to horrors which, when brought near, subdue even a constant mind.

The spirit of the Jacobites, which had been quelled for a time by the detection of Preston's plot, was revived by the fall of Mons.　The joy of the whole party was boundless.　The nonjuring priests　Joy of the ran backwards and forwards between Sam's Coffee House and　Jacobites at the fall of Westminster Hall, spreading the praises of Lewis, and laugh-　Mons ing at the miserable issue of the deliberations of the great Congress.　In the Park the malecontents were in the habit of mustering daily, and one avenue was called the Jacobite walk.　They now came to this rendezvous in crowds, wore their biggest looks, and talked sedition in their loudest tones.　The most conspicuous among these swaggerers was Sir John Fenwick, who had, in the late reign, been high in royal favour and in military command, and was now an indefatigable agitator and conspirator.　In his exultation he forgot the courtesy which man owes

---

[1] Narcissus Luttrell's Diary, April 11. 1691.

[2] Narcissus Luttrell's Diary, August 1691 ; Letter from Vernon to Wharton, Oct. 17. 1691, in the Bodleian.

[3] The opinion of the Jacobites appears from a letter which is among the archives of the French War Office.　It was written in London on the 25th of June 1691.

to woman.　He had more than once made himself conspicuous by his incivility to the Queen.　He now ostentatiously put himself in her way when she took her airing, and, while all around him uncovered and bowed low, gave her a rude stare, and cocked his hat in her face.　The affront was not only brutal, but cowardly.　For the law had provided no punishment for mere impertinence, however gross ; and the King was the only gentleman and soldier in the kingdom who could not protect his wife from contumely with his sword.　All that the Queen could do was to order the parkkeepers not to admit Sir John again within the gates.　But, long after her death, a day came when he had reason to wish that he had restrained his insolence.　He found, by terrible proof, that of all the Jacobites, the most desperate assassins not excepted, he was the only one for whom William felt an intense personal aversion.[1]

A few days after this event the rage of the malecontents began to flame more fiercely than ever.　The detection of the conspiracy of **The vacant** which Preston was the chief had brought on a crisis in eccle- **sees filled** siastical affairs.　The nonjuring bishops had, during the year which followed their deprivation, continued to reside in the official mansions which had once been their own.　Burnet had, at Mary's request, laboured to effect a compromise.　His direct interference would probably have done more harm than good.　He therefore judiciously employed the agency of Rochester, who stood higher in the estimation of the nonjurors than any statesman who was not a nonjuror, and of Trevor, who, worthless as he was, had considerable influence with the High Church party.　Sancroft and his brethren were informed that, if they would consent to perform their spiritual duty, to ordain, to institute, to confirm, and to watch over the faith and the morality of the priest-hood, a bill should be brought into Parliament to excuse them from taking the oaths.[2]　This offer was imprudently liberal : but those to whom it was made could not consistently accept it.　For in the ordina-tion service, and indeed in almost every service of the Church, William and Mary were designated as King and Queen.　The only promise that could be obtained from the deprived prelates was that they would live quietly ; and even this promise they had not all kept.　One of them at least had been guilty of treason aggravated by impiety.　He had, under the strong fear of being butchered by the populace, declared that he abhorred the thought of calling in the aid of France, and had invoked

---

[1] Welwood's Mercurius Reformatus, April 11. 24. 1691 ; Narcissus Luttrell's Diary, April 1691 ; L'Hermitage to the States General, June $\frac{18}{28}$. 1696 ; Calamy's Life. The story of Fenwick's rudeness to Mary is told in different ways. I have followed what seems to me the most authentic, and what is certainly the least disgraceful, version.

[2] Burnet, ii. 71.

God to attest the sincerity of this declaration. Yet, a short time after, he had been detected in plotting to bring a French army into England; and he had written to assure the Court of Saint Germains that he was acting in concert with his brethren, and especially with Sancroft. The Whigs called loudly for severity. Even the Tory counsellors of William owned that indulgence had been carried to the extreme point. They made, however, a last attempt to mediate. "Will you and your brethren," said Trevor to Lloyd, the nonjuring Bishop of Norwich, "disown all connection with Doctor Turner, and declare that what he has in his letters imputed to you is false?" Lloyd evaded the question. It was now evident that William's forbearance had only emboldened the adversaries whom he had hoped to conciliate. Even Caermarthen, even Nottingham, declared that it was high time to fill the vacant sees.[1]

Tillotson was nominated to the Archbishopric, and was consecrated on Whitsunday, in the church of Saint Mary Le Bow. Compton, cruelly mortified, refused to bear any part in the ceremony. His place was supplied by Mew, Bishop of Winchester, who was assisted by Burnet, Stillingfleet, and Hough. The congregation was the most splendid that had been seen in any place of worship since the coronation. The Queen's drawingroom was, on that day, deserted. Most of the peers who were in town met in the morning at Bedford House, and went thence in procession to Cheapside. Norfolk, Caermarthen, and Dorset were conspicuous in the throng. Devonshire, who was impatient to see his woods at Chatsworth in their summer beauty, had deferred his departure in order to mark his respect for Tillotson. The crowd which lined the streets greeted the new Primate warmly. For he had, during many years, preached in the City; and his eloquence, his probity, and the singular gentleness of his temper and manners, had made him the favourite of the Londoners.[2] But the congratulations and applauses of his friends could not drown the roar of execration which the Jacobites set up. According to them, he was a thief who had not entered by the door, but had climbed over the fences. He was a hireling whose own the sheep were not, who had usurped the crook of the good shepherd, and who might well be expected to leave the flock at the mercy of every wolf. He was an Arian, a Socinian, a Deist, an Atheist. He had cozened the world by fine phrases, and by a show of moral goodness: but he was in truth a far more dangerous

Tillotson Archbishop of Canterbury

---

[1] Lloyd to Sancroft, Jan. 24. 1691. The letter is among the Tanner MSS., and is printed in the Life of Ken by a Layman.

[2] London Gazette, June 1. 1691; Birch's Life of Tillotson; Congratulatory Poem to the Reverend Dr. Tillotson on his promotion, 1691; Vernon to Wharton, May 28. and 30. 1691. These letters to Wharton are in the Bodleian Library, and form part of a highly curious collection which was kindly pointed out to me by Dr. Bandinel.

enemy of the Church than he could have been if he had openly proclaimed himself a disciple of Hobbes, and had lived as loosely as Wilmot. He had taught the fine gentlemen and ladies who admired his style, and who were constantly seen round his pulpit, that they might be very good Christians, and yet might believe the account of the Fall in the book of Genesis to be allegorical. Indeed they might easily be as good Christians as he: for he had never been christened: his parents were Anabaptists: he had lost their religion when he was a boy; and he had never found another. In ribald lampoons he was nicknamed Undipped John. The parish register of his baptism was produced in vain. His enemies still continued to complain that they had lived to see fathers of the Church who never were her children. They made up a story that the Queen had felt bitter remorse for the great crime by which she had obtained a throne, that in her agony she had applied to Tillotson, and that he had comforted her by assuring her that the punishment of the wicked in a future state would not be eternal.[1] The Archbishop's mind was naturally of almost feminine delicacy, and had been rather softened than braced by the habits of a long life, during which contending sects and factions had agreed in speaking of his abilities with admiration and of his character with esteem. The storm of obloquy which he had to face for the first time at more than sixty years of age was too much for him. His spirits declined: his health gave way: yet he neither flinched from his duty nor attempted to revenge himself on his persecutors. A few days after his consecration, some persons were seized while dispersing libels in which he was reviled. The law officers of the Crown proposed to file informations; but he insisted that nobody should be punished on his account.[2] Once, when he had company with him, a sealed packet was put into his hands: he opened it, and out fell a mask. His friends were shocked and incensed by this cowardly insult: but the Archbishop, trying to conceal his anguish by a smile, pointed to the pamphlets which covered his table, and said that the reproach which the emblem of the mask was intended to convey might be called gentle when compared with other reproaches which he daily

[1] Birch's Life of Tillotson; Leslie's Charge of Socinianism against Dr. Tillotson considered by a True Son of the Church, 1695; Hickes's Discourses upon Dr. Burnet and Dr. Tillotson, 1695; Catalogue of Books, of the Newest Fashion, to be Sold by Auction at the Whig's Coffee House, evidently printed in 1693. More than sixty years later Johnson described a sturdy Jacobite as firmly convinced that Tillotson died an Atheist; Idler, No. 10. A Latin epitaph on the Church of England, written soon after Tillotson's consecration, ends thus: "Oh Miseranda Ecclesia, cui Rex Batavus, et Patriarcha non baptizatus." In a poem called the Eucharisticon, which appeared in 1692, are these lines:

" Unblest and unbaptised, this Church's son
Hath all his Mother's children half undone."

[2] Tillotson to Lady Russell, June 23. 1691.

JOHN TILLOTSON, ARCHBISHOP OF CANTERBURY

From an engraving by G. Vertue of a painting by Mary Beale (?) attributed to Sir G. Kneller had to endure. After his death a bundle of the savage lampoons which the nonjurors had circulated against him was found among his papers with this indorsement ; " I pray God forgive them : I do." [1]

The deposed primate was of a less gentle nature. He seems to have been also under a complete delusion as to his own importance. The **Conduct of Sancroft** immense popularity which he had enjoyed three years before, the prayers and tears of the multitudes who had plunged into the Thames to implore his blessing, the enthusiasm with which the sentinels of the Tower had drunk his health under the windows of his prison, the mighty roar of joy which had risen from Palace Yard on the morning of his acquittal, the triumphant night when every window from Hyde Park to Mile End had exhibited seven candles, the midmost and tallest emblematical of him, were still fresh in his recollection ; nor had he the wisdom to perceive that all this homage had been paid, not to his person, but to that religion and to those liberties of which he was, for a moment, the representative. The extreme tenderness with which the new government had long persisted in treating him had confirmed him in his error. That a succession of conciliatory messages was sent to him from Kensington ; that he was offered terms so liberal as to be scarcely consistent with the dignity of the Crown and the welfare of the State ; that his cold and uncourteous answers could not tire out the royal indulgence ; that, in spite of the loud clamours of the Whigs, and of the provocations daily given by the Jacobites, he was residing, fifteen months after deprivation, in the metropolitan palace ; these things seemed to him to indicate, not the lenity, but the timidity, of the ruling powers. He appears to have flattered himself that they would not dare to eject him. The news, therefore, that his see had been filled, threw him into a passion which lasted as long as his life, and which hurried him into many foolish and unseemly actions. Tillotson, as soon as he was appointed, went to Lambeth in the hope that he might be able, by courtesy and kindness, to sooth the irritation of which he was the innocent cause. He staid long in the antechamber, and sent in his name by several servants : but Sancroft would not even return an answer. [2] Three weeks passed ; and still the deprived Archbishop showed no disposition to move. At length he received an order intimating to him the royal pleasure that he should quit the dwelling which had long ceased to be his own, and in which he was only a guest. He resented this order bitterly, and declared that he would not obey it. He would stay till he was pulled out by the Sheriff's officers. He would defend himself at law as long as he could do so without putting in any

---

[1] Birch's Life of Tillotson ; Memorials of Tillotson by his pupil John Beardmore ; Sherlock's sermon preached in the Temple Church on the death of Queen Mary, 169$\frac{4}{5}$.

[2] Wharton's Collectanea quoted in Birch's Life of Tillotson.

FACSIMILE OF A LETTER FROM THOMAS KEN, BISHOP OF BATH
AND WELLS, TO GEORGE HARBIN

From the British Museum. (Add. MS. 32095, f. 401)

plea acknowledging the authority of the usurpers.[1]　The case was so clear that he could not, by any artifice of chicanery, obtain more than a short delay.　When judgment had been given against him, he left the palace, but directed his steward to retain possession.　The consequence was that the steward was taken into custody and heavily fined.　Tillotson sent a kind message to assure his predecessor that the fine should not be exacted.　But Sancroft was determined to have a grievance, and would pay the money.[2]

From that time the great object of the narrowminded and peevish old man was to tear in pieces the Church of which he had been the chief minister.　It was in vain that some of those nonjurors, whose virtue, ability, and learning were the glory of their party, remonstrated **Difference** against his design.　"Our deprivation,"—such was the reason- **between** **Sancroft** ing of Ken,—"is, in the sight of God, a nullity.　We are, **and Ken** and shall be, till we die or resign, the true Bishops of our sees.　Those who assume our titles and functions will incur the guilt of schism.　But with us, if we act as becomes us, the schism will die ; and in the next generation the unity of the Church will be restored. On the other hand, if we consecrate Bishops to succeed us, the breach may last through ages ; and we shall be justly held accountable, not indeed for its origin, but for its continuance."　These considerations ought, on Sancroft's own principles, to have had decisive weight with him : but his angry passions prevailed.　Ken quietly retired from the venerable palace of Wells.　He had done, he said, with strife, and should henceforth vent his feelings, not in disputes, but in hymns.　His charities to the unhappy of all persuasions, especially to the followers of Monmouth and to the persecuted Huguenots, had been so large that his whole private fortune consisted of seven hundred pounds, and of a library which he could not bear to sell.　But Thomas Thynne, Viscount Weymouth, though not a nonjuror, did himself honour by offering to the most virtuous of the nonjurors a tranquil and dignified asylum in the princely mansion of Longleat.　There Ken passed a happy and honoured old age, during which he never regretted the sacrifice which he had made to what he thought his duty, and yet constantly became more and more indulgent to those whose views of duty differed from his.[3]

Sancroft was of a very different temper.　He had, indeed, as little to complain of as any man whom a revolution has ever hurled down

---

[1] Wharton's Collectanea quoted in D'Oyly's Life of Sancroft ; Narcissus Luttrell's Diary.

[2] The Lambeth MS. quoted in D'Oyly's Life of Sancroft ; Narcissus Luttrell's Diary; Vernon to Wharton, June 9. 11. 1691.

[3] See a letter of R. Nelson, dated Feb. 21. 17$\frac{0.9}{1.0}$, in the appendix to N. Marshall's Defence of our Constitution in Church and State, 1717; Hawkins's Life of Ken ; Life of Ken by a Layman.

TOMB OF ARCHBISHOP SANCROFT

From an engraving by F. van Hove in the Sutherland Collection from an exalted station. He had, at Fressingfield in Suffolk, a patrimonial estate, which, together with what he had saved during a primacy

Hatred of Sancroft to the Established Church. He provides for the episcopal succession among the nonjurors

of twelve years, enabled him to live, not indeed as he had lived when he was the first peer of Parliament, but in the style of an opulent country gentleman. He retired to his hereditary abode; and there he passed the rest of his life in brooding over his wrongs. Aversion to the Established Church became as strong a feeling in him as it had been in Martin Marprelate. He considered all who remained in communion with her as heathens and publicans. He nicknamed Tillotson the Mufti. In the room which was used as a chapel at Fressingfield no person who had taken the oaths, or who attended the ministry of any divine who had taken the oaths, was suffered to partake of the sacred bread and wine. A distinction, however, was made between two classes of offenders. A layman who remained in communion with the Church was permitted to be present while prayers were read, and was excluded only from the highest of Christian mysteries. But with clergymen who had sworn allegiance to the Sovereigns in possession Sancroft would not even pray. He took care that the rule which he had laid down should be widely known, and, both by precept and by example, taught his followers to look on the most orthodox, the most devout, the most virtuous, of those who acknowledged William's authority with a feeling similar to that with which the Jew regarded the Samaritan.[1] Such intolerance would have been reprehensible, even in a man contending for a great principle. But Sancroft was contending for nothing more than a name. He was the author of the scheme of Regency. He was perfectly willing to transfer the whole kingly power from James to William. The question, which, to this smallest and sourest of minds, seemed important enough to justify the excommunicating of ten thousand priests and of five millions of laymen, was merely, whether the magistrate to whom the whole kingly power was transferred should assume the kingly title. Nor could Sancroft bear to think that the animosity which he had excited would die with himself. Having done all that he could to make the feud bitter, he determined to make it eternal. A list of the divines who had been ejected from their benefices was sent by him to Saint Germains with a request that James would nominate two who might keep up the episcopal succession. James, well pleased, doubtless, to see another sect added to that multitude of sects which he had been taught to consider as the reproach of Protestantism, named two fierce and uncompromising nonjurors, Hickes and Wagstaffe, the former recommended by Sancroft, the latter recommended by Lloyd,

[1] See a paper dictated by him on the 15th of Nov. 1693, in Wagstaffe's Letter from Suffolk.

RICHARD CUMBERLAND, BISHOP OF PETERBOROUGH

From a mezzotint by J. Smith, after a painting by T. Murray

the ejected Bishop of Norwich.[1]   Such was the origin of a schismatical hierarchy, which, having, during a short time, excited alarm, soon sank into obscurity and contempt, but which, in obscurity and contempt, continued to drag on a languid existence during several generations. The little Church, without temples, revenues, or dignities, was even more distracted by internal disputes than the great Church, which retained possession of cathedrals, tithes, and peerages.   Some nonjurors leaned towards the ceremonial of Rome : others would not tolerate the slightest departure from the Book of Common Prayer.   Altar was set up against altar.   One phantom prelate pronounced the consecration of another phantom prelate uncanonical.   At length the pastors were left absolutely without flocks.   One of these Lords spiritual very wisely turned surgeon : another deserted what he had called his see, and settled in Ireland ; and at length, in 1805, the last Bishop of that society which had proudly claimed to be the only true Church of England dropped unnoticed into the grave.[2]

The places of the bishops who had been ejected with Sancroft were filled in a manner creditable to the government.   Patrick succeeded the **The new** traitor Turner.   Fowler went to Gloucester.   Richard Cum-**Bishops** berland, an aged divine, who had no interest at Court, and whose only recommendations were his piety and his erudition, was astonished by learning from a newsletter which he found on the table of a coffeehouse that he had been nominated to the see of Peterborough.[3] Beveridge was selected to succeed Ken : he consented ; and the appointment was actually announced in the London Gazette.   But Beveridge, though an honest, was not a strongminded man.   Some Jacobites expostulated with him : some reviled him : his heart failed him ; and he retracted.   While the nonjurors were rejoicing in this victory, he changed his mind again ; but too late.   He had by his irresolution forfeited the favour of William, and never obtained a mitre till Anne was on the throne.[4]   The bishopric of Bath and Wells was bestowed on Richard Kidder, a man of considerable attainments and blameless character, but suspected of a leaning towards Presbyterianism.   About the same time Sharp, the highest churchman that had been zealous for

[1] Kettlewell's Life, iii. 59.

[2] See D'Oyly's Life of Sancroft, Hallam's Constitutional History, and Mr. Lathbury's History of the Nonjurors.

[3] See the autobiography of his descendant and namesake the dramatist.   See also Onslow's note on Burnet, ii. 76.

[4] A vindication of Their Majesties' authority to fill the sees of the deprived Bishops, May 20. 1691 ; London Gazette, April 27. and June 15. 1691 ; Narcissus Luttrell's Diary, May 1691. Among the Tanner MSS. are two letters from Jacobites to Beveridge, one mild and decent, the other scurrilous even beyond the ordinary scurrility of the nonjurors.   The former will be found in the Life of Ken by a Layman.

The most Reverend Father in God, John Sharp;
by Divine Providence, Lord Arch-Bishop of Yorke, Primate and
Metropolitan of England— Consecrat Iuly 5th 1691
Sold by C. Cooper at ye 3 Pigeons in Bedford Street. and H. Overton at ye White horse without Newgate.

JOHN SHARP, ARCHBISHOP OF YORK

From a mezzotint by F. Kyte

the Comprehension, and the lowest churchman that felt a scruple about succeeding a deprived prelate, accepted the Archbishopric of York, vacant by the death of Lamplugh.[1]

In consequence of the elevation of Tillotson to the See of Canterbury, the Deanery of Saint Paul's became vacant. As soon as the name of the new Dean was known, a clamour broke forth such as perhaps no ecclesiastical appointment has ever produced, a clamour made up of yells of hatred, of hisses of contempt, and of shouts of triumphant and half insulting welcome : for the new Dean was William Sherlock.

Sherlock, Dean of Saint Paul's

The story of his conversion deserves to be fully told : for it throws great light on the character of the parties which then divided the Church and the State. Sherlock was, in influence and reputation, though not in rank, the foremost man among the nonjurors. His authority and example had induced some of his brethren, who had at first wavered, to resign their benefices. The day of suspension came : the day of deprivation came ; and still he was firm. He seemed to have found, in the consciousness of rectitude, and in meditation on the invisible world, ample compensation for all his losses. While excluded from the pulpit where his eloquence had once delighted the learned and polite inmates of the Temple, he wrote that celebrated Treatise on Death which, during many years, stood next to the Whole Duty of Man in the bookcases of serious Arminians. Soon, however, it began to be suspected that his resolution was giving way. He declared that he would be no party to a schism : he advised those who sought his counsel not to leave their parish churches : nay, finding that the law which had ejected him from his cure did not interdict him from performing divine service, he officiated at Saint Dunstan's, and there prayed for King William and Queen Mary. The apostolical injunction, he said, was that prayers should be made for all in authority ; and William and Mary were visibly in authority. His Jacobite friends loudly blamed his inconsistency. How, they asked, if you admit that the Apostle speaks in this passage of actual authority, can you maintain that, in other passages of a similar kind, he speaks only of legitimate authority ? Or, how can you, without sin, designate as King, in a solemn address to God, one whom you cannot, without sin, promise to obey as King ? These reasonings were unanswerable ; and Sherlock soon began to think them so : but the conclusion to which they led him was diametrically opposed to the conclusion to which they were meant to lead him. He hesitated, however, till a new light flashed on his mind from a quarter from which there was little reason to expect

---

[1] It is not quite clear whether Sharp's scruple about the deprived prelates was a scruple of conscience or merely a scruple of delicacy. See his Life by his Son.

anything but tenfold darkness.   In the reign of James the First, Doctor
John Overall, Bishop of Exeter, had written an elaborate treatise on the
rights of civil and ecclesiastical governors.   This treatise had been

The Rev.ᵈ
William Sherlock D.D.
Dean of S.ᵗ Pauls.

R. White del. & sculp.

From an engraving by R. White

solemnly approved by the Convocations of Canterbury and York, and
might therefore be considered as an authoritative exposition of the
doctrine of the Church of England.   A manuscript copy had come

into Sancroft's hands ; and he, soon after the Revolution, sent it to the press.   He hoped, doubtless, that the publication would injure the new government : but he was lamentably disappointed.   The book indeed condemned all resistance in terms as strong as he could himself have used : but one passage, which had escaped his notice, was decisive against himself and his fellow schismatics.   Overall, and the two Convocations which had given their sanction to Overall's teaching, pronounced that a government, which had originated in rebellion, ought, when thoroughly settled, to be considered as ordained by God, and to be obeyed by Christian men.[1]   Sherlock read, and was convinced.   His venerable mother the Church had spoken ; and he, with the docility of a child, accepted her decree.   The government which had sprung from the Revolution might, at least since the battle of the Boyne and the flight of James from Ireland, be fairly called a settled government, and ought therefore to be passively obeyed till it should be subverted by another revolution and succeeded by another settled government.

Sherlock took the oaths, and speedily published, in justification of his conduct, a pamphlet entitled The Case of Allegiance to Sovereign Powers stated.   The sensation produced by this work was immense.   Dryden's Hind and Panther had not raised so great an uproar.   Halifax's Letter to a Dissenter had not called forth so many answers.   The replies to the Doctor, the vindications of the Doctor, the pasquinades on the Doctor, would fill a library.   The clamour redoubled when it was known that the convert had not only been reappointed Master of the Temple, but had accepted the Deanery of Saint Paul's, which had become vacant in consequence of the deprivation of Sancroft and the promotion of Tillotson.   The rage of the nonjurors amounted almost to frenzy.   Was it not enough, they asked, to desert the true and pure Church, in this her hour of sorrow and peril, without also slandering her ?   It was easy to understand why a greedy, cowardly, hypocrite

---

[1] See Overall's Convocation Book, chapter 28.   Nothing can be clearer or more to the purpose than his language.

"When, having attained their ungodly desires, whether ambitious kings by bringing any country into their subjection, or disloyal subjects by rebellious rising against their natural sovereigns, they have established any of the said degenerate governments among their people, the authority either so unjustly established, or wrung by force from the true and lawful possessor, being always God's authority, and therefore receiving no impeachment by the wickedness of those that have it, is ever, when such alterations are thoroughly settled, to be reverenced and obeyed ; and the people of all sorts, as well of the clergy as of the laity, are to be subject unto it, not only for fear, but likewise for conscience sake."

Then follows the canon.

"If any man shall affirm that, when any such new forms of government, begun by rebellion, are after thoroughly settled, the authority in them is not of God, or that any who live within the territories of any such new governments are not bound to be subject to God's authority which is there executed, but may rebel against the same, he doth greatly err."

should refuse to take the oaths to the usurper as long as it seemed probable that the rightful King would be restored, and should make haste to swear after the battle of the Boyne. Such tergiversation in times of civil discord was nothing new. What was new was that the turncoat should attempt to transfer his own guilt and shame to the Church of England, and should proclaim that she had taught him to lift his heel against the weak who were in the right, and to cringe to the powerful who were in the wrong. Had such indeed been her doctrine or her practice in evil days? Had she abandoned her Royal Martyr in the prison or on the scaffold? Had she enjoined her children to pay obedience to the Rump or to the Protector? Yet was the government of the Rump or of the Protector less entitled to be called a settled government than the government of William and Mary? Had not the battle of Worcester been as great a blow to the hopes of the House of Stuart as the battle of the Boyne? Had not the chances of a Restoration seemed as small in 1657 as they could seem to any judicious man in 1691? In spite of invectives and sarcasms, however, there was Overall's treatise: there were the approving votes of the two Convocations; and it was much easier to rail at Sherlock than to explain away either the treatise or the votes. One writer maintained that by a thoroughly settled government must have been meant a government of which the title was uncontested. Thus, he said, the government of the United Provinces became a settled government when it was recognised by Spain, and, but for that recognition, would never have been a settled government to the end of time. Another casuist, somewhat less austere, pronounced that a government, wrongful in its origin, might become a settled government after the lapse of a century. On the thirteenth of February 1789, therefore, and not a day earlier, Englishmen would be at liberty to swear allegiance to a government sprung from the Revolution. The history of the chosen people was ransacked for precedents. Was Eglon's a settled government when Ehud stabbed him? Was Joram's a settled government when Jehu shot him? But the leading case was that of Athaliah. It was indeed a case which furnished the malecontents with many happy and pungent allusions; a kingdom treacherously seized by an usurper near in blood to the throne; the rightful prince long dispossessed; a part of the sacerdotal order true, through many disastrous years, to the Royal House; a counterrevolution at length effected by the High Priest at the head of the Levites. Who, it was asked, would dare to blame the heroic pontiff who had restored the heir of David? Yet was not the government of Athaliah as firmly settled as that of the Prince of Orange? Hundreds of pages written at this time about the rights of Joash and the bold enterprise of Jehoiada are mouldering in the ancient bookcases of Oxford and Cambridge. While Sherlock was thus fiercely attacked by his old friends, he was not left unmolested by his old enemies. Some vehement Whigs, among whom Julian Johnson was conspicuous, declared that Jacobitism itself was respectable when compared with the vile doctrine which had been discovered in the Convocation Book. That passive obedience was due to Kings was doubtless an absurd and pernicious notion. Yet it was impossible not to respect the consistency and fortitude of men who thought themselves bound to bear true allegiance, at all hazards, to an unfortunate, a deposed, an exiled oppressor. But the political creed which Sherlock had learned from Overall was unmixed baseness and wickedness. A cause was to be abandoned, not because it was unjust, but because it was unprosperous. Whether James had been a tyrant or had been the father of his people was, according to this theory, quite immaterial. If he had won the battle of the Boyne we should have been bound as Christians to be his slaves. He had lost it; and we were bound as Christians to be his foes. Other Whigs congratulated the proselyte on having come, by whatever road, to a right practical conclusion, but could not refrain from sneering at the history which he gave of his conversion. He was, they said, a man of eminent learning and abilities. He had studied the question of allegiance long and deeply. He had written much about it. Several months had been allowed him for reading, prayer, and reflection, before he incurred suspension, several months more before he incurred deprivation. He had formed an opinion for which he had declared himself ready to suffer martyrdom : he had taught that opinion to others ; and he had then changed that opinion solely because he had discovered that it had been, not refuted, but dogmatically pronounced erroneous by the two Convocations more than eighty years before. Surely, this was to renounce all liberty of private judgment, and to ascribe to the Synods of Canterbury and York an infallibility which the Church of England had declared that even Œcumenical Councils could not justly claim. If, it was sarcastically said, all our notions of right and wrong, in matters of vital importance to the wellbeing of society, are to be suddenly altered by a few lines of manuscript found in a corner of the library at Lambeth, it is surely much to be wished, for the peace of mind of humble Christians, that all the documents to which this sort of authority belongs may be rummaged out and sent to the press as soon as possible : for, unless this be done, we may all, like the Doctor when he refused the oaths last year, be committing sins in the full persuasion that we are discharging duties. In truth, it is not easy to believe that the Convocation Book furnished Sherlock with anything more than a pretext for doing what he had made up his mind to do. The united force of reason and interest had doubtless convinced him that his passions and prejudices had led him into a great error. That error he determined to recant ; and it cost him less to say that his opinion had been changed by newly discovered evidence, than that he had formed a wrong judgment with all the materials for the forming of a right judgment before him. The popular belief was that his retractation was the effect of the tears, expostulations, and reproaches of his wife. The lady's spirit was high : her authority in the family was great ; and she cared much more about her house and her carriage, the plenty of her table and the prospects of her children, than about the patriarchal origin of government or the meaning of the word Abdication. She had, it was asserted, given her husband no peace by day or by night till he had got over his scruples. In letters, fables, songs, dialogues, without number, her powers of seduction and intimidation were malignantly extolled. She was Xanthippe pouring water on the head of Socrates. She was Dalilah shearing Samson. She was Eve forcing the forbidden fruit into Adam's mouth. She was Job's wife, imploring her ruined lord, who sate scraping himself among the ashes, not to curse and die, but to swear and live. While the balladmakers celebrated the victory of Mrs. Sherlock, another class of assailants fell on the theological reputation of her spouse. Till he took the oaths, he had always been considered as the most orthodox of divines. But the captious and malignant criticism to which his writings were now subjected would have found heresy in the Sermon on the Mount ; and he, unfortunately, was rash enough to publish, at the very moment when the outcry against his political tergiversation was loudest, his thoughts on the mystery of the Trinity. It is probable that, at another time, his work would have been hailed by good Churchmen as a triumphant answer to the Socinians and Sabellians. But, unhappily, in his zeal against Socinians and Sabellians, he used expressions which might be construed into Tritheism. Candid judges would have remembered that the true path was closely pressed on the right and on the left by error, and that it was scarcely possible to keep far enough from danger on one side without going very close to danger on the other. But candid judges Sherlock was not likely to find among the Jacobites. His old allies affirmed that he had incurred all the fearful penalties denounced in the Athanasian Creed against those who divide the substance. Bulky quartos were written to prove that he held the existence of three distinct Deities ; and some facetious malecontents, who troubled themselves very little about the Catholic verity, amused the town by lampoons in English and Latin on his heterodoxy. "We," said one of these jesters, "plight our faith to one King, and call one God to attest our promise. We cannot think it strange that there should be more than one King to whom the Doctor has sworn allegiance, when we consider that the Doctor has more Gods than one to swear by." [1]

Sherlock would, perhaps, have doubted whether the government to which he had submitted was entitled to be called a settled government, **Treachery of some of William's servants** if he had known all the dangers by which it was threatened. Scarcely had Preston's plot been detected, when a new plot of a very different kind was formed in the camp, in the navy, in the treasury, in the very bedchamber of the King. This mystery of iniquity has, through five generations, been gradually unveiling, but is not yet entirely unveiled. Some parts which are still obscure may possibly, by the discovery of letters or diaries now reposing under the

---

[1] A list of all the pieces which I have read relating to Sherlock's apostasy would fatigue the reader. I will mention a few of different kinds; Parkinson's Examination of Dr. Sherlock's Case of Allegiance, 1691; Answer to Dr. Sherlock's Case of Allegiance, by a London Apprentice, 1691; the Reasons of the New Convert's taking the Oaths to the present Government, 1691; Utrum horum? or God's ways of disposing of Kingdoms, and some Clergymen's ways of disposing of them, 1691; Sherlock and Xanthippe, 1691; Saint Paul's Triumph in his sufferings for Christ, by Matthew Bryan, LL.D., dedicated Ecclesiæ sub cruce gementi; A Word to a wavering Levite; The Trimming Court Divine; Proteus Ecclesiasticus, or Observations on Dr. Sh—'s late Case of Allegiance; the Weasil Uncased; A Whip for the Weasil; the Anti-Weasils. Numerous allusions to Sherlock and his wife will be found in the ribald writings of Tom Brown, Tom Durfey, and Ned Ward. See the Life of James, ii. 318. Several curious letters about Sherlock's apostasy are among the Tanner MSS. I will give two or three specimens of the rhymes which the Case of Allegiance called forth:

> "When Eve the fruit had tasted,
> She to her husband hasted,
>   And chuck'd him on the chin-a.
> Dear Bud, quoth she, come taste this fruit;
> 'Twill finely with your palate suit:
>   To eat it is no sin-a."

> "As moody Job, in shirtless case,
> With collyflowers all o'er his face,
>   Did on the dunghill languish,
> His spouse thus whispers in his ear,
> Swear, husband, as you love me, swear:
>   'Twill ease you of your anguish."

> "At first he had doubt, and therefore did pray
> That heaven would instruct him in the right way,
> Whether Jemmy or William he ought to obey,
>   Which nobody can deny.

> "The pass at the Boyne determin'd that case;
> And precept to Providence then did give place;
> To change his opinion he thought no disgrace;
>   Which nobody can deny.

> "But this with the Scripture can never agree,
> As by Hosea the eighth and the fourth you may see;
> 'They have set up kings, but yet not by me,'
>   Which nobody can deny."

dust of a century and a half, be made clear to our posterity. The materials, however, which are at present accessible, are sufficient for the construction of a narrative not to be read without shame and loathing.[1]

We have seen that, in the spring of 1690, Shrewsbury, irritated by finding his counsels rejected, and those of his Tory rivals followed, suffered himself, in a fatal hour, to be drawn into a correspondence with the banished family. We have seen also by what cruel sufferings of body and mind he expiated his fault. Tortured by remorse, and by disease the effect of remorse, he had quitted the Court : but he had left behind him men whose principles were not less lax than his, and whose hearts were far harder and colder.

Early in 1691, some of these men began to hold secret communications with Saint Germains. Wicked and base as their conduct was, there was in it nothing surprising. They did after their kind. The times were troubled. A thick cloud was upon the future. The most sagacious and experienced statesman could not see with any clearness three months before him. To a man of virtue and honour, indeed, this mattered little. His uncertainty as to what the morrow might bring forth might make him anxious, but could not make him perfidious. Though left in utter darkness as to what concerned his interests, he had the sure guidance of his principles. But, unhappily, men of virtue and honour were not numerous among the courtiers of that age. Whitehall had been, during thirty years, a seminary of every public and private vice, and swarmed with lowminded, doubledealing, selfseeking politicians. These politicians now acted as it was natural that men profoundly immoral should act at a crisis of which none could predict the issue. Some of them might have a slight predilection for William ; others a slight predilection for James : but it was not by any such predilection that the conduct of any of the breed was guided. If it had seemed certain that William would stand, they would all have been for William. If it had seemed certain that James would be restored, they would all have been for James. But what was to be done when the chances appeared to be almost exactly balanced? There were honest men of one party who would have answered, To stand by the true King and the true Church, and, if necessary, to die for them like Laud. There were honest men of the other party who would have answered, To stand by the liberties of England and the Protestant religion, and, if necessary, to die for them like Sidney. But such consistency was unintelligible to many of the noble and the

---

[1] The chief authority for this part of my history is the Life of James, particularly the highly important and interesting passage which begins at page 444. and ends at page 450. of the second volume. This passage was corrected by the Pretender with his own hand.

powerful. Their object was to be safe in every event. They therefore openly took the oath of allegiance to one King, and secretly plighted their word to the other. They were indefatigable in obtaining commissions, patents of peerage, pensions, grants of crown land, under the great seal of William ; and they had in their secret drawers promises of pardon in the handwriting of James.

Among those who were guilty of this wickedness three men stand preeminent, Russell, Godolphin, and Marlborough. No three men could be, in head and heart, more unlike to one another ; and the peculiar qualities of each gave a peculiar character to his villany. The treason of Russell is to be attributed partly to fractiousness : the treason of Godolphin is to be attributed altogether to timidity : the treason of Marlborough was the treason of a man of great genius and boundless ambition.

It may be thought strange that Russell should have been out of humour. He had just accepted the command of the united naval forces of England and Holland with the rank of Admiral of the Fleet. He was Treasurer of the Navy. He had a pension of three thousand pounds a year. Crown property near Charing Cross, to the value of eighteen thousand pounds, had been bestowed on him. His indirect gains must have been immense. But he was still dissatisfied. In truth, with undaunted courage, with considerable talents both for war and for administration, and with a certain public spirit, which showed itself by glimpses even in the very worst parts of his life, he was emphatically a bad man, insolent, malignant, greedy, faithless. He conceived that the great services which he had performed at the time of the Revolution had not been adequately rewarded. Everything that was given to others seemed to him to be pillaged from himself. A letter is still extant which he wrote to William about this time. It is made up of boasts, reproaches, and sneers. The Admiral, with ironical professions of humility and loyalty, asks permission to put his wrongs on paper, because his bashfulness will not suffer him to explain himself by word of mouth. His grievances he represents as intolerable. Other people got large grants of royal domains : but he could get scarcely anything. Other people could provide for their dependants : but his recommendations were uniformly disregarded. The income which he derived from the royal favour might seem large : but he had poor relations ; and the government, instead of doing its duty by them, had most unhandsomely left them to his care. He had a sister who ought to have a pension ; for, without one, she could not give portions to her daughters. He had a brother who, for want of a place, had been reduced to the melancholy necessity of marrying an old woman for her money. Russell proceeded

Russell (margin note)

to complain bitterly that the Whigs were neglected, and that the
Revolution had aggrandised and enriched men who had made the

From an engraving by W. Elder, after a painting by W. Wissing

greatest efforts to avert it. There is reason to believe that this complaint came from his heart. For, next to his own interests, those of his
party were dear to him ; and, even when he was most inclined to become

a Jacobite, he never had the smallest disposition to become a Tory. In the temper which this letter indicates, he readily listened to the suggestions of David Lloyd, one of the ablest and most active of the emissaries who at this time were constantly plying between France and England. Lloyd conveyed to James assurances that Russell would, when a favourable opportunity should present itself, try to effect by means of the fleet what Monk had effected in the preceding generation by means of the army.[1] To what extent these assurances were sincere was a question about which men who knew Russell well, and who were minutely informed as to his conduct, were in doubt. It seems probable that, during many months, he did not know his own mind. His interest was to stand well, as long as possible, with both Kings. His irritable and imperious nature was constantly impelling him to quarrel with both. His spleen was excited one week by a dry answer from William, and the next week by an absurd proclamation from James. Fortunately the most important day of his life, the day from which all his subsequent years took their colour, found him out of temper with the banished tyrant.

Godolphin had not, and did not pretend to have, any cause of complaint against the government which he served. He was First Commissioner of the Treasury. He had been protected, **Godolphin** trusted, caressed. Indeed the favour shown to him had excited many murmurs. Was it fitting, the Whigs had indignantly asked, that a man who had been high in office through the whole of the late reign, who had promised to vote for the Indulgence, who had sate in the Privy Council with a Jesuit, who had sate at the Board of Treasury with two Papists, who had attended an idolatress to her altar, should be among the chief ministers of a Prince whose title to the throne was derived from the Declaration of Right. But on William this clamour had produced no effect ; and none of his English servants seems to have had at this time a larger share of his confidence than Godolphin.

Nevertheless, the Jacobites did not despair. One of the most zealous among them, a gentleman named Bulkeley, who had formerly been on terms of intimacy with Godolphin, undertook to see what could be done. He called at the Treasury, and tried to draw the First Lord into political talk. This was no easy matter : for Godolphin was not a man to put himself lightly into the power of others. His reserve was proverbial ; and he was especially renowned for the dexterity with which he, through life, turned conversation away from matters of state to a main of cocks or the pedigree of a racehorse. The visit ended

---

[1] Russell to William, May 10. 1691, in Dalrymple's Appendix, Part II. Book vii. See also the Memoirs of Sir John Leake.

without his uttering a word indicating that he remembered the existence of King James.

Bulkeley, however, was not to be so repulsed. He came again, and introduced the subject which was nearest his heart. Godolphin then asked after his old master and mistress in the mournful tone of a man who despaired of ever being reconciled to them. Bulkeley assured him that King James was ready to forgive all the past. "May I tell His Majesty that you will try to deserve his favour?" At this Godolphin rose, said something about the trammels of office and his wish to be released from them, and put an end to the interview.

Bulkeley soon made a third attempt. By this time Godolphin had learned some things which shook his confidence in the stability of the government which he served. He began to think, as he would himself have expressed it, that he had betted too deep on the Revolution, and that it was time to hedge. Evasions would no longer serve his turn. It was necessary to speak out. He spoke out, and declared himself a devoted servant of King James. "I shall take an early opportunity of resigning my place. But, till then, I am under a tie. I must not betray my trust." To enhance the value of the sacrifice which he proposed to make, he produced a most friendly and confidential letter which he had lately received from William. "You see how entirely the Prince of Orange trusts me. He tells me that he cannot do without me, and that there is no Englishman for whom he has so great a kindness: but all this weighs nothing with me in comparison of my duty to my lawful King."

If the First Lord of the Treasury really had scruples about betraying his trust, those scruples were soon so effectually removed that he very complacently continued, during six years, to eat the bread of one master, while secretly sending professions of attachment and promises of service to another.

The truth is that Godolphin was under the influence of a mind far more powerful and far more depraved than his own. His perplexities had been imparted to Marlborough, to whom he had long been bound by such friendship as two very unprincipled men are capable of feeling for each other, and to whom he was afterwards bound by close domestic ties.

Marlborough was in a very different situation from that of William's other servants. Lloyd might make overtures to Russell, and Bulkeley to Godolphin. But all the agents of the banished Court stood aloof from the deserter of Salisbury. That shameful Marlborough night seemed to have for ever separated the false friend from the Prince whom he had ruined. James had, even in the last extremity, when his army was in full retreat, when his whole kingdom had risen against him, declared that he would never pardon Churchill, never, never. By all the Jacobites the name of Churchill was held in peculiar abhorrence ; and, in the prose and verse which came forth daily from their secret presses, a precedence in infamy, among all the many traitors of the age, was assigned to him. In the order of things which had sprung from the Revolution, he was one of the great men of England, high in the state, high in the army. He had been created an Earl. He had a large share in the military administration. The emoluments, direct and indirect, of the places and commands which he held under the Crown were believed at the Dutch Embassy to amount to twelve thousand pounds a year. In the event of a counterrevolution it seemed that he had nothing in prospect but a garret in Holland or a scaffold on Tower Hill. It might therefore have been expected that he would serve his new master with fidelity ; not indeed with the fidelity of Nottingham, which was the fidelity of conscientiousness, not with the fidelity of Portland, which was the fidelity of affection, but with the not less stubborn fidelity of despair.

Those who thought thus knew but little of Marlborough. Confident in his own powers of deception, he resolved, since the Jacobite agents would not seek him, to seek them. He therefore sent to beg an interview with Colonel Edward Sackville.

Sackville was astonished and not much pleased by the message. He was a sturdy Cavalier of the old school. He had been persecuted in the days of the Popish plot for manfully saying what he thought, and what everybody now thinks, about Oates and Bedloe.[1] Since the Revolution he had repeatedly put his neck in peril for King James, had been chased by officers with warrants, and had been designated as a traitor in a proclamation to which Marlborough himself had been a party.[2] It was not without reluctance that the stanch royalist crossed the hated threshold of the deserter. He was repaid for his effort by the edifying spectacle of such an agony of repentance as he had never before seen. " Will you," said Marlborough, " be my intercessor with the King ? Will you tell him what I suffer ? My crimes now appear to me in their true light ; and I shrink with horror from the contemplation. The thought of them is with me day and night. I sit down to table : but I cannot eat. I throw myself on my bed : but I cannot sleep. I am ready to sacrifice everything, to brave everything, to bring utter ruin on my fortunes, if only I may be free from the misery of a wounded spirit." If appearances could be trusted, this great offender was as true a penitent as David or as Peter. Sackville reported to his friends what had passed. They could not but acknowledge that, if the archtraitor, who had hitherto opposed to conscience and to public

---

[1] Commons' Journals, Mar. 21. 24. 1679 ; Grey's Debates ; Observator.
[2] London Gazette, July 21. 1690.

opinion the same cool and placid hardihood which distinguished him on fields of battle, had really begun to feel remorse, it would be absurd to reject, on account of his unworthiness, the inestimable services which it was in his power to render to the good cause. He sate in the interior council : he held high command in the army : he had been recently entrusted, and would doubtless again be entrusted, with the direction of important military operations. It was true that no man had incurred equal guilt : but it was true also that no man had it in his power to make equal reparation. If he was sincere, he might doubtless earn the pardon which he so much desired. But was he sincere? Had he not been just as loud in professions of loyalty on the very eve of his crime? It was necessary to put him to the test. Several tests were applied by Sackville and Lloyd. Marlborough was required to furnish full information touching the strength and the distribution of all the divisions of the English army ; and he complied. He was required to disclose the whole plan of the approaching campaign; and he did so. The Jacobite leaders watched carefully for inaccuracies in his reports, but could find none. It was thought a still stronger proof of his fidelity that he gave valuable intelligence about what was doing in the office of the Secretary of State. A deposition had been sworn against one zealous royalist. A warrant was preparing against another. These intimations saved several of the malecontents from imprisonment, if not from the gallows ; and it was impossible for them not to feel some relenting towards the awakened sinner to whom they owed so much.

He however, in his secret conversations with his new allies, laid no claim to merit. He did not, he said, ask for confidence. How could he, after the villanies which he had committed against the best of Kings, hope ever to be trusted again? It was enough for a wretch like him to be permitted to make, at the cost of his life, some poor atonement to the gracious master, whom he had indeed basely injured, but whom he had never ceased to love. It was not improbable that, in the summer, he might command the English forces in Flanders. Was it wished that he should bring them over in a body to the French camp? If such were the royal pleasure, he would undertake that the thing should be done. But on the whole he thought that it would be better to wait till the next session of Parliament. And then he hinted at a plan, which he afterwards more fully matured, for expelling the usurper by means of the English legislature and the English army. In the mean time he hoped that James would command Godolphin not to quit the Treasury. A private man could do little for the good cause. One who was the director of the national finances, and the depository of the gravest secrets of state, might render inestimable services.

Marlborough's pretended repentance imposed so completely on those who managed the affairs of James in London that they sent Lloyd to France, with the cheering intelligence that the most depraved of all rebels had been wonderfully transformed into a loyal subject. The tidings filled James with delight and hope. Had he been wise, they would have excited in him only aversion and distrust. It was absurd to imagine that a man really heartbroken by remorse and shame for one act of perfidy would determine to lighten his conscience by committing a second act of perfidy as odious and as disgraceful as the first. The promised atonement was so wicked and base that it never could be made by any man sincerely desirous to atone for past wickedness and baseness. The truth was that, when Marlborough told the Jacobites that his sense of guilt prevented him from swallowing his food by day and taking his rest at night, he was laughing at them. The loss of half a guinea would have done more to spoil his appetite and to disturb his slumbers than all the terrors of an evil conscience. What his offers really proved was that his former crime had sprung, not from an ill regulated zeal for the interests of his country and his religion, but from a deep and incurable moral disease which had infected the whole man. James, however, partly from dulness and partly from selfishness, could never see any immorality in any action by which he was benefited. To conspire against him, to betray him, to violate an oath of allegiance sworn to him, were crimes for which no punishment here or hereafter could be too severe. But to be ungrateful to his enemies, to break faith with his enemies, was not only innocent but laudable. The desertion at Salisbury had been the worst of crimes : for it had ruined him. A similar desertion in Flanders would be an honourable exploit : for it might restore him.

The penitent was informed by his Jacobite friends that he was forgiven. The news was most welcome : but something more was necessary to restore his lost peace of mind. Might he hope to have, in the royal handwriting, two lines containing a promise of pardon ? It was not, of course, for his own sake that he asked this. But he was confident that, with such a document in his hands, he could bring back to the right path some persons of great note who adhered to the usurper, only because they imagined that they had no mercy to expect from the legitimate King. They would return to their duty as soon as they saw that even the worst of all criminals had, on his repentance, been generously forgiven. The promise was written, sent, and carefully treasured up. Marlborough had now attained one object, an object which was common to him with Russell and Godolphin. But he had other objects which neither Russell nor Godolphin had ever contemplated. There is, as we shall hereafter see, strong reason to believe

Charles henri de Lorraine Prince de Vaudemont
Souverain de Commercy &c

NEC VIRTVTE FVIT NEC BELLO MAJOR ET ARMIS.

CHARLES DE LORRAINE, PRINCE OF VAUDEMONT

From an engraving by N. de Larmessin, after a painting by Ranc that this wise, brave, wicked, man, was meditating a plan worthy of his fertile intellect and daring spirit, and not less worthy of his deeply corrupted heart, a plan which, if it had not been frustrated by strange means, would have ruined William without benefiting James, and would have made the successful traitor master of England and arbiter of Europe.

Thus things stood, when, in May 1690, William, after a short and busy sojourn in England, set out again for the Continent, where the **William returns to the Continent** regular campaign was about to open. He took with him Marlborough, whose abilities he justly appreciated, and of whose recent negotiations with Saint Germains he had not the faintest suspicion. At the Hague several important military and political consultations were held ; and, on every occasion, the superiority of the accomplished Englishman was felt by the most distinguished soldiers and statesmen of the United Provinces. Heinsius, long after, used to relate a conversation which took place at this time between William and the Prince of Vaudemont, one of the ablest commanders in the Dutch service. Vaudemont spoke well of several English officers, and among them of Talmash and Mackay, but pronounced Marlborough superior beyond comparison to the rest. " He has every quality of a general. His very look shows it. He cannot fail to achieve something great." " I really believe, cousin," answered the King, " that my Lord will make good everything that you have said of him."

There was still a short interval before the commencement of military operations. William passed that interval in his beloved park at Loo. Marlborough spent two or three days there, and was then despatched to Flanders, with orders to collect all the English forces, to form a camp in the neighbourhood of Brussels, and to have everything in readiness for the King's arrival.

And now Marlborough had an opportunity of proving the sincerity of those professions by which he had obtained from a heart, well described by himself as harder than a marble chimneypiece, the pardon of an offence such as might have moved even a gentle nature to deadly resentment. He received from Saint Germains a message claiming the instant performance of his promise to desert at the head of his troops. He was told that this was the greatest service which he could render to the Crown. His word was pledged ; and the gracious master who had forgiven all past errors confidently expected that it would be redeemed. The hypocrite evaded the demand with characteristic dexterity. In the most respectful and affectionate language he excused himself for not immediately obeying the royal commands. The promise which he was required to fulfil had not been quite correctly understood. There had been some misapprehension on the part of the messengers. To carry over a regiment or two would do more harm than good. To carry over a whole army was a business which would require much time and management.[1] While James was murmuring over these apologies, and wishing that he had not been quite so placable, William arrived at the headquarters of the allied forces, and took the chief command.

The military operations in Flanders recommenced early in June and terminated at the close of September. No important action took place. The two armies marched and countermarched, drew near and receded. During some time they confronted each other with less than a league between them. But neither William nor Luxemburg would fight except at an advantage; and neither gave the other any advantage. Languid as the campaign was, it is on one account remarkable. During more than a century our country had sent no great force to make war by land out of the British isles. Our aristocracy had therefore long ceased to be a military class. The nobles of France, of Germany, of Holland, were generally soldiers. It would probably have been difficult to find in the brilliant circle which surrounded Lewis at Versailles a single Marquess or Viscount of forty who had not been at some battle or siege. But the immense majority of our peers, baronets, and opulent esquires had never served except in the trainbands, and had never borne a part in any military exploit more serious than that of putting down a riot or of keeping a street clear for a procession. The generation which had fought at Edgehill and Lansdowne had nearly passed away. The wars of Charles the Second had been almost entirely maritime. During his reign therefore the sea service had been decidedly more the mode than the land service; and, repeatedly, when our fleets sailed to encounter the Dutch, such multitudes of men of fashion had gone on board that the parks and the theatres had been left desolate. In 1691 at length, for the first time since Henry the Eighth laid siege to Boulogne, an English army appeared on the Continent under the command of an English king. A camp, which was also a court, was irresistibly attractive to many young patricians full of natural intrepidity, and ambitious of the favour which men of distinguished bravery have always found in the eyes of women. To volunteer for Flanders became the rage among the fine gentlemen who combed their flowing wigs and exchanged their richly perfumed snuffs at the Saint James's Coffeehouse. William's headquarters were enlivened by a crowd of splendid equipages and by a rapid succession of sumptuous banquets. For among the highborn and highspirited youths who repaired to his standard were some who, though quite willing to face a battery, were not at all disposed to deny

The campaign of 1691 in Flanders

[1] Life of James, ii. 449.

themselves the luxuries with which they had been surrounded in Soho Square. In a few months Shadwell brought these valiant fops and epicures on the stage. The town was made merry with the character of a courageous but prodigal and effeminate coxcomb, who is impatient to cross swords with the best men in the French household troops, but who is much dejected by learning that he may find it difficult to have his Champagne iced daily during the summer. He carries with him cooks, confectioners, and laundresses, a waggonload of plate, a wardrobe of laced and embroidered suits, and much rich tent furniture, of which the patterns have been chosen by a committee of fine ladies.[1]

While the hostile armies watched each other in Flanders, hostilities were carried on with somewhat more vigour in other parts of Europe. The French gained some advantages in Catalonia and in Piedmont. Their Turkish allies, who in the east menaced the dominions of the Emperor, were defeated by Lewis of Baden in a great battle. But nowhere were the events of the summer so important as in Ireland.

From October 1690 till May 1691, no military operation on a large scale was attempted in that kingdom. The area of the island **The war in Ireland** was, during the winter and spring, not unequally divided between the contending races. The whole of Ulster, the greater part of Leinster, and about one third of Munster had submitted to the English. The whole of Connaught, the greater part of Munster, and two or three counties of Leinster were held by the Irish. The tortuous boundary formed by William's garrisons ran in a north eastern direction from the bay of Castlehaven to Mallow, and then, inclining still further eastward, proceeded to Cashel. From Cashel the line went to Mullingar, from Mullingar to Longford, and from Longford to Cavan, skirted Lough Erne on the west, and met the ocean again at Ballyshannon.[2]

On the English side of this pale there was a rude and imperfect order. Two Lords Justices, Coningsby and Porter, assisted by a Privy **State of the English part of Ireland** Council, represented King William at Dublin Castle. Judges, Sheriffs, and Justices of the Peace had been appointed ; and assizes were, after a long interval, held in several county towns. The colonists had meanwhile been formed into a strong militia, under the command of officers who had commissions from the Crown. The trainbands of the capital consisted of two thousand five hundred foot, two troops of horse, and two troops of dragoons, all Protestants, and all well armed and clad.[3] On the fourth of November, the

---

[1] The description of this young hero in the list of the Dramatis Personæ is amusing : " Sir Nicholas Dainty, A most conceited fantastic Beau, of drolling, affected Speech ; a very Coxcomb, but stout ; a most luxurious effeminate Volunteer."

[2] Story's Continuation ; Proclamation of February 21. 169$\frac{0}{1}$; London Gazette of March 12.

[3] Story's Continuation.

LVDOVICVS PRINS VAN BADEN
Keiserlyke Generaal tegen de Turken.

I. Gole Feç: et Exc:

Cum Privil: Amstelodami

PRINCE LEWIS OF BADEN

From a mezzotint by J. Gole

anniversary of William's birth, and on the fifth, the anniversary of his landing at Torbay, the whole of this force appeared in all the pomp of war. The vanquished and disarmed natives assisted, with suppressed grief and anger, at the triumph of the caste which they had, five months before, oppressed and plundered with impunity. The Lords Justices went in state to Saint Patrick's Cathedral : bells were rung : bonfires were lighted : hogsheads of ale and claret were set abroach in the streets : fireworks were exhibited on College Green : a great company of nobles and public functionaries feasted at the Castle ; and, as the second course came up, the trumpets sounded, and Ulster King at Arms proclaimed, in Latin, French, and English, William and Mary, by the grace of God, King and Queen of Great Britain, France, and Ireland.[1]

Within the territory where the Saxon race was dominant, trade and industry had already begun to revive. The brazen counters which bore the image and superscription of James gave place to silver. The fugitives who had taken refuge in England came back in multitudes ; and, by their intelligence, diligence, and thrift, the devastation caused by two years of confusion and robbery was soon in part repaired. Merchantmen heavily laden were constantly passing and repassing Saint George's Channel. The receipts of the custom houses on the eastern coast, from Cork to Londonderry, amounted in six months to sixty seven thousand five hundred pounds, a sum such as would have been thought extraordinary even in the most prosperous times.[2]

The Irish who remained within the English pale were, one and all, hostile to the English domination. They were therefore subjected to a rigorous system of police, the natural though lamentable effect of extreme danger and extreme provocation. A Papist was not permitted to have a sword or a gun. He was not permitted to go more than three miles out of his parish except to the market town on the market day. Lest he should give information or assistance to his brethren who occupied the western half of the island, he was forbidden to live within ten miles of the frontier. Lest he should turn his house into a place of resort for malecontents, he was forbidden to sell liquor by retail. One proclamation announced that, if the property of any Protestant should be injured by marauders, his loss should be made good at the expense of his Popish neighbours. Another gave notice that, if any Papist who had not been at least three months domiciled in Dublin should be found

---

[1] Story's Impartial History ; London Gazette, Nov. 17. 1690.

[2] Story's Impartial History. The year 1684 had been considered as a time of remarkable prosperity, and the revenue from the Customs had been unusually large. But the receipt from all the ports of Ireland, during the whole year, was only a hundred and twenty seven thousand pounds. See Clarendon's Memoirs.

there, he should be treated as a spy. Not more than five Papists were to assemble in the capital or its neighbourhood on any pretext. Without a protection from the government no member of the Church of Rome was safe; and the government would not grant a protection to any member of the Church of Rome who had a son in the Irish army.[1]

In spite of all precautions and severities, however, the Celt found many opportunities of taking a sly revenge. Houses and barns were frequently burned : soldiers were frequently murdered ; and it was scarcely possible to obtain evidence against the malefactors, who had with them the sympathies of the whole population. On such occasions the government sometimes ventured on acts which seemed better suited to a Turkish than to an English administration. One of these acts became a favourite theme of Jacobite pamphleteers, and was the subject of a serious parliamentary enquiry at Westminster. Six musketeers were found butchered only a few miles from Dublin. The inhabitants of the village where the crime had been committed, men, women, and children, were driven like sheep into the Castle, where the Privy Council was sitting. The heart of one of the assassins, named Gafney, failed him. He consented to be a witness, was examined by the Board, acknowledged his guilt, and named some of his accomplices. He was then removed in custody : but a priest obtained access to him during a few minutes. What passed during those few minutes appeared when he was a second time brought before the Council. He had the effrontery to deny that he had owned anything or accused anybody. His hearers, several of whom had taken down his confession in writing, were enraged at his impudence. The Lords Justices broke out ; " You are a rogue : you are a villain : you shall be hanged : where is the Provost Marshal ? " The Provost Marshal came. " Take that man," said Coningsby, pointing to Gafney ; " take that man, and hang him." There was no gallows ready : but the carriage of a gun served the purpose ; and the prisoner was instantly tied up, without a trial, without even a written order for the execution ; and this though the courts of law were sitting at the distance of only a few hundred yards. The English House of Commons, some years later, after a long discussion, resolved, without a division, that the order for the execution of Gafney was arbitrary and illegal, but that Coningsby's fault was so much extenuated by the circumstances in which he was placed that it was not a proper subject for impeachment.[2]

[1] Story's History and Continuation ; London Gazettes of September 29. 1690, and Jan. 8. and Mar. 12. 169$\frac{0}{1}$.

[2] See the Lords' Journals of March 2. and 4. 169$\frac{2}{3}$, and the Commons' Journals of Dec. 16. 1693, and Jan. 29. 169$\frac{3}{4}$. The story, bad enough at best, was told by the personal and political

It was not only by the implacable hostility of the Irish that the Saxon of the pale was at this time harassed. His allies caused him almost as much annoyance as his helots. The help of troops from abroad was indeed necessary to him : but it was dearly bought. Even William, in whom the whole civil and military authority was concentrated, had found it difficult to maintain discipline in an army collected from many lands, and composed in great part of mercenaries accustomed to live at free quarter. The powers which had been united in him were now divided and subdivided. The two Lords Justices considered the civil administration as their province, and left the army to the management of Ginkell, who was General in Chief. Ginkell kept excellent order among the auxiliaries from Holland, who were under his more immediate command. But his authority over the English and the Danes was less entire ; and unfortunately their pay was, during part of the winter, in arrear. They indemnified themselves by excesses and exactions for the want of that which was their due ; and it was hardly possible to punish men with severity for not choosing to starve with arms in their hands. At length in the spring large supplies of money and stores arrived : arrears were paid up : rations were plentiful ; and a more rigid discipline was enforced. But too many traces of the bad habits which the soldiers had contracted were discernible till the close of the war.[1]

In that part of Ireland, meanwhile, which still acknowledged James as King, there could hardly be said to be any law, any property, or any State of the government. The Roman Catholics of Ulster and Leinster part of Ire- had fled westward by tens of thousands, driving before them land which was subject a large part of the cattle which had escaped the havoc of two to James terrible years. The influx of food into the Celtic region, however, was far from keeping pace with the influx of consumers. The necessaries of life were scarce. Conveniences to which every plain farmer and burgess in England was accustomed could hardly be procured by nobles and generals. No coin was to be seen except lumps of base metal which were called crowns and shillings. Nominal prices were enormously high. A quart of ale cost two and sixpence, a quart of brandy three pounds. The only towns of any note on the western coast were Limerick and Galway ; and the oppression which the shop-keepers of those towns underwent was such that many of them stole

enemies of the Lords Justices with additions which the House of Commons evidently considered as calumnious, and which I really believe to have been so. See the Gallienus Redivivus. The narrative which Colonel Robert Fitzgerald, a Privy Councillor and an eyewitness, delivered in writing to the House of Lords, under the sanction of an oath, seems to me perfectly trustworthy. It is strange that Story, though he mentions the murder of the soldiers, says nothing about Gafney.

[1] Burnet, ii. 66. ; Leslie's Answer to King.

The Right Honorable Baron DeGinckle, Generall of Their Majesties forces in Ireland &c,

T. Hill pinx.　　　　R. Williams fe.　　　Sold by R. Williams against ye Royall Bagnio in Long acre

GODARD VAN REEDE, BARON DE GINKELL, AFTERWARDS EARL OF ATHLONE

From a mezzotint by R. Williams, after a painting by T. Hill away with the remains of their stocks to the English territory, where a Papist, though he had to endure much restraint and much humiliation, was allowed to put his own price on his goods, and received that price in silver. Those traders who remained within the unhappy region were ruined. Every warehouse that contained any valuable property was broken open by ruffians who pretended that they were commissioned to procure stores for the public service ; and the owner received, in return for bales of cloth and hogsheads of sugar, some fragments of old kettles and saucepans, which would not in London or Paris have been taken by a beggar. As soon as a merchant ship arrived in the bay of Galway or in the Shannon, she was boarded by these robbers. The cargo was carried away ; and the proprietor was forced to content himself with such a quantity of cowhides, of wool, and of tallow as the gang which had plundered him chose to give him. The consequence was, that, while foreign commodities were pouring fast into the harbours of Londonderry, Carrickfergus, Dublin, Waterford, and Cork, every mariner avoided Limerick and Galway as nests of pirates.[1]

The distinction between the Irish foot soldier and the Irish Rapparee had never been very strongly marked. It now disappeared. Great part of the army was turned loose to live by marauding. An incessant predatory war raged along the line which separated the domain of William from that of James. Every day companies of freebooters, sometimes wrapped in twisted straw which served the purpose of armour, stole into the English territory, burned, sacked, pillaged, and hastened back to their own ground. To guard against these incursions was not easy ; for the peasantry of the plundered country had a strong fellow feeling with the plunderers. To empty the granary, to set fire to the dwelling, to drive away the cows, of a heretic was regarded by every squalid inhabitant of a mud cabin as a good work. A troop engaged in such a work might confidently expect to fall in, notwithstanding all the proclamations of the Lords Justices, with some friend who would indicate the richest booty, the shortest road, and the safest hidingplace. The English complained that it was no easy matter to catch a Rapparee. Sometimes, when he saw danger approaching, he lay down in the long grass of the bog ; and then it was as difficult to find him as to find a hare sitting. Sometimes he sprang into a stream, and lay there, like an otter, with only his mouth and nostrils above the water. Nay, a whole gang of banditti would, in the twinkling of an eye, transform itself into a crowd

---

[1] Macariæ Excidium ; Fumeron to Louvois, $\frac{\text{Jan. 31.}}{\text{Feb. 10.}}$ 1691. It is to be observed that Kelly, the author of the Macariæ Excidium, and Fumeron, the French intendant, are most unexceptionable witnesses. They were both at this time, within the walls of Limerick. There is no reason to doubt the impartiality of the Frenchman ; and the Irishman was partial to his own countrymen.

of harmless labourers. Every man took his gun to pieces, hid the lock in his clothes, stuck a cork in the muzzle, stopped the touch hole with a quill, and threw the weapon into the next pond. Nothing was to be seen but a train of poor rustics who had not so much as a cudgel among them, and whose humble look and crouching walk seemed to show that their spirit was thoroughly broken to slavery. When the peril was over, when the signal was given, every man flew to the place where he had hid his arms; and soon the robbers were in full march towards some Protestant mansion. One band penetrated to Clonmel, another to the vicinity of Maryborough: a third made its den in a woody islet of firm ground, surrounded by the vast bog of Allen, harried the county of Wicklow, and alarmed even the suburbs of Dublin. Such expeditions indeed were not always successful. Sometimes the plunderers fell in with parties of militia or with detachments from the English garrisons, in situations in which disguise, flight, and resistance were alike impossible. When this happened, every kerne who was taken was hanged, without any ceremony, on the nearest tree.[1]

At the headquarters of the Irish army there was, during the winter, no authority capable of exacting obedience even within a circle of a mile. Tyrconnel was absent at the Court of France. He had left the supreme government in the hands of a Council of Regency composed of twelve persons. The nominal command of the army he had confided to Berwick: but Berwick, though, as was afterwards proved, a man of no common courage and capacity, was young and inexperienced. His powers were unsuspected by the world and by himself;[2] and he submitted without reluctance to the tutelage of a Council of War nominated by the Lord Lieutenant. Neither the Council of Regency nor the Council of War was popular at Limerick. The Irish complained that men who were not Irish had been entrusted with a large share in the administration. The cry was loudest against an officer named Thomas Maxwell. For it was certain that he was a Scotchman: it was doubtful whether he was a Roman Catholic; and he had not concealed the dislike which he felt for that Celtic Parliament which had repealed the Act of Settlement and passed the Act of Attainder.[3] The discontent, fomented by the arts of intriguers, among whom the cunning and unprincipled Henry Luttrell

Dissensions among the Irish at Limerick

---

[1] Story's Impartial History and Continuation, and the London Gazettes of December, January, February, and March 169⁹⁰.

[2] It is remarkable that Avaux, though a very shrewd judge of men, greatly underrated Berwick. In a letter to Louvois dated Oct. $\frac{16}{26}$. 1689, Avaux says: "Je ne puis m'empescher de vous dire qu'il est brave de sa personne, à ce que l'on dit, mais que c'est un aussy mechant officier qu'il y en ayt, et qu'il n'a pas le sens commun."

[3] Leslie's Answer to King; Macariæ Excidium.

seems to have been the most active, soon broke forth into open rebellion. A great meeting was held. Many officers of the army, some peers, some lawyers of high note, and some prelates of the Roman Catholic Church were present. It was resolved that the government set up by the Lord Lieutenant was unknown to the constitution. Ireland, it was said, could be legally governed, in the absence of the King, only by a Lord Lieutenant, by a Lord Deputy, or by Lords Justices. The King was absent. The Lord Lieutenant was absent. There was no Lord Deputy. There were no Lords Justices. The edict by which Tyrconnel had delegated his authority to a junto composed of his creatures was a mere nullity. The nation was therefore left without any legitimate chief, and might, without violating the allegiance due to the Crown, make temporary provision for its own safety. A deputation was sent to inform Berwick that he had assumed a power to which he had no right, but that nevertheless the army and people of Ireland would willingly acknowledge him as their head if he would consent to govern by the advice of a council truly Irish. Berwick indignantly expressed his wonder that military men should presume to meet and deliberate without the permission of their general. The deputies answered that there was no general, and that, if His Grace did not choose to undertake the administration on the terms proposed, another leader would easily be found. Berwick very reluctantly yielded, and continued to be a puppet in a new set of hands.[1]

Those who had effected this revolution thought it prudent to send a deputation to France for the purpose of vindicating their proceedings. Of this deputation the Roman Catholic Bishop of Cork and the two Luttrells were members. In the ship which conveyed them from Limerick to Brest they found a fellow passenger whose presence was by no means agreeable to them, their enemy, Maxwell. They suspected, and not without reason, that he was going, like them, to Saint Germains, but on a very different errand. The truth was that Berwick had sent Maxwell to watch their motions and to traverse their designs. Henry Luttrell, the least scrupulous of men, proposed to settle the matter at once by tossing the Scotchman into the sea. But the Bishop, who was a man of conscience, and Simon Luttrell, who was a man of honour, objected to this expedient.[2]

Meanwhile at Limerick the supreme power was in abeyance. Berwick, finding that he had no real authority, altogether neglected business, and gave himself up to such pleasures as that dreary place of banishment afforded. There was among the Irish chiefs no man of sufficient weight and ability to control the rest. Sarsfield for a time took the lead. But Sarsfield, though eminently brave and active in the field, was little skilled

[1] Macariæ Excidium.   [2] Ibid. ; Life of James, ii. 422.; Memoirs of Berwick.

A Paris chez I. Mariette rue St Iacques aux Colonnes d'Hercule.

Iacques Duc de Berwick Maréchal de France,
Fils naturel de Iacques Second Roy d'Angleterre, et Chevalier
de la Iartierre.

JAMES FITZJAMES, DUKE OF BERWICK

From a French engraving in the Sutherland Collection

in the administration of war, and still less skilled in civil business. Those who were most desirous to support his authority were forced to own that his nature was too unsuspicious and indulgent for a post in which it was hardly possible to be too distrustful or too severe. He believed whatever was told him. He signed whatever was set before him. The commissaries, encouraged by his lenity, robbed and embezzled more shamelessly than ever. They sallied forth daily, guarded by pikes and firelocks, to seize, nominally for the public service, but really for themselves, wool, linen, leather, tallow, domestic utensils, instruments of husbandry, searched every pantry, every wardrobe, every cellar, and even laid sacrilegious hands on the property of priests and prelates.[1]

Early in the spring the government, if it is to be so called, of which Berwick was the ostensible head, was dissolved by the return of Tyr-

Return of Tyrconnel to Ireland
connel. The Luttrells had, in the name of their countrymen, implored James not to subject so loyal a people to so odious and incapable a viceroy. Tyrconnel, they said, was old : he was infirm : he needed much sleep : he knew nothing of war : he was dilatory : he was partial : he was rapacious : he was distrusted and hated by the whole nation. The Irish, deserted by him, had made a gallant stand, and had compelled the victorious army of the Prince of Orange to retreat. They hoped soon to take the field again, thirty thousand strong ; and they adjured their King to send them some captain worthy to command such a force. Tyrconnel and Maxwell, on the other hand, represented the delegates as mutineers, demagogues, traitors, and pressed James to send Henry Luttrell to keep Mountjoy company in the Bastille. James, bewildered by these criminations and recriminations, hesitated long, and at last, with characteristic wisdom, relieved himself from trouble by giving all the quarrellers fair words, and by sending them all back to have their fight out in Ireland. Berwick was at the same time recalled to France.[2]

Tyrconnel was received at Limerick, even by his enemies, with decent respect. Much as they hated him, they could not question the validity of his commission ; and, though they still maintained that they had been perfectly justified in annulling, during his absence, the unconstitutional arrangements which he had made, they acknowledged that, when he was present, he was their lawful governor. He was not altogether unprovided with the means of conciliating them. He brought many gracious messages and promises, a patent of peerage for Sarsfield, some money which was not of brass, and some clothing, which was even more acceptable than money. The new garments were not indeed very fine. But even the generals had long been out at elbows ; and there were few of the common men whose habiliments would have been

---

[1] Macariæ Excidium.　　　　[2] Life of James, ii. 422, 423.; Mémoires de Berwick.

Thomas Maxwell Esq.ʳ Major General of the
Army, and Commander of the Dragoons in Ireland. &c

I. Closterman pinx.   I. Smith fecit et excud.

MAJOR-GENERAL THOMAS MAXWELL

From a mezzotint by J. Smith, after a painting by J. Closterman

thought sufficient to dress a scarecrow in a more prosperous country.
Now, at length, for the first time in many months, every private soldier
could boast of a pair of breeches and a pair of brogues. The Lord
Lieutenant had also been authorised to announce that he should soon
be followed by several ships, laden with provisions and military stores.
This announcement was most welcome to the troops, who had long been
without bread, and who had nothing stronger than water to drink.[1]

During some weeks the supplies were impatiently expected. At
last, Tyrconnel was forced to shut himself up : for, whenever he appeared
in public, the soldiers ran after him clamouring for food. Even the beef
and mutton, which, half raw, half burned, without vegetables, without
salt, had hitherto supported the army, had become scarce ; and the common men were on rations of horseflesh when the promised sails were
seen in the mouth of the Shannon.[2]

A distinguished French general, named Saint Ruth, was on board
with his staff. He brought a commission which appointed him commander in chief of the Irish army. The commission did not
expressly declare that he was to be independent of the viceregal authority : but he had been assured by James that
Tyrconnel should have secret instructions not to intermeddle
in the conduct of the war. Saint Ruth was assisted by another general
officer named D'Usson. The French ships brought some arms, some
ammunition, and a plentiful supply of corn and flour. The spirits of
the Irish rose ; and the Te Deum was chaunted with fervent devotion
in the cathedral of Limerick.[3]

Arrival of a French fleet at Limerick: Saint Ruth

Tyrconnel had made no preparations for the approaching campaign.
But Saint Ruth, as soon as he had landed, exerted himself strenuously
to redeem the time which had been lost. He was a man of courage,
activity, and resolution, but of a harsh and imperious nature. In his
own country he was celebrated as the most merciless persecutor that
had ever dragooned the Huguenots to mass. It was asserted by
English Whigs that he was known in France by the nickname of the
Hangman ; that, at Rome, the very cardinals had shown their abhorrence of his cruelty ; and that even Queen Christina, who had little right
to be squeamish about bloodshed, had turned away from him with
loathing. He had recently held a command in Savoy. The Irish
regiments in the French service had formed part of his army, and had
behaved extremely well. It was therefore supposed that he had a
peculiar talent for managing Irish troops. But there was a wide difference between the well clad, well armed, and well drilled Irish, with

<hr />

[1] Life of James, ii. 433. 451.; Story's Continuation.

[2] Life of James, ii. 438. ; Light to the Blind; Fumeron to Louvois, $\frac{\text{April 22.}}{\text{May 2.}}$ 1691.

[3] Macariæ Excidium ; Mémoires de Berwick ; Life of James, ii. 451, 452.

whom he was familiar, and the ragged marauders whom he found swarming in the alleys of Limerick. Accustomed to the splendour and to the discipline of French camps and garrisons, he was disgusted by finding that, in the country to which he had been sent, a regiment of infantry meant a mob of people as naked, as dirty, and as disorderly as the beggars, whom he had been accustomed to see on the Continent besieging the door of a monastery or pursuing a diligence up hill. With ill concealed contempt, however, he addressed himself vigorously to the task of disciplining these strange soldiers, and was day and night in the saddle, galloping from post to post, from Limerick to Athlone, from Athlone to the northern extremity of Loughrea, and from Loughrea back to Limerick.[1]

It was indeed necessary that he should bestir himself: for, a few days after his arrival, he learned that, on the other side of the Pale, all was ready for action. The greater part of the English force was collected, before the close of May, in the neighbourhood of Mullingar. Ginkell commanded in chief. He had under him the two best officers, after Marlborough, of whom our island could then boast, Talmash and Mackay. The Marquess of Ruvigny, the hereditary chief of the refugees, and elder brother of that brave Caillemot who had fallen at the Boyne, had joined the army with the rank of major general. The Lord Justice Coningsby, though not by profession a soldier, came down from Dublin, to animate the zeal of the troops. The appearance of the camp showed that the money voted by the English Parliament had not been spared. The uniforms were new: the ranks were one blaze of scarlet; and the train of artillery was such as had never before been seen in Ireland.[2]

The English take the field

On the sixth of June Ginkell moved his headquarters from Mullingar. On the seventh he reached Ballymore. At Ballymore, on a peninsula almost surrounded by something between a swamp and a lake, stood an ancient fortress, which had recently been fortified under Sarsfield's direction, and which was defended by above a thousand men. The English guns were instantly planted. In a few hours the besiegers had the satisfaction of seeing the besieged running like rabbits from one shelter to another. The governor, who had at first held high language, begged piteously for quarter, and obtained it. The whole garrison was marched off to Dublin. Only eight of the conquerors had fallen.[3]

Fall of Ballymore

---

[1] Macariæ Excidium ; Burnet, ii. 78.; Dangeau ; The Mercurius Reformatus, June 5. 1691.

[2] An exact journal of the victorious progress of Their Majesties' forces under the command of General Ginckle this summer in Ireland, 1691; Story's Continuation ; Mackay's Memoirs.

[3] London Gazette, June 18. 22. 1691; Story's Continuation ; Life of James, ii. 452. The author of the Life accuses the Governor of treachery or cowardice.

Ginkell passed some days in reconstructing the defences of Bally-more. This work had scarcely been performed when he was joined by the Danish auxiliaries under the command of the Duke of Wurtemberg. The whole army then moved westward, and, on the nineteenth of June, appeared before the walls of Athlone.[1]

Athlone was perhaps, in a military point of view, the most important place in the island. Rosen, who understood war well, had always

Siege and fall of Athlone

maintained that it was there that the Irishry would, with most advantage, make a stand against the Englishry.[2] The town, which was surrounded by ramparts of earth, lay partly in Leinster and partly in Connaught. The English quarter, which was in Leinster, had once consisted of new and handsome houses, but had been burned by the Irish some months before, and now lay in heaps of ruin. The Celtic quarter, which was in Connaught, was old and meanly built.[3] The Shannon, which is the boundary of the two provinces, rushed through Athlone in a deep and rapid stream, and turned two large mills which rose on the arches of a stone bridge. Above the bridge, on the Connaught side, a castle, built, it was said, by King John, towered to the height of seventy feet, and extended two hundred feet along the river. Fifty or sixty yards below the bridge was a narrow ford.[4]

During the night of the nineteenth the English placed their cannon. On the morning of the twentieth the firing began. At five in the after-noon an assault was made. A brave French refugee with a grenade in his hand was the first to climb the breach, and fell, cheering his countrymen to the onset with his latest breath. Such were the gallant spirits which the bigotry of Lewis had sent to recruit, in the time of his utmost need, the armies of his deadliest enemies. The example was not lost. The grenades fell thick. The assailants mounted by hundreds. The Irish gave way and ran towards the bridge. There the press was so great that some of the fugitives were crushed to death in the narrow passage, and others were forced over the parapets into

[1] London Gazette, June 22. 25. July 2. 1691 ; Story's Continuation ; Exact Journal.

[2] Life of James, ii. 373. 376, 377.

[3] Macariæ Excidium. I may observe that this is one of the many passages which lead me to believe the Latin text to be the original. The Latin is, "Oppidum ad Salaminium amnis latus recentibus ac sumptuosioribus ædificiis attollebatur ; antiquius et ipsa vetustate incultius quod in Paphiis finibus exstructum erat." The English version is, "The town on Salaminia side was better built than that in Paphia." Surely there is in the Latin the particularity which we might expect from a person who had known Athlone before the war. The English version is contemptibly bad. I need hardly say that the Paphian side is Connaught, and the Salaminian side Leinster.

[4] I have consulted several contemporary maps of Athlone. One will be found in Story's Continuation.

PLAN OF THE FORT OF BALLYMORE

From George Story's Impartial History of the Wars of Ireland, 1693

the waters which roared among the mill wheels below. In a few hours Ginkell had made himself master of the English quarter of Athlone ; and this success had cost him only twenty men killed and forty wounded.[1]

But his work was only begun. Between him and the Irish town the Shannon ran fiercely. The bridge was so narrow that a few resolute men might keep it against an army. The mills which stood on it were strongly guarded ; and it was commanded by the guns of the castle. That part of the Connaught shore where the river was fordable was defended by works, which the Lord Lieutenant had, in spite of the murmurs of a powerful party, forced Saint Ruth to entrust to the care of Maxwell. Maxwell had come back from France a more unpopular man than he had been when he went thither. It was rumoured that he had, at Versailles, spoken opprobriously of the Irish nation ; and he had, on this account, been, only a few days before, publicly affronted by Sarsfield.[2] On the twenty-first of June the English were busied in flinging up batteries along the Leinster bank. On the twenty-second, soon after dawn, the cannonade began. The firing continued all that day and all the following night. When morning broke again, one whole side of the castle had been beaten down : the thatched lanes of the Celtic town lay in ashes ; and one of the mills had been burned with sixty soldiers who had been posted in it.[3]

Still however the Irish defended the bridge resolutely. During several days there was sharp fighting hand to hand in the strait passage. The assailants gained ground, but gained it inch by inch. The courage of the garrison was sustained by the hope of speedy succour. Saint Ruth had at length completed his preparations ; and the tidings that Athlone was in danger had induced him to take the field in haste at the head of an army, superior in number, though inferior in more important elements of military strength, to the army

[1] Diary of the Siege of Athlone, by an Engineer of the Army, a Witness of the Action, licensed July 11. 1691 ; Story's Continuation ; London Gazette, July 2. 1691 ; Fumeron to Louvois, $\frac{\text{June 28.}}{\text{July 8.}}$ 1691. The account of this attack in the Life of James, ii. 453., is an absurd romance. It does not appear to have been taken from the King's original Memoirs, or to have been revised by his son.

[2] Macariæ Excidium. Here again I think that I see clear proof that the English version of this curious work is only a bad translation from the Latin. The English merely says : "Lysander,"—Sarsfield,—"accused him, a few days before, in the general's presence," without intimating what the accusation was. The Latin original runs thus : "Acriter Lysander, paucos ante dies, coram præfecto copiarum illi exprobraverat nescio quid, quod in aula Syriaca in Cypriorum opprobrium effutivisse dicebatur." The English translator has, by omitting the most important words, and by using the aorist instead of the preterpluperfect tense, made the whole passage unmeaning.

[3] Story's Continuation ; Macariæ Excidium ; Daniel Macneal to Sir Arthur Rawdon, June 28. 1691, in the Rawdon Papers.

PLAN OF ATHLONE

From George Story's Impartial History of the Wars of Ireland, 1693

of Ginkell.   The French general seems to have thought that the bridge and the ford might easily be defended, till the autumnal rains, and the pestilence which ordinarily accompanied them, should compel the enemy to retire.   He therefore contented himself with sending successive detachments to reinforce the garrison.   The immediate conduct of the defence he entrusted to his second in command, D'Usson, and fixed his own headquarters two or three miles from the town.   He expressed his astonishment that so experienced a commander as Ginkell should persist in a hopeless enterprise.   " His master ought to hang him for trying to take Athlone ; and mine ought to hang me if I lose it." [1]

Saint Ruth, however, was by no means at ease.   He had found, to his great mortification, that he had not the full authority which the promises made to him at Saint Germains had entitled him to expect. The Lord Lieutenant was in the camp.   His bodily and mental infirmities had perceptibly increased within the last few weeks.   The slow and uncertain step with which he, who had once been renowned for vigour and agility, now tottered from his easy chair to his couch, was no unapt type of the sluggish and wavering movement of that mind which had once pursued its objects with a vehemence restrained neither by fear nor by pity, neither by conscience nor by shame. Yet, with impaired strength, both physical and intellectual, the broken old man clung pertinaciously to power.   If he had received private orders not to meddle with the conduct of the war, he disregarded them. He assumed all the authority of a sovereign, showed himself ostentatiously to the troops as their supreme chief, and affected to treat Saint Ruth as a lieutenant.   Soon the interference of the Viceroy excited the vehement indignation of that powerful party in the army which had long hated him.   Many officers signed an instrument by which they declared that they did not consider him as entitled to their obedience in the field.   Some of them offered him gross personal insults.   He was told to his face that, if he persisted in remaining where he was not wanted, the ropes of his pavilion should be cut.   He, on the other hand, sent his emissaries to all the camp fires, and tried to make a party among the common soldiers against the French general.[2]

The only thing in which Tyrconnel and Saint Ruth agreed was in dreading and disliking Sarsfield.   Not only was he popular with the great body of his countrymen ; he was also surrounded by a knot of retainers whose devotion to him resembled the devotion of the Ismailite murderers to the Old Man of the Mountain.   It was known

[1] London Gazette, July 6. 1691 ; Story's Continuation ; Macariæ Excidium ; Light to the Blind.

[2] Macariæ Excidium ; Light to the Blind.

Serenissimus Georgius, D. G. Hassiæ Landgravius Princeps Hirsfeldiæ, Comes in Cattimeliboco, Dietz, Kigenhaina, Nidda, Schauenburgo, Isenburgo et Budinga, Eques Nobilis Ordinis Aurei Velleris, Sacræ Cesareæ Majestatis Campi Mareschallus, Et Regiminis Catafractorum Præfectus, Hispaniæ Procer Anno Domini. MDCCIII.

PRINCE GEORGE OF HESSE DARMSTADT

From a mezzotint by J. Smith, after a painting by T. Murray

that one of these fanatics, a colonel, had used language which, in the mouth of an officer so high in rank, might well cause uneasiness. "The King," this man had said, "is nothing to me. I obey Sarsfield. Let Sarsfield tell me to stab any man in the whole army; and I will do it." Sarsfield was, indeed, too honourable a gentleman to abuse his immense power over the minds of his worshippers. But the Viceroy and the Commander in Chief might not unnaturally be disturbed by the thought that Sarsfield's honour was their only guarantee against mutiny and assassination. The consequence was that, at the crisis of the fate of Ireland, the services of the first of Irish soldiers were not used, or were used with jealous caution, and that, if he ventured to offer a suggestion, it was received with a sneer or a frown.[1]

A great and unexpected disaster put an end to these disputes. On the thirtieth of June Ginkell called a council of war. Forage began to be scarce; and it was absolutely necessary that the besiegers should either force their way across the river or retreat. The difficulty of effecting a passage over the shattered remains of the bridge seemed almost insuperable. It was proposed to try the ford. The Duke of Wurtemberg, Talmash, and Ruvigny gave their voices in favour of this plan; and Ginkell, with some misgivings, consented.[2]

It was determined that the attempt should be made that very afternoon. The Irish, fancying that the English were about to retreat, kept guard carelessly. Part of the garrison was idling, part dozing. D'Usson was at table. Saint Ruth was in his tent, writing a letter to his master filled with charges against Tyrconnel. Meanwhile, fifteen hundred grenadiers, each wearing in his hat a green bough, were mustered on the Leinster bank of the Shannon. Many of them doubtless remembered that on that day year they had, at the command of King William, put green boughs in their hats on the banks of the Boyne. Guineas had been liberally scattered among these picked men: but their alacrity was such as gold cannot purchase. Six battalions were in readiness to support the attack. Mackay commanded. He did not approve of the plan: but he executed it as zealously and energetically as if he had himself been the author of it. The Duke of Wurtemberg, Talmash, and several other gallant officers, to whom no part in the enterprise had been assigned, insisted on serving that day as private volunteers; and their appearance in the ranks excited the fiercest enthusiasm among the soldiers.

It was six o'clock. A peal from the steeple of the church gave the signal. Prince George of Hesse Darmstadt, and a brave soldier named Hamilton, whose services were afterwards rewarded with the title of

---

[1] Life of James, ii. 460.; Life of William, 1702.

[2] Story's Continuation; Mackay's Memoirs; Exact Journal; Diary of the Siege of Athlone.

Lord Boyne, descended first into the Shannon. Then the grenadiers lifted the Duke of Wurtemberg on their shoulders, and, with a great shout, plunged twenty abreast up to their cravats in water. The stream

GUSTAVUS HAMILTON, FIRST VISCOUNT BOYNE

From a painting in the possession of Viscount Boyne

ran deep and strong: but in a few minutes the head of the column reached dry land. Talmash was the fifth man that set foot on the Connaught shore. The Irish, taken unprepared, fired one confused volley and fled, leaving their commander, Maxwell, a prisoner. The conquerors clambered up the bank over the remains of walls shattered by a cannonade of ten days. Mackay heard his men cursing and swearing as they stumbled among the rubbish. "My lads," cried the stout old Puritan in the midst of the uproar, "you are brave fellows : but do not swear. We have more reason to thank God for the goodness which He has shown us this day than to take His name in vain." The victory was complete. Planks were placed on the broken arches of the bridge, and pontoons laid on the river, without any opposition on the part of the terrified garrison. With the loss of twelve men killed and about thirty wounded the English had, in a few minutes, forced their way into Connaught.[1]

At the first alarm D'Usson hastened towards the river ; but he was met, swept away, trampled down, and almost killed by the torrent of fugitives. He was carried to the camp in such a state that it was necessary to bleed him. "Taken !" cried Saint Ruth, in dismay. "It cannot be. A town taken, and I close by with an army to relieve it !" Cruelly mortified, he struck his tents under cover of the night, and retreated in the direction of Galway. At dawn the English saw far off, from the top of King John's ruined castle, the Irish army moving through the dreary region which separates the Shannon from the Suck. Before noon the rearguard had disappeared.[2]

Retreat of the Irish army

Even before the loss of Athlone the Celtic camp had been distracted by factions. It may easily be supposed, therefore, that, after so great a disaster, nothing was to be heard but crimination and recrimination. The enemies of the Lord Lieutenant were more clamorous than ever. He and his creatures had brought the kingdom to the verge of perdition. He would meddle with what he did not understand. He would overrule the plans of men who were real soldiers. He would entrust the most important of all posts to his tool, his spy, the wretched Maxwell, not a born Irishman, not a sincere Catholic, at best a blunderer, and too probably a traitor. Maxwell, it was affirmed, had left his men unprovided with ammunition. When they had applied to him for powder and ball, he had asked whether they wanted to shoot larks. Just before the attack he had told them to go to their supper and to take their rest, for that nothing more would be done that day. When he had delivered himself up a prisoner, he had uttered some words which seemed to indicate a previous understanding with the conquerors. The Lord Lieutenant's few friends told a very different story. According to them, Tyrconnel and Maxwell had suggested precautions which would have made a surprise impossible. The French General, impatient of all

---

[1] Story's Continuation ; Macariæ Excidium ; Burnet, ii. 78, 79. ; London Gazette, July 6. 13. 1689 ; Fumeron to Louvois, $\frac{\text{June 30.}}{\text{July 10.}}$ 1690 ; Diary of the Siege of Athlone ; Exact Account.

[2] Story's Continuation ; Life of James, ii. 455. ; Fumeron to Louvois, $\frac{\text{June 30.}}{\text{July 10.}}$ 1691 ; London Gazette, July 13.

THE STORMING OF ATHLONE

From an engraving by Tangena in the Sutherland Collection

interference, had omitted to take those precautions.　Maxwell had been rudely told that, if he was afraid, he had better resign his command. He had done his duty bravely.　He had stood while his men had fled. He had consequently fallen into the hands of the enemy; and he was now, in his absence, slandered by those to whom his captivity was justly imputable.[1]　On which side the truth lay it is not easy, at this distance of time, to pronounce.　The cry against Tyrconnel was, at the moment, so loud, that he gave way and sullenly retired to Limerick.　D'Usson, who had not yet recovered from the hurts inflicted by his own runaway troops, repaired to Galway.[2]

Saint Ruth, now left in undisputed possession of the supreme command, was bent on trying the chances of a battle.　Most of the

Saint Ruth
determines
to fight Irish officers, with Sarsfield at their head, were of a very different mind.　It was, they said, not to be dissembled that, in discipline, the army of Ginkell was far superior to theirs. The wise course, therefore, evidently was to carry on the war in such a manner that the difference between the disciplined and the undisciplined soldier might be as small as possible.　It was well known that raw recruits often played their part well in a foray, in a street fight, or in the defence of a rampart; but that, on a pitched field, they had little chance against veterans.　"Let most of our foot be collected behind the walls of Limerick and Galway.　Let the rest, together with our horse, get in the rear of the enemy, and cut off his supplies.　If he advances into Connaught, let us overrun Leinster.　If he sits down before Galway, which may well be defended, let us make a push for Dublin, which is altogether defenceless."[3]　Saint Ruth might, perhaps, have thought this advice good, if his judgment had not been biassed by his passions.　But he was smarting from the pain of a humiliating defeat.　In sight of his tent, the English had passed a rapid river, and had stormed a strong town.　He could not but feel that, though others might have been to blame, he was not himself blameless.　He had, to say the least, taken things too easily.　Lewis, accustomed to be served during many years by commanders who were not in the habit of leaving to chance anything which could be made secure by prudence, would hardly think it a sufficient excuse that his general had not expected the enemy to make so bold and sudden an attack.　The Lord Lieutenant would, of course, represent what had passed in the most unfavourable manner; and whatever the Lord Lieutenant said James would echo.

[1] The story, as told by the enemies of Tyrconnel, will be found in the Macariæ Excidium, and in a letter written by Felix O'Neill to the Countess of Antrim on the 10th of July 1691. The letter was found on the corpse of Felix O'Neill after the battle of Aghrim.　It is printed in the Rawdon Papers.　The other story is told in Berwick's Memoirs and in the Light to the Blind.

[2] Macariæ Excidium; Life of James, ii. 456.; Light to the Blind.　　　[3] Macariæ Excidium.

A sharp reprimand, a letter of recall, might be expected.   To return to Versailles a culprit ; to approach the great King in an agony of distress ; to see him shrug his shoulders, knit his brow, and turn his back ; to be sent, far from courts and camps, to languish at some dull country seat ; this was too much to be borne ; and yet this might well be apprehended.   There was one escape ; to fight, and to conquer or to perish.

In such a temper Saint Ruth pitched his camp about thirty miles from Athlone on the road to Galway, near the ruined castle of Aghrim, and determined to await the approach of the English army.

His whole deportment was changed.   He had hitherto treated the Irish soldiers with contemptuous severity.   But, now that he had resolved to stake life and fame on the valour of the despised race, he became another man.   During the few days which remained to him, he exerted himself to win by indulgence and caresses the hearts of all who were under his command.[1]   He, at the same time, administered to his troops moral stimulants of the most potent kind.   He was a zealous Roman Catholic ; and it is probable that the severity with which he had treated the Protestants of his own country ought to be partly ascribed to the hatred which he felt for their doctrines.   He now tried to give to the war the character of a crusade.   The clergy were the agents whom he employed to sustain the courage of his soldiers.   The whole camp was in a ferment with religious excitement. In every regiment priests were praying, preaching, shriving, holding up the host and the cup.   While the soldiers swore on the sacramental bread not to abandon their colours, the General addressed to the officers an appeal which might have moved the most languid and effeminate nature to heroic exertion.   They were fighting, he said, for their religion, their liberty, and their honour.   Unhappy events, too widely celebrated, had brought a reproach on the national character.   Irish soldiership was everywhere mentioned with a sneer.   If they wished to retrieve the fame of their country, this was the time and this the place.[2]

The spot on which he had determined to bring the fate of Ireland to issue seems to have been chosen with great judgment.   His army was drawn up on the slope of a hill, which was almost surrounded by red bog.   In front, near the edge of the morass, were some fences out of which a breastwork was without difficulty constructed.

On the eleventh of July, Ginkell, having repaired the fortifications of Athlone, and left a garrison there, fixed his headquarters at Ballinasloe, about four miles from Aghrim, and rode forward to take a view of the Irish position.   On his return he gave orders that ammunition

[1] Story's Continuation.   [2] Burnet, ii. 79. ; Story's Continuation.

should be served out, that every musket and bayonet should be got ready for action, and that early on the morrow every man should be under arms without beat of drum. Two regiments were to remain in charge of the camp : the rest, unincumbered by baggage, were to march against the enemy.

Soon after six, the next morning, the English were on the way to Aghrim. But some delay was occasioned by a thick fog which hung till noon over the moist valley of the Suck : a further delay was caused by the necessity of dislodging the Irish from some outposts ; and the afternoon was far advanced when the two armies at length confronted each other with nothing but the bog and the breastwork between them. The English and their allies were under twenty thousand ; the Irish above twenty five thousand.

Battle of Aghrim

Ginkell held a short consultation with his principal officers. Should he attack instantly, or wait till the next morning ? Mackay was for attacking instantly ; and his opinion prevailed. At five the battle began. The English foot, in such order as they could keep on treacherous and uneven ground, made their way, sinking deep in mud at every step, to the Irish works. But those works were defended with a resolution such as extorted some words of ungracious eulogy even from men who entertained the strongest prejudices against the Celtic race.[1] Again and again the assailants were driven back. Again and again they returned to the struggle. Once they were broken, and chased across the morass : but Talmash rallied them, and forced the pursuers to retire. The fight had lasted two hours : the evening was closing in ; and still the advantage was on the side of the Irish. Ginkell began to meditate a retreat. The hopes of Saint Ruth rose high. " The day is ours, my boys," he cried, waving his hat in the air. " We will drive them before us to the walls of Dublin." But fortune was already on the turn. Mackay and Ruvigny, with the English and Huguenot cavalry, had succeeded in passing the bog at a place where two horsemen could scarcely ride abreast. Saint Ruth at first laughed when he saw the Blues, in single file, struggling through the morass under a fire which every moment laid some gallant hat and feather on the earth. " What do they mean ? " he asked ; and then he swore that it was pity to see such fine fellows rushing to certain destruction. " Let them cross, however ; " he said. " The more they are, the more we shall kill." But soon he saw them laying hurdles on the quagmire. A broader and safer path was formed : squadron after squadron reached firm ground : the flank of the Irish army was speedily turned. The

---

[1] " They maintained their ground much longer than they had been accustomed to do," says Burnet. " They behaved themselves like men of another nation," says Story. " The Irish were never known to fight with more resolution," says the London Gazette.

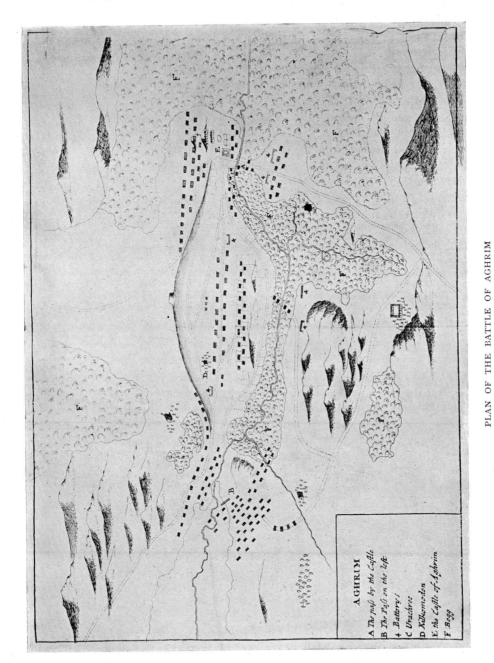

PLAN OF THE BATTLE OF AGHRIM

From George Story's Impartial History of the Wars of Ireland, 1693

French general was hastening to the rescue when a cannon ball carried off his head. Those who were about him thought that it would be dangerous to make his fate known. His corpse was wrapped in a cloak, carried from the field, and laid, with all secresy, in the sacred ground among the ruins of the ancient monastery of Loughrea. Till the fight was over neither army was aware that he was no more. The crisis of the battle had arrived ; and there was none to give direction. Sarsfield was in command of the reserve. But he had been strictly enjoined by Saint Ruth not to stir without orders ; and no orders came. Mackay and Ruvigny with their horse charged the Irish in flank. Talmash and his foot returned to the attack in front with dogged determination. The breastwork was carried. The Irish, still fighting, retreated from enclosure to enclosure. But, as enclosure after enclosure was forced, their efforts became fainter and fainter. At length they broke and fled. Then followed a horrible carnage. The conquerors were in a savage mood. For a report had been spread among them that, during the early part of the battle, some English captives who had been admitted to quarter had been put to the sword. Only four hundred prisoners were taken. The number of the slain was, in proportion to the number engaged, greater than in any other battle of that age. But for the coming on of a moonless night, made darker by a misty rain, scarcely a man would have escaped. The obscurity enabled Sarsfield, with a few squadrons which still remained unbroken, to cover the retreat. Of the conquerors six hundred were killed, and about a thousand wounded.

The English slept that night on the ground which had been so desperately contested. On the following day they buried their companions in arms, and then marched westward. The vanquished were left unburied, a strange and ghastly spectacle. Four thousand Irish corpses were counted on the field of battle. A hundred and fifty lay in one small enclosure, a hundred and twenty in another. But the slaughter had not been confined to the field of battle. One who was there tells us that, from the top of the hill on which the Celtic camp had been pitched, he saw the country, to the distance of near four miles, white with the naked bodies of the slain. The plain looked, he said, like an immense pasture covered by flocks of sheep. As usual, different estimates were formed even by eyewitnesses. But it seems probable that the number of the Irish who fell was not less than seven thousand. Soon a multitude of dogs came to feast on the carnage. These beasts became so fierce, and acquired such a taste for human flesh, that it was long dangerous for men to travel that road otherwise than in companies.[1]

[1] Story's Continuation ; London Gazette, July 20. 23. 1691 ; Mémoires de Berwick ; Life of James, ii. 456. ; Burnet, ii. 79. ; Macariæ Excidium ; Light to the Blind ; Letter from the

The beaten army had now lost all the appearance of an army, and resembled a rabble crowding home from a fair after a faction fight. One great stream of fugitives ran towards Galway, another towards Limerick. The roads to both cities were covered with weapons which had been flung away. Ginkell offered sixpence for every musket. In a short time so many waggon loads were collected that he reduced the price to twopence; and still great numbers of muskets came in.[1]

The conquerors marched first against Galway. D'Usson was there, and had under him seven regiments, thinned by the slaughter of Aghrim and utterly disorganised and disheartened. The last hope of Fall of the garrison and of the Roman Catholic inhabitants was that Galway Baldearg O'Donnel, the promised deliverer of their race, would come to

MEDAL ON THE BATTLE OF AGHRIM

the rescue. But Baldearg O'Donnel was not duped by the superstitious veneration of which he was the object. While there had been any doubt about the issue of the conflict between the Englishry and the Irishry, he had stood aloof. On the day of the battle he had remained at a safe distance with his tumultuary army; and, as soon as he had learned that his countrymen had been put to rout, he had fled, plundering and burning all the way, to the mountains of Mayo. Thence he

English camp to Sir Arthur Rawdon, in the Rawdon Papers; History of William the Third, 1702.

The narratives to which I have referred differ very widely from each other. Nor can the difference be ascribed solely or chiefly to partiality. For no two narratives differ more widely than that which will be found in the Life of James, and that which will be found in the memoirs of his son.

In consequence, I suppose, of the death of Saint Ruth, and of the absence of D'Usson, there is at the French War Office no despatch containing a detailed account of the battle.

[1] Story's Continuation.

sent to Ginkell offers of submission and service. Ginkell gladly seized the opportunity of breaking up a formidable band of marauders, and of turning to good account the influence which the name of a Celtic dynasty still exercised over the Celtic race. The negotiation, however, was not without difficulties. The wandering adventurer at first demanded nothing less than an earldom. After some haggling he consented to sell the love of a whole people, and his pretensions to regal dignity, for a pension of five hundred pounds a year. Yet the spell which bound his followers to him was not altogether broken. Some enthusiasts from Ulster were willing to fight under the O'Donnel against their own language and their own religion. With a small body of these devoted adherents, he joined a division of the English army, and on several occasions did useful service to William.[1]

When it was known that no succour was to be expected from the hero whose advent had been foretold by so many seers, the Irish who were shut up in Galway lost all heart. D'Usson had returned a stout answer to the first summons of the besiegers : but he soon saw that resistance was impossible, and made haste to capitulate. The garrison was suffered to retire to Limerick with the honours of war. A full amnesty for past offences was granted to the citizens ; and it was stipulated that, within the walls, the Roman Catholic priests should be allowed to perform in private the rites of their religion. On these terms the gates were thrown open. Ginkell was received with profound respect by the Mayor and Aldermen, and was complimented in a set speech by the Recorder. D'Usson, with about two thousand three hundred men, marched unmolested to Limerick.[2]

At Limerick, the last asylum of the vanquished race, the authority of Tyrconnel was supreme. There was now no general who could pretend that his commission made him independent of the Lord Lieutenant ; nor was the Lord Lieutenant now so unpopular as he had been for a fortnight earlier. Since the battle there had been a reflux of public feeling. No part of that great disaster could be imputed to the Viceroy. His opinion indeed had been against trying the chances of a pitched field, and he could with some plausibility assert that the neglect of his counsels had caused the ruin of Ireland.[3]

He made some preparations for defending Limerick, repaired the fortifications, and sent out parties to bring in provisions. The country,

---

[1] Story's Continuation ; Macariæ Excidium ; Life of James, ii. 464. ; London Gazette, July 30., Aug. 17. 1691 ; Light to the Blind.

[2] Story's Continuation ; Macariæ Excidium ; Life of James, ii. 459. ; London Gazette, July 30., Aug. 3. 1691.

[3] He held this language in a letter to Lewis XIV., dated the $\frac{5}{15}$th of August. This letter, written in a hand which it is not easy to decipher, is in the French War Office. Macariæ Excidium ; Light to the Blind.

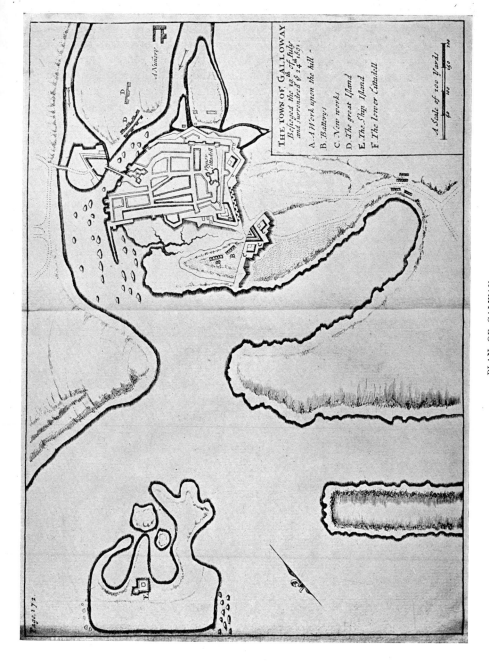

THE TOWN OF GALLOWAY
Besieged the 19ᵗʰ of July
and surrendered ye 24ᵗʰ 1691.

A . A Work upon the hill
B . Batteryʃ
C . New workʃ
D . The great Iʃland
E . The Ship Iʃland
F . The Lower Cittadell

A Scale of 100 Yards

PLAN OF GALWAY

From George Story's Impartial History of the Wars of Ireland, 1693

many miles round, was swept bare by these detachments, and a considerable quantity of cattle and fodder was collected within the walls. There was also a large stock of biscuit imported from France. The infantry assembled at Limerick were about fifteen thousand men. The Irish horse and dragoons, three or four thousand in number, were encamped on the Clare side of the Shannon. The communication between their camp and the city was maintained by means of a bridge called the Thomond Bridge, which was protected by a fort. These means of defence were not contemptible. But the fall of Athlone and the slaughter of Aghrim had broken the spirit of the army. A small party, at the head of which were Sarsfield and a brave Scotch officer named Wauchop, cherished a hope that the triumphant progress of Ginkell might be stopped by those walls from which William had, in the preceding year, been forced to retreat. But many of the Irish chiefs loudly declared that it was time to think of capitulating. Henry Luttrell, always fond of dark and crooked politics, opened a secret negotiation with the English. One of his letters was intercepted ; and he was put under arrest : but many who blamed his perfidy agreed with him in thinking that it was idle to prolong the contest. Tyrconnel himself was convinced that all was lost. His only hope was that he might be able to prolong the struggle till he could receive from Saint Germains permission to treat. He wrote to request that permission, and prevailed, with some difficulty, on his desponding countrymen to bind themselves by an oath not to capitulate till an answer from James should arrive.[1]

A few days after the oath had been administered, Tyrconnel was no more. On the eleventh of August he dined with D'Usson. The party

Death of Tyrconnel was gay. The Lord Lieutenant seemed to have thrown off the load which had bowed down his body and mind : he drank : he jested : he was again the Dick Talbot who had diced and revelled with Grammont. Soon after he had risen from table, an apoplectic stroke deprived him of speech and sensation. On the fourteenth he breathed his last. The wasted remains of that form which had once been a model for statuaries were laid under the pavement of the Cathedral : but no inscription, no tradition, preserves the memory of the spot.[2]

As soon as the Lord Lieutenant had expired, Plowden, who had superintended the Irish finances while there were any Irish finances to superintend, produced a commission under the great seal of James. This commission appointed Plowden himself, Fitton, and Nagle, Lords

[1] Macariæ Excidium ; Life of James, ii. 461, 462.

[2] Macariæ Excidium ; Life of James, ii. 459. 462. ; London Gazette, Aug. 31. 1691 ; Light to the Blind ; D'Usson and Tesse to Barbesieux, Aug. $\frac{13}{23}$.

Justices in the event of Tyrconnel's death. There was much murmuring when the names were made known. For both Plowden and Fitton were Saxons. The commission, however, proved to be a mere nullity. For it was accompanied by instructions which forbade the Lords Justices to interfere in the conduct of the war ; and, within the narrow space to which the dominions of James were now reduced, war was the only business. The government was, therefore, really in the hands of D'Usson and Sarsfield.[1]

On the day on which Tyrconnel died, the advanced guard of the English army came within sight of Limerick. Ginkell encamped on the same ground which William had occupied twelve months before. The batteries, on which were planted guns and bombs, very different from those which William had been forced to use, played day and night ; and soon roofs were blazing and walls crashing in every part of the city. Whole streets were reduced to ashes. Meanwhile several English ships of war came up the Shannon and anchored about a mile below the city.[2]

Second siege of Limerick

Still the place held out : the garrison was, in numerical strength, little inferior to the besieging army ; and it seemed not impossible that the defence might be prolonged till the equinoctial rains should a second time compel the English to retire. Ginkell determined on striking a bold stroke. No point in the whole circle of the fortifications was more important, and no point seemed to be more secure, than the Thomond Bridge, which joined the city to the camp of the Irish horse on the Clare bank of the Shannon. The Dutch General's plan was to separate the infantry within the ramparts from the cavalry without ; and this plan he executed with great skill, vigour, and success. He laid a bridge of tin boats on the river, crossed it with a strong body of troops, drove before him in confusion fifteen hundred dragoons who made a faint show of resistance, and marched towards the quarters of the Irish horse. The Irish horse sustained but ill on this day the reputation which they had gained at the Boyne. Indeed, that reputation had been purchased by the almost entire destruction of the best regiments. Recruits had been without much difficulty found. But the loss of fifteen hundred excellent soldiers was not to be repaired. The camp was abandoned without a blow. Some of the cavalry fled into the city. The rest, driving before them as many cattle as could be collected in that moment of panic, retired to the hills. Much beef, brandy, and harness was found in the magazines ; and the marshy plain

---

[1] Story's Continuation ; D'Usson and Tessé to Barbesieux, Aug. $\frac{18}{28}$. 1691. An unpublished letter from Nagle to Lord Merion of Aug. 15. This letter is quoted by Mr. O'Callaghan in a note on the Macariæ Excidium.

[2] Macariæ Excidium ; Story's Continuation.

of the Shannon was covered with firelocks and grenades which the fugitives had thrown away.[1]

The conquerors returned in triumph to their camp. But Ginkell was not content with the advantage which he had gained. He was bent on cutting off all communication between Limerick and the county of Clare. In a few days, therefore, he again crossed the river at the head of several regiments, and attacked the fort which protected the Thomond Bridge. In a short time the fort was stormed. The soldiers who had garrisoned it fled in confusion to the city. The Town Major, a French officer, who commanded at the Thomond Gate, afraid that the pursuers would enter with the fugitives, ordered that part of the bridge which was nearest to the city to be drawn up. Many of the Irish went headlong into the stream and perished there. Others cried for quarter, and held up handkerchiefs in token of submission. But the conquerors were mad with rage : their cruelty could not be immediately restrained ; and no prisoners were made till the heaps of corpses rose above the parapets. The garrison of the fort had consisted of about eight hundred men. Of these only a hundred and twenty escaped into Limerick.[2]

This disaster seemed likely to produce a general mutiny in the besieged city. The Irish clamoured for the blood of the Town Major who had ordered the bridge to be drawn up in the face of their flying countrymen. His superiors were forced to promise that he should be brought before a court martial. Happily for him, he had received a mortal wound, in the act of closing the Thomond Gate, and was saved by a soldier's death from the fury of the multitude.[3]

The cry for capitulation became so loud and importunate that the generals could not resist it. D'Usson informed his government that the

[1] Story's Continuation ; London Gazette, Sept. 28. 1691 ; Life of James, ii. 463. ; Diary of the Siege of Lymerick, 1692 ; Light to the Blind. In the account of the siege which is among the archives of the French War Office, it is said that the Irish cavalry behaved worse than the infantry.

[2] Story's Continuation ; Macariæ Excidium ; R. Douglas to Sir A. Rawdon, Sept. 28. 1691, in the Rawdon Papers ; London Gazette, Oct. 8. ; Diary of the Siege of Lymerick ; Light to the Blind ; Account of the Siege of Limerick in the archives of the French War Office.

The account of this affair in the Life of James, ii. 464., deserves to be noticed merely for its preeminent absurdity. The writer tell us that seven hundred of the Irish held out some time against a much larger force, and warmly praises their heroism. He did not know, or did not choose to mention, one fact which is essential to the right understanding of the story ; namely, that these seven hundred men were in a fort. That a garrison should defend a fort during a few hours against superior numbers is surely not strange. Forts are built because they can be defended by few against many.

[3] Account of the Siege of Limerick in the archives of the French War Office ; Story's Continuation.

PLAN OF LIMERICK

From George Story's Impartial History of the Wars of Ireland, 1693

fight at the bridge had so effectually cowed the spirit of the garrison
that it was impossible to continue the struggle.[1]　Some exception may

The Irish desirous to capitulate
perhaps be taken to the evidence of D'Usson: for undoubtedly
he, like every other Frenchman who had held any command in
the Irish army, was weary of his banishment, and impatient to
see his country again.　But it is certain that even Sarsfield had lost heart.
Up to this time his voice had been for stubborn resistance.　He was
now not only willing, but impatient to treat.[2]　It seemed to him that
the city was doomed.　There was no hope of succour, domestic or
foreign.　In every part of Ireland the Saxons had set their feet on
the necks of the natives.　Sligo had fallen.　Even those wild islands
which intercept the huge waves of the Atlantic from the bay of Galway
had acknowledged the authority of William.　The men of Kerry,
reputed the fiercest and most ungovernable part of the aboriginal population, had held out long, but had at length been routed, and chased
to their woods and mountains.[3]　A French fleet, if a French fleet were
now to arrive on the coast of Munster, would find the mouth of the
Shannon guarded by English men of war.　The stock of provisions
within Limerick was already running low.　If the siege were prolonged,
the town would, in all human probability, be reduced either by force or
by blockade.　And, if Ginkell should enter through the breach, or
should be implored by a multitude perishing with hunger to dictate his
own terms, what could be expected but a tyranny more inexorably
severe than that of Cromwell?　Would it not then be wise to try what
conditions could be obtained while the victors had still something to
fear from the rage and despair of the vanquished; while the last Irish
army could still make some show of resistance behind the walls of the
last Irish fortress?

On the evening of the day which followed the fight at the Thomond
Gate, the drums of Limerick beat a parley; and Wauchop, from one of

Negotiations between the Irish chiefs and the besiegers
the towers, hailed the besiegers, and requested Ruvigny to
grant Sarsfield an interview.　The brave Frenchman who was
an exile on account of his attachment to one religion, and
the brave Irishman who was about to become an exile on
account of his attachment to another, met and conferred, doubtless with
mutual sympathy and respect.[4]　Ginkell, to whom Ruvigny reported
what had passed, willingly consented to an armistice.　For, constant as
his success had been, it had not made him secure.　The chances were
greatly on his side.　Yet it was possible that an attempt to storm the
city might fail, as a similar attempt had failed twelve months before.

[1] D'Usson to Barbesieux, Oct. $\frac{4}{14}$. 1691.　　[2] Macariæ Excidium.

[3] Story's Continuation; Diary of the Siege of Lymerick.

[4] London Gazette, Oct. 8. 1691; Story's Continuation; Diary of the Siege of Lymerick.

If the siege should be turned into a blockade, it was probable that the pestilence which had been fatal to the army of Schomberg, which had compelled William to retreat, and which had all but prevailed even against the genius and energy of Marlborough, might soon avenge the carnage of Aghrim. The rains had lately been heavy. The whole plain might shortly be an immense pool of stagnant water. It might be necessary to move the troops to a healthier situation than the bank of the Shannon, and to provide for them a warmer shelter than that of tents. The enemy would be safe till the spring. In the spring a French army might land in Ireland : the natives might again rise in arms from Donegal to Kerry ; and the war, which was now all but extinguished, might blaze forth fiercer than ever.

A negotiation was therefore opened with a sincere desire on both sides to put an end to the contest. The chiefs of the Irish army held several consultations at which some Roman Catholic prelates and some eminent lawyers were invited to assist. A preliminary question, which perplexed tender consciences, was submitted to the Bishops. The late Lord Lieutenant had persuaded the officers of the garrison to swear that they would not surrender Limerick till they should receive an answer to the letter in which their situation had been explained to James. The Bishops thought that the oath was no longer binding. It had been taken at a time when the communications with France were open, and in the full belief that the answer of James would arrive within three weeks. More than twice that time had elapsed. Every avenue leading to the city was strictly guarded by the enemy. His Majesty's faithful subjects, by holding out till it had become impossible for him to signify his pleasure to them, had acted up to the spirit of their promise.[1]

The next question was what terms should be demanded. A paper, containing propositions which statesmen of our age will think reasonable, but which to the most humane and liberal English Protestants of the seventeenth century appeared extravagant, was sent to the camp of the besiegers. What was asked was that all offences should be covered with oblivion, that perfect freedom of worship should be allowed to the native population, that every parish should have its Roman Catholic priest, and that Irish Roman Catholics should be capable of holding all offices, civil and military, and of enjoying all municipal privileges.[2]

Ginkell knew little of the laws and feelings of the English : but he had about him persons who were competent to direct him. They had a week before prevented him from breaking a Rapparee on the wheel ; and they now suggested an answer to the propositions of the enemy. " I am a stranger here," said Ginkell : " I am ignorant of the constitu-

---

[1] Life of James, 464, 465.　　　[2] Story's Continuation

tion of these kingdoms : but I am assured that what you ask is inconsistent with that constitution ; and therefore I cannot with honour consent." He immediately ordered a new battery to be thrown up, and guns and mortars to be planted on it. But his preparations were speedily interrupted by another message from the city. The Irish begged that, since he could not grant what they had demanded, he would tell them on what terms he was willing to treat. He called his advisers round him, and, after some consultation, sent back a paper containing the heads of a treaty, such as he had reason to believe that the government which he served would approve. What he offered was indeed much less than what the Irish desired, but was quite as much as, when they considered their situation and the temper of the English nation, they could expect. They speedily notified their assent. It was agreed that there should be a cessation of arms, not only by land, but in the ports and bays of Munster, and that a fleet of French transports should be suffered to come up the Shannon in peace and to depart in peace. The signing of the treaty was deferred till the Lords Justices, who represented William at Dublin, should arrive at Ginkell's quarters. But there was during some days a relaxation of military vigilance on both sides. Prisoners were set at liberty. The outposts of the two armies chatted and messed together. The English officers rambled into the town. The Irish officers dined in the camp. Anecdotes of what passed at the friendly meetings of these men, who had so lately been mortal enemies, were widely circulated. One story, in particular, was repeated in every part of Europe. " Has not this last campaign," said Sarsfield to some English officers, " raised your opinion of Irish soldiers ?" " To tell you the truth," answered an Englishman, " we think of them much as we always did." " However meanly you may think of us," replied Sarsfield, " change Kings with us, and we will willingly try our luck with you again." He was doubtless thinking of the day on which he had seen the two Sovereigns at the head of two great armies, William foremost in the charge, and James foremost in the flight.[1]

On the first of October, Coningsby and Porter arrived at the English headquarters. On the second the articles of capitulation were
The capitu-
lation of
Limerick
discussed at great length and definitively settled. On the third they were signed. They were divided into two parts, a military treaty and a civil treaty. The former was subscribed only by the generals on both sides. The Lords Justices set their names to the latter.[2]

[1] Story's Continuation ; Diary of the Siege of Lymerick ; Burnet, ii. 81. ; London Gazette, Oct. 12. 1691.

[2] Story's Continuation ; Diary of the Siege of Lymerick ; London Gazette, Oct. 15. 1691.

By the military treaty it was agreed that such Irish officers and soldiers as should declare that they wished to go to France should be conveyed thither, and should, in the meantime, remain under the command of their own generals. Ginkell undertook to furnish a considerable number of transports. French vessels were also to be permitted to pass and repass freely between Britanny and Munster. Part of Limerick was to be immediately delivered up to the English. But the island on which the Cathedral and the Castle stand was to remain, for the present, in the keeping of the Irish.

The terms of the civil treaty were very different from those which Ginkell had sternly refused to grant. It was not stipulated that the Roman Catholics of Ireland should be competent to hold any political or military office, or that they should be admitted into any corporation. But they obtained a promise that they should enjoy such privileges in the exercise of their religion as were consistent with the law, or as they had enjoyed in the reign of Charles the Second.

To all inhabitants of Limerick, and to all officers and soldiers in the Jacobite army, who should submit to the government and notify their submission by taking the oath of allegiance, an entire amnesty was promised. They were to retain their property : they were to be allowed to exercise any profession which they had exercised before the troubles : they were not to be punished for any treason, felony, or misdemeanour committed since the accession of the late King : nay, they were not to be sued for damages on account of any act of spoliation or outrage which they might have committed during the three years of confusion. This was more than the Lords Justices were constitutionally competent to grant. It was therefore added that the government would use its utmost endeavours to obtain a Parliamentary ratification of the treaty.[1]

As soon as the two instruments had been signed, the English entered the city, and occupied one quarter of it. A narrow but deep branch of the Shannon separated them from the quarter which was still in the possession of the Irish.[2]

In a few hours a dispute arose which seemed likely to produce a renewal of hostilities. Sarsfield had resolved to seek his fortune in the service of France, and was naturally desirous to carry with him to the Continent such a body of troops as would be an important addition to the army of Lewis. Ginkell was as naturally unwilling to send thousands of men to swell the forces of the enemy. Both generals appealed to the treaty. Each construed it as suited his purpose, and each complained that the other had violated it. Sarsfield was accused

[1] The articles of the civil treaty have often been reprinted.
[2] Story's Continuation ; Diary of the Siege of Lymerick.

of putting one of his officers under arrest for refusing to go to the Continent. Ginkell, greatly excited, declared that he would teach the Irish to play tricks with him, and began to make preparations for a cannonade. Sarsfield came to the English camp, and tried to justify what he had done. The altercation was sharp. " I submit," said Sarsfield, at last: " I am in your power." " Not at all in my power," said Ginkell; " go back and do your worst." The imprisoned officer was liberated : a sanguinary contest was averted ; and the two commanders contented themselves with a war of words.[1] Ginkell put forth proclamations assuring the Irish that, if they would live quietly in their own land, they should be protected and favoured, and that, if they preferred a military life, they should be admitted into the service of King William. It was added that no man, who chose to reject this gracious invitation and to become a soldier of Lewis, must expect ever again to set foot on the island. Sarsfield and Wauchop exerted their eloquence on the other side. The present aspect of affairs, they said, was doubtless gloomy : but there was bright sky beyond the cloud. The banishment would be short. The return would be triumphant. Within a year the French would invade England. In such an invasion the Irish troops, if only they remained unbroken, would assuredly bear a chief part. In the meantime it was far better for them to live in a neighbouring and friendly country, under the parental care of their own rightful King, than to trust the Prince of Orange, who would probably send them to the other end of the world to fight for his ally the Emperor against the Janissaries.

The help of the Roman Catholic clergy was called in. On the day on which those who had made up their minds to go to France were required to announce their determination, the priests were indefatigable in exhorting. At the head of every regiment a sermon was preached on the duty of adhering to the cause of the Church, and on the sin and danger of consorting with unbelievers.[2] Whoever, it was said, should enter the service of the usurpers would do so at the peril of his soul. The heretics affirmed that, after the peroration, a plentiful allowance of brandy was served out to the audience, and that, when the brandy had been swallowed, a Bishop pronounced a benediction. Thus duly prepared by physical and moral stimulants, the garrison, consisting of about fourteen thousand infantry, was drawn up in the vast meadow which lay on the Clare bank of the Shannon. Here copies of Ginkell's

The Irish troops required to make their election between their country and France

[1] Story's Continuation ; Diary of the Siege of Lymerick.

[2] Story's Continuation. His narrative is confirmed by the testimony which an Irish Captain who was present has left us in bad Latin. " Hic apud sacrum omnes advertizantur a capellanis ire potius in Galliam."

The Triumph of IRELAND:

OR,

The Surrender of Limerick

To Their MAJESTIES FORCES under the Command of the Duke

Of *Wirtemberg*, and Lieutenant General *Scravenmore*, on *Sunday* the 27th. of *September* 1691. to the unspeakable joy
of the Protestant Army.

Tune of, *Let the Souldiers Rejoyce.*

Licensed according to Order.

LEt the Bells merrily ring,
Joy all tydings in-bring,
Great Limerick has now come at last to surrender,
To the Army of brave,
Who-roaes fight one proclaim,
Whilst William, great William were Rainbows defender.

'Twas in vain to hold out,
We that broke them about
Which Limerick too close-beset-ere like Hunter,
With the Walls of the Town,
We perforce batter down,
Great Limerick, great Limerick now grief to lie under,

We the Shannon did cross
Which our brave Foot and Horse,
Resolving to charge-a-a-charge and give fire,
We no sooner begun
But the Enemy run,
Into Limerick, to Limerick they strove to retire.

We the Teagues did persue,
Who to Limerick flew,
But for the French too-oi-oioioioh of all fire,
And expos'd them to fall,
To our brave General,
For they hars'd up, they hars'd up the Gates of the City.

Oh! for to take this poor Teague,
In a terrible twaage,
We French Dog if it oeoeterewe we come near him,
Bring forth my dear Joy,
We will kill and destroy,
For no longer, no longer we Dor will fear him.

Hubobobo they cry'd,
We are that we out fled,
To Day to the Conoeoeoe ain better shelter,
Whilst this plaguy Monsieur
Who has rude us here,
Quoth the City of Limrick by Creed for bienvenice.

Thus with a bone,
And a pitiful tone,
To Bumbrid we Creteioftcoiol did give quarter,
For our Generals bold,
Who are brave hearts of gold,
Who are never, are never More grieve for slaughter.

Then the Town in distress,
Did their sorrows express,
Struck by a bulbite Moi-oa-oa-a-ag of submission,
For, they could not withstand
Our bust Armed band,
Who had brought, t, t, ns to a low condition.

It was straightways agreed,
To surrender with speed,
Without any t-o-o oeo-onger delaying,
In the spight of Monsieur,
Who no trouble for fear
Of the Army, t, t Army whose flags were displaying.

Our brave Army they laid before,
And march'd out of the Town,
Poor Teagues with-a-e-e-e-e-o-e-oh they make,
Thus they on ragged Crew,
Bid Limrick adieu,
Say and Joyful, right Joyful they were to to take it.

Into Limrick we came,
Crown'd with Kroofies of fame,
Whilst Krumphies were loo-o-oi-oo-oui-ooining before us,
And our Dums they did beat
Thoroughly every street,
Whilst the Protestant families there the more us.

Printed for P. Brooksby, J. Deacon, J. Blare and J. Back.

---

proclamation were profusely scattered about; and English officers went through the ranks imploring the men not to ruin themselves, and explaining to them the advantages which the soldiers of King William enjoyed. At length the decisive moment came. The troops were ordered to pass in review. Those who wished to remain in Ireland were directed to file off at a particular spot. All who passed that spot were to be considered as having made their choice for France. Sarsfield and Wauchop on one side, Porter, Coningsby, and Ginkell on the other, looked on with painful anxiety. D'Usson and his countrymen, though not uninterested in the spectacle, found it hard to preserve their gravity. The confusion, the clamour, the grotesque appearance of an army in which there could scarcely be seen a shirt or a pair of pantaloons, a shoe or a stocking, presented so ludicrous a contrast to the orderly and brilliant appearance of their master's troops, that they amused themselves by wondering what the Parisians would say to see such a force mustered on the plain of Grenelle.[1]

First marched what was called the Royal regiment, fourteen hundred strong. All but seven went beyond the fatal point. Ginkell's **Most of the** countenance showed that he was deeply mortified. He was **Irish troops** **volunteer** consoled, however, by seeing the next regiment, which con- **for France** sisted of natives of Ulster, turn off to a man. There had arisen, notwithstanding the community of blood, language, and religion, an antipathy between the Celts of Ulster and those of the other three provinces; nor is it improbable that the example and influence of Baldearg O'Donnel may have had some effect on the people of the land which his forefathers had ruled.[2] In most of the regiments there was a division of opinion; but a great majority declared for France. Henry Luttrell was one of those who turned off. He was rewarded for his desertion, and perhaps for other services, with a grant of the large estate of his elder brother Simon, who firmly adhered to the cause of James, with a pension of five hundred pounds a year from the Crown, and with the abhorrence of the Roman Catholic population. After living in wealth, luxury, and infamy, during a quarter of a century, Henry Luttrell was murdered while going through Dublin in his sedan chair; and the Irish House of Commons declared that there was reason to suspect that he had fallen by the revenge of the Papists.[3]

[1] D'Usson and Tessé to Barbesieux, Oct. $\frac{7}{17}$. 1691.

[2] That there was little sympathy between the Celts of Ulster and those of the Southern Provinces is evident from the curious memorial which the agent of Baldearg O'Donnel delivered to Avaux.

[3] Treasury Letter Book, June 19. 1696; Journals of the Irish House of Commons, Nov. 7. 1717.

Eighty years after his death, his grave near Luttrellstown was violated by the descendants of those whom he had betrayed, and his skull was broken to pieces with a pickaxe.[1] The deadly hatred of which he was the object descended to his son and to his grandson ; and, unhappily, nothing in the character either of his son or of his grandson tended to mitigate the feeling which the name of Luttrell excited.[2]

When the long procession had closed, it was found that about a thousand men had agreed to enter into William's service. About two thousand accepted passes from Ginkell, and went quietly home. About eleven thousand returned with Sarsfield to the city. A few hours after the garrison had passed in review, the horse, who were encamped some miles from the town, were required to make their choice ; and most of them volunteered for France.[3]

Sarsfield considered the troops who remained with him as under an irrevocable obligation to go abroad ; and, lest they should be tempted to retract their consent, he confined them within the ramparts, and ordered the gates to be shut and strongly guarded. Ginkell, though in his vexation he muttered some threats, seems to have felt that he could not justifiably interfere. But the precautions of the Irish general were far from being completely successful. It was by no means strange that a superstitious and excitable kerne, with a sermon and a dram in his head, should be ready to promise whatever his priests required : neither was it strange that, when he had slept off his liquor, and when anathemas were no longer ringing in his ears, he should feel painful misgivings. He had bound himself to go into exile, perhaps for life, beyond that dreary expanse of waters which impressed his rude mind with mysterious terror. His thoughts ran on all that he was to leave, on the well known peat stack and potatoe ground, and on the mud cabin, which, humble as it was, was still his home. He was never again to see

Many of the Irish who had volunteered for France desert

---

[1] This I relate on Mr. O'Callaghan's authority. History of the Irish Brigades, Note 47.

[2] " There is," Junius wrote eighty years after the capitulation of Limerick, " a certain family in this country on which nature seems to have entailed a hereditary baseness of disposition. As far as their history has been known, the son has regularly improved upon the vices of the father, and has taken care to transmit them pure and undiminished into the bosom of his successors." Elsewhere he says of the member for Middlesex, " He has degraded even the name of Luttrell." He exclaims, in allusion to the marriage of the Duke of Cumberland and Mrs. Horton, who was born a Luttrell, " Let Parliament look to it. A Luttrell shall never succeed to the Crown of England." It is certain that very few Englishmen can have sympathised with Junius's abhorrence of the Luttrells, or can even have understood it. Why then did he use expressions which to the great majority of his readers must have been unintelligible? My answer is that Philip Francis was born, and passed the first ten years of his life, within a walk of Luttrellstown.

[3] Story's Continuation ; London Gazette, Oct. 22. 1691 ; D'Usson and Tessé to Lewis, Oct. $\frac{4}{14}$., and to Barbesieux, Oct. $\frac{7}{17}$. ; Light to the Blind.

the familiar faces round the turf fire, or to hear the familiar notes of the old Celtic songs.　The ocean was to roll between him and the dwelling of his greyheaded parents and his blooming sweetheart.　There were some who, unable to bear the misery of such a separation, and finding it impossible to pass the sentinels who watched the gates, sprang into the river and gained the opposite bank.　The number of these daring swimmers, however, was not great ; and the army would probably have been transported almost entire if it had remained at Limerick till the day of embarkation.　But many of the vessels in which the voyage was to be performed lay at Cork ; and it was necessary that Sarsfield should proceed thither with some of his best regiments.　It was a march of not less than four days through a wild country.　To prevent agile youths, familiar with all the shifts of a vagrant and predatory life, from stealing off to the bogs and woods under cover of the night, was impossible.　Indeed many soldiers had the audacity to run away by broad daylight before they were out of sight of Limerick Cathedral. The Royal regiment, which had, on the day of the review, set so striking an example of fidelity to the cause of James, dwindled from fourteen hundred men to five hundred.　Before the last ships departed, news came that those who had sailed by the first ships had been ungraciously received at Brest.　They had been scantily fed : they had been able to obtain neither pay nor clothing : though winter was setting in, they slept in the fields with no covering but the hedges ; and many had been heard to say that it would have been far better to die in old Ireland than to live in the inhospitable country to which they had been banished.　The effect of these reports was that hundreds, who had long persisted in their intention of emigrating, refused at the last moment to go on board, threw down their arms, and returned to their native villages.[1]

　　　Sarsfield perceived that one chief cause of the desertion which was thinning his army was the natural unwillingness of the men to leave their families in a state of destitution.　Cork and the neighbouring villages were filled with the kindred of those who were going abroad.　Great numbers of women, many of them leading, carrying, suckling their infants, covered all the roads which led to the place of embarkation.　The Irish general, apprehensive of the effect which the entreaties and lamentations of these poor creatures could not fail to produce, put forth a proclamation, in which he assured his soldiers that they should be permitted to carry their wives and children to France.　It would be injurious to the memory of so brave and loyal a gentleman to suppose that when he made this promise he meant to break it.　It is much more probable

The last division of the Irish army sails from Cork for France

---

[1] Story's Continuation ; London Gazette, Jan. 4. 169½.

PATRICK SARSFIELD, EARL OF LUCAN

From an engraving by F. Tilliard of a painting by Lady Bingham that he had formed an erroneous estimate of the number of those who would demand a passage, and that he found himself, when it was too late to alter his arrangements, unable to keep his word. After the soldiers had embarked, room was found for the families of many. But still there remained on the waterside a great multitude clamouring piteously to be taken on board. As the last boats put off there was a rush into the surf. Some women caught hold of the ropes, were dragged out of their depth, clung till their fingers were cut through, and perished in the waves. The ships began to move. A wild and terrible wail rose from the shore, and excited unwonted compassion in hearts steeled by hatred of the Irish race and of the Romish faith. Even the stern Cromwellian, now at length, after a desperate struggle of three years, left the undisputed lord of the bloodstained and devastated island, could not hear unmoved that bitter cry, in which was poured forth all the rage and all the sorrow of a conquered nation.[1]

The sails disappeared. The emaciated and brokenhearted crowd of those whom a stroke more cruel than that of death had made widows and orphans dispersed, to beg their way home through a wasted land, or to lie down and die by the roadside of grief and hunger. The exiles departed, to learn in foreign camps that discipline without which natural courage is of small avail, and to retrieve on distant fields of battle the honour which had been lost by a long series of defeats at home. In Ireland there was peace. The domination of the colonists **State of Ireland after the war** was absolute. The native population was tranquil with the ghastly tranquillity of exhaustion and of despair. There were indeed outrages, robberies, fireraisings, assassinations. But more than a century passed away without one general insurrection. During that century, two rebellions were raised in Great Britain by the adherents of the House of Stuart. But neither when the elder Pretender summoned his vassals to attend his coronation at Scone, nor when the younger held his court at Holyrood, was the standard of that House set up in Connaught or Munster. In 1745, indeed, when the Highlanders were marching towards London, the Roman Catholics of Ireland were so quiet that the Lord Lieutenant could, without the smallest risk, send several regiments across Saint George's Channel to reinforce the army of the Duke of Cumberland. Nor was this submission the effect of content, but of mere stupefaction and brokenness of heart. The iron had entered into the soul. The memory of past defeats, the habit of daily enduring insult and oppression, had cowed the spirit of the unhappy nation. There were indeed Irish Roman Catholics of great ability, energy and ambition : but they were to be

[1] Story's Continuation ; Macariæ Excidium, and Mr. O'Callaghan's note ; London Gazette, Jan. 4. 169½.

found every where except in Ireland, at Versailles and at Saint Ilde-
fonso, in the armies of Frederic and in the armies of Maria Theresa.
One exile became a Marshal of France. Another became Prime
Minister of Spain. If he had staid in his native land, he would have
been regarded as an inferior by all the ignorant and worthless
squireens who had signed the Declaration against Transubstantiation. In
his palace at Madrid he had the pleasure of being assiduously courted
by the ambassador of George the Second, and of bidding defiance
in high terms to the ambassador of George the Third.[1] Scattered
over all Europe were to be found brave Irish generals, dexterous Irish

TWO MEDALS CELEBRATING THE CAPTURE OF LIMERICK

diplomatists, Irish Counts, Irish Barons, Irish Knights of Saint Lewis
and of Saint Leopold, of the White Eagle and of the Golden Fleece,
who, if they had remained in the house of bondage, could not have been
ensigns of marching regiments or freemen of petty corporations. These
men, the natural chiefs of their race, having been withdrawn, what
remained was utterly helpless and passive. A rising of the Irishry
against the Englishry was no more to be apprehended than a rising of
the women and children against the men.[2]

[1] Some interesting facts relating to Wall, who was minister of Ferdinand the Sixth and
Charles the Third, will be found in the letters of Sir Benjamin Keene and Lord Bristol, published
in Coxe's Memoirs of Spain.

[2] This is Swift's language, language held not once, but repeatedly and at long intervals. In
the Letter on the Sacramental Test, written in 1708, he says: "If we were under any real fear
of the Papists in this kingdom, it would be hard to think us so stupid as not to be equally
apprehensive with others, since we are likely to be the greater and more immediate sufferers:
but, on the contrary, we look upon them to be altogether as inconsiderable as the women
and children. . . . The common people, without leaders, without discipline or natural courage,

There were indeed, in those days, fierce disputes between the mother country and the colony : but in such disputes the aboriginal population had no more interest than the Red Indians in the dispute between Old England and New England about the Stamp Act. The ruling few, even when in mutiny against the government, had no mercy for any thing that looked like mutiny on the part of the subject many. None of those Roman patriots, who poniarded Julius Cæsar for aspiring to be a king, would have had the smallest scruple about crucifying a whole school of gladiators for attempting to escape from the most odious and degrading of all kinds of servitude. None of those Virginian patriots, who vindicated their separation from the British empire by proclaiming it to be a selfevident truth that all men were endowed by the Creator with an unalienable right to liberty, would have had the smallest scruple about shooting any negro slave who had laid claim to that unalienable right. And, in the same manner, the Protestant masters of Ireland, while ostentatiously professing the political doctrines of Locke and Sidney, held that a people who spoke the Celtic tongue and heard mass could have no concern in those doctrines. Molyneux questioned the supremacy of the English legislature. Swift assailed, with the keenest ridicule and invective, every part of the system of government. Lucas disquieted the administration of Lord Harrington. Boyle overthrew the administration of the Duke of Dorset. But neither Molyneux nor Swift, neither Lucas nor Boyle, ever thought of appealing to the native population. They would as soon have thought of appealing to the swine.[1] At a later period Henry Flood excited the dominant class

being little better than hewers of wood and drawers of water, are out of all capacity of doing any mischief, if they were ever so well inclined." In the Drapier's Sixth Letter, written in 1724, he says : "As to the people of this kingdom, they consist either of Irish Papists, who are as inconsiderable, in point of power, as the women and children, or of English Protestants." Again, in the Presbyterians' Plea of Merit, written in 1731, he says : "The estates of Papists are very few, crumbling into small parcels, and daily diminishing ; their common people are sunk in poverty, ignorance and cowardice, and of as little consequence as women and children. Their nobility and gentry are at least one half ruined, banished or converted. They all soundly feel the smart of what they suffered in the last Irish war. Some of them are already retired into foreign countries : others, as I am told, intend to follow them ; and the rest, I believe to a man, who still possess any lands, are absolutely resolved never to hazard them again for the sake of establishing their superstition."

I may observe that, to the best of my belief, Swift never, in any thing that he wrote, used the word Irishman to denote a person of Anglosaxon race born in Ireland. He no more considered himself as an Irishman than an Englishman born at Calcutta considers himself as a Hindoo.

[1] In 1749 Lucas was the idol of the democracy of his own caste. It is curious to see what was thought of him by those who were not of his own caste. One of the chief Pariahs, Charles O'Connor, wrote thus : "I am by no means interested, nor is any of our unfortunate population, in this affair of Lucas. A true patriot would not have betrayed such malice to such unfortunate slaves as we." He adds, with too much truth, that those boasters the Whigs wished to have liberty all to themselves.

THE STATUE OF WILLIAM III ON COLLEGE GREEN, DUBLIN

From a photograph

to demand a Parliamentary reform, and to use even revolutionary means for the purpose of obtaining that reform. But neither he, nor those who looked up to him as their chief, and who went close to the verge of treason at his bidding, would consent to admit the subject class to the smallest share of political power. The virtuous and accomplished Charlemont, a Whig of the Whigs, passed a long life in contending for what he called the freedom of his country. But he voted against the law which gave the elective franchise to Roman Catholic freeholders, and he died fixed in the opinion that the Parliament House ought to be kept pure from Roman Catholic members. Indeed, during the century which followed the Revolution, the inclination of an English Protestant to trample on the Irishry was generally proportioned to the zeal which he professed for political liberty in the abstract. If he uttered any expression of compassion for the majority oppressed by the minority, he might be safely set down as a bigoted Tory and High Churchman.[1]

All this time hatred, kept down by fear, festered in the hearts of the children of the soil. They were still the same people that had sprung to arms in 1641 at the call of O'Neill, and in 1689 at the call of Tyrconnel. To them every festival instituted by the State was a day of mourning, and every trophy set up by the State was a memorial of shame. We have never known, and can but faintly conceive, the feelings of a nation doomed to see constantly in all its public places the monuments of its subjugation. Such monuments every where met the eye of the Irish Roman Catholic. In front of the Senate House of his country, he saw the statue which her conquerors had set up in honour of a memory, glorious indeed and immortal, but to him an object of mingled dread and abhorrence. If he entered, he saw the walls tapestried with the most ignominious defeats of his forefathers. At length, after a hundred years of servitude, endured without one struggle for emancipation, the French revolution awakened a wild hope in the bosoms of the oppressed. Men who had inherited all the pretensions and all the passions of the Parliament which James had held at the King's Inns could not hear unmoved of the downfall of a wealthy established Church, of the flight of a splendid aristocracy, of the confiscation of an immense territory. Old antipathies, which had never slumbered, were excited to new and terrible energy by the combination of stimulants which, in any other society, would have

---

[1] On this subject Johnson was the most liberal politician of his time. "The Irish," he said with great warmth, "are in a most unnatural state: for we see there the minority prevailing over the majority." I suspect that Alderman Beckford and Alderman Sawbridge would have been far from sympathizing with him. Charles O'Connor, whose unfavourable opinion of the Whig Lucas I have quoted, pays, in the Preface to the Dissertations on Irish History, a high compliment to the liberality of the Tory Johnson.

GVLIELMVS III
ANTIQVAM ET FIDELEM
HIBERNIÆ METROPOLIN
HOC INDVLGENTIÆ SVÆ MVNERE
ORNAVIT.
BARTH VAN HOMRIGH ARM.
VRB. PRÆTORE.
MDCXCVIII.

MEDAL PRESENTED BY WILLIAM III TO THE CITY OF DUBLIN

counteracted each other. The spirit of Popery and the spirit of Jacobinism, irreconcilable antagonists every where else, were for once mingled in an unnatural and portentous union. Their joint influence produced the third and last rising up of the aboriginal population against the colony. The greatgrandsons of the soldiers of Galmoy and Sarsfield were opposed to the greatgrandsons of the soldiers of Wolseley and Mitchelburn. The Celt again looked impatiently for the sails which were to bring succour from Brest; and the Saxon was again backed by the whole power of England. Again the victory remained with the well educated and well organised minority. But, happily, the vanquished people found protection in a quarter from which they would once have had to expect nothing but implacable severity. By this time the philosophy of the eighteenth century had purified English Whiggism from that deep taint of intolerance which had been contracted during a long and close alliance with the Puritanism of the seventeenth century. Enlightened men had begun to feel that the arguments, by which Milton and Locke, Tillotson and Burnet, had vindicated the rights of conscience, might be urged with not less force in favour of the Roman Catholic than in favour of the Independent or the Baptist. The great party which traces its descent through the Exclusionists up to the Roundheads continued, during thirty years, in spite of royal frowns and popular clamours, to demand a share in all the benefits of our free constitution for those Irish Papists whom the Roundheads and the Exclusionists had considered merely as beasts of chase or as beasts of burden. But it will be for some other historian to relate the vicissitudes of that great conflict, and the late triumph of reason and humanity. Unhappily such a historian will have to relate that the victory won by such exertions and by such sacrifices was immediately followed by disappointment; that it proved far less easy to eradicate evil passions than to repeal evil laws; and that, long after every trace of national and religious animosity had been obliterated from the Statute Book, national and religious animosities continued to rankle in the bosoms of millions. May he be able also to relate that wisdom, justice, and time did in Ireland what they had done in Scotland, and that all the races which inhabit the British isles were at length indissolubly blended into one people!

END OF VOLUME IV

GLASGOW: PRINTED AT THE UNIVERSITY PRESS BY ROBERT MACLEHOSE AND CO. LTD.